Prison Disturbances April 1990

Report of an Inquiry

by

THE RT HON LORD JUSTICE WOOLF
(PARTS I and II)
and
HIS HONOUR JUDGE STEPHEN TUMIM
(PART II)

Presented to Parliament by the Secretary of State for the
Home Department by Command of Her Majesty
February 1991

LONDON: HMSO

£38.00 net

Cm 1456

The Rt Hon Kenneth Baker MP PC
Secretary of State for the Home Department
Home Office
50 Queen Anne's Gate
LONDON   31 January 1991
SW1H 9AT

Dear Home Secretary

This is the Report of the Inquiry into Prison Disturbances in England
and Wales in April 1990 which was commissioned by your predecessor,
now Lord Waddington of Read.

The Report starts with an Overview. The Overview summarises
disturbances at six prison establishments. It explains also the Inquiry's
approach to preventing a recurrence. It identifies 12 specific
recommendations. The subsequent sections of the Report make a
range of proposals which follows on from those recommendations.
Part I of the Report examines in detail the disturbances at the six
prison establishments. Part II examines the wider issues arising out of
the disturbances.

I was appointed by the then Home Secretary on 6 April 1990 and have
been solely responsible for preparing Part I of the Report. Judge
Stephen Tumim joined the Inquiry on 27 July 1990. We have been
jointly responsible for preparing Part II of the Report.

The Report makes no reference to the names of prisoners. It would be
most unfortunate if their identities were discovered. Section 1 urges
the media not to publish any names which the Report omits.

I now submit the Report to you.

Yours ev

Harry Woolf

The Rt Hon Lord Justice Woolf

CONTENTS

	Paragraph	Page

SECTION 1: OVERVIEW

	Paragraph	Page
Introduction	1.1	1
An Outline of What Happened at Six Disturbances		
Manchester (Strangeways)	1.16	3
Glen Parva	1.60	7
Dartmoor	1.70	8
Cardiff	1.97	11
Bristol	1.113	13
Pucklechurch	1.129	15
The Central Problems of the Prison Service	1.142	16
What Should be Done to Prevent Repetition of the Riots?	1.157	18
The Structures for Consultation Across the Criminal Justice System	1.169	20
The Head of the Prison Service	1.173	21
The Relationship Between Headquarters and Establishments	1.179	22
The Enhanced Status of Prison Officers	1.180	22
Relations With Prisoners	1.183	23
Standards Within Prisons	1.186	23
The Control on the Number of Prisoners Within a Prison	1.188	23
Sanitation	1.192	24
Links with the Community	1.194	24
Small Units	1.197	25
Remand Prisoners	1.204	25
A Grievance Procedure and Disciplinary Proceedings	1.207	26
Conclusion	1.210	26

SECTION 2: THE WAY WE WORKED

	Paragraph	Page
Terms of Appointment	2.1	28
The Team is Formed	2.5	28
Guiding Principles	2.18	30
The Early Days	2.19	32
Preliminary Hearing	2.30	34
Part I	2.33	34
Part II	2.39	35
Conclusion	2.59	38

PART I – THE DISTURBANCES IN DETAIL

SECTION 3: MANCHESTER (STRANGEWAYS) PRISON

	Paragraph	Page
Introduction	3.1	41
The State of the Prison, Its Population and Staff Prior to 1 April 1990		
i) The Physical Setting	3.10	42
ii) Access to the Roofs	3.21	43
iii) Training and Contingency Planning	3.24	44
iv) The Prison Population	3.32	45
v) Staffing	3.45	47
The Atmosphere and Regime Prior to 1 April	3.55	48
i) Food	3.57	48
ii) Kit	3.61	49
iii) Employment	3.62	49

	Paragraph	Page
The Number of Prisoners Allowed to Assemble at the Same Location	3.67	50
Religion	3.68	50
Manchester Visitors' Centre	3.76	51
Inmates' Evidence	3.78	51
Staff Attitudes	3.87	53
Signs of Tension	3.90	53
Warnings of the Disturbance	3.93	54
The Disturbance – Sunday 1 April		
i) Morning Preparations	3.114	57
ii) The Chapel Service on 1 April 1990	3.124	59
iii) Withdrawal of Staff from the Prison	3.139	61
iv) A Wing	3.157	65
v) B Wing	3.159	65
vi) C Wing	3.161	65
vii) D Wing	3.164	66
viii) E Wing	3.165	66
ix) The Remand Prison	3.172	67
x) The Communications Room	3.182	68
xi) The Loss of the Remand Prison	3.185	69
xii) The Prison Hospital and the Injured	3.192	70
xiii) The Release of Mr Proctor	3.200	71
xiv) The Plight of the Prisoners on Rule 43 Still in the Prison	3.201	71
xv) The Evacuation of Prisoners	3.206	72
xvi) Co-ordinating the Evacuation	3.217	73
xvii) The Arrival of Staff From Other Establishments	3.223	74
xviii) The Arrival of the Media	3.224	74
xix) The First Incursion into E Wing	3.226	75
xx) The First Night (1/2 April 1990)	3.230	75
The Disturbance – Monday 2 April 1990		
i) Retaking the Remand Prison	3.233	76
ii) The Discussions on Whether to Prepare a Plan to Retake the Main Prison	3.234	76
iii) The Plan to Retake the Main Prison	3.236	76
iv) The Decision Not to Attempt to Retake the Main Prison	3.250	78
v) The Attack on the Kitchen	3.273	83
The Siege		
i) From the Afternoon of Monday 2 April to Saturday 7 April	3.278	83
ii) From Sunday 8 April to Easter Monday 16 April	3.304	86
iii) Tuesday 17 April to Tuesday 24 April	3.318	88
The Forceful Intervention on Wednesday 25 April	3.330	90
Surrender Arrangements	3.339	91
Staff and Families	3.342	92
Inmates' Families	3.346	92
The Media	3.349	93
The Board of Visitors	3.375	96
The Greater Manchester Probation Service	3.380	97
The Greater Manchester Police Service	3.387	98
The Greater Manchester Fire Service	3.401	100
The Greater Manchester Ambulance and Hospital Services	3.416	102
Conclusions Specific to the Manchester Disturbance	3.432	104

SECTION 4: GLEN PARVA YOUNG OFFENDER INSTITUTION AND REMAND CENTRE

Introduction	4.1	113
The Institution	4.5	113
The Population and its Accommodation	4.8	114
Industrial Relations	4.14	114
The Regime	4.15	114
Kit	4.29	116
Food	4.31	117
Problems for Inmates	4.35	117
Drugs and Treatment Rooms	4.39	118
Contingency Planning	4.41	118
Background to the Disturbance	4.47	119
Warnings of the Disturbance	4.52	120
The Disturbance	4.57	120
The Role of Midland Regional Office and Headquarters	4.99	125
The Involvement of the Emergency Service	4.103	126
The Media	4.106	126
The Consequences of the Disturbance	4.109	126
Conclusions Specific to the Glen Parva Disturbance	4.115	127

SECTION 5: DARTMOOR PRISON

Introduction	5.1	130
The Prison	5.2	130
The Prison Population	5.13	131
Dartmoor's Reputation	5.17	132
The Regime	5.28	134
Industrial Relations	5.33	134
The Local Agreement	5.50	137
Warnings of the Disturbance	5.54	137
The Disturbance	5.69	139
The Situation Within C and D Wings	5.80	140
The Progress of the Disturbance	5.82	141
The Disturbance in the Old Chapel	5.88	141
The Decision Not to Intervene	5.93	142
The Fire on D4 Landing and the Role of the Fire Service	5.97	142
The Night of 7/8 April	5.105	144
Sunday 8 April	5.108	144
The Inmate Who Died	5.134	147
The Roof Protest Until 14 April	5.138	148
The A Wing Incident	5.146	149
The Role of Headquarters and South West Regional Office	5.151	149
Inmates' Comments on the Disturbances	5.154	150
The Prison Officers' Association Points on the Disturbance	5.163	151
The Board of Visitors	5.168	151
The Involvement of the Fire Service	5.184	153
The Involvement of the Ambulance and Medical Services	5.189	154
The Involvement of the Devon and Cornwall Constabulary	5.195	155
The Consequences of the Disturbance	5.197	156
Conclusions Specific to the Dartmoor Disturbance	5.199	156

SECTION 6: CARDIFF PRISON

	Paragraph	Page
Introduction	6.1	161
The Prison	6.2	161
The Regime and Staffing	6.6	161
The Remand Regime	6.15	163
Kit	6.17	163
Food	6.18	163
Prisoners' Letters	6.19	163
Contingency Planning	6.20	164
Background to the Disturbance	6.22	164
Warnings of the Disturbance	6.25	164
The Disturbance	6.37	166
Extinguishing Fires	6.52	168
The Surrender	6.57	169
The Role of Headquarters and the South West Regional Office	6.62	169
Command of the Incident	6.65	170
The Involvement of the South Wales Police	6.67	170
The Involvement of the Ambulance Services	6.70	170
Inmates' Evidence	6.71	170
The Consequences of the Disturbance	6.74	171
Conclusions Specific to the Cardiff Disturbance	6.78	171

SECTION 7: BRISTOL PRISON

	Paragraph	Page
Introduction	7.1	175
The Prison	7.3	175
The Prison Population	7.8	175
The Atmosphere Within the Prison	7.12	176
Warnings of the Disturbance	7.15	176
The State of the Prison Prior to 8 April	7.20	177
Contingency Planning	7.42	179
The Dartmoor Prisoners	7.48	180
Sunday 8 April: the Morning and Afternoon	7.54	181
The Evening and Start of the Disturbance	7.64	182
The Progress of the Disturbance	7.83	184
The Rescue of Prison Officer Santley	7.90	185
The Evacuation of B and C Wings	7.104	187
Attacks by Inmates	7.115	188
Surrender Arrangements	7.117	188
The Role of Headquarters and the South West Regional Office	7.118	188
Mr Wall's Role	7.123	189
The Retaking of the Prison	7.130	190
The Surrender	7.132	190
The Board of Visitors	7.144	192
The Consequences of the Disturbance	7.148	192
Conclusions Specific to the Bristol Disturbance	7.158	193

SECTION 8: PUCKLECHURCH REMAND CENTRE

	Paragraph	Page
Introduction	8.1	197
The Centre	8.3	197
The Regime	8.9	198
The Management at Pucklechurch	8.27	200
The Effect of the Bristol Disturbance	8.33	201
Warnings of a Disturbance	8.35	201
Staff on Duty over the Weekend 21/22 April 1990	8.37	201

		Paragraph	Page

The Disturbance

i)	The Attack on Prison Officer Leary	8.47	202
ii)	The Sounding of the Alarm	8.55	203
iii)	The Association Room	8.58	203
iv)	Mr Woolford Takes Charge	8.60	204
v)	The Evacuation and Spread of the Incident	8.64	204
vi)	The Arrival of Reinforcements	8.71	205
vii)	Preparation to Try and Retake the Male Block	8.78	206
viii)	The First Intervention	8.88	207
ix)	The Lull Before the Second Intervention	8.93	207
x)	The Second Intervention	8.97	208
xi)	The Kitchen/Dining Room Incident	8.103	209
xii)	The Surrender	8.121	211
xiii)	The Board of Visitors	8.124	211
xiv)	The Treatment of Inmates in the Female Block and Hospital	8.137	212

The Regional Director's Surrender Plans	8.171	216
The Governor's Recommendations for the Future	8.174	216
Media	8.176	217
The Consequences of the Disturbance	8.177	217
Conclusions Specific to the Pucklechurch Disturbance	8.188	218

SECTION 9: LESSONS FROM PART I

Introduction	9.1	224
The Importance of Security, Control and Justice to a Stable Prison System	9.19	225
The Disturbances Demonstrate a Need to Pay More Attention to Justice Within Prisons	9.24	226
The Disturbances Demonstrate the Importance of Maintaining Security and Control	9.38	228
A Control Categorisation for Prisoners is Not Practicable	9.43	228
Security Information Reports Must Be Completed and Properly Submitted to Governors	9.51	229
The Disastrous Effect of the Loss of an Officer's Keys Must be Reduced	9.56	230
Staff Must Initially Be Expected to Withdraw From the Immediate Scene of a Serious Disturbance	9.58	230
There Should be Security Firebreaks to Which Staff Can Withdraw and Which Staff Can Hold	9.61	231
Physical Security Should be Checked and, Where Necessary, Upgraded	9.67	231
There Must be Improved Methods of Communication	9.77	232
There Must be Better Contingency Planning and Training	9.81	233
Boards of Visitors Should Have a Central Role	9.85	233
The Prison Service Should Have the Capacity to Deploy Water During a Disturbance	9.87	234
Control and Restraint Techniques Will Need to Continue to be Reinforced and Cooperation With the Police Maintained	9.88	234
Conclusion	9.98	235

PART II: – THE PREVENTION OF DISTURBANCES

SECTION 10: IMPRISONMENT

Introduction		10.1	239
Identifying the Task of the Prison Service			
i)	The Convicted Prisoner	10.4	239
ii)	Remand and Unsentenced Prisoners	10.45	245
The Prison Rules		10.65	248
Limiting the Role of the Prison Service		10.67	248
Diversion from Prison			
i)	The Remand Prisoner	10.75	249
	a) The Courts	10.80	250
	b) Bail Information Schemes	10.88	251
	c) Prison Bail Schemes	10.92	251
	d) Bail Hostels	10.96	252
	e) Special Hostels	10.97	252
	f) Secure Hostels	10.99	252
ii)	Offenders		
	a) Hostels for Offenders	10.102	253
	b) Public Interest Case Assessment	10.104	253
	c) Young Offenders	10.107	253
	d) Fine Defaulters	10.108	254
	e) Money Payment Supervision Orders	10.114	254
	f) The Mentally Disordered Offender	10.115	255
iii)	Conclusion	10.139	258
Providing the Sentencing Court with More Information		10.141	258
A Forum for Consultation Within the Criminal Justice System		10.157	260
The Local Committees		10.181	263

SECTION 11: BUILDINGS

Introduction		11.1	265
The Broad Principles and How to Give Effect to Them		11.7	266
i)	The Size of Accommodation Units and of Prisons	11.7	266
ii)	Separate Units in Relation to Security	11.24	268
iii)	Locking Systems and Keys	11.34	269
iv)	Community Prisons	11.49	271
v)	Visits	11.69	273
vi)	Accommodating Remand Prisoners	11.72	274
vii)	Shared Accommodation	11.81	275
viii)	Access to Sanitation	11.97	276
ix)	Hygiene	11.113	278
x)	Accommodation for Board of Visitors	11.122	279
xi)	Conclusion	11.124	280
The Relationship between the Prison Service and Professional Consultants		11.126	280
Overcrowding		11.133	281

SECTION 12: MANAGEMENT

Introduction	12.1	285
Senior Management Reorganisation	12.8	286
The Director General	12.26	288
The Relationship Between Ministers and the Prison Service	12.35	290
The Prisons Board	12.61	293

	Paragraph	Page
Relations Between Headquarters and Establishments	12.66	294
The Prison Service's Planning Document	12.80	296
The Area Manager's "Contract" With Establishments	12.88	297
A Code of Standards	12.98	298
The Prisoner's "Contract"	12.120	301
Prison Staff's "Contract"	12.130	303
Medical Services	12.131	303
Race Relations	12.135	304
The Management of Intervention During Serious Incidents	12.143	305
Escort Duties	12.158	307
Board of Visitors	12.169	308
Prison Visitors	12.182	310
The Management of Sex Offenders	12.185	311
The Management of Disruptive Offenders	12.221	316
i) Current Options		
a) A Transfer Under Circular Instruction 37/90	12.240	318
b) Transfer from a Category C Prison to the Local Prison	12.261	321
c) Segregation Under Rule 43 of the the Prison Rules (Rule 46 of Young Offender Institution Regulations)	12.264	321
d) Allocation to a Special Unit for the Control of the Disruptive Prisoner	12.272	322
e) Conclusion	12.292	325
ii) The Use of New Generation Prisons	12.297	325
The Management of the Remand Population	12.306	326
The Management of Young Offenders and Young Remands	12.325	329
The Management of Drug Abusers	12.339	331
The Management of HIV/AIDS	12.354	333
Conclusion	12.374	335

SECTION 13: STAFF

	Paragraph	Page
Introduction	13.1	337
The "Fresh Start" Package	13.12	338
i) The Nature of the "Fresh Start" Package, Why It Was Necessary and Its Objectives	13.17	339
a) The New Working Arrangements and Management Structures	13.26	340
b) Unification of the Governor and Officer Grades	13.28	340
c) The Abolition of Overtime to be Compensated for by Increased Pay	13.30	340
ii) The Scope for Efficiency Savings	13.39	342
iii) How "Fresh Start" Was Implemented	13.50	343
iv) Regime Effects	13.71	346
v) Effects on Non-unified Staff	13.74	347
vi) Evidence from the Prison Governors' Association	13.76	347
vii) Conclusion	13.79	347
A Framework for Determining Appropriate Staffing Levels	13.84	348
Staffing Levels at Weekends	13.94	349
Training and Education to Enhance the Role of Prison Officers	13.107	351
The Conditions Within Prison Establishments	13.148	356
The General Recruitment of Staff	13.151	356

	Paragraph	Page
The Accelerated Promotion Scheme	13.169	358
The Prison Officer Development Scheme	13.178	360
The Chief Officer	13.185	360
Uniforms	13.188	361
"Contracts" Between Staff and Management	13.199	362
Non-Unified Staff	13.207	363
Cross Postings	13.223	365
Industrial Relations	13.227	366
Conclusion	13.255	369

SECTION 14: PRISONERS

	Paragraph	Page
Introduction	14.1	371
Incentives and Disincentives	14.23	374
Induction, Discharge and Sentence Planning	14.57	378
Education	14.84	382
Physical Education	14.111	385
Work	14.117	386
Pay and Private Cash	14.149	391
Kit	14.177	395
Food	14.198	397
Family Ties	14.220	400
Visits	14.225	401
Home Leave	14.236	403
Family Visits	14.246	404
Telephones	14.251	405
Censorship of Correspondence	14.263	407
Communication with Prisoners	14.275	409
Remedies	14.289	411
Reasons for Decisions	14.300	412
Grievance Procedures	14.309	414
i) The History	14.311	414
ii) The New System	14.320	415
iii) Our Proposals	14.326	416
a) Confidential Access	14.330	417
b) Access to the Governing Governor	14.336	418
c) Board of Visitors	14.339	418
d) A Complaints Adjudicator: An Independent Element	14.342	418
e) The Complaints Adjudicator's Role in Relation to Grievance Procedures	14.355	420
Disciplinary Procedures		
i) The History	14.363	421
ii) The Present Situation	14.374	422
iii) Our Proposals	14.398	426
Conclusion	14.436	431

		Page
SECTION 15: RECOMMENDATIONS AND PROPOSALS		433
SIGNATORIES		455

ANNEXES

SECTION 2: THE WAY WE WORKED

		Page
Annex 2A: Letter to target establishment staff		459
Annex 2B: Letter to target establishment inmates		463
Annex 2C: Letter to non-target staff		467
Annex 2D: Letter to non-target inmates		469
Annex 2E: Letters from prison: A summary of letters from prisoners and staff		472

Annex 2F: Statement from preliminary hearing and
     guide to Part I issues   513
Annex 2G: List of those giving oral evidence at the
     public hearings   521
Annex 2H: Statement about the Part II seminars   524
Annex 2I: List of those submitting written evidence   526
     to the Inquiry
Annex 2J: Discussion Guide – Seminar A   530
Annex 2K: Discussion Guide – Seminar B   533
Annex 2L: Discussion Guide – Seminar C   536
Annex 2M: Discussion Guide – Seminar D   538
Annex 2N: Discussion Guide – Seminar E   541
Annex 2O: List of those who participated at the
     public seminars   544
Annex 2P: Discussion Guide – Lincoln Seminar   548
Annex 2Q: List of those who had meetings with
     the Inquiry   550
Annex 2R: List of visits made by the Inquiry   553

SECTION 3: MANCHESTER PRISON

Annex 3A: Plan of Manchester Prison
     at 1 April 1990   555
Annex 3B: Photographs of the roof spaces   556
Annex 3C: North Region Document on Major
     Incidents   558
Annex 3D: Chronology of Operational Events in
     April 1990   563
Annex 3E: Plan of the redevelopment of
     Manchester   573

SECTION 4: GLEN PARVA YOUNG OFFENDER INSTITUTION AND REMAND CENTRE

Annex 4A: Plan of Glen Parva YOI & RC   574

SECTION 5: DARTMOOR PRISON

Annex 5A: Plan of Dartmoor Prison   575
Annex 5B: Illustration of prisoners' access to
     D Wing Roof   576
Annex 5C: Board of Visitors Major Incident
     Procedure   577

SECTION 6: CARDIFF PRISON

Annex 6A: Plan of Cardiff Prison   581

SECTION 7: BRISTOL PRISON

Annex 7A: Plan of Bristol Prison   582
Annex 7B: Photographs of damage   583

SECTION 8: PUCKLECHURCH REMAND CENTRE

Annex 8A: Plan of Pucklechurch RC   588
Annex 8B: Procedure for Dealing With the
     Surrender of Prisoners After a Major Incident   589

SECTION 13: STAFF

Annex 13A: List of industrial disputes from
1 January to 30 October 1990 592
Glossary 595

Section 1

Overview

Introduction

1.1   The first 25 days of April 1990 saw the worst series of prison riots in the history of the British penal system. The Home Secretary set up an Inquiry. This is the Report of that Inquiry. The Report attempts to provide the answers to four questions connected with those riots. They are:

    i)   what happened during the six most serious riots?

    ii)   were those six riots properly handled?

    iii)   what were the causes of those riots?

    iv)   what should be done to prevent riots of this type happening again?

1.2   The Inquiry was conducted in two parts. Part I concentrated primarily on questions one and two. It examined the six most serious riots. They were at Manchester (Strangeways), Glen Parva, Dartmoor, Cardiff, Bristol and Pucklechurch. Part II of the Inquiry dealt with the answers to questions three and four. This Report is also divided into Part I and Part II in order to reflect the way in which the Inquiry was conducted.

1.3   There are two more questions which I should mention. They are:

    i)   why did the riots not happen earlier?

    ii)   why were the consequences of those riots not even more serious?

1.4   The answer to these two questions is clear. It is that the members of the Prison Service as a whole, against heavy odds, have managed over a number of years to contain an almost impossible situation by showing immense dedication, courage and professionalism.

1.5   I wanted to draw attention to the answer to those two questions at the outset of this Report because the Report contains a number of critical comments about the Prison Service. It is important that those comments do not obscure or detract from the fact that the public have every reason to be extremely grateful to the members of the Prison Service. They have coped, usually successfully, with what could have been very many explosive situations. Despite all the stresses to which the members of the Prison Service have been subjected, the vast majority have remained steadfastly loyal to the Prison Service and have continued to show a remarkable degree of professionalism.

1.6   Ironically, when the riots struck in April 1990, the Prison Service had already started to tackle some of the worst features of the prison system which had been in existence for many years. Long term problems were, for the first time, being confronted. However, as often happens at times of change, the improvements which were being introduced brought with them periods of increased instability which made the prison system particularly vulnerable to disturbances. The riots interrupted that process of improvement.

1.7   During the period in which this Inquiry was being conducted, the Prison Service resumed its programme of change. It is a programme designed to improve the prison system. The Prison Service is, however, well aware that there still remain a great many problems which need to be addressed. In providing answers to the foregoing four questions, the Inquiry's aim has been to assist the Prison Service to continue its programme for the reform of the prison system.

1.8   To help achieve this objective, the Report will erect a series of signposts identifying the route which the Inquiry believes the Prison Service should follow. The journey will take some time. There is a great deal of ground to be made up because of neglect in the past. However, if the members of the Prison Service have the confidence in themselves which I believe they should have, and if they receive the support that they deserve, then this country will have a prison system of which it can be proud. This would be a very different situation from that which exists at present.

1.9   The Inquiry has received an extraordinary volume of evidence. In addition to the 170 witnesses who gave evidence orally at the formal hearings, the Inquiry has had numerous meetings with staff and prisoners, individuals and organisations, both in this country and abroad. To the 1,730 letters from prisoners and prison staff which the Inquiry has received, there needs to be added the numerous letters from former members of the staff, ex-prisoners, the public and organisations. The Inquiry received written expert evidence in abundance from organisations and individuals. The quality of the evidence naturally differed, but it was all of value. Some items of evidence were of value because they gave an insight into some small aspect of the conditions in a particular prison. Others were of value because they helped to create the global picture of the working of the prison system which the Inquiry needed in order to answer the four questions to which I have referred.

1.10   Part I of the Report examines what happened during the six riots. The Inquiry has had to consider both the detail and the general effect of this evidence. The detail has enabled the Inquiry to draw attention to events which occurred during each riot which call in some cases for commendation and in other cases for criticism. The evidence as a whole has enabled the Inquiry to identify underlying problems which exist throughout the Prison Service and which, if they are to be tackled, require action to be taken which relates not only to individual prisons but to the whole of the prison system.

1.11   It will be noted that I make no reference to the names of prisoners. This is to avoid prejudicing them in the event of a prosecution or their being still in prison. It would be most unfortunate if their identities should be disclosed by the media. I appreciate that it may be possible for those who already know the identities of the prisoners to whom I refer to make the connection. However, if this is the case, I urge them not to publish the names which I have omitted.

1.12   The Inquiry deals with the underlying problems and the remedies which they require in Part II of this Report. Part II is in five sections. The five sections are headed: Imprisonment, Buildings, Management, Staff and Prisoners. Each Section concentrates on more than one of the underlying problems and sets out recommendations or proposals for remedying them. The scale of the problems and the full significance of each recommendation or proposal can only be appreciated, however, if they are considered collectively. A number of the recommendations and proposals are dependent upon the implementation of others. In other words, the picture must be looked at as a whole. For this purpose, it is essential to have an overview of the whole Report. It is that overview which this Section of the Report seeks to provide.

1.13   The overview is divided into three parts. The first part is a thumbnail sketch of each of the six disturbances. This should provide a backcloth of what happened during the disturbances against which the remainder of the overview can be considered.

1.14   The second part of this Section draws attention to the central problems of the Prison Service. These problems explain the instability which results in the prison system being disrupted by disturbances, of which the April 1990 riots are so far the most serious.

1.15   The third part of this Section identifies the principal changes which are needed if the Prison Service is to be able to tackle its underlying problems. Twelve recommendations are made. But no reference is made here to the proposals which are set out in the succeeding sections of this Report. They are summarised with the recommendations in Section 15. The distinction which the Inquiry has drawn between its recommendations and its proposals is that, while both are important, the recommendations identify the major changes which the Inquiry would like to see made. The proposals identify the detailed improvements which the Inquiry regards as necessary. The recommendations are the signposts to which I referred earlier. The proposals are the steps which, over a period of time, the Prison Service should take in order to follow those signposts.

An Outline of What Happened at Six Disturbances

Manchester (Strangeways)   1.16   This was the initial and most serious by far of the six disturbances. It started on 1 April and continued to 25 April 1990. The disturbance could have been avoided. When it occurred it should not have been allowed to engulf the whole prison. The disturbance should have been brought to an end earlier.

1.17   The rioters involved gutted the interior of the prison. Injuries were caused to 147 members of staff and 47 prisoners (including those affected by smoke or fumes). One prisoner received injuries which may have contributed to his death. Another young prisoner who was involved was later to take his own life. It is estimated that the damage caused to the buildings will cost £60m to repair (though a substantial part of this cost would have been incurred in any event, if the refurbishment which was very necessary had been carried out).

1.18   Largely as a consequence of the destruction which took place within the prison, police cells had to be used during the remainder of 1990 to house prisoners. The cost was over £20m. Strangeways acted as a beacon which provided the signal for unrest and disturbances across many parts of the prison system.

1.19   Strangeways was the largest prison in England and Wales and one of the largest prisons in Europe. It was a local prison. It was designed to cater primarily for prisoners remanded or sentenced by Courts in the Manchester area. When it was built in 1868, it was a fine Victorian building. It was of radial design with a central rotunda from which emanated six wings. They were A, B, C, D, and E Wings, which contained the cells, and F Wing, which contained administration offices and the Church of England Chapel (a plan is at Annex 3A).

1.20   At a later date, another block had been added. This was the remand prison. This was in a cruciform shape with four wings, G, H, I and K, containing cells. There were two internal routes from the main prison to the remand prison. In addition, there was a further area known as the Croft. This was built across the road from the main prison. A high level bridge connected the two areas.

1.21   The prison was overcrowded. The certified normal accommodation (CNA) for the whole of Strangeways was 970. The total population on 1 April 1990 was 1,647. In the past, the prison population had been even larger. In March 1988, the prison population had reached 1,803. The population included in April 1990 adult and young prisoners who were convicted and serving their sentences. In addition, it included adult and young prisoners on remand. There were 97 adults and young prisoners who, for their own protection, were not allowed to associate with other prisoners. They were held under the provisions of Prison Rule 43. There were ten prisoners who were segregated on Rule 43 in the interest of the good order and discipline of the prison. Of the sentenced 15 were category A prisoners, 105 were category B prisoners, 500 were category C prisoners and 64 were category D prisoners.

1.22 Improvements had been made to the living conditions at the prison during the previous three years. However, on 1 April 1990, the physical conditions, in addition to being grossly overcrowded, were still insanitary and degrading. Despite the efforts of the staff, prisoners were spending far too long in their cells. There were frequent problems about shortage of kit. Sometimes, for example, prisoners had to go without socks or wear ill-fitting second-hand shoes. When prisoners had their one weekly shower, it was often impossible even to provide them with clean towels.

1.23 There was at least one area, however, where the prison was flourishing. This was in relation to its religious activities. The Reverend Noel Proctor, the senior Church of England Chaplain, could claim a substantial part of the credit for this. The services at the Church of England Chapel on a Sunday were regularly attended by between 300 and 400 prisoners. By any standards, this was an exceptionally large congregation to have in a prison.

1.24 There was an abundance of warnings that there could be trouble in the prison Chapel during the Church of England Service on the morning of Sunday 1 April 1990. The warnings had to be judged against a background of a tense prison in which warnings of this sort were not unusual. Their collective message, however, was clear. Trouble in the Chapel that Sunday morning was planned.

1.25 There was a breakdown in communications between staff and governors. The full significance of the warnings was not appreciated by those in charge of the prison. While some precautions were taken, those precautions were not on the scale they would or should have been if the full significance of the warnings had been appreciated. The prisoners who were on Rule 43 for their own protection did not attend the service. 309 prisoners, however, did attend.

1.26 The service started at 10.00 on 1 April. Mr Proctor conducted it in conjunction with a Church Army Captain. Initially, he was able to control the service. But part-way through, a prisoner took hold of the microphone and began to address the congregation. Shortly afterwards, pandemonium broke out. Notwithstanding the extremely courageous action of Mr Proctor, the situation quickly became completely out of control. The prison officers who were present had to withdraw.

1.27 Seven prison officers had been placed in the vestry during the service as a precaution. These officers tried to intervene after the situation became out of control. They were not successful. One prison officer had his keys taken by a prisoner. That officer and Mr Proctor were only able to leave the Chapel by the door into the vestry as a result of the assistance of some of the prisoners. Prison officers were, however, able to escort the young inmates from the Chapel. In all the circumstances, the officers who were present initially acquitted themselves satisfactorily.

1.28 The majority of the officers vacated the Chapel from one of the two doors at the back of the Chapel. While doing so, a second prison officer lost his keys. The rear Chapel doors gave access to the Centre of the prison. The officers did not remain on the landing outside the Chapel doors. They withdrew. Prisoners at the beginning did not try to leave through those doors. They barricaded themselves in the Chapel.

1.29 Some prisoners made their way into the roof area. They got through an unprotected gap which had been left in the roof protection in the eaves of the Chapel roof at the groin between the Chapel and the Centre. By using this route, prisoners were able to obtain access to the top of the wire grid. This was fixed above the landings to protect the roof. They also proceeded initially into A Wing and then to the other wings of the main prison. Access to the wings was obtained by making a hole in the ceiling of an office on the top floor of A Wing which, like similar offices on other wings, was not fully protected. Once on the wings, prisoners were able to release all the other prisoners by using the keys which had been taken from officers.

1.30   The disturbance had started at about 11.00. By 11.13, the Governor who was in charge of the main prison decided that all staff should vacate the Centre of the main prison. There were then probably about 20 to 30 officers present in the Centre. At the time this decision was taken, the Centre was under no immediate threat. There had been no hostile action by any prisoner towards the prison officers on the Centre. But there was a "tidal wave" of noise. The Centre was vacated prematurely.

1.31   The adult Rule 43 prisoners held for their own protection were on C wing. 71 were on C1 landing (the ground floor). About seven were on C2 landing. With commendable courage, officers on C Wing were able to evacuate the Rule 43 prisoners who were on the C1 landing. They were not able to evacuate those on C2.

1.32   There were also Rule 43 prisoners held for their own protection on E4 landing. Those prisoners were left in their cells. No orders were given for the evacuation of those prisoners. More action could have been taken to protect the Rule 43 prisoners in E Wing.

1.33   The whole of the main prison was evacuated by staff shortly after 11.15. A substantial number of prisoners who had not yet been released by other prisoners, were left in their cells.

1.34   At about 12.20, prisoners who were on the loose in the main prison broke through one of the doors leading into the separate remand prison. The staff in the remand prison then vacated that prison. Only delaying tactics had been taken to prevent the loss of the remand prison. It should have been made secure and held.

1.35   Shortly before the loss of the remand prison (at about 11.55) the governing Governor, Mr O'Friel, who had been off duty, arrived at the prison and took charge. By that time the situation within the prison was chaotic. Mr O'Friel introduced a sense of order and purpose among the staff. The police and other emergency services were promptly on the scene and they took appropriate action.

1.36   Nothing could by then be done for the Rule 43 prisoners who had been left in the prison. They were subject to appalling treatment by other inmates.

1.37   It was extremely difficult to evacuate those prisoners who did not wish to be involved in the disturbance. Some prisoners had climbed onto the roofs. From that advantage point they threw slates, scaffold poles and bricks into the area inside the perimeter of the prison.

1.38   C&R (Control and Restraint) equipment was delivered to the prison (shields, helmets and other protective wear for prison officers). Prisoners were then evacuated from the main prison in large numbers. They were protected by officers forming a cordon of overhead shields under which the prisoners could pass, safe from the missiles hurled from above. Some prisoners helped other prisoners. Without such help some prisoners would not have been able to escape from the violence and destruction which was then taking place within the prison. Keys were even given to a category A prisoner by staff on his promise, which he kept, to return those keys after he had released other prisoners.

1.39   During the initial period of the disturbance, the Regional Office gave all the support they could. They helped with the arrangements for the transfer from Manchester of the prisoners who had surrendered. This transfer was a remarkable achievement. By 07.06 on 2 April 1990 about 1,289 prisoners had been moved out of Manchester. Not one prisoner escaped during this process.

1.40   With the help of reinforcements from other prisons, an exploratory incursion was made into E Wing at 20.00 on 1 April. The wing was taken back by the staff and held for some hours. They did not withdraw until 00.22 the following morning.

1.41   During the night of 1/2 April the Deputy Director General, Mr Emes, had a long discussion with Mr Boon. Mr Boon was the Governor who had relieved Mr O'Friel during that night. Mr Emes was in command at Prison Service Headquarters in London. They discussed the prospects of retaking the main prison. Mr Boon and Mr Emes were pessimistic about the prospects.

1.42   On the morning of 2 April, it was estimated that there were still approximately 142 prisoners loose in the prison. Mr O'Friel came back on duty. At about 09.00 on 2 April there was a discussion between Mr O'Friel and Mr Emes. C&R units subsequently entered the remand prison and retook that prison without opposition.

1.43   Mr O'Friel began to prepare a plan to retake the main prison. He was advised by members of his staff and a national C&R instructor. By 14.00 a plan had been prepared. It involved entering the prison from a number of different positions. The objective was to draw the prisoners on to the low ground by a series of diversionary attacks. It was planned then to trap the prisoners below roof level by making a main thrust through the Chapel on to the Centre at the fourth (top) landing.

1.44   Mr O'Friel was unable to speak to Mr Emes immediately. He was given a message from Mr Emes making it clear that there was to be no attack without Mr Emes' authorisation.

1.45   Just before 15.00, Mr Emes was able to telephone Mr O'Friel and speak to him. Mr Emes had just left a meeting with Ministers and was not in his own office when he made the telephone call. Neither he nor Mr O'Friel was in the ideal setting to make a long and detailed assessment of the intervention plan. They did not do so. Mr Emes decided that the attack should not take place.

1.46   The discussion then turned to an alternative plan which Mr O'Friel had prepared in case the main attack was not authorised. The object of this alternative plan was to destroy or remove food and stores which were in the kitchen. Mr Emes gave his approval to the alternative plan.

1.47   During the telephone conversation, Mr Emes was under the misapprehension that Mr O'Friel agreed with his decision not to proceed with the main attack. Although he failed to make this clear to Mr Emes, Mr O'Friel was strongly in favour of proceeding with the main attack.

1.48   A decision of this importance should not have been taken in this manner. If Mr Emes had appreciated he was taking a different view from Mr O'Friel, it would have been wrong to have overruled Mr O'Friel. The plan should have been allowed to proceed. Mr Emes said that he was strongly influenced in his view by the fact that prison staff would be at a lower level than the inmates on the wire grid and therefore at a disadvantage. He had not told Mr O'Friel of the weight he attached to this. He overestimated its importance. There would have been a reasonable prospect of a large number of inmates being trapped at the lower levels as a result of the initial attack and of all but a small minority of the remaining inmates surrendering very rapidly. There was not an unacceptable risk of injuries to staff. If the intervention was unsuccessful, it could have been stopped and the staff could have withdrawn.

1.49   The alternative plan to enter the kitchen was put into operation and achieved its objective. A diversionary attack on F Wing, which was situated below the Chapel, met with serious resistance from prisoners. They threw missiles down upon the staff from the roof of the Chapel. In the course of the diversionary attack, one member of staff received an injury to his leg.

1.50   Almost 400 staff had been ready to launch the main attack. Only a part of that number was involved in the alternative attack on the kitchen. The cancellation of the main attack proved to be a damaging blow to the morale of the staff.

1.51 There followed a long siege until 25 April 1990. Initially there was a steady flow of surrendering prisoners. By the night of 5 April there were probably not more than 25 prisoners still in the main prison. By Good Friday, 13 April, the number of prisoners in the prison was reduced to ten. The trickle of prisoners who up to that time had been surrendering then ceased.

1.52 On 16 April, however, a prisoner suffering from gastroenteritis was brought out of the prison by two other prisoners. All three were apprehended. After that, no further prisoners were captured or surrendered until 23 April. On 23 April one prisoner was captured, reducing the number still in the main prison to six.

1.53 During the intervening period, there had been a number of exploratory interventions. Despite the small and reducing number of prisoners in the prison, and the attention they were attracting from the media, no attempt was made to retake the prison. There should have been a decision to prepare a plan for a full scale intervention before that decision was made on 23 April. The disturbance should not have been allowed to drag on as long as it did.

1.54 On 22 April, a high level conference was convened to discuss the possibilities of a successful intervention. During that conference, those present were informed of the route from the Chapel to A Wing through the roof. This was the route which had been initially used by the prisoners on 1 April to get through into the wings. This information was regarded as being of the greatest significance. It answered Mr Emes principal objection to intervening on 2 April. It was the means by which prison staff would be able to capture the high ground from the prisoners. The route was well known to senior members of staff at Strangeways (but probably not to Mr O'Friel). But they did not appreciate its importance.

1.55 On 23 April, with the approval of the Home Secretary, instructions were given for the preparation of a plan to retake the prison.

1.56 Just before 09.00 on 25 April, an intervention was made. It involved approximately 100 staff (eight C&R units). The C&R units rapidly regained possession of the prison. One prisoner surrendered at 10.02. The remaining five prisoners made their way on to the roof. The last prisoner was not recaptured until 18.20.

1.57 A thorough investigation was made of the interior of the prison. It was found that, contrary to the fears which had existed at one time, there were no bodies within the prison. The prison was, however, very badly damaged.

1.58 Fortunately the strength of the Victorian structure was such that it is practical to renovate the prison. A plan has been prepared by the Prison Service which will enable this to be done. This plan reflects improvements in the design of the prison which the Inquiry favoured.

1.59 The scale and length of the disturbance was in part due to the way in which it was handled. But the nature of the disturbance was also influenced by the number of prisoners who were prepared to become involved. Those who initiated the disturbance claimed that it was the only way to draw attention to their perceived grievances about the way they had been treated by the Prison Service, and the physical conditions in which they were required to live.

Glen Parva 1.60 Glen Parva is both a Young Offender Remand Centre and a Young Offender Institution (a plan is at Annex 4A). The disturbance began on Friday 6 April 1990 at about 19.20. It was the only one of the six disturbances investigated which did not start on a Saturday or a Sunday. However, the commencement of the disturbance was probably planned for Sunday 8 April. It was probably brought forward because the inmates found out that the management had been forewarned of the trouble expected on the Sunday.

1.61   The disturbance started for different reasons from the other disturbances. It was not a disturbance to bring attention to alleged grievances. It developed from a plan to escape which was foiled.

1.62   The shortcomings at Glen Parva were not as great as those in the other five establishments examined. But the remand inmates, in particular, had some reason for complaint. There was overcrowding. The CNA for the remand inmates was 192. There were 330 remand inmates in Glen Parva on 6 April. The redeeming feature at Glen Parva was the regime which was provided for remand inmates. They could work. There were opportunities for education and for association. There was a full physical education programme. But, with the increased overcrowding of remand inmates, the opportunities available to each inmate became more restricted.

1.63   The inmate who wanted to escape had been transferred from Strangeways following the start of the riot there. His motive, he says, was that his mother was too far away to enable him to have visits. He persuaded the inmate with whom he shared a cell to join him. They were both inmates on remand.

1.64   Shortly before 20.00 on Friday 6 April, a prison officer went to release one of the two inmates for association. He was not in sight or hearing of another officer (as in future such an officer performing this duty should be). The two inmates attacked the officer and obtained his keys. Fortunately, another inmate intervened. He attacked the officer's assailants and successfully freed him. The officer radioed for assistance. When the alarm was sounded, other officers came to the unit in time to prevent the escape. By then, the keys had been used to let other inmates out of their cells.

1.65   It is not clear precisely how many inmates were involved in the ensuing disturbance, but it was probably up to about 60. These inmates took part in the disturbance probably, in part, because they were influenced by what was happening at Strangeways. In part it was because of the reduction in the quality of their regime in recent months because of the increase in overcrowding. The disturbance was probably also fuelled by the inmates being carried away for a time by the excitement of finding themselves unexpectedly on the loose in the unit.

1.66   Some staff assembled rapidly in C&R equipment. They were prevented from proceeding beyond the first floor landing by barricades and because the inmates were spraying them from hoses. The lower barricades were dismantled. By 21.15 the disturbance was isolated on the third landing. There were about 50 to 60 inmates behind further barricades. The tactics were to negotiate with those inmates. At 00.16 the inmates who were on the third landing started to surrender. All had done so by 02.46.

1.67   As a result of the disturbance, five officers were injured. None required treatment, apart from the officer whose keys had been taken at the beginning of the incident. One inmate was also injured.

1.68   Minor damage was caused to two other accommodation units by inmates who were supporting those who were involved in the main disturbance. All the damage was repaired by early May 1990, at a total estimated cost of about £32,000.

1.69   This disturbance was well handled. It was brought to an end within a reasonable period of time. The uniformed staff and the governors acted as a team to achieve this result, with appropriate support from the Regional Office.

Dartmoor   1.70   The disturbance at Dartmoor began on Saturday 7 April 1990. Dartmoor was the main Category B training prison for the whole of the South West Region. It was used to accommodate long term prisoners, including prisoners serving life sentences. It also had a vulnerable prisoners unit (VPU). On 7 April, Dartmoor held 601 prisoners, including those in the VPU.

1.71   The prison was built originally in about 1809 in an elevated and isolated position. It has seven wings, A to G (the plan is at Annex 5A). Five of the wings are on either four or five levels. E and F Wings are on only two levels. There are 650 cells. They have no integral sanitation, except for 12 cells in B Wing. But that wing had been empty for some time.

1.72   Dartmoor has an awesome reputation. Its buildings are affected by damp. It has a long tradition of bad relations between officers and management. The staff are regarded by prisoners as being illiberal, the regime as being rigid.

1.73   In 1960, the Government decided that Dartmoor should be closed. That decision was never acted upon, despite the fact that the May Committee in 1979 recommended its closure.

1.74   In their evidence, both staff and inmates referred to Dartmoor as being the dustbin of the system. It was said, disparagingly, to receive the prison system's "rubbish", including an unduly large number of young, badly behaved prisoners. At the time of the disturbance, a substantial proportion of the prisoner population was disgruntled.

1.75   There was, however, no overcrowding at Dartmoor. Each prisoner occupied his own cell. The amount of employment and, more recently, education available had been increased considerably. During the working day, work or education classes were available for 95% of the prisoners.

1.76   The state of relations between governor grades and uniformed staff was bad. For five years, the prison had had an energetic governor of high calibre in Mr May. But he had been subject to a number of votes of no confidence by uniformed staff.

1.77   During the week prior to 7 April, there had been an abundance of security information reporting that a disturbance could be expected during the weekend of 7/8 April. The information was not, however, consistent as to when and where trouble could be expected. Precautions were taken by segregating certain inmates. The Governor considered bringing in extra staff for the weekend. He decided not to do so. He was influenced by the fact that under "Fresh Start" working arrangements, extra hours performed by the staff would have had to have been repaid over subsequent weekends. This was an appropriate decision for the Governor to reach.

1.78   Saturday 7 April 1990 was Grand National day. On D Wing the prisoners were allowed to watch the race. After the race was over, the prisoners started to return to their cells quite normally. But then one prisoner threw a dustbin down towards the landing below. This was followed by dustbins, cell furniture and other equipment. The staff withdrew from the landing into the adjoining wing, which was C Wing. They were accompanied by about 40 prisoners.

1.79   Very shortly after the incident started, prisoners were seen wearing hoods and masks. It appears these must have been prepared in advance. The prisoners were able to break through the protection which was intended to prevent access to the roof. At 17.50, the first prisoners were seen on the roof. Once on the roof, substantial quantities of ammunition, in the form of slates, coping stones and debris, were available. This was used to bombard anyone who ventured into the vicinity of the wing. It was also used to cause damage to adjoining wings.

1.80   Mr May was present at the prison at the time the disturbance started. He decided that he should evacuate the prisoners from C Wing. He was concerned that there could be a fire in D Wing which might spread into C Wing.

1.81   The prisoners who were evacuated from C Wing were relocated in the Old Chapel. It was intended then to rehouse them in A Wing. But some prisoners were unwilling to go there. Authority was given by the South West Regional Office instead to transfer 40 prisoners to Bristol Prison and 40 to Gloucester Prison.

1.82   Trouble broke out in the Old Chapel. This was because the prisoners who were to be transferred to the other prisons were told they could not take their belongings with them. The prisoners damaged the Chapel and some broke out through an unsecured window. C&R units captured them. This part of the disturbance was brought to an end when three principal officers decided to take the initiative and started allowing prisoners to collect their personal effects from C Wing.

1.83   At about 20.40 some prisoners from C Wing were transferred to Bristol and Gloucester Prisons. Those who were transferred to Bristol were to play a part in the disturbance which took place at that prison.

1.84   Shortly after the disturbance began, C&R units began to arrive from other prisons within the South West Region. With the assistance of C&R instructors, a plan was devised for making a forceful re-entry to D Wing. The earliest time at which an intervention could be made was 02.00 on 8 April. Having considered the plan, Mr May came to the conclusion that there should not be an intervention during that night (of 7/8 April). This was a reasonable conclusion for Mr May to reach.

1.85   During that night, there were a number of fires. One was on D Wing on the fours landing. The fire was in the area of a cell in which a prisoner was subsequently found to have died as a result of a fire. He had probably been responsible for lighting the fire himself. Two fire appliances accompanied by a prison officer started to make their way towards the fire, but withdrew, partly because of the difficulty of manoeuvring and partly because someone shouted that the fire was only someone brewing up his tea.

1.86   Negotiations were held during the night. The following morning, Mr May held a meeting at about 06.00. Having considered a report from the negotiating team, Mr May decided not to intervene, but to continue with negotiations.

1.87   The prisoners re-appeared on the roof of D Wing at about 07.40. They moved from D Wing onto C Wing roof and started to drop burning material into C Wing through the roof. The deployment of water could have prevented prisoners moving across the roof. Three C&R units, however, deterred the inmates from actually entering C Wing.

1.88   Some prisoners made clear to staff in C Wing that they wanted to surrender. Other prisoners deterred them from doing so. They were throwing tiles and other objects into C Wing to such an extent that, just after 14.30 on 8 April, C&R units had to be sent in to C Wing again, as a show of force.

1.89   The arrival of the C&R teams in C Wing caused a change of mood on the part of the prisoners who where next door in D Wing. After prisoners had been given an assurance that they would be safe, prisoners removed the barricades which had been erected at the entrance to D2 landing. They then started to surrender. To begin with they surrendered in a trickle, but later this became a flood. Staff then entered the wing. It was cleared of prisoners, apart from one prisoner who remained on the roof. By 18.00, apart from that one inmate, the incident was over.

1.90   The prisoner who remained on the roof caused some disruption within the prison, but the decision was taken not to risk injury to him or to staff by trying to recapture him. He eventually surrendered on 14 April 1990. This prisoner was particularly disgruntled to have been transferred to Dartmoor. He had recently been transferred from Long Lartin to Cardiff under an arrangement known by the circular instruction which introduced it (10/74). He wanted to go to a prison in the North.

1.91   On 11 April, while that inmate was still on the roof, three inmates from A Wing managed to climb onto the roof of that wing. They used the same method as had been used in D Wing during the major disturbance. On this occasion, however, no other inmate was prepared to join them. The whole incident lasted only about two and a half hours.

1.92   Considerable damage was done to D Wing during the main disturbance. A number of prisoners were clearly intent on causing as much damage as possible. The cost of repairing the 139 cells which were damaged would have been approximately £3.5m. The work would have taken a year to complete. However, the wing needed refurbishing anyway. It was decided to carry out this work at a cost of £5.1m. The cost of repairing the riot damage which would not otherwise have been incurred is assessed at £600,000. No member of staff was injured.

1.93   From the commencement of the incident at Dartmoor until it came to an end, both the Regional Director and Mr Emes adopted an advisory role. They made no attempt to dictate how the incident should be handled, though they made it clear that they wanted the disturbance to be brought to an end as soon as possible.

1.94   Dartmoor was a divided society. The conditions within the prison meant that a riot could happen at any time. The continuation of the Strangeways disturbance contributed to what happened at Dartmoor. The prisoners who were interviewed and gave evidence made it clear that their major complaints were about slopping out, the inadequacy of the recesses (lavatories and wash areas), the fact that they had to eat food in their cells and that there was trouble with infestation by vermin. There was also a suggestion that prisoners were not treated like human-beings or adults. A frequent complaint was the pettiness of some rules and the way they were enforced.

1.95   Mr May's decision on the morning of 8 April not to intervene was questionable. C&R units could have entered D Wing from C Wing at all levels. Once it was daylight, the difficulties which might have caused problems the previous night could have been overcome. The prisoners were showing little signs of wanting to negotiate. There was a danger of the disturbance being drawn out like that at Strangeways. Fortunately, the fact that C&R units entered C Wing early in the afternoon of 8 April brought about the necessary change in atmosphere, so Mr May's decision had limited consequences.

1.96   There was continuous tension between uniformed staff and governors as to how the disturbance should be handled. This was due to the uniformed staff having no confidence in the ability of the management to handle the disturbance. It was a reflection of the bad relations between the two groups of the staff in the prison.

Cardiff   1.97   The disturbance at Cardiff began on the morning of Sunday 8 April 1990. It started before the Dartmoor disturbance had finished. Like Manchester, Cardiff is a city centre Victorian Category B local prison which primarily serves the Courts in its immediate locality. It is, however, substantially smaller than Manchester. It has a certified normal accommodation (CNA) of 337 prisoners.

1.98   The prison is divided into three Wings, A, B and D (the plan is at Annex 6A). A and B Wings are constructed in the conventional Victorian style. They are galleried and linked at right angles to a Centre from which they can be separated on each landing by locked gates.

1.99   The cells do not have integral sanitation. The regime, however, was generally relaxed. There was normally a good relationship between staff and inmates. Prisoners were let out of their cells whenever this was practicable. A problem at Cardiff was the number of staff who were off work for health reasons.

1.100   As a result of the Strangeways disturbance, 58 Manchester prisoners were transferred on 2 April 1990 to Cardiff. This increased the total population within the prison to 485 prisoners. At the time of the disturbance at Cardiff there was, therefore, a substantial amount of overcrowding. On 6 April, a prisoner was transferred from Bristol to Cardiff. His transfer was because he was regarded as being a troublemaker at Bristol. However, Cardiff was informed by Bristol that, in a new setting, he was unlikely to be difficult. He was placed on A2 landing with another inmate who was not the ideal companion.

1.101   The disturbance took place on A Wing. That wing has a CNA of 115 prisoners. On 6 April, it was accommodating 203 prisoners.

1.102   Bearing in mind that the Strangeways disturbance was still continuing and that the Dartmoor incident had started, it was not surprising that trouble was to be expected at Cardiff - as it was at many other prisons on the weekend of 7/8 April. But the initial information which was received by staff at Cardiff prison suggested that the trouble would occur in the Chapel rather than on A Wing.

1.103   On 7 April, a woman prison officer, who was part of the regular staff on A Wing, was told by a prisoner that she should not come to work the following day because he did not want to see her hurt. She understood the trouble was to be on her landing. Unfortunately, the woman prison officer was told by a superior officer to deliver the information the following morning. The governor in charge of that wing, Miss Ring, did not receive this information until 08.15 to 08.30 on 8 April. Up to that time, Miss Ring thought that the disturbance was most likely to occur in the Chapel. At about 08.40 the disturbance started. This was before Miss Ring was able to take any action on the information from the woman prison officer.

1.104   Just after the inmates had returned from collecting their breakfast, two inmates began a dispute in a cell doorway on A2 landing. Officers tried to intervene. They possibly over-reacted to the situation. The principal officer on duty calmed matters. For a moment, it appeared that he might have succeeded in defusing the situation.

1.105   A prisoner, however, then threw a bucket of tea along the landing. He was the companion of the prisoner from Bristol. The prisoner from Bristol threw a dustbin down a flight of stairs. The disturbance erupted. The staff were forced to withdraw to the Centre. As they did so, they were doused with water from a hose reel on the landing. One officer was left behind. Prisoners took his keys. The officer made his way to the Centre, assisted by other officers. The keys were used to release other prisoners.

1.106   There were a number of Rule 43 prisoners on A Wing. They were removed from their cells by staff and led to the adjoining hospital. Padlocks and chains were obtained. They were used to secure the gates from the landing on A Wing to the Centre. The gates did not have locks which could be doubled (a way of ensuring the lock could not be opened by the ordinary key). But other gates which could be double locked were doubled. This meant that the wing could be secured. There was time to do this because the prisoners who were rioting decided first of all to break into and ransack the canteen on the wing.

1.107   Although various objects were thrown at them, the staff remained on the Centre. This prevented the riot spreading to other wings. Later, a prisoner returned the keys to a member of staff. The prisoners were able to obtain possession of some tools, including an electric drill, from a cell on the wing which was being refurbished. The prisoners attempted to use the drill to gain access to the roof. But the governor in charge had the power turned off in time to prevent them obtaining access. The prisoners then removed sections of metal railing and attempted to smash their way through the roof. They were unsuccessful. Fires were also started but, when they spread, they were extinguished by the Fire and Rescue Service.

1.108   Reflecting the generally good relations between prisoners and staff, throughout the disturbance some prisoners did not wish to be involved. They wanted staff to release them on to the Centre. Other prisoners, however, were trying to prevent their evacuation. There was a danger that, if the gates onto the Centre were opened, staff would be rushed. Initially, therefore, the prisoners who were not involved, were not allowed out of the wing.

1.109   Eventually those who wanted to leave the wing persuaded the other prisoners not to interfere. The prisoners who wanted to be evacuated were then allowed to leave the wing onto the Centre, ten at a time. After some prisoners had surrendered, the attitude of the remainder changed. They wanted to surrender as well. By 11.40 there were only about 28 prisoners left. By 12.10 the wing was finally cleared. The riot had been brought to a speedy conclusion.

1.110   Prior to the start of the disturbance, the prison was in a unsettled state. The riots at the other prisons contributed to this. However the arrival of the Manchester prisoners probably was not a direct cause of the disturbance. Some prisoners on A Wing had probably decided to create an incident on A Wing on 8 April 1990. The Bristol prisoner and his companion probably took advantage of the possible over-reaction of staff to the dispute between the two inmates in a cell doorway to provide the spark which caused the disturbance to flare up in earnest. This would not have happened without the support of a number, but by no means all, of the prisoners.

1.111   The cost of repairing the damage caused during the disturbance is approximately £30,000. Four officers were injured. Fortunately their injuries were not severe. One prisoner sustained a broken ankle.

1.112   The most serious consequence of the disturbance was its effect on staff morale. The staff lost confidence in themselves. They were very reluctant to restore the relaxed regime which had previously existed. By the time of the hearing into the disturbance on 12 and 13 July 1990, however, the position had considerably improved.

Bristol   1.113   The riot at Bristol (Horfield) Prison took place on Sunday 8 April 1990. It was not long after the riots at Dartmoor and Cardiff had come to an end. Like Strangeways and Cardiff Prisons, Bristol is a Victorian local prison. (The plan is at Annex 7A). The prison is situated two miles north of Bristol City Centre. It serves the Courts in Avon, Somerset and Wiltshire. It had nothing like the overcrowding of Strangeways or Cardiff. The CNA of the prison as a whole was 557. On 7 April 1990, the total population was about 572.

1.114   There was scaffolding erected in the prison (as there was in Manchester). On 22/23 March 1990, two remand prisoners had gained access to the roof using that scaffolding. There had also been rumours of a possible disturbance in the prison, but the information was not precise. It was thought by the Governor that the riot at Strangeways was unlikely to be repeated at Bristol.

1.115   Just before midnight on 7 April, prisoners who had been transferred from C Wing of Dartmoor arrived at Bristol. They had broken some, at least, of the windows in one of their coaches. The prisoners from Dartmoor who were to remain at Bristol were accommodated on A Wing. The wing contained primarily remand prisoners. Space was made for the Dartmoor prisoners by transferring from the Wing the prisoners who were on Rule 43 for their own protection.

1.116   During the following day, 8 April, the prisoners from Dartmoor contributed to a state of considerable tension on A Wing. The uniformed staff and governors, however, did their best to reduce tension and assist the Dartmoor prisoners to settle in.

1.117   Just after 18.00 on 8 April, the trouble started. An ex-Dartmoor prisoner threw a bowl of water into the face of a senior officer. This was followed by a struggle in which others became involved. In spite of the efforts of the principal officer in charge, the commotion became worse. Eventually the staff had to withdraw. During this period, one officer lost his keys and another officer had to be taken by some prisoners into a cell for his own safety.

1.118   With the keys which had been taken, it was possible for other prisoners to be released. Very soon there was uproar in the wing. As a precaution, a C&R unit had been on standby. But because of the scale of the disturbance, it was not sensible for this unit to intervene on A Wing. Instead, the unit was used in an effort to prevent the disturbance spreading to the other two main accommodation wings, which were B and C Wings. B and C Wings were connected to A Wing by a high-level bridge.

1.119   The roof of A Wing was of very similar design to the roof of Strangeways, but it was not penetrated directly from the wing. The prisoners did, however, reach the roof of A Wing. They obtained possession of tools which were being kept for maintenance work in a cell on the wing. Using those tools, the prisoners were able to break out of A Wing and make their way onto the Chapel roof. From that roof, they were able to reach the roof of A Wing. Once on the roof of A Wing, they were in a commanding position. They were able to throw missiles from that roof to almost every part of the prison.

1.120   Great difficulty was experienced in trying to rescue the prison officer who had been taken into the cell by two prisoners. Initially, courageous attempts were made to break into that cell from outside using oxy-acetylene equipment. But the members of staff engaged in the rescue attempt came under horrendous bombardment from the roof. Although a number of staff were injured in the rescue attempt, it was extremely fortunate that no member of staff was killed. Eventually, the officer was freed through one of the entrances to the wing. He was taken there by prisoners, who had dressed him in prisoners garb. These prisoners commendably prevented the officer from being harmed.

1.121   The prisoners crossed from the roof of A Wing to B and C Wings by using the flat roof of the overhead bridge. The staff on those wings withdrew, leaving the prisoners locked in their cells. The staff did not seek authority to withdraw, as they should have done. Although the situation may have appeared alarming, the staff were under no immediate threat. The prisoners in B and C Wings had no difficulty in breaking out of their cells. Considerable damage was done to those wings.

1.122   Although the governing Governor remained in overall control of the prison, Mr French, Governor 4, effectively commanded the incident. Later the South West Regional Office arranged for the Governor of Leyhill Prison, Mr Wall, to take over command of the prison. This he did shortly after midnight.

1.123   During the course of the night, a plan was prepared to retake the prison. It was approved by the SWRO. After some successive delays, it was to be implemented at 06.00 on 9 April.

1.124   During the night, however, some prisoners made it apparent that they wanted to give themselves up. Next morning, by the time that the C&R units were ready to launch the attack on the prison, a large number of prisoners had already surrendered. When the C&R units entered A Wing, they met no opposition. Other C&R units were not so fortunate. In particular, a unit which used a police vehicle to reach the far end of A Wing, came under heavy attack from the roof.

1.125   The C&R units then turned their attention to B and C Wings. They again met no real resistance. Those wings were secured by 10.03 on 9 April. By then, all the prisoners had surrendered, apart from five prisoners. They remained on the roofs of A and B Wings. They surrendered at 14.44 the same day.

1.126   Altogether, 17 staff and 12 prisoners were injured. 300 prisoners had to be transferred to 13 other establishments.

1.127   An immense amount of damage was done. It would have cost approximately £1m to reinstate A Wing. However, plans have been made to refurbish A Wing in accordance with current standards. That will cost £3.5m. In addition, the cost of refurbishing B and C Wings will be approximately £100,000. Because of the scale of work, the actual cost of refurbishment was not materially affected by the damage.

1.128   The conditions on A Wing were unacceptable. It was the Dartmoor prisoners' arrival at Bristol which was the catalyst which set off the disturbance. Once it started, the Bristol prisoners were all too ready to join in. There were a number of examples of prisoners showing considerable courage in going to the assistance of staff. Unfortunately, there were a sufficient number of hostile prisoners to turn what could have been a minor incident into a major riot.

Pucklechurch   1.129   The riot at Pucklechurch Remand Centre began on Sunday 22 April 1990. It was the last of the serious incidents which occurred that month. Pucklechurch held primarily youths on remand and not mature criminals. However, the violence which occurred was probably as bad, if not worse, than that which occurred during the other riots.

1.130   The male section of Pucklechurch had a CNA of 103. At the time of the disturbance the Centre was overcrowded. It held 124 male inmates. In addition, Pucklechurch had a separate block of accommodation for 56 adult and young women prisoners. They were not directly involved in the riot. They were moved from Pucklechurch shortly after the disturbance began. (The plan of the Centre is at Annex 8A.)

1.131   Pucklechurch had no workshop or vocational training courses. There had been some attempt made to build up the educational programme. The most successful side of the regime was that provided by the physical education staff.

1.132   Pucklechurch is close to Bristol. Many of the inmates had connections in Bristol. They were therefore very much influenced by what had happened during the riot at Bristol Prison. After the Bristol riot, there were general rumours that there would be a disturbance at Pucklechurch. Following more specific information in the week preceding the Pucklechurch riot, the number of staff on duty over the weekend of 21 and 22 April 1990 was increased.

1.133   On the evening of 22 April, at about 18.35, a member of staff was serving tea to inmates who were locked in their cells on A Wing. The officer was accompanied by two orderlies (prison inmates). There was not another officer in sight or hearing (as there could have been and in future there should be). When the officer unlocked a cell on the 2's landing, he was grabbed by two inmates. He shouted to the orderlies to sound the alarm, but they did not do so. In the course of the struggle, the officer lost consciousness. He recovered to find himself locked in a cell and his keys gone.

1.134   By that time, most of the inmates in A Wing had been let out by other inmates. They were creating considerable noise. The senior officer on duty heard the noise. He went towards A Wing. He was surrounded by inmates who told him to get his men and get out. The senior officer sounded the alarm. He organised the release of the officer whose keys had been taken.

1.135   By 18.50 Mr Woolford, the Head of Custody, had arrived at the prison. He took command of the incident. He remained in immediate command until the incident finished. He tried to contain the disturbance in A Wing, but was unsuccessful. Some inmates obtained access to the Works Department. At Pucklechurch, as at Cardiff and Bristol, they obtained possession of tools, including oxy-acetylene cutting equipment. This was used to break through the skylights in the corridors, allowing inmates to bombard C&R units when they later entered the building.

1.136   C&R teams were sent to Pucklechurch from other establishments. Just before 00.30 hours on 23 April, an assault was launched. The initial intervention was unsuccessful, because of the barricades which the inmates had erected and the smoke from fires. There were also attacks by inmates on C&R units when they were both on open ground. This had not happened at any previous riot.

1.137   During the night, a further intervention plan was drawn up. This involved using 11 C&R units. At 06.00 on 23 April, the second attack began. Again, the units had to put up with intense opposition. This time the attack was eventually successful, after what one senior officer described as hand to hand fighting in the kitchen/dining area. Shortly after midday, all the inmates had surrendered.

1.138   The length of time which the riot lasted, and the vigour of the inmates' resistance, was probably influenced by the inmates' fear that they would be assaulted by staff when they surrendered. This fear could have been partly induced by the unnecessary and indiscriminate use by staff of C&R holds when moving inmates who had surrendered.

1.139 The degree of violence which the inmates displayed was still disturbing. Part was due to the conditions in which the inmates were contained. Part was due to an element of the sort of hooliganism which has been associated with football matches.

1.140   The preparations which were made for the surrender of the inmates were unsatisfactory. The inmates were not treated after they had surrendered in the way that they should have been. There was delay in providing them with clothing after they had been strip searched. They were placed in cells, from which the mattresses had been removed. Personal possessions were taken from them unnecessarily. The personal clothing and possessions which were removed were not properly looked after. There were suggestions, about which the Inquiry makes no findings, that unjustified violence was used.

1.141   Bearing in mind the size of Pucklechurch, the injuries were high. 47 members of staff and 35 inmates were injured. The future of Pucklechurch as a Remand Centre is uncertain. It has not yet been reopened. The cost of repairing the damage would be about £1m.

The Central Problems of the Prison Service

1.142   The riots which the Inquiry investigated were not isolated incidents. Other lesser, but still serious disturbances occurred in April 1990. They stem from a long history of violent disturbances in the prison system. On the evidence, prison riots cannot be dismissed as one-off events, or as local disasters, or a run of bad luck. They are symptomatic of a series of serious underlying difficulties in the prison system. They will only be brought to an end if these difficulties are addressed.

1.143   There was a considerable degree of consensus among those who provided evidence as to the causes of these successive disturbances. Differences tended to be ones of degree. The emphasis frequently depended on the perspective of the person providing the evidence. If it was a prisoner or a pressure group, the focus would usually be on: (i) the insanitary and overcrowded physical conditions to which prisoners were subjected; (ii) the negative and unconstructive nature of the regime; (iii) the lack of respect with which the prisoners were treated; (iv) the destructive effects of prison on the prisoner's family ties and the inadequacy of visits; and (v) the lack of any form of independent redress for grievances.

1.144   If the evidence was from uniformed staff, it would recognise a need to improve the conditions for prisoners, but would stress additional causes which staff felt were frustrating them in performing their duties. The evidence would draw attention to the lack of staff, lack of training, a sense of being undervalued, isolation from other staff and the divide between different grades and classes of staff. It would refer also to a lack of leadership within the Service.

1.145 Evidence from governors would agree that all the causes so far identified required attention. It would also draw attention to a lack of support and assistance from Headquarters. Governors lacked confidence in Headquarters. They felt powerless to implement the changes which they know were needed within their establishments.

1.146 Some witnesses drew attention to a further problem. They identified a lack of co-ordination between the different parts of the Criminal Justice System. As the system operated at present, there was no link or established means of communication between the Judges who were responsible for sending prisoners to prison, and the Prison Service which was responsible for holding them there. Some of those giving evidence suggested that the result of this breach in the chain of communication was chronic overcrowding. Unless a link were established, overcrowding would continue. Overcrowding led to an inherently instable prison system and resulted in disruption and riot.

1.147 I accept that these lists identify the majority, but not all, of the possible underlying causes of the riots. Each of these causes contributed to the present problems of the Prison Service. In the Report, there are recommendations or proposals which directly relate to them. They are dealt with under the respective headings of the Sections in Part II of this Report.

1.148 It is possible, however, to identify one principal thread which links these causes and complaints and which draws together all our proposals and recommendations. It is that the Prison Service must set security, control and justice in prisons at the right level and it must provide the right balance between them. The stability of the prison system depends on the Prison Service doing so.

1.149 Security here refers to the need to prevent prisoners escaping. Control refers to the obligation, ultimately, to prevent prisoners causing a disturbance. Justice encapsulates the obligation on the Prison Service to treat prisoners with humanity and fairness and to act in concert with its responsibilities as part of the Criminal Justice System.

1.150 The April riots occurred because these three elements were out of balance. There were failures in the maintenance of control. There were failures to achieve the necessary standards of justice. There could easily have been a collapse in security.

1.151 These factors are each dependent on the other. If there is an absence of justice, prisoners will be aggrieved. Control and security will be threatened. This is part of what happened in April. The scale of each of the riots indicates that in each establishment there was a substantial number of prisoners who were prepared to turn what otherwise could have been a limited disturbance into a full scale riot. This was, at least in part, because of the conditions in which they were held and the way in which they were treated. If a proper level of justice is provided in prisons, then it is less likely that prisoners will behave in this way. Justice, therefore, contributes to the maintenance of security and control.

1.152 Lapses in control affect both security and justice. Prisoners did not escape during the April disturbances. But they might easily have done so. They were very close to achieving this at Long Lartin prison on 2 April 1990. The April disturbances also clearly demonstrated that, with a breakdown in control, prisoners suffer as well as the Prison Service. No-one can claim that the prisoners attacked in Strangeways, and intimidated in Cardiff, Pucklechurch and Dartmoor were at that time being treated in prison with justice. The breakdown in control led in many senses to a breakdown in justice in prisons.

1.153 Security, control and justice will not be set at the right level, and will not be held in balance, unless there are changes in the way the Prison Service structures its relations, both between management and staff, and between staff and prisoners. There is a fundamental lack of respect and a failure to give and require responsibility at all levels in the prison system. These shortcomings must be tackled if the Prison Service is to maintain a stable system.

1.154   The evidence from Part I of the Inquiry makes this clear. Industrial relations at Dartmoor were notoriously poor. The handling of the disturbance was hampered as a result. The sense of hostility by inmates at Pucklechurch was very marked. There were failures in communication among management and with headquarters which affected the handling of and which probably prolonged the Strangeways siege.

1.155   A central objective in our proposals and recommendations, therefore, is to ensure that relations within the prison system are based upon respect and responsibility. To do this we have addressed the structures and procedures which operate in the Prison Service. We have considered the nature and standard of provision for prisoners and for those who work in the Prison Service. If, through the operation of these structures, management show that they respect their staff and are ready to give them greater responsibility for their own work, then staff are the more likely to treat prisoners in the same way. At the same time, prisoners will not respect staff if they know that staff have no respect for or confidence in their managers. Headquarters must give a lead, but it has a right also to expect that leadership to be followed.

1.156   These then should be the fundamental objectives of the Prison Service. If they are to be achieved, the Prison Service will need to be an integral part of a Criminal Justice System which co-operates to meet the objectives of all parts of that system. The recommendations and proposals in this Report are directed to these ends.

What Should be Done to Prevent Repetition of the Riots?

1.157   The Prison Service is well aware of a need to improve the present situation in its prisons. Over recent years, the Prison Service has instituted a series of fundamental changes within the Service of the greatest importance.

1.158   First, there has been a vast rebuilding and refurbishment programme which was long overdue. In 1990/91, roughly £300m is to be spent on new prisons and almost £150m is to be spent on refurbishment. That programme necessarily takes time. It will transform the physical conditions within the prisons. This will both increase stability within prisons and improve relations between prisoners and staff and staff and management.

1.159   The Inquiry has had two aims in relation to the building and refurbishment programme. The first is to stress the importance of ensuring that the progress is as fast as is practicable. The second is to ensure that, where it is not already too late, the programme takes fully into account the lessons which are to be learnt from the recent disturbances and the principles which should apply for the future. The most important of these principles are that prisoners should be accommodated in small units and in community prisons.

1.160   Secondly, the Prison Service has introduced, since 1987, two different and radical managerial reforms. The first was a package designed to reform the organisation of staff and management within prison establishments. It was sorely needed. There were undoubtedly deeply embedded work practices within the Prison Service which were grossly inefficient and which needed to be addressed. There were structural difficulties which needed attention. There were organisational problems which required change. "Fresh Start" was an attempt to achieve the necessary changes.

1.161   Under "Fresh Start", the excessive periods of overtime which prison officers were working, and were having to work in order to earn a reasonable wage, were to be phased out. The uniformed grades of staff and the governor grades were to be unified. The tasks within each prison establishment were to be grouped and were to be performed by teams of management and staff. These were all important changes for the better.

1.162   The manner in which the changes have been implemented, however, has meant that "Fresh Start" has not succeeded in improving relations in many prisons. Staff feel that they were misled as to what was involved in the "Fresh Start" package. They do not believe that the Prison Service has delivered what it promised. The objectives of the "Fresh Start" package have been imperilled by a widely held belief that it has resulted in still more inadequate staffing levels.

1.163   Whether this last belief is justified or not can only be ascertained if some way is found of objectively ascertaining what is the proper staffing level within each prison establishment. The Prison Service is at present carrying out a process to enable this to be done. The merits of that process were in dispute before the Inquiry. The Prison Officers' Association at the present time are not prepared to be associated with the process. This is a reflection of the unhappy state of industrial relations between the Prison Officers' Association and the Prison Service. While the present approach for determining staffing levels may not be perfect, no better method of achieving the objective has been suggested to the Inquiry. If undertaken properly, the present exercise cannot but improve the position. It is for this reason that the Report urges the Prison Officers' Association to rethink their attitude to it.

1.164   The second managerial reform was implemented in September 1990. It involved the reorganisation of management above establishment level. There are aspects of this reorganisation which have been strongly criticised by governors and other staff. However, the reorganisation has been implemented. The Inquiry took the view that, this having been done, it should have an opportunity of proving its worth before its merits were assessed. The Inquiry has assumed, therefore, that, for the time being at any rate, this structure of management above establishment level will remain.

1.165   The changes which the Prison Service has already attempted and is attempting to bring about are important. However, they are primarily directed to the physical conditions within the prison system, and to the management of that system. There needs now to be greater attention paid to the way in which prisoners and staff are treated. The way prisoners are treated can often be a reflection of the way staff themselves feel they are treated by management. An important lesson of the riots is that they would either not have taken place, or, if they had, they would have been on a different scale, if a substantial body of inmates had not been prepared to support those who instigated the initial disturbance which developed into a riot at each establishment. What is now required is a planned programme of change which will address the substantial problems which remain.

1.166   The planned programme should address the lack of stability and the unsatisfactory state of relations within the prison system. The programme has to take into account the need for a balance between security, control and justice. In Part II of this Report, together with His Honour Judge Tumim, I identify such a programme.

1.167 Our programme is based on 12 central recommendations. These are that there should be:

    i)   closer co-operation between the different parts of the Criminal Justice System. For this purpose a national forum and local committees should be established;

    ii)   more visible leadership of the Prison Service by a Director General who is and is seen to be the operational head and in day to day charge of the Service. To achieve this there should be a published "compact" or "contract" given by Ministers to the Director General of the Prison Service, who should be responsible for the performance of that “contract” and publicly answerable for the day to day operations of the Prison Service;

iii) increased delegation of responsibility to Governors of establishments;

iv) an enhanced role for prison officers;

v) a “compact” or “contract” for each prisoner setting out the prisoner's expectations and responsibilities in the prison in which he or she is held;

vi) a national system of Accredited Standards, with which, in time, each prison establishment would be required to comply;

vii) a new Prison Rule that no establishment should hold more prisoners than is provided for in its certified normal level of accommodation, with provisions for Parliament to be informed if exceptionally there is to be a material departure from that rule;

viii) a public commitment from Ministers setting a timetable to provide access to sanitation for all inmates at the earliest practicable date not later than February 1996;

ix) better prospects for prisoners to maintain their links with families and the community through more visits and home leaves and through being located in community prisons as near to their homes as possible;

x) a division of prison establishments into small and more manageable and secure units;

xi) a separate statement of purpose, separate conditions and generally a lower security categorisation for remand prisoners;

xii) improved standards of justice within prisons involving the giving of reasons to a prisoner for any decision which materially and adversely affects him; a grievance procedure and disciplinary proceedings which ensure that the Governor deals with most matters under his present powers; relieving Boards of Visitors of their adjudicatory role; and providing for final access to an independent Complaints Adjudicator.

1.168   In the following paragraphs and in the remainder of the Report we describe these recommendations more fully. They are central to resolving the problems which have been identified from the April disturbances. They are also a package. They need to be considered together and moved forward together if the necessary balance in our prison system is to be achieved.

The Structures for Consultation Across the Criminal Justice System

1.169   The Prison Service must co-ordinate its activities with those of the other sections of the Criminal Justice System. In the course of this Report we identify many areas which require co-operation, co-ordination and consultation between the various parts of the Criminal Justice System. At the present time, there is no body in existence in which all those responsible for the different sections of the Criminal Justice System can consult together so as to perform more effectively their role in the system.

1.170   There are special conferences which make a contribution. There are trilateral meetings between the Lord Chancellor, the Home Secretary and the Attorney General, complemented by regular meetings among officials. However, there is no body in which all the important interests are represented. In the Inquiry's judgment, there is a need for a forum in which information of mutual interest to the different sections of the Criminal Justice System can be exchanged and proposals for improvement can be considered. There is clearly room for debate as to what form this committee or forum should take, who should be involved, and what its terms of reference should be. However that a forum is needed, this Inquiry does not doubt. It therefore recommends that a national forum for this purpose should be created.

1.171   It is for those who would have the responsibility for setting up the forum to determine its precise nature. A possible model which the Inquiry would favour would involve creating a forum composed of a very senior Judge to represent the Lord Chief Justice, and possibly the permanent heads of the Home Office, the Lord Chancellor's Department, and the Head of the Crown Prosecution Service, together with a distinguished policeman and probation officer, who would be likely to command the respect of their colleagues. The Director General of the Prison Service would also be a member. The Council would co-opt other members when the business made this necessary. For example, the permanent head of the Department of Health would attend if there were a problem with regard to mentally disordered offenders. The forum might be called the Criminal Justice Consultative Council.

1.172   In addition to the national forum, there should be Local Committees reflecting similar interests and responsible for achieving similar objectives at a local level. Again, there is room for debate about the level at which the Local Committee should be pitched and as to what its precise terms of reference should be. We consider, however, that a local Judge should sit on each Committee. The Committees which exist in some parts of the country at present do not involve Judges. The experience of these Committees, however, shows clearly the value of a Committee of this sort. We consider that value can be increased by broadening their membership and scope, and by bringing them within the ambit of the national forum. It should be the responsibility of the national forum to determine what would be the preferable model of Local Committee, to set up the appropriate organisation for the Local Committees and to supervise them.

The Head of the Prison Service

1.173   During the April disturbances, and in particular during the disturbance at Strangeways, there was a widely held sense of a lack of visible leadership of the Prison Service. This was substantially due to the structure at the top of the Prison Service at that time. There was then, as now, a Director General who, subject to Ministers, was in overall charge of the Service. There was also a Deputy Director General. The Deputy Director General was in charge of the operational side of the Prison Service. The way the Director and Deputy Director General divided their responsibilities resulted in the Deputy Director being in overall charge of the handling of the disturbances.

1.174   The consequence of this division in responsibility was that the Director General adopted a low profile during the disturbances. He hardly featured in the evidence during Part I of the Inquiry, while the Deputy Director General's role was examined in detail.

1.175   One of the changes made by the recent reorganisation has been to remove the office of Deputy Director General. The Inquiry regards this as a move in the right direction. But this, by itself, is not enough. The Director General must be and be seen to be the visible operational head in day to day charge of the Prison Service. He must also give the leadership which is expected of the head of an operational service.

1.176 In the course of the evidence, it was suggested that this objective could best be achieved by making the Prison Service a separate agency. However, the Inquiry does not consider it necessary to take a position on that issue. The necessary role and responsibilities can be given to the Director General within the present structure (as they could within an agency structure). Ministers have special responsibilities in relation to the Prison Service because of its role of having to keep in custody those sent to prison by the courts. Whatever the structure or status of the Prison Service, the Inquiry appreciates that Ministers are likely to want to ensure that their responsibilities are adequately reflected.

1.177 The necessary relationship between Ministers and the Director General should be marked by Ministers giving annually to the Director General a "compact" or "contract". This would identify the resources which were to be provided to the Prison Service. It would establish the priorities for the Prison Service. And it would set out the tasks which were to be performed by the Prison Service during the period covered by the "contract". The "contract" would be published so that the responsibilities of the Director General were known. Its performance would be supervised by Ministers and at any time they would be entitled to vary or add to its terms. But it would be seen that it was the obligation of the Director General as the operational head of the Service to ensure that the Prison Service fulfilled the published objectives set out in the "contract". He would expect to explain in public the Prison Service's performance in meeting those objectives. He would continue to fulfil his other role as adviser to Ministers on Prison Service issues. He would also seek to develop the necessary co-operation with other parts of the Criminal Justice System.

1.178 I use the word "contract" to describe this document because that is a word which is in current use within the Prison Service to describe the document between an Area Manager and the Governor of a prison setting out the annual objectives for each prison. However, neither document would be legally enforceable. A "compact" may be a preferable name for these documents and the equivalent documents which we suggest should be provided for staff in prison and for prisoners.

The Relationship between Headquarters and Establishments

1.179 If a prison is to operate to maximum efficiency, then the governor must be given the responsibility which he needs to run the establishment. There is a need for increased delegation. The Headquarters of the Prison Service must see its primary role as being to set out the policy and objectives to be achieved by the prison and then to support and monitor the efforts of those working in prisons to give effect to that policy and achieve those objectives. The role of Headquarters should be an enabling one: enabling Governors to govern and providing support for staff. This will involve a substantial change in the attitude of Headquarters.

The Enhanced Status of Prison Officers

1.180 The quality of the prison system ultimately depends on the quality of the performance of the prison officers who have the day to day responsibility for dealing with prisoners. The status of prison officers needs to be raised. They should be better trained with better prospects of promotion and they should generally only be deployed on duties appropriate to their status. In order to attract candidates of the appropriate calibre, the Inquiry approves opportunities for accelerated promotion. The promotion of uniformed staff through the ranks to senior managerial posts will make a substantial contribution to improving relations between different levels of staff.

1.181 If prison officers are to be able to perform their enhanced role, then other staff will have to take over responsibility for those tasks which can no longer be sensibly performed by prison officers. To unify the Service, the increased opportunities for uniformed staff need to be matched by a re-assessment of the role of non-uniformed staff which was not sufficiently considered in "Fresh Start".

1.182 Prison staff, including prison officers, should receive from the Governor a "contract" which sets out what the establishment will provide for the member of staff and the duties he has to fulfil in return.

Relations with Prisoners

1.183   As an extension of the "contractual" arrangements which we recommend should exist between Ministers and the Prison Service, and which already exists between Area Managers and prisons, the prisoner should receive a "compact" or "contract" from the prison at which he is held. It would be provided to both remand and sentenced prisoners. It should identify what the prison expects to provide for the prisoner, and it should set out what the prison requires from the prisoner in return. The "contract" would be discussed with the prisoner. It would include details relating to the features of the prison regime which are important to the prisoner. If the prisoner were still in the same prison after 12 months, the "contract" would be reviewed with him then.

1.184   If the prisoner's expectations were not fulfilled, he would be entitled to enlist the aid of the Board of Visitors or to invoke the grievance procedures to ensure that the prison did not unreasonably depart from the "contract". As a last resort, the "contract" could provide a platform for judicial review. If the prisoner misbehaves then, as a result of disciplinary proceedings, he could be deprived of certain of his expectations under the "contract".

1.185   The "contract" would be a recognition of the respect to which the prisoner is entitled and the responsibility which is required from him in return. In due course, as sentence planning for all prisoners develops, the "contract" would, in the case of a prisoner serving more than 12 months, be co-ordinated with his or her sentence plan. The provisions in the "contract" would change as the prisoner progresses through his sentence.

Standards Within Prisons

1.186   In order to achieve justice within prisons there must be required standards of conditions and regime within prisons. After proper consultation, the Home Secretary should establish a series of national Accredited Standards applicable to all prisons. It would then be the responsibility of every prison establishment to reach at least that standard. Area Managers, by encouragement and using the "contract" which they have with individual prisons, would be responsible for ensuring that, over a period of time, each prison in their area fulfils all the national Accredited Standards.

1.187   The Area Manager would certify when a prison had reached a required standard. When it fulfilled all the standards, it would be granted Accreditation Status by the Home Secretary, on the recommendation of HM Chief Inspector of Prisons. For the time being, the national standards would have to be aspirational. Once they are achieved, that would be the time to consider whether it was necessary to make them legally enforceable. We would, however, expect that at that stage they would be incorporated in the Prison Rules and so would be legally enforceable by judicial review.

The Control on the Number of Prisoners Within a Prison

1.188   Each prison has a certified number of prisoners it can hold without overcrowding. That provides each prison's level of Certified Normal Accommodation (CNA). The validity of the CNA formula as a measure for establishing the point at which overcrowding starts is disputed. However, it has the great advantage that it is a formula already in use. While its shortcomings are recognised, the Inquiry considers that, for the time being, it should be the formula which is used to indicate the maximum number of prisoners who should be accommodated at any one time in a prison. As it is unlikely that all cells within a prison will be capable of being used at any particular time, even at the CNA figure, there may be a degree of overcrowding. Sensibly, therefore, a prison should normally be occupied under its CNA. That should also allow for some capacity to deal with variations in the size of the population week by week.

23

1.189 The Inquiry has noted that, by the end of 1992, the Prison Service expects the total prison population to equal the total prison accommodation available. If properly managed, overcrowding should then become a thing of the past. But this needs to be regularly and closely monitored and controlled if overcrowding is not again to become endemic. That system of control needs to make some formal provision for any occasion when, because of circumstances which cannot be anticipated, it might be necessary for a prison to exceed the CNA figure.

1.190 It is therefore recommended that there should be a new Prison Rule. The Rule should come into effect at the end of 1992, if by then the system is in equilibrium. The new Rule should provide that no establishment should hold prisoners in excess of its CNA. It should be possible, however, for an establishment to exceed its CNA by no more than 3% for no longer than seven days in any three months. Where there are exceptional circumstances in which such a saving is not sufficient to accommodate the prison population, the Secretary of State should be required to issue a certificate specifying the precise requirement and the reasons. The certificate would last up to three months and be renewable. The Secretary of State would be required to lay a copy of the certificate before both Houses of Parliament.

1.191 This recommendation would not by itself abolish overcrowding in prisons, but it should substantially inhibit that overcrowding and would require Parliament to be informed of the situation.

Sanitation

1.192 After overcrowding, the most destructive feature of the prison system at the present time is the lack of sanitation and the degrading process of slopping out which is its consequence. It destroys the morale of prisoners and staff. It is uncivilised and a symptom of an archaic prison system. The Prison Service accepts that slopping out has to be eradicated, but as yet there is no public commitment to a date on which this practice is to end and all prisoners are to have integral sanitation.

1.193 Ministers should announce the date by which such sanitation can be provided. It should be the earliest practicable date. It should not be later than that already recommended by HMCIP - February 1996. Such an announcement could send the clearest signal possible that the Prison Service is to be committed to bringing the prison system up to acceptable and just standards.

Links with the Community

1.194 As conditions within prisons improve, the Inquiry would like to see greater emphasis being placed throughout a prisoner's sentence on his eventual return to the community. If the destructive effects of imprisonment are to be reduced so that the prospects of the prisoner not re-offending can be improved, it is critical that, where this is possible, the prisoner's links with his family and the community should be maintained. The Report, therefore, recommends more extensive provision for visits and leave. Most prisoners attach the greatest importance to visits and leave and the opportunity to have them is a significant incentive to responsible behaviour.

1.195 It is also highly desirable for the stable running of a prison and for the prospects for the prisoner leading a law abiding life after release that, whenever practicable, he should be accommodated as near to his home and community as possible. The problem of holding prisoners remote from their homes and visitors was a very evident factor during the disturbances. So was the number of prisoners transferred from other prisons which were nearer to their homes.

1.196 We therefore recommend a system of community prisons. These would be either prisons near to the main centres of population, as many local prisons are now, with the facilities and accommodation capable of holding most prisoners throughout most of their sentence. Or they could be arranged in clusters of separate prisons within a locality through which the prisoner could progress. We recognise that there would still be a need for some specialist prisons. We recognise also that this is a recommendation which cannot be implemented in full immediately. It is a signpost which the Prison Service should follow and which should influence its management and use of its existing and new buildings.

Small Units

1.197   The implementation of the last recommendation would be facilitated if prisoners were to be accommodated in small units. Small units would also assist in the security and management of prisoners. A lesson of the April disturbances is that, within a large prison establishment, there need to be "firebreaks" which can be readily secured by prison staff so as to prevent prisoners overwhelming the whole prison.

1.198   It is preferable, therefore, for prisoners to be accommodated and managed in units containing about 50/70 prisoners. Larger wings in existing and new prisons should be divided so as to hold approximately the desired number of prisoners. The ability to incorporate this approach into an existing prison is clearly demonstrated by the plans which the Prison Service has drawn up for the refurbishment of the main prison at Manchester.

1.199   It is also desirable that the number of prisoners treated as being in the same prison should not exceed 400. This does not mean that a prison should never accommodate more than 400 where there is the space to do so. On the contrary, it is fully recognised that if proper use is to be made of the prisons at present available, many more prisoners than 400 will have to be accommodated in some prisons.

1.200 However, where this is the situation, the Inquiry's recommendation would be met by operating two or more prisons within the same prison perimeter. They would share the common facilities within that perimeter.

1.201   The days when it is appropriate for all the cells in a prison the size of Manchester to be able to opened by the same key are over. There should be different locks on the cells of each unit so that the loss of a set of keys will only give access to the cells of one unit. The units should be divided from each other by secure gates, preferably electrically operated. In the case of other areas in a prison where large numbers of prisoners congregate, there should be similar opportunities for containing prisoners within a defined area.

1.202   The security and management advantages of small units should result in a greater feeling of security for prisoners and for prison staff. They should therefore result in improved relations and in better justice for prisoners.

1.203   They should also enable the requirements of security and control, and the range of regimes offered, to be better attuned to the requirements of each part of the prison population. The result should be better relations, better control, better justice and a better balance between all three.

Remand Prisoners

1.204   It must be beyond dispute that only those for whom prison is essential should be there. This approach has influenced the Inquiry's consideration of whether there are groups of offenders who could be diverted from prison in greater numbers if alternative facilities were more fully available. The Inquiry has concentrated particularly on the position of remand prisoners. This is because they represent a significant proportion of the prison population and because they unjustly suffer some of the worst conditions in the prison system.

1.205 The Inquiry proposes the extension of the initiatives which are already being implemented in some, but not all, areas of the country to avoid unnecessary remands in custody. Those who have to be remanded in prison, as a matter of justice should be contained in conditions which, as far as this is possible, reflect the prisoner's remand status. These conditions must acknowledge that the remand prisoner is innocent unless and until proved guilty. They must reflect too the reasons for which the remand has been granted under the Bail Act 1976.

1.206 To emphasise the importance of these matters, the Inquiry recommends that there should be a separate Statement of Purpose setting out the Prison Service's responsibilities relating to remand prisoners. This Statement of Purpose should reflect the principle that remand prisoners should normally be accommodated, treated and managed separately from convicted prisoners. It should reflect also the fact that it should be part of the policy of the Prison Service to ensure that a remand prisoner spends his time while in custody in as constructive a manner as possible and that, to the extent that this is practicable, his employment, family and community connections should be kept intact. In order to further this policy, it is recommended that all remand prisoners, unless there is good reason for treating them otherwise, should be regarded as being equivalent to Category C rather than Category B prisoners.

A Grievance Procedure and Disciplinary Proceedings

1.207 Prisoners should know why a decision which materially and adversely affects them is being taken. This is essential to achieving satisfactory relations within prisons. If prisoners consider they have a genuine grievance, they should be able to have resort to a grievance procedure which has at its final stage the necessary degree of independence.

1.208 There should also be a more appropriate distinction drawn between disciplinary and criminal proceedings. Disciplinary proceedings should be capable of being appropriately disposed of by the exercise by a prison governor of his existing powers of punishment, subject to an appropriate right of appeal. It is not consistent with the Board of Visitors' watchdog functions for the Board of Visitors to be involved in adjudicatory proceedings.

1.209 The Inquiry's recommendation therefore involves:

i) prisoners normally being given reasons for any decisions which adversely affect them to a material extent and the Prison Rules being amended to set out the details of that requirement;

ii) there being a legally qualified and independent Complaints Adjudicator who should be able at the final stages of the grievance procedure to make recommendations and, in cases of disciplinary proceedings, to determine an appeal;

iii) the adjudicatory role of Boards of Visitors being abolished; and

iv) serious criminal offences committed in prison being heard by the normal criminal Courts.

Conclusion

1.210 What has been set out in this overview indicates the general approach of the Inquiry to the four questions with which this Section began. It is not intended to give an indication of all the issues considered by the Inquiry, or all the proposals which the Inquiry has made. It is intended to identify the main signposts which the Inquiry considers the Prison Service should follow for the future.

1.211   In making its recommendations and in making its proposals the Inquiry has tried to be realistic and practical and to take into account the likely financial consequences. Some recommendations and proposals have financial implications, but not all should lead to greater expense.

1.212   It is partly with a view to avoiding unnecessary expense that the Inquiry has concentrated on methods of diverting from prison those who need not be there - although that was not the sole reason. There should be cost savings in reducing the involvement of prison officers in fields where their enhanced status is not required - although, again, cost savings are not the primary justification. The Inquiry has proposed the curtailing of censorship, partly because it recognises that the expense involved in censoring is out of proportion to the benefits. The proposals of the Inquiry to reduce the security status of remand prisoners, and the proposals which should have the effect of reducing the number of prisoners unnecessarily held within the highly secure dispersal system, should also lead to a reduction of expense. The alterations which the Inquiry proposes should be made to the grievance procedures and to disciplinary proceedings are deliberately designed to avoid unnecessary and disproportionate expenditure, although some additional costs would be incurred.

1.213   Finally, and most importantly, when drawing up the balance sheet of the cost of the improvements which the Inquiry believes should be implemented, it is necessary to remember that the objective is to remove the features of the existing prison system which result in instability and which lead to riots. The cost of the April disturbances here speak for themselves.

Section 2

The Way We Worked

Terms of Appointment

2.1 On 5 April 1990, I was appointed by the Home Secretary, then the Rt Hon David Waddington QC MP, to conduct this Inquiry. The Home Secretary announced my appointment to the House of Commons in an oral statement on 5 April. As the Home Secretary told me in my letter of appointment the following day, my terms of reference at that time were:

> "To inquire into the events leading up to the serious disturbance in Her Majesty's Prison Manchester which began on 1 April 1990 and the action taken to bring it to a conclusion."

2.2 The Inquiry was a departmental Inquiry, a category of Inquiry which, when it is conducted by a judge, is also known as a Judicial Inquiry. The Home Secretary said that he would consider the alternative of establishing the Inquiry under the Tribunals and Inquiries Act 1921 if I were to form the view that my investigations were being seriously hampered by lack of the powers which the 1921 Act would confer. In the event, I received full co-operation from all those with a contribution to make and never found that I needed to ask for the statutory powers under that Act.

2.3 The Home Secretary gave me no date for completing the Inquiry, but I knew I was required to proceed with all possible speed. The Home Secretary told the House of Commons on 5 April 1990 that he intended that the report should be published.

2.4 After the series of riots and disturbances at other prisons during the weekend of 7 and 8 April, I was consulted about extending the terms of my Inquiry to the further serious disturbances which had taken place at other prison establishments. I agreed to this. The Home Secretary wrote to me on 10 April with my revised terms of reference which are those which have governed the conduct of this work. They are:

> "To inquire into the events leading up to the serious disturbance in Her Majesty's Prison Manchester which began on 1 April 1990 and the action taken to bring it to a conclusion, having regard also to the serious disturbances which occurred shortly thereafter in other prison establishments in England and Wales."

The Team is Formed

2.5 I was extremely fortunate to have an outstandingly able Secretary to the Inquiry in Mr John Lyon who has organised and guided the Inquiry with immense skill. He has been supported by a small and very dedicated staff who have worked together magnificently throughout the Inquiry, regularly until late at night – Ms Rachael Reynolds, Miss Kathleen Cooper, Mr Noorel Haque, Miss Pauline Skinner, and for part of the Inquiry, Mrs Beverley Onashoga. I brought with me my Clerk, Mr Neville Hinsley, who was fully integrated into the team and has provided invaluable assistance.

2.6 An Inquiry of this nature required Assessors who had considerable experience of the Prison Service and who were well equipped to advise on the wider issues. I was grateful, therefore, to the Home Secretary for agreeing to the appointment of three assessors: Mr Gordon Lakes CB MC, who, until 1988 was the Deputy Director General of the Prison Service; Professor Rod Morgan, professor of criminal justice at Bristol University, who was able to combine very considerable knowledge and learning of Prison Service matters with past membership of a Board of Visitors; and Mrs Mary Tuck CBE who, until 1989, was head of the Home Office Research and Planning Unit and who is particularly well versed in the social sciences as well as the Home Office's administrative procedures. Together they provided a remarkably broad range of experience and knowledge of the penal scene. They have given unstintingly of their time and their very considerable talents. Their role has gone well beyond that of normal assessors. They have been closely involved in all stages of the Inquiry and played an important part in the evidence gathering process. They are entitled to a large part of the credit for any virtues (but not the shortcomings) of this report.

2.7 It was clear at the outset that it would be necessary to conduct public hearings into the circumstances of the Manchester and other disturbances, and to invite witnesses to give formal written and oral evidence to the Inquiry. I was provided, therefore, with a team by the Treasury Solicitor, led by Mr Peter Whitehurst and assisted by Mr Roddy Jones, Mr Laurence O'Dea and Miss Kim Brudenell. They had considerable experience in assisting inquiries of this sort, and they made an invaluable contribution.

2.8 Her Majesty's Attorney General appointed as Counsel to the Inquiry: Mr David Latham QC, Mr Anthony Morris and Mr David Evans. They all bore a heavy burden in preparing for and conducting the public hearings. The submissions which they made to me were of particular assistance in the preparation of the first part of the Report. If it had not been for the confidence they inspired in those who wished to take part in the Inquiry as to their impartiality and as to the care and skill with which they would present the evidence, the Inquiry would have lasted considerably longer than it has.

2.9 Once I had started work, and had begun to examine the reports of the disturbances and to visit some of the prisons involved, I recognised the peculiar complexity of the task with which I was faced. Prisons are closed institutions. Apart from those who have worked in prisons, little is known about how they should operate, what records should be kept and what evidence of a disturbance should be available. I needed a specialist team of experts who were well versed in prison matters to visit the prisons, to look at the papers, to talk to those involved, including prisoners, and to check carefully the Prison Service's own account of events. They were necessary to help identify points of dispute and the aspects of the disturbance which would need to be explored at the public hearings.

2.10 With Mr Lakes' help, and with the agreement of the Home Secretary, I therefore appointed an Investigative Team to look at each of the incidents on which I wished to focus. They were all former prison governors. They were Mr Geoffrey Lister who, until he retired in 1985, was Regional Director of the Midland Region of the Prison Service; Mr John Richardson OBE who, before his retirement, had been Governor of HM Prison Liverpool; Mr Brian Hayday, a former Governor at South East Regional Office; and Mr Don Long OBE, a former Governor of HM Prison The Verne.

2.11 The Investigative Team – affectionately known as the Saga Team – produced full and careful reports within a very short space of time which commanded our respect and admiration. The reports were shown to all the parties who were represented and were subject to correction and comment. The Investigative Team was supported by a serving prison Governor, Dr Madeline Moulden, who assisted in the preparation of the reports under Mr Lakes' guidance, and who separately worked for the Inquiry in helping to analyse the letters we received from prison inmates and staff. Mr Lister also took on the additional task of examining the records of some of the inmates involved in the disturbances.

2.12 The Inquiry had to consider whether the design and condition of the prisons in which the disturbances took place had contributed to the disturbances. The Inquiry needed expert assistance on these matters. We were fortunate in being able to appoint Mr John Lynch, an architect who was, at the time, seconded to the Prison Service from the Property Services Agency (PSA) and who had considerable experience in the design of prisons. He prepared detailed reports and recommendations on each of the prisons on which I was to focus. These were made available to the represented parties. I have adopted some of his recommendations in this report. His reports have also influenced the Prison Service's plans for the reconstruction of some of these and other prisons.

2.13 When I was first appointed, I hoped that my task could be confined primarily to fact finding. But it quickly became clear to me that this was impossible if I was to produce a report which would explain why the disturbances took place and which would make useful recommendations. There were underlying issues relating to the management and operation of prisons which needed to be examined if there was to be any prospect of reducing the risk of such riots in the future.

2.14 I was aware that HM Chief Inspector of Prisons, His Honour Judge Stephen Tumim, had given considerable thought to these issues. His authoritative and independent reports are highly respected. At the time of my appointment, he was already undertaking an examination of the very serious problem of suicide in prisons which would involve an examination of some of the issues with which I would be concerned. (This report was published on 19 December 1990.) The Chief Inspector had at his disposal a fund of experience and expertise on a wide range of prison matters. It made clear and obvious sense that I should have the benefit of his help in considering the wider aspects of this Inquiry.

2.15 I therefore proposed to the Home Secretary, with Judge Tumim's agreement and support, that Judge Tumim should join the Inquiry. The Home Secretary, Mr Waddington, wrote to me on 9 May 1990 agreeing with my proposal that Judge Tumim should be joined to the Inquiry once I had completed the first part of the Inquiry in relation to the facts of the individual disturbances and before I moved to the second part involving consideration of the wider issues. The Home Secretary announced this to the House of Commons in response to a Written Question from Sir John Wheeler MP on 10 May 1990.

2.16 Judge Tumim was formally appointed to the Inquiry by the then Home Secretary in a letter of 27 July 1990. I gratefully acknowledge Judge Tumim's contribution to the work of the Inquiry and the value of his forthright and wise advice. I should also acknowledge the help of two members of his staff, Mr David Jenkins and Mr Anthony French. Judge Tumim had to continue to bear the responsibilities of his office as well as assisting the Inquiry. I know that the combined burden was a heavy load indeed. Fortunately we were able to discuss fully together each of the wider issues. I am glad to be able to record that he is fully in accord with the conclusions set out on these issues. However, I suspect that if he had been responsible for the way our conclusions are expressed, they would be much more succinct and far more felicitously crafted.

2.17 I owe a deep debt of gratitude to the whole team.

Guiding Principles

2.18 I decided at the outset that in conducting the Inquiry, I should be guided by the following principles:

    i)   *the Inquiry should as far as possible be in public:* this seems to me the sine qua non of an Inquiry of this sort. The fact that prisons are unavoidably closed institutions made it all the more important that there should be full public discussion, not just in relation to the facts of each disturbance, but also of the wider issues. However there were times when it was unfortunately necessary to take evidence in private. In addition, so as to consult as broad a cross section of views as possible, I had many meetings on the wider issues with people whom I believed could assist the Inquiry.

ii) *a broad canvass:* I was grateful to the Home Secretary for telling the House of Commons during answers to his statement on 5 April that:

> "It will be up to Lord Justice Woolf to interpret the terms of reference".
> [Hansard 5 April 1990, col 1342.]

I have taken up that invitation and decided that I should address the wider issues the disturbances raise. However, in judging whether an issue was a matter which I should consider, I have paid particular attention to the contribution, if any, which the issue might make to fomenting or avoiding disturbances in prison. The statement I made at the preliminary hearing on 14 May 1990, to which I will refer later, contains my conclusions as to what was to be my approach. It is a broad approach. It involves trying to identify underlying problems and suggesting solutions. It is not however an inquiry into the whole of the prison system, let alone the Criminal Justice System. The important matters which I decided it would not be right to investigate or make findings about were:

a) the responsibility of named prisoners for acts of violence or other criminal conduct. I was well aware that parallel with my Inquiry police investigations were being conducted which would most likely result in prosecutions. A number of these prisoners have now been charged but not yet tried. Quite apart from prejudicing those individuals, my Inquiry was likely, if I did not adopt this course, to prejudice those prosecutions. If I had not come to this decision, there would have been no alternative but to adjourn the Inquiry until after the prosecutions. The Inquiry would also have been considerably prolonged and turned into a series of what would have been in effect trials of particular incidents during the disturbances;

b) for the same reasons, the responsibility of members of the prison staff who were alleged by inmates to have been guilty of assaults or other criminal conduct. If these allegations were true they raised matters which justified prosecution;

c) the merits of the reorganisation of the Prison Service above establishment level. This reorganisation, which was on a very significant scale, was implemented in September 1990. The decision to implement it was announced on 11 January 1990. Following the disturbances, the then Home Secretary wrote to the Prison Governors' Association on 21 May 1990 saying that he intended to proceed with the implementation of the reorganisation. The Home Secretary could have postponed the implementation, but he decided not to do so. The merits of the reorganisation were highly controversial. Unless I made it clear that I was not going to examine the reorganisation, the Inquiry would have prolonged the controversy. It appeared this would have been very undesirable and would have led to uncertainty which would have adversely affected the Prison Service. Once the decision had been reached to implement the reorganisation, it appeared to me that it was important, as has happened, that management and staff should reserve judgment on the merits of the reorganisation until it had been tested in practice, and to give it their support in the meantime. The expense involved in implementing the reorganisation meant it would be folly to reverse the process before that test had taken place;

d) sentencing policy, by which I mean the length of sentences passed by judges for different classes of offences;

e) problems which solely relate to women prisoners, none of whom was involved in the disturbances;

f) the position of those prisoners from Northern Ireland (or indeed the Republic of Ireland) who may wish to return to a Northern Ireland prison following their conviction for serious offences in England and Wales. The Irish Prisoners Support Group have advanced forceful submissions on their behalf suggesting they should be transferred to prisons in Northern Ireland. However, this issue was not directly or indirectly involved in any of the disturbances and none of the prisoners in the prisons with which I was concerned fell within this group. I do, however, deal generally with the need for prisoners, where possible, to serve their sentences near their homes.

iii) *wide consultation:* many people have given much thought to prison matters, from many different starting points. I wanted to make sure that I benefited from such varied experience and wisdom. I was grateful for the evidence I received from the Prison Service, and from a wide range of representative bodies and organisations. But I set considerable store on the views of those with direct experience of the front line of prison life – the staff in prisons and the inmates;

iv) *speed:* I was mindful of the Home Secretary's wish that I should proceed with all possible speed. I was also conscious that it was important that the Inquiry's findings and recommendations should be made known as soon as possible because until this happens there will be uncertainty about aspects of the Prison Service's policy for the future. I have aimed, therefore, to move as quickly as is consistent with fairness and thoroughness.

The Early Days

2.19 My initial tasks were to identify those prisons, in addition to Manchester, which had suffered serious disturbances and on which I wished to focus. I needed to brief myself on those establishments, and to set in train the arrangements for the public hearing into each of the relevant disturbances.

2.20 I received from the Prison Service a summary of all the serious incidents which had occurred from 1 to 9 April. Including Manchester, that initial list identified 26 different prisons. More disturbances were to follow, in particular the serious disturbance in Pucklechurch Remand Centre, which started on 22 April 1990. I did not consider it was practicable, or necessary, to examine in public the circumstances of each of these disturbances. I decided to focus consideration on those that appeared on the evidence available to me at the time to be the most serious, taking account of the length of time which they took to resolve, the injuries which may have been suffered and the damage caused. I also took into account the nature of the establishment so that the Inquiry could reflect as far as it was necessary different types of prisons in which serious disturbances had occurred.

2.21 Following the resolution of the Manchester disturbance on 25 April, I decided to focus on six prisons in all – HM Prison Manchester (Strangeways); HM Young Offender Institution and Remand Centre Glen Parva; HM Prison Dartmoor; HM Prison Cardiff; HM Prison Bristol; and HM Remand Centre Pucklechurch.

2.22 I wrote to the Director General of the Prison Service on 30 April 1990 asking for evidence in relation to these six establishments, and to a further three in which there had been serious disturbances – HM Prison Hull, HM Prison Long Lartin, and HM Young Offender Institution Stoke Heath. Having examined the Prison Service's evidence in relation to those further three prisons, I was satisfied that I had properly identified the leading six.

2.23 I wrote also personal letters from 2 May 1990 onwards to some 95 individuals and organisations whom I believed might wish to contribute evidence to the Inquiry – either in respect of the particular disturbances I was investigating, or in respect of the wider issues, or both. I asked both the Prison Service and the other individuals and organisations to send me evidence in relation to the first part of the Inquiry by 21 May; and in relation to the second part by 1 September 1990.

2.24 My letter to interested organisations announced also that I would be holding a preliminary public hearing on 14 May at the Royal Institution of Chartered Surveyors in London. I drew public attention to that hearing through a press advertisement issued between 4 and 8 May in national newspapers, and in a number of regional newspaper serving the areas in which the disturbances had taken place.

2.25 My aim was that the public, and in particular concerned organisations and individuals, as well as the Prison Service itself, should have the earliest indication possible of my intentions. I was able to do so not much more than a week after the Manchester disturbance had ended.

2.26 I was especially anxious to bring home to Prison Service staff and to inmates themselves that I needed their help. I therefore wrote on 1 May 1990 personally to each member of staff who was in one of the six target prisons at the time of the disturbance; and personally to each of the prisoners whom we had reason to believe was present in one of the prisons at the time of the disturbance. That was a very considerable undertaking, involving nearly 1,350 letters to prison staff and some 4,050 letters to prison inmates. I am most grateful for the assistance of the Prison Service in identifying the staff and inmates, and in working long hours over the course of two or three days to help the Secretariat in addressing and despatching the envelopes. I reproduce the text of the letters at Annex 2A and Annex 2B. I asked for replies by 18 May (although some of the earlier forms asked rather more ambitiously for replies by 11 May). Inevitably, not all these letters were delivered; and some of them arrived late. But, nevertheless, I received over 600 replies from prison inmates and about 260 replies from prison staff. Their responses were invaluable to me in the preparation of my Report, as I shall show.

2.27 I wrote also a letter dated 1 May to all the members of staff in the Prison Service – including those working in prisons, the regions and headquarters – and to all prison inmates. I reproduce copies at Annexes 2C and 2D. I asked the Director General to ensure through his Governors and managers that these letters were shown to or displayed where they would be seen by staff and inmates. Again, with an undertaking of this magnitude, there were bound to be variations in the degree to which staff and inmates were made aware of my invitation, but, nevertheless, I received over 700 letters from inmates and some 170 letters from staff. The size of the response from staff, may appear poor when compared with that of inmates, but, aside from the fact that there are fewer of them, the explanation for this is probably that the staff could make their response through the Prison Officers' Association. Again, their contributions were of considerable value, as the subsequent chapters of this Report will show.

2.28 I and my team read carefully all the letters we received. We considered also that it would be helpful to the Inquiry, and of wider public interest, to prepare an analysis of these responses. The Inquiry therefore prepared such an analysis with the help of Dr Moulden and of Miss Ann Dunlop, an experienced researcher at one time with the Home Office Research and Planning Unit. I am particularly grateful to Mrs Tuck who contributed much also to this task. I refer to the analysis at various parts of this Report and reproduce it at Annex 2E.

2.29 In the days leading up to the preliminary hearing on 14 May, I started my programme of visiting prisons. I visited eight prisons before the hearing, including the six upon which I had decided to focus, and all four of the then Regional Offices. I also had meetings with the Director General of the Prison Service, the Deputy Director General of the Prison Service, representatives of the Prison Governors' and Prison Officers' Associations, representatives of bodies representing the Boards of Visitors and Prison Visitors, representatives of the Howard League, the Prison Reform Trust and the National Association for the Care and Resettlement of Offenders, and others including the Chaplain to Prisons, the Bishop of Lincoln.

Preliminary Hearing

2.30 The preliminary hearing was held in London on 14 May 1990. I set out at the hearing, as is the normal practice, the way in which I proposed to approach the Inquiry, the issues which I wished to address, and the procedures I would follow. I dealt with questions of representation and costs. In particular, I issued a guide as to the issues which would be considered for the purpose of Part I of the Inquiry. I reproduce my statement and the guide at Annex 2F.

2.31 The parties who were to appear at the hearing and their representatives were identified at this stage. They were:

i) for the Home Office – Mr Andrew Collins QC and Mr Robert Griffiths, instructed by the Treasury Solicitor;

ii) for the Prison Officers' Association – Mr John Hendy QC and Mr Barry Cotter, instructed by Mishcon de Reya;

iii) for the Prison Governors' Association – Mr Malcolm Lee QC and Mr John Saunders, instructed by Pinsent & Co.

2.32 These parties were represented for Part I of the Inquiry. I subsequently granted the Crown Prosecution Service the right to appear and be represented. Mr Peter Openshaw instructed by the Crown Prosecution Service held what I think can properly be described as a watching brief during the hearings in Manchester. In view of the nature of the evidence about the Pucklechurch disturbance, I decided that Mr Anthony Morris should represent the Pucklechurch inmates during that part of the Inquiry. It was not necessary for any of the parties to continue to be represented for Part II of the Inquiry, and no such representation was granted. No other party sought or was granted representation at any stage.

Part I

2.33 The public hearing into the disturbance at Manchester Strangeways Prison opened at the Freemasons Hall, Manchester on Monday 11 June. This part of the hearing ended on Friday 29 June, after 15 days. The hearings were intended to start at 10.00 and to rise at 17.00 with a break of an hour for lunch. While some days were a little shorter, others were considerably longer. During the course of this part of the hearing evidence was taken from 70 witnesses. I am grateful to the co-operation and stamina of all those involved.

2.34 The public hearings resumed at the Castle Hotel, Taunton, Somerset on Monday 9 July. The hearings in Taunton continued until Monday 23 July. There were three days of hearings into the Dartmoor disturbance; two days each into the Cardiff and Bristol disturbances; and four days into the Pucklechurch disturbance. In all, evidence was taken from 93 witnesses during the proceedings in Taunton.

2.35   The Inquiry resumed in London at the Royal Aeronautical Society for two days on 31 July and 1 August. Evidence was taken in relation to the disturbance at Glen Parva, from others who had not been heard during the Taunton hearings and from the Deputy Director General, Mr Emes, for a second time. In all, evidence was taken from eight witnesses during the proceedings in London.

2.36   The great majority of all this evidence was taken at sessions in public. The evidence was able to be limited and time saved because potential witnesses submitted statements to the Inquiry which I read beforehand and which were seen by the represented parties. Some witnesses did not need to be called to give evidence. Others were able to give their evidence briefly because Counsel to the Inquiry were able to ascertain that their evidence was not disputed. A list of those who gave oral evidence is attached at Annex 2G.

2.37   I was grateful to the Prison Service for its co-operation in ensuring that prison inmates whom we wanted to call were made available at the hearings. At times it was a major logistical exercise which was carried out with considerable efficiency and skill. It was essential, in my view, to have evidence from inmates where they could address matters of dispute or controversy. However their evidence raised the issue as to whether criminal proceedings would be prejudiced by the Inquiry. Therefore, if a possible inmate witness was considered to be a potential defendant in a criminal prosecution on a serious charge, he was not normally called to give evidence. He was, however, interviewed by one of my Assessors so that the Inquiry would know his account of the events.

2.38   There were some other inmates, however, who, while they were prepared to give evidence to me, did not wish to be identified in public. In deference to their wishes, and because I did not believe that their identification was material to the Inquiry, each inmate was identified only by an initial – thus Inmate DA was the first inmate giving evidence about the disturbance at Dartmoor. Other inmates were prepared to give evidence to me, but not in public session. They did not feel up to recounting in public some of the horrific incidents they had witnessed, or, despite the precautions as to their names, they feared identification and victimisation either by other inmates or staff. I respected those wishes. I therefore took evidence from some 14 inmates in private session. I made sure that each inmate – whether he gave evidence in public or in private – had available to him the services of a solicitor. Each inmate who gave evidence orally – whether in public or in private – did so in front of the represented parties and was open to cross-examination by them.

Part II

2.39   Soon after my appointment to conduct the Inquiry, I was conscious that Part II posed a particular problem as to how to gather evidence in public. I therefore discussed the problem with the Rt Hon Sir John May, who had been Chairman of a previous Inquiry into the prisons (The Committee of Inquiry into the United Kingdom Prison Services). The report of this Inquiry was published in October 1979. Sir John May was himself also considering the same problem in relation to the Inquiry he is conducting into proceedings following the Guildford and Woolwich bombings. Sir John suggested the possibility of holding seminars in public. On the basis of this suggestion, and my experience of seminars conducted at the Institute of Advanced Legal Studies, Judge Tumim and I considered most carefully the best way of conducting the second and wider stage of the Inquiry.

2.40   It is the normal procedure for Inquiries to consider submissions in private session and to take evidence from their authors in private session and on a bi-lateral basis. An Inquiry will identify those whom it would like to give oral evidence. They come before the Inquiry one by one to do so.

2.41   Judge Tumim and I considered that was not the right way forward for this Inquiry. We wanted to continue the public element of the hearings which was an integral part of Part I. The nature of the issues we wished to address also seemed to us to require that the views of one party should be tested in public against the views of the other. It should not and need not be an accusatorial setting. We wanted instead to pool ideas and proposals and to see how separate insights and contributions could contribute to what all the evidence had shown was an agreed goal – better prisons.

2.42   We therefore formulated what I believe is a new procedure for judicial inquiries – the public seminar. I announced my intention to conduct the second part of the Inquiry on seminar lines at the preliminary hearing on 14 May. As Judge Tumim and I developed our thinking with the assistance of our Assessors, we kept the public informed. I made a statement during the public hearing in Manchester on 29 June. A copy of that statement is at Annex 2H. In that statement, I set out the principles which had governed our choice of seminar topics: the matter should be relevant to disturbances; it should be central to considering how to prevent them; it should be something on which there was no consensus and where public discussion would be helpful in finding a way through; and it should hold out the prospect of practical and affordable recommendations.

2.43   In accordance with these principles, I identified the five topics which would form the subjects of the public seminars. They were:

   i)   the tactical management of the prison population – the seminar was held at the City University, London on 26 and 28 September;

   ii)   active regimes – the seminar was held in the Westminster Theatre, London on 2 and 5 October;

   iii)   relationships with the Criminal Justice System – the seminar was held at the City University on 19 October;

   iv)   the administration of the prison service – the seminar was held at the City University on 22 and 23 October; and

   v)   justice in prisons – the seminar was held at the City University on 30 and 31 October.

2.44   I emphasised on 29 June that these seminars would form only part of our examination of the wider issues. We would be considering other matters which fell outside these subjects, and we would give equal and full consideration to all the written submissions which we received.

2.45   I wrote on 29 June to about 70 organisations and individuals whom we considered were likely to be interested in these seminars, with a copy of my statement, so that they would know how our minds were moving. I wrote to them again on 28 August with further details.

2.46   We had asked to receive written submissions in relation to the wider issues by 1 September. We are grateful to those, including the Prison Service, who sent in written evidence – especially those who met the deadline. All together, we received over 150 submissions from organisations and individuals with experience in prison matters – in addition to those from staff and inmates which I have identified above – and over 180 letters from members of the public. Judge Tumim and I considered all these submissions and letters. Annex 2I provides further details of those who submitted evidence.

2.47   Given this volume of evidence, it would not have been practicable for the Inquiry itself to have published what we received. In addition, some individuals wished to give submissions or information to us in confidence. We did, however, make available at the public seminars a list of all those who up to 18 September had provided written evidence, with addresses so that those who wished to see these submissions could approach the authors or organisations direct. I understand that, as a result, a high proportion of the submissions sent to us are already in the public domain, including the submission from the Prison Service.

Others decided to publish their evidence. Judge Tumim and I very much welcomed this exchange of submissions as a valuable contribution to the public debate.

2.48   The format for the seminars was as follows: in advance of the seminars, and on the basis of the written submissions which we had received, I wrote on 19 September on behalf of Judge Tumim and myself to all those individuals and organisations whom we wanted actively to participate in each of the seminars. The aim was to keep the number of participants at each seminar to around 30. Most organisations were, therefore, invited to send one representative; the Prison Service and the trade unions two or, in some cases, for the Prison Service, three representatives; others, including academics and two former prisoners, were invited in their own right. With the invitation, I sent a discussion guide for the relevant seminar prepared by the Inquiry. These guides are reproduced at Annexes 2J to 2N. Their intention was to provide a framework for the discussion, and to assist participants in preparing their contributions. From the way the discussion developed at the seminars, Judge Tumim and I believe they were very effective in meeting these objectives.

2.49   The press, and any other organisation or member of the public, were welcome to attend the seminar. The participants and the members of the Inquiry were seated round a large table. The press and public were behind them.

2.50   In introducing each seminar, Judge Tumim and I made clear that all those who spoke were speaking in a personal capacity. Their views did not necessarily represent, in the case of the Prison Service, the views of their Minister, or in the case of organisations, the official views of their organisation. Where they wished to speak in an official capacity, they were invited to say so.

2.51   The discussion guides and the list of those submitting written evidence were available to everyone who attended the seminar. The proceedings were transcribed by verbatim reporters and the transcripts were sent to each of the participants.

2.52   At the start of the seminar, Judge Tumim or I invited one of the participants to open the discussion. Others were invited to signal to the Chair when they wished to speak. All participants were invited to keep their contributions to about five minutes, or at most ten – and they gallantly did so. At the end of each segment of the discussion, Judge Tumim and I would throw open the discussion to the floor and invite those who were not participants to make any contribution they wished. As with the public hearings, the seminars lasted from 10.00 until 17.00, with a break of an hour for lunch. Those seminars spread over two days ended at the lunch time on the second day.

2.53   I have gone into some detail on the arrangements for these public seminars because some of those who attended have suggested that there might be wider public interest in the approach Judge Tumim and I adopted. Others must judge for themselves, but we found them of very considerable value in moving the discussion forward and in helping us to test out the strength of particular ideas. I found on a number of occasions that provisional views which I had formed had, as a result of the debate, to be varied or discarded. We are grateful to all those who took part and hope that they will see something of their own contributions in the pages of this report. A list of those who participated at the public seminars is attached at Annex 2O.

2.54   The public seminars also meant that we were able to have wide ranging consultations with a very large number of people over a comparatively short period. In all, there were some 145 separate people who attended as participants or who contributed to the discussion.

2.55   Judge Tumim and I considered that, as well as these public seminars, we should provide a direct opportunity to hear the contributions of prison inmates and of prison service staff within the same format. We therefore held a seminar for prison inmates at Lincoln prison on the morning of 16 October 1990; and a seminar for Prison Service staff, principally from Lincoln and Stocken prisons, also at Lincoln prison on the afternoon of the same day. A discussion guide was prepared for both seminars which is at Annex 2P. The topics we asked to be discussed were the provision of incentives for prison inmates, and ways of improving relationships between inmates and staff. Contributions ranged widely. They showed clearly the depth of thought which both inmates and staff had given and were prepared to give to these issues. We were much helped by their contributions.

2.56 As well as these seminars, Judge Tumim and I considered fully and carefully all the written evidence we received. We also had a range of meetings with those whom we thought would be able to assist us. We were very grateful for their contribution. A list of those with whom we had meetings is attached at Annex 2Q.

2.57 I also visited prison establishments in the United Kingdom. Judge Tumim, as Chief Inspector, was already, of course, very well familiar with the field. I had meetings with the Director of the Scottish Prison Service and visited prisons in Scotland. I paid visits to prisons and spoke to prison administrators in France, the Netherlands, West Germany (as it then was), Spain, Canada and the United States of America. Altogether, during the course of the Inquiry, I visited 43 prisons in Great Britain and abroad. I set out fuller details of my visits at Annex 2R.

2.58 I believed it was important during my visits to see more than simply the geography of each prison. Wherever time and circumstance allowed, therefore, as well visiting parts of the establishment, including the living units, the segregation unit and often the hospital, I had separate meetings with the Governor and his senior managers, with the Board of Visitors, with representatives of the Prison Officers' Association, with members of staff, and with prison inmates. As a result, I was able to augment the information which we were receiving from staff and inmates in their written correspondence. I found the discussions I had in prisons of immense value. There was a well of energy and goodwill on the part of staff which gave me considerable confidence in the future of our Prison Service; and a degree of realism and understanding on the part of inmates which needs to be harnessed for the future.

Conclusion

2.59 A consequence of the way we have worked, or so I am told, is that we have unavoidably raised expectations about this Report. We have consulted very widely and many people have given much time and effort in briefing us and in giving us their views and advice. They rightly expect to see something come from all their efforts. It will be for others to judge how far those expectations have been met. But fortunately prisons are not run by judicial inquiries. The quality of our prisons in the future will primarily depend on the energy and ability of all those involved, in whatever capacity, in running our prisons. If they can take what we have to say, and use it to assist in producing a prison system in which the country can take pride, then the team will be satisfied and I hope that the Home Secretary will feel his predecessor's decision that there should be a judicial public inquiry into the prison disturbances in April 1990 was fully justified.

PART I

THE DISTURBANCES IN DETAIL

Section 3

Manchester (Strangeways) Prison

Introduction

3.1   Strangeways is one of the largest prisons in Europe. The disturbance which took place there between 1 and 25 April 1990 was the worst in the history of this country's prison system. This was because of the scale of the disturbance, the extent of the damage which was done and the period of time over which it continued.

3.2   Regrettably the death of one inmate may be connected with the disturbance. One prison officer died from pneumonia. Subsequently another young inmate, who played a prominent part in the disturbance, was to take his own life when at another establishment. 147 members of staff received injuries or were affected by smoke or fumes, and 47 prisoners were injured. The number of deaths and the extent of the injuries which occurred, were, however, nothing like as great as was dramatically portrayed in the media at the time of the disturbance. Also it is estimated that it will cost £60 million to repair and refurbish the prison, although much of that cost would have been incurred anyway through refurbishment.

3.3   The timing of the disturbance was particularly unfortunate. While conditions for prisoners and staff in Strangeways were still far from satisfactory, an able governor supported by his management and staff had been tackling the problems. As a result the regime for the inmates and the working conditions for the staff had substantially improved. In addition, work was about to start on some of the improvements in the physical conditions at the prison which were desperately needed.

3.4   During the week before the incident, a report was published into Strangeways by Her Majesty's Chief Inspector of Prisons (HMCIP). It had been submitted to the Secretary of State in September 1989. That report set out the findings of HMCIP as a result of an inspection which took place between 17 and 22 July 1989. In its conclusions the report states:

> "There was a feeling in Manchester that in the last three years the prison had emerged from the doldrums. This was confirmed by all that we saw. Management are to be congratulated for providing the successful impetus for this. The governor had put in place a management structure which worked for Manchester and he had used it strongly to promote efficient use of staff and the beginnings of a reasonable regime for inmates. It was striking to see the degree of ownership exhibited by staff at all levels and much useful energy expended searching for more constructive ways to complete tasks. Specialist staff were well integrated."

3.5   The improvements to which that report refers had continued since the time of the inspection on which it was based. The damage which was caused to the structure of the prison during the disturbance and the dispersal of the prisoners which inevitably followed mean that these efforts have been squandered.

3.6   The effects of the disturbance were not, however, limited to Manchester. Its vibrations affected the whole prison system of England and Wales. At other prisons serious disturbances took place which were linked to the disturbance at Manchester. There was a reduction of staff confidence in many areas of the service. The loss of accommodation at Manchester and other establishments mean that, until that accommodation can be restored or replaced, the conditions under which many prisoners have to live are far worse than they otherwise would have been. In the meantime prisoners have had to be accommodated in police cells at a cost to the Prison Service of over £20,700,000.

3.7   The consequences of the disturbances at Manchester were therefore grave. It is with regret that I have to report that the evidence which has been considered by this Inquiry clearly indicates that if there had not been a combination of errors by the Headquarters of the Prison Service and the management and staff at Strangeways:

i)   the disturbance which took place on 1 April could and should have been avoided;

ii)   the disturbance could and should have been confined to part only of the prison instead of engulfing the whole establishment;

iii)   the disturbance could and should have been brought to an end long before 25 April 1990.

3.8   The scale of the disturbance cannot however be attributed solely to this combination of errors. A substantial cause of the disturbance lies in the failures of the past. The Governor and his present staff cannot be held responsible for these. Despite the efforts of the Governor and his staff the conditions in which the prisoners were being contained were still intolerable. Because of this, even if the appropriate measures had been successfully taken to prevent the disturbance on 1 April, this would probably only have had the effect of postponing the disturbance.

3.9   The consequences of the disturbance could have been even more catastrophic. More prisoners could have been injured or there could have been a mass breakout of prisoners. That neither occurred is due to acts of great courage and initiative by the governors and staff of the prison. All ranks of the Prison Service worked with dedication for very long hours. It was due to their efforts, supported by the Regional Office and Headquarters and the police, which enabled the majority of the inmates, well over 1,200, to be evacuated by 07.00 on 2 April without a single serious incident. This was a remarkable achievement. In addition there were individual acts of great responsibility by some prisoners, but for which, more serious injuries could have been suffered by members of staff and fellow inmates.

The State of the Prison, its Population and Staff Prior to 1 April 1990

i) The Physical Setting   3.10   Strangeways is a local prison. That means it is designed to cater primarily for prisoners remanded or sentenced by courts in the Manchester area. It was built in 1868 to a design of Alfred Waterhouse, the distinguished architect of the Victorian period. The original buildings are solidly constructed, using red bricks and stone lintels. They dominate the surrounding locality.

3.11   A plan of the prison is at Annex 3A. The main part of the prison occupies a site of 9.5 acres. It is enclosed by a perimeter wall. The two main accommodation blocks are in this area. One block is the main prison. It is of typical Victorian radial design with a central rotunda (the "Centre") from which emanate the six wings, A, B, C, D and E (which contain the cells) and F (which contains the offices which were used for administration purposes and the Church of England Chapel). The other accommodation block is the Remand Prison. It is cruciform in shape, with four wings of varying length, G, H, I and K. There are two internal routes between the Main Prison and the Remand Prison. At the ground floor level there is a passage which joins the kitchen to G Wing of the Remand Prison. At first floor level in G Wing there is a door to a staircase. The staircase leads to the gymnasium which serves both prisons.

3.12   In addition to the Main and Remand Prisons, there are a number of buildings of more recent origin which are not of the same impressive design.

3.13   In the Main Prison all the wings are four storeys high. The cells are very much as they were originally designed, with vaulted ceilings. They are 13 feet in length, seven feet wide and eight feet high. Whilst some of the cell windows have been enlarged, most are in their original state, with vertical bars behind which there is a cast-iron frame window, with the central pane opening inwards for ventilation. The cells have doors which are of a wooden frame construction with metal cladding on the inside. The cells are ventilated and heated through brick-lined ducts which are connected to a highly decorative tower which rises some 164 feet above the Centre of the prison.

3.14   Three sets of buildings are linked to the Main Prison. To the East, both adjoining E Wing, are the hospital and the communications room and men's reception and to the West of F Wing there is a series of rooms which are used for visits. Linked to the perimeter wall is the gatehouse and other buildings which are part of the original design.

3.15   The prison wings are of the conventional galleried design. From the Centre there is normally excellent visibility into each of the wings and of the four landings. These landings give access to the cells which run along either side of the central well.

3.16   The wings have pitched roofs covered with Welsh slate on timber with glazed peaks running along their entire length. There are also extensively glazed gable ends.

3.17   F Wing differs from the other wings. The upper floor contains the Chapel and the lower floor contains offices which are used for administrative purposes. The floor of the Chapel slopes upwards towards the Centre. This means that access is obtained to the Chapel from the Centre at the fourth landing level through two separate entrances. There are also two entrances at the lower end of the Chapel, which is on the same level as the second landing in the wings. Looking towards the Centre, from the Main Gate, the entrance at the right of the Chapel is at the end of the passage which gives access both to the communications room and to E Wing. The entrance on the left gives access into the vestry and into the buildings which are used for visits.

3.18   The northern perimeter wall abuts on to Sherborne Street. A high level bridge connects the main part of the prison to a further area of 7.25 acres known as The Croft, on the far side of Sherborne Street. This area contains a number of workshops and a new laundry as well as other buildings.

3.19   Outside the perimeter there is a staff mess, an estate of staff quarters and a visitors centre.

3.20   It is accepted by the Prison Service that improvements to the establishment, including a new gatehouse, were overdue. They had been delayed by protracted negotiations to acquire the land which lay immediately to the South West of the prison and which was the site of a former Police Court. The site was acquired in March 1990, shortly before the disturbance. In E Wing a simple form of sanitation had been installed in some cells as an experiment. There had also been an experiment using chemical lavatories. At the time of the disturbance work had already taken place on C Wing, preparatory to installing internal lavatories. Equipment was on site ready for that installation.

ii) Access to the Roofs   3.21   The possibility of prisoners gaining access to roofs had been a longstanding problem at Strangeways. Substantial precautions had been taken to prevent access being obtained from outside the buildings. Within the wings extensive work had also been carried out. In each wing a wire grid had been fixed across the open gallery above the 4s landing at cell ceiling height. The grid was made from substantial ¼" gauge steel mesh. It had integral locked gates for maintenance work. The cell ceilings on the 4s landings are constructed of arched brickwork which, although solid, could be breached using heavy tools. On each of the 4s landings there was also a room used as an office. These offices had ceilings constructed of plasterboard covering expanded wire mesh nailed to the ceiling rafters. These rooms were normally kept locked but, if access was obtained, these ceilings could be easily breached. (They could be even more easily breached from above when it would be simple to force down the mesh and plaster board.) Breaching these ceilings would give access to the roof space above. Once there, it would be a comparatively easy matter to break through to the outside of the roof. It was intended to concrete over these ceilings but, although authority to carry out this work had been sought since October 1985, the work was still outstanding at the time of the riot. This left a very real weakness in security. It meant that the protection provided to prevent access between the top floor landing and the roof could be by-passed.

3.22   The Chapel roof was also protected by a lighter gauge steel mesh. The mesh was fixed immediately below the felt and slate covering of the roof. Below that there was an unprotected suspended false ceiling. At the top of the Chapel near the Centre there were small rooms, one of which was used as a projection room. Access could be obtained to the top of the projection room through the false ceiling. From there it was by no means difficult to obtain access to the roof space of A Wing. This was because some time earlier a wall in the roof space which had prevented access from the Chapel area to A Wing had been partially demolished and this had not been replaced at the time of the disturbance. (The work was to be carried out at the same time as the work to the ceilings.) From the roof space of A Wing it was possible to obtain access to the wire grid and to attack the roof, which had no additional protection. In addition it was also possible to break into the roof spaces of the other wings. (Photos of the roof spaces appear in Annex 3B.) The defects in the protection of the roof were discussed at a security meeting at Manchester prison on 28 March 1990, but the importance of carrying out the rectification work as a matter of urgency does not appear to have been appreciated.

3.23   At the time of the riot, extensive scaffolding had been erected from the ground floor to the top of the Centre. This was in order to carry out a programme of internal decoration. The scaffolding had been protected against access from the landings by wire mesh on the 2s and 4s landings at ceiling height. This protection had been strengthened shortly before the riot and it was never penetrated during the disturbance. During the riot access to the scaffolding was gained from above. The vast number of scaffold poles which made up the scaffold were then available to the prisoners and were used as both weapons and ammunition.

iii) Training and Contingency Planning

3.24   At the time of the incident, the previous method of dealing with disturbances, MUFTI (minimum use of force tactical intervention) had been replaced by control and restraint techniques (C&R). C&R training is divided into three parts. C&R1 teaches staff in three-man teams how to control and restrain individual prisoners. C&R2(a) teaches staff methods of self-defence, C&R2(b) and C&R3 are progressive systems of training where staff learn the techniques to defend and to deal with prisoners who are acting in concert and with force against prison staff. Since C&R had been introduced 350 of the Manchester staff had been trained in C&R1, but only 125 of these were fully up to date after attending recent refresher courses.

3.25   In April 1989 the Prison Service embarked on a substantial programme to train officers in C&R2 and 3. 58 members of staff at Strangeways had attended C&R3 training. This was fewer than it should have been.

3.26   The contingency plans for dealing with emergencies at Strangeways had been revised but not replaced since 1984. It was the Governor's responsibility to make sure that the plans were updated regularly and sent to the Regional Office. The Manchester plans were updated in September 1988 and January 1989 and additional plans (covering links with other services) were created during 1989 and were sent to the Regional Office.

3.27 Before the incident there had also been satisfactory liaison between the emergency services - the police, ambulance, fire and medical services.

3.28 In October 1989 the Operations Assistant Regional Director visited Manchester prison. He examined the establishment's contingency plans and noticed that they failed to separate minor incidents from major incidents. He spent some time discussing with the Head of Custody the need to modify the deficiency.

3.29 A conference was held in December 1989 for the North Region Governors at which the Operations Assistant Regional Director focused upon the requirement of dealing with a major incident. Thereafter, each prison received a handout which indicated the types of management structure, role specification and strategy needed for managing major incidents. Under the heading "Roles" this provided that "in consultation with the Director, (the Commander) will determine the strategy to deal with the incident and ensure a successful conclusion as soon as possible". A copy of this document appears in Annex 3C.

3.30 Neither the handout nor the contingency plans in use at the time of the disturbance at Manchester mention the importance of trying to limit the area affected by the incident. Nor do they mention the need to identify the place where staff should muster after the beginning of an incident.

3.31 There was also a shortage of equipment. On 1 April 1990 Manchester prison had available only 47 sets of the old type of MUFTI equipment, and four sets of the new C&R equipment (which was much superior) together with a few odd items of equipment which had been used for training. There is no doubt that at the early stage of the incident, the staff at Strangeways were without adequate equipment to protect themselves from the attacks of rioting prisoners.

iv) The Prison Population 3.32 The certified normal accommodation for the whole of Strangeways was 970 inmates. The total population on 1 April was 1,647 (an overcrowding factor of 1.69). There were 902 prisoners in the Main Prison that weekend. The Main Prison had an operational capacity of 906 according to an agreement reached following industrial action taken by the Prison Officers' Association (POA) in 1988.

3.33 Towards the end of March 1990, when the population was 1,639, the prison contained 819 sentenced adults, 127 sentenced young prisoners, 108 convicted but not sentenced adults and 85 convicted but not sentenced young prisoners. In addition there were 180 adults and 61 young prisoners waiting to appear at the Crown Court and 157 adults and 102 young prisoners waiting to appear at the Magistrates Courts.

3.34 Of the total population, 97 adults and young prisoners were on Rule 43 for their own protection. There were also ten inmates who were placed on Rule 43 as being a threat to the good order or discipline of the establishment.

3.35 Prisoners are divided into four categories, depending on the security risk they pose. The categories start at "A", for those needing the highest degree of security, and descend to "D".

3.36 The prison contained among its sentenced population 15 Category A prisoners, 105 Category B, 500 Category C and 64 Category D prisoners. The remaining sentenced adults, presumably, had not been categorised. Young prisoners are not categorised. However, 76 of those sentenced were destined for medium term closed accommodation, 18 for long term closed accommodation and 19 were scheduled to go to open accommodation.

3.37 The unsentenced adult population, in accordance with the usual practice, was treated as being equivalent to Category B. The unsentenced young prisoners were treated as awaiting allocation to closed accommodation.

3.38 In the Main Prison, adult convicted prisoners were accommodated in A, B, C and D Wings. Convicted young offenders were held in E Wing, which was physically divided from the Main Prison at the Centre end of the wing by gates. The convicted prisoners held under Rule 43 for their own protection, were on C1 landing and overflowed onto C2 landing, where there were seven prisoners. The remand prisoners who were on Rule 43 were held on the 4s landing on E Wing. On 1 April there were approximately 50 prisoners of all categories in the separate prison hospital.

3.39 In the months prior to the incident there had been an influx of Liverpool based prisoners in exchange for a group of Manchester inmates segregated under Rule 43 for their own protection. It is estimated that on 1 April 1990, 135 of the 801 sentenced prisoners were of Liverpool origin.

3.40 Part of the role of Strangeways, as a local prison, was to allocate sentenced prisoners to different establishments. Not all stayed in their allocated prison. Some were returned to Manchester. Over the six months, prior to 1 April, the number of prisoners returned because they did not fit in at their training prisons had varied between 26 and 52 per month. The figure was normally in the 30's. These figures are of significance because this category of prisoner is often the most troublesome in the system. As a result of being returned and the manner of that return they often have deep feelings of resentment. At Manchester, those prisoners included ten prisoners returned by the Prison Service Headquarters Dispersal Prison Steering Group for a six months period because of the disruption they were causing in their dispersal prisons. (The dispersal prisons are high security training prisons. They are designed to hold category A prisoners for the main part of their sentences, dispersed among lower category prisoners.)

3.41 The prison also had an increased number of Category C prisoners who were regarded as being unsuited to dormitory accommodation and required to be housed in cells. They totalled 252 and were an extremely large group of potentially difficult inmates for a local prison to handle. The increase in number was partly the result of a decision (in January 1990) to change Preston Prison from a category C prison into a local prison. This meant it was no longer possible to transfer prisoners of this category to Preston.

3.42 In the weeks leading up to the disturbance there had been concern in the prison as to the numbers and the mix of prisoners. With justification these matters were regarded by local management and staff as a possible cause of disruption, but no steps had been taken to deal specifically with this possibility in the handling or location of inmates. Mr O'Friel, the governing Governor, was concerned that he did not have the resources to make a proper assessment of the problem. His request for a psychologist had not been met and without a psychologist he felt he was unable to adopt a more sophisticated approach to population management - a conclusion that I do not consider to be entirely justified.

3.43 Mr Fullwood, the Chief Probation Officer for Greater Manchester, also refers to the fact that the probation service regarded the mix of prisoners as being highly inappropriate. He said the mix included mentally disordered offenders (some of whom at times had experienced psychotic episodes), sex offenders, remand prisoners, large numbers of short time fine defaulters and a handful of highly volatile and disturbed lifers.

3.44 Although the certified normal accommodation (CNA) of the prison was 970, for many years the prison had held substantially more prisoners than that number. For example, in March 1988 the figure had reached 1,803. In the summer of 1988 the prison population had averaged about 1,750 prisoners (this was the figure agreed with the POA, after industrial action, as being the maximum capacity for Strangeways). Historically therefore, the population of 1,647 on 1 April was not particularly large. However, there had been an increase in numbers of inmates from the end of January 1990, when the figure had been 1,417, to a peak on 27 March, when the figure was 1,658. This undoubtedly had an affect on the conditions within the prison. For example, late in January, 103 prisoners were held one to a cell and 111 three to a cell. On 11 March only 39 prisoners were sleeping one to a cell and 174 were sleeping three to a cell. The mix of prisoners also made the prison more difficult to manage. These factors contributed to the instability of the prison, engendered hostility on the part of inmates and overburdened the staff.

v) Staffing   3.45   Strangeways had been in the vanguard in implementing Fresh Start. Immediately prior to 1 April, there were 550 uniformed grades in post as against an authorised complement of 552. They were preponderantly of some maturity. Just over 83% were aged 31 or over and over 50% were 41 or above. On 1 April there were 175 governor and uniformed grades, including specialists, on duty. This was not significantly fewer than should have been on duty, although a number of officers had to "act up", that is perform the duties of a more senior officer.

3.46   On 31 March/1 April, in the Main Prison the staffing position was as follows:

> A Wing – there should have been a Senior Officer and eight Officers on duty. There were nine officers on duty, one of whom (Mr Richardson) acted as the Senior Officer;
>
> B Wing – there was the full complement of nine officers, but instead of a Senior Officer there was a Principal Officer in charge;
>
> C Wing – there was the full complement of a Principal Officer, (Mr Zegveldt), two Senior Officers and eight Officers;
>
> D Wing – while there should have been two Senior Officers and 14 Officers on duty, there was a Senior Officer, (Mr Bancroft), an Acting Senior Officer, (Mr Platt) and 13 Officers - an overall shortage of one Officer.

3.47   There was a full complement also assigned to Central Services (three Senior Officers and two Officers), although two of the senior officer posts were being filled by officers acting up.

3.48   On the Observation, Classification and Assessment Unit there should have been a Senior Officer and four Officers. In fact there were five Officers.

3.49   On 1 April Miss Stewart, a Governor 5, was responsible for E Wing and the Remand prison in the absence of the Governor 4 who was normally in charge, Mr Duggan. Miss Stewart probably had on duty on 1 April on E Wing 12 or 13 Officers and two Senior Officers. In the remand prison, she had on duty on G Wing nine Officers and one Senior Officer; on H and I Wings, she had ten Officers and two Senior Officers for each wing; and on K Wing she had ten Officers, one of whom was acting up as a Senior Officer. In addition Miss Stewart was assisted by two Principal Officers.

3.50   The Deputy Governor, Mr D McNaughton, took the view that the prison "could carry out the functions of the establishment without any real undue stress with its establishment of staff". However this was far from being the view of Mr Serle, the local Chairman of the POA, or of many of the staff. In support of that view it is right to draw attention to the fact that Mr Collins in his written submissions on behalf of the Prison Service says:

> "there was some support for some of the complaints from Mr O'Friel who was concerned that proper account was not taken of the need to cater for foreseeable but irregular demands on staff. It is certainly possible that perceived staff shortages affect the staffs' confidence and morale.

Furthermore there is force in the submission on behalf of the Prison Officers' Association (POA) that at weekends there was too much reliance on cross deployment (using an officer to do different duties than those on which he is normally engaged) and acting up (using officers of a lower rank temporarily in a higher rank)".

3.51 Whether during the week a similar comment is justified is impossible for the Inquiry to determine on the evidence it has heard and in the absence of an objective standard for assessing what staffing levels are required. The need for such a standard is considered in Part II of this report.

3.52 The number of staff on duty affects the ability to provide a satisfactory and consistent regime for the inmates. The apparent shortcomings which existed at Manchester from time to time undoubtedly increased tension and created hostility. In local prisons one of the most acute problems is the burden of escort duties. This burden is very difficult to predict precisely since it is influenced by the Courts' listing of cases which can materially effect the anticipated demand for prisoners in custody. When an unexpected call is made for staff for escort duties what suffers is usually the regime (whether it be association, classes, work or exercise) or the training of staff.

3.53 The Manchester disturbance (as was the pattern in other establishments) took place at a weekend. This was almost certainly no coincidence. The inmates knew that fewer staff would be on duty at a weekend and there would be less activity. However I do not regard a shortage of staff on 1 April as having any significant influence on events on that day. If there had been more staff on duty this would not have made any difference unless, possibly, they had been deployed differently, for example on additional tasks such as to provide a greater show of force or to search prisoners as they entered the Chapel or to ensure that any disturbance was contained there by guarding the exits.

3.54 If however the overall complement of staff was inadequate, as the POA suggests, this could have contributed to instability within the prison. Over-taut staffing levels would make it more difficult to provide a consistent and constructive regime which would have helped to alleviate the dehumanising effects of the insanitary and unsatisfactory physical conditions within the prison. Furthermore the strong belief of staff that they were undermanned had adversely affected morale.

The Atmosphere and Regime Prior to 1 April

3.55 Although the management and staff of the prison could take pride in the progress which had been made, conditions within the prison were still of a wholly unacceptable standard. Prisoners, and in particular remand prisoners, were being locked up for excessive periods of time in overcrowded cells, the vast majority of which had no internal sanitation.

3.56 When the prisoners were unlocked in the morning there were problems caused by the fact that there was only one wash-hand basin for between 15 and 20 prisoners. Most prisoners therefore had to use the wash bowl and plastic jug provided to collect water from the recesses and return with it to their cells, which were frequently shared, to complete their ablutions. It was virtually impossible for an inmate to achieve a level of personal hygiene which was in accordance with modern standards. Furthermore, in the main prison wings where there could be 70 prisoners to each landing, there would be at most four WCs for their use. In the remand centre there were only two WCs to each landing.

i) Food 3.57 It is almost inevitable that prisoners complain about the food. Strangeways was no exception. Some of the complaints were vociferous. Mr R Frost, a Governor 5, was in charge of the kitchens at Strangeways. There can be no doubt that Mr Frost did his best with the resources available to provide the best food that was possible in the circumstances. He had, however, to provide a huge number of meals. They had then to be transported in heated containers to the wings where they were served to the inmates. The inmates then took their trays of food to their cells where the food was eaten.

3.58 One of the regular complaints of the inmates was that they were provided with nothing but stews. Mr Frost disputed this and was deeply upset by the fact that he had lost his menu book in the riot. The food was probably not as bad as was made out by the inmates. Nonetheless, food which is prepared a long time beforehand and is handled in the way that food had to be handled at Strangeways, is not going to be appetizing when served, particularly if it is eaten in unsatisfactory and unhygienic conditions in the inmates' cells.

3.59 Another problem was the timing of meals. Like the majority of English prisons the timing of meals is far from satisfactory and interferes with what should be the morning activities. At Strangeways the timings were as follows:

Breakfast	– 07.45
Lunch	– 11.25 - 11.45
Tea	– 16.00 - 16.45

(the last meal of the day)

3.60 A hot drink was served at approximately 18.30. The dominant factor in fixing the timing of inmates' meals is the structure of staff shifts and their associated meal breaks. These can reduce the manning levels at more normal meal times, so prisoners have to be locked away.

ii) Kit   3.61 Inmates were meant to receive a change of kit once a week. Kit was changed when prisoners had their weekly bath or shower. There were six bathhouses for the whole prison. Each bathhouse had twelve showers and one bath (showers were also available in the gymnasium). Considerable friction was caused between inmates and staff because, through no fault of the staff, there was frequently a shortage of kit. Sometimes prisoners had to go without socks or had to wear second hand shoes which were the wrong size, or a shirt without buttons, or trousers which were far too large. What is more, after the once weekly shower, on numerous occasions it was impossible even to provide a clean towel or clean underwear and socks. During the three months prior to the disturbance, the clothing position had improved, partly as a result of a kit committee and a kit recovery programme being instituted. Nonetheless, the shortage of kit remained a genuine source of grievance for prisoners.

iii) Employment   3.62 There had been a considerable improvement in the provision of employment for adult sentenced prisoners. Although many of these inmates had to work part-time, all but about 89 adult prisoners in the main prison were provided with some employment for at least part of the day. In Mr O'Friel's view, before the increase in the population in 1990, they had been down to the hard core of unemployed prisoners.

3.63 The position was different for remand prisoners. They were not employed except for cleaning. Mr O'Friel described their position as "grossly inadequate" although it had been substantially improved. They had some PE, day and evening association, a small amount of group work and some education classes.

3.64 No work other than cleaning was provided for young prisoners. The Acting Senior Officer in their wing considered that about 50% of the young prisoners preferred to spend their day lying on their bed and shouting out of their windows at night. Mr O'Friel was probably right in describing this as "a slight exaggeration", but he agreed that, while progress was being made, there was still a long way to go. The main activities for the young prisoners were PE and education, the education being available for about 50 of the 210/220 young prisoners. Twenty at a time also had PE in the gym in the morning or afternoon for up to one and a half hours.

3.65 So far as the regime provided for the prisoners is concerned Mr O'Friel succinctly summed up the total situation when he said:

> "although we had an enormously long way to go.......we had come an enormously long way."

3.66 The conditions in which they were being held clearly caused some prisoners to become frustrated and angry. The position became worse as a result of the deterioration in conditions caused by the increase in numbers before the beginning of April. In his evidence to the Inquiry, on behalf of the Greater Manchester Probation Service, Mr Fullwood, the Chief Probation Officer, summarised the view of the Probation Officers in these terms:

> "Manchester Prison has for many years been a human warehouse, doing its best to protect and control too many men in conditions which sap rather than enhance human dignity."

This description certainly does not overstate the position.

The Number of Prisoners Allowed to Assemble at the Same Location

3.67 It was nothing unusual for large numbers of prisoners to congregate in one place at one time at Strangeways. At meal times some 300 to 400 prisoners would either be collecting their meals or be in transit to different serveries at the one time. There would be 200 to 300 prisoners in the workshops at the Croft. When outdoor exercises were taking place there would be at least 100 prisoners at each location. During evening classes, 120 prisoners could congregate in a comparatively small area at any one time. The Chapel was used for a number of activities besides worship and it was in the Chapel that the largest gatherings would take place. Film attendances in the Chapel were limited to one wing at a time, but there was no such restriction on religious services.

Religion

3.68 Chaplains have a long and distinguished history of service within Her Majesty's Prisons. I am informed that the history goes back to 1773. Originally, in addition to their religious duties, they were responsible for welfare and education. Nowadays they are able to concentrate on the spiritual and rehabilitative aspects of prison life, although they still do a considerable amount of welfare work. It is unlikely that during the long and distinguished history of the chaplaincy work in prisons, a prison has been better served by their chaplaincy than was Strangeways. The prison was served by two Church of England chaplains, one Roman Catholic chaplain and three Methodist chaplains. In addition there was an Imam who visited the Muslim prisoners twice weekly and a Jewish Rabbi who visited the jewish inmates. A Buddhist minister had also recently been appointed.

3.69 During the year to September 1989, the prison had been visited by Christian Scientists, Mormons, Jehovah Witnesses, Sikhs and Quakers.

3.70 In addition to holding services and bible classes, and general parochial duties, the chaplaincy was very much involved in assisting inmates to find jobs and accommodation. They had also formed strong links with religious congregations outside the prison.

3.71 The energy and enthusiasm of the chaplaincy is illustrated by their involvement with the Billy Graham Mission in 1989. During the period of the Mission the chaplains were assisted by over 20 missioners each day. They showed video films of the meetings held by Billy Graham to over 1200 inmates and as a result over 150 made a commitment to the church. There were 29 services and religious classes each week which was supported by part-time staff.

3.72 The chaplaincy encouraged other activities, including the making of boards for blind people to enable them to play bingo and fund raising for charities.

3.73 The Reverend Noel Proctor, the senior Church of England chaplain, normally conducted three services on Sunday. At the first early morning service only between 45 and 55 prisoners would attend, but the main service would be well attended by 300 or even 400 inmates.

3.74 I have emphasised the energy and activity of the chaplaincy because it explains why there was nothing unusual on 1 April in a large attendance at the main service. It is true that the size of the attendance was substantially influenced by the fact that if the inmates did not attend they would be "banged up". Nonetheless it is clear that religion was playing a significant part in the lives of many of the inmates of Strangeways. The lack of alternatives no doubt encouraged many to attend for the first time, but the evidence indicates that a large proportion of those who attended found the services rewarding. This reaction was no doubt assisted by Mr Proctor's personality and the fact that he was able to involve many outside organisations and individuals in the service. If the nature of the main Church of England service had been fundamentally changed by limits on attendance, many inmates would have felt deprived.

3.75 After the riot started, the chaplaincy, with the support of the local churches led by the Bishop of Manchester, was very involved in providing counselling and welfare for those who had been caught up in the riot.

Manchester Visitors' Centre

3.76 Prior to 1987 the facilities for visitors to the prison were wholly unsatisfactory. A centre was then established outside the main gate which was run by the SELCARE (Greater Manchester) Trust. The building is modest. However they had set up a canteen and child care facilities and had tried to establish a queuing system for visitors. Visitors at the centre are able to ask for advice on a range of subjects from the Citizens Advice Bureau and on health matters from the Health Visitor.

3.77 The centre is staffed entirely by employees of voluntary agencies and volunteers. They play an important part in making visits less stressful and more meaningful. The centre is supported by central Government finance. It is clearly important that adequate finance for these centres is available. They play an important part in making a success of visits which, in a local prison, are probably the most important aspect of the prisoner's life.

Inmates' Evidence

3.78 In their letters to the Inquiry and in their written and oral evidence, the inmates made a large number of complaints. The majority of the complaints were associated with the conditions in which the prisoners were having to live. Some writers however blamed the riot on a hard core of prisoners. A minority suggested that some prison officers wanted a riot and encouraged inmates to riot in order to justify their dispute with management on staffing levels. The letters are analysed in Annex 2E.

3.79 In oral evidence to the Inquiry, Inmate F said the clothes that he was given to wear made him look like a tramp. He thought that inmates were banged up far too long and that the food was no good. Another inmate (Inmate G) gave evidence that he had been told that he had to wait three months for association. Inmate L, a former policeman, said that prison officers had their own system of control which was nothing to do with Home Office guidelines. There was no redress against prison officers and in his view the situation was so serious that those outside the prison had to be involved. He pointed out that, although only a very small minority of prison officers were bullies who verbally abused and degraded people, it was difficult to go to a prison officer to complain about another prison officer.

3.80 Inmate I, who was on Rule 43, regarded Preston, which was the prison he was then at, as being like a five-star hotel when compared with Strangeways. He indicated that it was difficult for Rule 43s to take exercise at Strangeways because of the treatment they were subjected to by other prisoners. Another inmate (Inmate J) who was also on Rule 43, said he used to be locked up 23 hours a day and only had one hour for exercise on days when the weather was fine; he was also allowed to attend a film show once a week. There were no education classes available to him.

3.81 One prisoner described the Board of Visitors as just prison officers in suits. Another inmate who, according to the affidavit he provided to the Inquiry, was the true leader of the riot (although this does not accord with a substantial quantity of other evidence) stated:

> "The disturbance was intended as a protest not so much against prison conditions in terms of overcrowding, lack of privacy, "slopping out", lack of exercise and so on but more a protest against the oppressive regime conducted within the prison by prison officers. The oppression consisted of abuse by the officers of their powers and violence from the officers to inmates together with a complete failure by senior prison officers to fairly conduct the laid down grievance procedures."

Later in his affidavit the same inmate goes on to complain about how disciplinary proceedings were conducted.

3.82 On the evidence before the Inquiry it is impossible to make any findings with regard to these allegations, but these examples reflect the general tone of the complaints which were being made.

3.83 Repeatedly in their response to questions as to what steps should be taken to avoid disturbances in the future, inmates reply with "If you treat us like animals, we'll behave like animals". The same response was given by an inmate of a foreign prison whom I asked about the time he had spent at Strangeways.

3.84 Suggestions made for improving the situation included the introduction of a wing based discussion group. One prisoner suggested:

> "Maybe have a member of the BOV sitting in on it instead of an officer to hear what wants changing and looking into. Maybe even a representative of the inmates taking notes and putting them forward to the Board. This could make people aware of problems concerning that particular wing."

Another prisoner suggested more incentives and responsibilities for prisoners. Another suggested that smaller prisons would be better. Finally a few prisoners recommended more woman officers. "The lady officers do a better job and plus they listen to your problems and try to help with them. And in the riot while the male officers were running about worrying, the lady officers were all calm and did their job."

3.85 In accord with what he regarded as the underlying principles of Fresh Start and good management, Mr O'Friel had delegated the handling of prisoners' grievances to the subordinate manager best placed to deal with the issues raised. This was not understood by the inmates, many of whom felt they had been deprived of their entitlement to have their complaints dealt with by the Governor. There was a lack of confidence in the system of justice within the prison. A number of prisoners attributed the riot which took place to the fact that no-one appeared to be taking any notice of their complaints.

3.86 Prisoners in a prison of the size of Strangeways cannot reasonably expect to have ready or frequent access to the Governor 1. It is however essential that the governing Governor should be seen in and about the prison. It is also essential that everyone knows who is the governing Governor. The fact that Mr O'Friel, in common with other governing Governors, had no means of identifying himself other than by word of mouth during his tours of the prison, may explain why more inmates were not aware of the visits which Mr O'Friel was in the habit of making to all parts of the prison.

Staff Attitudes

3.87   While some prisoners complained of arbitrary and oppressive behaviour, and even mental and physical brutality, the complaints were in very general terms. There were very few specific complaints of acts of brutality by particular officers. It was suggested that one prisoner in the punishment cells had been forcibly injected with drugs, but our investigation failed to establish the truth, or otherwise, of what had been alleged. However, at that time Manchester, as will be explained later, was short of its senior medical staff. A full-time medical officer of the prison, Dr Somasunderam, when giving evidence, quite inappropriately suggested that drugs could be used for controlling prisoners when they were no more than a nuisance. It is possible therefore that the control of the administration of drugs was not as strict as it should have been.

3.88   When an inmate complained of prison officers' attitudes, he usually also made the point that it was only a minority involved. An individual probation officer was, however, concerned by the lack of sensitivity and poor professional standards of certain prison officers. His experience accords with evidence from a number of inmates who referred to a minority of officers who were adopting bad practices. The same probation officer indicated that:

> "intense anger and frustration has been a major feature in many of the prisoners with whom I have worked and has often been a dominant feature of work".

3.89   I have little doubt that while the majority of officers' attitudes could not be described as other than correct and some officers were sympathetic in their attitude, a small minority of officers were still by their actions creating a divide between staff and prisoners and spoiling the good work of the majority. They created the impression among prisoners, whether justified or not, that staff could behave oppressively.

Signs of Tension

3.90   While some of the prison staff spoke of a period leading up to the disturbance when they had been aware of heightened tension between staff and inmates, this was not confirmed by others who should have been in a position to know. The probation officers were, however, of the opinion that during the three weeks before the disturbance there was "a noticeable increase in the level of tension within the prison".

3.91   Some confirmation of the increase in tension was provided by events which occurred during the second half of March. On 15 March there was an incident in which a prisoner had to be brought under control using control and restraint (C&R) techniques. Another prisoner, who was later to be one of the alleged leaders in the disturbance, became involved and he also had to be restrained. On 17 March one prisoner caused a fire in his cell and another threatened Mr Morrison, a Governor 4, that he would start a riot unless he was transferred to another prison. Both those prisoners played a prominent part in the riot which began on 1 April. Finally, on 26 March two prisoners climbed the scaffolding which had been erected in the Centre of the Main Prison to enable re-decoration to take place. By so doing they gained access to the rotunda gallery and from that gallery, through one of the rotunda windows, to the roof. It was almost 20 hours before two prison officers brought them down, using the route over the projection room to which reference has already been made and will be made later.

3.92   Interviews with those who played a prominent role in the riot indicate that, for differing reasons, they were labouring under an intense sense of grievance. These inmates encouraged others to become involved in the riot which started on 1 April. This encouragement no doubt explains why the majority of the inmates who gave evidence had been aware that there could well be an incident on that date and were confident that staff were aware of this as well.

Warnings of the Disturbance

3.93   Mr O'Friel was at the prison in the morning of Saturday 31 March 1990, although he does not normally attend the prison at weekends. It was the day on which the media were carrying reports of the demonstrations against the community charge in London the previous day. Similar disturbances had taken place in Manchester. Mr O'Friel was standing in for Mr Wallace, who was the Governor 4 responsible for the Operations Group, which includes the prison's security section. During the morning Mr O'Friel conducted disciplinary adjudications. He did not notice anything amiss.

3.94   In the afternoon prisoners from D Wing attended a film show in the Chapel. When the film was over there was some reluctance to leave. However, the very experienced Senior Officer on D Wing, Mrncroft, was able to deal with the situation and persuaded the prisoners to return to their cells. Mr Bancroft was struck by the fact that the inmates were behaving very differently from normal. He formed the impression "that something was brewing". This was confirmation of previous warnings of trouble that he had had. The previous day Prison Officer Fagen, the D Wing Censor, had handed him a note – which he had collected from a letter box on D Wing – which said either there would be "trouble" or there would be a "riot" in the Chapel on Sunday. In addition, Mr Bancroft had received "general tip-offs" from prisoners on the Wing indicating that they were not going to Chapel on Sunday. The note was taken to the prison Security Office and Mr Bancroft passed on the information he had received to the Governor 4, Mr Morrison, who had overall responsibility for the main prison, and who was the senior Governor on duty at the time and to Governor 5, Mr Holliday. He also told Mr Holliday and Mr Morrison that when there had been a previous disturbance in the Chapel (in October 1986) prison officers had been stationed in the roof above the projectionists room. He suggested the same procedure should be followed that Sunday. The suggestion was not followed.

3.95   The officer in charge of A Wing that weekend was Acting Senior Officer Richardson (an officer of some 13 years service). On Saturday 31 March, some time before 14.30, he was told by a member of the church choir that he was not going to the Chapel in the morning because it was "going up". When Mr Richardson suggested that there were always reports of that sort the inmate replied "This is it." He went on to say that notes originating among the Category A prisoners who were in cells on D1 were circulating the jail. The notes urged prisoners "to arouse the scouser, to smash the Chapel and take the roof off the place". This was more precise information than Mr Bancroft had received. Unlike Mr Bancroft's information it was not from an anonymous source but from an inmate known to Mr Richardson. Mr Richardson therefore took the information seriously and reported it to the officers who were in charge of the Control Room, Mr Ferns and Mr Cook. The fact that the information came from a member of the choir who was not prepared to go to Chapel makes it of particular significance.

3.96   There were two principal officers who were responsible for security at the prison. One of those officers was Mr Rutson. He had been a principal officer responsible for security for three years prior to the disturbance. He had attended a two-week course for security officers at the Prison Service Staff College, but he regarded the most important training as that learnt as the result of experience and the information obtained from a partner. Mr Rutson undoubtedly had a flair for security work. He is an extremely strong personality and energetic. His approach was unorthodox – although it is fair to say that the security officer job description left considerable scope for individual discretion. He recognised that the Security Information Report forms (SIRs) which had been specially prepared to facilitate the collating and recording of security information, should be completed. However by temperament Mr Rutson was a person who preferred action to writing, and this would have contributed to a situation where security information tended to be dealt with informally. Mr Rutson considered that all information reported to Control should be recorded in the control room log. However an examination of the log makes it clear that it was completed only spasmodically. This meant that while Mr Rutson said it was the practice of Security Principal Officers to check the log when they came on duty, this was of little value.

3.97   Mr Rutson was firmly of the opinion that if he had been on duty on 1 April he would have told Mr O'Friel of the information that had been received. His advice to Mr O'Friel would have been that nobody from the punishment block should go to Chapel and that there should have been "ad hoc rub-downs to people going to the Chapel". He would have also placed more staff in the Chapel and on the landings. If Mr Rutson had been on duty the riot in the Chapel may well not have started.

3.98   The other Security Principal Officer, Mr Palmer, although he had been in the service for over 28 years, had only been one of the Security Officers for a month. Like Mr Rutson he was responsible to Mr Wallace. On 31 March he was the Security Principal Officer on duty. His approach to events over the weekend was clearly affected by the fact that he had spent six or seven years working in the main prison. He knew that there was frequently information to the effect that there might be trouble in the Chapel on Sunday. Mr Palmer, unlike Mr Rutson, had not received any training and, as he said in evidence, he was "learning on the job". He agreed that in the period immediately preceding 1 April, the co-ordination of security information was inadequate and the "practices were lax".

3.99   On 31 March Mr Palmer was called to the Control Room as a result of Mr Richardson reporting the information he had received from a member of the choir. When he arrived at the Control Room he was told the full story. Mr Richardson was so concerned about the situation that he suggested that the Church Service should be cancelled. But Mr Palmer considered he could not possibly do this. Nor was he prepared to accept the suggestion which Mr Richardson made that Category A prisoners should not be allowed to go to Church. No SIR was completed about the information from the member of the choir and it does not appear to have been recorded anywhere. If Mr Palmer had had Mr Rutson's experience he may have responded differently. Mr Rutson said the information "would have made the hairs at the back of your neck stand up". If he had been the recipient of the information, I am confident there would have been more action taken.

3.100   In addition, Prison Officer McCormick passed information to Control that he had been told there would be trouble in Chapel on Sunday. This, however, was done in a light-hearted manner. It would not necessarily have been taken seriously by those who received the message. No action appears to have been taken as a result of this report.

3.101   Before Mr Morrison went off duty on 31 March he left a message for Mr Zegveldt, the Principal Officer who would be in charge of C Wing on 1 April, to draw up some contingency plans for Chapel the following morning. Mr Zegveldt is a very experienced Principal Officer of some 23 years service. At that time all that Mr Morrison had in mind was the possibility of a sit-in next day.

3.102   Mr Zegveldt had been on detachment and had only returned to the prison five days before the riot. But he sensed that there was a difference in the behaviour of the prisoners. He received the message from Mr Morrison when he returned from tea on 31 March. Mr Zegveldt decided to give instructions to all the staff on duty that they should carry out the process of unlocking the prisoners for the purpose of slopping out that evening in a way which would not involve an "unhealthy" number of inmates being out at the same time. He did not intend the staff to impose what is technically known as a controlled unlocking. Nevertheless, the inmates on D Wing were let out excessively slowly. As a result there was tension on that wing, with the inmates banging on their doors.

3.103   When Mr Morrison went off duty on 31 March, a Principal Officer was left in charge of the prison as Night Orderly Officer and a Duty Governor was on call. On the night of 31 March the Principal Officer was Mr Robertson who had come on duty between 19.30 and 20.00. He took over from Mr Zegveldt who had been the Principal Officer on the previous shift.

3.104   Assisting Principal Officer Robertson that night was Senior Officer Verrall. During the course of the evening Mr Verrall was told by an Auxiliary Officer (Mr Bateman) that an inmate in D Wing had told him that there was to be a riot the following day. Mr Verrall reported the information to Mr Robertson and Mr Robertson asked him to get any further information he could. Mr Bateman then went back to the cell of the inmate who had given him the information and passed him a piece of paper to write on. This course was adopted because an interview with the inmate after he had been locked up for the night would have drawn attention to the inmate. The note which the inmate provided stated:

"There's going to be a riot in the Church of England using weapons such as PP9's and hoods against officers regarding treatment towards inmates."

3.105   The reference to PP9's is a reference to a battery used for radios. Batteries in an inmate's sock can make an effective cosh.

3.106   Mr Verrall attached to the note a memorandum addressed to the Governor which read:

"Sir,

Whilst on live night duty on Sat 31-3-90 I was handed the attached piece of paper reference an incident that was to occur on 1-4-90 in the C of E Chapel."

3.107   After the note had been obtained, Principal Officer Robertson rang the Communications Room and passed on the information. This was duly logged against the time, 22.47, as:

"PO Robertson rang with information that a riot situation may occur in the chapel tomorrow 1-4-90. Inmates will be using PP 9 batteries and may be wearing hoods/masks."

3.108   The following morning, 1 April, Principal Officer Robertson regarded his duties as being taken over by Acting Senior Officer Johnson. Mr Johnson was in charge of the Centre. The handover was not to an officer of equivalent rank to Mr Robertson because during the day a Governor (on 1 April Mr Morrison) is in charge of the Main Prison. Mr Robertson says that before he went off duty he handed the note and memorandum to Mr Johnson with instructions that it was to be given to the Duty Governor as soon as he came in.

3.109   It is not in dispute that Mr Morrison, who was the Duty Governor in the Main Prison, was not handed the note or memorandum, nor was he told of its contents. Mr Morrison did not see the entry in the log and no-one told him about it. He knew nothing of the information which Mr Richardson received, or of the note which Mr Fagen had found and handed to Mr Bancroft. Mr Morrison on coming on duty apparently followed the normal practice in not checking the log which had been kept overnight at the Centre. The practice at weekends was for the Night Orderly Officer's reports, including information of any particular incident during the previous night, to be given next morning by the Principal

Officer who was the Night Orderly Officer to the Senior Officer in charge of the Centre. It was that officer's responsibility to pass the reports on for the attention of the Duty Governor.

3.110   Mr Johnson says that he mentioned the existence of the note to whoever he came in contact with. However, contrary to his recollection, it appears he did not do so to Mr Zegveldt. Nor did he mention it to Mr Morrison or to the duty Governor of the whole prison, Mr Wallace. He did however hand it to Governor 5, Mr Holliday.

3.111   Mr Holliday was under the impression that he had mentioned the note to Mr Zegveldt, but Mr Zegveldt was adamant that he did not know of the note. Mr Zegveldt suggested that, because he was already taking action that morning because of what had happened the previous day, everybody assumed that he knew of the note. In my view Mr Zegveldt is probably right about this. However, Mr Zegveldt was anxious to hold a staff briefing meeting as soon as the staff came on duty and it is possible he did not take in what he was told. Another possibility is that because Mr Holliday thought that the note had come from an anonymous source, Mr Holliday did not attach the importance to it that he would have done if he had known its true history.

3.112   At least two other officers received information (Mr Collins and Mr Oliver), but they did not attach particular importance to what they heard. Their evidence only goes to indicate the extent to which warnings were available. Mr Collins passed his information to Mr Johnson who said he was already aware of it. Mr Oliver did not take any action since he thought the information was common knowledge.

3.113   Although the warnings should have been recorded in SIR's this was not done. Informal methods of communication were relied on.

The Disturbance – Sunday 1 April

i) Morning Preparations

3.114   At approximately 07.50 on Sunday 1 April the staff who had come on duty were called together in the Centre. Without checking with the Centre Senior Officer or any Governor as to recent developments, Mr Zegveldt, who had come on duty at about 07.40 (which was late for him although his shift did not start until 08.00) addressed them. He told them about the events of the previous evening so far as he was aware of them. He gave them instructions about being careful as to the manner in which they unlocked inmates for breakfast. He told the senior officers on A, B, C and D Wings that he wished them to put an extra officer in the Chapel and said that the officers in the Chapel should move in pairs, not become isolated and if there was any trouble they should evacuate the Chapel.

3.115   Mr Zegveldt anticipated, on the information which was available to him, that if there was trouble in the Chapel (he thought there was a greater prospect of trouble during afternoon exercise by D Wing prisoners on B yard), it might take the form of a sit-down with the possibility of a hostage-taking. He did not wish the staff therefore to be isolated. Mr Zegveldt said that, if he had been aware of the information which was in fact available, he would certainly have wanted to see the Governor in Charge to discuss the matter with him.

3.116   After the staff meeting Mr Zegveldt reported to Mr Morrison. He told him of the arrangements which he had made at the staff meeting. During that discussion Mr Wallace came into the room. Mr Wallace had come on duty at about 07.45 and had gone to his office, which was in F Wing below the Chapel. Having looked at the papers that were waiting for him there, he went into the Governor's office. He saw there the journal which summarised the matters of which Mr Morrison was aware which had taken place the previous evening. Mr Wallace entered the Centre just in time to hear the end of Mr Zegveldt's briefing. After the briefing was finished, Mr Zegveldt informed him of the steps he had taken and why he had taken them. Mr Holliday mentioned the note to Mr Wallace, but did so in terms which indicated, as he thought was the case, that it was a note from an anonymous source and therefore Mr Wallace did not regard it as being important. Mr Holliday also handed the note and memorandum to Mr Wallace. At the time this did not register with Mr Wallace. He never looked at the note. Indeed, he had no recollection of having received it until Mr Holliday told him well after the riot started that he was certain that he had handed it to him. Mr Wallace then searched for the note and the memorandum and found them both stapled together. It was unfortunate that the note was not drawn more forcefully to Mr Wallace's attention because he accepts that if it had been he would have set in process enquiries as to the origin of the note. This should have led to a greater appreciation of the dangers of trouble that morning.

3.117   At 08.30 there was a meeting between Mr Palmer and Mr Wallace. There is a dispute between Mr Palmer and Mr Wallace as to whether Mr Wallace was informed by Mr Palmer of the information which had been given by Mr Richardson and of the note handed in to Mr Robertson. However, Mr Palmer's assessment of this information was very low key. The probabilities are that even if he is right in his recollection, his dismissive approach would have meant that Mr Wallace would not have attached importance to what he had to say on the subject. Mr Palmer agreed however that Mr Wallace did ask him to make his staff available to assist. Mr Palmer interpreted this as a request to assist in moving the prisoners in and out of the Chapel. Mr Palmer arranged for this to be done.

3.118   Mr Wallace also asked Mr Zegveldt and Mr Holliday to find out whether they could obtain any "hard information". This produced the name of a particular inmate as an instigator. But he could be ruled out as being a cause of possible trouble at the Chapel since he was a Roman Catholic who would not attend the Church of England service.

3.119   Although further information was not given to Mr Wallace, some additional steps were taken. In particular those Rule 43 inmates segregated at their own request and located in C Wing, were advised not to attend the Chapel service. None did so. The same action was not taken in respect of the Rule 43's on E4, but fortunately they also decided not to attend. Additional staff were sent into the vestry of the C of E Chapel. Their instructions were that if there was any trouble in the Chapel they should make sure the staff and the preachers were evacuated.

3.120   Mr Holliday also raised with Mr Wallace the possibility of staff being placed in the roof of the Chapel. He was aware that if there was trouble the prisoners could well try to get on to the roof. Although he had only been at Manchester about nine months, he had heard something about the previous occasion when there had been trouble in the Chapel when staff had been placed in there. He had heard that the route which had been used by the prisoners on that occasion was through the false ceiling near the projection room and onto the top of the projection room and into the roof space in that way. Mr Holliday's assessment at that time was that, if there were trouble, they could cope with the entrances, but without staff in the roof-space, they would not be able to stop the prisoners making for the roof. Mr Wallace however rejected his suggestion because he considered it would not be safe.

3.121   Bearing in mind the breakdown which had taken place in communicating all the warnings received, the precautions which were taken were fairly substantial. They would, however, have been on a wholly different scale if all the information available had been appreciated by those in charge that Sunday morning. Indeed Mr Wallace's evidence was that if he had been aware of the information which had been provided to Mr Richardson, and the full information as to the provenance of the note which had been handed to Mr Robertson, he would "have considered seriously whether to cancel the whole of the service and......would most certainly have contacted the Governor at home and discussed the issue with him." Mr Morrison took a similar view. He too would have spoken to Mr O'Friel and might have advocated cancellation of the service. He accepted that the precautions taken were wholly inadequate.

3.122   Mr O'Friel would have been reluctant to cancel the whole service, if he had been consulted, as his aim would have been to try and keep the prison running normally. However Mr O'Friel would not have allowed the young prisoners or the prisoners on D1, that is the prisoners who were in the segregation unit, to attend the service. He would have had staff on the E4 landing and in the vestry wearing the MUFTI protective clothing which was available. He would also have required random searches of prisoners entering the Chapel.

3.123   It is clear that there was a lack of co-ordinated organisation that Sunday morning. Although there was a meeting of the Governor grades and Principal Officers there was no attempt to coordinate the information which was available or the action which should be taken. The Governors and Principal Officers on duty appear to have been acting on their own individual assessment of the situation and on their own initiative. Even Mr Bancroft, the Senior Officer who was to be in charge of the service in the Chapel, was only told he was to be in charge about 15 minutes before the service began.

ii) The Chapel Service on 1 April 1990

3.124   The Church of England service in the main prison started very much (but not quite) as normal. The prisoners, but no Rule 43's, were taken to the Chapel in the normal way at about 10.00, except that the landing was more heavily supervised by staff than usual. There were statements that it was thought the prisoners from D1 who were segregated for disciplinary reasons or because they were category A prisoners, were searched. Evidence from two officers to this effect was placed before the Inquiry after the hearing at Manchester. But the probabilities are that few, if any, prisoners were searched. In the light of the information received there should at least have been a large number of random "rub down" checks.

3.125   The Chapel is 124.5 feet long and 41 feet wide. There were 309 prisoners in the Chapel. This was not an excessively large number by Manchester standards (where as set out above the Church of England service was normally extremely well attended by about 300 to 350 inmates). However the mix of prisoners could well have been different from usual. There were no Rule 43 prisoners (usually 8-12 attended). The evidence before the Inquiry indicates that a number of other inmates who would normally have attended the service did not do so, including the prisoner who had spoken to Mr Richardson. The prisoners who did attend were supervised by 14 officers in the Chapel instead of the usual eight. In addition there were the seven officers outside on the vestry stairs. The officers who Mr Palmer had arranged to supervise the inmates going to Chapel dispersed after the prisoners had entered the Chapel.

3.126   Towards the front of the Chapel, that is at the lower level, there were about 90 young prisoners who occupied the first five rows from the front of the Chapel. There was then a gap of two rows. The adult prisoners occupied the rows from the seventh row upwards. Mr Proctor, the Chaplain, estimated there were about 190-200 adult prisoners. This was a slight under-estimation.

3.127   The Category A prisoners, the prisoners from the punishment segregation unit and the prisoners identified as being on the E (for escape) list, arrived late that morning, just as the first hymn was about to be sung. Their arrival clearly caused a stir among the inmates who were already in the congregation. There are descriptions given (which are not entirely satisfactory) of how some of those prisoners who came in late showed others that they were carrying chair legs and other weapons, concealed in their clothing.

3.128   Mr Proctor, who was conducting the service in conjunction with a Church Army Captain (Mr Ferguson), had been forewarned that there might be trouble. Because of this he began the service by reminding the congregation that he expected them to behave themselves as they were in God's House.

59

3.129 During the solo singing of a hymn there was a certain amount of noise. Mr Proctor warned inmates that if they wanted to "act up" he would bring the service to a close and let them go back to their cells. He was under the impression that the congregation settled down and when the solo was finished there was clapping. There was however trouble with a subsequent hymn with some of the inmates refusing to stand.

3.130 This was followed by a sermon from an Army Scripture Reader which was not well received and attracted a few catcalls.

3.131 Then, as Mr Proctor rose to announce the final hymn, an inmate came down the centre aisle and took the microphone from a position in front of the choir. He began to address the congregation, talking about the hardness of the prison system. A tape recording was made of this part of the service and fortunately it survived the subsequent disturbance. This gives the best indication of what was happening. It makes it clear that pandemonium broke out. It is not surprising therefore that the accounts given by witnesses of precisely what happened differ.

3.132 It is clear that Mr Proctor, who is of slight build, was the first person to try and deal with the situation. He wrestled the microphone away from the inmate who had been using it to address the congregation. He then attempted, by addressing the prisoners, to restore order. For a time he felt that he might be successful, as he had been in the past, in doing so. But an inmate among those who had arrived late shouted out words to the effect that "You've heard enough, let's do it, get the bastards" and brandished two sticks. This brought the lull to an end. Other prisoners also brandished weapons and put on masks. Some of the prisoners pressed towards the back of the Chapel where most of the prison officers were. Those prison officers, in accordance with the instructions they had been given by Mr Zegveldt, then started to leave.

3.133 What then happened at the Chapel is clearly described by Mr Bancroft. He was at the back and had been standing in approximately the centre of the Chapel. There were two prison officers down near the two exits at the front of the Chapel, but there were none down the sides of the Chapel. Mr Bancroft tried to give an urgent message on his radio to the Communications Room and he gave instructions to open the gates at the rear of the Chapel so staff could retreat. He intervened with one inmate, while other officers were being attacked with missiles including sticks. In addition he saw a hooded prisoner smashing a bookcase. He was then hit by some sort of missile, which could have been a hymn book. A fire extinguisher was hurled over his left shoulder narrowly missing him. He was doused with water from a fire bucket and struck on the right elbow by another extinguisher. He was then pushed out of one of the rear doors of the Chapel, like "a cork from a bottle". By then, the other officers, who had been at the rear of the Chapel, had already left.

3.134 Another officer, Mr McInerney, had been leaving by the other rear exit. He was confronted by a prisoner who grabbed his keys. They came away, enabling the prisoner to take possession of them.

3.135 In the meantime, at the front of the Chapel, the two officers who were in charge of the young prisoners, Mr Liddle and Mr Mawdsley, were moving them out of the Chapel through the passage which gives access to E Wing. They showed considerable presence of mind and courage. They were attacked by other prisoners. Mr Liddle was grabbed by the throat and struck on the head by a table leg, causing him to fall to the ground where he was struck again, kicked and had his spectacles broken. He got to his feet and was again struck, but he managed to get to the door and into the passage which led to E Wing. He was pushed down the stairs and had his arm very badly broken. Mr Mawdsley was also attacked. He tried to close the door but was trapped behind it, he was beaten with sticks and, like Mr Liddle, was pushed down the stairs.

3.136 While this had been happening, the seven officers who had been in the vestry, were trying to get into the Chapel. But they were impeded by those who were seeking to get out, including Mr Ferguson, the Church Army Captain and Mr Harris, the Army Scripture Reader. In the vanguard of the officers from the vestry was Prison Officer McCormick. While making his way towards the centre of the Chapel to assist Mr Proctor, Mr McCormick was struck and knocked to the ground. Prisoners, who then gathered round, assaulted and kicked Mr McCormick and another officer. In the melee which ensued, Mr McCormick's keys were taken from him by the prisoner who had first hit him and who had seized the microphone during the service. That prisoner then shouted "I've got the keys" and started to make for the back of the Chapel, pursued by Mr Proctor. Mr Proctor was stopped by another prisoner wielding a fire extinguisher above his head. Mr Proctor told him to drop it, which he did. In the meantime three prisoners, in order to protect Mr McCormick, dragged him towards the door into the vestry preceded by the officers who had entered the Chapel with him. Mr Proctor had also been rescued by inmates who were members of the choir, who persuaded Mr Proctor to leave with them.

3.137   One of the prisoners who helped both Mr McCormick and Mr Proctor, a former police officer, described how Mr McCormick had been on the floor of the Chapel at the time when all the prison officers withdrew. The withdrawal of these officers is confirmed by a prison officer, Mr Pogson, who had been one of the officers in the vestry. However, on Mr Pogson's account, it would be wrong to criticise the prison officers for this. Some of the prison officers in the vestry had been diverted by the need to look after prisoners who had left the Chapel through the same exit as the officers were seeking to enter. In addition to Mr McCormick, Prison Officer McLean had been injured. Mr Pogson explains how he was overwhelmed and pushed back down the stairs into the vestry by those trying to get out of the Chapel. Finally the seven officers were a motley force. They had no MUFTI or C&R equipment. They included two officers who had angina and one with a back problem. They did their best in the circumstances.

3.138   There is no doubt however that Mr McCormick could well have sustained even more serious injuries if it had not been for the action of the inmates who rescued him. Mr Proctor probably also owes his safety to other prisoners who intervened and guided him into the vestry. It is also fair to say that other inmates could have prevented Mr McCormick and Mr Proctor being taken from the Chapel but they, including the inmate who originally seized the microphone, did not do so. Indeed this inmate (the one who seized the microphone) was clearly agreeable to Mr Proctor and Mr McCormick being taken to safety. The prisoners were content to get the prison officers out of the Chapel and obtain keys, but they were not interested in taking hostages, as they could have done.

iii) Withdrawal of Staff from the Prison

3.139   At the time the incident occurred, Mr Holliday was returning to the Chapel by the spiral staircase in A Wing. He was on the spiral staircase between the 2nd and 3rd landings when he first heard the noise. He arrived outside the Chapel on the 4th landing just as the gate to the Chapel was being closed behind Senior Officer Bancroft. Both gates were then closed. There were about 15 officers around the gates. The entrances had doors, as well as the gates, and the left hand door was jammed ajar by a fire extinguisher. There was a massive noise of banging, shouting and screaming. Mr Holliday could hear Mr Proctor trying to control things. Mr Holliday left since he considered that he would be more use elsewhere in preventing a possible escape from the other end of the Chapel. He did not, as he now accepts he should have done, give any orders to the staff to try and contain the prisoners in the Chapel and prevent them getting into the Centre.

3.140   Shortly after Mr Holliday left, Mr Zegveldt must have arrived outside the Chapel on the fourth landing. At that time he was aware of only one officer being present. That officer was Officer McInerney. Mr McInerney's key chain, without the key, was wedged in the locked metal gate of the entrance to the Chapel which is nearest to A Wing and which had the wooden door which was partly open. It appears probable that the other officers had left the wing by that time. Why they had left is not clear because they had not been ordered to do so and the prisoners initially made no attempt to leave the Chapel. On the contrary they were barricading the doors into the Chapel, no doubt because they were under the misapprehension that the officers would try to re-enter.

3.141 Acting Senior Officer Johnson was still in charge in the Centre. This was a situation for which he was quite unprepared. He had no training and very limited experience of being controller in the Centre. He had no contingency plans of any relevance immediately available. As the disturbance broke out, Mr Morrison joined him in the Centre. Mr Johnson had, during the course of the morning prepared his own check list of what should be done in the event of an incident. He promptly took action in accordance with that check list. He sent a radio message that the Chapel "had gone," while Senior Officer Rigby went round to each wing telling the staff to report to the Centre. Shortly afterwards Senior Officer Bancroft arrived, soaking wet, and according to Mr Johnson said "We have lost the prison". However it appears more likely that what was said was that the Chapel was lost and that the prisoners had got keys. This is Mr Morrison's recollection and is also more consistent with Mr Rigby's recollection.

3.142 Those in the Centre were in a difficult position because the planks on the scaffolding obscured their view of the higher levels. Mr Johnson was under the impression that he saw through the planks inmates streaming out of the Chapel, but it is most unlikely that he is right about that. He then phoned the main gate to make sure that it was fully sealed, phoned main reception to prevent the movement of inmates, and informed the staff on C1 and D1 that the incident was taking place. On his own initiative, he later told them that they should evacuate the prison. He had heard on the radio that the inmates had keys and he also told staff on A1 to leave. Mr Morrison heard what he was saying, but did not intervene. Mr Johnson asked Mr Morrison more than once whether he should sound the klaxon and when Mr Morrison agreed to his doing so, the klaxon (which is usually used for giving a warning of an escape) was sounded.

3.143 Mr Johnson's impression was that there were probably 20-30 officers at the Centre at that time. Apparently no instructions were given to them as to what action they should take. This was unfortunate because Mr Holliday estimated 15-20 officers could have held the main prison. There is no doubt that those in the Centre were under the impression that a number of prisoners were on the landings in the Centre and elsewhere. But it is more likely that they were confused by the noise which Mr Morrison accurately described as horrendous. In the early stages it is probable that only isolated inmates were out of the Chapel, and they were not on the Centre at the higher levels or on the scaffolding, but initially in A Wing on the fourth landing. Even if they were on the scaffolding, having got on at the top from the rotunda, they could not have got from there into the Centre because of the protective mesh around the scaffolding which was never at any time penetrated. Nor would they have been able to throw objects at the staff. The 4s level had protection above it and it was of much closer gauge than that above the wing landings.

3.144 Nevertheless, Mr Morrison came to the decision that the Centre should be evacuated. He ordered the staff to withdraw down F Wing. At the time Mr Morrison had not taken any steps to obtain direct information that prisoners were on the Centre. He assumed they were because of the "tidal wave" of noise and the information he had been given that keys had been taken. However he himself had seen officers going towards the chapel on the 4s. If a check had been made, it would have been revealed that the Centre was then under no immediate threat. The most reliable information Mr Morrison apparently had about the movement of inmates was that Mr Zegveldt had seen inmates dropping down on the 4s in A Wing. (The way they did so has already been explained.) Mr Zegveldt had said that it would be impossible to retake the area that the prisoners had occupied.

3.145 Mr Morrison's recollection of events is not very clear. However, with the assistance from the incident log which was being kept in the Communications

Room, what probably happened is as follows. Mr Morrison first informed the Communications Room that it would be necessary to withdraw staff from the main Centre but Mr Wallace told him at that time (11.11) not to withdraw. Shortly thereafter, Mr Morrison decided that staff *should* withdraw and he reported this to the Communications Room. The staff then withdrew, and Mr Morrison reported that they had done so at 11.13.

3.146 In the course of his evidence Mr Johnson made it clear that he considered that Mr Morrison was not giving him the lead that he should and not taking command of the situation. Indeed he made it clear that he considered that Mr Morrison had panicked. This was a charge which Mr Morrison strongly denied. He said:

> "I did the very best that I could to stay as calm as I could in the circumstances. I remember at the time telling myself mentally that I would not be any help to other people if I failed to stay as calm as possible. So I welcome the opportunity to respond to the charge and I reject it."

3.147 Mr Morrison had entered the Prison Service in 1977 as a direct entrant Assistant Governor. Before coming to Manchester as a Governor 4 in 1987 he had been Assistant Governor at Lincoln Prison for five years. At Manchester Mr Morrison was, under Mr O'Friel, the Governor responsible for running the main prison. His responsibilities included security and control. When the disturbance broke out it was his responsibility, under the general control of Mr Wallace, to take charge of the main prison and exert control over the staff in the prison.

3.148 Having had the advantage of hearing Mr Morrison give evidence, I have no doubt that he is a Governor of considerable ability who has qualities which are of great value to the Prison Service. I also accept that he did not panic as had been suggested. However, I equally have no doubt that he was totally unprepared for and shocked by the situation with which he was faced that morning. This was partly because of the breakdown in the communication of information which should have made it clear that the risk of a disturbance during the Chapel service was much greater than Mr Morrison believed to be the case. It was also because there was no contingency plan to which Mr Morrison could turn to gave him any assistance. In particular he did not appreciate the importance of trying to contain the prisoners in as limited an area as possible of the main prison, nor the significance of withdrawing staff from the main prison which had the effect of giving the prisoners control of that prison. He should have exercised, but did not exercise, more control over the actions which Mr Johnson was taking.

3.149 Up to the time of the disturbance, Mr Morrison had been required to act only as administrator and manager, a role which he performed well. On that Sunday morning he was suddenly required to act as an operational commander without previous experience or training. In the few minutes before he ordered the withdrawal from the Centre he was not in a position to provide the sort of leadership which was needed if the staff who were present were to become an effective force. As he said towards the end of his evidence at the Inquiry:

> "The thing that was really paramount in my mind from a very early stage was the safety of staff because I could see with my own eyes what had happened to Mr Bancroft and from the noise above me it was abundantly apparent that something absolutely major was going on."

He therefore took the action, which would ensure their safety, of withdrawing.

3.150 Mr Morrison, however, had other responsibilities, including responsibilities to the inmates who would be left within the main prison. He should not have given the order that he did without ensuring that it was necessary to do so. At the time it was not necessary to leave. He should himself have ascertained, or ordered a member of staff to ascertain, the true situation before giving the order. If he had done so he would have learnt that there was no immediate danger.

3.151   The situation could, however, have changed rapidly if a substantial number of mutinous prisoners had obtained access to any of the wings apart from E Wing. There were no security gates separating the other prison wings from the Centre. The only barriers were small (four feet six inches high) wire mesh control gates, which could not be double locked and which were too flimsy to withstand a moderately severe attack. E Wing was the exception. From E Wing access to the Centre was by a substantial timber framed door which could be double locked.

3.152   There was also a problem with keys. As all the cells could be opened by using the same bunch of keys, there was nothing to stop the prisoners going to each wing and unlocking all the prisoners there. These prisoners then had the run of the prison.

3.153   There were means, however, to stop prisoners using a prison officer's keys to gain access from the wings to the outside areas of the prison. This was achieved by a doubles key which, when applied, deadlocked the doors and so made the ordinary key ineffective. At the opposite side of the Centre in a safe was the doubles key which could have been used for securing external doors and gates. At one time Mr Johnson said that he considered obtaining the doubles key, but he decided that it was not safe to do so. He indicated later, however, that he had not really thought about the doubles key and that seems to be the more likely position.

3.154   As Counsel to the Inquiry submitted:

> "The evidence from the prisoners suggests that the fact that the prison officers had, as we submit is clear from the evidence, vacated the fours before there had been any significant infiltration of prisoners into the roof spaces seems to have had a profound psychological effect on the prisoners themselves. It immediately gave the indication to them that the prison was theirs. Whether or not a determined attempt to hold the fours would have been successful will always remain a matter of speculation. But there is no doubt that by deserting the fours the prison officers effectively handed the prison to the prisoners".

3.155   Within a short time of the staff withdrawing from the Centre, Mr Holliday, together with other staff, went back into the Centre from F Wing. At that time there were some prisoners running about the 2s landings. Some were armed and some were wearing masks. The officers with Mr Holliday were not in MUFTI or in C&R equipment. They were attacked by some prisoners. Before they were attacked, however, Mr Holliday was able with other members of the staff to take various articles out of the Centre, including mobile or two-way radios. Mr Holliday's impression at that time was that if they had had C&R equipment available, it would still have been possible to have held the Centre, unless and until the decking (which was laid across scaffolding between the 2 and 3 landings and which prevented inmates descending the scaffolding to the Centre) was removed by prisoners.

3.156   At the time the disturbance in the Chapel started, Mr Wallace had been in his office on F Wing under the Chapel. He noticed a small amount of noise on two occasions during the service but attached no particular importance to this. However shortly before the service was due to finish at 11.00 he decided to go and observe the preparations being made for the inmates to leave the Chapel. It was just as he was leaving his office that he heard the noise which indicated that trouble had started. On hearing the noise his immediate reaction was to go to the Centre, but on opening the door from the west wing into the Centre he realised that because of the scaffolding he could not see anything other than staff running across the Centre towards the stairways going up to the 4s level. He therefore decided it was important that he went and took charge in the communications room, or as it is sometimes described, the control room, and that is what he did. He arrived, according to the incident report, at about the same time as Mr Holliday, at 11.05. At that time the police and fire brigade had already been notified. Just after Mr Wallace arrived, the Regional Office was informed. Reports began to be received of inmates on the F/Chapel Wing roof and (11.07) on E Wing roof. By 11.08 the Governor 1 had been paged.

iv) A Wing 3.157   The officer in charge of A wing that weekend was acting Senior Officer Richardson, a situation which the POA submits was not appropriate. He is the officer who had been informed by the member of the choir that he was not going to chapel, and who, as already described, had reported his concerns to Mr Palmer. Mr Richardson was therefore well prepared for trouble on the Sunday. His fears were confirmed when the inmates started to go into the Chapel from A wing because he said the inmates were "strangely silent". When the disturbance started, he was waiting for the inmates to come out of Chapel. He immediately ran, as did other staff, towards the Chapel. The inmates in A wing who had not attended the Chapel Service were then secure in their cells. He says that he was two thirds of the way towards the Chapel when he heard a voice from above saying that they, the inmates, "are getting out at the front", (that is to the forecourt). The group of staff he was with then went out to the forecourt and milled about in the area in the vicinity of the vestry door. He had not himself seen any inmates on the loose inside the prison.

3.158   The other officers who were on A wing appeared also to have vacated the wing at an early stage. This meant that when the inmates from the Chapel came one at a time from the roof space and through the hole they had made in the office ceiling, they found A Wing unsupervised by staff. They could therefore release the prisoners who were there at will.

v) B Wing 3.159   On B wing the inmates who were not at chapel had also been locked in their cells by about 10.45. The last inmates to be locked up were ones that Mr Andrews, a prison officer, had brought back from the sick bay. He found there were no other officers present on the wing apart from the senior officer who was on duty (Senior Officer Danbury).

3.160   He then went to the tea room on A Wing, where he was when the disturbance started. He started to make his way to the Centre when he was told by an officer to go to the back door of the Chapel to cut the inmates off if they tried to break out on to the forecourt. He went to a position outside the vestry. B Wing therefore appears also to have been almost immediately left without officers.

vi) C Wing 3.161   The senior officer in charge of C 1 landing on C Wing was Mr Collins. At the time of the disturbance, he had with him prison officers Duffield and Hoad. Mr Collins was the officer who had been told the previous day by an inmate "there's going to be trouble in the chapel tomorrow boss, I'm not going". Nevertheless, on the Sunday he had found that the situation appeared quite normal. However when Mr Zegveldt suggested that he should advise the Rule 43s not to go to Chapel, he had done so. He had, however, allowed approximately 15 of the Rule 43s prisoners to have exercise. They were on exercise when Mr Duffield received a message that there had been a disturbance in the Chapel and that keys had been taken. The inmates were then brought in and locked up.

3.162   According to Mr Collins' recollection what then happened was as follows: he rang Mr Johnson at the Centre and told him that the Rule 43s were locked up. He asked for instructions. Mr Johnson said that he would ring back. Shortly afterwards he heard through his radio that D1 staff were going to evacuate, so he telephoned control and asked for instructions. He was told "wait out". The next thing that happened was that the warning klaxon went. He also heard a message come over the radio that "main prison staff were unable to contain. Main prison staff to withdraw". He then rang control again and was told to evacuate his staff. The officers on C Wing then started to leave in accordance with this order. However, having walked a few yards from C Wing doors, Mr Collins was concerned about the Rule 43 prisoners. He told Mr Duffield to radio control and ask about the 71 Rule 43s locked up on C1. They received a message back from the communications room control that, if at all possible, they should get the Rule 43s out. (According to the incident log, this would have been about 11.16.)

3.163 The three Officers, Collins, Duffield and Hoad, then went back on to C1 landing and attempted to evacuate the inmates. Unfortunately, because they were terrified, a number of inmates had barricaded themselves in their cells. The officers had some difficulty in persuading them to allow the officers into the cells. However, they were eventually successful and they unlocked all the prisoners on C1. By that time the noise was horrendous. Mr Collins had to decide what to do about the seven Rule 43s on the C2 landing. He was sure from what he had heard that there were prisoners loose either on the 2s or the 3s. He came to the conclusion that it was not possible to try and release the seven inmates on the second landing and so unfortunately they were left behind. This was not Mr Collins' fault. He and the other two officers acted with a commendable sense of duty and professionalism in raising the safety of the Rule 43 prisoners with the communications room and in going back into C Wing after previously being asked to leave. Mr Collins was not a young man. He was 59 years of age and was due to retire on 3 October 1990. With the noise by then taking place it must have been a harrowing experience trying to persuade the inmates on C1 to evacuate the wing. As Mr Collins said in evidence, he did not feel that it would be safe to go on to C2 himself so as to try and repeat the same exercise with the seven Rule 43s who were on that landing. He was not prepared to order other officers to do what he was not prepared to do himself. The inmates from C1 however were safely escorted to the Croft area with the assistance of two dog handlers who had joined the officers earlier.

vii) D Wing 3.164 During the chapel service five category A inmates from D Wing were having exercise. Prison Officer Parr was supervising them. He heard about the disturbance over the radio and tried to bring the exercise to an end. However the prisoners saw a helicopter flying over the prison and realised that something was happening. They refused to return. The three officers who were on duty were not in a position to force the inmates to come in. Having heard the radio messages about evacuating the prison (to which reference has already been made) they locked the entrance to the exercise yard. The inmates were left there while the officers withdrew from the wing. At the time that they did so, according to Mr Parr, inmates were already loose on D2 and D3 landings. The officer in charge, Acting Senior Officer Platt, left D wing and positioned himself at the end of C wing so that he could keep the five category A prisoners who were in the exercise yard under observation. He remained there until he was relieved by a dog handler.

viii) E Wing 3.165 On E wing there were two senior officers, one of whom was acting Senior Officer Reynolds, and 12 or 13 other members of staff. About 100 of the young prisoners on the wing had gone to chapel. There had been no advice given to the officers on E wing that the Rule 43s should not go to chapel. Indeed when Miss Stewart, who was the governor responsible for the remand wing, had visited E wing, while she warned the staff of possible trouble in the chapel, she had assumed that any Rule 43s who wanted to go to chapel would do so. She had therefore told the staff that after the service was ended they should take the Rule 43s straight out and put them straight back in the cells. However, in the event no Rule 43s went to the service.

3.166 Because of the suspected trouble, staff on E Wing went down the passageway to E wing to meet the young prisoners when the service finished. Mr Reynolds said in evidence that the first he knew of trouble was when approximately 20 of the young prisoners came running down the passageway. When the inmates were back in the wing, followed by Officers Liddle and Mawdsley, the gates in the passage were locked.

3.167 After the inmates had been secured, Mr Reynolds went to the Centre and asked for instructions from Senior Officer Johnson about whether he should double lock E wing passage. He was told "yes" but having removed the double keys from the safe he replaced them. He considered that it would be unsafe to transport the double key to E wing because of the risk of losing it to inmates. He was told to return to E wing and hold the passageway from E Wing for as long as he could. Preparations were then made by the staff to defend the gate in that passage.

3.168   Shortly after that Mr Reynolds heard the instruction to evacuate the prison. He instructed the staff to retreat through the door leading to the hospital on E1 landing. He next heard a loud noise from level 4. He saw some inmates run along that landing, only to run back when they saw the officers. All the officers then retreated into the hospital and closed the gate.

3.169   Contrary to what happened in C wing, the Rule 43s were left on the wing. It would have been a more difficult task to evacuate the E Wing Rule 43s, because those inmates were on the 4s landing. The Rule 43s who were evacuated from C Wing were on the ground floor.

3.170   The other senior officer on the wing took some of the staff from E Wing to the kitchen. He considered that kitchen officers and inmates might still be there. The staff who had been with Mr Reynolds stayed in the hospital for a time until they were told to muster near the main reception, which they did. But an hour later, they had still not received any instructions as to what to do.

3.171   Mr Reynolds in his evidence made it clear that E Wing had been evacuated because of the instructions that had been received. When asked whether there could have been time to evacuate the Rules he candidly said "there may have been time to get them out but I couldn't swear to it". This was probably as fair an assessment of the position as is possible. The position would have been clearer if orders had been given earlier to evacuate all the inmates on Rule 43 from the wing. However it appears the danger to them was not appreciated until inmates were breaking into E Wing.

ix) The Remand Prison   3.172   Miss Jennifer Stewart had joined the prison service in November 1979 and had been at Strangeways since 1986. She was the Governor 5 who was normally responsible for the remand prison's central services group. Over the weekend of 31 March and 1 April she had been responsible for the remand prison and for E Wing, the Governor 4 of the remand prison being off duty. She had come on duty on Sunday 1 April at about 07.40. The first advance warning of trouble that she received was when Mr Holliday came to the remand prison at about 08.00. He told her that there was some concern that there may be problems in the Chapel and asked for additional staff.

3.173   The staff which she had available has been set out earlier. Miss Stewart considered that the staff available was adequate to carry out the routines on the respective wings. She provided four of her staff for use in connection with the main chapel service.

3.174   Miss Stewart says that Mr Wallace visited her during the morning. They were both "slightly bemused" by the suggestions of trouble since there was nothing significant about the atmosphere in the remand prison. She adds that, because it was 1 April, "we wondered if there was some kind of wind up going on, because that would not have been unheard of either. We did not feel that there was any serious cause for concern."

3.175   At the time of the start of the disturbance there were 37 adults on exercise in H yard. The other remands were all in their cells locked up. Miss Stewart received a telephone call from Mr Wallace asking her to send staff to assist. By that time she had already instructed the senior officer in G Wing and his staff, apart from one officer, to report to the communications room. At the time of the telephone call she had allowed the exercise to continue so as to avoid an adverse reaction from the prisoners. She explained this to Mr Wallace, but she received a second telephone call from him shortly after at about 11.10 to bring the exercise in. This she did without incident with the assistance of her staff. She then instructed all her staff, apart from a principal officer, a senior officer and four or five other staff, to go to the Centre. She herself left the remand prison about 11.20.

3.176   At that time Miss Stewart had given no specific instructions to the remaining staff as to what they were to do. She did not take any steps to secure the two entrances to the remand prison from the main prison. However an officer had suggested that a padlock and chain should be placed on the gate at the entrance which gave access to the kitchen and this was applied to that gate. The wooden door on the far side of the gate was not, as it could have been, double locked. Miss Stewart's explanation for not taking this precaution was that that the remand prison "was at risk did not seem a possibility at that stage".

3.177   Shortly after she reached the communications room area, Miss Stewart learnt about the evacuation that was taking place of the convicted Rule 43s. She asked Mr Wallace whether anything could be done about the Rule 43s on E4. He told her it was too late because prisoners were already on E wing. From the communications room, Miss Stewart instructed her staff in the remand prison that if any prisoners came into the remand centre they should evacuate.

3.178   Surprisingly, no doubles key was available in the remand prison. Miss Stewart had some idea that there was a doubles key in the main Centre but she said she "could not have got to it....with complete assurance". In any event, while the door at G1 from the kitchen could be double locked, the door at G2 from the gymnasium had only a single lock which could be opened by the keys available to the prisoners.

3.179   A doubles key was however obtained from a safe in the governing Governor's office. The gates leading out from the remand prison were double locked. The gate at I1, however, although initially "doubled", was subsequently unlocked to allow an evacuation route for the staff who remained in the remand prison.

3.180   Nothing was done to defend the remand prison apart from the use of a chain and padlock on the gate on G1 and doubling the external locks. Only a skeletal staff was left in the remand prison, although a substantial number of staff were in the vicinity of the main gate waiting to be told what to do.

3.181   Miss Stewart was taken completely by surprise as to the scale of the incident. She had never been fully briefed about the information which was available relating to the risk of an incident in the Chapel that morning. She felt that the information of which she was aware could well amount to no more than an April fool. There were no contingency plans which gave guidance as to the desirability of securing the remand prison in the event of a serious incident in the main prison. The physical protection of the remand prison from the main prison was limited. While a substantial gate had been recently put in position inside the wooden door on G1, this could not be doubled. Apparently this was because it was positioned part way along the last cell wall on G1, so that it would have been possible to by-pass that gate by making a hole in the wall of that cell.

x) The Communications Room

3.182   Mr Wallace was in command until Mr O'Friel arrived at the prison just before 12.00. Mr Wallace exercised control perfectly appropriately from the control/communications room. (In a local prison there is not technically a control room.) The communications room had been sited previously in the Gate Lodge. There the facilities had been totally inadequate. It had been transferred into temporary accommodation in the building known as the Back Reception. This was linked with the passage which runs between the Chapel and E wing. Two years previously plans had been submitted for it to be refurbished and rebuilt as a purpose built command suite, but authority for the work to proceed was still awaited.

3.183   The communications room provided no visibility. Video equipment gave only a view of the pedestrian entrance at the main gate. The room was equipped with three telephones and an outside direct line to the police. In addition there was a radio net. As the inmates at an early stage obtained possession of a radio, they were able to jam the radio net for a time and to overhear communications. Furthermore, when the prisoners obtained access to offices, they were able to interfere with the telephone lines. The result was that the communications room was confined to using a single outside line until a mobile phone could be provided. This was subsequently backed up by additional lines laid by British Telecom.

3.184   In the words of Mr Wallace, the communications room itself was too small. There were no separate areas from which governor grades could command an incident. There was no room to take any executive decisions without being surrounded by everybody else who was in there. There was no room for police liaison or for other services and although cameras had been asked for for years they had not been supplied. However, with the facilities which they had, the controllers in the communications room, in Mr Wallace's words, "performed excellently".

xi) The Loss of the Remand Prison

3.185   One of Mr Wallace's concerns was that the communications room could be attacked by inmates coming from the Chapel along the corridor to E wing. He therefore stationed staff in MUFTI in that corridor. This was successful. Staff were also placed in F wing (under the Chapel) to protect F wing from attack. However no staff were deployed in MUFTI in the remand prison. Mr Wallace's explanation for this is that there were not sufficient staff. However Mr Nicholson, the C&R instructor to whom reference will be made later, thought the Remand Prison could have been held by one trained C&R3 unit (12 men and a commander). Although Mr Wallace may not have been aware of this at the time, the other evidence indicates that there were in fact plenty of staff who could have been used for this purpose. Only ten officers had been used in F Wing. There were a dozen in the gate area. The remainder were in the forecourt and vestry area. While it was important to have staff in this area in case the inmates who got out of the Chapel made directly for the gate, some could have been safely deployed in the remand prison.

3.186   The likely reason the staff were not so deployed is that once Mr Wallace knew that the inmates were secure in the remand prison, he regarded the remand prison as being safe. He overlooked the risk of the inmates, who had keys, trying to release all the prisoners, which is what subsequently happened. Some confirmation of this is provided by the instructions Mr Wallace gave to Mr Rigby. These instructions were to double the external doors of the prison. He made no mention of the door at G1 from the kitchen. Mr Rigby fulfilled Mr Wallace's instructions, returning to take the double lock off the I1 exit as already explained.

3.187   One of Mr Wallace's first priorities once staff withdrew from the main prison should have been to hold the Remand Prison. He should have given this his attention but he did not. Miss Stewart should have been told to return and take command. But until Mr O'Friel arrived, nothing was done, apart from applying the doubles to the external locks and putting a padlock and chain on the gate on G1.

3.188   The officer on duty as the remand centre co-ordinator was Prison Officer Oliver. He had been in the Service some 17 years. He thought it right to get in touch with Senior Officer Rigby on the telephone and ask whether any particular steps should be taken. He was told that none was necessary.

3.189   When the other staff left with Miss Stewart, Mr Oliver was one of the six prison officers who remained in the remand centre. According to the log, Mr Morrison reported inmates proceeding to the remand prison at 11.43. However it was not until after 12.00 – about 12.20 – that they actually broke in through the wooden door leading from the kitchen into G1. Mr Oliver states that the iron gate which had been padlocked and chained as "a sort of delaying tactic" was completely smashed off. Mr Oliver and the other officers had built a barricade on G1 and another on I1, but these also were intended only as delaying tactics.

In fact on inspection, it is apparent that it would have been relatively simple to have erected an effective barricade between the wooden door and the gate on G1 which would have made access to that route almost impossible. It would have been more difficult to erect a barricade on G2 to prevent access from the gym. This however was a route which was much less well known, though it had been recently used by category A inmates who were using the gym. It was not the route (at least initially) used by the inmates to obtain access from the Main Prison to the Remand Prison.

3.190   Fortunately, with the assistance of the barricades which were created, the staff in the Remand Prison were able to evacuate safely, although Mr Oliver's impression was that within five or six seconds there must have been 50 or 60 inmates on the landing.

3.191   Mr O'Friel had arrived at the prison at 11.55 and one of the first orders he had given, having been briefed as to the position, was that steps should be taken to try and retain the remand prison. Miss Stewart therefore returned to the remand prison to try and organise this. But she reached only the unlocked door at the end of I wing before she was met by the staff who were leaving. By now it was too late to save the remand prison and Miss Stewart was therefore able only to double lock that exit. She then returned to the communications room.

xii) The Prison Hospital and the Injured

3.192   Before the riot the Prison's Medical Services had been weakened because for about 12 months the Hospital Governor 4 post was vacant. Also, at the time of the riot, the Senior Medical Officer, who has unfortunately since died, was off duty because of illness. The prison did however have a modern purpose built hospital wing.

3.193   What happened in the hospital during the riot was as follows: on the morning of 1 April there were two Senior Officers on duty and an acting Principal Officer, Mr Ashworth. Mr Ashworth had heard there might be trouble in the Chapel so he had asked the medical officer on duty, Dr Somasunderam to remain. Fortunately the doctor did so, and during the day he was able to set up a treatment centre at the main gate of the prison.

3.194   Early in the incident Mr Ashworth left the hospital with staff to give assistance to the discipline staff. He left Mr Callaghan, one of the senior officers, in charge.

3.195   Among the first patients brought in to the hospital were four prison officers. One was Mr Liddle from E Wing, who had been injured when evacuating prisoners from the Chapel. He had a very bad fractured arm. Another officer had a fractured or dislocated shoulder. Mr McCormick was brought in with injuries to his face and back, as was Prison Officer Benstead, who had a head injury. They were all very badly shocked. In addition there were about 50 inmates who were brought to the hospital by prison officers. They had not been injured, but were taken to the hospital as a safe haven. They were put into the hospital out-patients waiting room.

3.196   Mr Callaghan was particularly concerned about the condition of Mr Liddle whom he knew had a heart condition. Mr Liddle was looking very unwell. He therefore decided that the injured officers should be evacuated from the hospital. He took them first to the gate. He then took the officers who were most seriously injured to the North Manchester General Hospital in his own car. When he returned he found that there was no first aid equipment at the gate lodge. He made arrangements for the ambulance service which was already present to provide the items which were necessary.

3.197   At about 12.00 Mr Callaghan was able to turn his attention to the prisoners who had been in the hospital before the disturbance. They had remained in the hospital under the supervision of three female hospital officers and a young male discipline officer. Having regard to what he had been told of the situation, Mr Callaghan decided that the hospital should be evacuated. He therefore returned to the hospital, which was still secure. Some of the inmates who were detained there did not appreciate the situation in the prison and were therefore not cooperative. But Mr Callaghan, with the help of other officers, managed to remove all the inmates to the remand visits area. While this was happening a considerable amount of noise could be heard coming from E Wing, which has two access doors leading to the hospital. The incident log records Mr Morrison as having confirmed the transfer of the prisoner patients at 12.29 and that the hospital was clear at 12.30.

3.198   As set out in more detail later in this section under the heading "The Ambulance and Hospital Services", about 13.00 the ambulance service provided a major accident equipment vehicle for use by the prison hospital staff. This was used to tend to both injured prison officers and inmates. The Prison Service were also provided with a paramedic who, in Mr Callaghan's words, "did a magnificent job for us". Those officers and inmates who required hospital attention were taken either to the North Manchester General Hospital or to the Manchester Royal Infirmary.

3.199   At the North Manchester Hospital the consultant in intensive care who was called in was Dr McCartney. As a result of information gained from the radio of the Greater Manchester Ambulance Service, it was appreciated that there was a major riot. Arrangements were made for an emergency surgical resuscitation team to be on duty in the Casualty Department. The major incidents procedure was initiated. Because there was difficulty in obtaining information as to what precisely was happening, Dr McCartney went to the prison himself. He organised with the officer who was in charge of the ambulance service for a triage of potential patients (that is a system for sorting out priorities in terms of treatment). In the event because the patients came out in only small numbers, it was not necessary to make use of this.

xiii) The Release of Mr Proctor

3.200   During the whole of this time Mr Proctor was still in the vestry. He was doing his best to look after the inmates who were with him. The incident log recalls that at 12.37 he had telephoned to say that he and the ten inmates with him wished to be released. At 13.06 it is recorded that they were still locked in the vestry, but safe. Eventually Mr Rigby, Mr Holliday and Mr Hancox rescued them. In order to do this they had to face a barrage of slates and missiles, even though they had worked out the safest route. They found Mr Proctor in a distraught state in his office. Staff then escorted them from the vestry, by which time it was about 15.00.

xiv) The Plight of the Prisoners on Rule 43 Still in the Prison

3.201   By about 12.00, therefore, the whole of the prison accommodation had been lost, but all the staff had managed to leave the wings, with some injuries but no deaths. So far as the prisoners were concerned, whether they wanted to be involved or not, they were caught up with what was happening in the prison. If they were one of the unfortunate Rule 43 prisoners who were not evacuated, their position was indeed perilous.

3.202   One inmate (Inmate F) described in evidence how he sat in his cell, believing the officers were bound to come any minute. Eventually, however, he tried to get out of the wing only to find that those who were doing so were being attacked by the other "cons". Inmate M was situated on C2 where Rule 43's were occupying four cells. He was in a cell with another inmate and they put their beds against the door as a sort of barricade. His cell-mate was petrified. They could see officers in the yard and tried to shout for help. Then other inmates came to the door and shouted at them, calling them names and saying they wanted to get in. He heard the cell next door having its door broken down and went to the spyhole to try and see what was happening. When Inmate M looked round he found his cell-mate was hanging himself. He managed to get his cell-mate down and onto the bed. Eventually other inmates arrived and helped him to take his cell-mate into A Wing, from where they eventually managed to escape.

3.203   Inmate I could hear inmates outside his cell on C2 discussing how they had just castrated another inmate. He was abused through the cell door and implements were pushed through the door. Then water came pouring into the cell up to his ankles. He became unconscious and was semi-conscious while being carried through the Centre.

3.204   Inmate J was one of the Rule 43s on E Wing. In his evidence he said he could see from his cell inmates smashing the windows. They then came to his cell and told him, "we're going to kill you, you beast". They said they were going to chop him up, that there was a couple of dead already and he was next. He described the noise of screams and doors being broken down. He barricaded his door and tried to dig his way out of the cell through the exterior wall. Using a table leg, he managed to get about half way through the wall, such was his desperation. While he was doing so some prisoners attacked his door with an axe. They told him they were going to chop his fingers off. Eventually they broke in. He was viciously assaulted and knocked unconscious. When he regained consciousness, he was guided by another inmate down to A Wing, where he was released.

3.205   Inmate N probably had the most terrifying experience. He was sharing a cell with another inmate on Rule 43 on the E4 landing. They barricaded their doors but four inmates, two masked, started breaking the door down. They shouted that they were going to kill them. When they broke in they found a set of depositions. These did not actually belong to N, but they would not believe N when he told them this. He was hit with table legs and stabbed with a pair of scissors in his side. He was eventually thrown over the balcony from the landing. He landed on the wire netting between the 2s and the 1s. Things were then thrown upon him. He lost consciousness. As he regained consciousness he was being dragged off the netting by inmates, who threw paint over him. Another inmate came to his rescue and took him to the A1 landing, where he was able to get out and was carried away on a stretcher.

xv) The Evacuation of Prisoners

3.206   It was very difficult for the prison staff to evacuate from the prison those prisoners who wanted to be released. The exits had been doubled from 13.21. There was the problem of inmates bombarding officers from the roofs, including the remand roof.

3.207   Mr Rigby was however able to let out 15 prisoners from the end of H1, after fires had been observed in the remand prison both on G and H wings at 13.33 and 13.35. Mr Rigby also went with Mr Holliday to the end of A wing after inmates shouted down that there were prisoners severely injured (they referred to two dead) that needed to come out. The two members of staff shouted to the inmates that they were not able to get them out because of the many prisoners on the roof throwing slates, scaffold poles and bricks. The staff said that if this stopped, they would evacuate the prisoners out of A Wing. The bombardment did stop. Mr Rigby and Mr Holliday were able to release inmates from A Wing. The inmates were let out in batches of six. Some of the inmates were in a bad condition and had to be carried out on stretchers; others were suffering from an overdose of drugs which may or may not have been self-inflicted (there was talk of inmates being forcibly injected).

3.208   The bombardment restarted once the injured had been released. In order to evacuate other prisoners, officers had to form a cordon of over-head shields under which the inmates could pass. At one stage the double lock at the end of A Wing gate, which was being locked and unlocked between each batch, jammed. Mr Holliday decided to allow that lock to be broken off the gate by inmates. They did this in a matter of seconds with a scaffold pole.

3.209   Mr Aubrey, a hospital officer, assisted Mr Holliday and Mr Rigby. He was of particular value because he was able to make an instantaneous assessment for Mr Holliday as to the extent of injuries.

3.210   This task of releasing the inmates involved Mr Aubrey, Mr Rigby and Mr Holliday going back and forth to the visits area. During the course of this, in addition to the bombardment, they were urinated and spat upon and had milk poured upon them. The only protection that Mr Aubrey and Mr Rigby had at that time were shields. Mr Holliday had no protection whatsoever.

3.211 At another stage, a category A prisoner was twice given a set of keys by Mr Holliday, with Mr O'Friel's approval, after the prisoner had promised to return them. The prisoner wanted the keys to release other prisoners whom he said were still locked in their cells. After the prisoners had been released, the prisoner complied with his promise and returned the keys.

3.212 The decision to hand keys over to the category A prisoner was heard by staff on the radio net and similar action was taken by other members of staff on H1 remand landing. Again the keys were returned.

3.213 In addition to asking for the cell keys on two occasions, the category A prisoner also asked for breathing apparatus. Mr Holliday, having consulted Mr O'Friel about the request, was not prepared to allow him to have this. The prisoner wanted the breathing apparatus because he said that there were prisoners who were trapped in cells which were either on fire or full of smoke. However he had no experience of using breathing apparatus and that is why the request was refused. Instead Mr Holliday offered to enter with breathing equipment if he was given a guarantee of safety. The prisoner said that he could not give that guarantee. The prisoner therefore did his best to release the inmates without the apparatus.

3.214 That prisoner at that stage of the riot acted in a most commendable manner. Mr Holliday, Mr Rigby and Mr Aubrey acted with conspicuous courage and a remarkable devotion to duty. Without their actions there could have been even graver consequences to the inmates who had been injured. It was one of the happier aspects of the incident that, notwithstanding the riot that was taking place, Mr Holliday, with Mr O'Friel's consent, was able to trust a category A prisoner in the way which he did, and find that trust justified. This is one of the episodes in the course of the prolonged disturbance which makes it clear that before the riot, notwithstanding the physical conditions in Strangeways, some of the relationships between prisoners and staff were what they should be.

3.215 In addition to being evacuated from A and H Wings, prisoners were able to leave from the end of D Wing. In order to do this they had to break through the side brick work of a passageway and then descend from the wing on knotted sheets. Subsequently the gate at the gable end of that wing was opened and some 300 prisoners were let out.

3.216 Because of the number of prisoners who were now surrendering (between 14.00 and 17.00 some 800 prisoners surrendered) the organising and the controlling of these prisoners became a major problem. Initially they were housed in the visits area. However it was impossible to accommodate all the prisoners in this area. The prisoners who surrendered were therefore taken out of the prison by the main gate and transported round the perimeter wall to the Croft area. They were housed in the Croft until arrangements could be made to transfer them to other establishments.

xvi) Co-ordinating the Evacuation

3.217 The organisational problem involved in dealing with such a large number of prisoners was immense. Mr O'Friel had to deploy staff to deal with the situation. Arrangements had also to be made for the prisoners to be accommodated at other establishments. For this task Mr O'Friel needed the full co-operation of the North Regional Office and the Deputy Director General's office at Headquarters. This he received. The Assistant Regional Director had previously spoken to Mr Wallace and was made aware of the magnitude of the disturbance and of the need for staff reinforcements at 11.12. He in turn had paged the acting Regional Director, Mr Bone, in the absence on holiday of the Regional Director, Mr Papps. He also contacted the other Assistant Regional Director, Mr Rudgard, who activated the regional contingency plans for primary and secondary support groups to be provided from a large number of local establishments. Mr Stapleton, the Assistant Regional Director of the North Region, then set off from home to open the incident control room at the regional office, having alerted a member of the Deputy Director General's office in London of what was happening.

3.218   The Deputy Director General, Mr Emes, arrived at Cleland House at about 14.00. He opened the Headquarters control room. National co-ordination was needed to find places in different parts of the country to which the Manchester prisoners could be evacuated. That work was based on the headquarters control room. The control room was also involved in assembling staff from outside the North region to be sent to support the Manchester staff.

3.219   By 15.30 the prison had been given a comprehensive account of what accommodation was available in the North Region. Coaches were made available by Greater Manchester Buses. The police began to make an assessment of the availability of police cells. Plans were also being formulated to provide space for inmates in other regions. The Midland Region offered over 300 places, the South West region were able to offer 180 places and the South East Region 75 places.

3.220   There was also a problem in providing food for the ever increasing number of staff and prisoners. The officers' mess could not cope with problems of this size, although it was doing its best. A temporary kitchen was set up in the Croft and "air line type" meals were obtained.

3.221   The coach drivers found it by no means easy to get to the prison. But when they arrived, prisoners were put on the coaches under the supervision of both prison officers and police officers. An attempt was made to keep records, but conditions were chaotic and it was not possible to do it accurately. Some prisoners gave the wrong names and the computer was not operating. At times the atmosphere in the Croft workshops where the prisoners were kept was extremely tense and some vandalism took place.

3.222   The first coach left the prison at about 15.00 with 30 prisoners bound for Preston prison. Thereafter coaches continued to leave the prison under police escort until the next morning at 07.06. By that time some 1,289 prisoners had been evacuated. Having regard to the conditions under which everyone was working, this was an achievement in which the Prison Service can take real pride. Not one prisoner escaped during this process, or at any time during this prolonged disturbance.

xvii) The Arrival of Staff From Other Establishments

3.223   The Regional Office made arrangements for staff from other establishments in the Region to go to Manchester to give support. Initially there was some confusion in their deployment when they arrived at Manchester. Some had come with C&R equipment, others had not. It was not clear where they were to go or what they were to do. However the Principal Officer responsible for C&R training for the North Region, Mr Brian Nicholson, arrived at the prison at about 14.45 and he took charge. C&R equipment also arrived from the regional stores.

xviii) The Arrival of the Media

3.224   By the end of the afternoon, the media had arrived in large numbers and television cameras were being operated from hydraulic hoists. To begin with liaison with the media was unsatisfactory (this is a subject examined later). Following a brief official statement at 15.40, at 17.00 a further press statement was issued. It said that 500 prisoners had already surrendered. Steps were being taken to disperse them to other prisons. No escapes were known to have occurred but the serious disturbance was continuing. It was too early to report on casualties or on the extent of the damage, but this was thought to be considerable.

3.225   By 18.00 the regional office began to hear reports of fatalities from the media, but there was no evidence to support this from the prison.

xix) The First Incursion into E Wing

3.226   By 20.00 Mr O'Friel and Mr Nicholson had agreed that prison officers should enter E Wing. In Mr O'Friel's mind the incursion was in the hope of retaking accommodation which could be used for housing prisoners when they surrendered. Mr Nicholson regarded it as an exploratory incursion with the object of finding out what sort of opposition they would meet.

3.227   Approximately ten C&R units of 12 men each were used. They were able to retake E Wing without any significant difficulty or casualties. According to the communications room's Incident Log, the incursion began at 20.05. By 20.10 all four landings had been secured. It was not intended that the incursions should go beyond retaking E Wing, but at 20.25 at least one C&R unit had entered the main Centre, where some fighting took place. When this was reported to Mr O'Friel, he instructed them that they were not to move beyond the E Wing doors to the Centre. This probably is the explanation for the entry in the Headquarters Operation Log at 21.15 that there had been "a distinct over-reaction from the staff to start with but this has now been retrieved".

3.228   Some staff at any rate believed that the Centre could have been retaken. If this had happened, the progress of the disturbance would have been very different. The staff did, however, from time to time come under attack from inmates. The inmates had access into the roof area above the 4s landing and were able to stand on the wire grid in order to attack the staff above the 4s landing with scaffold poles and other objects. Mr Boon, the Governor of Risley who had been sent to Manchester to assist Mr O'Friel, visited E Wing at about 21.30. He said in evidence that the staff were holding the 4s landings at the Centre, but with some difficulty. "Conditions there were quite appalling".

3.229   However, the staff remained in E Wing until about 00.22 on 2 April, when inmates again broke through onto the wing. The staff then withdrew. By that time Mr Nicholson regarded the purposes of the incursion as having been achieved. He considered that while it would have been possible for the units to have remained, it would clearly have been uncomfortable for them to have done so. He said that at one time there were about 60 inmates on the overhead wire grid. The withdrawal was made without incident. No officers were injured during the period E Wing was occupied.

xx) The First Night (1/2 April 1990)

3.230   Mr Boon relieved Mr O'Friel overnight. Mr O'Friel went off duty at 00.10, shortly before it was decided to vacate E Wing. Before he had gone off duty, Mr O'Friel had indicated to the Regional Office that he intended to try and retake the prison early the following morning.

3.231   During the night Mr Emes, the Deputy Director General, kept in close contact with Mr Boon. Among other matters, they considered the possibility of the bodies of dead prisoners being in E Wing or in the Centre. Mr Boon indicated this was unlikely, but he made it clear that because of the quantity of rubble and rubbish on the anti-suicide netting which hangs below the landings, it was impossible to say that there were no bodies in those areas.

3.232   At 05.44, Mr Emes had a long discussion with Mr Boon about the prospects of retaking the prison by an attack later that morning. There was no doubt that Mr Boon was very pessimistic as to the likely outcome. He contemplated first re-entering E Wing, then taking the Centre and then taking the other wings. He thought about 480 staff would be needed. According to the record of the telephone conversation he stated that "the risks are considerable. Primarily because in E Wing prisoners have got those very long scaffolding poles which they were able to poke through the wire netting which is lining the roof." Mr Boon added that the "C&R people really cannot say whether they could withstand that but they would certainly have to". Mr Emes commented that "it looks as though the prospects of any staff getting in without the risk of serious injury up to the point of death is very considerable". Mr Boon agreed with this and added that "he certainly would not suggest that we try to take the wire netting with staff – that would be extremely dangerous". Mr Emes asked Mr Boon to reflect further on the situation but not to contemplate putting an operation into effect without reference to him.

The Disturbance – Monday 2 April 1990

i) Retaking the Remand Prison

3.233   At 07.00 Mr O'Friel came back on duty. At that time it was estimated that approximately 142 prisoners were still on the loose inside the prison. After discussions between Mr O'Friel and the Deputy Director General, C&R units entered the remand prison at about 10.00 and retook it without difficulty. In the course of the operation six prisoners were apprehended. The remand prison was very badly damaged, but there were a few cells which could be used. The initial assessment of damage to the remand prison suggested that between 30% and 50% of the roof wire had been removed. The remand reception area was completely burned out and there was severe damage to all internal fittings. No bodies were found, but the six inmates who surrendered indicated that they thought two prisoners had been killed in the main prison, one hanged on the Centre and another thrown on to the netting in E Wing.

ii) The Discussions on Whether to Prepare a Plan to Retake the Main Prison

3.234   Normally when a disturbance occurred in a prison, the establishment communicated with the Regional Office and when necessary the Regional Office communicated with Headquarters. In the case of a serious incident not only would the Regional Office open an operations room, an Headquarters operations room would open as well.

3.235   Because of the seriousness of the riot at Manchester and the difficulties with communications, the operations room at Headquarters and Mr O'Friel were in direct communication with each other. On the morning of 2 April at 10.25, there was a conversation between the Headquarters and Regional Office when it was decided that there should be a return to the normal structure. However in practice this was not adhered to. At 12.57 there was once more a conversation between Mr Emes and Mr O'Friel during which Mr O'Friel told Mr Emes that the best information was that there were still 120 inmates unaccounted for. Mr O'Friel also told Mr Emes that in contemplating the best way of entering the main prison they were considering all the options, including postponing re-entry until the following morning. Mr O'Friel said they were trying to make sure that they had enough forces to make the operation as risk free as possible, but the trouble was that the longer they waited the more opportunity the inmates had for reinforcing their defences.

iii) The Plan to Retake the Main Prison

3.236   By 14.00 Mr O'Friel and his C&R commanders had agreed a plan. The plan was to enter the Chapel by the two lower doors and for the teams then to make their way through the Chapel to the doors at the top end of the Chapel, which gave access to the 4s landing of the Centre. It was intended to send in 12 units, 150 C&R equipped officers, by that route. Before that thrust was made, however, there were to be diversionary attacks from a number of different positions. These were to be on F Wing (that is below the Chapel) and from the Remand Wing through the kitchen, with a view to taking the Centre at ground floor level. There was to be yet a further attack through the hospital into E Wing. The object of the diversionary attacks was to draw prisoners onto the low ground so that the main attack would trap prisoners below roof level. The main attacking force through the Chapel would have an additional 70 C&R trained Manchester staff to deal with the captured or surrendering prisoners.

3.237   Through Mr Rudgard, Region, and subsequently Headquarters, were initially informed that it was hoped that the attack would take place at 14.30. As part of the preparations for the attack, the proposed entry points had been reconnoitred. It was known that the barricades which had been erected by the prisoners at that time were weak. In particular, it was known that the barricades in the Chapel, which was to be the principal point of attack, were not "very strong". In addition the information available indicated that the inmates had not yet broken down landings or stairs which would hinder the progress of the attack. There remained the fact that some inmates could be in the roof areas on the wire grids and would be in a position to throw scaffold poles and other missiles on the advancing prison officers. However, as Mr Nicholson pointed out, C&R techniques (using shields above the heads of the units) are designed to cope with this.

3.238   The plan for intervention on the afternoon of 2 April had been prepared primarily by the C&R commanders and by Mr Halward who was an Assistant Regional Director of North Region and who was at the prison to assist Mr O'Friel. Mr Halward's assessment of the plan was that it had a good chance of success, subject to the limitation that there was a risk that a number of prisoners would retreat to the roof and the plan did not encompass the taking of the roof area. Mr Halward recognised, however, that there was inevitably a risk of injury associated with the plan because it involved "going into a building controlled by 130 odd prisoners who had recently demonstrated that they were aggressive towards staff". On the whole he would have been against intervention.

3.239   In addition to Mr Nicholson there were three other C&R commanders. Their view, like that of Mr Nicholson, was that the plan would be successful. Mr Nicholson did not think there was any risk of death, but so far as injuries were concerned, while they could not guarantee there would be no injuries, the view was that there would not have been serious injuries. As Mr Nicholson said in evidence "We had enough units, enough trained men to flood the prison and do the job".

3.240   Mr O'Friel was confident initially that the plan would be authorised by the Deputy Director General. Because of the time constraints, he gave Mr Nicholson permission to brief the commanders of the C&R units and thereafter to form the units up ready to implement the plan as soon as it was authorised.

3.241   In coming to his conclusion that the plan should be implemented, Mr O'Friel was naturally influenced by the views of the C&R commanders. But he was also in a position to form his own judgment of the merits of the attack. He had not before had operational command in a riot situation, but he had previous experience of a number of prison riots and had himself had to deal with a disturbance which took place in the Chapel at Strangeways in 1986. Mr O'Friel was an extremely experienced Governor 1 and the current Chairman of the Prison Governors' Association. He was widely regarded as one of the most able governors in the Prison Service. He was entitled to expect that his opinion of the prospects of the intervention being successful would carry great weight with Mr Emes.

3.242   Mr O'Friel knew that he could not speak to Mr Emes immediately because Mr Emes had told Mr O'Friel during their telephone call at 12.57 that Mr Emes would be seeing the Home Secretary at 13.30.

3.243   The plan was communicated to Mr Peter Rudgard, who was an Assistant Regional Director and who had been sent to the prison to liaise with the Governor and, if necessary, Headquarters. Mr Rudgard informed the Acting Regional Director, Mr Bone. He, in turn and in the absence of Mr Emes, spoke at 14.09 to Mr Peter Leonard, a Governor 2 at Headquarters. The record of that conversation does not make it clear that the main attack was to be through the Chapel and wrongly records that two teams, not 12, were to go through the Chapel. It does however note that the Acting Regional Director, Mr Bone, had agreed with the Governor that the teams should be prepared to withdraw if the assault proved to be more difficult than anticipated. The note also does not make it clear that part of the exercise was to draw the inmates from the high ground to the low ground so that they would be cut off from the high ground when the main thrust through the Chapel was made.

3.244   Mr Leonard spoke to Mr Emes at 14.18. Mr Emes emphasised that he was not prepared to authorise any plan until he had talked to the Governor. The instruction from him and from Mr Bone to the Governor at that stage was to be "No". The log records that "Mr Emes would initiate". This message was transmitted by Mr Bone to Mr O'Friel. Mr O'Friel explained to Mr Bone that the prisoners were busy building fortifications which was one of the reasons in favour of an early intervention. While there were risks attached to an intervention (nobody could minimise that) the risks were calculated. Both Mr O'Friel and Mr Bone was firmly of the opinion that the risks involved in an intervention on that day were less than they would be the following day.

3.245   Mr Bone then made a further report to Headquarters. The record of that telephone conversation again misrecords the proposed action. It suggests that the attack on the Chapel was to be the diversion and not the main attack. The record also indicates that there was a clear difference of opinion between Mr Bone and Mr Leonard. Mr Leonard suggested that there was no prospect of "grabbing" the 119 prisoners, who were then thought to be in the main prison, and that more difficult prisoners would merely go to the higher ground. Against that, Mr Bone pointed out that unless they intervened the riot would be more protracted. During that conversation it was emphasised that Mr O'Friel would need a decision by 16.00 otherwise it would be too late. The reason for this was that any intervention needed to be completed before it became dark.

3.246   At Region, Mr Bone, the Acting Regional Director, regarded himself as little more than an intermediary in relation to the attack. The information that Region was passing to Headquarters was therefore regarded as being no more than a rough outline of what was involved in the attack. However, on the information which was available to him, it was Mr Bone's view that, although there were problems in the attack, they had been taken into consideration and it was a good plan.

3.247   However, as a result of the conversations which Mr Bone had had with Mr Leonard, he had formed the impression that Mr Emes was likely to disapprove of the plan. He conveyed this impression to Mr O'Friel. At 14.37, according to the Governor's Log, Mr O'Friel had a further conversation with Mr Bone during which he assured him "that the position is winnable if we go in now". However, having been warned of the likely reaction, Mr O'Friel took the precaution of briefing the commanders of the C&R unit that, if permission was not forthcoming for the attack on the prison as a whole, a raid would be made on the prison kitchen with a view to preventing inmates obtaining food.

3.248   According to the Governor's log, at 14.55 Mr O'Friel instructed Mr Wallace to pull back staff.

3.249   Mr Leonard spoke to Mr Emes again. He then reported back to Mr Bone (at 14.57). He said that Mr Emes had posed two questions. The first was what were the chances of success? When Mr Leonard had told Mr Emes better than 50%, Mr Emes had said that was not good enough, he wanted a 100% guarantee. The second question was why was it necessary for the attack to take place that day? Why should they not wait a couple of days? The answer given by Mr Bone was "because it was going to be increasingly difficult because of the size and geography of the place. Once they become totally entrenched, it could be more than a couple of days it would be a very long period". The note of this conversation also records that there was information that "there was a concerted plan behind this – which amounts to the fact that as prisoners were dispersed to other prisons they would create similar disturbances at every prison that they go to".

iv) The Decision Not to Attempt to Retake the Main Prison

3.250   The reason that Mr Emes was not able to speak to Mr O'Friel direct, and messages had to be passed in this unsatisfactory way through Mr Bone and Mr Leonard, was that Mr Emes was, for the second time that day, not at the command room at Prison Service Headquarters but with Ministers in the Home Office at Queen Anne's Gate (QAG). However, just before 15.00, Mr Emes and the Director General, Mr Train, left the meeting with Ministers. Mr Emes spoke to Mr O'Friel direct from the Home Office. By this time the units were already in position for the attack – although they may have been "called back" as a result of the conversation between Mr O'Friel and Mr Wallace at 14.55.

3.251   Mr O'Friel received the phone call from Mr Emes in a cell behind the communications room which had been converted into an office. It was also occupied by the Police Superintendent who was the liaison officer and his assistant, the Home Office Press Officer and the Assistant Regional Director. There could well have been other people who were in earshot, but Mr O'Friel could not be sure of this.

3.252   Mr O'Friel's recollection of the conversation is that Mr Emes started by saying words to the effect that he understood or he knew that Mr O'Friel had a plan for a major attack on the main prison. Mr O'Friel confirmed that this was right. Mr Emes then asked Mr O'Friel what were the prospects or likelihood of staff casualties. Mr O'Friel replied that there was a real likelihood, a strong probability, that in an operation of that size there would be casualties. Mr O'Friel believes he stressed the number of staff involved and the size of the operation – that is that the operation would involve 382 staff, apart from the supporting groups, including the 70 staff from Manchester.

3.253   The conversation then moved on to weapons and the fact that there had been difficulties on E Wing the night before. However, Mr O'Friel believes he made it clear that the position would be different from the night before because of the scale of the plan. He then believes that Mr Emes asked him whether there could be fatalities. He replied that he could not rule it out. Mr Emes then said that the attack was not to be launched. It was not worth it, given the risk of staff casualties. Mr O'Friel believes that on this occasion, and possibly on a later occasion, Mr Emes added that the buildings were not worth casualties. On his version, Mr O'Friel's assessment of the prospects of success and his reasons for this assessment were never properly discussed.

3.254   Mr O'Friel said in evidence that he was concerned that if the major attack were to be stood down, there would be a difficult morale and management problem for the forces. He was therefore anxious that they should be seen to achieve something. He therefore told Mr Emes about his plan for an attack on the kitchen. Mr O'Friel said that Mr Emes agreed to that attack, after he had closely questioned Mr O'Friel about it.

3.255   Because Mr Emes spoke to Mr O'Friel from the Home Office and not from Cleland House (which is the Prison Service Headquarters) his telephone conversation was not recorded, as it should otherwise have been. However, late that afternoon, or during the evening, Mr Emes made a note of the telephone conversation, which was subsequently typed out. That note reads as follows:

> "NRO rang to say that Brendan O'Friel has 400-500 staff who could now be used to attempt to retake prison. Would I contact him and discuss it.
>
> Spoke to Brendan from QAG immediately after meeting with S of S. He confirmed that he now had in excess of 400 staff. We discussed possibility of using them to mount an assault.
>
> Situation at Manchester well in excess of 100 prisoners – probably 200 hold the high ground, 4s roofs and roof spaces in all five wings of main prison. Are armed with landing rails and scaffolding poles and have masonry and cell doors to drop on staff below.
>
> Very extensive damage: buildings probably unsafe in places: landing rails torn away: many barricades – location unknown.
>
> Discussed prospects of success. Barricades and debris will prevent staff momentum. Area to be retaken huge. Chances of success less than 50/50. High probability of heavy staff injuries, with fatalities likely from masonry doors and scaffolding poles.
>
> Inter prisoner violence no longer being reported. No lives at risk in main prison. Extensive damage to buildings already inflicted.
>
> *Gains* from successful assault – only time and reduce some further damage.
>
> *Losses.* High Staff and prison casualties, likelihood of fatalities.

Agreed with Brendan no point in working up a plan for total retake, but he could mount probing raids to maintain pressure on prisoners and get better intelligence – provided they would not pose unacceptable risk to staff."

3.256   Unfortunately, this note provides no guidance of what Mr Emes and Mr O'Friel said during the conversation. Indeed, the reason for its preparation after the conversation would be a matter of concern, because of its lack of accuracy, were it not for the fact Mr Emes genuinely misunderstood what Mr O'Friel's state of mind was. He wrongly thought that Mr O'Friel was agreeing with the strong views he held about the inadvisability of intervention. On the other hand, the note provides useful confirmation as to how Mr Emes was assessing the question of intervention. What is significant is that he was concentrating on what would be the advantages and disadvantages in a Manchester context. He was not attaching importance in reaching his decision to the impact on the prison system as a whole. In particular, he did not consider the effect on other vulnerable establishments of prisoners for the first time demonstrating that not only could they take control of virtually the whole of the largest prison in the country, but that they could continue to hold that prison. The possible domino and public order consequences of the riot were not mentioned. They do not appear to have featured prominently in Mr Emes' assessments of the pros and cons of intervention.

3.257   Mr Emes regarded the note as being a mixture of points made in the conversation and his own conclusions. For example "Chances of success less than 50/50" is Mr Emes' assessment. It is not based on anything which was said by Mr O'Friel, who took a different view of the prospects. The statement "Agreed with Brendan no point in working up a plan for a total retake" had no factual basis.

3.258   What apparently misled Mr Emes as to Mr O'Friel's state of mind, was Mr O'Friel's surprising lack of advocacy in support of the plan and his rapid deployment of the proposal of the alternative plan to attack the kitchen. Mr O'Friel's failure to respond can no doubt partly be explained by the circumstances in which the conversation was held. A crowded converted cell is not the ideal situation in which to have an argument with the Deputy Director General. Furthermore, it is possible that, as a result of the earlier conversations, Mr O'Friel recognised that Mr Emes was hostile to the plan even before he spoke to him and he decided to leave the discussion to Mr Emes. Mr Emes is in the habit of positively expressing his views and undoubtedly did so during the conversation. However, making all allowances for the circumstances, Mr O'Friel should have made his own position clearer. In an interview with the media, Mr O'Friel repeated the word "poleaxed", which was the word used by a member of the Board of Visitors to describe the effect of the decision upon the Governor. If he was as strongly affected by Mr Emes' decision as that, he should have left Mr Emes in no doubt as to what his opinion was. He was, after all, a very senior governor and the riot was taking place in his prison.

3.259   Mr Emes believes the conversation ended, so far as the plan was concerned, by his saying something to the effect that "Really it is not a runner, is it Brendan?" That is a statement couched in the terms of a question. Mr Emes says that at that point Mr O'Friel went on to ask about the attack on the kitchen. Mr Emes, in the absence of any statement to the contrary by Mr O'Friel, assumed, and continued to assume until 21 April, that Mr O'Friel agreed with his assessment that the chances of success were not great and that the risks were disproportionate to the prospect of success.

3.260   It was extremely unfortunate that Mr Emes was labouring under misapprehensions about Mr O'Friel's support for the plan, the details of that plan, and the state of the prison; and that he did not appreciate that the staff were drawn up and ready to enter the prison. Mr Emes, in his evidence to the Inquiry, emphatically insists his decision was correct and that it was the only possible decision. It is therefore almost inevitable that, whatever Mr O'Friel had said during the conversation, Mr Emes would have come to exactly the same decision.

3.261   Mr Emes' explanation for allowing Mr O'Friel, in these circumstances, to proceed initially with his preparation of a plan was that he did not know whether Mr O'Friel would be able to devise a plan to deliver staff to the roof space. This would have enabled them to tackle the prisoners on the same level, instead of from the landing below. However, it is common ground that this was not one of the matters that was at any time raised with Mr O'Friel. If it was of the significance that Mr Emes now indicates, then he should have raised it expressly with Mr O'Friel at the outset. While I accept that Mr Emes was trying to give me as accurate an account as he could of what occurred during the conversation, I have little doubt that by the time Mr Emes made his telephone call to Mr O'Friel shortly before 15.00, he had already decided that there should not be an attack. Although he asked Mr O'Friel questions during the course of that conversation, Mr Emes was primarily interested in obtaining confirmation of the decision to which he had already come, a decision which was based on inadequate, inaccurate and out of date information.

3.262   The way in which Mr Emes saw his role is clearly indicated in one answer he gave in evidence at the Inquiry when it was sitting in Manchester. The question which was asked was:

> "How far did you expect a Governor in Mr O'Friel's position to go in relation to a plan before asking you for the permission to commit the staff to an attack such as this was obviously likely to be contemplated?"

The answer was:

> "I expect him to work out a plan as well as he could and to offer it to me, so that we could then consider it together. Then I could make a decision."

3.263   The answer makes it clear that Mr Emes regarded it as his task to make the decision. He did not at that stage limit his role to scrutinising the decision taken by Mr O'Friel, and only intervening if he considered Mr O'Friel's decision was wrong. Instead, he regarded the decision as being one for him to take on information provided by Mr O'Friel. The distinction may appear to be a narrow one, but it is nonetheless significant. It is obviously easier for an official at Headquarters to exercise the scrutinising role, albeit that role includes the right of veto, than for him actually to make the decision.

3.264   It is necessary to have this distinction in mind because at the later disturbances, Mr Emes appears to have adopted the monitoring or scrutinising role. Mr Emes gave evidence in London on the last day of the Inquiry about his role in relation to the later disturbances. By that time, evidence had been given by Mr Dunbar, the Regional Director of the South West Region, who saw his role and that of Headquarters as supervisory. Mr Emes was asked about this. The question was:

> "As I understood Mr Dunbar's evidence, it was that he was saying that the primary decision has to be taken by the man on the spot, although there has to be a residual right as senior to veto or to suggest alternative courses of action?"

Mr Emes' answer to that question was:

> "I am sure that that is right."

3.265   At a later stage I will have to express my conclusions as to what are the appropriate roles of Headquarters and the Governor of an establishment where there is an incident of this seriousness and as to the appropriateness of Mr Emes' decision. However, at this stage it is useful to draw attention to certain features relating to Mr Emes' decision. First, it was highly unsatisfactory that Mr Emes should have had to take the decision in the circumstances which he did. A hurried conversation just after coming out of a meeting with Ministers was not the way this important issue should have been dealt with.

3.266   Secondly, Mr Emes needed a full and detailed description of the plan from Mr O'Friel. He did not ask for this and it was not volunteered. Mr Emes had not at any time sufficient information to make the appropriate decision. Instead, he relied in part on an inaccurate report by Mr Rudgard to Mr Bone of what Mr O'Friel had said to Mr Rudgard, which Mr Bone had reported to Mr Leonard so that he could report it to Mr Emes. To make a decision on information passed in this way was a recipe for disaster and this it proved to be.

3.267   Thirdly, Mr Emes, unlike Mr O'Friel, did not have at hand the expert C&R advice Mr Nicholson could give. (He could, however, have obtained expert general guidance from the PE Branch situated at Headquarters which had been responsible for devising and developing C&R3 techniques.) Mr Emes had visited the prison only once and had not worked there. He did not have Mr O'Friel's knowledge of the then state of the prison or its inmates. He was unaware of the preparations which had been made and of the destructive effect his decision would have on the morale of the staff from many establishments who had assembled at Manchester and were poised to enter the prison.

3.268   Fourthly, Mr Emes knew that Mr Boon was against intervention (Mr Boon remained of the opinion that intervention would be unsuccessful and gave evidence of this at the hearing). But Mr Emes did not, at least fully, appreciate the distinction between Mr Boon's plan of the previous evening and the more sophisticated plan which had been devised for the intervention which was proposed by Mr O'Friel. The instructions which Mr Emes had given to Mr Boon were to prepare the plan in case there was a need to rescue prisoners next day. He had been told by Mr Boon at least the outline of that plan. Mr O'Friel had not prepared his plan with this limited objective. His plan was designed to retake the prison because it was clear there was not going to be any speedy resolution of the disturbance. There was now a hard core of inmates left. Unless an intervention was made that day, the prisoners would undoubtedly strengthen their defences and make an intervention more difficult.

3.269   Fifthly, Mr Emes, although he did not communicate this to Mr O'Friel, was, according to his evidence, critically concerned about the fact that the inmates held the high ground. However, the strength of the plan which had been devised was that it was intended by the diversionary moves to draw the inmates to the lower ground, so that the staff in the main attack would be above them. It is true some of the inmates would almost certainly have remained on the high ground, but this need not have been of the crucial importance that Mr Emes believed.

3.270   In order to assess the risks which the plan involved, it is necessary to know how C&R units operate. They use their shields very much in the same way as did the Roman legions to create a testudo. They rely on being able to advance slowly notwithstanding all the ammunition which can be hurled upon or at them. A C&R unit uses the linked shields of its members held in front of and above the unit as a protective wall. The tactics which they would have been using would have been very similar to those which had been used successfully the previous evening on E Wing, but on a larger scale against inmates who were dispersed as a result of having to attack the units on a number of fronts. Bearing in mind the number of directions from which the advancing units would be coming, the ability of the inmates to repel the advance would have been much reduced from that of the previous evening. However, even if this did not prove to be the case and the plan was unsuccessful, it would have been possible for the units, having advanced, to have withdrawn, if necessary, from any part of the prison where they were subject to particularly heavy attack.

3.271   It has to be remembered that if inmates were above the wire grid on the 4s landing, while the staff would not have been able to reach them, neither would the prisoners have been able, except in a few positions, to drop down from that wire grid or readily to get back above it. In addition, if staff were to withdraw into cells on the lower landings, there would have been no danger of their being trapped by doing this if those landings had been previously cleared of inmates and the entrances to the landings were guarded. As for the Centre, the same problem of the high ground did not arise. There was no wire grid on which the prisoners could stand. Because of the wire mesh round the scaffolding, it would have been impossible for the prisoners to attack the staff unless the mesh was first penetrated or they came on to the landing from the wings.

3.272 By abandoning the attack, the opportunity for at least testing the reaction of the inmates was lost. It could well have been that a determined attack would have resulted in an immediate loss of heart by inmates and a surrender. Instead, the decision communicated a message to the prisoners that they need not fear a full attack by the prison staff. In the course of the negotiations which took place later, the chief negotiator said that it was a considerable handicap that inmates were not under the threat of the prison being stormed. In addition, the opportunity was lost of regaining at least part of the prison.

v) The Attack on the Kitchen

3.273 With the main plan vetoed, Mr O'Friel gave instructions for the attack on the kitchen to proceed. It began at 15.30. It involved a diversionary attack on F Wing deploying six C&R units. Although the kitchen had a number of skylights which would have enabled inmates to attack staff from above and the kitchen was vulnerable to attack from both E and D Wing, there was no resistance to the staff entering the kitchen. However, the staff were forced to withdraw from the kitchen at about 15.40 because fires in the kitchen were causing considerable smoke. There was also a risk of the roof collapsing.

3.274 A short time after that withdrawal, the staff re-entered the kitchen, supported by a diversionary attack on F Wing. This time it was possible to take and hold the kitchen until the food and stores which were still in the kitchen had been removed or destroyed. When this had been done the staff, withdrew from the kitchen at approximately 16.15.

3.275 While the kitchen operation was continuing the diversionary attack on F Wing met serious resistance from prisoners. They threw missiles down upon the staff from the roof of the Chapel. The bombardment was so heavy that staff engaged on the diversionary attack were forced to withdraw at 15.50, after one member of staff had been injured by a blow to his leg.

3.276 Although this operation had been reasonably successful, only part of the staff who had been assembled for the main task of retaking the main prison were involved. The cancellation of the main attack was a very serious blow to the morale of the staff. It was not understood why "Headquarters" had cancelled the attack. Mr O'Friel did his best to explain the reasons, but it was apparent to those who were present that he was far from happy about the decision.

3.277 The successful operation in the kitchen was reported to Mr Emes and he congratulated all concerned.

The Siege

i) From the Afternoon of Monday 2 April to Saturday 7 April

3.278 After this operation events progressed at a slow pace until 25 April.

3.279 At 16.30 on 2 April a banner was unfurled by inmates which bore the words "no dead". This was in response to what was already being said in the media about a large number of inmates having met their death. Shortly after 17.15 on 2ril, the discussions with the inmates who were still in the main prison were resumed. Between then and 20.30 15 inmates surrendered, despite some of them being bombarded as they surrendered by prisoners who were on the roof. One of the inmates who surrendered had previously been injured and needed to be taken to hospital. It was hoped that a large-scale surrender would take place. There were negotiations with a view to such a surrender, but the negotiations broke down. That evening it was calculated that there were still 102 prisoners in the prison who had not surrendered.

3.280 Overnight, Mr Boon again took over from Mr O'Friel. At 23.50 a fire broke out in the remand Chapel, which resulted in part of that Chapel collapsing, although the fire service took the necessary action. It was discovered that the prisoners had found a way of going from the main prison to the remand prison through the undercroft (a maze of passages running below the prison buildings) and using ventilation shafts which ran the full height of the building. The following day the undercroft was secured, the ventilation ducts blocked and staff posted to prevent further intrusions.

3.281   Mr O'Friel resumed command of the prison at about 07.00 on Tuesday 3 April. At 08.00 he gave authority for contractors to start work clearing debris from the remand prison. A major problem facing Mr O'Friel was a suggestion by surrendering prisoners that an escape was planned through the sewers. It would involve Category A prisoners. Precautions were taken, but no actual escape was attempted.

3.282   During the morning of 3 April an attempt was made to calculate the numbers who were left in the prison. It was thought that 1556 prisoners had been transferred out of the prison, that 17 remained in the Croft, and that 9 were in the officers' mess. The computer printout showed an inmate roll on 1 April of 1,646. (This number did not however include a prisoner who had arrived late on the morning of 3 April and the correct number was 1,647.) It was calculated, therefore, that 64 prisoners were still in the prison. This proved to be an under-estimation of the prisoners still free because the numbers transferred out had been miscalculated. It was later discovered that on Tuesday 3 April there had been 85 prisoners who were still at large in the prison. The problem was that in the confusion which existed the staff had found it impossible to keep proper records. As a result the Prison Service was not sure how many inmates had surrendered, how many were still in the prison and whether any inmates were missing.

3.283   Negotiations continued during the morning of Tuesday 3 April. It was hoped that at least the injured prisoners would be able to be released. Just after 11.00 on Tuesday 3 April, prisoners who were in the Chapel dug a hole in the floor of the Chapel in an attempt to enter F Wing. They began to attack staff with scaffolding poles and other weapons. The staff in F Wing were holding the barricades which led from F Wing into the Centre. There was a danger of their being outflanked from above and the confidential records relating to prisoners which were stored in F Wing being put at risk. It was therefore decided to counter-attack and to try and re-take the Chapel.

3.284   Over the previous night, however, the prisoners had strengthened the barricades in the Chapel. The C&R teams were unable to enter the Chapel because of the barricades and because the gates to the Chapel were jammed. There was therefore a change of plan. Under the command of Mr Nicholson, an attack was made on E Wing. During the next 1 1/2 hours staff established control of all four landings on E Wing right up to the Centre, although many prisoners stayed on the roof or above the wire grid in E Wing and threw missiles down on the staff.

3.285   The attack on E Wing was successful in diverting the attention of the prisoners who had previously been attempting to enter F Wing. In his evidence, Mr Nicholson described as vicious the attack on the 12 C&R Units. Nevertheless, the staff were able to take all four landings. They were able also to test the barricades onto the Centre and find that they were flimsy. The staff did not however proceed beyond E Wing because of the orders they had received.

3.286   During this particular incident, one of the prisoners recognised Mr Nicholson. He shouted that he did not want this sort of situation. Mr Nicholson had replied that they should pack it in then and the attacks upon the staff gradually ceased.

3.287   There was then for a time a sort of truce. It seemed that a large number of prisoners might be prepared to surrender and arrangements were made for this. Twelve prisoners surrendered on A Wing at about 13.30, but the large-scale surrender never took place.

3.288 At 13.22 some prisoners appeared on the roof of E Wing with a prisoner who appeared to be a hostage. He had a rope around his neck. There was a threat to throw him off the roof if staff were not withdrawn. This was certainly a hoax and was not treated as a serious incident. After a time the prisoner went back inside the prison. During this period there was a further outbreak of violence at the third landing level of E Wing.

3.289 As a result of the attacks on staff in E Wing, one member of staff suffered from severe concussion, another a back injury, a third an arm injury and the fourth an injured calf. All four had to be taken to hospital.

3.290 Despite the viciousness of the attack to which they were subjected during the period they were in E Wing, Mr Nicholson was still of the view that, bearing in mind that the planned attack on the main prison would have involved entering the prison from a number of different points, the abandoned attack on the main prison of 2 April would have been successful.

3.291 At 15.00 on 3 April, Mr D White, one of the Rule 43 remand prisoners who had been evacuated on Sunday night from A Wing, died at the North Manchester General Hospital. He had been admitted with a dislocated shoulder, head injuries and a bruised right eye but in hospital he suffered a severe coronary attack.

3.292 Negotiations continued with the assistance of local solicitors as well as the Editor of the Manchester Evening News. As a result, by about 18.00, 26 prisoners surrendered. During the evening, 5 further prisoners surrendered.

3.293 Mr O'Friel reported progress to Mr Emes at 19.44 on 3 April. At that time, in addition to holding E Wing, other staff were patrolling at ground level under cover of the landings in B and D Wings. There was however concern by that time about possible booby traps and about structural dangers, because of the possible weakened state of the fabric of the prison. Because of this Mr O'Friel was considering pulling back the staff overnight to a holding position. This is what happened. So far as E Wing was concerned, the staff withdrew to the access points on the first and second landings. The staff did not re-enter E Wing again until the end of the siege.

3.294 Over the night of 3/4 April, Mr Boon was once more the Governor in charge. During the night the situation was reasonably quiet. However, there was a fire on A Wing. Mr Boon organised the recovery of the records and other confidential documents from F Wing in the early hours. The staff undertaking this operation were subjected to some attacks from the roof.

3.295 So far as staff injuries were concerned, there were now 26 members of staff who had received injuries, nine had been treated as outpatients in hospital and two had been admitted. One, Officer Jones from Bristol, had a punctured lung and another, Officer Berrall from Risley, had head injuries. Officer Walter Scott, who had been duty on 1 April, and had subsequently suffered from pneumonia, died in Bury General Hospital on 4 April.

3.296 On Wednesday 4 April it was thought that there were at least 35 prisoners present in the prison. However, later analysis of the inmate roll of the prison indicated that there were still 54 prisoners present. (The number should have been 55.) The Governor decided that the policy should be to carry on negotiations with a view to reducing that number.

3.297 During the day another 29 prisoners surrendered. Although there was still some doubt as to the number of prisoners who remained in the prison, the highest figure which was suggested was 25 (26 was the correct number). During that night, 11 of the prisoners who remained in the prison were identified by name. There was little activity on the part of the prisoners, though at one time there was an incident when a prisoner threw slates at staff.

3.298   On Thursday 5 April there was concern as a result of information received from negotiators that the prisoners might stage a dramatic incident. They might try to set fire to the whole prison or break out. It was also believed that there was a possibility that booby traps had been prepared. In answer to the threat of fire, for the first time certain areas of the prison were doused with water by the fire service as a preventative measure. No other active steps were taken. Staff remained in control of the remand prison and guarded the access points to the main prison.

3.299   The main event on Thursday 5 April was the efforts of one prisoner to address the public at large and the media in particular, including television crews, using a loud hailer. The Governor and his staff responded devising methods of making a noise in an attempt to drown what the prisoner was trying to communicate. However the activities of the prisoners continued to receive extensive coverage on television, the radio and in the press, despite the prison's efforts.

3.300   Also on 5 April the Home Secretary made a statement in the House of Commons about the disturbance and announced the setting up of this Inquiry. Towards the end of the afternoon two prisoners surrendered (reducing the number in the prison to 24) but, although there was again talk of the surrender of larger numbers, this did not materialise.

3.301   During the night of 5 April and the following night the prison adopted tactics designed to prevent the prisoners from sleeping. These involved the use of powerful lights and noise, including officers hammering on their shields with their batons. During the course of this exercise on the night of 6/7 April some of the officers shouted jeering remarks at the inmates who were in the prison. The abuse included calling the prisoners beasts. This behaviour was very properly regretted publicly by Mr O'Friel at the first opportunity at a press conference on the morning of Saturday 7 April.

3.302   At 17.20 on 7 April three more prisoners surrendered. This left 21 in the prison.

3.303   Leading up to the first weekend after the start of the riot, the Governor and Headquarters were concerned about the adverse comments which had been appearing in the media suggesting that the whole incident had been badly handled. To try and meet the criticism, arrangements were made to improve the briefing of the media which from then on included regular statements by the Governor.

ii) From Sunday 8 April to Easter Monday 16 April

3.304   On Sunday 8 April, a week after the incident had started, Mr O'Friel and Mr Bone discussed the possibility of obtaining military assistance. This question was subsequently raised with Mr Emes. Mr Emes came to the conclusion that the situation did not justify military intervention since there was no immediate risk to life and the disturbance was confined within the perimeter of the prison.

3.305   Mr O'Friel then raised the question of whether the Fire Service could direct water on the prisoners without restriction. Mr O'Friel also asked for an expert negotiator to back up the local negotiators and for expert advice as to how to place more pressure on the prisoners. The Fire Service made it clear that they could only use their units for the purpose of controlling fires. As a result, two Green Goddesses (Home Office stand-by fire fighting vehicles) arrived at the prison. They were not accompanied by trained crews and they could not be deployed until the prison staff had learnt how to use them. Prison fire officers trained prison staff in the use of the equipment. In addition an experienced negotiator was at the prison from 4 April, but he then had to leave for a short time. He was, however, in full-time attendance from 9 April.

3.306   During the next week, and over the following Easter weekend, the principal tactics which were adopted were continued negotiations, with water being used in considerable quantities, ostensibly to avoid fires. The Regional Director, Mr Alistair Papps had arrived back on 9 April from holiday abroad. (He had suggested an earlier return but Mr Emes had not felt this was necessary.) Mr Papps authorised the use of water from the Green Goddesses above ground level. This meant that they could be used to create a barrier to stop prisoners entering an area where they might cause injury to staff or further damage to the prison. The discussions between Headquarters and Region made it clear that it did not matter if prisoners were to become wet in the process, as long as water was not being used on them directly in a position where they could slip and fall.

3.307   Initially noise, including loud music, was relied upon to disturb the inmates at night. From 9 April, however, music was no longer used as the result of a Ministerial decision. Instead it was intended to use mechanical means to make a noise. However, the equipment which was delivered was initially not effective.

3.308   From time to time, limited entries were made into the prison to gather information. On Tuesday 10 April, in the early hours of the morning, a team of 50 officers entered C Wing. Their objectives were to cut the wire grid above the top landing and to find out whether it was possible by the use of ladders for staff to get above the wire. The entry had been preceded by a team with dogs who had entered one of the wings at 15.00 to make a noise and unsettle the prisoners. Initially the entry into C Wing was successful. A barricade was removed. But when the staff attempted to cut away the wire and clear access to the roof space, they were attacked by inmates with scaffolding poles. One officer was injured in the stomach by a pole. Two other officers were injured when one officer lost his footing and fell on top of a second officer, who fell some ten feet to the landing below. Mr Nicholson, who was leading the intervention, also suffered a minor injury when he was hit by a weapon.

3.309   Although fortunately none of the injuries was serious, they clearly caused concern to the Governor, the Acting Regional Director and Headquarters. That concern was increased by talk of the prisoners having cross-bows and darts. There was also the fear of booby traps. One of the last seven prisoners to surrender alleged that this fear was deliberately engendered by disinformation spread by surrendering prisoners. In addition the staff thought that one prisoner was HIV positive and that there might be some attempt to infect them.

3.310   On Wednesday 11 April Mr Emes, together with Mr Papps, visited the prison. They had discussions with the Governor. It was agreed that the tactics of negotiation together with measures to probe the prison and put pressure on the remaining prisoners should continue.

3.311   The steady surrender of prisoners continued. On 8 April one prisoner, on 9 April two prisoners, and on 10 April three prisoners surrendered (by which time it was estimated that 15 prisoners were still at large in the prison). Then on 11 April three prisoners surrendered. On Friday 13 April, which was Good Friday, two more prisoners surrendered, reducing the number in the prison to ten. The intermittent surrenders then ceased, although on 16 April a prisoner suffering from gastro-enteritis was brought out of the prison by two other prisoners, and all three were then apprehended. After that, no further prisoner was captured or surrendered until 23 April. Until then, the number of prisoners at large therefore remained at seven.

3.312   Although negotiations continued after Good Friday 13 April, they were not having any serious effect on prisoners. Nevertheless the same tactics continued to be used.

3.313   When at the hearing Mr Emes was asked about this he said in his evidence:

"I think the hard answer to that was because our focus was away from

Manchester on the rest of the Service. Manchester was at that stage continuing with these negotiations, and we allowed those negotiations and probing to continue, in other words we did not ask Manchester to change what it was doing or work a plan because we allowed Manchester to continue with the agreed activities throughout that weekend, whilst we at Headquarters focused on other things. It may be that that was an oversight which should have been rectified."

3.314   Mr O'Friel's explanation for his not taking the initiative was, in his words:

"Once that decision had been taken about no major attack being launched, and the fact that the message that I constantly got throughout the rest of the operation was a consistently high level concern about staff casualty as these mounted through the 25 days. It seems to me, that the option of a major assault had been effectively ruled out, and my energies, for much of the rest of the siege were turned towards what I was allowed to do and that was first negotiation, and as the situation developed, to develop pressure tactics to try and ensure that the prisoners came out."

3.315   However, as early as 5 April Mr O'Friel had made it clear during discussions with the Minister of State that he and the Acting Regional Director were of the view that "the structural problems of the main prison, the fire risk and the inevitability of very serious booby trappings meant that intervention, in their view, was actually entirely impractical by the forces that he had available to him at present."

3.316   The practicability of intervention had also been reduced by the fact that the C&R trained staff who had arrived from other establishments had been returning to those establishments. Manchester's own C&R trained staff were far from fresh. Finally, by then staircases had been destroyed by inmates and the landings were in what Mr Nicholson described as "a pretty poor state".

3.317   This was a very difficult period for Mr O'Friel and his staff. His negotiators knew that progress would be very very slow. The prison was under constant scrutiny by the media with television cameras filming from hydraulic gantries every activity of the prisoners. The prisoners were enjoying the attention of the media and indulging in all sorts of performances for the benefit of the cameras.

iii) Tuesday 17 April to Tuesday 24 April

3.318   On 17 April a discussion took place between Mr Emes and Mr Papps. Mr Emes suggested that as the number of prisoners at large was now reduced to seven on five wings, they should plan a method of taking one wing of the prison at a time. They should hold that wing so that they could reduce the area available to the prisoners.

3.319   The following day, Wednesday 18 April, Mr Emes made his second visit to the prison with Mr Papps. Mr Emes formed the view that matters seemed to have ground to a halt and that the remaining prisoners were not responding to negotiations. However, having spent two hours with Mr O'Friel and with Mr de Frisching from the Midland Region, who was supporting Mr O'Friel, Mr Emes reluctantly came to the conclusion that it was not possible to take and hold E Wing, which was the wing which it was easiest to assault.

3.320   On the following day, Thursday 19 April, discussions took place between the Home Secretary, the Minister of State, Mr Mellor, and officials. Mr Emes reported on his assessment of the situation as a result of his visit to the prison the previous day. Having considered various possibilities, it was decided that the Chief Constable of Greater Manchester should be asked for his assessment of the options for ending the disturbance. This should be without prejudice to the question of whether the Prison Service should mount the operation or whether control should be passed to the police.

3.321   Following telephone conversations with the Permanent Under Secretary at the Home Office, Sir Clive Whitmore, on 19 and 20 April, the Chief Constable attended a meeting chaired by Mr Emes on Saturday 21 April. As a result of those discussions, it was decided that it was not necessary at that stage for control to be handed over to the Chief Constable in view of the fact that the prisoners could not escape, the Governor was containing the situation and there was no risk of loss of life or serious injury.

3.322   By that time, there was general discussion in the media about whether or not there was to be a military intervention. On Friday, 20 April, the Secretary of the local branch of the Prison Officers' Association, during a television interview, called for the use of troops and expressed his opinion that the prison should be retaken by force. He also stated categorically that Mr O'Friel had been stopped from mounting an attack on the main prison on the second day of the disturbance.

3.323   The following morning, 21 April, there was a radio interview with the Director General, Mr Train, on the BBC Today programme. Mr Train made his first reported statement about the disturbance. Mr Train tried to explain the Prison Service's handling of the disturbance. One of the matters he was asked was whether the Governor had been over-ruled about intervention. Mr Train responded that "The Governor's view was the one that prevailed. The Governor was the man on the ground who knew exactly what the situation was".

3.324   Mr O'Friel was concerned when he heard this statement. It was not in accord with what he believed had happened. However, when Mr Emes was asked about this matter in evidence, he said that at the time that Mr Train gave the interview, it was "his belief at that time, as was mine,.... at the end of the conversation on the 2nd Brendan O'Friel and I had been in agreement." Mr Emes however agreed that the interview was unfortunate in that it created the impression that the decision had been taken by the Governor and not by Headquarters. Mr Train's comment about Mr O'Friel being the man on the ground is relevant to the question as to who should be the appropriate person to take a decision of this sort.

3.325   On Friday 20 April an intervention was made into the Chapel by four C&R units. They took down a barricade which contained considerable quantities of combustible material. They advanced as far as the Centre. There they met prisoners and used water pumped by the Green Goddesses to prevent the prisoners attacking them. Another C&R unit also dismantled the barricade in F Wing. The following morning a further incursion was made into the Chapel and F Wing to remove material.

3.326   On Sunday, 22 April, the Home Secretary visited the prison and inspected the scene for himself. Later that day there was a conference at the Prison Service Staff College, chaired by Mr Emes, in which a group of experts, including the police and the army, discussed what tactical intervention might be possible. During the conference, the possibility of obtaining access onto the wire grid above the 4s landings on the wings from the Chapel was discussed. Although this was not appreciated by the majority of those present, this route was the one used initially by prisoners to obtain access to the Wings from the Chapel (that is through the groynes from above the projection room). Mr Wallace, who was at the meeting, was well aware that access could be obtained in this way. He had seen it himself when slates were removed in F Wing roof for the negotiation to bring to an end the incident on 26 March. He was also aware that there had been a wall which originally prevented access into the groynes and then into the A Wing roofspace and that the wall had been broken down some time earlier and not yet repaired.

3.327   On Monday 23 April the Home Secretary, who had been briefed about the meeting which had taken place the previous day, agreed that the time had come to take the initiative to bring the incident to a conclusion and that a plan should be drawn up to retake the prison. Later that day, the Deputy Director

General, Mr Emes, and the Permanent Secretary returned to the prison and instructed the C&R commanders to devise a plan to retake the prison. That afternoon the negotiators enticed a leading member of one group of prisoners to the door of E Wing for discussions. C&R staff were lying in ambush there and he was captured.

3.328 C&R units later entered C Wing as far as the Centre at ground level, the barricades on B Wing were removed and D Wing was also explored. After the units had withdrawn, the prisoners started a large fire which continued to burn from about 16.25 to 18.00 on 23 April, when it was brought under control. During the night, other C&R units removed most of the barricades in F Wing. Minor injuries were received by two members of staff.

3.329 On Tuesday 24 April, the intervention plan was rehearsed in the remand prison. Other prisons provided seven additional C&R units and four more Green Goddesses were provided. There were therefore a total of seven Green Goddesses available. The plan of attack involved two units entering C Wing. One unit would go to the 4s landing and climb through a hole in the wire grid which had already been cut. It would then advance along the wire to the Centre. The other unit was to block off the lower landings at the Centre end of the Wing. Two units would enter E Wing and go up to the 4s landing using a contractors ladder and then on to the wire grid using a step-ladder. One unit was then to move on to D Wing. Three C&R units were to enter the Chapel, and one of these units was to gain access to A Wing via the left hand Chapel roofspace, that is via the ceiling of the projection room. The other unit was to gain access by the right hand Chapel roofspace and proceed to B Wing. The third unit was to attack the barricades at the Centre using water hoses. Finally, a unit was to secure the entrance to the Centre from F Wing using hosepipes in support. This was a fairly complex strategic exercise involving over 100 staff to recover a prison which was by then held by six prisoners.

The Forceful Intervention on Wednesday 25 April

3.330 At 08.55 on Wednesday 25 April Mr O'Friel gave the signal to start the planned operation. After 25 minutes the staff had managed to secure the positions on the wire grid as planned. Five prisoners, however, managed to escape to the roof. From there the prisoners threw down planks. At 10.02 the sixth prisoner, who had become isolated from the others, surrendered in B Wing.

3.331 Attempts were then made to isolate the prisoners who were on the Chapel roof in the area of the Rotunda. The initial efforts, using wire to create barriers, were not successful. Staff came under severe bombardment. It was then decided to try and build a barricade, but one of the most active of the remaining prisoners managed to impede this. At 17.20, Mr Emes gave approval for water to be used to drive him away. Water was used on the groyne linking F Wing to A and E Wings. A large hole was then made inside the Rotunda which effectively prevented the prisoners moving from the Chapel roof. At 18.13 the prisoners made it known that they would come down if three named officers were present. At 18.20 all five remaining prisoners were brought down using a hydraulic platform.

3.332 At 20.35 at the prison the Home Secretary and Deputy Director General congratulated the Governor, his staff and the emergency services on the success of the operation.

3.333 During the course of the disturbance 147 injuries were incurred by members of staff, some of which were minor and some of which included the ill effects of inhaling smoke and fumes. 47 prisoners were also injured. Among their number were prisoners who were taken to hospital suffering from drug overdoses.

3.334 The following day the prison was thoroughly searched and no bodies were found. The emergency was declared over.

3.335   The final re-taking of the prison was rapid and successful (though the capturing of last five prisoners took some hours) and its very success raises the question as to why an attack was not made earlier. After all, from the weekend of 13 April there were no more than ten prisoners at large.

3.336   It was suggested to Mr Emes in evidence that the activities of the Prison Officers' Association and the media had caused a change of heart at the Prison Service Headquarters and but for this the Prison Service would have been content to continue with the siege tactics apparently indefinitely. Mr Emes would not accept that this was the case. He contended that it was the meeting which took place the preceding weekend on 22 April at the Prison Service Staff College which for the first time provided the critical information. This information was the identification of the route into the roof spaces of the wings from the Chapel. Mr Emes had not appreciated until he gave evidence at the last day of the hearing at Manchester that this was the very same route as had been taken by the inmates from the Chapel. He was also not aware that the existence of that route was known to members of the staff at Manchester prior to the start of the disturbance.

3.337   Because of this question, Mr O'Friel was recalled to give evidence. Initially, in that evidence, he suggested that, if he had realised the importance that Mr Emes attached to gaining access to the roof space on 2 April, he would have told him there and then about that means of access. However, later in his additional evidence, the position did not appear as clear cut. Apparently it was only as a result of the Staff College meeting of 22 April that Mr O'Friel learnt of the extent to which access could be obtained from the Chapel into the roof voids on the wings. This is more likely to be the accurate situation.

3.338   What, however, was not in dispute was that Mr Emes had not informed Mr O'Friel until shortly before the disturbance was brought to an end of the critical importance he attached to the question of access to the roof space. It is equally clear that, until Mr Emes' final visit before the change of policy took place on 23 April, no indication was given to Mr O'Friel that an outright attack on the whole of the prison would be acceptable. Up to that time the most aggressive policy which was contemplated was taking one wing at a time if the opportunity arose.

Surrender Arrangements

3.339   I have already referred to the successful evacuation of the large number of prisoners who surrendered within the first two days of the disturbance. The inmates who surrendered or who were recaptured at a later date, were treated in a perfectly proper manner. As the disturbance progressed a standard procedure was adopted. An independent observer, usually a member of the Board of Visitors but occasionally a solicitor as well, would be present when an inmate was taken into custody. The observer would accompany the prisoner through the reception area to the hospital where he would be seen by a medical officer. Each prisoner was allowed to take a bath and have a meal and was then transported from Manchester.

3.340   Most of the prisoners were transferred to other prison establishments, but some had to be transferred to police custody until space could be found. Of the 1,647 prisoners in Strangeways at the start of incident, 1,235 were transferred to other prison establishments and 367 were transferred to police custody. One prisoner was discharged having completed his sentence and, apart from the inmate who unfortunately died, the remainder stayed at Strangeways. They were employed in a number of supporting roles which they performed well.

3.341   The prisoners who were transferred to other establishments in many cases made existing problems in those establishments more acute. In some cases this resulted in industrial action being taken by some prison officers who refused to accept any more prisoners at their establishment. Some of the prisoners who were transferred to police cells, who included inmates on remand, spent considerable periods of time contained in wholly unsuitable conditions.

Staff and Families

3.342   There was a major problem in providing information for staff and families during the early stages of the disturbance. The progress of the disturbance was televised and this caused the families considerable anxiety. Their anxiety was increased by the reporting of the incident, both on television and in the press, in terms which, fortunately, subsequently proved to be grossly exaggerated. Naturally families in these circumstances wanted information. Many telephone calls were made to the prison. Some members of the families of staff called at the prison. The lack of available telephones added considerably to the scale of the problem. There were only two phones available to officers to enable them to phone home. One was in the Officers' Club. The second was in the Staff Mess. There were long queues for the use of these phones.

3.343   The chaplaincy and the Prison Officers' Association's local committee did their best to assist, but their task was extremely difficult. On 4 April two officers were specifically detailed for family welfare tasks and they were given lists of staff members who had been injured.

3.344   A number of the members of staff understandably exhibited symptoms of stress and acute anxiety. Fortunately, the Principal Training Officer had done some useful preparatory work in this area and a stress management package was prepared which proved to be valuable. One of the two teams of psychologists who were assembled at Strangeways helped with the debriefing of staff. The debriefing process identified the symptoms of stress. As a result, the Governor sent a bulletin to members of staff and their families advising them that stress could be expected and how it could be dealt with. After the incident came to an end, one psychologist remained at Strangeways. In co-operation with the Principal Training Officer the psychologist set up a series of sessions aimed at coping with post-incident stress. By 25 May, 109 officers had attended these sessions.

3.345   Many extra hours were worked by staff during the incident. They were compensated by ex gratia cash payments of £8 per hour instead of the usual time off in lieu. All staff who had taken part in the incident were given five days special leave.

Inmates' Families

3.346   Because of the nature and length of the disturbance, a number of the inmates' families came to the prison to see whether they could assist or find out about their relatives. In the initial stages of the riot there was obviously immense difficulty in keeping them informed of the situation. In the later stages, those difficulties should not have existed, but at times there appears to have been a breakdown in communications. During a period of considerable stress, families were considerably assisted by the activities of Partners of Prisoners and Families Support Group (POPS) and Lifeshare.

3.347   In the early stages of the incident the then visitors centre was being used by the police and the probation service and so could not be used by families. POPS and Lifeshare, with the help of the Bishops of Manchester and Salford, were able to obtain a room at the back of St Clement's Church, a short walk from the prison. With the support of the City Administrator and Social Services, they gave considerable assistance to families. Telephones were manned and such information as was available was provided.

3.348   There were considerable difficulties in tracing inmates who had been dispersed throughout the country. In some cases it took up to 14 days to trace the whereabouts of a particular inmate. This was far too long. In the case of a disturbance of this scale, it is important that proper lines of communication are maintained between the prison authorities and responsible voluntary organisations who are assisting. A family centre such as that provided by POPS and Lifeshare is a very valuable support unit. However, there are other bodies who seek to capitalise on a riot-type situation and whose influence will not be helpful. By having a system of accreditation for appropriate bodies, it should be easier for the emergency services to isolate mischief makers.

The Media

3.349   The media regarded the disturbance as an event of immense public interest. They deployed considerable personnel and energy to ensure that it was as extensively reported as possible. The media's response is fully understandable. The extent of the interest shown by the media, however, and what was published, give rise to a number of areas of concern.

3.350   The first area of concern is the effect which the presence of the media, and the audience which it offered, had on the length of the disturbance. The probabilities are that the prospect of appearing on television, being heard on the radio and photographed and written about in the press, almost certainly encouraged the hard core of the inmates to prolong the disturbance. It encouraged them also to indulge in dangerous and destructive activities which they would not have done otherwise.

3.351   Having regard to the public interest in the disturbance, however, it would be quite unrealistic to expect the media voluntarily to adopt a self-denying ordinance. It was to be expected that they would publish accounts of what occurred which, after reasonable enquiries, were understood to be accurate and which did not offend professional standards. Under existing law there are no steps which the Prison Service could take to prevent the media publishing what they did. I do not consider that there are any grounds for suggesting a change in the law. It follows that no complaint can be made in relation to the vast majority of accounts which were published of the progress of the disturbance on television, radio or in the press. Considerable publicity must be accepted as being an inevitable consequence of a disturbance on the scale of Strangeways.

3.352   The next two areas of concern are linked. They relate first to the sensational statements which were made in the press and on radio and television which were subsequently shown to be wholly inaccurate and which caused considerable distress to the families of members of staff and inmates. And they relate secondly to the manner in which the prison service dealt with the media and provided spokesmen to brief the media.

3.353   The problem was particularly acute in the early stages of the disturbance. On 2 April there were dramatic headline reports indicating that between 12 and 20 prisoners were dead. These reports were based on rumours. There were also suggestions of castration and the mutilation of inmates which were equally inaccurate.

3.354   It is contended on the part of the media, and in particular Mr Unger, the Editor of the Manchester Evening News, that some at least of the responsibility for the speculative reporting must be laid at the door of the Prison Service. They failed to provide satisfactory spokesmen or a proper briefing. Mr Unger considered the arrangements made by the Prison Service were inept.

3.355   There was also a feeling among the staff at Strangeways, and prison officers in particular, that the Prison Service's case with regard to the way inmates had been treated at Strangeways prior to the disturbance and the way in which the disturbance itself was being handled, was not being properly presented on the media. Mr Serle, the Secretary of the local POA Branch in particular, felt it necessary himself to grant interviews so that the prison officers' case could be heard.

3.356 There was undoubtedly a real problem from the prison's point of view in providing information to the media of the sort that they wanted. First of all, in the initial period of the incident very senior staff could not be spared to conduct briefing sessions. When they could, there was the difficulty that in the early stages of the disturbance the Prison Service did not itself know whether there was truth in the dramatic accounts which were being given by some of the inmates who surrendered of what was occurring inside the prison (which matched those made by the media). Some inmates were known to have had appalling injuries. Inmates who surrendered were genuinely under the impression that even worse injuries had been inflicted. Possibly because the situation inside the prison was so chaotic, no one really knew what was happening. Some inmates had pretended to have suffered possibly fatal injuries in order to avoid being attacked further.

3.357 Some steps were, however, taken by Headquarters with reasonable promptness. At 16.35, arrangements were made for Mr Stephenson, a Governor 4, to travel to Manchester. He was to act as a press liaison officer pending the arrival of an information officer from London. Contact was also maintained with the Greater Manchester Police. As quickly as could be expected, an information officer was sent to Manchester. He arrived at the prison at 18.40 on 1 April.

3.358 In addition, by about 14.30 an emergency press office was opened in London, staffed by four officers. Two of these officers (a senior information officer and an information officer) were members of the prison's desk (that is the section of the Home Office press office which deals with prisons). This press office was under intense pressure from the time it commenced operations. It received an unending flow of incoming calls. Initially direct communications with the prison were impossible. The office had to rely on information coming from the North Regional Office.

3.359 Nevertheless, the first official statement was released at 15.40. It gave in broad terms the nature of the incident. A further statement was issued at 17.00 as already described. Thereafter statements continued to be made using the press facility point set up by the Greater Manchester Police.

3.360 The first ministerial interview took place early on 2 April. It was followed by a second ministerial interview at lunchtime and a statement by the Home Secretary to the House of Commons at 16.11 the same day. Further ministerial statements were made thereafter and Ministers were interviewed frequently on the radio and television.

3.361 At about 17.10 on 1 April the Prison Service received its first rumours of fatalities. The sources of the stories was understood to be the Cavendish News Agency. That news agency was contacted and said that the deaths had occurred at the Crumpsall Hospital. The hospital was contacted and it was learnt that the report was wrong. This information was relayed to the press office for dissemination. The press desk was also told by ITN that the ambulance staff and subsequently a fireman had confirmed fatalities at Manchester. However no support for these alleged confirmations could be found and this was made clear.

3.362 At 21.50 a statement was issued by the information officer at Manchester which set out in brief terms a summary of the day's events. When the statement was issued the information officer was questioned by the press. His response was: "We have no information of any fatalities". This response was undoubtedly regarded by members of the media as unsatisfactory. But, bearing in mind the limited information which the Prison Service had of what was happening within Strangeways, it was difficult to be more categoric.

3.363 A further statement was issued at midnight by the information officer and the press office closed at 01.15 on 2 April. A statement was issued by the information officer at 06.45 and the press office re-opened at 07.00. Full details of the information available was subsequently provided by Ministers, the press officers and the Prison Service. It does appear that, having regard to the difficulty in obtaining hard facts, as much information as could responsibly be provided was being made available.

3.364 It is, however, now accepted by the Prison Service, and in my view correctly accepted, that from the beginning of any trouble of this nature a reasonably senior governor grade official must be available to act as official spokesman. If an official of that seniority had been handling questions from the media and had been able to explain why no firmer information could be given, that may have prevented the more extreme and totally inaccurate reports which appeared on the media. At Headquarters, it is intended that in future a nominated official, normally a senior governor, should undertake regular press briefing. In addition that there will be a nominated member of the Prison Board available for interviews at briefings. This again will be a substantial improvement on the position which existed at the time of the Manchester disturbance.

3.365 This action is also important because, as already indicated, many members of the Prison Service throughout the country were aggrieved about the media reporting. They felt that their side of what was happening at Manchester, and at the other establishments where trouble occurred, was not being properly portrayed. They felt this was due to a lack of leadership within the Prison Service. There was a feeling that the head of the service should be providing through the media the leadership which they were seeking at what was a stressful and difficult time. Their feeling is understandable since it was not until 21 April that the Director General was interviewed by the media. That interview was not as helpful as it would otherwise have been because the Director General shared Mr Emes' misapprehension as to Mr O'Friel's agreement to the calling off of the intervention on 2 April. He also unfortunately and wrongly suggested that the decision to do this had been Mr O'Friel's. This leadership problem will be addressed in part II of this Report.

3.366 It is also accepted by the Prison Service that, for an incident of this seriousness, they should establish a media monitoring unit so that misconceptions and inaccuracies can be picked up and challenged immediately. This is undoubtedly right. It is also important that if senior staff are to be used for briefing they should be are given access to the latest information.

3.367 Mr Unger, the editor of the Manchester Evening News, was closely questioned when he gave evidence to the Inquiry about the propriety of the reporting of the incident by his newspaper. He denied the suggestion that his newspaper had fallen below proper standards of journalism. The Inquiry did not investigate the propriety of statements which were subsequently proved to be inaccurate which appeared in other sections of the media. This being the case, it would not be right to seek to form any judgment of the reporting by the Manchester Evening News alone. The appropriate body to adjudicate on the reporting by the press was the Press Council. That body carried out an investigation and its report was published on 17 January 1991. (The matters it considered would now be the responsibility of the Press Complaints Commission).

3.368 In relation to reporting on the radio and television, the evidence with which I was presented would not justify my making any criticism of any specific programme. In so far as there are matters of concern they should be considered by the Broadcasting Complaints Commission.

3.369 What happened during the incident does, however, stress the huge importance of the media recognising the sensitivity of incidents of this nature. They need to recognise the consequences of their conduct and the dangers of their causing unnecessary worry and anxiety. It also emphasises the need for the media to appreciate that, with the best will in the world, sometimes it will be impossible for the Prison Service to give any indication off or on the record, for example, as here, as to whether or not there had been fatalities. This is because the Prison Service itself does not actually know.

3.370 There is a further aspect of the media's handling of the incident which was referred to in evidence. That was their use of long range microphones. These can be highly effective over remarkably long distances and the media had established themselves in a number of buildings close to the perimeter of the prison and overlooking the prison. When tending casualties at the incident, the ambulance service obtained the clear impression that their conversations with the injured were being overheard. They therefore felt inhibited in inquiring into matters with their patients in the way that otherwise they would have done. If this type of intrusion was happening, I am sure editors will agree it should not have occurred and will wish to take the appropriate action to avoid repetition.

3.371 An additional feature of the media's handling of the incident arises because they interviewed members of the Prison Service, the fire service, the ambulance service and the Board of Visitors in order to obtain newsworthy stories. During the course of an incident such as at Manchester, it would be inconsistent with their responsibilities for members of those services and of the Board to give information with regard to matters relating to the conduct, or the tactical or strategic management of the incident. The temptation to do so must be resisted. This creates particular problems for those who are the local or national representatives of unions.

3.372 At Manchester the Branch Secretary of the POA was Mr Serle. He had high regard for the way Mr O'Friel handled the incident. Mr Serle gave a number of interviews to the media. He consulted both the press officer and Mr O'Friel about what he intended to say. On occasions he modified what he actually said as a result of the views they expressed. Mr O'Friel was not able himself to give an interview until 4 April and he appreciated the efforts which Mr Serle was making to boost the morale of the staff in the prison.

3.373 Mr Serle believed that, while he owed an equal loyalty to his members and to the Governor, he must remain autonomous from prison management. He felt free to say what he considered should be said on behalf of his members, even though this related to operational matters. While I fully accept the sincerity of Mr Serle's actions and bear in mind that he wanted to counter the risk of individual officers giving media misinformation, it was not right for Mr Serle during the course of the incident to make the statements which he did which related to operational, tactical and strategic matters. In particular it was quite wrong for him as a member of a disciplined service to give the briefings to the press which he did on 20 and 23 April. It was wrong to indicate as he did then that a major operation was imminent. This could have had adverse consequences. It could not be justified by a desire to boost the morale of officers or to persuade inmates to surrender.

3.374 Mr Serle did what he considered was right in the circumstances because, as he himself pointed out, he was without any proper guidance. To avoid similar problems arising in the future, it is most important that clear guidelines should be agreed and published by the Prison Service. The guidelines should identify the matters on which it is appropriate for union members to comment during the currency of an incident. The guidelines should be prepared by the Prison Service after consultation with the Prison Officers' Association and the Prison Governors' Association.

The Board of Visitors

3.375 The Board of Visitors were not informed, as they should have been by the Prison, of the outbreak of the disturbance. They soon learnt about it as a result of television and radio reports. From 19.00 on 1 April they were at the prison, though it was initially not thought safe for them to enter.

3.376 The Manchester Board has 20 members, of whom nine took no part in the Board's "watchdog role" at the prison so that they could deal with subsequent adjudications. The remainder performed their role admirably. One member of the Board who had been heavily engaged suffered seriously in her health, possibly because of the strain involved. Two Board members, Mrs Stewart and Mrs Redfern, gave valuable evidence to the Inquiry.

3.377   The evidence from the Board confirmed that an allegation by inmates that prison staff had used catapults was very unlikely to have had substance. The evidence also assisted with regard to an inmate who was said to have had a serious leg injury. Mrs Stewart made 20 personal recommendations which were also of value.

3.378   Mrs Stewart was concerned about the danger of members of the Board being under a liability to pay damages. Accordingly, the Inquiry sought clarification from the Home Office. The response indicated that, provided that the member of the Board had been acting in good faith, it would be difficult to conceive of a case when the Home Office would not be prepared to bear the costs and damages which a member was liable to pay. This was not quite the clear and unqualified statement that might be expected, bearing in mind that the Board provide their services without being remunerated. As long as the member of the Board was acting in good faith, the Home Office should accept responsibility and make it clear that this is the position.

3.379   The only aspect of the Board's activities which gives rise to any concern is Mrs Stewart's involvement with the media over the dispute as to what had occurred during the critical telephone conversation between Mr O'Friel and Mr Emes on 2 April. The media were intensely interested in that telephone conversation. Mrs Stewart says that she saw Mr O'Friel receive the message and he looked "stunned" or "poleaxed". She therefore, out of loyalty to Mr O'Friel, wanted to place his side of what happened before the media and to say what he felt unable to say at that stage. For the reasons I have explained above, she was unwise to do so during the disturbance. There were, however, matters on which it would have been appropriate for Mrs Stewart to comment as part of the watchdog role of the Board. Mrs Stewart had had no guidance or training on what she could or could not comment on. My present purpose is to avoid a reoccurrence in the future of what happened and not to criticise Mrs Stewart for what she said to the media.

The Greater Manchester Probation Service

3.380   The staff complement at Manchester consisted of two senior probation officers and 13 probation officers. In addition the service managed and provided staff for the prison visitors centre.

3.381   I have already referred to the Chief Probation Officer's views on the mix of the population at Manchester prison. In addition, the Probation Service pointed out that lifers needed to feel they were progressing through the system and not to perceive their treatment and movement round the system as regressive. They draw attention to the fact that one of the prisoners considered to have played a principal role in the riot up until the last few days was, on 30 March, in a distraught condition complaining vociferously of his transfer from another establishment. He declared "I have nothing to lose".

3.382 The Probation Service refer also to increasing delays in the case of young offenders going to court and to prisoners being given no reason for the delays or explanations which were unsatisfactory.

3.383   Shared working initiatives between prison officers and probation officers are said to have been frustrated because the prison officer had to deal with what was regarded as a more pressing priority. The Probation Service cite the example of an officer who should have been available for 75 days but who was able only to contribute 19 days during that period.

3.384   The Probation Service said that the overcrowded state of the prison was aggravated by "1,000 fine defaulters" passing through the prison each year. The

Service had been developing fine teams to work with the courts and reduce the numbers. However they considered that some fines were still at an unrealistic level. The inappropriate use of suspended committals when more constructive pro-active work could be utilised aggravated the situation. It could be helped by the judicious use of money payment supervision orders and debt counselling.

3.385 I regard these comments by the Probation Service as justified and have taken them into account during part II of this Report and in making my comments hereafter.

3.386 During the disturbance, the Probation Service provided support for prison authorities and advice and information to the families of prisoners. In addition the Probation Service provided counselling visits and group sessions for the many prisoners who were in a distressed state as a result of the disturbance. They also provided assistance to prison officers and their families and set up a help line for this purpose. In performing this work, the Probation Service co-operated with the chaplaincy. The contribution which the Service made was extremely valuable.

The Greater Manchester Police Service

3.387 The Greater Manchester police were alerted to the disturbance by a call from the prison to their operations room at 10.56 by Senior Officer Bennett. The police log records Mr Bennett as saying:

> "We've a serious incident, 300 prisoners, they've got keys, they're rioting in the chapel, they could be in the grounds, so we request assistance as soon as possible please".

3.388 Mr Bennett also asked the police to contact the Fire Brigade.

3.389 As a result of the call, the Greater Manchester police brought into action their contingency plan. The Chief Constable of the Greater Manchester police sent me details of the contingency plans used. Part of the force emergency procedures manual deals specifically with emergency procedures relating to escapes or serious incidents involving Manchester prison. One section of that procedure deals with rioting or serious disturbance within the prison. That plan appears to have been closely followed and to have enabled the police to act efficiently and quickly. The plan did not, however, provide for the mass evacuation of prisoners from Strangeways. The Greater Manchester police have themselves identified this as a point which will have to be addressed for the future.

3.390 At 10.58 on 1 April, a police vehicle was despatched to the prison to act as a radio control post. This was in accordance with the contingency plan. Nine dog handlers were deployed at 11.00 to provide an immediate external cordon against escapes while further police assistance was summoned. The first serial of 11 officers was deployed to reinforce the perimeter cordon at 11.10. The cordon was strengthened as further reinforcements arrived. By 12.29, all police support units were in position at the prison. Meanwhile, the police force helicopter had been alerted. This arrived at the scene at 11.06. The roads around the prison were closed by 11.29, providing what the police report to the Inquiry described as a sterile area which was maintained until 07.00 on 27 April 1990.

3.391 By 13.00 on 1 April, 138 police officers were manning the perimeter, with nine dog handlers. Other officers controlled the traffic. There was, in addition, a tactical aid group of 49 officers, including a Superintendent, on standby at the prison.

3.392 All these police officers were provided by the Greater Manchester police. Neighbouring forces, from Merseyside, Lancashire and Cheshire were each asked to provide 50 constables with supervision, and they arrived at about 20.30

on 1 April. In the event it was not necessary to deploy them and they were stood down at 11.00 on 2 April.

3.393   As this was a major incident, the Greater Manchester police put in place their normal command and communication arrangements. A strategic control room was opened at 14.31 in the force major incident room and remained in operation until 11.00 on 9 April. A tactical command point was established at Collyhurst police station and that remained open throughout the disturbance.

3.394   During the course of the disturbance, the police continued to provide perimeter security and to maintain the traffic cordon. The police tactical aid group assisted prison officers in managing the movement and containment of prisoners in the Croft area in the first 36 hours before the prisoners were evacuated to other prisons and to police cells. The police helicopter was in the air for a total of 35 hours, providing illumination at night, diversionary tactics and aerial reconnaissance. From the morning of 2 April, police medics were available to C&R units within the prison. Police evidence gatherers also assisted throughout the disturbance. And the police provided a considerable quantity of equipment, including 200 long shields, 26 sets of body armour, 150 riot helmets, 90 long batons, 150 pairs of handcuffs, three generators and five lighting units. In addition, they arranged for the supply and installation of two British Telecom exchange lines in the prison entrance.

3.395   The police casualty bureau was also able to play a significant part in the early days. This was opened at 16.58 on 1 April and was finally closed at 19.00 on 6 April. Its primary purpose was to take calls from the public about relatives. The police estimate that they handled over the five days nearly 5,000 calls, deploying 70 officers in the first three days. The bureau also provided a central consultation point for information on the whereabouts of inmates evacuated from the prison, which the Prison Service was not in a position to provide.

3.396   Finally, the police established a major incident room at 15.30 on 2 April to investigate the criminal offences which were committed during the course of the disturbance.

3.397   It is clear from the evidence which the police submitted to the Inquiry that, despite the very considerable assistance which they necessarily provided throughout the disturbance, they were rarely involved or consulted by the prison authorities. According to their evidence, on only one occasion were the police on the spot consulted about the operational strategy adopted by the Governor. Mr Boon held a meeting at 04.00 on 3 April when, according to the police, there was a general discussion about the possibilities of intervention attended by an Assistant Chief Constable.

3.398   The Chief Constable himself, who had received daily briefings about the situation from his officers, was not directly involved until, as previously described, he received a telephone call from the Permanent Under Secretary of State at the Home Office at 18.40 on 19 April in which he was asked to consider options involving the police for bringing the disturbance to an end. The Chief Constable subsequently confirmed, at a meeting with Mr Emes on 21 April, his initial assessment which was that it was not necessary at what the Chief Constable described in his evidence as "this late stage" to hand over control of the scene to the police. The police were, however, involved in a meeting on 22 April to consider in more detail the tactical options.

3.399   The call on police resources was considerable. On 1 April, 730 police were deployed as a result of the disturbance. By 8 April, the number had fallen to 235. The number stabilised at about 140 from 12 to 17 April and fell to just over 90 from 18 April before rising again to 163 on the last day, 25 April. In his written evidence the Chief Constable said that the initial police response on 1 April was, in his opinion, "correct, sufficient, and in accordance with established guidelines and contingency plans. The police could not have done anything more." I accept that assessment.

3.400 Police contingency plans proved their worth – but there is clearly a feeling among the Greater Manchester police that they could have been given a greater opportunity to advise on the tactical options available to the Prison Service as the disturbance wore on. It may have been they would have had little more to contribute than they were already providing, but on the basis of the evidence I have seen, I consider that the police service was consulted too little and too late.

The Greater Manchester Fire Service

3.401 At 10.59 on 1 April the control room for Greater Manchester County Fire Service received a message from the police that there was a possible riot or serious incident at Strangeways. In accordance with a pre-determined attendance plan for just such an eventuality, the Fire Service immediately mobilised three fire pump engines, one mobile hydraulic platform and an emergency salvage tender, with the necessary fire officers. All appliances arrived at the prison within about four minutes. At the same time, in accordance with the Fire Brigade orders for such incidents, two Assistant Divisional Officers and one Divisional Officer also arrived at the prison to take command.

3.402 According to the evidence of the Deputy Chief Officer, Mr Gordon Price, the first intimation of a fire in the prison came at about 11.42 when fires were seen in B and D Wings. Ten minutes later, at 11.52, the Divisional Officer asked for two further pump engines. Over the following hours, the Fire Service dealt with a number of comparatively small fires by directing water from a hydraulic platform outside the prison walls.

3.403 There were two serious fires, however, which occurred later on 1 April. The first was on the ground floor of K Wing, in the remand block, in the central stores. Two fire officers and two firemen entered the prison grounds at 16.45 to contain that fire. The fire officers did not need to enter the cell accommodation to deal with this fire: they tackled it through the cell windows from outside the cell block. This was the first occasion on which the Fire Service entered the prison grounds. They were protected by shields carried by prison officers. They withdrew as soon as the main fire was extinguished.

3.404 At 17.13 on 1 April, there was a fire in G Wing of the remand prison and the gymnasium. To deal with this fire it was necessary to bring the hydraulic platform into the prison and to set it up between G Wing and the hospital block. All fire service personnel inside the prison wore visors and the fire officer working from the platform was protected by a prison officer with a shield.

3.405 Fire Service appliances and staff were on duty outside the prison throughout the rest of the disturbance. The Inquiry's investigative team found that throughout the disturbance there was a minimum of five and a maximum of seven appliances at the prison, together with emergency tenders, an hydraulic platform, a turntable ladder and a central control unit vehicle. They found that 2,400 fire service officers were deployed at some time throughout the disturbance.

3.406 Fire brigade personnel protected by prison officers dealt with a large fire between D Wing and the kitchen area early on the morning of 5 April. The Manchester Fire Service log, which they sent the Inquiry, records this at 01.58. Much later that day, recorded at 20.42, the Deputy Chief Fire Officer reported that fire crews were being deployed to soak through a large amount of timber in the central core of the prison. More water was put on these barricades the following day. The soaking of these barricades was to reduce what the Fire Service described in their log as, a "severe fire hazard" created by the wood being soaked with oil by the inmates. In oral evidence to the Inquiry the Deputy Chief Officer, Mr Price, confirmed that throughout the disturbance Fire Service personnel and their equipment were not used for any purpose other than for dealing with or preventing fires.

3.407   The Fire Service log records further damping down of barricades on 10 April (23.41). Action was taken on the night of 11 and 12 April to extinguish a fire in the Chapel (between 23.55 and 00.08)); on 12 April (at 23.47) to deal with molotov cocktails being thrown by prisoners from, according to the Investigative team, A Wing; and on the night of 15/16 April between about 02.00 and 03.40, to deal with a much more serious fire in E Wing which required bringing fire service equipment, including a turntable ladder, into the prison grounds.

3.408   Fire Service personnel had again to deal with a fire in E Wing on 18 April (recorded at 14.13) plus some small fires in cells later that day. The Fire Service log records that on 23 April at 16.53 there was a fire in C Wing and that the fire crew which was sent to deal with it was bombarded by prisoners on the roof. Mr Price said that the Fire Service crew came under attack by prisoners on a number of occasions. But he thought the reasons were "because we were under the protection of the prison officers – I think they were really after the prison officers".

3.409   There were further serious fires on the morning of 24 April when fire was spreading from D Wing towards the Centre and, later that morning, involving A Wing. According to the log, this was to be the last major involvement of the Fire Service before the disturbance was brought to an end. On 25 April the log records Fire Service personnel dealing with small pockets of fire as the last prisoners were removed from the roof. Two hours later, at 21.00, the Fire Service forward control was discontinued and all the appliances and officers withdrew from the prison area. For the Fire Service as well, the incident was over.

3.410   The Greater Manchester Fire Service submitted to me its operational procedures order and plan of the prison and its operations brigade orders. The brigade orders set out clearly and at some length the operational procedures and the principles which must be followed. These principles include the statement that "the safety of fire fighters must be considered a major priority at any incident in a Prison Service establishment, second only to the rescue of persons in danger from fire". It added that, notwithstanding this, "officers in charge should not hesitate to withdraw personnel if their life or safety is clearly at risk". I am aware of no circumstances in respect of the Manchester disturbance where that was necessary.

3.411   The operational procedures also confirm Fire Service policy that: "Fire Service attendance to penal institutes during a riot situation is to deal *solely with incidents which result in a fire or rescue*, this after consultation with Prison Authorities" (their underlining). This principle too appears to have been followed closely by the Fire Service during the disturbance.

3.412   Mr Price confirmed that liaison with the Prison Service during the disturbance was "excellent". The ability to co-operate in this way would have been assisted by the fact that, as Mr Price reported in his evidence, before the disturbance the Divisional Commander had had meetings with prison management and liaised closely with them. The Fire Service's Prisons Operational Procedure had been formulated in conjunction with the Governor and his staff. A series of exercises had been held to prove the operational procedures, the last of which had been held about two months prior to the incident.

3.413   As a result of his experience during the riot, Mr Price suggests that the Fire Service Divisional Officers should have their own room in the reception area of the prison for briefing fire brigade officers on arrival. This clearly makes good sense.

3.414   Another example of good co-operation and preparedness was given to the Inquiry by the County Fire Officer, Mr A J Parry, who said that some years previously the Prison Service had, on the fire brigade's recommendation, installed a dry ring main on the prison walls. This allowed the main to be charged from outside the prison. It had, during the disturbance, provided a good supply of water to supplement the internal hydrants.

3.415 Careful pre-planning with the Fire Service proved its worth throughout the length of this disturbance.

The Greater Manchester Ambulance and Hospital Services

3.416 The part played by the prison hospital staff in dealing with those injured in the riot has already been considered earlier in this section of the Report under the heading "The Prison Hospital and the Injured". The hospital staff, as is there set out, warmly acknowledged the assistance they received from the Manchester Ambulance and Hospital Services. It is now necessary to consider that assistance in more detail.

3.417 The Greater Manchester Ambulance Service was first alerted to the riot at 11.22 on 1 April 1990 by an emergency call from a police officer at Collyhurst Police Station, near Strangeways Prison. He stated that there was a serious incident at the prison and requested five ambulances be sent. The vehicles were despatched to the prison at 11.24 and the first arrived at 11.33.

3.418 The Ambulance control called out the duty officer, Mr Bateman, at 11.45. He arrived at Manchester Prison at 12.10. He introduced himself to the police and fire officers present and started to make arrangements for the deployment of the ambulances and to warn hospitals in the area. Mr Bateman decided that six vehicles were required, plus one major accident equipment vehicle. He deployed three ambulance paramedics to treat patients within the prison and, in response to a request from the prison hospital, provided stretchers, carry sheets and six chests of medical equipment. He also arranged during the course of the day for drugs to be provided by North Manchester General Hospital (recorded in the Ambulance radio log at 16.43) and, for a supply of body bags (recorded at 17.10). In oral evidence to the Inquiry, the Assistant Senior Ambulance Officer, Mr Gordon Underhill, said that the bags were delivered in a yellow plastic sack and that they "remained just inside the main gate until the disturbance was over and they were then removed".

3.419 At 14.01 on 1 April, the first casualties began to be brought out. North Manchester General Hospital, Manchester Royal Infirmary and Hope Hospital were put on alert. Both North Manchester General Hospital and Manchester Royal Infirmary implemented their major incident procedure. Between 14.01 and 23.50, 45 casualties were taken out of the prison. Injuries included over-doses, lacerations, broken arms and legs, head injuries and chest and stomach injuries, and the effects of inhaling smoke and of an attempted hanging.

3.420 The first 24 hours were particularly difficult for the ambulance and medical services. I have already referred to Dr McCartney's role. Ambulances could not be parked at the entrance of the prison because of the danger from slates thrown by prisoners from the roof. The injured had to be carried on stretchers or helped to the ambulances waiting some way from the main gate. Communications within the prison were at this stage rudimentary.

3.421 By 2 April, however, there were discussions between the Assistant Senior Ambulance Officer, Mr Underhill, the Site Medical Officer, Dr McCartney, and the police and prison hospital staff. Arrangements were made for casualties to be brought out by police medics and for ambulances to be reversed into the gate house at the front of the prison, thus making it difficult for the television cameras and photographers to get pictures of the injured as they left the prison. The North Manchester General Hospital was identified as the receiving hospital for all the injured from the prison – and two secure wards were set aside for this purpose. The Manchester Royal Infirmary was invited to stand down. Dr McCartney said in his evidence to the Inquiry that they did so at about mid-day on 3 April.

3.422 According to Mr Underhill's evidence, the Ambulance Service provided four ambulances and crews at the prison on 2, 3 and 4 April, although, according to the ambulance service log of radio messages, six extra ambulances were called for in anticipation of the assault which took place on 3 April on E Wing and there appears to have been five ambulances on the scene until shortly after 15.00. On 4 April, ambulance cover was reduced to two vehicles and, at 17.00, to one vehicle, manned by a paramedic crew.

3.423 Mr Underhill told the Inquiry that he requested at 07.00 on 6 April that three extra vehicles be put on stand-by (the radio log records a request for two such vehicles), because he understood that the prison authorities were to seek to regain the prison. But this operation was not proceeded with and when Mr Underhill was informed at 11.00 that the prison authorities were scaling the incident down, all the ambulances were withdrawn shortly before mid-day on 6 April. They were not to return until 10 April.

3.424 On 10 April, two prison officers were injured and required hospital treatment. As a result of this incident, the Ambulance Service decided that one vehicle and crew would remain on call at Strangeways until the end of the disturbance. This remained the position until the Ambulance Service were informed at 18.15 on 24 April that it was intended to begin an assault on the prison between 06.30 and 09.00 the following morning, 25 April. The Ambulance Service were requested by the prison to provide extra vehicles.

3.425 Mr Underhill in his evidence said that on 25 April he attended a briefing of the prison staff and outside agencies at 06.30 "where we were informed as to exactly what was to take place". This showed good co-ordination and planning by the Prison Service. As a result, on 25 April there were three ambulances and a major accident vehicle deployed at various points around the prison. During the course of the day, the ambulance cover was scaled down, and the last vehicle left Manchester Prison at 19.30 on 25 April.

3.426 The Greater Manchester Ambulance Service reported to the Inquiry that throughout the incident its ambulance staff and officers had attended Manchester prison for a total of 669 hours, at a cost of £10,846.50.

3.427 To this must be added the cost of disruption to the local hospitals. In his evidence to the Inquiry, Dr McCartney said that in the first four days of the riot two hospital theatres at North Manchester General Hospital were cleared to deal with possible casualties. By 5 April that was reduced to one theatre. As he said, "this obviously had an affect on the waiting list of patients coming to the hospital, and the staff standing around wondering if they could be doing something more useful".

3.428 Dr McCartney described the generality of injuries which were treated as being those one normally sees after a Saturday night brawl, though some of the injuries were serious. Dr McCartney emphasised that he was looking at the injuries from the point of a consultant normally involved in intensive care.

3.429 Dr McCartney made clear in his evidence that he was not satisfied with the level of liaison during the course of the riot. He said in evidence that the hospital had itself activated its major accident procedure without being asked to do so by the emergency services. He was concerned about the lack of information given to him when he acted as the hospital's site medical officer at Manchester Prison. He spoke to the police and to the prison hospital staff, and relied otherwise on overhearing matters being discussed on the internal radio and on what he described as "the rumours that were prevalent in the prison at the time". The result was that hospital staff were keyed up for injuries resulting from interventions which never happened, and that the hospital routine was unnecessarily disrupted.

3.430 Members of the ambulance service who manned the control room did not share this perception of poor liaison. They said in written evidence that liaison between the ambulance service and hospital control was effective. In any event, it appears no action was taken by the hospital authorities to improve the quality of the briefing they were given. Dr McCartney in his oral evidence to the

Inquiry, accepted that "looking back it would have been correct to point out to the Governor the situation at the hospital". He felt, however, "that the Governor had probably enough on his plate without". It might, however, have been prudent to have raised the matter with a more junior governor. This is something which the hospitals in the area, including the North Manchester General Hospital, and the Greater Manchester Ambulance Service will wish to consider further in consultation with the Prison Service so as to ensure more effective co-operation and the best use of medical resources in any future incident.

3.431 The Ambulance Service, and it must be said the hospital, had no previous experience of dealing with a prison riot on the scale of Strangeways. The Greater Manchester Ambulance Service's major incident plan was followed by the Ambulance Service, but, according to Mr Underhill, the plan did not take into account a protracted incident. In their recommendations to the Inquiry, the Greater Manchester Ambulance Service proposed as a matter of urgency to develop a plan to cover prison riots. They kindly showed me a copy of the plan on 22 August 1990. The plan gives a brief general summary of the likely emergency arrangements for Manchester Prison, together with a more detailed control action card identifying the specific steps which must be taken and requiring the time each action is taken to be inserted on the card. Such plans are useful. They should be discussed and ideally tested with the co-operation of the hospital authorities and the prison to ensure that all parties know clearly what is required of them and so that in any future incident hospital services to the community are disrupted as little as possible.

Conclusions Specific to the Manchester Disturbance

3.432 These conclusions and comments must be read together with Section 9 of the Report which deals with the lessons to be learnt from the disturbances which took place in April 1990.

1. The disturbance which took place in the Chapel had been planned. That is clear from the evidence given formally and informally to the Inquiry. It is also confirmed by the extent to which it was known beforehand that the disturbance was to take place and the fact that there were some inmates at the Chapel with weapons and masks. However, the number of inmates who attended the service with the intention of creating a disturbance was probably no more than 12 and possibly a smaller number than that. The remainder of those involved took advantage of the situation which developed to give vent to their own frustration.

2. The object of those who initiated the disturbance was to draw attention to their perceived grievances, which in the case of some inmates were of long standing. They related to the way they were treated by the Prison Service and the conditions in which they were required to live, not only at Manchester but at other prisons as well. These inmates contend that they had no other effective method of ventilating their grievances. It is unlikely that they contemplated taking over the whole prison. Their initial objective was probably limited to causing a violent disruption and damage to the Chapel and a rooftop demonstration in the area surrounding the Rotunda. They were almost certainly astonished that they were so successful and that they were able to take control of the whole prison. Indeed, this was achieved so very easily that some of the inmates involved concluded that the prison staff had voluntarily vacated the prison, in effect had handed the prison over, perhaps because this would assist them in their disputes with management over manning levels. Reports to this effect have also appeared in the media. It is important that I make clear that I have throughout the Inquiry had this suggestion very much in mind. I am satisfied that there is absolutely no truth in the suggestion. I do however accept that inmates could have genuinely misinterpreted what happened and some would, with justification, feel that they had been abandoned by staff.

3. The reason why the disturbance developed so rapidly was in particular because of the lack of preparedness of the prison staff and management and the inept handling of the early stages of the disturbance. This was largely attributable to totally inadequate training of the prison management and staff as to how to handle an incident of this sort. It was also due in part to the scale of the support which the instigators of the disturbance received from other inmates.

4. A large proportion of the inmates in the prison were sympathetic to the instigators of the disturbance and antagonistic towards the Prison Service because of the conditions in which they were housed at the time at Strangeways. Although there had been substantial improvements over the last two years in those conditions, they were still, so far as the vast majority of the inmates were concerned, with justification regarded as being wholly unacceptable and inhumane. As the inmates repeatedly told the Inquiry, if they were treated like animals they would behave like animals. The prison was overcrowded, and the inmates were provided with insufficient activities and association. The inmates were spending too long in their cells without sanitation and without the opportunity, with reasonable frequency, to bathe and to change their clothes, including their underwear. In addition, some of the inmates had come to expect to benefit from the improvements which had taken place in the prison, but these benefits were reduced or withdrawn in the weeks leading up to the incident because of overcrowding and problems relating to staffing levels. This increased the discontent among inmates. The action which is needed to prevent inmates being in this antagonistic state is considered in part II of this Report.

5. The conditions which contributed to the antagonism of the majority of the inmates towards the prison system in general was not the responsibility of the staff and management of the prison. Well led by the Governor 1, Mr O'Friel, the overwhelming majority had done their best to improve the position of the inmates. However, in addition to the undermining of what they had achieved as a result of the additional pressures to which the prison was subjected in the period leading up to the disturbance, the management and staff at the prison were faced with immense problems due to the failure of Governments in the past to provide the resources to the Prison Service which were needed to enable the Service to provide for an increased prison population in a humane manner. The long overdue improvements in the prison which were recognised as being needed at the time of the riot should already have been implemented.

6. Headquarters and the North Regional Office bear a substantial responsibility for the extent to which the management and staff of the prison were unprepared for the disturbance. Security and contingency planning was given too low a priority by both bodies. The risks of a major incident at a local prison such as Manchester were seriously underestimated. In consequence the resources which were made available to local prisons for training and handling a serious disturbance were inadequate. A proper control room of the type which exists at dispersal prisons should have been provided with adequate means of communication. The security improvements needed to the Chapel and the roof ceilings of the offices on the wings should not have been delayed because of lack of resources. More C&R equipment should have been available. More attention should have been given to locking systems. Staffing levels should have made more generous provision for training. Additional guidance for and monitoring of contingency planning should have been provided.

7. The prison should also have given higher priority to security and control. The way security records were kept was unsatisfactory. The contingency plans should have been more developed. A higher priority should have been given to operational and C&R training (particularly as to how to contain a disturbance). Full plans of the establishment should have been available for the commander of any incident. The informality and

irregularity with which security information was recorded was unsatisfactory. A properly maintained up-to-date written record of relevant security information should be kept by the senior governor on duty at the prison. He should be responsible for ensuring the record is properly maintained and the information disseminated during his period of duty. The Governor or his substitute should be responsible for ensuring that other governors and officers are given any information it contains relevant to their duties. He should be personally responsible for handing it to the person taking over from him. If, in the event, no governor is on duty, the senior member of staff should have the responsibility. To rely upon an oral exchange of information alone is not satisfactory.

8. The route from the Chapel over the projection room ceiling into the roof space above A Wing should have been blocked long before 1 April 1990. There was no possible justification for leaving such a glaring gap in security to be carried out in conjunction with other works.

9. It is tempting to conclude from this disturbance that far too many inmates were allowed to be in the Chapel at the one time and that there should be a set limit placed on the number of inmates which can congregate at any one place at any one time. However any figure which is chosen as being the limit would be arbitrary. The state of prisons is infinitely variable. A limit could be too restrictive and unnecessarily interfere with a worthwhile aspect of prison life. Alternatively it would encourage the prison to permit more people to be present than would be justified on a proper consideration of the circumstances. I am not therefore in favour of laying down an arbitrary limit on the number of prisoners who should be allowed to attend a particular Chapel service. It is preferable to leave decisions of this sort to the Governor of the prison. He should know the mood of his prison. It should be his responsibility to decide and, as long as he considers the problem properly, his decision should be beyond criticism. Nevertheless, as a general rule for an ordinary weekly service on Sunday, for a prison with a mixed population such as that at Manchester, it would be preferable if the number of prisoners attending were less than 300. 200 would be a sensible working rule for a stable prison (this last requirement of a stable prison means that in many of our larger prisons the norm should be lower than 200). However I would emphasise that there can be circumstances where the Governor could regard a figure in excess of 300 prisoners as perfectly acceptable. If, for example, the service is a carol service before Christmas, the Governor could authorise a very much larger attendance.

10. Given the state of tension which existed at Strangeways in the spring of 1990, it would undoubtedly have been preferable that there should have been at least two ordinary Church of England services for the main prison. Having regard to the information which should have been available on 1 April, the numbers attending any service on that day should have been reduced to half and preferably to a third, although this would have meant two or three services. What happened at Manchester can be criticised because there was an excessive reluctance to restrict the numbers and no proper consideration was given to the question of what numbers should attend. A large number of prisoners were known only to be going to the main service on Sunday because it was regarded as being preferable to being locked up. An additional exercise would have been equally attractive to them. The principle of freedom of worship need not involve allowing more prisoners to congregate at one time at one place than is desirable in the interests of security and control.

11. The prisoners, or at least a large random sample, should have been subjected to a rub-down search as they entered the Chapel on 1 April 1990. More officers should also have been deployed in the Chapel. I do not accept that this would have provoked the inmates. In the light of the rumours working around the prison, a show of strength would have been understood and would have been welcomed by the majority of inmates. Placing officers

out of sight in the vestry served little purpose. The officers provided by Mr Palmer should have not left the Chapel after escorting the prisoners into the Chapel. They should have remained in the Chapel during a large service of this nature, particularly in the conditions which prevailed. At least one and preferably two Governors should have attended the service supported by a Principal Officer. A Senior Officer, however experienced, should not have been the most senior member of the Prison Service present.

12. The probabilities are that if there had been the precautions taken which Mr O'Friel said he would have wanted had he been consulted, this would have avoided the action which initiated the disturbance, at least during the Chapel service. Certainly the steps referred to in conclusions 10 and 11 would have achieved this result.

13. When the disturbance did start, the action which the prison officers took in vacating the Chapel cannot be criticised. They probably would have had to have taken exactly the same steps even if the number of inmates present in the Chapel had been substantially less and there had been still present the same number of inmates determined to create a disturbance.

14. The staff should have been instructed, either before the service or when they evacuated the Chapel, to remain in the passage outside the Chapel on the 4s landing. A Governor on duty should have ensured that such instructions were given. The staff's presence in the Centre at the 4s level would have deterred the prisoners from trying to leave the Chapel by the doors on to the Centre. It would not have prevented inmates trying to enter A Wing and then the other wings by the overhead route, but if officers had remained in the wings the prisoners might have been deterred from dropping down through the office ceiling into the wing and this could have resulted in the prisoners being dealt with by the officers on the wings if they did try to enter the wing in this way. With the help of chains and padlocks or even handcuffs or jamming the lock, the staff should have been instructed to try to contain the inmates within the wings at the gates until staff equipped with MUFTI could be deployed. The fact that MUFTI equipment was out of date did not mean it was of no use. A show of force could have had a sobering effect on at least the majority of the inmates. A sensible precaution would have been to have let the prisoners see that at least one unit of officers in MUFTI was deployed during the service.

15. If the officers had been forced to withdraw from the Centre and from the whole of the main prison, some of their numbers should have been redeployed in the Remand Prison to hold that prison once other staff had been deployed in MUFTI at the other exits from the Chapel.

16. Miss Stewart should not have left the Remand Prison. She was in charge of that prison and should have done more to arrange for its defence. It was her place to be at that prison supervising the evacuation of the remand prisoners on Rule 43. Mr Wallace should have given her instructions to this effect when she arrived at the communications room. Action to evacuate those prisoners should have been taken earlier. If prompt action had been taken, the Remand Prison should not have been lost and the Rule 43 inmates on E4 should have been able to have been protected.

17. The fact that relatively junior governors were on duty, who had not received any training in the handling of a major disturbance, contributed to the riot spreading to the whole prison. Training and an up to date contingency plan are vital when a disturbance of this nature occurs. While the training and the contingency plan must be general in nature, they should enable those in command to know what action to take during the period of initial shock which follows such an event. The failure to take the right action and instead to withdraw far too rapidly from the prison was not due to any lack of steadfastness of purpose on the part of those involved. It was due to their inability to provide the necessary leadership and control during the initial period of the disturbance.

18. Subsequently, and especially after Mr O'Friel had taken command, the staff's behaviour was commendable. However the lack of proper contingency planning and the difficulties of communication caused by the lack of facilities, meant that it was not possible to manage the reception of staff from other establishments satisfactorily. A Centre should have been established to which they could have reported and where they could have been fully briefed.

19. Bearing in mind the limited facilities for communications, both the Regional Office and Headquarters provided excellent support with regard to the evacuation of the inmates. Management at the prison deserve to be commended for the way inmates were moved out of the wings to safety and held until they could be evacuated. It would have been preferable to have correctly recorded the names of the inmates who were being evacuated, but the failure to keep a proper record is fully understandable having regard to the conditions existing in the prison.

20. The commander at Headquarters during a serious disturbance should avoid, so far as this is possible, being away from Headquarters, even to brief Ministers, while he is on duty. The establishment of a briefing room for Ministers at Headquarters since the riot is to be welcomed.

21. The person in command at Headquarters in respect of a serious disturbance should be kept fully informed of what is occurring. But he should recognise that his role is primarily supportive and supervisory, although in the final analysis he has the right of veto in relation to any particular proposed action. He can also, if this is necessary, replace the commander at the establishment. He should recognise the practical limitations which arise from his being far away from the scene of the disturbance. He cannot command the incident. He will be in a position to take a broader view than the commander on the scene and there will be less danger of his being affected by what is occurring at the scene. However he will not be in control of the establishment or the staff. He will be unaware of the detail of what is happening or the atmosphere within the establishment. If he has lost confidence in the ability of the commander of the establishment to deal with the disturbance, he should replace that commander.

22. Mr Emes showed great strength of character and leadership in being prepared to take a clear and firm decision against intervention on 2 April. However, during the telephone conversation just before 15.00 that day, he was in no position to take the decision which he did. He had not been correctly or fully briefed. He had no advice available to him as to what the C&R teams under fully trained commanders would be likely to be able to achieve. Neither he nor Mr Leonard had witnessed a demonstration of C&R3 except on a video film and he had only the most general of briefings. He should have taken technical advice. If he was not able to discuss more fully the matter with Mr O'Friel at 15.00, he should have deferred a decision to nearer the deadline of 16.00.

23. The plan prepared by Mr O'Friel with the help of his C&R advisers and in particular the very experienced Principal Officer Instructor, Mr Nicholson, had sufficient prospect of success to justify Mr O'Friel's judgment that there should be an intervention. This conclusion is reinforced by the successful entry into E Wing on 1 April and the holding of that wing for a substantial period; the information which Mr Nicholson had obtained as to the state of the barricades; what happened when there was an intervention into the kitchen, and the subsequent re-entry into E Wing. Mr Emes was correct in stressing that there was already substantial damage to the prison and little likelihood of immediate danger to any inmate from other inmates. But he failed to take sufficiently into account in his assessment of the situation the importance of not allowing the mutiny, for that is what it was, to continue for longer than was necessary. The inmates had already

created a most unfortunate precedent in showing that they were able to take over the whole of a large local prison. It was important that they should not also be able to show that they could continue to hold that prison, notwithstanding the assembly of a very large force of trained and equipped C&R officers. The continued control by the inmates of the prison was likely to add to the tensions which already existed at other establishments. It should have been appreciated that they could well hold out against a siege for a long time. It is true that there would have been a serious risk of injury if not of death to the members of staff involved. Any intervention where the inmates control the establishment will inevitably carry such a risk. This is a risk which regrettably prison staff sometimes are required to face. However, that risk was not as materially affected by the inmates' control of the wire grid above the 4s as was suggested by Mr Emes. The staff would have been very seriously at risk on entering the wings and the Chapel when they were in the open and under bombardment from the roof. It was then that the masonry and cell doors referred to by Mr Emes in his note could be dropped on them and not when they were under the wire grid. They were under such a bombardment when rescuing inmates, when they entered E Wing on 1 April and when they entered the kitchen on 2 April. The plan should have been allowed to proceed. If it had done so there was a reasonable prospect of a large number of inmates being trapped at the lower levels as a result of the initial attack and of all but a small minority of the remaining inmates surrendering very rapidly. The teams may have been forced to withdraw. This was an eventuality which Mr O'Friel accepted, but one which I regard as being unlikely. It would anyway have been preferable to not intervening.

24. I suspect Mr Emes may have been influenced in his approach by the different situation which exists in a hostage-taking. There the inmates have the hostages in their power and can be provoked by intervention into taking innocent life. That has to be borne in mind when taking a decision whether or not to intervene. The danger in a riot situation is different.

25. Mr O'Friel should have made clear to Mr Emes that he did not agree with Mr Emes' decision not to allow intervention and the reasons why. It was unfortunate Mr Emes' mind had been coloured by Mr Boon's adverse assessment of a different plan. If Mr Emes had appreciated that Mr O'Friel did not agree with his assessment, he would no doubt have explored the matter further with Mr O'Friel. If he had done so he should have come to the conclusion there were insufficient grounds to justify over-ruling Mr O'Friel.

26. The alternative attack on the kitchen was a sensible tactic if the prison was not to be retaken. In any major incident it is important to try and deprive those taking part of food and water. Unfortunately, by the time the attack took place, the prisoners had acquired ample food and they had no difficulty in obtaining water.

27. Having rejected the plan to retake the prison by force on 2 April, the strategy which was then adopted involved alternating periods of negotiation and pressure. This followed the techniques used for dealing with hostage situations. However the convincing evidence from the senior negotiator strongly suggests that for negotiations to be effective in a riot situation the negotiator must be able to make it clear to the prisoners involved that if they do not surrender within a limited period forceful intervention will take place. In Manchester this was not possible because the C&R forces which had assembled dispersed and the negotiator suggests this prolonged the disturbance. Further study should take place as to whether different negotiation tactics can be developed for use in riot situations which do not require an intervention force to be overtly waiting to intervene.

28. Having taken the decision not to intervene, within a few days it should have been clear that unless there was a forceable intervention, or at the

least the threat of such an intervention, the disturbance was likely to continue for many days. The continuance of the disturbance was affecting and would continue to affect other establishments. The disturbance was a blatant display of unlawful conduct which was receiving wide publicity. Certainly not later than 13 April, by which date the number of mutinous prisoners had been reduced to ten, it should have been appreciated that negotiations were not going to succeed and that alternative tactics were needed. Mr Emes should have then reconsidered the situation. Although his failure to do so is understandable because of the many other disturbances with which he was having to deal (a schedule of which appears in Annex 3D), Mr Emes should have ensured that positive steps were taken at a high level to try and devise a plan of which he could approve. He should at least have explained to Mr O'Friel what were his requirements. If this had been done, the method of entry to the roof void of the prison would probably have been identified at a much earlier date.

29. I make these comments about Mr Emes' personal role because as Deputy Director General in charge of operations he takes personal responsibility for what happened at the Headquarters level. He agreed at the Inquiry that in reaching his decisions as to what action should be taken he was not acting under the instructions of Ministers and the decision was his alone. The reason for this is that while Mr Train as Director General had overall responsibility for advising Ministers on the policy for the Prison Service, Mr Emes was treated by Mr Train as being in charge of operations and in fact acted as the operational head of the Service. During the major part of the disturbance, he was carrying a very heavy burden indeed, probably far greater than any individual should have had to carry. Since April 1990 a management reorganisation has taken place which abolished the office of Deputy Director General. If it had not been for this it would have been necessary to make detailed criticisms of the management structure. This would now be a purposeless exercise, but attention is drawn to it in fairness to Mr Emes, who perhaps was faced with an almost impossible task. What should be the role of the Director General is considered in part II of the Report.

30. The scale of the disturbance made it clear that it is necessary to reconsider what should be the approach to C&R training and the arrangements which should be made for the expeditious provision of C&R reinforcements. This is a subject which will be considered in Section 9.

31. The use of loud noise and other methods of disturbing the prisoners during the night appear to have been ineffective and to have caused substantial inconvenience to the members of the public in the locality. Where prisons are in built up areas such tactics should not be used in the future until there has been a full evaluation of the value of such tactics and it is concluded that their use justifies the inconvenience they cause.

32. With regard to the media, attention is drawn to the part of the section which is headed "Media" and the improvements in the arrangements for providing information for the media accepted to be needed by the Prison Service. Guidelines should be drawn up after consulting the Prison Officers' Association, the Prison Governors' Association and the Board of Visitors as to what matters it is appropriate for their members to make comments on during the currency of a serious incident.

33. The adverse effects of the disturbance on the inmates and staff who were caught up by it emphasises the importance which in the future should be attached to debriefing and stress counselling.

34. A different system with regard to locks should have been adopted at Manchester. This subject is considered further in Section 9.

35. The scaffolding in the Centre was needed in order to carry out redecorating

work. Although scaffold poles provided formidable weapons it would be unrealistic to ban scaffolding in an establishment when there is no reasonably economic way of performing the work without it. However, the scaffolding should be erected for the minimum period and in no circumstances should scaffolding be left lying around the establishment when not in use. When scaffolding is erected, it should be as well protected as reasonable. This was the situation at Manchester at the time of 1 April incident. While the prisoners were able to obtain access to the scaffolding from above, a remarkable feature of the disturbance was the fact that at no time was the protection of that scaffolding from the landings penetrated, though no doubt the prisoners could have done so if they had made a determined effect.

36. The whole question of manning levels and activities at weekends needs to be reviewed. The fact that the incident occurred at Manchester at a weekend was no coincidence. This matter will be more fully considered in Part II of this report.

37. Although the media questioned the wisdom of rebuilding Strangeways, the right decision was reached to restore Strangeways for use as a prison. Strangeways is well situated to serve the courts in the Manchester area and it could prove to be a model for community prisons in the future. The restoration, which I am pleased to note is to be completed by mid-1993, will give an opportunity to bring the prison up to contemporary standards. It should then be capable of providing light and airy prison accommodation of a satisfactory standard, as long as the recommendations and proposals in other parts of this report are borne in mind. In particular the cells should once more be used for the single occupation for which they were intended, except in the case of a small number of cells which, for operational reasons, such as the risk of suicide, should be occupied by more than one inmate. They should have integral sanitation or alternatively they should be provided with an electronic locking system which enables access to sanitary arrangements without the involvement of unnecessary staffing during the day and at night. The windows should be enlarged if possible and modern metal doors and frames with pivot hinges fitted. The wings should be divided into units holding not more than 80 inmates. There should be separate and secure routes to enable staff to gain access into each unit and into the roof voids. All cells should be wired for TV, radio and personal alarms. Gates giving access to units should be capable of being operated electronically from a central point under surveillance by closed circuit television. The refurbishment should include facilities for each unit to have washing machines for the washing of inmates' clothing. Consideration should also be given to extending the indoor sports facilities and to the construction of a swimming pool – when resources permit. Telephones for inmates' use should be installed on each landing. A new heating system should be installed. There should be sufficient facilities for management, probation officers and staff both on and off duty. A separate room should be provided for the use of the Board of Visitors. There should be a new visitors centre. The services to any unit should be capable of being turned off without affecting the services in any other unit and where possible this should be operable from a position close to the Main Gate – or some other accessible and secure location. There should also be water points together with a suitable appliance for delivering water for defensive purposes in the case of a disturbance. I have been kept informed of the Prison Service plans for the "new" Strangeways and have been encouraged and impressed by the way in which they are catering for the matters to which I refer. A plan of the new prison appears at Annex 3E.

38. The existing restrictions on the circumstances in which water can be used and the authority which is needed for its use may be too restrictive and should be reviewed.

39. Liaison between the prison management and the emergency services was generally excellent but maintaining the necessary preparedness and ability to co-operate requires continuous consultation and joint training. The lessons referred to in the parts of this section of the report dealing with the emergency services should be heeded.

Section 4

Glen Parva Young Offender Institution and Remand Centre

Introduction

4.1   The disturbance at Glen Parva occurred on Friday 6 April 1990. It was the first establishment to have a serious disturbance after the start of the riot at Manchester.

4.2   Glen Parva had none of the obvious defects of the other establishments which had disturbances and which have been targeted by this Inquiry. The physical conditions were adequate. The Governor provided the leadership which was needed. The staff in general worked well with the inmates. They co-operated with management to ensure that, within the limitations imposed by the resources which were available, there was a varied regime. Glen Parva was therefore an unlikely site for the next serious disturbance after Manchester. It is, however, probable that a disturbance would not have occurred if an inmate had not been transferred to Glen Parva from Manchester because of the riot there.

4.3   Glen Parva is a Young Offender Institution and Remand Centre near Leicester. It occupies a spacious site which was once the Royal Leicestershire Infantry Depot. It was built in stages. Originally it was a Borstal and an allocation centre. It first became operational in 1974. Hospital and sport complexes were added in 1979. In 1981 a remand centre and a young offenders prison was established on the site. Glen Parva then contained three quite separate establishments within a common security fence – a Borstal, a remand centre, and a young offenders prison.

4.4   In 1988 legislation resulted in major changes in the sentencing of young offenders. All young offenders between the ages of 14-21 became liable to be sentenced to detention in a young offenders institution. The detention centres and youth custody centres, which had replaced the Borstals, were renamed young offender institutions. Glen Parva became one of these institutions. In conjunction with this role, it also continued its role as a remand centre.

The Institution

4.5   A plan of Glen Parva is at Annex 4A. The accommodation is divided into separate living units. At the time of the disturbance, there were six units being used, at the southern end of the establishment, namely units 7, 8, 9, 10, 11 and 12. Unit 7 ((7) on the plan) was a punishment or segregation unit. Units 8, 9 and 12 ((3), (4) and (9) on the plan) were remand units (unit 9 was also used for allocation). Units 10 and 11 ((6) and (8) on the plan) were occupied by sentenced young offenders. There were a further five living units at the northern end of the site which were occupied by sentenced young offenders.

4.6   The units with which the Inquiry is concerned all follow broadly the same design. The main accommodation containing the cells is three storeys high. The main entrance to each unit is off a single storey enclosed corridor. The corridor links all the units and other facilities and gives access in each living unit to a single storey association room with television, staff offices, washing facilities and servery. It is necessary to go through the association room to reach the sleeping accommodation. There are flat roofs throughout the establishment, with roof lights over the association rooms. Most accommodation is in cells, which have integral sanitation. In addition, each unit has a small four bedded dormitory. There are dining areas but, because the units housing remand inmates are overcrowded, the remand inmates ate in their cells.

4.7   The design of the living units was such that officers in the association and living areas had no vision and little idea of what was going on in the three storey cell units. Officers on duty there can feel – and are – very remote. This made it difficult to maintain staff confidence and control in these units. (There was not the same problem in the two new units, which had been built as units 14 and 15, where visibility is excellent. These were not in use before the disturbance.)

The Population and its Accommodation

4.8   The certified normal accommodation (CNA) of Glen Parva in April 1990 was 612. On 6 April the population was 778. The total overcrowding factor for the whole establishment was 1.27.

4.9   The overcrowding was primarily among the remand inmates. Cells had to be doubled up. On 6 April 1990 the overcrowding factor for these inmates was 1.72 (in other words, nearly three quarters of the inmates had to share cells). The CNA for remand inmates was 192 and there were 330 inmates.

4.10   Those serving their sentences were not so badly placed. The overcrowding factor was 1.07. The CNA for young offenders was 420 and there were 448 inmates.

4.11   On the remand side, the cells are equipped to take two inmates. Since they are designed for only one inmate, they are far from spacious. The remand inmates are therefore less well off for accommodation than those who are convicted. The Governor, Mr Rumball, said that remand prisoners prefer not to be alone in a cell. While this may be so, the remand inmates had no choice as to whether they shared a cell or not. Had these remand inmates only been using their cells to sleep in, they could have taken a different view about the desirability of having to share a cell.

4.12   The furniture for remand inmates is fixed and made of steel. This overcomes the problem which occurs in some remand establishments in this country (but not usually abroad) that on the day inmates leave the centre, they break up the furniture.

4.13   In his report in 1985 the then Chief Inspector of Prisons described Glen Parva as a well equipped establishment with good accommodation. However, while the buildings may have been perceived as adequate at the time they were built, for current control purposes they are not ideal, for reasons I will explain later.

Industrial Relations

4.14   Industrial relations at Glen Parva were generally satisfactory. The local POA Committee had no complaint to make about the facilities given them to carry out their work. They told the Inquiry that they supported the Governor's efforts to maintain a positive regime within the establishment.

The Regime

4.15   The Governor of Glen Parva ran an unusual regime for remand inmates. He gave them a choice between "opting in" to a full programme, including work and education, or "opting out". Remand inmates have the right not to work.

Glen Parva dealt with this by offering remand inmates an all or near nothing approach. If remand inmates did not work, they were not paid. While those who opted out could attend education, and gym classes of at least one hour and possibly two hours a week (if spaces were available), it is clear that when, as often happened, there were more people than places, they were likely to be at the end of the line.

4.16   Those opting out of work were entitled to association on week-end days only. By contrast, at the time of the disturbance, association was available for "opt ins" every evening of the week (subject only to a limit of a maximum of 40 inmates at any one time). Both those who opted in to the full programme, and those who opted out could earn association on Friday afternoon, if they came high enough up in a regular competition for keeping their cells clean and in good order. Mr Rumball explained this as follows:

> "We believe.....that a standard of cleanliness and inmate turnout and cell cleanliness is important in an establishment....In order to encourage that, and particularly with young people, you need to offer them some incentives. We offer them this incentive (additional association) in return for trying to maintain good standards."

4.17   It is perhaps not surprising, therefore, that the great majority of remand inmates opted in to the full programme. Out of an average remand population of about 200, 20 or fewer opted out.

4.18   The Glen Parva remand regime does, therefore, achieve its objective. It deters the majority of inmates from opting out of activities entirely and spending their time wholly unproductively in their cells. They can earn a better standard of living. The approach is however unusual and vulnerable to criticism. It may be justified if those who opt out are provided with a standard of life which is consistent with their status as remand inmates, that is people who are to be presumed innocent until proved guilty. It is debatable whether Glen Parva was able to achieve this standard for those opting out. However, subject to it doing so, I regard the approach as being infinitely preferable to the position described at Manchester of youngsters spending far too long lying on their beds during the day and creating noise at night.

4.19   All sentenced young offenders were assessed during their first week and an appropriate sentence plan was devised. This identified that work, courses, and community activities the inmate would undertake. A personal officer was appointed to help and encourage the sentenced inmate in achieving objectives. It is the personal officer's job to make himself familiar with the inmate's background, see him at regular intervals and keep notes on his progress, so that he will be able to report appropriately to the Probation Service and other agencies. An induction course and a personal officer would also have been of value for remand inmates, but they were not provided.

4.20   There is no doubt, however, that Glen Parva provided a good range of activities for remand inmates. Remand inmates could work in the contract services workshop, or as orderlies or cleaners. There was a full physical education programme providing, on 6 April, 322 places a week for remand inmates in one hour sessions (the number of places was raised to 420 shortly afterwards). There were opportunities to go to the canteen and Library. There was access to daily visits (except Saturday). These visits, the investigative team found, often lasted longer than the statutory 15 minutes.

4.21   There were also opportunities for association. 40 inmates in each unit could be given association at any one time (out of a CNA of 60, and a possible maximum occupation of 105). There was association during the day. There was also association each evening – except that, as a result of the Fresh Start requirement to make staff efficiency savings, from 1 April 1990 the Governor had decided to cut all evening association for remand inmates at the week-ends, providing instead association for some on Saturday and Sunday mornings.

4.22   In a remand centre, education staff have to cope with the varying needs of a changing population. Every remand inmate was required to have a compulsory session of health education during his time at the establishment. On reception, inmates were issued with a proforma in which they were asked whether or not they wished otherwise to participate in education, and what aspects of the programme particularly interested them. From this, priorities for attendance at classes were worked out. Those under school leaving age were automatically placed on classes. Special consideration was given to those whose reading and abilities were low or non-existent. Other remand inmates, however, did not have as good a chance as sentenced inmates of being given access to classes.

4.23   There were other opportunities for remand inmates who could not or did not wish to attend classes. It was possible for him to be put in contact with a distance learning tutor. Also, where an inmate showed severe learning difficulties or was illiterate, but again did not wish to attend education classes, his needs were dealt with by an adult basic education volunteer tutor, under the direction of the basic education team leader. Any remand inmate under school leaving age undergoing punishment in the segregation unit, received a visit from the remand education team leader each morning and afternoon and was provided with work.

4.24   Altogether, the remand education programme, including health education, provided 28 sessions of education for remand inmates each week, and some 280 student places. All classes were full. High standards of discipline and mutual co-operation were achieved. Not long before the disturbance, prison officers were taken off the task of supervising classes. It seems that the majority of inmates were unaware that this had happened. There was no loss of classroom discipline or control.

4.25   Overall, and by admittedly unexacting standards, this was a relatively good regime for remand inmates. Many remand inmates in other establishments would be astonished by these opportunities. But Glen Parva was still falling short – considerably short – of its own targets for keeping remand inmates out of their cells. The target was 9.5 hours each day, a target which, the Governor told the inquiry, was governed by the current staff levels. The actual figure, however, for the financial year 1989/90 fell short. Remand inmates were out of their cells for 6.7 hours on week days and 4.7 hours on week-ends. (These figures do not however include time spent going to court or on visits.)

4.26   One of the Assessors to the Inquiry learnt, when he interviewed remand inmates at Glen Parva, that even these figures masked a very wide disparity in individual treatment. Remand inmates felt they did not do as well as convicted inmates.

4.27   Although there were clear differences in standards between remand and other inmates, the Governor and his staff are to be congratulated on their efforts to provide a mixed regime for remand inmates. Despite their efforts, however, the delivery was not constant. Nor did the opportunities increase to meet the increased number of remand inmates received by Glen Parva in the early months of 1990.

4.28   Mr Rumball, the Governor, said in his evidence to the Inquiry, that as a result, there were longer queues for meals, less frequent showers, and reduced association. This all created a feeling among remand inmates of a steady erosion of conditions. The fact that inmates *could* be doubled up – and may even have *wanted* to be doubled up – should not obscure the reality that this reduced each inmate's chances of taking part in the activities on offer. It was bound to deny some inmates the activities which would otherwise have been available to them. It was bound to lead to discontent, for which the staff would be blamed.

Kit

4.29   Remand inmates at Glen Parva were strongly discouraged from wearing their own clothes. Mr Rumball explained this to the Inquiry as a tradition built up at Glen Parva over the years. It was clearly successful since he could recall only two inmates who had ever insisted on wearing their own clothes. Mr Rumball said the wearing of prison clothes allowed inmates to appear tidily in their own clothes in Court and it avoided discrimination against the less well off.

4.30   The inquiry's investigative team found the standard of prison clothing on issue satisfactory. It was helped by an efficient laundry. There was still the usual prison problem of discarded clothing – thrown out of the windows or deposited in dustbins – a problem which was being tackled by a well motivated reclamation party. However, I am not convinced by Mr Rumball's reasons for so firmly discouraging inmates from wearing their own clothes. These, or arguments like them, are used whenever uniforms are defended: and they are rarely shown to be overwhelming or insurmountable when a change is made. Certainly, other prison establishments seem to find ways of dealing with them.

Food

4.31   All food at Glen Parva was prepared in a central kitchen. There was a Principal Catering Officer in charge, assisted by a Senior Officer and five Catering Officers. Since there were so many separate units, food was transported in heated trolleys to serveries, manned by prison officers and selected inmates. Neither these officers nor the inmates had any particular training in basic food hygiene or in methods of serving.

4.32   Remand inmates dined in their cells; sentenced inmates in each unit dined together.

4.33   The Governor told the Inquiry that, while there was more than one view on dining in association, it provided an opportunity for staff to talk to the inmates and for inmates to talk to each other. While he kept it under review, in his view dining communally was preferable to dining in cells. Cell dining was necessary for remand inmates because of the larger numbers in the remand units.

4.34   The quality of the food did not appear to loom large amongst the inmates' complaints to negotiators during the disturbance, or in the subsequent interviews between my Assessors and inmates. There was the problem common to many establishments that the food was served too far from those who actually prepared it. The POA Committee commented adversely about this and thought that the officer caterers should have more face to face contact with their "customers". Food did not appear, however, to be a major problem at Glen Parva.

Problems for Inmates

4.35   The traditions of Glen Parva could make it difficult for those coming from others part of the prison system. The establishment's Borstal origins are not too far beneath the surface. The best of the Borstal tradition is seen in many aspects of the regime, including the education programme and the personal officer scheme for sentenced inmates. However, there was a risk that inmates with experience of other remand establishments could find it difficult to adjust to the Glen Parva traditions. Some inmates could find the approach behind the opting in scheme too regimented.

4.36   There was also the position of the 10% of remand inmates who opted out and so did not conform. Some of them would be a dissatisfied, under-employed and potentially disruptive influence.

4.37   There was a further unsettling factor. Glen Parva held a significant number of inmates who were convicted but not yet sentenced. Mr Rumball drew attention to their position in his evidence to the Inquiry. From the establishment's point of view, they were difficult to deal with because they fell between the remand and the sentenced inmates. They were unsure about their future. They did not know what their sentence would be.

4.38   It is clearly undesirable that these inmates should be kept in this situation longer than necessary. Between 4 March and 24 June 1990, however, there were an average of 68 inmates in this position – 23% of the total average remand population. There was a time when the number of such inmates was as high as 87. Of the inmates in Glen Parva on 1 March 1990 and convicted before that date, 20 inmates had waited at least a month before sentence. The average wait for those 20 inmates was two and a half months; the longest nearly five months (10 of those 20 eventually received non-custodial sentences, mostly probation). These periods of waiting are longer than some sentences. They are entirely unacceptable – for the inmates and for the reputation of the court system. This requires urgent attention.

Drugs and Treatment Rooms

4.39   At Glen Parva, as elsewhere, there was a continuing problem of preventing the inmates from receiving illicit drugs. A programme of searching was maintained. The number of finds was small. For the six months prior to 1 April 1990, there were twenty incidents of possession or use of cannabis. There was no evidence of any other type of drug being found or used. Those who were identified as having received drugs on a visit were subject to closed visiting arrangements. Furthermore, any inmate suspected of attempting to receive drugs during a visit was placed close to a supervising officer. The Governor, in his evidence, considered that he was on top of the situation.

4.40   During the disturbance itself, the two treatment rooms adjacent to the living units were not in any way violated. But their physical security would have given them little protection from attack. I understand that all controlled drugs were kept in the pharmacy in the hospital and only pharmaceutical products of a bland nature were kept in the treatment rooms. Though much more secure than the treatment rooms, the hospital pharmacy would not have been able to withstand a serious attack. This is a matter of concern.

Contingency Planning

4.41   Contingency planning at Glen Parva on the whole was satisfactory. The response to concerted indiscipline was one of 11 emergency routines prepared by the establishment and last revised in August 1988. It was out of date in its reference to MUFTI teams rather than C&R units, but in all material respects appears to have been clear and well-formulated. It was not so voluminous as to be unmanageable. Nor was it so inflexible as to be unadaptable to particular circumstances. It provided a clear check list of the action to be taken. It instructed that the Governor, the communications officer, the police, the Board of Visitors and, if necessary, the Midland Regional Office should all be informed by identified people. It also gave some brief, but useful tips on the handling of a disturbance – for example it counselled the operations principal officer to:

> "isolate the incident, keep the atmosphere as calm as possible, and prevent escalation.....establish dialogue with demonstrators; establish cause of disturbance; identify ringleaders".

4.42   The local police had a contingency "Operational Order" available to assist them during a disturbance. While this included a description of the establishment, it was not really up to date. It did not include the most recent new buildings. The police said that it had been their intention to visit Glen Parva to familiarise senior officers with the lay out, but they regretted that this had not taken place before the disturbance.

4.43   Control and restraint training seems to have been given a high priority, to some extent at the expense of other subjects. Thirteen principal officers, 39 senior officers and 161 officers had been trained up to C&R1 standard. A Governor 5, three principal officers and 49 senior officers and officers had also been trained up to C&R3 standard.

4.44   On the night of the disturbance, Glen Parva held only a mixed bag of C&R equipment: six helmets; six fire resistant overalls; six pairs of gloves; 24 sets of shin guards; and two shields. In addition, they had 24 complete sets of the old type MUFTI equipment. However other C&R equipment was made available once the disturbance had started, and C&R units from other establishments brought their own equipment. There never seems to have been a time during the course of the disturbance when shortages of this type of equipment caused any problem. (Shortly after the disturbance, 60 complete sets of C&R equipment were delivered to the establishment – a satisfactory allocation.)

4.45   During the earlier part of the disturbance, there were problems in controlling the mains water supply to the unit involved. The inmates were using the internal unit fire hoses against staff and to cause damage. Until control of the ground floor was recovered, where the stop-cock for both the hose reels and the domestic water supply is located, nothing could be done to prevent them. This situation clearly needs attention.

4.46   It is possible to control the supply of electricity and gas externally to the units, but during the disturbance, there was no need to do so.

Background to the Disturbance

4.47   The evidence suggests that from December 1989 Glen Parva had to weather a number of unsettling events which would have made the establishment more vulnerable to a disturbance. These developments were:

    i)   in December 1989, Glen Parva accepted 23 young offenders from Grendon Underwood (which specialises in disturbed prisoners and whose population was dispersed while Grendon was being repaired). It was expected these inmates would be at Glen Parva for only a short period – but some remained until March 1990;

    ii)   81 young offenders were transferred to Glen Parva from Wellingborough in January 1990 (Wellingborough was being used to take the majority of inmates from Grendon). The sentenced inmates could only be accommodated by converting one of the remand units to a unit for sentenced prisoners, thus increasing the pressure on remands;

    iii) on 2 April Glen Parva received 14 remands and 2 sentenced young offenders from Manchester following the start of the riot there;

    iv)   on 3 April it received 17 sentenced inmates from Stoke Heath (15 of them via Birmingham) following the disturbance at Stoke Heath;

    v)   on 4 April a total of 30 former Manchester inmates were transferred to Glen Parva via Lincoln and Birmingham – 18 were on remand and one of these was to figure prominently in the disturbance at Glen Parva two days later;

    vi)   in addition, the situation was made worse by a steady increase in the number of remand prisoners coming from the Courts.

4.48   These developments led to an increase in the remand population from 220 in January 1990, to 307 by the end of March, to 322 by 6 April – and with a loss of one remand unit to the sentenced inmates, there were 48 fewer cells in which to accommodate them. In addition, on 1 April 1990 Glen Parva had a shortfall of 14 officers.

4.49   The Inquiry's investigative team examined possible indicators of tension.

They noted that the incidence of reported indiscipline was high among remand inmates. It amounted to the equivalent of four offences against discipline for each inmate during the 12 months before 1 April 1990.

4.50　The team noted that on 6 April – the day of the disturbance – an ex-Manchester inmate in unit 12 had lodged a complaint about conditions and about having to wear prison clothes. But there was nothing otherwise in the pattern of applications to the Governor from inmates to suggest that complaints were increasing – indeed there were 300 applications in January 1990, and 251 in March – a falling trend. On the other hand, there was an increase in applications to the Board of Visitors (six in January, 26 in March) but no indication from these applications that inmates were significantly dissatisfied with their conditions or treatment.

4.51　Nor was there any indication of impending trouble in the register of petitions to the Home Secretary, in the number of inmates reporting sick or the level of staff absences. And only five inmates had been segregated under Rule 43 at their own request in the three months prior to 6 April.

Warnings of the Disturbance

4.52　The first concrete sign of trouble was received by Glen Parva on 3 April 1990. The Corby police had heard from an inmate that there would be a disturbance at Glen Parva on the coming *Sunday* 8 April. The prediction was therefore two days *after* the incident in fact happened. The informant said that an officer would be assaulted when he unlocked inmates from their cells. The trouble would be on the remand unit 8 (the unit which was in fact involved). On the same day (3 April), information was received from another establishment which had seen a letter smuggled out from Glen Parva which said that an incident would occur before 10 April.

4.53　On 4 April, the stories appeared to be hardening. An inmate told an officer that there was going to be trouble in the church on 8 April. There was corroboration for this in a report from another officer. A third officer reported that there would be a "sit-in" at medical treatments on 5 April.

4.54　The following day, 5 April, the sit-in did not take place. But an officer reported that he had heard two former Strangeways inmates saying that they were going "kick off in the chapel on Sunday". Another officer reported a possible incident in unit 9 after canteen on 6 April.

4.55　The following day (6 April) there was intelligence from an officer suggesting that there were problems in unit 10 – a unit with sentenced prisoners.

4.56　The Head of Custody, with the approval of the Governor, took action in response to this build up of intelligence – which did not, of course, all point the same way. He sought to get further information from unit 8, and kept a potentially disruptive inmate from that unit in the segregation unit. He ensured that association in unit 9 on 6 April was carefully monitored. He defused the problems in unit 10 by allowing inmates to spend their own cash in the canteen on 6 April. Finally he sent a memorandum to the Midland Regional Office setting out precautionary arrangements for church services on 8 April. These included the staff inside the chapel not carrying keys. This was a sensible precaution not taken at Manchester.

The Disturbance

4.57　How the disturbance started is not in dispute. The two inmates and the officer involved tell roughly the same story. An inmate transferred from Strangeways wanted to escape, according to him because his mother lived too far away to visit him. The investigative team found that the inmate had told the chaplain of this. For reasons which I do not criticise this information was not fed into the security intelligence system.

4.58   The Manchester inmate thought he would persuade his cell-mate to join him in the escape attempt. This second inmate felt aggrieved because the recent increase in the number of inmates at Glen Parva had lead to a reduction in the regime.

4.59   This second inmate had a "bad reputation", according to the inquiries made by the investigative team. His record showed that some nine months previously he had intended to take a member of staff hostage and seize his keys to effect his escape. This was information available to the establishment which was of greater importance.

4.60   The result of an unfortunate allocation was that two would-be escapees were put together in a cell. In the heated climate following Strangeways, they were able to persuade themselves that, by overcoming an officer and taking his keys they could, with the support of other inmates, effect their escape. It was perhaps a forlorn hope – but for the Prison Service it proved to be an expensive escapade.

4.61   At about 19.15 on Friday 6 April, Officer Richmond was detailed by the Senior Officer in charge of unit 8, to go to the number 2 landing to unlock three inmates for association. One inmate, who had been punished, was located in a cell on his own. Officer Richmond unlocked him first. This inmate came out of his cell, closed the door and went off to the association area. A second inmate had stayed late in bed that morning and as a result had forfeited one hour of association. He was in cell 2/8 with another inmate who had lost two hours for throwing water and so was not yet due to be released. They were the two inmates referred to earlier.

4.62   Officer Richmond went to cell 2/8 and let out the one due for association. The other asked the officer if he could get a cigarette from next door. The officer agreed and the inmate went to an adjoining cell. Officer Richmond then moved to another cell to let out the third inmate who was due for association. Like the first, this inmate closed his cell door behind him and walked to the association area.

4.63   At this time there were only two inmates out on the landing, the one due for association and the other who was due to go back in his cell but who had gone to get a cigarette. Officer Richmond told that inmate to go back into his cell. As he tried to close the door on him, the inmate held it open from the inside and the other inmate jumped on Mr Richmond's back. They fell forward into the cell, and on to the cell floor. The inmate on Mr Richmond's back held him in a head lock. Mr Richmond was holding his keys in his right hand under his body. The inmate who had first gone into his cell, then started to jump up and down on Mr Richmond's shoulder and arms, shouting "get his fucking keys". The officer was in pain from the assault on his shoulder and was unable to use his radio because his left arm was incapacitated. He thought at that point that he was going to be taken hostage inside the cell.

4.64   Officer Richmond managed to struggle to his feet, with one inmate still round his neck punching him and the other inmate trying to get his keys. He then forced his way backwards and they all fell out of the cell on to the landing. At this point, Officer Richmond lost his keys. He remembers seeing the inmate running down the landing and starting to unlock the doors. At this moment, another inmate jumped on top of him. He then saw the very first inmate he had let out of his cell, standing by the entrance to the landing. He told him to press the alarm bell. He did not do so and ran off down the stairs.

4.65   Officer Richmond was still struggling to get away from the two inmates holding him down when he saw an inmate running down the landing towards him. This inmate, who is to be highly commended for his courage and sense of responsibility, dived on top of Mr Richmond's assailants and started punching them. He successfully freed the officer, who managed to get to his feet and run towards the entrance to the landing. Three times he radioed for assistance. The time was 19.20.

4.66   Mr Richmond was met by Officer Evans at the bottom of the steps. Mr Richmond told Mr Evans that the inmates had his keys and that most of the inmates on the number two landing were already out of their cells. Mr Evans locked the door on the ground floor.

4.67   A few seconds later, officers responding to the alarm came into the unit. Mr Evans stopped them going up to the landings as he considered there were too few officers to deal with the number of inmates involved.

4.68   The inmate who intended to escape made his way towards the exit door. When he saw the officers, he withdrew to the third landing to join other inmates who had been released from their cells. According to the inmates, only one of those who did not want to be involved was assaulted by other inmates, although others who were unwilling were intimidated.

4.69   Within minutes of it starting, the incident had been turned by the inmates from a frustrated escape attempt to a destructive disturbance. This was achieved by the inmate with the keys releasing inmates in their cells on the second and third landings (but not on the ground floor).

4.70   The precise number of inmates who were directly involved is difficult to establish. It could have been about 60. There were other inmates on association in the unit at that time. They were not involved. They were initially evacuated to the nearby education block, and later to unit 14.

4.71   After the alarm was raised, the police and fire service were informed by 19.28. The police arrived at the establishment by 19.38.

4.72   Governor 3, Mr Shaw, the Head of Custody, arrived at the establishment before Mr Rumball. He put into action the contingency plans on which he had been working earlier that day in preparation for the coming weekend. When the Governor, Mr Rumball, arrived at 20.00 he was briefed on the situation and ensured that the police, fire and ambulance services had been called and that Midland Regional Office had been informed and had been asked for C&R reinforcements. He ensured also that staff did not go off duty at the end of their shifts.

4.73   By 20.02 the inmates in all the other living units had been locked away. Double locks had been applied to the external doors to all the units. By 20.18 two C&R units had been deployed to sweep through the grounds.

4.74   Mr Rumball designated Governor 3, Mr Shaw, as the forward incident commander to be located in unit 8, and in effect, to take tactical command of the incident there. Mr Rumball established himself in the Board room and used the adjacent offices for the senior officers of his support staff and the emergency services. He liaised with these services and took command of running the rest of the establishment, including incipient disturbances in other units, in particular unit 9 and unit 12. At 20.55 Mr Brown, the Chairman, and Mr Clutton, a member of the Board of Visitors, were contacted and asked to come in: they were to play important roles later in the incident.

4.75   Governor Shaw had taken control at the forward command post at unit 8 at about 20.20. He had about 20 staff in riot gear and a number of other staff who were without protection. At that stage the staff were not properly organised. Mr Shaw instructed Officer Tower, a C&R instructor, to form units from those who were properly equipped.

4.76   Mr Shaw discovered that some 31 inmates who had been on association in unit 8 had by then been located in the south education block. A further 14 inmates, who had never become involved, were locked in their own cells on the first (ground floor) landing. The second and third floor landings were in the control of the inmates and protected by barricades at the south stairwell on the ground floor and at the north stairwell on the second and third landings. There were sounds of destruction, and the internal fire hoses were being used against staff.

4.77 By 20.44, Midland Region had given authority to use the new empty unit (unit 14) to take surrendering inmates from unit 8. The Region had also called up support staff from Leicester, Stocken, Nottingham and Onley, together providing 56 further staff. By 20.56 the first support C&R unit from outside the establishment arrived. It was despatched to unit 8.

4.78 By about 21.00, therefore, management were ready to start positive management of the incident. They needed to complete the sweep of the grounds; to isolate the disturbance in unit 8 and to start to try to resolve it; to manage the inmates in the other units so as to avoid the contagion spreading; to ensure that arrangements were in place for the relocation of the rioting inmates; and to get in place and if necessary deploy prison service reinforcements from other establishments, together with the police, fire and ambulance services. They needed also to clear their lines with the Region and, through them, Headquarters; to ensure the Board of Visitors were deployed; and to respond to press interest. Above all they needed a plan.

4.79 The evidence suggests that in almost all these respects, Glen Parva staff and management acquitted themselves well. They were assisted by the contingency plans which I have earlier described.

4.80 It was of the greatest importance in this first period – and indeed throughout the incident – to meet the injunction of the contingency plan and isolate the incident. The aim was to isolate it within unit 8 and, if possible, within one landing on unit 8.

4.81 The design of Glen Parva made this extremely difficult, as Mr John Lynch pointed out in his structural report on the establishment which he prepared for the Inquiry. There were two main problems. The structure was not of sufficiently stout construction to withstand determined attempts to destroy it. Mr Lynch reported that the living units:

"fall short of the robust security standards required for young offender institutions".

4.82 The second main problem in isolating the incident was that inmates could have easy access to the flat roofs. By smashing out landing windows they could have got on to the single storey roofs above the association room of each unit and used them, if they so wished, as a way of getting more easily to the top of the roofs of the living units. The roofs of the corridors linking the units would also have provided an express way to most other parts of the establishment.

4.83 In his report Mr Lynch concluded that:

"In view of the fragile and vulnerable nature of these buildings, and the easy access to roofs, it is surprising the damage was largely confined to fittings, and that the disturbance was of such a limited nature. In the circumstances, the control and tactics exercised by managers and staff must have been most effective".

4.84 I accept Mr Lynch's assessment. In the event, the seat of the disturbance was held to the third floor of unit 8. The physical weaknesses of Glen Parva were not to prove the establishment's undoing. This is to the credit of staff and management.

4.85   At about 21.12, while Governor Shaw was still assessing the situation, three inmates appeared at the south stairway barricade on the ground floor and asked to surrender. They were encouraged to remove part of the barricade. In a matter of minutes, staff protected by C&R units had dismantled that barricade. The units then moved on to the second landing. They took control of it and dismantled the barricade at the north end. Only one inmate was found on this landing; he wanted no part in the disturbance and immediately surrendered.

4.86   By about 21.15 the disturbance had been isolated on the third landing of the unit. There were about 50 to 60 inmates behind the third floor barricades. Mr Rumball said in evidence to the Inquiry that of these he estimated that about 15 formed the "hard-core". Mr Shaw decided that the proper course was to seek to negotiate the end of the disturbance.

4.87   Mr Shaw secured the Governor's agreement to this tactic. It was based on Mr Shaw's judgement that to attempt to break through the barricades, which were exceptionally well constructed, would put officers at too great a risk. There were live electrical wires and water at the south end. The north end barricade could only be traversed by one officer at a time, who would therefore have been very vulnerable. In addition, the south stairwell was in total darkness. This assessment of the situation was sound. Mr Shaw kept the staff informed about the tactics which were going to be adopted.

4.88   The arrangements for negotiation were well thought out. Officer Downs, who had been on a negotiators course, was made the lead negotiator with Senior Officer Young as his back up. Two officers – Officer Thomas and Officer Ward were log keepers. Officer Ingham was responsible for the telephone link between Governor Shaw and the negotiators.

4.89   The inmates had at this stage demanded a radio. Perhaps reflecting what they knew of what had happened at Strangeways, they said that they had hanged an inmate and threatened further hangings if their demands were not met. Officer Downs was able to see that two inmates had nooses around their necks which were not attached to anything. They were grinning. He passed on to Mr Shaw his assessment (which proved to be correct) that this was a hoax.

4.90   The negotiators were able to identify the ringleaders of the disturbance. They opened up discussions with them at various locations in conditions which were always noisy and at times chaotic. These negotiations continued until the eventual surrender.

4.91   During the course of the negotiations, complaints were made by inmates about the standard of food, the lack of association, and that inmates in unit 8 in particular were kept locked up in their cells too long. Mr Rumball told the Inquiry in evidence that inmates had also complained about the attitude of staff. He believed – and I have no evidence to doubt this – that this was a reflection of the staff having to deal with the increased population in the early part of 1990 rather than anything intrinsically unhelpful in the attitude of the staff themselves.

4.92   There were also problems in other parts of the establishment. In unit 12 (another remand unit) there was some smashing of windows at about 21.54. The situation quietened down, however, when a C&R unit was positioned outside the unit, clearly visible to the inmates inside.

4.93   In unit 9, a remand and allocation unit within sight and earshot of unit 8, there had been some unrest and noise at the start of the disturbance. More seriously, at about mid-night, a small fire was reported on the ground floor in unit 9 and several barricades were made in the cells. Eight inmates were removed shortly afterwards to the segregation unit (unit 7) and some others were removed later. As a result, the problems were controlled and contained.

4.94   At about mid-night, the negotiators were joined at the barricade by the Chaplain and by a Medical Officer. Their task was to reassure the inmates that they would not be badly treated if they surrendered. At 00.16 two inmates surrendered. They were followed by two further inmates at 00.33. But the main surrenders did not start until a little under an hour later. At about 01.14, ten inmates surrendered; followed by 14 inmates at 01.49 and a further 13 at 02.20. The remainder – 30 or so – came out some twenty minutes later. Mr Richmond's keys were finally handed over by an inmate to Officer Smith.

4.95 The surrender of the inmates was delayed because a substantial group was prevented from giving themselves up by the stronger and more disaffected elements among the inmates. The negotiations were, however, helped by an inmate of stronger character than the rest. He persuaded 12 of the inmates to give themselves up.

4.96 When the Inquiry visited Glen Parva on 25 April, they saw graffiti on the wall of unit 8 saying that:

"you cannot beat the system, but you can have a good laugh trying".

Perhaps that reflected the mood of some of the inmates at the time.

4.97 The arrangements for the surrender worked satisfactorily. There have been no allegations made to the Inquiry of the use of undue force. As well as the Chaplain and the Medical Officer, two members of the Board of Visitors, (Mr Brown, the Chairman, and Mr Randall) were in the office on the ground floor of unit 8. They saw the inmates being taken out of the unit. The surrendering inmates were handcuffed to a prison officer, but were not under C&R restraint. Mr Brown told the investigative team that he saw no undue force used.

4.98 Inmates were taken by vans provided by the police to unit 14. Their reception there was observed by another member of the Board of Visitors, Mr Clutton.

The Role of Midland Regional Office and Headquarters

4.99 Mr Rumball told the Inquiry that, throughout the incident, he felt well supported by the Midland Region. The Regional Office were clearly anxious, however, that the disturbance should be brought to a conclusion as soon as possible. At about 23.54, the Midland Regional office telephoned Mr Rumball to say, on the Regional Director's instructions, that the barrier in unit 8 should, if possible, be removed. The inmates should be told that if they did not come out quickly, staff were prepared to go in and risk possible injury.

4.100 The Midland Regional Office log records that at 23.59, the Deputy Director General's office were informed that a time limit was to be given to the inmates after which the barricades would be removed if they had not come out voluntarily. In fact, no such ultimatum was given to the inmates. No attempt was made to storm the barricades, though several probing operations were mounted.

4.101 Mr Rumball interpreted – no doubt accurately – the burden of his conversation with the Regional Office as a suggestion and not as an order. He believed that negotiations were likely to lead to a speedy resolution. And at around mid-night he assessed that the negotiations were getting results. There is no doubt that inmates would have seen C&R units, both when the units were testing the barricades and through the cell windows, so they have may been in no doubt that forceful intervention was on the cards. Nevertheless, it seems likely that the Deputy Director General's Office would have had from their discussion with the Midland Regional Office at 23.59 an impression about the conduct of the negotiations which did not accurately reflect the reality of the situation. This impression should not however have lasted for long. The Midland Regional Office gave the Deputy Director General's Office regular up-dates during the three hours after mid-night – based on reports to them by Mr Creese in Glen Parva.

4.102 Mr Rumball informed the Midland Regional Office at 02.46 that all the inmates were out of unit 8. This information was passed by the Regional Office to the Deputy Director General's Office – logged at 02.48. The Deputy Director General's Office authorised the closure of the Midland Regional Office incident room about an hour later. The incident was over.

The Involvement of the Emergency Services

4.103   The response of emergency services to the disturbance was excellent. The police in particular were very supportive. There was a police superintendent, an inspector and a sergeant in the Governor's command room. They arranged for 80 police officers to secure the perimeter. They also provided six transit vehicles to move the surrendering inmates from unit 8 to unit 14.

4.104   The police commented very favourably on the way the disturbance had been handled by the Prison Service and by the Governor. They considered that the Governor had set up a clear communications system which enabled the police to be kept fully informed. They were very impressed by the arrangements made by the Governor to log the incident. They also considered that the liaison between the Prison Service staff of all grades and the police officers was excellent.

4.105   The Fire Service provided four appliances, though fortunately they were not needed. An ambulance was also at the establishment throughout the incident. All the emergency services were regularly briefed as to what was going on.

The Media

4.106   Mr Rumball appointed a Governor 4, Mr Creese, to liaise with the media and with the police press officer. This made good sense. Mr Creese had been on a training course at the Prison Service College in Wakefield about dealing with the media.

4.107   Mr Creese's handling of the media was very effective. Throughout the night he kept in touch with the Home Office press office and the media.

4.108   Press statements were issued at 00.25 on 7 April, at 02.30 and at 02.48. Mr Rumball gave a press conference in the Gate Lodge at 04.30. On the evidence I have seen, the arrangements for briefing the press – with the assistance of the police press officer – appeared to have worked well.

The Consequences of the Disturbance

4.109   The Prison Service reported to the Inquiry that four officers were injured during the disturbance. The most serious injuries were to Mr Richmond, who received injuries to his shoulder requiring out-patient treatment. Despite this injury, after attending hospital, Mr Richmond returned to Glen Parva. His arm was in a sling, he had a black eye, a cut lip and was still suffering considerable pain. Nevertheless he remained at the establishment until 02.40 on 7 April trying to give what help he could.

4.110   One officer received an electric shock, one sustained an injured toe. Another cut his hand on broken glass. None, except Mr Richmond, required treatment.

4.111   Only one inmate was injured. He is reported to have broken a knuckle while breaking up property in the unit.

4.112   Unit 8 sustained damage to sanitary ware, windows and doors, and to floors and decorations by flooding. Units 9 and 12 had damage to sanitary ware and window glass. All were repaired by early May, at a total estimated cost of about £32,000.00.

4.113 Following the disturbance, Mr Rumball sent personal letters of thanks to the emergency services and to all the staff. He also took Mr Richmond and his wife to visit unit 8 on the following day, 8 April – which Mr Rumball told the Inquiry was appreciated by Mrs Richmond. I commend him for this thoughtful action.

4.114 Mr Rumball himself was boosted by receiving a personal letter of thanks from the Home Secretary. He did not, however, receive a message or a visit from either the Director General or the Deputy Director General. The Deputy Director General, Mr Emes, said in evidence at the Inquiry that he had personally written on Easter Sunday, 15 April, to all the Governors involved in disturbances, but he regretted if, in the event, Mr Rumball had not received his letter or had been over-looked: that would have been an oversight.

Conclusions Specific to the Glen Parva Disturbance

4.115 The following conclusions and comments must be read with Section 9 of the Report which considers lessons to be learnt from all the disturbances.

1. Although I have comments to make as to certain aspects of this disturbance, my general conclusion is that the disturbance was not the fault of the Governor, management or staff of Glen Parva, or of the Midland Regional Office or Headquarters.

2. The contrast in the conditions of the remand and sentenced inmates illustrates the need for special steps to be taken to protect the position of remand inmates. If their conditions of containment had been better protected they would not have been less favourable than those provided for sentenced inmates.

3. Glen Parva also demonstrates that sentenced inmates, at least, can safely dine in association. I regard this as a desirable objective, particularly for those establishments holding young inmates: however, there was not, as there should have been, regular face to face contact between the catering officers and the inmates at meal times.

4. I do not criticise the staff or management for putting in the same cell the two inmates who appeared to have sparked off the disturbance. I agree with the Governor that the fact that one of the two inmates had been at Strangeways at the start of the riot was not a sufficient indicator of trouble in itself to justify special action being taken. Even if the chaplain's information about the inmate who wanted to escape had been fed into the security intelligence system, on its own I would not have expected much attention to have been paid to it.

5. I consider that security intelligence was properly submitted by staff, and that management took all reasonable steps on the basis of that intelligence to respond to it. It was perhaps understandable, given the general direction of the intelligence and the example of the Strangeways disturbance, that the main concentration should have been on the church services on 8 April. Knowing what we now know, greater credence might have been given to the initial intelligence highlighting trouble in unit 8 -but even that would have provided a plan for 8 April (in accordance with that intelligence) for an incident which, in the event, occurred on 6 April. In addition it is interesting to note that one of the inmates interviewed stated that the "plan" for Sunday was called off because it was realised that staff knew of it.

6. As at Pucklechurch (where there was more tension prior to the disturbance and additional staff were on duty) the incident raises the question whether a single officer should unlock a cell holding two inmates with no other officer in sight or within calling distance. My conclusion is that this should

not happen in this type of establishment. The officer need not be accompanied by another officer but he should be in sight or hearing of another officer or at least have a personal alarm.

7. What happened to Mr Richmond illustrates that there should be an examination as to whether there is a need for personal alarms to be carried by officers performing duties of the type Mr Richmond was carrying out. Personal alarms are now used by officers in many other countries. Their viability and their advantages and disadvantages as against carrying a mobile radio, should at least be tested by the Prison Service.

8. That so many were prepared to take advantage of the situation and join in smashing up their living accommodation, was probably partly a reflection of the climate in prison establishments generally created by the Strangeways disturbance. It is significant that of the 75 letters received by the Inquiry from inmates at Glen Parva (the analysis of which appears in Annex 2E) 57 said the riot at Glen Parva "kicked off because of Strangeways". The riot could therefore be described as a "copy-cat" incident. But I do not like that term, however, because it trivialises what was a major incident and the dangerous effect which a serious disturbance can have in other establishments, even when, like Glen Parva they had previously been relatively stable.

9. That the initial escape bid developed into a riot was also partly a reflection of the circumstances at the time in Glen Parva itself. The increasing number of remand inmates from the Courts and from other establishments, including Strangeways, and the resultant decline in opportunities for activities, provided fertile ground for the disturbance to develop. The majority of the young inmates were undoubtedly carried away for a time by the excitement of finding themselves unexpectedly on the loose in the unit.

10. The inmates who were seen by the Inquiry Team acknowledged that they had no deep grievances about the conditions or staff at Glen Parva. They rather shamefacedly acknowledged that they had allowed themselves to be led astray by "two nutters".

11. Some inmates' perception of staff attitudes is, however, alleged to have been one factor in some inmates taking part in this disturbance. The analysis of the inmates letters at Annex 2E, however, makes it clear that this was not a universal perception. At least ten of the inmates who were prepared to write to me made it clear that they thought a riot at Glen Parva was not justified. One correspondent, regrettably with considerable experience of other establishments, made the point that the officers at Glen Parva are "the best I've ever come across".

12. The normal attitude of the bulk of the inmates in unit 8 was indicated by the intervention of one of their number courageously taking on the two inmates who were attacking Mr Richmond. It is also illustrated by the attitude of the inmates who were out on association. They were locked into a room very much as at Pucklechurch, but unlike at Pucklechurch they did not take advantage of the incident to cause a secondary disturbance. It is also significant that the sentenced inmates, who had better conditions and had not suffered a deterioration in their conditions of confinement, gave no indication of wishing to join in the disturbance.

13. The history of the incident makes it clear how important is good leadership in controlling a disturbance. While there was some initial and undesirable confusion among staff, it also shows how professional and effective prison staff can be in containing a disturbance if properly led by a management which is well prepared and has taken, in advance, the steps necessary to set out how an emergency should be handled.

14. It appears that the media were properly briefed. This is probably connected with Governor 4 Creese having recently attended a Prison Service course on this subject. At all establishments there should be at least one and preferably two Governor grades who have attended such a course.

15. The existence of physically separate living units was significant in helping to contain the disturbance to only part of the establishment.

16. The establishment's physical security is not what it should be. The problem of the flat roofs needs tackling. The protection to the treatment rooms and hospital pharmacy need strengthening. There should be greater protection in the units. The Prison Service should consider the detailed recommendations on these matters in Mr Lynch's report to the Inquiry in the light of its buildings priorities and of the type of inmate it intends in future to hold at Glen Parva.

17. There is also the problem of keys shared by most other establishments in the prison system. They can too readily come into the possession of inmates. When they do so they provide indiscriminate access to cells and other parts of the establishment.

18. The attitude of the Strangeways inmate who wanted to escape illustrates that being confined near home can be extremely important in avoiding disruption and disturbances.

19. The evidence at Glen Parva indicates that staffing levels can be too taut and that there is need for an objective assessment. The Inquiry's attention was drawn to the effect of escort duties on the proper management of an establishment. The staff's positive attitude and flexibility was acknowledged, but there were still adverse effects on regimes due to staff shortages.

20. The time spent by young inmates on remand and in particular, in the case of a minority of inmates, between conviction and sentence is a matter of considerable concern. It illustrates the need for close co-operation between the Prison Service and the Courts. Something must be done to reduce the long waiting times for those convicted, but not yet sentenced.

Section 5

Dartmoor Prison

Introduction

5.1   The disturbance at Her Majesty's Prison Dartmoor began on Saturday 7 April 1990. It was six days after the disturbance at Strangeways had commenced. It followed on from the disturbance at Glen Parva on 6 April and was part of a weekend of disruption which must have been one of the most stressful weekends in the Prison Service's history.

The Prison

5.2   Dartmoor is situated on an elevated and isolated moorland on the edge of Princetown in Devon. Its site and location means it is subject to extremes of climate, including very wet conditions. It was built originally in about 1809. The construction is extremely solid with walls over 600 mm thick. But there have been many additions, extensions and other buildings added over the last two centuries. The early buildings are faced with granite and subsequent buildings have either been built in stone or in concrete blockwork using a granite aggregate.

5.3   Dartmoor has four main living areas for prisoners. They are sub-divided into seven wings (see Plan at Annex 5A). The wings are connected by corridors. The three main living areas are each divided into two wings, known as A and B Wing, C and D Wing and F and G Wing. In addition there is segregation unit in E Wing. A, B, C, D and G Wings are on either four or five levels. Together they provide about 650 cells (128, 144, 109, 109 and 156 respectively). E Wing, with 56 cells, and F Wing, with 52 cells have only two levels. All cell windows are positioned at high level and the inmates are unable to see out.

5.4   In April 1990, B Wing was empty pending refurbishment. Twelve of the cells in this wing had been fitted with integral sanitation on an experimental basis for the guidance of the contractors who were to be responsible for the full-scale installation.

5.5   None of the cells in the occupied wings had integral sanitation. In some wings such sanitary facilities as were available were wholly unsatisfactory. In D Wing (where the principal disturbance took place) there were only eight lavatories, washbasins, sluices and urinals for 134 prisoners. In addition, the recesses were in a poor state of repair and, like much of the fabric, suffered from damp. In A Wing, where a subsidiary disturbance took place, the conditions were better.

5.6   The Department commenced its written evidence to the Inquiry about the Dartmoor disturbance with these words:

> "HM Prison Dartmoor is a forbidding establishment in an isolated location on the outskirts of Princetown, Devon. Its isolation and grim reputation led to a decision in 1960 that it should be closed. However a rising inmate population since then has meant that it has been kept open and there are plans for extensive rebuilding."

5.7   The Inquiry was mindful of the recommendation made by the May Committee in 1979 (at paragraph 6.41 of their Report) that Dartmoor should be closed. The May Committee described the prison as "nowadays simply against nature". I consider later whether, having regard to its location, the condition of its buildings and the attitude of its staff and prisoners, now is the time to repeat the May Committee's recommendation. I set out here the historical background.

5.8   The then Home Secretary, Mr Butler, in explaining his reasons for coming to his decision in due course to close Dartmoor, told the House of Commons in 1960 that "it was because of the inconvenience of its site for staff and their families, and the limitations which its isolated position imposes on the development of constructive methods of penal treatment": these he regarded as being the decisive factors.

5.9   In November 1962 his successor (Mr Brooke) reiterated that it was his intention to transfer the prisoners elsewhere when other accommodation became available. He indicated that he could not give a fixed date for this, but that he would give at least three years notice. During the 1960's, on several occasions, the Department was on the point of giving that three years' notice. It did not do so because of population considerations.

5.10   In 1974, the Prisons Board decided on a progressive rundown of Dartmoor. One wing (B Wing) was closed, leaving accommodation for some 450 prisoners. However, in 1977 it was decided that the empty wing should be refurbished and that this should be followed by a rolling programme of refurbishment of the remaining accommodation.

5.11   In 1979 the lease of the site from the Duchy of Cornwall fell due for renewal. The then Home Secretary (Mr Whitelaw) decided that the prison should remain open indefinitely because there was no prospect of the prison population being reduced. A new 99 year lease was agreed. In the light of this decision, it became necessary to plan the full refurbishment and modernisation of Dartmoor. A staged programme, including installation of integral sanitation in all the wings and a new kitchen, was drawn up and was due to be completed in early 1994.

5.12   By the autumn of 1990 preliminary work had just been finished. The major contract to refurbish D, B and A Wings, to build a new kitchen and to provide new visits and administration facilities had recently been entered into. The cost of this work is expected to be £24.65 million. None of the promised refurbishment had therefore taken place by April 1990. Physically, Dartmoor still fully justified its awesome reputation.

The Prison Population

5.13   Dartmoor is the main Category B closed training prison for the whole of the South West Region. It has a certified normal accommodation of 606 prisoners. In April it was used to accommodate medium to long term prisoners, including 60 life prisoners. On Saturday 7 April, the date the disturbance began, there was a population of 607 prisoners, of whom approximately 27 were serving sentences of life imprisonment.

5.14   In early 1989, a vulnerable prisoner unit (VPU) was established in G Wing. The VPU accepts short-term prisoners if they have at least six months to serve. It normally holds 156 prisoners. On 7 April it held 150. The remainder of the 607 prisoners were in the Main Prison.

5.15   A breakdown of the population, according to length of sentence, was available for 1 April 1990. It was as follows:

Up to 18 months:	44	=	7.3%
Over 18 months to 4 years:	255	=	42.4%
Over 4 years to 10 years:	244	=	40.6%
Over 10 years but not life:	31	=	5.2%
Life imprisonment and custody:	27	=	4.5%
TOTAL:	601	=	100.0%

5.16   At the time of the disturbance, the upper landings of D Wing housed a large number of subversive and disruptive prisoners. Part of the explanation for this is that when the VPU was established in G Wing (approximately 18 months earlier) the "better" prisoners who had to move were able to transfer to other establishments. But the more difficult were not and they came to D Wing. In addition staff on D Wing contend that after prisoners have been on Rule 43 (GOAD) there is a tendency to send them to D Wing when they return to the landings. This could have been connected with the fact that the sanitary conditions on D Wing were the least satisfactory. It is fair to record, however, that only a minority of the prisoners on D Wing actively took part in the disturbance on 7 April.

Dartmoor's Reputation

5.17   The evidence suggests that if Dartmoor is the first training prison to which Category B prisoners are allocated, they might regard that allocation as reasonable. But prisoners who are allocated to Dartmoor from other training prisons look upon the allocation as being a punishment. Some prisoners are transferred from dispersal prisons (usually Long Lartin) and from other Category B training prisons to Dartmoor because they have failed to adjust to the regime in their previous establishment. Category C prisoners who are allocated initially to Dartmoor regard themselves as being deprived of the more liberal regimes of Category C prisons. Those who are transferred from Category C prisons are usually transferred for disciplinary reasons. In addition, life sentence prisoners transferred to Dartmoor for the second stage of their sentence object to not being transferred to a more liberal prison. They often find that, far from the transfer resulting in their regime being improved, it has resulted in their freedom being curtailed.

5.18   In their evidence to the Inquiry, both staff and inmates referred to Dartmoor as being the dustbin of the system. It was said to be the prison which received what some described as "the rubbish" (including an unduly large number of young badly behaved prisoners). One inmate (Inmate DM), who, at 46 was much older than the average inmate, said in evidence:

> "When you arrive there you are told this is the end of the line......You are told this and made to feel this way. There's nothing constructive in it, right from getting up in the morning......to locking up at night......ones like me, who they think or assume might be trouble they fire us all into that pit Dartmoor......the average age is about 25 years old......If you put them all together in a situation like that......it's degenerate......It's going to blow some time isn't it?"

5.19   This aspect of its reputation is partly due to the physical state of the establishment, in particular the damp. In winter some cells, regularly, cannot be used. The damp also affects the decor. Dartmoor's reputation is also the result of its isolated position, which makes visiting difficult; a matter to which inmates always attach the greatest importance. It is also partly due to the fact that it is regarded as having an illiberal regime and a rigid and unsympathetic staff. The Inquiry's own investigative team reported on "impassive, somewhat belligerent and cynical attitudes which we found most deterring".

5.20   A number of inmates refer to the fact that you can tell the "bad officers" because of the slashed peaks on their caps and the metal toe caps on their boots. A prisoner, who was serving a life sentence, thought that the Governor was trying to improve things, but that he was out-manoeuvred and out-gunned by the POA. One inmate who was on D Wing referred to the fact that the majority of staff were unpleasant. They got away with bullying because the "quiet life" officers did not make waves to try to stop them. He took the view that there would be a real change if the other staff were to refuse to tolerate the behaviour of the bad officers.

5.21   A frequent complaint is the pettiness of some rules and the way they are enforced. A prisoner who had served a number of sentences at other establishments, including Strangeways, cited as an example that when he arrived at Dartmoor he put up a curtain to his window to stop the cold. Most other prisoners had curtains, but an officer (who did not like him, as a result of a previous sentence the inmate had spent at Dartmoor) told him to take it down. Inmates were not allowed to change television channels, but one Saturday this inmate was asked by others to change channel to prepare for the football that was coming on. He did so and, as a result, lost three days remission and received seven days cellular confinement. He said they were treated like "kids".

5.22   Mr May said that he regarded the punishments which were being imposed at Dartmoor before he became governor as being over severe. He agreed that the use of the special cell at Dartmoor had also been excessive. He said that as a matter of course, if a prisoner came into the segregation unit having been involved in a violent incident he was put in the special cell. He added, however, that the regime at present in the unit was much more in accord with that in other establishments.

5.23   I received a number of complaints about the quality of food. In the three months immediately preceding the riot, there had been a total of 35 formal complaints – which did not seem to be excessive. But in otherwise positive evidence, Inmate DH told the Inquiry that the food was very bad. Other inmates made the same complaint about the food, including Inmate DE. He stated that one of the problems was the fact that, by the time it arrived in the wings, it was freezing cold. There were problems associated with the distribution of food. Heated trolleys could be used to deliver food to only E, F and G Wings. The food had to be carried to the other wings and, not surprisingly, this gave rise to complaints that, by the time it arrived, it was cold and unappetising. The arrival of a new Principal Officer Caterer had led to an improvement in the quality of food which the investigative team found to be "wholesome, sufficient and invariably well presented".

5.24   A major complaint was in connection with slopping out and the fact that a large number of prisoners shared the same recesses, and then had to eat in cells in which there was trouble with infestation by vermin.

5.25   Furthermore every weekend there is what Mr Mawson, the Chairman of the POA Branch at Dartmoor, described as a "close down" procedure: no association on Friday evenings, and no visits on Mondays.

5.26   It is not surprising in these circumstances that the evidence before the Inquiry indicates that a substantial proportion of the population of Dartmoor are disgruntled. This is supported by the prisoners' letters which are analysed in Annex 2E.

5.27   It is important to remember these accounts by prisoners were not given on oath. They have not, unless they were given in oral evidence, been subject to cross examination. In fact, the picture was not entirely negative. Inmate DH found it preferable to Channings Wood. He found the officers more friendly and approachable and was in a better position to fulfil his educational ambitions. He associated the increase in tension at Dartmoor prior to 7 April to what was happening at Strangeways.

The Regime

5.28 There was no overcrowding at Dartmoor. Each prisoner occupied his own cell. Furthermore, in recent years, the amount of employment and (more recently) education available had been increased considerably. By 1990, 95% of the prisoners had employment or education classes during the working day. The provision of education was continuing to improve as the result of the appointment of an education officer. A start had been made by the Probation Service in involving Prison Officers in group work with inmates. A training course had been held which was well received, but there was difficulty in freeing officers from their ordinary duties to do welfare tasks.

5.29 Unfortunately, because of alleged shortages of staff, restrictive attitudes on the part of the staff and the lack of suitable prisoners who could work outside the prison, it was possible on a particularly bad day for up to 100 inmates to find themselves unemployed.

5.30 This was a particular problem for Dartmoor's own Rule 43 prisoners (those held under this rule for their own protection). They were not housed in the VPU in G Wing but on the upper of the two landings of E Wing. In April 1990 they were approximately 30 in number. They had no employment, mainly because of the lack of a separate work place. They could not be employed in the wing because it also housed the prisoners under punishment, including the Rule 43 inmates held for reasons of good order or discipline (GOAD). A building had been identified seven years ago in which they could conveniently be employed, but regrettably the Regional Office had not regarded the project as being of sufficient urgency to justify the allocation of finance. Ironically, no doubt purely by coincidence, an allocation has now been made. Until the building is refurbished, however, Rule 43 prisoners in E Wing remain underemployed.

5.31 The position of the inmates in the VPU in G Wing was much better. Jobs in the textile workshop making prison clothes, warning flags and mattress covers were available for 90 inmates. Altogether there were jobs for a possible 143 inmates out of the maximum of 156 who could be in G Wing.

5.32 It was however not only the Rule 43's (own protection) who missed out on what was available. A life prisoner, Inmate DF, who had bad eyesight and was therefore regarded as unemployable, gave evidence that he still spent 22 to 23 hours a day banged up in his cell, although unsuccessful attempts had been made to employ him as a carpenter in the craft workshop and as a cleaner.

Industrial Relations

5.33 I have no doubt that the governing Governor for the last five years, Mr May, is a liberal and energetic manager of high calibre. He has been the subject of votes of no confidence by the prison staff. Far from being to his discredit, they are probably a reflection of his efforts to improve the situation at Dartmoor. These efforts were against considerable opposition from some of the staff. They were concerned by his liberality, in particular with what they considered was insufficient staff.

5.34 Having arrived at Dartmoor in 1985 on promotion to Governor 2, Mr May left Dartmoor on promotion, in September 1990, to Governor 1. He acknowledged that industrial relations were one of his failures at Dartmoor. He could not explain it. However it was undoubtedly partly due to arguments over staffing levels, which soured relations between the Governor and the POA. The Governor was the "pig in the middle" between the POA's demands and the manning levels imposed by Headquarters.

5.35 In the course of his evidence Mr Mawson, the Chairman of local branch of the POA, said:

> "Relations between the prison officers and the Governor at Dartmoor are not good. I find it difficult to talk to the Governor, and I believe the Governor finds it difficult to talk to me. Over the five years the Governor has been in the establishment, I honestly believe there is an area of mistrust on both sides and that mistrust has created local problems, not national problems, local problems, for the smooth running of the establishment."

5.36 Mr Mawson cited as an example of the problems with regard to the relationship between himself and Mr May the period of time it took to reach an agreement as to the calling in of additional staff when staffing levels fell below the MSL (minimum staffing levels). It took two years to put together the local agreement and it was only signed after regional intervention.

5.37 Mr Mawson was asked whether the difficult relations with the Governor was because of a clash of personalities. He said no:

> "I am only a mouthpiece for the staff of Dartmoor, so it is not personal. It is a question that I am being instructed by the staff to say certain things, and do certain things, which the Governor does not agree with and the mistrust that is there breaks down any sort of end result."

5.38 Mr May did not entirely endorse Mr Mawson's view that there was a lack of trust on both sides. He said:

> "I have to accept that he may not trust me, but I don't think it is a case of lack of trust on my part. I think we have tried, certainly I have tried, a variety of strategies in order to work with the POA and with the staff. We have had some successes but by and large I have to conclude after the time I had been at Dartmoor that has not been something I am too delighted with."

5.39 Mr May in his evidence referred to some improvements which had already been made with the agreement of the POA officials. For example, there was a prison officer led pre-release course run entirely by uniformed staff, which was very successful. There was also what Mr May described as "a very sound proposal" for changing the pattern of supervision in workshops, which the officials of the POA supported but which was not accepted when put to the membership by the POA.

5.40 It is fair also to record in this context that Mr Mawson said, and Mr May agreed, that staff would have been prepared to come in on duty before the riot on 7 April if they had been asked. I consider this aspect later.

5.41 Towards the end of his period at Dartmoor, Mr May had a new Deputy Governor whom he regarded as extremely able. He said that he was able, therefore, to withdraw from face to face discussion himself. He had come to the conclusion that that was paying dividends. He had also tried to improve relationships by having full staff meetings. But they did not work. They had become occasions for what he "felt was a sort of gun-slinger phenomena". He had tried an alternative strategy of "using joint working parties on a number of issues".

5.42 In his first submission to the Inquiry, dated 26 April 1990, Mr Mawson put at the forefront of the causes of the disturbance the shortage of staff as a result of "Fresh Start". He took the same view in his evidence before the Inquiry. The figures which he put forward, which Mr May accepted as being "absolutely spot on", were straight-forward. Dartmoor's complement for basic grade officers on 31 August 1987 was 134 plus 2 kitchen staff – a total of 136 staff. By 1 April 1990, through the framework agreement and optancy (the right to opt out of working additional hours), the number should have risen to 154.75. In fact it stood at 135, a deficit of 19.75. There was also a shortage of one senior officegrade and one hospital officer grade. The result was a total deficit of 21.75 staff.

5.43   This shortage of staff, it was suggested, had led to closed workshops and restricted association time. In his evidence, Mr Mawson said that every day as many as 12 tasks on average had to be closed. As well as shutting workshops, there might be no cleaning officer, or fewer officers checking locks, bolts and bars or engaged on other security tasks.

5.44   Some confirmation of this evidence was given by one of the members of the Board of Visitors. She said that it was sad that the craft centre was not used because of a shortage of uniformed staff to escort and supervise.

5.45   While accepting Mr Mawson's figures, Mr May emphasised that an underlying problem was that there had never been any proper evaluation of the manpower needed. He felt that if there had been an objective evaluation of the work of the prison, this could have made a very real difference. He did not think it was necessary to import outside evaluators for this task and he recognised that the calculation would involve a certain degree of negotiation. What he was looking for was a base which would be acceptable to both sides from which future staffing could be derived.

5.46   Mr May did not, however, put the problems all down to a lack of staff. He was correct not to do so. He identified an undercurrent or counter-culture at Dartmoor which is "a bit negative and a bit sort of backward looking". An example of the "counter culture", referred to by Mr May and which was given to the Inquiry's investigative team, was the cancellation of a football match which the staff of the VPU were planning with the inmates of the unit. It was cancelled because of pressure from other staff. Another example was the initial refusal of the staff to cooperate after the riot in the reopening of B Wing, although there were ample staff.

5.47   Mr May told the Inquiry:

"People talked about the necessity to have in place sufficient staff resources in order to liberalise the regime. My own view is that that is very over simplistic, but whether a regime is liberal or whatever, it is not to be directly correlated with the number of staff. It is about all sorts of things."

He also said:

"there are a number of staff at Dartmoor whose attitude to the job was probably formed some years ago when undoubtedly Dartmoor's role was a very different one, and I think it is for some of them a bit difficult to make the sort of major changes that the Prison Service is now expecting of them. But I would actually depart from the use of the word hostile. I think there are a number of my colleagues who I have seen over the years whose attitude and behaviour towards prisoners, I think, is absolutely first class. They are genuinely able to do the fatherly role which some of us are less able to do."

5.48   Mr May did not consider the underlying problem was limited to the older officers. Some of the younger officers could become the new "Dartmoor dinosaurs" ready to occupy the reserved seats in the tea room which came vacant through retirement. The problem, however, was one which Mr May believed was capable of change. He said that this would involve:

i)   improving physical conditions, as the daily degradation of slopping out contributes to a perception of prisoners being inferior;

ii)   the removal of confrontation on matters such as staffing levels and the POA's resistance to change and innovation, which has its roots in a chronic sense of being undervalued and under threat;

iii)   the recruitment of candidates who are able to identify with the Prison Service's statement of purpose and a sufficient number of candidates of the calibre to fill the most senior jobs in the future;

iv) reviewing the promotion system so that the able people and not "duffers" are promoted;

v) providing rewards – there has to be established a relationship between performance and reward – perhaps with a locally based bonus payment scheme reviewed on a three yearly basis.

5.49   It would be wrong therefore to attribute all the troubles in industrial relations merely to the existence of a militant POA at Dartmoor. The evidence indicates that this was not the case, and that, if tackled in the right way, the office holders in the POA may be more prepared to join in with the management of Dartmoor so as to achieve improvements. However, even then, the office holders may have difficulty in carrying their membership with them.

The Local Agreement

5.50   A number of prisons, including Dartmoor, have entered into local manning level agreements. The Dartmoor agreement makes provision for staff to be called in, if the staff on duty would otherwise fall below the minimum staffing level (MSL). The staff are then called in from their rest days. Mr Mawson said that if staff were going to be called in on their rest days, normally they would not want to be called in just to allow inmates, for example, to watch the Grand National. The agreement therefore does not in ordinary circumstances permit the calling in of staff to enable association to take place.

5.51   The Inquiry was fortunate to receive evidence from Mr Alan Taylor about the working of these local agreements. Mr Taylor was the senior vice-Chairman of the Prison Officers' Association. He explained that the local agreements were intended to introduce an element of flexibility to accommodate particular local circumstances. They set out two different situations where a Governor would be entitled to call in extra staff. One would be where there was an operational emergency. The other would be to ensure MSL were maintained.

5.52   Mr Taylor said that what the minimum staffing level should be depended on what was considered locally to be the minimum level of staff necessary to provide the essential services for the establishment. The definition of what were essential services was again a matter for local agreement.

5.53   I conclude from Mr Taylor's evidence that in practice the local agreements relating to the calling in of staff to maintain the MSL do not provide staff for association, exercise or classes. These are activities which could be very much needed to maintain the equilibrium of the prison.

Warnings of the Disturbance

5.54   Up until the commencement of the Strangeways disturbance, there was no special indication of impending trouble. There had been no marked change in the pattern of adjudications. The same was true with the regard to the frequency and nature of petitions to the Home Secretary.

5.55   The number of prisoners reporting sick appeared high, but the pattern was consistent. There was an exceptionally high number of staff who were off work. 46 officers took 477 days sick leave in January 1990, 35 officers took 431 days in February, and 33 officers took 128 days in March. But those who were off included a number of staff who were long term sick and were being considered for medical retirement.

5.56   But there were more tangible signs of unrest after the Strangeways disturbance. It was significant that the majority of the prisoners on D Wing who were seen by the Inquiry said that they knew there was going to be a disturbance, although they did not know when.

5.57   The information available to staff corroborates this evidence. During the week prior to 7 April there was an abundance of Security Information Reports (SIRs) and other information available, which gave clear warning that a disturbance could be expected during the weekend of 7/8 April.

5.58   Among the warnings was information which identified precisely the place and time when the incident would occur, namely, at the end of association on D Wing on the afternoon of Saturday 7 April. Certain of the other information did however indicate differing times and places.

5.59   The Security Officer at Dartmoor was Principal Officer Comber. He had instigated a satisfactory system for recording and collating security information. At least 27 SIR's were filled in prior to the disturbance. In his oral evidence to the Inquiry, Mr Comber acknowledged that the SIRs were "above the scale that we would normally get". But he pointed out that there were a number of different types of incidents referred to. Having regard to what was happening at Strangeways, intelligence of this sort was to be expected.

5.60   There was mention in the SIRs of an incident which occurred on Thursday 5 April, when an officer heard an inmate shouting down from D5 landing "Let's start the riot". His memorandum refers to the atmosphere being "explosive". However, Mr Comber regarded this information with some scepticism because he knew the inmate concerned and he regarded him as being in the "idiot" class. I would not subscribe to this assessment having heard the inmate give oral evidence at the hearing in Taunton.

5.61   In his report to the Inquiry, Detective Superintendent Quick of the Devon and Cornwall Constabulary, states that 17 of the reports which were submitted during the week 2 to 7 April 1990, had been identified by the police investigation as being relevant to the riot. That was not the limit to the information which was available. The Superintendent is wholly justified in stating:

"I do feel that..... given the Strangeways incident which was just a few days old, the perceived increase in tension and the specific nature of some of the information, that positive action was required."

5.62   Mr Comber took action. He caused investigations to be made on the basis of the SIRs in order to ascertain who the ringleaders were likely to be. He identified seven inmates as being potential ringleaders. With Mr May's concurrence, they were segregated as a precautionary measure. (Mr May considered that this action which, in particular, removed potential troublemakers from C Wing could be the explanation why other wings did not join the disturbance when it started in D Wing).

5.63   Notwithstanding this action, the atmosphere remained tense. On the Friday morning, 6 April, a search took place. The search resulted in four lethal homemade knives being found dumped outside a cell window on C Wing. But it did not result in any definite information being obtained or in any reduction in the tension in the prison. That the tension existed is corroborated by the decision of the Senior Probation Officer to withdraw probation staff from the wings that Friday, 6 April.

5.64   Other information that was received included a warning on 6 April which was given to the officer who was performing the duties of censor. He was told not to remain in the wing during the afternoon of Saturday 7 April. There was also a request made to Mr May on 6 April by a prisoner that he should be placed on Rule 43 because he believed a disturbance would take place on Saturday or Sunday. He said that, the prisoners were planning to overpower an officer in the exercise yard. (As a result of this officers were told not to carry keys on exercise.)

5.65   On 6 April Mr May considered whether to call in more staff for the weekend. The matter had been raised previously at a meeting on 5 April between Mr Comber and other Governors. It was decided at the meeting on 6 April not to call in any additional staff. In reaching this decision, Mr May was influenced by the fact that bringing in staff "is a high cost option". This is because, if he called in staff, he would be obliged to repay the hours with time off over subsequent weekends. Instead, it was arranged that F and G Wings would be locked up a little early so that the staff could be available at the Centre to help deal with any trouble which might occur in any of the other wings. (In the event, however, there was insufficient time for the staff to assemble at the Centre.) The Governor also warned the police and the SWRO of possible trouble over the weekend.

5.66   Mr May considered the matter further on 7 April with Governor 5 Mr Upton, and Principal Officers Hitchins and Seaborne. It was decided that if there were serious trouble on any wings, prisoners on other wings should be evacuated to the Old Chapel. It was also decided that all knives not being used in the kitchen should be removed. As a further precaution it was decided that Principal Officer Hitchins should keep the double keys in the Control Room. In the event of trouble he would double the gates leading into F Wing, which gave access to the Vulnerable Prisoners Unit. In addition it was decided that the gate to the Segregation Unit should be doubled because of the presence in the unit of possible ringleaders.

5.67   Mr May's impression over the Friday and most of Saturday was that the crisis had passed. He had not seen what he considered were the classic indicators of tension – the refusal of food and inmates seeking to avoid being on the landing by getting themselves put on report or applying for Rule 43 (there was in fact a request, as already indicated, on 6 April). Furthermore, no information had been provided about the names of the potential ringleaders from other inmates. Mr May said that the perception of staff "was that at half-past-three we were in the clear and then at twenty-to-four we were not".

5.68   When the disturbance occurred, therefore, the staff and management were caught by surprise, despite all the warnings and precautions taken. Mr May repeated in evidence what one of his colleagues had said to him after the event. The prison staff and management's "reflex reactions" were not working in the right way.

The Disturbance

5.69   The morning of Saturday 7 April passed normally.

5.70   On D Wing, Senior Officer Harris was in charge over the weekend during the day. The staff were well aware of the many rumours of impending trouble, but they were unsure whether the disorder, if it did happen, would occur on the Saturday or the Sunday. Senior Officer Harris considered that it was right that association should continue in the normal way. He was, however, concerned that there were no staff on standby who would be ready to give immediate support if needed. He says that the staff felt isolated. It was decided to keep as close together as possible and not leave any colleague on his own where he might be taken hostage by prisoners.

5.71   Saturday 7 April was Grand National day. During afternoon association the inmates on D Wing were allowed to watch the race. Initially, after the Grand National finished, the inmates returned to their cells normally. Senior Officer Harris was supervising and had two officers on each landing. He was also assisted by the Censor Officer.

5.72   Just as the Senior Officer and the staff were beginning to think that the crisis had passed for that afternoon, the situation suddenly changed dramatically and without warning. The time was 15.40. An inmate on landing 5 threw a dustbin down towards the landing below. This was accompanied by inmates shouting either, according to officers, "it's off, it's off" or, according to prisoners, "get off, get off". A number of prisoners joined in. Buckets of water, dustbins, cell furniture and equipment were thrown down on to the wire which was stretched below the landing.

5.73   Officer Sharp, who was on the second landing, gave evidence that he heard the Senior Officer shout for the staff to leave. By then, cell doors had been wrenched from their hinges and were coming down onto the wire as well. Mr Sharp's evidence was that he retreated to the door on the ground floor between C and D Wings and held that door open for some time so that the staff and prisoners who wished to do so could get clear. A prisoner in his oral evidence singled out a woman prisoner officer whom he described as being particularly brave. This was Officer Mrs Draper-Rush. Apparently, without regard for her own safety, she ushered inmates who wanted to leave out through the same door.

5.74   Altogether about 20 inmates left D Wing into C Wing through doors which connect between the two wings on the various landings. In addition, all the officers were able to evacuate safely. The doors were then locked. (They cannot be double locked.) Before the doors between the two wings were closed, however, some inmates from C Wing made their way into D Wing. Among them was the inmate who was to stay on the roof after the other inmates had surrendered.

5.75   There is evidence both from prison officers and inmates that, immediately the disturbance started, a number of inmates donned masks and put T-shirts over their heads. This indicates that there was a degree of preparation.

5.76   The Communications Officer, Mr Mawson was in charge of the communications room that Saturday. (He is also the Chairman of the local POA.) When the alarm bell was activated, he started to notify the various agencies, including the South West Regional Office (SWRO), the police and the fire brigade. The necessary action was promptly taken, except that, due to an error for which Mr May takes responsibility, the Board of Visitors were not informed, as they should have been.

5.77   Mr May was on duty and he established a command suite.

5.78   Within a few minutes Mr May felt he had to evacuate C Wing. He took this decision because he was concerned that the inmates could set fire to D Wing and a fire could spread to the adjoining C Wing. He also considered that it was possible that the inmates who were already on the roof of D Wing could make their way to C Wing.

5.79   At 16.05 about 100 prisoners from C Wing, together with those who had escaped from D Wing, were evacuated from the wing to the Old Chapel in the grounds of the prison. This was in accordance with the plan Mr May had agreed on earlier that day. Five prisoners from C Wing who initially refused to move were prevailed upon eventually to do so.

The Situation Within C and D Wings

5.80   Among the staff who were summoned to the prison was Principal Officer Pinhey. He arrived at the prison at about 16.15. He was briefed by Mr May and took charge of C&R. He was able to form one C&R Unit immediately. The unit enterered C Wing to assess the situation. Mr Pinhey found that the prisoners had made a hole in the wall between D4 and C3 Landings (D4 and C3 are on the same level). Through this hole, he was able to observe what was going on inside D Wing. He could see prisoners wearing hoods and towels round their faces and smashing furniture. Other prisoners were just standing around.

5.81   Principal Officer Pinhey was seen by the prisoners and, having had his shield doused with urine, the hole was blocked up by a bowl. The unit then withdrew and the gate was double locked. Principal Officer Pinhey arranged for the unit to guard the entrance to C Wing. He then reported to the governor. He assembled another C&R unit and despatched them to provide additional support.

The Progress of the Disturbance

5.82   The police, fire and ambulance services attended the scene promptly and in adequate numbers. There were however features of the police and fire service involvement to which I will have to refer later.

5.83   Two C&R units from Exeter prison arrived at Dartmoor with commendable speed by 17.02. They were followed by C&R Units from Channings Wood prison, the first of which arrived at 17.40.

5.84   At 17.22 some four inmates were sighted on D Wing roof. By 17.55 there were ten more prisoners on D Wing roof. 20 minutes after that, smoke was seen coming through that roof.

5.85   Access to the roof had been obtained by two routes. The first route demanded a remarkable degree of agility and involved considerable risk. It involved using the bridge which crossed above the landings at level 5 in D Wing. This bridge enabled the inmates to climb onto water tanks which were cantilevered from the wall (as shown on the illustrations at Annex 5B). The tanks were then used as a platform from which to break through the glazing of the roof. The glazing was protected by bars. These were prised away from the timber frame into which they were fixed.

5.86   The other means of access was also from the landing which gave access to the roof spaces shown in the drawing (Annex 5B). The access to the roof space from the landing was protected by an iron security gate and an iron door inside that gate. The gate was fitted with a security lock operated by a double master key, which was not normally in the possession of prison officers. The gate was opened by prising out of the granite wall a substantial granite block, approximately 12″ by 15″ x 9″, to which the plate of the lock was secured. The iron door was then forced. The force required was considerable.

5.87   Once onto the roof the prisoners found ready ammunition. Areas of the original roofing had been replaced with asbestos sheeting, but there were still substantial areas of slating. The slates, coping stones and other debris were used to bombard anyone who ventured into the vicinity of the wing. The same ammunition also caused damage to the adjoining wings.

The Disturbance in the Old Chapel

5.88   It was initially decided that the prisoners who had been moved from C Wing to the Old Chapel should be re-located in A Wing, where they could be doubled up and kept secure. The movement of the prisoners was being supervised by Governor 5 Mr Upton and was under the control of Principal Officer Hitchins. Mr Upton became worried about the time which was being taken to rehouse the prisoners. He gave instructions that they should no longer be given tea before being relocated. However, this attempt to accelerate the process caused the prisoners to become agitated. 74 prisoners remaining in the Old Chapel appeared to be refusing to go to A Wing.

5.89   Mr May responded by making a request to SWRO for authority to transfer the prisoners to other establishments. Authority was given for 40 prisoners to be transferred to Bristol and 40 to Gloucester prisons. When the prisoners were informed of the intention to send them to these other prisons they initially refused to go unless they could first remove their property from C Wing. Mr May, following advice from PO Pinhey, decided that he should not give the prisoners permission to do this. He went to the Chapel and explained that he considered that it was unsafe for the inmates to return to C Wing. The inmates refused to accept his explanation. In Mr May's words one of the inmates "anointed him" with tea. A disturbance then occurred in which lights and electrical fittings were smashed, and doors and stained glass in the former altar area were damaged. Inmates began to break out of the Old Chapel through an unsecured window. C&R Units were deployed around the building and the inmates who broke out were captured.

5.90 Three Principal Officers, Mr Pinhey, Mr Tucker and Mr Comber, decided that immediate action had to be taken to deal with the situation. They agreed to take three inmates into C Wing to collect their possessions, using C&R shields to provide protection. If this method proved successful, they agreed to allow the other inmates to collect their possessions in the same way. This tactic proved successful. What could have proved to be an awkward development was defused. Mr May accepted that this was the appropriate action to take and retrospectively endorsed what was being done.

5.91 Some members of the uniformed staff criticised Mr May for his initial decision not to let the prisoners go back to C Wing. They alleged Mr May had underestimated the attachment which the inmates had to their few personal effects, which included budgerigars and photographs.

5.92 Having collected their possessions, 80 inmates were transferred to Bristol and Gloucester by coaches which left the prison at about 20.40. After that exercise was completed, C Wing was sealed.

The Decision Not to Intervene

5.93 On the instructions of the Governor, Mr Pinhey and the Regional C&R Instructor, Principal Officer Benge, with the assistance of two C&R Instructors, Senior Officer Carter and Senior Officer Green, prepared a plan for a possible intervention. It was decided that the earliest time at which an intervention could be made was at 02.00 on 8 April.

5.94 The plan which was devised required units to enter D Wing at all levels from the corresponding landings in C Wing. The dividing wall between the two wings was not of substantial construction and there were doors which gave access from each landing in C Wing into D Wing. The entry was to be preceded by a diversionary attack at the other side of D Wing.

5.95 Having considered the plan, Mr May came to the conclusion that there should not be an intervention that night. His decision was influenced by his concern that the staff would have to make an entry into D Wing in the dark when "there was extremely minimal intelligence about the situation inside the wing". Water, electricity and heating had been cut off. Mr May knew that the Fire Service had offered to make arc lights available. He knew also that the C&R units would be carrying dragon lights. But he did not consider that this lighting would overcome the disadvantage caused by the dark. (The electricity could not be restored because of the fear of fire or electrocution.) In addition, Mr May was not satisfied that the forces which were available were sufficient. They did not outnumber the estimated number of hostile inmates in the wing and they were very tired.

5.96 Mr May decided to reconsider the position the following morning. Only a holding force was therefore deployed for the night. His decision was accepted as being appropriate by Mr Dixon at SWRO and by Mr Gander at Headquarters.

The Fire on D4 Landing and the Role of the Fire Service

5.97 There were a number of minor fires both in C and D Wings. For example, in the Dartmoor incident log there is a reference to a cell fire in C Wing at 21.42.

5.98   The most serious fire referred to in the records occurred in a cell on the 4th landing of D Wing. The prison incident book has two entries relating to the fire. The first reference is timed at 02.50 and reads: "cell fire on D4 kitchen side". The second reads: "02.55 fire appliance timed to D Wing".

5.99   According to the evidence submitted in writing by the Chief Fire Officer of the Devon Fire and Rescue Service, their log entries relating to this fire, read as follows:

8 April 1990

02.55 hrs – a message from an appliance at the incident to Brigade Control indicated that there was a report of a fire in a cell. The full pre-determined attendance was requested. This was duly despatched at 02.56 hrs;

03.07 hrs – a further message from the incident to Brigade Control indicated that the fire was reported to be in D Wing of the prison. Because that wing was occupied by the inmates causing the disturbance, all appliances were instructed to remain outside the prison by the prison staff;

03.15 hrs – a message from an appliance at the incident indicated that the fire service were not required to deal with the cell fire because of its inaccessibility due to the wing being occupied. The message also requested that the fire service attendance should be restricted to (2) appliances and the turntable ladder. Supporting appliances were therefore returned to the station by Brigade Control.

5.100   In his written statement to the Inquiry, Mr Alan Dudley, a prison officer, states:

"Then there was a report that there was a fire coming from the side of D Wing and that they wanted the fire engines to be taken down there. I was volunteered to take the fire engines down to D Wing but unfortunately when we got around there, there was a shout from one of the cells that it wasn't a cell fire and that somebody had actually set fire to a dustbin to brew up some water for some tea in one of the cells, but the Fire Brigade said it wouldn't have mattered because we couldn't have got in there anyway. With the new fencing etc they couldn't swing the fire engine around so they couldn't actually get into the yard to put the fire out. When they actually realised that it wasn't a major fire, the fire brigade decided they would withdraw because it would have been too dangerous for them anyway, even if they could have got into there, because they could quite easily have come under fire from anybody on the roof."

5.101   In his oral evidence at the hearing, Mr Dudley gave a similar description. He went on to say that the fire was in the area of cell number 36 on D4, which was a cell in which an inmate was subsequently found to have died. Mr Dudley added:

"I don't believe it was actually that cell; it might have been a couple of cells further along, say, about 34. But it was in that direction yes."

5.102 He added that he was not able to identify the precise cell. As there was no evidence of any other serious fire in close proximity on D4 to D4.36, the inference is that this was in fact a fire in D4.36. If this is so, it is clear that it was unfortunate that there was a remark made by an inmate on D Wing (according to Mr Dudley's oral evidence) that "it is not a cell fire – we are burning up for tea". It is possible that the remark was not of great significance as, according to Mr Dudley, the officer in charge of the fire appliances had decided that he could not drive two fire appliances to the appropriate position to deal with the fire. This was because there was no room to manoeuvre and because of the danger of bombardment from the inmates. Mr Dudley took the view that it would have been difficult, but not impossible, for the two fire appliances to have proceeded further. Furthermore, having observed the fire for a few minutes, the officer in charge of the appliances did not see it as a threat.

5.103 According to the Fire Service Log at 03.07 a number of prison staff had given instructions that fire appliances were to remain outside the prison. Mr Dudley was not aware of any such instructions. In fact it appears that the Fire Service Log entry is not accurate. This is corroborated by the Chief Fire Officer's letter of 11 August 1990.

5.104 In the event the fire appliances withdrew and no action was taken to put out the fire. (I have referred to two fire appliances on the basis of Mr Dudley's evidence, but the same letter suggests that only one fire appliance entered the prison – whether it was one or two appliances does not matter.)

The Night of 7/8 April

5.105 Apart from the fire, the situation appears to have been generally quiet during the night. Such activity as there was, was mainly on the 3rd and 4th landings. Inmates smashed the skylight in C Wing from D Wing roof. It was thought that some of the inmates were under the influence of drugs or alcohol.

5.106 There was also intermittent contact between D Wing inmates and prison staff who had been appointed to act as negotiators. An inmate describing himself as TIN TIN (whose real identity was known) represented the inmates. He indicated that they did not want violence. He said that that was why "they had pushed officers out of the wing".

5.107 The attempts to negotiate were ineffective. During such negotiations as there were, between 04.30 and 05.00, inmates attributed the disorder to the conditions, food and alleged brutality on E Wing. Inmates repeated these allegations to the Inquiry. The Inquiry's investigative team reported that the "Segregation unit is more severe than most but we saw no evidence of any physical brutality". The Probation Officer, Mr Thacker, said, "In recent times they (that is staff) have been under considerable provocation and in very difficult situations, such as dealing with a dirty protest, they have shown remarkable restraint and patience". This view was subsequently endorsed by Mr May.

Sunday 8 April

5.108 A meeting was held by the Governor on the morning of 8 April at about 07.00. That meeting considered a report from the negotiating team who had opened negotiations with the inmates. Mr May again decided against making an intervention. This was against the advice of the members of uniformed staff who were present. The Governor's decision was, however, supported by Mr Upton, a Governor Grade 5 who was the only governor at Dartmoor who had received training in C&R up to Grade 3. (Mr May had only observed C&R training.)

5.109 Once Mr May had decided against intervention, a team of negotiators was again established from the uniformed staff. At that time, only one member of the team had been trained in negotiating techniques. Mr Hogue, a senior psychologist, was placed in charge of the negotiating tactics and the team.

5.110 After the meeting, Mr Upton attempted to speak to the inmates on the roof through a loud hailer, but the inmates' response was to shout abuse and to hurl tiles at him.

5.111 This was followed by a serious escalation in the disturbance. From about 07.40 onwards on the morning of 8 April the inmates reappeared on the roof. They managed to move from D Wing roof onto C Wing roof. They were making a determined attack on C Wing from the roof. During the course of this, burning material was dropped onto C Wing through the roof. However, three C&R units put in the wing deterred the inmates from actually entering.

5.112   By 09.10 a note in the SWRO office log records that:

"Inmates now doing so much damage to C Wing roof that staff have had to be pulled out – governor holding conference to consider best strategy".

5.113   The Governor's log does not confirm that the C&R units were actually withdrawn from C Wing. It acknowledges that "C Wing now under major threat". But it is unlikely that the staff withdrew from C Wing.

5.114   In response to the situation in C Wing, Principal Officer Pinhey requested permission to use water over C Wing to push back the inmates to D Wing. The Governor decided against this. The Governor did however instruct Senior Officer Grice to go up in the police helicopter and broadcast a message to the prisoners that "we want a peaceful end".

5.115   Not surprisingly, this message had little impact on the inmates on D Wing. They continued to cause considerable difficulties for the uniformed staff and management of the prison. From time to time staff seeking to move round the prison had to put up with a hail of debris from the roof. A land-link was set up, but it was subsequently destroyed by the inmates' activities at about 14.19. It is clear that inmates were at risk of attack by others if they tried to surrender or were thought to be acting as "a grass" (one of the inmates who talked to Mr Dudley was brutally assaulted).

5.116   It was impossible for the kitchen to be used to feed the considerable number of inmates in other parts of the prison. Because of this problem, the regional catering manager in London, was contacted. He arranged to provide for temporary kitchens.

5.117   Unfortunately, conflicting arrangements were made for the mid-day meal on 8 April. The Region asked Plymouth Airport to provide 500 airline style meals. The prison made arrangements with Exeter prison to provide meals and a civilian driver was sent to collect them. When the driver arrived at Exeter prison he learnt that the regional catering manager had cancelled the order. To add to the difficulties, the airline meals were late in arriving.

5.118   The staff were also without a proper meal. A local fish and chip shop, however, came to the rescue. The shop provided 90% of the staff with a very acceptable meal. Within 35 minutes they provided another 105 portions of pie and chips for inmates. I agree with Mr Shepherd, the Governor 4 Head of Works Services, that that must be some sort of record.

5.119   At 14.16 an inmate was captured, after apparently falling through a roof. By that time, a number of prisoners had made it clear that they wanted to surrender. To prepare for the expected surrender, some 50 prisoners were moved out of A Wing to Cardiff, Winchester and Reading prisons. The space they made available was to be used as a collection area. However, a surrender was delayed by the activities of other prisoners who built barricades against the wall dividing C from D Wing.

5.120   Senior Officer Haley, who was in charge of one of the C&R units in C Wing, had for some time been conducting negotiations from the C4 landing with an inmate who had been playing a prominent role. (The incident log at 10.46 records good negotiations going on. However the progress was by no means constant.) Mr Haley had been joined by Prison Officer Dudley at about 11.00. Then, around 14.00, a large quantity of missiles were thrown into C Wing, so that Mr Haley and Mr Dudley were virtually trapped with their unit on C4. It was therefore decided to bring in additional C&R units into the wing. The aim was to cause a diversion and a show of force to enable Mr Haley, Mr Dudley and the unit which was already there to withdraw. However, the arrival of the C&R teams in the wing, just after 14.30, was to change the mood of the inmates.

5.121   Governor 5 Mr Upton was in nominal control of the C&R units and was the incident area commander. He found considerable difficulty in exercising command. One of his problems may have been that, as his C&R kit did not display any identifying insignia, staff from other establishments did not appreciate his status. Another difficulty was that he was constantly having to make telephone calls to the Governor in the control room in order to keep Mr May in the picture. This illustrates the need in an incident of this sort, for a command radio net as well as an ordinary one.

5.122   The problems of exercising overall control resulted in a sense of frustration on more than one occasion. A C&R unit would take what it regarded as a useful initiative only to be brought back by Governor Upton in order to ensure that Mr May's instructions were carried out. There is little doubt that some uniformed staff had little respect for the Governor's ability to control the incident.

5.123   Mr May in evidence candidly confesses that during this particular period of time there was "some confusion". He said that at the time he was unaware of the diversion, but he was aware that Mr Upton was increasing the numbers of C&R units in C Wing with the view to gaining some intelligence. Mr Upton gives a rather different picture in his statement. He says that he sought and obtained permission from Mr May to "storm the wings". Subsequently, however, he received a message to contact the Governor by telephone. When he did so, Mr May informed him the wing was not to be stormed because negotiations had been commenced.

5.124   Senior Officer Green, who was in charge of a C&R unit on C1 landing under Principal Officer Pinhey, appears to have taken the initiative which changed the course of the disturbance. He took a sledgehammer and broke open the connecting door on that landing. The other C&R units who were available were then brought onto that floor as a show of strength.

5.125   After the door between C1 and the comparable landing in D Wing, D2, had been removed, the unit removed a barricade and advanced into D Wing. At that moment, Governor 5 Upton arrived on the scene and ordered the unit to stop. He regarded what they were doing as being contrary to the policy of the Governor.

5.126   However by then, Senior Officer Green had managed to establish a dialogue with a hooded prisoner who was on top of the barricades. That prisoner, with others, told Mr Green that they had had enough and wanted to come out, but they were frightened as to what might happen to them. Mr Green assured them that they would be safe. Mr Pinhey, the Principal Officer in charge of the unit, also arrived on the scene. He assured an inmate who wanted a solicitor present that he would arrange this. The Chaplain, who also came onto the wing at that time, said that he would be there if an inmate surrendered.

5.127   A small group of prisoners then went back into the wing to discuss the situation with others. The prisoner who had first spoken then returned with his personal possessions. From then on prisoners began to surrender. At first it was a trickle, but it developed into a flood. About 80 prisoners came out that way from D2 to C1 landing.

5.128   Mr Green then removed the barricade and started to clear the cells in D wing. In this way, what had started out to be a diversion and a show of force, became the means of bringing the disturbance virtually to an end.

5.129   Mr Dudley (who had been conducting the negotiations on C4) was particularly struck by the extent of the change of mood. He said that once entry started, the attitude of the inmates on the roof was "how are we going to get out of here?" Mr Benge put it more strongly, "Negotiations seemed to be getting nowhere until some C&R activity was seen.... many Governors just do not have an idea how C&R teams work and what they are capable of".

5.130   However, while Mr Dudley recognises the benefit which accrued from Mr Green's unauthorised activities, he also points out the difficulties that can be caused by untrained staff wanting to do "their bit". The inmates he was negotiating with became nervous as a result of the activities on the floors below. He felt the negotiations which he was then conducting could have been adversely affected. He was also concerned about the fact that other staff were conducting their own negotiations, although they were not trained. Reassurances were being given which, as a negotiator, he could not guarantee. If the disturbance had not collapsed as quickly as it did, his position could have been undermined.

5.131   The important assurance which the inmates wanted was an assurance that they would not be ill-treated if they surrendered. A number of officers (including Principal Officer Pinhey) were able to give this assurance. The inmates were also reassured by the presence of the chaplain, particularly as it had not been possible by that stage to meet the prisoners' requests for an independent observer.

5.132   As prisoners in D Wing surrendered, Prison Officer Benge reported that prisoners on the roof were also giving themselves up. Following this, C&R units were deployed at each entrance. They entered D Wing simultaneously. The wing was retaken at about 16.30. The C&R units who swept D Wing found some inmates locked in their cells. They were released. All inmates were then taken out of the wing, apart from the one who was to remain on the roof.

5.133   At 18.00 Mr May met the press and gave them an account of the events of the day.

The Inmate Who Died

5.134   Staff first knew that an inmate might have died at about 14.32 on 8 April. They were told by inmates shouting from D Wing. Shortly after the C&R units had swept D Wing, the duty Doctor, accompanied by a police forensic expert, a representative of the Fire Services and the chaplain went to cell D4.36. The cell was at the end of the landing and the door of the cell was covered by a barricade which had been constructed across the access to the Wing. The barricade was not designed to prevent admission to the cell but to prevent admission to the wing. The cell door was locked. The inmate was found to be burnt beyond recognition.

5.135   It appears probable that the fire which Mr Dudley referred to in his evidence was the one that caused the deceased's death. Assuming this is the case, it would not be right to condemn the Fire Service or Mr Dudley, though it is a matter for regret the position was not fully investigated. Although the scale of the fire may have been surprising, they had no reason to question the information which was shouted to them about the reason for the fire. Indeed the information could have been initially true and the fire could have become worse later.

5.136   One inmate who gave evidence (Inmate DH) described the deceased lighting a fire in the censor's office. This was just after someone, whose identity he did not know, started a fire in the office of the senior officer. At 10.00 the next day (Sunday 8 April) Inmate DH went to the cell of the deceased and saw him there, badly burnt. He was unable to help as to when he had died.

5.137   The general consensus among the inmates to whom the Inquiry spoke, tends to confirm that the prisoner who died had started the fire in the senior officer's office, which caused dense smoke. It appears from what these inmates said that he was criticised for having started that fire. That may be why he locked himself in his cell.

The Roof Protest Until 14 April

5.138   The inmate, who did not surrender on Sunday 8 April, remained on the roof until Saturday 14 April. On 8 April (before the incident came to an end), he had been seen climbing onto the roof taking water with him. He may also have had Complan, which he had purchased before the incident. This may explain why he was able to hold out for so long.

5.139   Although he did not give oral evidence, that inmate made a very long statement to one of the Assessors when he was interviewed at Dartmoor prison on 19 June. At the time of the incident he had served four and a half years of a ten year sentence. He had already lost nearly two years remission because of offences against prison disciplinary rules. He had only arrived at Dartmoor eight days before the disturbance, on 7 April. He had been transferred under CI 10/74 from Long Lartin to Cardiff. From there he had expected to be moved back to the north, but when Long Lartin would not have him back, he was sent to Dartmoor. He felt aggrieved about his transfer to Dartmoor, because his mother had been told that he was to be transferred to Full Sutton. He was also concerned about the fact that his family would be unable to visit him in Dartmoor. He says that prior to the disturbance starting in D Wing, he had no knowledge that it was going to occur.

5.140   What happened during the remaining days he spent on the roof was as follows. After the rest of the prisoners had surrendered the inmate began by demanding a transfer to the North Region. He was told that the Governor would do all he could to obtain a transfer for him to Full Sutton, provided he came down within the next 15 minutes. But the deadline passed and he did not come down. During the following days he was subject to swings of mood. If the Prison Service indicated that a demand could be met, he would make more demands. His main themes were that he wanted to see a solicitor and he wanted to be transferred to the north.

5.141   Tuesday 10 April was relatively uneventful. On Wednesday 11 April he showered debris down on to C Wing whilst staff were trying to serve food. He threw missiles at the kitchen and raised a banner which said "stop brutality". From time to time, he encouraged other inmates to take action themselves, including the three inmates who managed to demonstrate on A Wing roof (to whom I will refer later).

5.142   About 21.35 on Wednesday 11 April his solicitor arrived from Liverpool. He talked to him for over an hour, but was unable to persuade him to come down.

5.143   The South West Region gave permission to wet the roof of D Wing at the C Wing end, to prevent the inmate from disrupting the routine on C Wing. On the following morning, Thursday 12 April, the operation to wet that roof commenced, but the prison fire appliance was not sufficiently powerful to do the job and the inmate pretended to take a shower in the spray. The operation kept him away from C Wing. It also wet him thoroughly, which was not the intention. The inmate, however, remained a nuisance, (as I was able to observe when I visited the prison that day). Even after he received a telephone message from his mother telling him to come down, he did not respond.

5.144   On Saturday, 14 April, he was spreading disaffection in E Wing by shouting. A compressor was located in the vicinity to drown out what he was saying. Later on that day he was observed tying a rope around his blankets. At 12.40 Principal Officer Comber was able to persuade him to give himself up.

5.145   The inmate was located in the prison hospital for two days, but he was none the worse for his experience. After he left the hospital, until he was interviewed on behalf of the Inquiry, he was in almost continuous conflict with staff on E Wing. He admitted that he was refusing food and water and he later carried out a dirty protest (in which he left his excrement on the floor and walls of his cell). He did however have visits from his mother who persuaded him to eat again.

The A Wing Incident

5.146   The inmate's continued presence on the roof was a disruptive influence on the prison. On 11 April, three inmates from A Wing managed to climb on to the roof of that wing. They used the water tanks as a platform to obtain access to the raised windows, as had occurred previously in D Wing during the major disturbance. On this occasion, other inmates were not prepared to join them. The whole incident lasted only about two and a half hours from 20.05 to 22.32.

5.147   The roof was hosed down so that the three inmates could not move around the roof. Negotiations were started by Senior Officer Green. He ascertained that the alleged reason for this protest was that the three inmates thought another inmate, who had been on the roof of D Wing, had been subjected to brutality and had had his arms and legs broken. To establish that this was untrue, arrangements were made to take one of the three prisoners from the roof to see that the inmate was perfectly all right. When the other inmates were informed of this, they came down.

5.148   Mr Green, in the course of his negotiations, agreed that the three inmates would be allowed to spend the night of 11 April in A Wing. His agreement to allow this was subsequently countermanded by a senior officer, who insisted that the three inmates should go to the segregation unit in E Wing. It is not clear why the arrangement made by the negotiator was countermanded. Unless there are good reasons for going back on such undertakings, this should not happen.

5.149   This incident was therefore limited both as to the numbers involved and to its length. However, the situation could have become more serious because the staff of A Wing partly withdrew. Governor 5, Mr Johnson, happened to be at the prison for other reasons when the trouble broke out. He immediately mustered as many staff as possible in C&R equipment with the intention of intervening quickly.

5.150   The C&R unit arrived at A Wing. The unit evacuated the 100 or so prisoners who were not involved in the dispute to the lower classroom area. The Church of England Chaplain and the Methodist Minister, who had heard about the disturbance on the radio, went to the prison and joined the prisoners in the classroom area. They played a very important role in reassuring the prisoners, many of whom were concerned that they could be burnt in their cells because of the incident. The clergy made endless cups of tea and coffee and were able to relieve the tension by involving the prisoners in stories.

The Role of Headquarters and South West Regional Office

5.151   From the commencement of the incident, the South West Regional Office (SWRO) and the Deputy Director General's Office had been kept fully informed about what was happening. Communication was normally via the Regional Office, who in turn kept Headquarters informed of what was happening.

5.152   Mr Emes, the Deputy Director General, and his office adopted very much an advisory role. There was no attempt by Mr Emes to intervene directly or to dictate how the incident should be handled. Mr Emes made clear, however, that he would like the incident brought to an end as soon as possible. As the disturbance continued during Sunday 8 April, Mr Emes is recorded as indicating on the telephone to the Regional Director, Mr Dunbar, to "hurry that one up". During the afternoon he pressed the Regional Office to let him know the position with regard to intervention. He also spoke to Mr May direct.

5.153 Apart from providing a link between Headquarters and the establishment, the SWRO were closely involved in co-ordinating the provision of support from other establishments. They arranged the movement of inmates from Dartmoor, including those from C Wing who were in the Old Chapel.

Inmates' Comments on the Disturbances

5.154 A particularly articulate and well educated inmate on D Wing regarded most of the prison officers as being "OK". However he also referred to the minority of staff who were very self-conscious and insecure. He said they appeared to have a chip on their shoulder and got away with bullying. At the time of the incident, he was already locked up on D Wing on the 3s. Within ten minutes there was dense smoke coming under his door. He tried to prevent its entry by jamming towels underneath the door. After about half an hour, friends released him from his cell (he does not specify how). He said that he and a number of other inmates were trying to escape from the wing, but there was no way of doing so until the incident ended.

5.155 The inmate says in his evidence that, after the incident, he was on C Wing. Initially he was treated satisfactorily. However, a number of officers began to be more belligerent. There was no association. Only three prisoners would be released at a time for slopping out. He says that on 19 April he made a complaint about a foul mouthed officer. The next morning he was unlocked by that officer and was told that he was going down to the block (E Wing). He asked why. He was told "Governor's orders for further questioning".

5.156 The inmate said that the cell he was put in on E Wing was filthy. He was allowed no property. He therefore refused to do anything he was told. He was informed he was there for police interviews. He saw the police on Monday 23 April, but the interview took only three minutes. After the interview, he was not moved back to C Wing.

5.157 The inmate was seen by Mr May, who asked him what his grievance was. He said that he was not prepared to accept any punishment because he had done nothing wrong. There was no reason for keeping him down the block. Mr May responded that he had been charged with being on the roof. The inmate denied this.

5.158 The inmate developed serious piles. He was then taken to the hospital. After that he was re-located on A Wing and then transferred to F Wing, which, the inmate said, is a "good wing".

5.159 The inmate concludes his evidence by saying that he expected to be treated with respect. The whole of his difficulties since the disturbance were totally the result of the bad attitude of a minority of officers. He adds "you are not left with much dignity in prison but you cannot allow officers such as these that you get here to take your last shred of dignity away from you".

5.160 I refer also to the interview with a life sentenced prisoner who before coming to Dartmoor in January 1990 had already served 16 years. He had served parts of his sentence in Durham, Wakefield, Leeds, Hull, Wormwood Scrubs, Bristol and Exeter prisons. His view of Dartmoor was "about the best place I have been in. I am a Principal Officer's wing orderly which is about the best job. While I was at Bristol I had a heart attack and I have been able to get fairly good jobs ever since. The staff here are OK. I have not met a real bastard here. If you behave like a fool you get treated like one. But if you treat them OK here, then you get treated OK. You must not demand things, you have to ask for things."

5.161 Although this inmate spent most of the time on A Wing, at the time of the disturbance he was housed on D Wing. He was out of his cell when the dustbins came down the stairs. He said that he was able to get out with the female Officer Lynn Draper-Rush. What happened was because of Strangeways. Mostly it involved "young lads". He regarded the whole disturbance as being ridiculous, pointless. It was the inmates who suffered. Their possessions were raided by the other inmates.

5.162 These accounts have not been tested and there has been no opportunity for evidence in rebuttal to be called. I refer to them because they give some indication of the varying attitudes to Dartmoor. They give a flavour of the inmates' perceived grievances which help to provide the background against which the disturbance has to be considered.

The Prison Officers' Association Points on the Disturbance

5.163 In the POA's opinion, the management of the prison had not attached sufficient importance to the risk of a riot. Mr Mawson, the chairman of the Dartmoor POA Branch, referred to the 27 SIRs from staff warning of the riot. He referred also to the search on 6 April which found home made knives and razor blades fixed onto toothbrush handles.

5.164 Mr Mawson make it clear that, irrespective of the terms of the local agreement, if Mr May had asked for staff to come in on the Saturday afternoon before the incident (on 7 April), staff would have come in. This was because they would have recognised the danger of the situation. Mr May agreed with this judgement. Mr Mawson criticised Mr May for not bringing in additional staff. Mr May's response was that he would have asked for additional staff if he had thought that a riot was likely, as opposed to simply possible.

5.165 Mr Mawson refers as well to what he said was the management's failure throughout the incident to follow the advice which had been given by staff. There were 36 trained C&R men who were ready to enter D Wing when the incident first broke out, but they were ordered not to do so. Then there was the refusal to allow the C Wing inmates to remove their possessions before being transferred out of the prison, which resulted in the interior of the Old Chapel being destroyed. Mr Mawson refers also to the interference by Mr Upton with the initiative which led to the surrender. Finally, he refers to what he regarded as being the too rapid return to normal, particularly in A Wing, after the main incident, and to the allowing of association, which led to the roof climbing episode on 11 April.

5.166 Mr Mawson regards these matters as all indicating an inability on the part of management to listen to staff and a "them and us" attitude which he suggests is wholly inconsistent with the philosophy of "Fresh Start".

5.167 I agree with Mr Mawson that these are all examples of the way poor industrial relations before the disturbance made it difficult for staff and management to act cohesively in the face of a crisis. I consider the responsibility for such a state of affairs must be shared equally between the two sides. I shall return to the wider issues this raises in Section 13.

The Board of Visitors

5.168 As already indicated, Mr May takes responsibility for the fact the Board of Visitors were not notified of the outbreak of the disturbance as they should have been. This had the consequence, as Mr Doidge, the Chairman of the Board of Visitors, pointed out in his incident report, that the prison was deprived of independent observers for over three hours during the most critical and formative period of the confrontation.

5.169 The Board has recommended that, in future there should be call-out rotas for members of the Board of Visitors when an incident occurs. These should be available to the Duty Governor and on display in the orderly room. It should then be automatic, and part of the contingency plan of the establishment, that the appropriate member of the Board is telephoned as part of the prison's standard operating procedures. I would have thought it was irrefutable that arrangements on these lines should have been in existence.

5.170   Although the Board of Visitors had not been informed of the start of the disturbance, Mr Doidge and the Vice-Chairman, Lieutenant Commander Evatt, attended as soon as they heard about the incident from television reports. The Chairman arrived at 19.15 and the Vice-Chairman at 19.30. They found that there was nobody detailed to brief them. They managed to obtain information only by themselves approaching staff. This is not satisfactory. I accept the Board of Visitors' recommendation that there is need for a laid down procedure for briefing the Board representatives who attend an incident.

5.171   The Board members were in time to witness the inmates escaping from the Old Chapel. Together with another member of the Board, Mr Reynolds, who attended later, they kept a careful log of what they observed. Later a rota was established so that a member of the Board was present throughout and until the last inmate surrendered.

5.172   The Board had a major incident procedure, a copy of which appears in Annex 5C. This in simple language sets out the role of the Board and how they should act. The procedure is apparently based on one devised by the Board of Visitors of Wormwood Scrubs. I include it as an Annex because it seems to me that, while all procedures of this sort must be constantly reviewed, the one adopted by the Dartmoor Board provides a useful precedent for other establishments.

5.173   Unfortunately the Board of Visitors incident procedure assumes that the Governor will resort to his "Governor's incident box" as part of his handling of a major incident. This did not happen in this disturbance. The Governor's incident box is intended, according to the procedure, to hold the BOV incident box, which will be extracted by the Board of Visitors member who first arrives. However, as the Governor's incident box was not being used on 7 April 1990, its location had to be established before the Chairman and the Vice-Chairman of the Board were able to obtain the necessary orders and stationery. Again, this is a problem which has to be tackled.

5.174   It is important for the members of the Board of Visitors to be able to use a telephone, even if it cannot be for their exclusive use. Here they had no telephone allocated for them. Again they had to rely on their own local knowledge and go to the gate house where they were able to use a line.

5.175   These are all matters which should be resolved in the course of contingency planning. Arrangements should be made to enable the Board to play its very important role in any future disturbance without having to rely on the Board taking its own initiatives.

5.176   The logs which were kept by the members of the Board of Visitors very helpfully record what they observed. After the incident was over, and throughout the following week, members of the Board were present at all times. The Chairman told them he did not consider it necessary to keep a log. This was a mistake. So far as possible those prisoners who were seen and the complaints, if any, which they made should have been recorded. Unless this is done, it is difficult to perform the task of protecting both inmates and officers.

5.177   After the incident, a number of inmates were kept for a long period of time under segregation on E Wing. There has been a chorus of complaints from these inmates that they did not see members of the Board during this time.

5.178   After the incident, on 25 April 1990, there were some 35 inmates held under Rule 43 for reasons of good order or discipline (GOAD). Authority was given for their detention by Mr Hill (another member of the Board) but no record was kept of the names of the inmates concerned. The same is true of the authority given by Mr Doidge on 27 April in respect of one inmate.

5.179   Mr Doidge was absolutely confident that each inmate would have been seen. It is possible therefore that the evidence which was given by inmates that they had not been seen is incorrect. It would, however, have been preferable if there had been some record to which Mr Doidge could refer to show the inaccuracy of the inmates' evidence. Without it, it is difficult accurately to respond to complaints.

5.180   The Board's records indicate that on 31 May 1990, a member of the Board had seen six Rule 43s GOAD and that each, without exception, complained that no-one from the Board of Visitors had seen them. The prisoners claimed that they did not know why they were being segregated. The record, however, notes the fact that they had previously been seen by another member.

5.181   It is usual for the inmates to be seen at Board meetings. Mr May said that on the visits of the Board after the disturbance, however, it had been necessary to cut corners. Board meetings had been held to consider those held in E Wing under Rule 43 (GOAD) without the prisoners being present or being seen.

5.182   It is also far from clear that the Board followed up the prisoners' complaints as well as they should. In addition to the "clinics" which are held once monthly by three members, rota visits are made on a weekly basis by one member of the Board. The records which are made of the rota visits are much more informative than those made at the clinics. For example, on 4 June 1990, it is recorded that an inmate was complaining that he had been assaulted on A Wing by an officer. The comment beside this was "warned and advised". Mr Doidge explained that entry on the basis that Mr Heppell, the member of the Board concerned, probably was not aware that it was no longer a disciplinary offence to make a malicious allegation, he being a relatively inexperienced new member of the Board. However this suggests a lack of training and instruction of members of the Board. Furthermore, it was not Mr Doidge's practice to read all reports of visits. He was, for example, unaware of this entry, which clearly required action.

5.183   In evidence, Mr Doidge agreed that it would be useful if a standard document were to be given to an inmate when he arrived at Dartmoor telling him the different ways in which he could communicate with and arrange to be seen by a member of the Board. Mr May referred to the fact that there is a document in the course of production. It is called "The Dartmoor Information Booklet". It has taken some six months to be printed. It will explain to an inmate about his life in Dartmoor. It may well be that the necessary information will be or can be incorporated into this booklet. From the information which Mr Doidge has sent to the Inquiry since he gave evidence, it appears that the majority of the matters to which I have drawn attention have already been dealt with by the Board.

The Involvement of the Fire Service

5.184   The Devon Fire Rescue Service have what they call a "pre-attack plan" for Dartmoor prison. The plan identifies different incidents, including "riot conditions (major disturbance)" and specifies what attendance there should be for the different categories of incident. The plan appears to be satisfactory and to have worked in the case of this incident. A letter dated 7 June 1990 to the Inquiry, from the Chief Fire Officer states:

"The arrangements contained within the plan worked extremely well throughout the incident. The co-operation and liaison between the emergency services, and the prison Governor and his staff were first class. The Governor conducted regular briefing and up-dating sessions throughout the incident which resulted in the services being fully aware at all times of the current situation and what would be required of their resources if called upon."

5.185 I have no reason to question these conclusions and, like the Chief Fire Officer, I am sure that adequate pre-planning and the liaison before and during the incident were of the greatest importance.

5.186 In the same letter, the Chief Fire Officer says that no de-briefing sessions occurred following the disturbance. He draws attention to this because, apparently, it is normal practice to conduct a de-briefing session following incidents and training exercises in which there has been a considerable involvement of the brigade's manpower and resources. Here there does not appear to have been an involvement on that scale. However, one inmate lost his life because of fire. Bearing in mind that the Fire Service probably attempted to take action to deal with that fire but then desisted from doing so, this does appear a matter which called for de-briefing.

5.187 In an earlier letter to the inquiry dated 23 May 1990, the Fire Service provided a chronology of their involvement on 7 and 8 April. This stated that the only request that was made on 7 April for the Fire Service's involvement was to provide portable lighting to illuminate D Wing during the hours of darkness. The provision of such equipment to the prison would clearly have been of the greatest importance if there had been an intervention during the hours of darkness of 7/8 April. However the supply of the lights would not fit in with the terms of paragraph 6.4 of the pre-attack plan which states:

"The use of personnel and equipment should be confined to those activities which constitute normal fire service procedures and practices."

5.188 While paragraph 6.4 is in accord with the policy adopted by other Fire Services, I consider that a distinction should be made between the provision of personnel and the provision of equipment in the case of a riot or disturbance. I can well understand why fire officers should not be involved and why fire appliances which can be easily identified as belonging to the Fire Service should also not be involved. But lighting equipment does appear to fall within a different category. Consideration should be given as to whether the pre-attack plan should recognise this distinction.

The Involvement of the Ambulance and Medical Services

5.189 Dr O'Hanlon, the senior medical officer, was at the prison throughout the disturbance. He attended all the Governor's briefings and was responsible for alerting the Ambulance Services, two casualty departments at local hospitals and local doctors who were willing to come and help.

5.190 The first ambulance from the Devon Ambulance Service, according to a report submitted by the Chief Ambulance Officer, arrived at the prison at 16.39. This was backed up by a further four vehicles which were despatched in accordance with the assessment of the need by the ambulance service's Duty Officer who attended the prison.

5.191 The Chief Ambulance Officer considered that there was close liaison between the police, the fire service and the prison authorities under the auspices of the Governor. He reported that the Governor made arrangements for the officers from other services to be kept up-to-date on the situation.

5.192 A de-briefing exercise was held on 9 April by the Ambulance Service. It produced the following recommendations:

    i)   two ambulance incident officers should be at the scene at any one time;

ii) the telephone line direct into central ambulance control should be made available to be used for such incidents;

iii) "talk through" facilities should be available to enable the outstations on the radio net to communicate with each other without going through control;

iv) an ambulance officer should visit the scene and then return to central ambulance control to brief the control staff so that they are fully aware of the situation;

v) cellular telephones had a very important role to play; they were more effective than radio;

vi) a separate officer should be duty officer for any other incidents which may occur in the division at the same time as the major incident;

vii) the presence of an adequate mix of qualified ambulance personnel and paramedics was felt to be essential;

viii) ambulance personnel should be positioned well back from the firing lines of such incidents allowing casualties to be brought to them.

5.193   Dr O'Hanlon referred to the treatment room on D Wing being broken into. This resulted in a number of surrendering prisoners being identified as being "intoxicated". These inmates were admitted to hospital. He pointed out, however, that the prison hospital staff had anticipated the possibility of the treatment room being broken into. They had removed all controlled drugs from such locations and had kept the amount of medication stored there to a minimum.

5.194   By 10 July 1990, the date on which Mr Shepherd, the Head of Works Services at Dartmoor, gave evidence to the Inquiry, steps had already been taken by him to make the treatment room more secure by the provision of a security gate at the entrance. In addition, when the wings are refurbished, there is to be a reinforced door, reinforced security of the windows, and stronger lockable cabinets.

The Involvement of the Devon and Cornwall Constabulary

5.195   The Devon and Cornwall Police attended the incident, but did not become directly involved. They had previously been warned that there could be an incident and were on standby. When the disturbance started, they sent two police special units (of an inspector, two sergeants and 12 constables). A special control room was opened at Headquarters at Plymouth and a control room with radio and telephone lines, with an Assistant Chief Constable in charge, was set up in the prison. Other police officers closed roads and kept the public away.

5.196   Detective Superintendent Quick of the Devon and Cornwall Constabulary made a valuable report to the inquiry. In the course of that report he indicated, among other matters, that the police should bear in mind that they have not only to assist in the containment of the situation but also to investigate a serious criminal offence. Consideration should therefore be given to the employment at an early stage of photographers with video and still cameras. Prisoners should also be photographed as soon as they come down from the roof, so as to show how they were dressed and appeared. There should be facilities for urgent interviews to take place, particularly where there has been loss of life. Adequate interviewing facilities needed to be made available within the prison for interviews under caution. There was a need also to arrange for proper de-briefing.

The Consequences of the Disturbance

5.197   During the main incident one inmate regrettably lost his life. Otherwise no officers or staff received other than minor injuries.

5.198   The bill for repairs is heavy. It is estimated that the cost of repairing the 139 cells lost from D Wing would be approximately £3.5m and take 12 months. However, it has been decided to refurbish the whole wing at a cost of £5.1m. As the refurbishment of the wing was necessary in any event, the cost of repairing the riot damage, which would not otherwise have been incurred, is assessed at £600,000. Fortunately for the timing of this work, B Wing had not been in use pending refurbishment. This wing was brought back into operation so as to enable D Wing to be refurbished first.

Conclusions Specific to the Dartmoor Disturbance

5.199 The following conclusions and comments must be read together with Section 9 of the Report, which deals with the lessons to be learned from all the disturbances.

1.   Counsel to the Inquiry, in his concluding submission on Dartmoor, commenced by stating:

> "In April, Dartmoor was a divided society. The Prison Officers Association mistrusted the Governor over staffing levels. He was frustrated over their lack of co-operationwith his attempts to liberalise the regime. As always the people on the receiving end of this power struggle were the prisoners, who saw their regime diminished in a prison where few, if any, of them wanted to be. Dartmoor was a prison waiting for a riot to happen. Strangeways was the spark required to ignite it."

This is an admirable and accurate summary of the situation at Dartmoor when the disturbance commenced.

2.   The Governor and his staff were all aware that there was a considerable risk of a disturbance at Dartmoor during the week ending 7 April. Bearing in mind the constraints on staffing levels to which the establishment was subject, the action taken to prepare for trouble over the weekend was reasonable. The management and staff of the prison were not at fault in not preventing the start of the disturbance.

3.   While the use of SIRs was satisfactory, the general contingency planning needs considerable attention. There were no evacuation plans nor drawings or photographs of the different parts of the prison. More detailed attention to security might have led to the routes to the roof being made less accessible.

4.   The absence of a satisfactory communications room was a significant handicap in the handling of the disturbance. The absence of any proper radio communications meant that Mr Upton, instead of being the "field" commander of C&R, was reduced to the status of the Governor's runner. There needs to be a means of telling the status of anyone wearing C&R kit.

5.   Some degree of planning by prisoners for a riot clearly existed. This can be seen from the SIRs warning of the riot taking place at the time and place it did, and the wearing of masks by those who joined in. Probably only a small number of the participants, however, were involved in that planning. The probabilities are that the throwing of the dustbin on D Wing was a signal.

6.   If as Mr Mawson suggested there had been 36 men trained in C&R and ready to enter D Wing at the start of the disturbance, then I have little

doubt that an immediate entry into D Wing would have been sufficient to restore order there and then, apart from a few hardliners who might have made a roof top protest. This was not the position however. Once Mr May, in accordance with the contingency arrangements which had been made, started to evacuate prisoners from C Wing, then that action had to have priority and the staff who were available were needed for that purpose. Once the rioters had become established, an intervention by a small force would have been hazardous. No-one can criticise Mr May, in so far as he was responsible, for not authorising an early intervention. In the circumstances the staff, who were in the wing behaved perfectly reasonably and appropriately in vacating the wing.

7. So far as the incident in the Old Chapel is concerned, it was a mistake not to allow the inmates to collect their possessions from C Wing, as some of the staff wanted. Mr May made an error of judgement in the heat of the moment.

8. The second possibility of intervention arose at 22.00 on 7 April. At that time Mr Benge, an experienced regional C&R instructor, had helped to formulate an intervention plan. He considered that an intervention would be successful. Others took the same view. Had the intervention had taken place it may very well have been successful. But an intervention in the dark would have been necessary. Mr May was concerned that he had not sufficient information as to the conditions inside D Wing to justify intervention. He was particularly concerned as to whether balustrades may have been removed which would add to the hazard. By no means all the inmates on the wing were supporting the riot and in the dark (it was not practical to restore the electricity), even with the lamps which were available, it would have been difficult to have distinguished those who were rioting from those who were not. There was no suggestion that anyone was at risk if an intervention was not made. Mr May had limited knowledge of what could be achieved by C&R units, particularly in the dark. Although it is possible to take two views as to whether or not it was reasonable to intervene at that stage, I do not consider there is any justification for criticising Mr May for deciding not to intervene at that time.

9. By the morning of 8 April, Mr May had ample resources to intervene if he had wanted to do so. His adviser was confident that an intervention could be made. Mr May was still concerned about the situation within D Wing. He preferred to rely on negotiations, notwithstanding the fact that clearly region and Headquarters would have preferred a more forceful policy. Bearing in mind the initial response to negotiation and the fact that the rioters were showing every intention of extending their activities to C Wing, I regard this decision by Mr May as being highly questionable. It was possible for him to ascertain more about the state of D Wing relatively easily once it was light. The response to Mr Upton's approach with the loud-hailer indicated that there was unlikely to be a rapid surrender by the ring-leaders through negotiations alone.

10. If negotiations was the preferred route, the policy should have been negotiation backed up by a show of force. The inmates should have been under no misunderstanding that, unless they were to come out peacefully within a limited period, there would be a forceful intervention.

11. Although Mr May was concerned about the outcome of intervention, having heard his evidence, I have little doubt that the real reason for his decision not to intervene that morning is that he firmly believes that intervention should only be used as a last resort after negotiation has failed. He is conscious of the effect on his prison of a forceful intervention. In my view, this approach, while understandable, does not make sufficient allowance for the effect that the prolongation of the incident could have had on the other Dartmoor prisoners, on other prison establishments and on the Prison Service as a whole. By reaching the decision which he did,

Mr May was running the risk of a repetition of a Manchester type situation. Fortunately that was avoided by what happened in the afternoon, when there was an unintended intervention. However, in fairness to Mr May, it has to be pointed out that it is difficult for a Governor who is not fully familiar with the novel C&R techniques which were still being rapidly developed to appreciate what could be achieved.

12. Region and Headquarters were kept fully informed by the prison as to how the disturbance was being handled. Both the Regional Director and the Deputy Director General encouraged Mr May to intervene. However, when he decided not to do so they were justified in accepting his decision. It is not practical, except in the most exceptional circumstances, to order a Governor to retake a prison establishment or part of that establishment by force if he has decided, after discussing the issue with his superiors, that this is the wrong policy. It is Mr May who would have had to command the intervention by force and it would be extremely difficult for him to command an intervention which he considered was unjustified. There was no justification for replacing Mr May and there was no one available who could command an intervention under Mr May's overall control.

13. Sufficient steps were not taken earlier to protect C Wing. Mr May implied that water was not used on the roof of C Wing because the inmates got there first. They should not have done so. Staff should have been deployed to use water to try and prevent inmates getting on to C Wing roof. Water could also have been used to stop the inmates returning to D Wing roof after they had left the roof for the night.

14. The length of the disturbance was probably influenced by the inability of the prisoners to obtain food as the kitchen was in a different building.

15. The Devon Fire and Rescue Service had generally a good pre-attack plan. The Governor had apparently conducted regular briefings and updating sessions throughout the incident. Apparently no de-briefing was conducted because the Fire Services considered its involvement during the incident was "fairly minimal". I find this reaction to the Fire Services involvement surprising bearing in mind that the brigade control had a report of a cell fire in the wing where the inmate met his death. What happened illustrates the problems which can arise because of the vulnerability of firemen to attack from inmates. It indicates that there is a need for clarification of the respective roles of the Fire Service and the Prison Service as to extinguishing a fire inside part of the prison establishment which is occupied by rioting inmates. It would have been preferable if the Fire Service had not decided to withdraw merely because of a shout from an inmate. A closer investigation could have been made even if it involved a combined operation between the Fire Service and a C&R unit.

16. The allegations which were made by inmates of brutality in, and the excessive use of, the segregation unit were uncorroborated. As in the case of other disturbances, it is not possible for me to make any finding. However it is to be noted that Mr May accepts that special cells appear to have been used too frequently in the past. Whether justified or not, the "block" at Dartmoor has an unenviable reputation within the prison system. If a change in attitude of staff is achieved at Dartmoor it is to be hoped that the reputation of the block will also change. This is an aspect of life at Dartmoor which requires the closest personal attention and monitoring by the new Area Manager, the Governor and the Board of Visitors.

17. The barrier between staff and management must be broken down. Nothing could be more illustrative of the harmful existing situation than the reaction of uniformed staff to the activities of management in relation to the incident on 7/8 April. There was an obvious and regrettable breakdown in communications during the riot. This gave the impression of ineffective attempts by management to give leadership which were in turn interpreted

by staff as frustrating their initiatives and rejecting the sound advice of staff.

18. Relationships are being poisoned by arguments over staffing levels. At Dartmoor, as with other establishments, it is essential that tasks are defined and an objective in-depth assessment is made of the staffing needs. More flexibility needs to be built in to attendance patterns to enable manning levels to be increased at weekends, particularly where, as over the critical weekend, there is a real prospect of disruption. Mr Mawson considered that what was needed was about nine extra staff and then Dartmoor "would have no staffing problems. Dartmoor would run efficiently." Mr Mawson cannot, without the examination I have proposed, know whether this figure is correct or not. However, his estimation of the numbers indicates that this problem should not be insurmountable.

19. The Board of Visitors at Dartmoor have shown themselves to be committed to playing an important role in the prison. However, at the present time they do not have the confidence of the inmates. What is needed is a better method of explaining to inmates what they can do and what they cannot do. There needs also to be a more proficient approach by members to their task coupled with the appropriate training. Better records must be kept, complaints followed up and the inmate concerned informed of the result. The attitude of staff needs to be monitored more vigorously. It must be clearly understood that it is part of the Board's task to express its disapproval of any behaviour which is not in accord with proper standards.

20. On the evidence which is available, it appears that, while segregation was being authorised by the Board of Visitors, visits to the block were not being made with the regularity which is desirable. Good practice requires that authorization of segregation and monthly extensions should not take place without personal visits. Part of the problem may be that, after the riot, E Wing's normal role was suspended and prisoners were placed in that wing without being on Rule 43. This was not, however, properly explained to the prisoners.

21. The time lag between the preparation of food and its consumption must be drastically reduced. Consideration should be given to the staggering of meal times, to the introduction of eating in association and to the provision of dining rooms where this is possible. The catering staff should not be faced with their present impossible task.

22. On the assumption that the need for prison accommodation is such that Dartmoor is required to house prisoners, then drastic action is required if Dartmoor is to be retained as a prison establishment.

23. I agree with what Governor 4 Mr McLean said in his evidence: what is needed is for prisoners (if they are to be imprisoned) to want to be at Dartmoor.

24. Dartmoor has always had the disadvantage of its geographical location and its massive and intimidating exterior. However its cellular accommodation could be vastly improved by the refurbishment programme which is already planned and which should be given the highest priority. If the prison is to remain in use, facilities designed to reduce the impact of the climate should be included, such as a sports hall. The refurbishment should include the division of the existing wings, integral sanitation and the enlargement of the existing ventilation grills into secondary windows so that inmates can see out of their cells. Every effort should be made to ensure that damp is kept at bay and that the cells are warm and dry.

25. Consideration should be given to how to improve prisoners' family links. Transport could be arranged from the main urban centres from which Dartmoor's population is drawn so as to make visiting easier.

Arrangements could be made for overnight accommodation for visitors as suggested by the Prison Governors' Association. Telephones could play a part in reducing a sense of isolation. This could be the prison to pioneer private family visits.

26. Dartmoor's present reputation, both among staff and inmates, must be eradicated. It is harmful to the morale of both. Dartmoor needs to be given a clearly defined and positive role within the prison system in which prison officers can be closely involved. It could, for example, be a prison centre of excellence in education. The VPU function, which it already has, could be developed.

27. If the staff are given the right leadership, if they have a clearly defined role and if the physical conditions in which they are required to work are of an acceptable standard, then the counter-culture should wither. It should be encouraged to do so by making it clear that management will not tolerate reactionary attitudes. The policy towards promoting staff should support the need to encourage a change of attitude by staff. The uniformed staff must recognise that unless the counter culture does wither, Dartmoor has a limited future. They cannot continue (as I believe they have in the past) to frustrate needed improvements by arguments over staffing levels.

28. If, but only if, there is a fresh approach by uniformed staff and management and if a fresh role can be created for Dartmoor, then Dartmoor should be capable of making a positive contribution to the prison system of this country. There is no reason why all its wings should not be fully occupied and why its inmates and its staff should not feel that it has advantages which make it worthwhile being there, despite the disadvantages of its location. If there is no fresh approach, the present planned expenditure would be better spent elsewhere. This should be Dartmoor's last chance.

Section 6

Cardiff Prison

Introduction

6.1   The riot at Cardiff prison occurred on 8 April 1990. This was a week after the start of the disturbance at Manchester prison; just over 24 hours after the riot at Glen Parva; the second day of the disturbance at Dartmoor; and five hours before there was to be an outburst of violence at Bristol.

The Prison

6.2   Like Manchester, Cardiff is a city centre Victorian local prison which primarily serves the Courts in the immediate locality. It has a distinctly Welsh character.

6.3   A plan of the prison appears at Annex 6A. The main accommodation at the prison is divided into three Wings, A, B and D. These wings are the original Victorian buildings and were built in about 1830. A and B Wings are constructed in the conventional Victorian style. They are galleried and linked at right angles to a Centre from which they can be separated by gates on each landing, which can be locked. D Wing is separate from the other two wings. The prison also has a number of other buildings interspersed irregularly within the perimeter wall and a new gatehouse complex built in 1987. The adult prisoners, whether on remand or convicted, are housed in A and B Wings. D Wing is the remand centre for young offenders in South East Wales. It contains some young persons held for their own protection under Rule 46 (the young offender equivalent of Rule 43).

6.4   The disturbance took place on A Wing. At the lower ground floor level of that wing, the landing is separated into two halves by lockable gates at the foot of each of two flights of steps. At the end nearest the Centre is a segregation unit. The other half of the landing contained vulnerable prisoners held under Rule 43 at their own request. A2 landing contained the adult prisoners who were on remand and A3 and A4 held the convicted prisoners.

6.5   The prison has a certified normal accommodation (CNA) of 252 inmates in the main prison and 85 in the remand centre for young offenders (a total of 337). In the early part of 1990 the prison usually held about 250 sentenced and 200 unsentenced inmates. On 8 April there were 458 prisoners at Cardiff; 203 were accommodated in A Wing, which had a CNA of 115.

The Regime and Staffing

6.6   Cardiff, like most local prisons, was grossly overcrowded. The cells did not have integral sanitation and what sanitary facilities there were were limited (eg there was one WC for 13 cells in the segregation unit). There was, however, normally a good relationship between the staff and inmates. The regime was generally relaxed. An example of this is that prisoners on remand were allowed a visit each day which lasted substantially longer than the statutory entitlement of 15 minutes. In addition the prisoners were let out of their cells whenever this was practicable.

6.7   There were active educational and PE programmes at the prison. The main problem with maintaining these programmes were cancellations because of lack of discipline staff.

6.8   The industries at Cardiff include a large tailoring complex, two metal recovery workshops and the laundry. The workshops can provide 175 full time workplaces for adult convicted inmates and normally operate Monday to Friday each week. There was no shortage of workshop places. During the year ending March 1990 the average working week for tailoring was 24.4 hours, for laundry it was 23.5 hours and for metal recovery it was 22 hours.

6.9   The number of inmates employed in each workshop was affected by the ability of the establishment to provide two discipline officers to patrol the workshops' areas. In the absence of patrolling officers, workshop manning levels were reduced to a ratio of eight inmates per instructor. During the year ending March 1990 it was not possible to provide shop patrols on 81 days. Employment in the metal recovery industry was also affected by the long term absence on sick leave of the Senior Officer instructor. During the first three months of 1990, the metal recovery workshop No.2, with an effective minimum complement of 20 inmates, was completely closed due to instructor and staff shortages. In the tailoring industry during the same period, the workshops were only fully operational for 28 out of 64 days. On 36 days they were operating on reduced manning levels. As a result 2,168 hours were lost. The metal recovery workshop No.1 had an effective minimum complement of 35. Over the same period it was fully operational for 20 days, completely closed for six days and operating on a reduced manning level for 38 days. 4900 inmate hours were lost.

6.10   Among the suggested causes of the lack of staff were: the implementation of "Fresh Start", the unpredictability of the demand for staff for escort duties, an above average sickness problem and, finally, possible absenteeism.

6.11   Cardiff, has unfortunately a bad record for officers being away from work. During the year ended 31 March 1989, from some 200 uniformed staff a total of 2735 officer days were lost. During the year ending 31 March 1990, 4254 days were lost by the same group of staff.

6.12   The effect on regimes of staff shortages was explained by the Governor, Mr Alan Rawson, in evidence as follows:

"For example, from the week beginning 6 February up until the week beginning 2 April, in fact there were 45 week days. Of those 45 days, on ten occasions there was no education at all because of shortage of an officer to supervise and on eight of those days there was education for only half a day and during the period from 1 January to the end of March, there were 64 possible working days during that period. Of those, the workshops were only operational for 28 days and the workshops operated on reduced prisoner manning levels on the other 36 days in the tailoring industry and in the metal recovery industry the workshops were only operational for 20 days, closed completely for six days and operated on reduced manning levels for 38 days. The problems which these figures indicate are connected with Cardiff's problem in relation to staff being off duty for sickness. Under Fresh Start the allowance for sick leave is 3% of the hours which should be provided by the staff. For the year ending March 1989 the figure for Cardiff was 7.6%, over twice the hours allowed."

6.13   The management has tried to tackle the staff sickness problem at Cardiff by monitoring and appropriate intervention. This resulted in 11 officers being medically retired, dismissed or deciding to resign during the year ending 31 March 1990. A factor contributing to the sickness problem at Cardiff was the age profile of officer grades. 66% were over 40 and 28% were over 50 years of age. The number of older officers was linked to the desire of many officers of Welsh origin to return to their home area towards the end of their period of service.

6.14 A concern of staff, which is not limited to Cardiff, is that Fresh Start, in addition to creating tight manning levels, has for operational reasons divided the staff into discrete groups which the staff say tend to become isolated from each other, causing a fall in morale. The oral evidence before the Inquiry, however, does not suggest that there was anything wrong with the morale of staff on A Wing. This may have been due to the continuity of work by staff within the wing which helped to develop a good relationship among the staff and between the staff and the majority of prisoners.

The Remand Regime

6.15 Remand prisoners were on A2. Their landing was boarded over and this provided a considerable amenity area. They did not have the same opportunities of employment as the convicted prisoners, but were able to spend much of the day out of their cells. This gave them access to showers, PE, table tennis, TV and videos. This mitigated the effects of the lack of integral sanitation in the cells and of overcrowding.

6.16 More could have been done, however, to provide remand prisoners with opportunities to attend educational classes and employment. A construction industry training course (CIT) was provided for convicted prisoners. It was never offered to remand prisoners, because it was thought they would not be interested. But as Mr Smith, the head of Works Services, accepted in evidence, they might have been interested in at least a limited decorating course for part of a day. However when, shortly before the hearing, they were offered work in the tailoring shop only six out of 70 were prepared to work.

Kit

6.17 Kit, as in many local prisons, was a problem at Cardiff. However, even here Cardiff was better placed than most local prisons because it has its own laundry. This meant that it was possible for shortages of kit to be compensated for by the laundry giving precedence to laundering its own kit. At the hearing, the Governor gave evidence that he had made arrangements to introduce a personal kit system for remand prisoners. But he recognised that there would still be problems because of the turn over of remands in a local prison and the difficulty of imposing any sanctions if their kit was missing.

Food

6.18 The quality of food in Cardiff, by prison standards, was exceptionally good. This apparently was due to the calibre of the Principal Officer in charge of catering (Principal Officer Davies BEM) who used the cash allowances with which he was provided particularly imaginatively and effectively. The evidence provided to the Inquiry by the prisoners in letters is exceptional. There were only five complaints about food and even those complaints have to be set against complementary comments by two prisoners.

Prisoners' Letters

6.19 Annex 2E provides an analysis of letters from 47 prisoners from Cardiff. Of those, 20 identified one or more aspects of the prison which contributed to the build up of tension and made a riot more likely. Among the complaints (in addition to those about food) were that there was too much time spent in cells (which conflicts with what is said above about the position on A2 landing), too little exercise, inadequate wages, a poor attitude among staff and inadequate visiting arrangements.

Contingency Planning

6.20   Cardiff had a set of contingency plans. They were out of date in relation to the names and addresses of Regional Staff. They did not have an action list to ensure that key people such as the Board of Visitors were notified of a disturbance. The plans were available in the Governor's Office, in the Communications Room and in the Centre. But a number of staff were not familiar with the plan. Nevertheless, prior to the weekend of 7/8 April arrangements had been made to ensure that in the event of a disturbance each wing would be secured and the double locks applied to the external doors and gates.

6.21   As in other local prisons the Communications Room was not well equipped. There were no cameras to provide a visual display of what was occurring within the prison compound, although there were cameras which gave a view of the main gate area. There were only three telephone lines, including a direct line to the police which was a shared line with the internal emergency phone. The Room was also undermanned once the disturbance had started. It was operated by a single officer, Mr Thomas Jones, for over half an hour. Despite his excellent work, this made the passing and receiving of telephone messages difficult. Mr Jones had to operate the switchboard taking external and internal calls, the UHF radio and the direct line to the police. During the incident the Governor used the Board Room as his command post.

Background to the Disturbance

6.22   As a result of the Strangeways disturbance 50 ex-Manchester prisoners were transferred to Cardiff on 2 April 1990. Each of those prisoners was seen by a Governor grade shortly after reception to ensure that he was not suffering from trauma after the disturbance. They were distributed around both A and B Wings. The majority of the Manchester prisoners were relieved to have been moved to Cardiff after their experience, but a few were agitating to return to the North. They were worried about when their cases would come up for hearing. The Probation Service helped with the integration of the Manchester prisoners and interviewed each of them, leaving them where appropriate an article on stress based on that used after the Bradford Fire Disaster. Mrs Benedict, the Chairman of the Board of Visitors, played a most helpful role in assisting the prisoners to settle down at Cardiff.

6.23   The arrival of such a large number of prisoners was in itself a significant event. The normal population of the prison is Welsh, though from many different backgrounds, including a number of black prisoners. The Manchester prisoners were of a different character. However the decision to spread them throughout the prison meant that their impact was much less than otherwise it would have been.

6.24   On 6 April 1990 a prisoner was transferred to Cardiff from Bristol, where he had been identified as a trouble maker. Miss Ring, a Governor 5 at Cardiff, was informed that the difficulties this prisoner had caused in Bristol were connected with other prisoners there and that in a new setting he was unlikely to be difficult. Inmates are housed either two or three to a cell in Cardiff, and the Bristol prisoner was placed with an inmate on A2 landing. This proved not to be the ideal choice. However, in view of what she had been told by Bristol, Miss Ring did not pay specific attention to where he was located and the staff on the landing were not told of his reputation.

Warnings of the Disturbance

6.25   The Security Principal Officer, Mr Lockley, was supported by a Security Committee and security matters normally received close attention. However, as in other establishments, the correct procedures with regard to SIR forms were not always followed and sometimes information was not seen by those who should have seen it, including Mr Rawson, the Governor. It is, as Mr Lockley was driven to accept, extremely important that procedures with regard to the completion and consideration of SIRs are properly followed and that this is constantly brought home to the staff. Over the days leading up to the incident, there were SIRs completed, entries made in the staff observation book and an informal written memorandum all of which were designed to perform the role which would be more appropriately performed by the SIR. The Head of Custody should have given clear attention to ensuring the proper procedures were adhered to.

16.26   Not surprisingly, after the commencement of the disturbance in Strangeways on 1 April, rumours of trouble were circulating in Cardiff. On 3 April the Security Committee considered a report about the possibility of a disturbance at the Church of England Service on 8 April. Later there were a number of other reports from inmates that trouble could be expected on Sunday morning 8 April at the beginning of or during the Chapel service. It was suggested that the prisoners from Manchester would be involved. On Saturday 7 April a prisoner received off bail indicated to a member of the disciplinary staff, Mr Hutton, that he knew something was due to happen "In the Chapel tomorrow". This was recorded in the Staff Observation Book kept on the Centre.

6.27   An inmate repeated a similar warning on the Sunday morning of 8 April. He gave evidence to the Inquiry. He said he was told by inmates on A2 that it was "kicking off today so watch" in the chapel. This information was given to Principal Officer O'Brien.

6.28   The prison officer who was regularly on duty on A2 landing was Mrs Megan Jones. She had been concerned after the riot at Strangeways started about the way nine inmates had got into a group together in a cell. She had Manchester prisoners on her landing but they caused no trouble. She found the prisoner transferred from Bristol, however, "a hard case and a bit of a nutter". Mrs Jones said in evidence that before she went off duty on the evening of 7 April, she had been told by an inmate that "he had a wife and a mother and he did not want to see me being hurt". He said that she should not come to work the following day. She understood the trouble was to be on her landing.

6.29   Mrs Jones gave evidence that she mentioned this conversation to Mr O'Brien at a meeting of staff before she went off duty on 7 April. There was a pooling of information at that meeting and the tactics for the next day were discussed and agreed. Mr O'Brien told her that she should put the information in writing and pass a message to the duty Governor about it. Mr O'Brien however had no recollection of being told anything about, in particular, trouble on A2.

6.30   Overnight, Mrs Jones wrote out her message. She did not see the Governor 5, Miss Ring, until 08.15 to 08.30 the following morning, 8 April, when she handed her the message. It stated:

"At approx 20.10 hrs on Saturday 7th April [a remand inmate] stated to me that the prisoners intended to cause problems today for staff and he wanted me out of the way when it started."

6.31   On 7 April Miss Ring was the Governor in charge of the prison. She decided in the light of the information that she had then received, (including information from the Staff Observation Book, but not what had been to said to Mrs Jones), to arrange that all shifts should be extended the following day. She secured the agreement of the South West Regional Office (SWRO) to this decision. This should have had the effect that there would be the equivalent of ten additional officers on duty on the morning of 8 April. However, there were fewer than this because a prisoner had to be guarded at a hospital.

6.32   Miss Ring thought at that time, as did the remainder of the staff, that the most likely place for a disturbance would be in the Chapel during the Church of England service on 8 April. Arrangements were therefore made for the number of inmates attending that service to be carefully monitored. If there were signs that many more were going to try and attend than the normal number (approximately 40) action was to be taken to limit the numbers attending. Chapel was not cancelled in advance. It was felt that the right tactic was to keep things as normal as possible in order to avoid exacerbating the situation.

6.33 Cardiff held the regional stock of C&R training equipment. When the Dartmoor disturbance occurred on 7 April, SWRO wished to transfer the regional training equipment held at Cardiff to Dartmoor. Apparently the SWRO were under the impression that this equipment was at Cardiff to assist only with training programmes and that Cardiff would have its own equipment as well. This was not the case. The SWRO equipment was virtually the only equipment at Cardiff. No enquiry was made as to whether the removal of this equipment would leave Cardiff bereft of equipment.

6.34 A message was received on 7 April at 17.30 by Principal Officer O'Brien that he should send some C&R equipment to Dartmoor (the SWRO log says "1 section of training equipment") and, if available, a C&R instructor. Mr O'Brien consulted Miss Ring on the telephone at her home and made arrangements for the transfer of the equipment to Dartmoor, accompanied by a C&R instructor who was off duty. The SWRO log records the transfer by the following entry "Cardiff informs *all* C&R equipment sent to Dartmoor".

6.35 Because Miss Ring suspected there might be problems on the following day, she returned to the prison at about 20.00 on 7 April. She found the prison generally quiet, but also that all the C&R equipment had been taken. Miss Ring was unhappy about the transfer and so she later telephoned Mr Rawson the Governor. She discussed the matter with him and also the arrangements which were being made for the following day. Mr Rawson shared her concern, but felt the position with regard to the equipment had to be accepted. He was content with the precautions which were planned, but decided to go into the prison himself the following morning.

6.36 Miss Ring came on duty at 07.45 on 8 April. She received the memorandum from Mrs Jones at 08.15 to 08.30. By then she had found the prison normal and had arranged for Mr O'Brien to brief staff. She decided to discuss the memorandum with Governor 5, Mr Winters, who was Head of Residential on A and B Wings. She met Mr Winters halfway to the Administration Block. After speaking to him, Miss Ring went on to the Governor's Office. Mr Winters made his way directly to the Centre.

The Disturbance

6.37 In accordance with instructions which had been given by Principal Officer O'Brien, the prisoners on A Wing were that morning more closely supervised than usual. On landing A2, at about 08.40 and just after the inmates had returned from collecting their breakfast from the hotplate area at the under-centre, two inmates began a noisy dispute in a cell doorway. They were conducting what appeared to be a dance, after one of their trays had been thrown out of the cell. A number of witnesses described their activity as being a pretended fight. Mrs Jones tried to intervene, but without success.

6.38 Another officer, Mr B J Jones, then rushed to the scene. He became involved with another inmate who is alleged to have punched him in the chest and pushed him away. Principal Officer Williams, who was also on the landing, then intervened. He came to the conclusion that whatever the rights or the wrongs of the matter, the presence of Officer B J Jones was aggravating the situation. Mr Williams told Mr Jones to go to the Centre, which he did. He also told another officer who was giving orders to the prisoners to move away. As a result of this intervention there was a "pregnant pause while the prisoners seemed perplexed". Principal Officer Williams thought he might have succeeded in defusing the situation.

6.39 It was not to be. The inmate with whom the prisoner from Bristol was sharing a cell threw a bucket of tea along the landing, muttering abuse at the same time. The inmate from Bristol threw a dustbin down the flight of stairs at the centre of the landing. This caused the disturbance to break out in earnest. A broom was thrown which just caught Principal Officer Williams on the head. Under a barrage of missiles, the staff retreated along A2 to the Centre.

6.40 Prisoners on A3 and A4 then joined the disturbance. Staff on those landings also had to withdraw to the Centre. As they did so, they were dowsed with water from a hose reel which had been obtained by the prisoners from a locked cupboard on landing A2. The water continued to be used by the inmates until it was turned off by the Works Department at the request of Principal Officer Williams.

6.41 Unfortunately another officer, Mr Hutton, was left behind trying to lock up A3. He was accosted by a prisoner who shouted at him incoherently, grabbed him by the shoulders and turned him round. Other prisoners then grabbed Mr Hutton from behind in a stranglehold, causing his glasses to fly off. They pulled at his belt and forced him down on to the landing. A necklock was applied to the officer who says he was blacking out as he heard an inmate say "We have got his keys, let him go, don't hurt him he is all right". The hold was released and Mr Hutton, very shaken, was able to get to his feet and walk along the landing. Two officers came towards him and assisted him back to the Centre. Another officer, Mr Davies, who had replaced Mr Jones, was also assaulted and injured, but he was able to make his own way back to the Centre. He subsequently required hospital treatment for a wound on the back of his head.

6.42 Governor 5 Winters and Principal Officer Williams entered A Wing in the hope of dispersing the inmates, but they had to retreat from the wing as a result of the debris being thrown at them.

6.43 When Mr Winters learnt from Principal Officer Williams that Mr Hutton's keys had been taken, he gave instructions for the doubles key to be collected and for the doubles lock to be put on all gates around A Wing. He then (shortly after 09.00) sent Senior Officer Eddy and a group of staff to evacuate the Rule 43 prisoners from their cells through the gate which led from A1 to the hospital. These prisoners were situated in the hospital as a temporary measure and later moved to police cells.

6.44 In the meantime, Principal Officer Williams had asked the Works Department to supply sufficient padlocks and heavy chains to secure the gates from the landings on A Wing to the Centre. These gates did not have locks which could be doubled. This was done and the combined effect of applying the double locks to the external exits and chaining and padlocking the gates to the Centre meant that the inmates were unable to get out of A Wing. Fortunately, although the doubles key had been removed to the Main Gate as a precaution after what had happened at Strangeways, the chains and padlocks and the doubles key were obtained before the inmates made any concerted attack on the Centre. There was time to do this because when the staff withdrew from the landings, the disruptive inmates turned their attention first of all to breaking into and ransacking the canteen. If these inmates had immediately attacked the Centre, the outcome could have been very different.

6.45 Although the inmates were throwing objects at staff, the staff did not withdraw. In accordance with the instructions from Mr Winters and Mr Williams, they stayed at the Centre, by the gates on each landing, taking note of what the inmates were doing. The inmates taunted the officers by displaying the keys. They unlocked cells and broke up everything which they could lay their hands on. In addition fires were started. However it was clear that a number of inmates did not want to be involved and were anxious to be released. This could not be achieved straightaway, however, because it involved removing the chains and running the risk of the other inmates rushing the gates. In addition they could not be released until other accommodation had been identified to hold them.

6.46 There were no disturbances in the other wings, although the inmates must have been aware from the noise of what was happening in A Wing.

6.47 Mr Winters was concerned that there was no C&R equipment available because it had been taken away the previous evening. However, as soon as the trouble started at Cardiff, SWRO directed staff en route to Dartmoor to Cardiff. They also arranged for a number of establishments, including Bristol and Swansea, to send C&R equipped officers to Cardiff.

6.48 The problem of finding space for the surrendering A Wing prisoners was met by moving out all the young inmates from D Wing. This left D Wing empty for the A Wing prisoners. SWRO arranged for the young D Wing inmates to be moved to other establishments.

6.49 While the staff were waiting for these arrangements to be made, an inmate returned the keys to a member of staff. Subsequently some of the inmates broke into cell number A3/36, which was being refurbished. Principal Officer Williams observed them removing an electric drill and an extension cable, which they carried to the roof access area in A Wing. When Governor Winters was informed of this, he instructed the electric power to be turned off by the Works Department. This was done in time to prevent the inmates using the drill to obtain access to the roof.

6.50 Prisoners then began removing sections of metal railing and the vertical support bars on the A4 landing. These objects were used in an attempt by the prisoners to smash their way through the roof access. (The roof access is reached by one of the short open stairways situated on each side of A4 landing. There are iron gates at the top of the stairways. They have ordinary single locks and are secured also by a padlock and chain. These gates give access to a landing underneath a steel trap door in the roof.)

6.51 In addition to using the vertical support bars from the railings, the inmates also obtained acrow-props from cell A3/36, which had been used in connection with the refurbishment. Fortunately, even using these weapons, the inmates were unable to penetrate the trap door.

Extinguishing Fires

6.52 At one stage the prisoners who were rioting began to fear for their own safety because of the fires which had been lit. They asked that the water should be turned on again in order to fight them. This was agreed, on the understanding that the water would not be used against members of the staff or the fire brigade. A fire was then extinguished by the prisoners. The water was then turned off again.

6.53 Most of the fires, however, were dealt with by the County of South Glamorgan Fire and Rescue Service. They had been informed of the disturbance at 09.15 on 8 April. Two appliances attended the scene and were initially stationed within the sterile area (ie the area between the outer and inner walls of the prison). Within a short time of their arrival the senior operational officer, Mr David Martin, took command.

6.54 Mr Martin saw that there was already smoke, some black, issuing from six cell windows. He therefore readied one appliance by attaching it to a hydrant. At that stage it was impossible to approach the wing because inmates were throwing missiles from the cells. As the fire was getting worse, Mr Martin decided that an attempt to fight the fire had to be made if the deaths of prisoners were to be avoided. He therefore tried to make contact with the prisoners. He spoke to a prisoner who appeared to be a spokesman of the inmates and explained the danger. As a result the prisoner agreed that the attacks on fire fighters would cease in return for a number of assurances, which Mr Martin gave. These assurances were that the only function of the fire service was to protect lives; that the fire service formed no part of the operations of the prison or police services; that the fire service would not use or allow its equipment to be used against prisoners; and that anyone in fire-fighting uniform would be a bona fide fire-fighter.

6.55 A crew under the direction of Assistant Divisional Officer Carder, accompanied by a number of prison officers, then began to tackle the fires from outside the building through cell windows. The barrage of missiles was much reduced. Such missiles as were thrown were directed at prison staff. Mr Martin therefore asked the prison officers to withdraw. The throwing of missiles then virtually ceased.

6.56 The fires were brought under control and Mr Martin returned to the Centre. From then on he played an observer's role until A Wing was cleared.

The Surrender

6.57 By about 11.00, D Wing was ready to receive inmates surrendering from A Wing. Shortly after, the inmates who wished to be evacuated were initially allowed through the gate from A3 onto the Centre. Some rioters tried to prevent this evacuation. They hurled missiles at the gate way and threatened staff with spears from behind nearby lockers. However by this time (11.16) prisoners on A2 landing also wanted to be allowed out. They prevailed upon the other inmates not to interfere with the evacuation. Inmates were then also let out onto the Centre from the A2 landing in groups of about ten at a time.

6.58 Once the evacuation was under way, other inmates decided to give up, and eventually there was a mass surrender.

6.59 By this time C&R teams and equipment had arrived at the prison. However the surrender was handled without the need to use C&R equipped staff or C&R techniques. At 11.40 there were approximately 28 inmates left in the wing. By 11.50 the last inmates were ready to surrender. By 12.10 the wing was finally cleared. Police investigations commenced at about 13.45.

6.60 For a part of the time during the incident, the kitchen was evacuated and secured. Later, as the situation was being resolved, the catering staff returned to the kitchen and, without employing any inmates, ensured that every prisoner was properly fed throughout the day.

6.61 The C&R staff who had been sent to reinforce the Cardiff staff, were used to escort to other establishments some of the Cardiff prisoners who had surrendered. Later in the day, some of the inmates who had been moved to police cells were returned to the prison.

The Role of Headquarters and the South West Regional Office

6.62 The Deputy Director General, Mr Emes, clearly considered it was important that this incident should be speedily concluded. He had been kept informed of progress by the Director of the South West Region, Mr Ian Dunbar. Mr Dunbar had a telephone conversation with Mr Emes during which Mr Emes stressed the need for a victory. Mr Emes emphasised that, as the prisoners had not obtained access to the roof, it should be possible to enter the wing and push the inmates out.

6.63 Mr Emes' desire that the incident should be speedily resolved was understandable bearing in mind the other incidents with which the Prison Service had to deal and that the Strangeways disturbance was still in progress.

The previous day (7 April) the disturbances at Glen Parva and, apart from one prisoner, at Dartmoor had been resolved. The same day there had also been an attempted escape by inmates at Bristol, and two inmates had spent the day on the roof of Stafford prison. Through the night an escape attempt had been thwarted by staff at Canterbury prison; and there was a probable suicide at Highpoint prison. While the Cardiff disturbance was going on there was a demonstration at Leeds prison and a minor disturbance at Brixton prison, during which two staff were injured.

6.64   Cardiff was given all the support it needed by Headquarters and SWRO. In the event, the prison's own staff, with the help of the emergency services, were able to do almost all that was necessary.

Command of the Incident

6.65   Mr Rawson, the Governor of Cardiff, had set up his command post at the commencement of the incident. The actual handling of the incident, however, was left in Mr Winters' hands. Mr Rawson played an overall co-ordinating role. Mr Rawson was responsible also for dealing with the media. At one time it was hoped that the media might be encouraged to play down the Cardiff incident. This was found to be impractical. At the instigation of the Deputy Director General and the Regional Office, Mr Rawson gave a briefing about the riot to the media shortly after the incident was concluded.

6.66   The Chairman of the Board of Visitors was only contacted at a very late stage, and the Vice-Chairman was not spoken to until 12.30. The Governor accepts that if in future there should be a disturbance of this scale, arrangements will have to be made for promptly contacting the Board of Visitors.

The Involvement of the South Wales Police

6.67   During the incident the South Wales police were in attendance and had implemented their contingency plan. The prison wall was guarded by 28 officers, supplemented by two dog handlers and a traffic motorcyclist. An incident room was established at the central police station. The divisional police liaison officer was in the prison throughout the disturbance.

6.68   After the incident was over, the police conducted an investigation and, as a result, charges were brought against certain inmates.

6.69   The Chief Constable of the South Wales Constabulary provided valuable background information to the inquiry.

The Involvement of the Ambulance Services

6.70   The ambulance services attended the incident but, because of the way in which it was resolved, they were not required to play an active role.

Inmates' Evidence

6.71   I have already referred to some of the views of inmates. The following additional points were made by inmates who gave evidence.

6.72   The mock fight had been arranged as a signal for the commencement of the disturbance. The witness who gave this evidence, however, made a conflicting statement in a letter addressed to the inquiry. He explained this by saying that this was all part of a collective response to the letter from the inquiry and that he had not been able in the letter to tell the truth because of inmate pressure. His evidence as to this was not convincing.

6.73   Another inmate who was on A2 landing, stated that the first he was aware of a possible riot was approximately half an hour before it started. He understood it was connected with a rumour about the proposed arrival at Cardiff of 50 more Strangeways prisoners. It was feared that this would make the already overcrowded conditions worse and adversely affect the period the inmates were allowed for visits. He understood that initially the disturbance was only to take the form of a protest, but the idea changed because of the presence of officers on the landing who were not the regulars. He said that if the regular officers had been on duty they would not have been attacked. If there had been any such attempt, the other prisoners would have stopped it.

The Consequences of the Disturbance

6.74   Five staff and one inmate were injured. Officer Hutton had injuries to his neck, throat, elbow and left leg and other minor injuries. Officer Davies was cut on his head; Officer Latham was cut and had bruising to his upper back; Senior Officer Northey was cut and bruised; and Officer Martin was also cut. One inmate received hospital treatment for a broken ankle.

6.75   The damage caused included the destruction of the recesses and their fittings, 27 cells doors ripped off their hinges, and five cell fires. The costs of the repairs were approximately £30,000.

6.76   By the time A Wing was ready for reoccupation, Pucklechurch had been badly damaged and so the Pucklechurch inmates together with the appropriate staff were transferred to Cardiff.

6.77   As a result of the disturbance the staff lost confidence in their ability to maintain control. They were therefore reluctant to restore the relaxed regime which had previously existed. By the time of the hearing on 12/13 July at Taunton, however, the position had considerably improved.

Conclusions Specific to the Cardiff Disturbance

6.78   These conclusions and comments must be read together with Section 9 of the Report which deals with the lessons to be learnt from all the disturbances.

1.   Prior to the disturbance, the striking feature of Cardiff prison was the relaxed atmosphere and the comparatively satisfactory relations between staff and inmates. But conditions at Cardiff were far from ideal with slopping out and gross overcrowding (A Wing had a CNA 115 and a population of 203 prisoners). The influx of Manchester prisoners had had an adverse affect on the regime. But they had been wisely split up, had integrated well and the general approach of the Governor, the staff and the Board of Visitors appears to have been very satisfactory.

2.   The evidence as a whole suggests that the disturbances at other establishments may have affected the attitude of inmates at Cardiff. The presence of the Manchester inmates probably had no direct connection with the start of the disturbance. At most, the arrival of the Manchester prisoners provided some credibility for the rumour, which was entirely without foundation, that additional Strangeways' inmates were about to arrive.

3.   The inmate from Bristol may well have been very much involved. The question therefore arises as to whether more care should have been taken with his placement and his handling. However, while he might have been treated differently, I do not criticise Cardiff for the action which was taken. The inmate was transferred from Bristol without any finding of misconduct having been made against him and the information given by Bristol was not in terms which would cause anxiety. The person with whom he shared a

cell had a reputation of being unstable, but nothing was known which suggested the two inmates would be an especially inflammable combination. Cardiff prison staff should, however, have been provided with fuller information by the Bristol prison staff about the reasons for transferring the Bristol prisoner. That information should not and need not have been used unfairly at Cardiff prison to label that prisoner as a troublemaker or to deny him the opportunity to earn a better reputation. But without such information, the receiving prison cannot make informed judgements. The wider aspects of this are discussed more fully in Sections 9 and 12.

4.   The preponderance of the evidence strongly suggests that some inmates planned to have a disturbance on A Wing on 8 April. Whether the initial fight was part of that plan is very questionable. The two inmates who were actually involved were interviewed on behalf of the inquiry. They denied this was the case and suggested it was a genuine dispute. What could well have happened was that the struggle between the two inmates resulted in an over-reaction by staff, who were naturally tense that morning. This resulted in staff misinterpreting the situation and in one officer over-reacting. However Principal Officer Williams handled the situation admirably. If it had not been for the fact that the wing was in an unusually unsettled state, he would probably have defused the situation. However, an inmate's action in throwing a dustbin, and that of his cell-mate in throwing a bucket of tea along the landing, defeated Mr Williams' efforts. These actions provided the spark which caused the disturbance to flare up in earnest.

5.   The staff were right to withdraw to the Centre. Fortunately, having done so, instead of abandoning the Centre (as happened at Strangeways) they stayed at the Centre under the command of Mr Winters and Principal Officer Williams. This contributed to the incident being brought to an end reasonably rapidly. Governor Winters and Principal Officer Williams are to be commended for their actions. The rapid chaining and padlocking of the gates at the Centre was important since this prevented the inmates having access to the Centre. Considerable damage was done to A Wing. But the scale of the damage was nothing like that which would have occurred if the incident had spread to other parts of the prison or onto the roofs of the wings. Although chains and padlocks provided the security which was needed, what happened still underlines the need for there to be separate locks on to a Centre from the wings, which cannot be opened by keys which can be obtained from staff on the landings.

6.   There was also a problem in relation to keys. Although the scale of the incident was limited, it would have been even more limited if the inmate with the keys had not been able to use them to let out other inmates in the wing. Although cell doors could be and were removed, if inmates had not had access to keys, the scale would have been smaller and the incident probably would have ended even quicker. This raises the question as to the extent to which all the cells in a large wing should be capable of being unlocked by the same key. This subject will be dealt with in more detail in Section 11 of the Report. The method of attaching keys to officers' clothing needs to be reviewed.

7.   A further difference between Cardiff and the riots at some other establishments is that a larger proportion of the prisoners did not wish to be involved. This reluctance to get involved could have been influenced by the fact that inmates could be observed at all times by the staff who had not left the Centre. It was likely also to have been influenced by the generally good relations between staff and inmates (there were of course exceptions). This enabled staff to influence inmates to surrender quickly. Once a substantial number of prisoners started surrendering, then other inmates joined them.

8.   The Fire Service played a significant role in keeping the consequences of

the disturbance within limits. The fires were kept under control and there was no injury or loss of life due to fire. The incident indicates that there are times when direct negotiations by a Chief Fire Officer can be more effective than negotiations by the Prison Service in obtaining the cooperation of the inmates with fighting fires. Mr Martin is to be commended for his role.

9. Works tools should not have been left in a cell. As at other establishments, this was shown to be a security weakness. The use of the acrow-props in the work was understandable, but a drill should not need to be left in a cell. But for the power being cut off promptly, the drill could have changed the course of the incident by assisting the prisoners to get on to the roof. It should be normal routine to remove from a wing all removable works equipment at the end of the day's work.

10. The arrangements for accommodating the Rule 43 inmates in A Wing was not satisfactory. Fortunately, however, their evacuation to a place of safety was promptly carried out and the Rule 43's do not seem to have been an immediate target.

11. The Board of Visitors should have been notified earlier. Their contribution was still significant in helping the prison to return to normality.

12. The procedure for collating security information was unsatisfactory. Prison Officer Megan Jones' warning was of great importance. It should have been conveyed to the Governor in charge the same evening she received it and before she went off duty. An SIR should have been used. This should have been the required procedure and should have been made clear to Mrs Jones. However this failure of communication probably did not affect the outcome.

13. The fact that the disturbance started among remand prisoners underlines the need to improve their regime. The delay before their cases are heard and their feeling that they had been unnecessarily remanded in custody may add to their sense of frustration.

14. At Cardiff, as at the other establishments, there is a real problem with regard to the exchange of kit. Some method has to be devised to meet this problem.

15. The extent of staff sickness at Cardiff (more than double the notional allowance under the staff attendance system) caused considerable problems for management in maintaining a consistent regime. The age profile of the Cardiff staff and of the staff at other Welsh establishment's should be examined. The examination should consider whether there is not at Welsh establishments an undue number of older staff (many transferred at their own request to a Welsh establishment) more prone to illness than is desirable. Where an establishment has a high sickness level, this must be taken into account in assessing its staffing needs, subject to the establishment doing everything it can to reduce the levels of sickness.

16. As in other establishments, the external commitments of the prison affected its ability to provide a consistent programme of activities.

17. The confusion in relation to the transfer of C&R equipment did not affect the outcome of the disturbance.

18. The contingency plans should have been more up to date, better practised and more generally understood.

19. The Communications Room was ill-equipped and under-manned. In particular, there should have been a dedicated telephone link to police headquarters. The single communications officer should not have been left

without support for the first 30 minutes of the incident.

20. The local incident command and communications structure should now be reviewed with particular attention being given to the location, organisation and manning of the incident command post.

21. The staff's morale was badly affected by the disturbance. There needs to be a greater follow up in staff and family care after an incident of this seriousness.

22. The works staff provided valuable support to the discipline staff during the disturbance, for example they very quickly provided the chain and padlocks to protect the centre and they controlled the services. Other non-discipline staff also made an important contribution.

Section 7

Bristol Prison

Introduction

7.1   The riot at Bristol prison started on Sunday 8 April 1990. It was a week after the start of the disturbance at Strangeways and later on the same day as the riot at Cardiff. The events at Bristol followed closely on the eruption of trouble at Dartmoor the previous day and the transfer of prisoners from Dartmoor to Bristol the previous night.

7.2   Like Manchester and Cardiff prisons, Bristol is a local prison. It was opened in 1882 and is situated in the densely populated suburb of Horfield, by which name it is also known. Horfield is two miles north of Bristol City Centre. The prison serves courts in Avon, Somerset and Wiltshire. It has a vulnerable prisoners unit (VPU) and one of its wings is used for prisoners serving life sentences.

The Prison

7.3   The original buildings of the prison are primarily constructed out of red brick. The prison has a reasonably imposing facade including a campanile or clock tower. The front of the Chapel forms part of the facade. Running under the chapel is what is known locally as the Governor's passage. A plan of the prison is at Annex 7A. The chapel and passage are shown on the block numbered 25 on the plan. (The numbers which follow are those on the plan.)

7.4   Running behind the chapel (25) to the north west is A Wing (24). A Wing is one of the two wings which date from the opening of the prison. It is of typical gallery construction, with landings going down either side of the wing. There are approximately 23 cells opening on to each landing. Above the fourth landing, just below the pitched roof, there is iron mesh protection similar to that at Strangeways. The mesh prevents access to the roof voids (to which, unlike at Strangeways, prisoners never gained access).

7.5   Linked to the chapel (by E Wing) and to the north-east of it, is D Wing (20). D Wing is the other wing which dates from the opening of the prison. D Wing overlooks residential buildings beyond the perimeter wall. It is connected to E and F Wings (21 and 25).

7.6   B and C Wings (6 and 4) are connected to A Wing by a high level bridge (7). They lie to the north-west of A Wing. They were completed in 1967 and 1976 respectively.

7.7   A new gate house complex (39) has recently been completed. It includes facilities for visits and administration and has an excellent control room.

The Prison Population

7.8   The CNA (certified normal accommodation) of the prison as a whole is 552. On 7 April 1990, the total population was 572. There was, therefore, nothing like the scale of overcrowding which existed at Manchester.

7.9   A Wing contained mainly remand prisoners awaiting trial. There were also some sentenced prisoners, prisoners who had been transferred from other prisons under CI 10/74 because they were control problems and some Rule 43 inmates, who were on remand or not yet allocated to the VPU. Among the inmates in A Wing there were both remand and convicted Category A inmates. B Wing accommodated long term prisoners, including up to 30 "lifers". C Wing was an overflow for A Wing and contained a very similar mix of prisoners. The segregation unit was on E Wing. In addition there was a pre-release employment hostel outside the prison walls.

7.10   The VPU is housed in D and F Wings. Before the arrival of prisoners from Dartmoor on 7 April there were 113 inmates in the VPU.

7.11   During the period leading up to the disturbance at Bristol on 8 April 1990, the number of prisoners in the prison who presented particular security or control problems had increased. Between January and the end of March 1990 there were three category A prisoners. In the days before 8 April 1990, that number had risen to eight (of whom three were located in the hospital). Up to the end of March there had been one prisoner who was regarded as an escape risk; now there were four. There had been three prisoners held on Rule 43 for reasons of good order or discipline (GOAD); now there were five. There were also five prisoners who had been transferred to Bristol under CI 10/74 and who were being held in segregation.

The Atmosphere within the Prison

7.12   There was little to indicate before the end of March 1990 that a major disturbance might occur. There had been some slight increase in disciplinary offences; in January there were 38 cases, in February 37 cases and in March 63 cases. But subsequent analysis shows that, compared to the long term average, the March figure was not unduly high. Neither the numbers nor the nature of the cases gave any indication that serious or widespread disorder was likely.

7.13   There was a roof top incident on 22/23 March 1990 when two remand prisoners gained access to the roof of A Wing. They climbed the scaffolding erected for the repair of the clock tower. The prisoners wanted to attract media attention to their claims that they were innocent of a murder charge. The incident ended without injury or damage. Though there was a superficial similarity to a similar incident which preceded the Strangeways disturbance, the Bristol incident had no direct connection with the disturbance of 8 April.

7.14   There were no significant changes in other possible indicators of tension.

Warnings of the Disturbance

7.15   Rumours of possible trouble were circulating in the prison from the end of March. Towards the end of March the staff received reports of a possible disturbance on A Wing amongst trial and remand prisoners following the cancellation of exercise. As a result of these reports, one prisoner was segregated under Rule 43 GOAD and another was charged under prison rules.

7.16   On 2 April two prisoners on A Wing were identified as possible instigators of disruption. One of them was segregated on the same day on Rule 43 GOAD.

7.17   On 3 April, an anonymous telephone call was made to the gate which said "you're next, arsehole". This was understood to mean that Bristol was to experience a riot like that which had occurred at Strangeways.

7.18   On 4 April, an officer on A Wing submitted a security information report

(SIR) to the effect that a major disturbance would occur in the prison within the next few days. This disturbance had apparently been planned to take place the previous weekend, but it had been prevented by some of the remand prisoners who were awaiting trial. It was understood, however, that the incident had only been postponed not cancelled. This resulted in an investigation being carried out and number 4, the top landing of A Wing, was identified as being the likely centre of the trouble. Action was taken. One of the prisoners identified as being a possible cause of disorder was transferred to Cardiff prison (he was subsequently at the centre of the disturbance there). Another was segregated under Rule 43 GOAD. The following day, 5 April, another prisoner was charged with using threatening language and located in the segregation unit.

7.19   While these incidents indicated an increase of tension, particularly in A Wing, they were not particularly surprising, in view of what was going on in other prisons. The prisoners would have been aware of the Strangeways riot and the other incidents from the vast publicity which they were receiving.

The State of the Prison Prior to 8 April

7.20   The Governor of the prison was Mr Roy Smith. He is a Governor 2. He had arrived at Bristol some nine months before the incident. Bristol was the first local prison of which he had been in charge. He had no experience of commanding a serious incident.

7.21   He regarded the relationship between the various disciplines working within the prison as good. He also regarded the relationship between staff and inmates as good. In his statement he said that "although there were many inmates who spent a lot of time, sometimes in excess of 20 hours, in their cells each day, there were other inmates who were out of their cells for much of the day. There were a number of activities taking place in the prison with opportunities to work but these did not apply to everyone."

7.22   Undoubtedly the staff were playing a constructive role in the prison. They were responsible, for example, for running a highly successful pre-release hostel. But the fact remains that, according to the regime monitoring data, the sentenced inmates in C Wing had only one to two hours out of their cells each day (although the record may have understated the position). By contrast, the prisoners in the VPU were spending the majority of the day with their cells unlocked.

7.23   The escort commitment, as with most local prisons, made it difficult to maintain the programme of regime activities. Mr Smith said there was "not a week which went by without a workshop or activity having to close at some stage".

7.24   Mr Smith pointed out that while Bristol did not have a proper gym, the PE programme was very good. The exercise yard was used. So was the chapel even, for example for bowls. This was an indication of the way the staff made the most of limited facilities to enhance the regime for prisoners.

7.25   When the riot at Strangeways prison commenced on 1 April, Mr Smith considered that the general opinion was that it was unlikely to be repeated at Bristol. The information coming from key figures among the long stay inmates was that there would be no problem there.

7.26   Mr Smith felt, however, that the incident on 22 March had acted as a signal to other inmates that if they managed to obtain access to the roof they would get media coverage. That, of course, is what had happened at Strangeways.

7.27   Mr French, the Governor 4 who was head of custody, confirmed to the Inquiry the general position that, notwithstanding the security information reports (SIRs) which were being received, there were no exceptional indications of tension in the prison prior to Strangeways. During the week leading up to 8 April he recognised, of course, that what was known to be happening at Strangeways was very much in the thoughts of both staff and inmates. However his view was that, while the information which was available required careful consideration, there was nothing which called for exceptional measures.

7.28   Bristol prison had well established lines of command for security matters. Below Mr French was Mr Darch, the Governor 5 who was head of operations. Below him was Mr Knott, a very experienced principal officer. Mr Knott was supported by senior officers. When a SIR was completed, it would be seen by Mr Knott. He would attach to it advice to Mr Darch. Mr French, in his evidence, describes how, because of the events at Strangeways, there was a meeting every morning of principal officers to discuss manning problems. At the end of the meeting there would be a discussion about the situation generally within the prison and the current security information.

7.29   So far as SIRs are concerned, the correct procedure for completing them was routinely followed at Bristol. In respect of the warnings which were received before the disturbance, the SIRs were completed and properly acted upon.

7.30   A Wing was, apparently, always a somewhat volatile wing. The senior probation officer points out that A Wing "is a microcosm of the national prison population......the sentenced - including lifers - recalled lifers and failed parolees, fine defaulters, civil prisoners and those who sought the security of Rule 43," who had not yet been allocated to D Wing. He adds that "within this population there are inmates whose behaviour has caused them to be placed on GOAD and there is always the presence of potential escapers and category A men". From the information he provides, the regime on A Wing and the population contained in A Wing in the first week of April 1990 were very similar to those which existed in April 1986 on D Wing at Bristol when a disturbance occurred which resulted in that wing being devastated.

7.31   The senior probation officer commented (though no evidence was produced to support this) that one effect of sentencing policies and probation service diversion schemes was that there had been an increase, in prisons such as Bristol, in the number of criminally sophisticated inmates, of whom a high proportion were violent offenders.

7.32   The senior probation officer also refers to the fact that a new wing principal officer had only taken up his appointment some two days before the disturbance occurred. He reports that other staff grades had been moved and that there was "a high degree of anxiety at all levels of staff concerning the reduction of working hours in April" in connection with the "Fresh Start" arrangements. He concludes that "this must have communicated to the inmates who considered that their already limited time out of cells might be further limited".

7.33   A probation officer who had worked at the prison for three years up to February 1990 said that she was conscious that the management of the prison was being affected by the lack of experience of the junior governor grades. She suggested that this led to insensitive and inappropriate interactions for both staff and inmates, the undermining of wing management and uniform staff, and faulty decision making. There was also a lack of consistency and clarity in dealing with staff and prisoners.

7.34   So far as A Wing was concerned, she was very conscious of the restricted activities, the lack of association and the constant complaints about the quality of food.

7.35   She also noted that there appeared to be a change in the type of prisoner being allocated to B Wing, with increasingly more violent inmates being accommodated there. She felt that, in consequence, when she left the prison in February 1990, the atmosphere was tense and the level of morale of both staff and inmates was low.

7.36   One of the Rule 43 prisoners on A Wing gave evidence as to the atmosphere in the Wing after the Strangeways disturbances had started. He described the atmosphere as tense. But he added that "a good deal of time there is tension within the prison, sometimes higher and sometimes lower, but that particular week it was much higher. Media coverage and such like, I think, was a contributing factor to it". He went on to say that he felt it was a situation of "the sheep waiting for the shepherd at Horfield". Another inmate, who was also on A Wing, said in evidence; "there was a bit of tension due to the Strangeways riot because it was being televised and on the radio and everything and everyone was getting keyed up because of this". He also referred to activities being cancelled.

7.37   Letters were received from 116 (20%) prisoners who were at Bristol at the start of the disturbance on 8 April. An analysis of the contents of those letters is set out in Annex 2E. The letters confirm the other evidence received by the Inquiry which indicates that, until after the arrival of the Dartmoor prisoners, while it was possible that there could still be a disturbance, this was thought by the prisoners to be unlikely.

7.38   Despite this, staff in their evidence referred to the presence among the prisoners of a more disruptive element than was formerly the case. They believed there were more prisoners who, if the situation were not to their liking, would threaten to "smash up".

7.39   Mr Marshall, a prison officer who had spent most of the last five years working on A Wing, gave evidence that he had not noticed any special increase in tension during the first week of April: "it had gone up and down, which it generally does in A Wing". Mr Marshall's evidence to this effect was particularly valuable because he had been responsible for two of the SIRs which had been filled in, one of which referred to the possibility of the major disturbance which had been postponed.

7.40   The new principal officer who was in charge of A Wing on the weekend when the disturbance occurred was Mr Harris. Although he had been in the prison service for some 19 years he had only been promoted to principal officer on 19 March 1990. During the week before the incident, while he was amazed at the mix of categories on the wing, he was not conscious of any tension and he was impressed by the manner in which the staff carried out their duties.

7.41   There are, therefore, different judgements about the degree of tension arising from relationships and the regime in the prison. The preponderance of the evidence suggests, however, that while there were unsatisfactory aspects of the regime, which gave inmates legitimate grounds for complaint, they were due to external constraints rather than to faults of the local management and staff.

Contingency Planning

7.42   A range of contingency plans had been prepared by the management of the prison to cover different emergencies. The documents were held in the control room. The documentation was well presented and up-to-date. They included a range of photographs and drawings of different parts of the prison. The plans did not, however, stress the importance of trying to localise any serious disturbance.

7.43   The prison also had a collator of security information. For this purpose a card index system was in use which showed at a glance important information about every prisoner. This card would accompany the prisoner when he left the prison.

7.44   128 members of staff had received C&R1 training and 44 had been trained up to C&R3. Only two governors, grade 5, were fully C&R trained – and their training did not include training for command above unit level.

7.45   The prison held 25 sets of the out-of-date MUFTI equipment, but only 12 sets of C&R equipment. (Since the disturbance each trained uniformed member of staff has been issued with his own set of C&R equipment.)

7.46   Relationships and liaison between the prison and the police, fire, and ambulance services were excellent. The police visited the prison each day and a Detective Sergeant is a standing member of the Prison Security Committee. Two major fire exercises are conducted annually and monthly evacuation exercises have been arranged. Six months prior to the disturbance, an exercise had been held to practice the complete evacuation of A Wing. The local fire service had made visits to familiarise themselves with the prison early in 1990. In addition, ambulance crews visit the prison regularly and have some idea of the layout of the buildings. During the incident there was excellent co-operation between the prison and the emergency services.

7.47   As in other prisons, it is not possible at Bristol to control all the utilities from a central point. For water and electricity there are a number of stop-cocks and switch rooms in different locations. The control point for switching off high pressure gas is in the boiler room, which during the disturbance was under attack. (To overcome this the Gas Board had to excavate outside the perimeter of the prison to cut off the supply. The gas supplied to the kitchen could, however, be cut off without this problem.)

The Dartmoor Prisoners

7.48   When the Dartmoor incident occurred on Saturday 7 April, Governor 4 Mr French was in charge of the prison in the absence of the governing Governor Mr Smith, who was at his home in Yorkshire that weekend. At about 18.00 Mr French received a message at home about the need to transfer prisoners from Dartmoor to other prisons in the region. He understood that Bristol would receive up to 40 prisoners. He therefore rang the prison. He spoke to the orderly officer and made the necessary arrangements for the Dartmoor inmates to be received and fed. Mr French then returned to the prison.

7.49   Mr French also warned the police that the Dartmoor prisoners would be coming. In the event, it was fortunate that the police arranged for some 30 police officers to be stationed outside the prison for the prisoners' arrival.

7.50   The impression that Mr French had been given was that the prisoners who were coming had not been involved in the disturbance in Dartmoor. In fact they were the prisoners who had been transferred from C Wing to the Old Chapel at Dartmoor and who had been involved in the disturbance in the chapel. However, while the Regional Office was at fault in not giving a better briefing to Bristol as to the background of the inmates coming from Dartmoor, this did not affect the way they were dealt with once they arrived at Bristol.

7.51   The two coaches containing the Dartmoor prisoners arrived just before midnight. Many of the windows of the coaches were broken. A window in one of the coaches was probably broken by stones thrown at it when it was passing through Bristol. But there is no doubt that it was the Dartmoor prisoners who broke the majority of the windows in the coaches. On arrival at the prison, the coaches were surrounded by the police and escorted into the prison. The prisoners from one coach were taken to A Wing. (The space for them in A Wing had been found by transferring the Rule 43 prisoners from A Wing to D Wing.) The second coach proceeded to Gloucester prison.

7.52   The Dartmoor prisoners were understandably concerned that their families and relatives should be notified of their transfer from Dartmoor. However, it was not until the afternoon of the following day that those who wished to do so were permitted to telephone relatives about their transfer. This gave rise to resentment. The prisoners were unaware that the probation service in Dartmoor had been informing relatives of their transfer.

7.53   Governor French remained on duty throughout that night. He used the time to revise the next morning's routine for exercise and chapel. A Wing convicted and remand inmates were exercised separately. Special arrangements were made for exercise on other wings and for chapel. A C&R unit with a principal officer in charge was placed on stand-by and an extra three governor grades were brought in for duty.

Sunday 8 April: the Morning and Afternoon

7.54   When staff came on duty at 07.30 on Sunday 8 April, Mr French briefed them about the situation and the new routines. Staff were redeployed to cover for the people who were to make up the C&R unit.

7.55   Mr French, was approached by the Regional Office to provide staff to assist in the handling of the Dartmoor disturbance. Mr French made it clear that he was not in a position to do so. However, he later complied with a request to send one senior officer and six officers to help at Cardiff.

7.56   The morning started quietly and Mr French went off duty, handing over the command of the prison to Mr Day, who is also a governor 4.

7.57   Governor 5, Mr McAllister, was in charge of A Wing. He had arranged for six extra staff to be deployed on A Wing during the day and two extra staff in the evening. Mr McAllister also spoke to the night staff on A Wing before they went off duty. They reported that everything was normal at that stage but the staff said that during the night there had been a lot of noise and a few doors had been kicked.

7.58   The principal officer of A Wing then briefed the staff on the wing. His watchword to the staff was that they should be cautious. In Mr McAllister's words "we went cannily". However, when the Dartmoor inmates in particular were unlocked, there was a great deal of tension. The atmosphere "was sullen, a sullen dragging of feet, a few mutters etc".

7.59   At the Roman Catholic service that morning, instead of the usual ten inmates, 26 inmates attended. However the service passed off normally. Because of what had happened at Strangeways, there was naturally particular concern about the service in the Church of England chapel that morning. Arrangements had been made to ensure that there were separate small congregations for the Anglican services. It is significant that when a group of the Dartmoor prisoners entered the chapel and saw that there were only a few prisoners attending and that they were supervised by a considerably increased number of staff, they left the chapel before the service started.

7.60   The signs of tension remained as the day passed. A number of minor confrontations occurred. There was also a scuffle. Mr McAllister, however, regarded the staff on A Wing as working very hard and very skilfully to contain the situation. He said that quite often the staff were having "to stand toe to toe with prisoners". Prisoners did not refuse to go back to their cells when required to do so, but were being very slow about it. They were being very aggressive. Throughout the whole day there was a series of tension filled mini-incidents. The Dartmoor prisoners played a prominent role in this with a lot of shouting, a lot of swearing and a lot of threats.

7.61   At about 16.45, the day staff went off duty and the evening staff took their place. Mr McAllister remained in charge of A Wing under the Governor, Mr Smith. Mr Smith had returned to the prison and had taken over from Mr Day at about 11.30. Governor 5 Mr Darch was in charge of B and C Wings, and Governor 5 Ms Wilks was circulating generally in the prison and reporting to

Governor Smith.

7.62 When Mr Smith had toured the prison during the afternoon, he had found that the Dartmoor prisoners were having their kit changed and all seemed well. The physical education instructors had been supervising five-a-side football on the exercise yard and this was allowed to continue for longer than usual. During the afternoon the Dartmoor prisoners had attended the canteen. They were allowed to make telephone calls, and to write a "free" letter (that is a letter which does not come out of their allowance of letters). Mr McAllister also wisely arranged for them to receive pay, whether or not that was strictly due, so that they could make purchases from the canteen.

7.63 At 17.00, Governor 4 Mr Day went off duty. Governor 5 Ms Wilks then took charge of the control room.

The Evening and Start of the Disturbance

7.64 On the evening of 8 April, there was a total of 46 officers on duty at the prison, compared with 28 on a normal evening. In A Wing there were nine staff on duty. There was Principal Officer Harris (who had specially stayed on duty from the previous shift), one senior officer and seven other officers. The usual staffing level was a senior officer and six other officers.

7.65 Mr McAllister spoke to his staff and to various inmates and then went to his office which adjoined A Wing.

7.66 Just after 18.00, association started on A Wing. The third landing was on association. They had descended to the ground floor where they were watching television. There were about 30 to 35 of them. In accordance with the normal rotation of association, the Dartmoor prisoners on the second landing, were not due for association at that time. They were, however, allowed out of their cells to slop out and to shower. This was conducted under the supervision of Principal Officer Harris. He allowed four cells - that is eight men – to go out at a time.

7.67 At first all appeared to be going well. However, at about 18.15 an inmate from Dartmoor went down and joined those on association. He was ordered back to his cell by Senior Officer Mackrill. There was then an argument in which a Bristol prisoner intervened in support of the staff. The Dartmoor prisoner then left the association area.

7.68 A few minutes later the same prisoner returned to the association area with a washing bowl. He tried to obtain hot water from the urn which is used for the supper time drinks for the wing. Officer Jones told the prisoner that he could not have a bowl of hot water as there would not be enough for supper. The prisoner became abusive and walked along the wing, with Senior Officer Mackrill and Officer Jones in close attendance. Notwithstanding their presence, he filled his bowl with water and, when again challenged by the senior officer, he threw the bowl of water into his face. Mr Mackrill and the inmate then grappled with each other and they both ended up on the floor. A number of other prisoners then joined in. The senior officer was kicked about the head and body. The Dartmoor prisoner was able to get away. The senior officer tried to follow him, but his path was blocked by a number of other inmates.

7.69 Principal Officer Harris, who was in his office, heard the commotion and ran out in time to see an inmate with a broom handle striking Officer Marsh. He immediately pressed the alarm bell for assistance (it does not sound in the wing but in the control room) and then tried to calm down the situation. With the help of an inmate he was temporarily successful. Mr Harris ordered the Dartmoor inmates who were on the second landing to return to their cells. However they would not do so. Mr Harris tried to coax them back to their cells, but they obviously had no intention of going. One inmate then tried to seize Mr Harris' keys.

7.70 One of the extra staff on duty that night was Prison Officer Helmore. He was engaged in supervising the slopping out on the fourth landing. These prisoners were not being as strictly controlled for slopping out as the prisoners on the second landing. About 15 inmates at a time were allowed out. When the trouble started, Mr Helmore and the other officers on the fourth landing locked up their inmates.

7.71 Mr Helmore noticed that Mr Harris was in trouble and went to assist him. He too attempted to persuade the Dartmoor inmates to go back to their cells, but was equally unsuccessful. He was being harassed by prisoners, so he decided that the best thing to do was to make his way down to the ground floor. As Mr Helmore passed an inmate, his key chain was grabbed and ripped from his belt.

7.72 Mr Harris had by now realised that the situation was becoming out of control. He gave the order for the staff to withdraw to the other side of the barrier which divides part of the first landing from the cells and the treatment room. When Mr Harris was behind the barrier, he learnt that Officer Helmore had lost his keys. He learnt too that one member of the staff, Officer Santley, was missing.

7.73 The prisoner who had obtained keys from Officer Helmore was by this time unlocking the other cell doors on the second landing.

7.74 Mr Marsh had also gone to Mr Mackrill's assistance. He had grabbed the inmate by the wrist, but he had lost control of him. He formed the impression that the inmate had greased his wrists so that it was difficult to hold them. Another inmate then struck him with a broom handle and it was probably this attack on him that Mr Harris saw.

7.75 The inmate who struck Mr Marsh had also struck Officer Santley on his arms and legs. Fortunately two inmates, who were prison cleaners, intervened and ushered Officer Santley to safety in a cell. Another inmate had come to the assistance of Woman Officer Flavel and had ushered her clear of the violence.

7.76 When the alarm had been sounded, the control room immediately put into effect its contingency plans and the police and ambulance services were informed. Mr Smith went to the control room to take charge. Off duty staff, including Governor 4 Mr Day and Governor 4 Mr French, were called in. D Wing was double locked.

7.77 The general alarm was heard by Mr McAllister in his office on his radio. He immediately, to use his words, "trotted" to A Wing, where he found "pandemonium". There were inmates on the second landing holding bed ends, wooden table legs and other weapons. Some were hooded. Some were throwing things down to the landing below. The inmates from the third landing (remand prisoners) were still milling around on the first landing watching what was going on and not taking too much of a part in it. Most of the staff were already behind the barrier gate, but one or two members of staff were still making for that gate.

7.78 Mr McAllister contacted control on the radio and told them to get the C&R unit which was on stand-by to the Governor's passage. He told Mr Harris that the staff should come off the wing and that the gate should be locked. He withdrew with the staff through the gate to the Governor's passage. The orderly officer was waiting with the doubles key and he double locked the gate into the wing.

7.79 Mr McAllister was then told that a set of keys had been taken and that Mr Santley was unaccounted for. An immediate attempt to re-enter the wing to rescue Mr Santley was repulsed by a group of prisoners hurling missiles.

7.80 Mr Santley, having been taken into a cell on the ground floor (A1/38), was dressed in prison clothes by the inmates. The window of the cell was broken so that attention could be drawn to where he was.

7.81   Mr McAllister decided that it was not possible to intervene immediately with the single C&R unit that had assembled in the Governor's passage. There were about 60 to 70 inmates actively involved in rioting and that number was growing all the time as more inmates were unlocked. Mr McAllister was aware from his own experience that the Bristol remand inmates who had been on association were themselves quite capable of causing mayhem. He decided that, with the number of inmates actively involved and the possibility of a similar number of inmates joining in, it would not be right to send in one C&R unit of 12 men to face them.

7.82   Mr McAllister then went to B and C Wings and found the inmates locked in their cells. The wings were quiet, apart from the noise of some cell doors being kicked. Mr McAllister decided that, to prevent the disturbance spreading, it was essential to hold the high level bridge between those Wings and A Wing. He therefore deployed the C&R unit on the bridge, having carefully briefed Principal Officer Yeomans who was in charge of the unit. The bridge which provides the link between A, B and C Wings adjoins A Wing at the fourth landing level. There are two sets of doors at the entrance to A Wing: a single door which gives immediate access to A Wing and double doors set back a few yards along the bridge towards C Wing. The other end of the bridge joins a corridor running between B and C Wings at the third level. The corridor and the bridge form a T-shape, with the bridge the body of the T. The bridge, the corridor and both B and C Wings have flat roofs and are not as solidly built as the Victorian A Wing.

The Progress of the Disturbance

7.83   Inmates from A Wing managed to get onto the roof of that wing. They displayed considerable ingenuity and recklessness in doing so. Maintenance work was being carried out in A Wing. Among the cells to which the inmates obtained access was one in which the tools being used for this work were kept. Making use of these tools and parts of the balustrading which they had broken away from the landing, the inmates attacked the three windows in the wall of A Wing adjacent to the chapel. The windows had only cast-iron frames, which are not very robust, but they were protected by seven horizontal security bars which were firmly built in to the brickwork on either side. This challenge to the prisoners was soon overcome. In the case of one window the bars were removed by breaking away the brick work. This is shown in photograph 1 in Annex 7B.

7.84   After removing these bars, the inmates were able to get through that window and drop down some six feet to the flat roof of the passage which runs below the window. From that flat roof, they were able to climb on to the tiled roof of the chapel and to the campanile or clock tower which forms part of the facade of the chapel. The clock tower was scaffolded at that time for repairs. The inmates used the scaffold boards to make a bridge between the roof of A Wing and the roof of the chapel. Once inmates were on the roof of the chapel and A Wing, they were in a commanding position because they were able to throw missiles from the roof to almost every part of the prison. The prison log records that prisoners were breaking out of A Wing on to the chapel roof at 18.57.

7.85   The prisoners also broke through the wall at the other end of A Wing. This required them to break through the 19 inch brick work above the iron gate leading on to the bridge to B and C Wings. The hole is shown in photograph number 2 in Annex 7B. This gave the inmates access to the roof of the bridge.

7.86 Once the inmates had access to the roof of the link bridge, they had a route which enabled them to reach the roofs of B and C Wings from where they could then attack those wings.

7.87   The incident log records that at 18.41 inmates were on the bridge. Although a double lock had not been applied to the bridge gate, access across the roof would any way have allowed them to by-pass the gate. Mr Helmore refers to having seen inmates going through the gates on the fourth landing onto the bridge to B and C Wings and smashing out all the windows of the bridge. He reports that they then returned to A Wing and barricaded the entrance to the bridge.

7.88   The log records that the police arrived at the prison at 19.00. In the first instance, the police presence consisted of a sergeant and ten officers, with a Duty Inspector who was located in the control room. Subsequently, the Deputy Divisional Commander, Superintendent Standen, attended. He eventually deployed 20 officers inside the prison. Their function was to give immediate support to the Prison Service and to protect fire service personnel. The police also provided a quantity of protective clothing and equipment.

7.89   Mr French returned to the prison between 19.00 and 19.15. Thereafter, Mr Smith played a background role as overall commander. Mr French acted as the tactical commander until Mr Wall, the Governor of Leyhill prison, assumed formal command at 00.50 on 9 April.

The Rescue of Prison Officer Santley

7.90   Once the cell which Mr Santley was occupying had been identified, Mr Helmore spoke to him from outside the wing. Plans were then made to release him. It was decided to cut through the bars of the cell window from outside. This was by no means an easy task as the cell floor was about 8 to 12 feet above the outside ground level.

7.91   The first attempt came to an end prematurely because the oxygen bottle ran out before it was possible to cut the double set of bars; the inner being of cast iron and the outer manganese steel. By the time the team returned with fresh supplies of oxy-acetylene, prisoners were already visible outside the building climbing across from the chapel onto the main A Wing roof.

7.92   It was decided to recall the C&R team from the overhead bridge to provide protection while the bars were being removed. Before the C&R team left the bridge, Mr McAllister gave instructions to the Governor 5, Mr Darch, to barricade the gates which gave access from the link bridge to C Wing. Mr McAllister intended to take the same action with regard to B Wing. He did not do so because he found that the gate between B Wing and the bridge had been double locked. Mr McAllister considered this was sufficient as he was aware that the inmates in A Wing had by then barricaded their side of the entrance to the bridge and were therefore unlikely to enter the bridge.

7.93   Mr McAllister then took charge of the attempt to free Mr Santley. This was an extremely perilous exercise.

7.94   In order to cut through the bars a member of the works staff, Mr Wills, had to stand on a table to use the equipment. The team came under heavy bombardment from the roof. Mr McAllister, although C&R3 trained, had no protective clothing. Despite the risk of injury, he directed three further attempts to cut the bars. On one occasion Mr Wills was knocked from under the shields of the C&R unit. The oxy-acetylene torch was extinguished and had to be relit. Then the oxy-acetylene bottles were struck and began to leak, so it was no longer safe to use the equipment. A final attempt was made to break the weakened bars by using a scaffold pole. This failed because the team was driven back by the bombardment from above.

7.95   During the attempts, two officers received severe injuries. Mr Stone, who was without a helmet, was struck on the head from a slate. The other officer, Mr Reid, was injured during the third attempt on the bars, having taken charge of the scaffold pole from Mr Wills. Mr Reid was knocked unconscious and had to be dragged back to safety. For a time he appeared to have stopped breathing and to have swallowed his tongue. Fortunately, although the team was without any medical back-up, they were able to restart his breathing and remove his tongue from his throat. Mr McAllister called for assistance, but when that was not immediately forthcoming, it was decided to take Mr Reid to the gate.

7.96 When the attempts to free Mr Santley from outside had failed, the inmates who had been protecting him decided to try and bring him out of the wing themselves. One of the inmates who gave evidence (Inmate BA) explained how he telephoned control and made the arrangements for the release of Mr Santley. He and other inmates then obtained the keys which the inmates had taken from the prison officers. They used the keys to release Mr Santley. They took him to the gate of the wing. While they were doing this they came under attack from other inmates who were throwing down objects upon them from the third and fourth landings. They were also subject to abuse.

7.97 Mr McAllister, who knew that Mr Santley was to be brought out by the prisoners, took what remained of the C&R team to the Governor's passage entrance to A Wing. That entrance is protected by a wooden door and then a gate. Mr McAllister opened the wooden door into A Wing and saw that there were a number of armed inmates surrounding Mr Santley at the other side of the gate. Mr McAllister had the difficult decision to make as to how to release Mr Santley without giving the inmates an opportunity to escape, if that was their intention. However, with the aid of the orderly officer, Mr Santley and about 16 inmates were released before the gate was slammed closed again and once more doubled locked. The outer wooden door was then locked.

7.98 Fortunately Mr Santley, although extremely shocked, was not otherwise injured. For this he has to thank the commendable and courageous action of the inmates who at some risk to themselves protected him and enabled him to be evacuated. By that time it was 20.27.

7.99 Although a number of injuries were sustained by other members of staff in the attempt to release Mr Santley, it is both fortunate and fortuitous that no member of staff was killed. There were slates, coping stones and blocks of masonry being thrown down upon them. The height from which these missiles were thrown meant they were travelling with considerable velocity. These missiles were still lying on the ground when I inspected the scene on 11 April. They told their own story as to the murderous nature of the attack to which staff were subjected.

7.100 Each member of the staff involved in the attempted release acted with immense courage. Mr McAllister deserves to be singled out for special praise for the admirable manner in which he directed events from the time that the incident started in A Wing until Mr Santley was released.

7.101 It would have been of considerable assistance if water could have been used to protect the staff during the attempt to remove the bars from the cell in which Mr Santley was taking refuge. The Fire Brigade were by then at the prison under the command of Divisional Commander Townley. The severity of the disturbance, however, prevented the fire service personnel entering the secure perimeter. They did, however, lay hose pipes through the main gate into the vehicle compound. In addition four hand held hose lines, two ground monitors and one bi-pod monitor were provided for the use of prison staff. Unfortunately, the water pressure within the prison was inadequate for the water to be used to deter and control the movement of prisoners.

7.102 To overcome this problem the fire service subsequently provided relays from up to half a mile distance from the establishment. The fire service took this action because of Mr Santley's perilous situation and in order to deal with small fires in A Wing. The Chief Fire Officer points out, however, that it might be difficult for the fire service to provide this sort of assistance in the future and that it would be preferable if the prison service had its own equipment and trained personnel. In any event, it is necessary that there should be a considerable improvement in the water supply if, in the future, similar tactics are to be used. The practicality of improving the water supply needs to be investigated.

7.103   With this assistance from the fire service, by the time that Mr Santley was released, hoses were being sprayed on the clock tower and the chapel roof by prison staff. This effectively deterred prisoners from throwing down missiles onto the area around the main door to A Wing. This was of assistance in taking Mr Santley and the prisoners who came out with him to a place of safety.

The Evacuation of B and C Wings

7.104   The staff left B and C Wings while the efforts were being made to release Mr Santley. The Department's statement delivered to the inquiry reports:

> "At 20.08 it became necessary for staff to leave B and C Wings. Under a noisy and frightening attack B Wing staff using a table as a shield came under fire as they left and again as they neared the reception in front of the chapel. C Wing staff withdrew via the perimeter. However as inmates were on the chapel roof at the clock tower end of the wing, it was difficult for staff to reach the compound near the gate. Inmates were by now on the roof of both B and C Wings. Staff were also evacuated from D wing at 20.11."

7.105   The statement that staff were evacuated from D Wing is inaccurate. Staff remained in charge of D Wing throughout. It is also questionable whether or not it was "necessary for staff to leave B and C Wings".

7.106   Although Mr McAllister recollects speaking to the governor in command of C Wing about erecting a barricade to prevent prisoners coming from the bridge into C Wing, nothing appears to have been done about it. As Mr French pointed out in his evidence, this could have been because the door to the bridge opened outwards and so would be difficult to barricade.

7.107   Inmates did not, however, enter C Wing from the bridge, but from the roof of the link between B and C Wings having come across from A Wing on top of the bridge. The way that entrance was obtained is shown in photograph 3 in Annex 7B. That photograph shows that part of the brickwork has been broken away. The brickwork was 11 inches thick and would not have provided the same impediment as the brickwork in A Wing.

7.108   The inmates were probably able to enter B Wing by breaking open the trap door in the roof of the wing. Governor 4, Mr Day, who is the head of works services, regarded the trap door as being of quite sound construction. There was a gate and a door which appeared to have been forced from above.

7.109   At some stage after Mr McAllister had taken the C&R team from the bridge, Mr Darch left C Wing. Mr Everleigh who was normally responsible for E Wing was then the senior officer in charge of C Wing. He had with him in C Wing six other officers and about 170 inmates.

7.110   At the time the alarm went up on A Wing, some of the inmates on C Wing were on association and some were bathing. Association was brought to an end early on instructions from the control room and the inmates were all successfully returned to their cells.

7.111   The staff on C Wing could see what was happening in A Wing and the damage that the inmates were doing. They also could see inmates coming across to C Wing and they could hear a lot of banging from upstairs. Mr Everleigh thought inmates had entered C Wing. He therefore, without contacting control or seeking assistance, told the staff to evacuate. It is not by any means clear that inmates had in fact by then obtained the access which is shown in Annex 7B, photograph number 3. The probabilities are that they had not. The inmates on C Wing were no doubt making a considerable noise and the whole situation must have been extremely frightening. There was no more than seven staff in C Wing and a very large number of prisoners. Mr Everleigh said it was reported to him that the inmates had in fact entered the wing and so far as Mr Everleigh was concerned that was the deciding factor.

7.112   It was unfortunate that Mr Everleigh did not seek instructions or check to see if inmates had entered the wing before withdrawing the staff. According to the log, at 20.03, and five minutes before the wing was vacated by staff, seven C&R staff are reported as arriving from Pucklechurch and other reinforcements would have arrived shortly thereafter. However Mr Everleigh had received no precise orders as to what to do. He took the action which he thought was appropriate at the time.

7.113   When the C Wing staff withdrew they came under attack with missiles and this was seen by the staff in B Wing. The senior officer in charge of B Wing tried to get through to control on his radio net but was unsuccessful. He told his staff also to evacuate. After the staff had evacuated, they were seen by the orderly officer Mr Dumbrell. He arranged for the gates to B and C Wings to be double locked.

7.114   After the staff withdrew, the inmates in B and C Wings had no difficulty in breaking out of their cells. The 9 inch brickwork was broken away. Considerable damage was done in those wings prior to the end of the disturbance.

Attacks by Inmates

7.115   During the course of the evening, inmates attempted to break in to the hospital. Mr French instructed Mr McAllister to take his C&R unit to the hospital. Mr McAllister deployed eight members of the C&R unit in the hospital to prevent the inmates breaking in there. Mr McAllister's unit, with Principal Officer Yeomans, had earlier rescued from the hospital an inmate who had suffered a stroke about six months previously and who was very ill. When the unit opened the gate from the passage, they came under a very heavy rain of debris from the skylights above. They located the inmate's cell and found him comatose. The inmate was initially transported in a wheelchair, but subsequently he had to be carried in the midst of the C&R unit under shield cover and evacuated to the compound.

7.116   At about 22.10 Senior Officer Leadbeater and four other officers, who had gone to the main stores in order to look for C&R equipment, were trapped by inmates. Mr McAllister sent two C&R teams, one led by Mr Yeomans, to carry out a rescue. They used their shields to provide protection against the missiles which were being thrown, which included scaffolding poles. The attacks on Mr Yeomans' unit were of such ferocity that the unit's shields were split.

Surrender Arrangements

7.117   During the night further provision was made for the prisoners who were expected to surrender as a result of the attack. 38 of those who had already surrendered were moved to Bridewell Crown Court cells. Forty Rule 43 prisoners were transferred from D Wing to Gloucester. A further 73 Rule 43 prisoners were moved to the visits waiting room. In this way, D Wing was emptied of inmates.

The Role of Headquarters and the South West Regional Office

7.118   South West Regional Office (SWRO) and the Deputy Director General's Office had been informed promptly of the disturbance. Their respective incident command rooms were already open because of the disturbances at other establishments that Sunday. In addition to the problems at Dartmoor and Strangeways, there was the disturbance at Cardiff, the report of a suicide at HMP Highpoint, the report of a demonstration at Leeds and a disturbance at Brixton. In the afternoon there was an attempt by remand prisoners to overwhelm staff at Hull and at 18.50 a disturbance at Stoke Heath.

7.119 By 18.59 Mr Emes (the Deputy Director General) had given permission for the use of water on the roof. He was clearly anxious that the incident should be brought to a speedy conclusion. In a conversation recorded at 19.28 Mr Emes asked for a plan to be drawn up for staff to enter the wing and he suggested tactics which could be adopted for this purpose. The transcript of the call indicates that Mr Emes said: "As soon as he's got the troops I want that place taken". At 18.39 he is recorded as suggesting water should be put on to the bridge to prevent inmates from getting on to other wings. When there is a suggestion at 20.56 that inmates were crossing the bridge, Mr Emes is recorded as indicating they should "get staff in to hold the bridge and push inmates back".

7.120 While considerable interest was being shown by Mr Emes as to what was happening at Bristol, the usual lines of communication and control were maintained. SWRO performed the line management role in relation to the incident and kept Mr Emes informed of what was happening.

7.121 The SWRO was concerned about Mr Smith's qualifications to control the incident. They arranged for the Assistant Regional Director, Mr Dixon, to be sent to Bristol to support Mr Smith and for Mr Wall later to replace Mr Smith as the governor in overall charge of the incident at the prison. In the meantime, Mr French remained in tactical command of the incident.

7.122 As a result of instructions which had been received from Mr Emes, Mr Hunter of the Regional Office, spoke to Mr Smith at Bristol at 21.05 about a possible intervention. He was told that a plan was being drawn up to re-enter the prison using about 100 C&R officers, with the movement of inmates on the roof being restricted with water. This plan had been devised by Mr French. At that time the plan was to try and retake the prison at 22.00. Mr Hunter wanted to bring the time of intervention forward but he was told that this was not possible. In the event, the suggested time of 22.00 proved over-optimistic. The attack was delayed until much later, though this delay was in part due to the fact that Mr French had to brief first Mr Dixon and then Mr Wall on the plan when they arrived at the prison.

Mr Wall's Role

7.123 When Mr Wall arrived at the prison at about 21.30, one of his first tasks after he had been told about the situation was to brief the press. He then spent a considerable time with Mr French making himself familiar with the layout of the prison, which he did not know. He also had to be told about the arrangements which had been made and the plan which had been drawn up. Mr Wall, during his period in the service, had had experience of a number of serious disturbances going back to 1972. In general Mr Wall decided that Mr French had done extremely well in preparing his plan. However, Mr Wall decided that there were matters which needed further development and investigation before the plan could be implemented. He regarded intervention of the sort proposed as a highly sophisticated operation which needed a high degree of preparation.

7.124 Mr Benge, the Regional C&R Instructor, also played a significant role in helping to formulate the plan and in the discussions with Mr French, Mr Dixon and Mr Wall. By that stage, he had already assisted at the disturbances at Dartmoor and then Cardiff.

7.125 After he had given his evidence to the Inquiry, Mr Wall provided a list of 20 matters which he regarded as being significant in considering the viability of a plan to retake a prison which was in the hands of inmates. He wished to be satisfied of these matters before he would accept "ownership" of the plan and be ready to implement it. Mr Wall's evidence illustrates the complexity of the planning which should go into a major intervention of the sort which was contemplated at Bristol. Among the complications with which Mr Wall was faced was a lack of information about the situation in the wings which had been taken by the inmates. There was also the problem about where to house inmates once they had surrendered.

7.126   The need to make detailed plans for the intervention meant that Mr Wall was not in a position to telephone the Deputy Director General's office until 03.28. He gave Mr Leonard, in the absence of Mr Emes, his assessment of the prospects of success. At about the same time, 03.30, Mr French described the plan to region.

7.127   Mr Wall spoke on the telephone to Mr Emes at 04.51. Mr Emes gave permission for the plan to be implemented. At one stage during his discussions with headquarters, Mr Wall estimated that the proposed plan had a 90% chance of success with a casualty rate of 5 to 10%. Mr Emes was prepared to accept that. Mr Wall also reported a threat by prisoners to throw bodies off the roof if there was any attempt to retake A Wing.

7.128   The plan which Mr Emes approved was as follows. A police helicopter was to be used as a diversionary tactic (in the event it was not deployed). C&R units were then to enter A Wing. Three units were to go in at 2 levels from the south. Three more units were to go in at one level from the north. A diversionary attack was also to be made at the side of A Wing. It was estimated that, including units held in reserve, about 20 C&R units (approximately 300 staff) would be needed, with 35 police officers on the perimeter and another 40 in support. The proposed timing of the attack (06.10) enabled staff to obtain some rest and also enabled the police to relieve their officers who had been on duty.

7.129   After Mr Wall had taken command of the prison at 00.50, Mr Dixon the Assistant Regional Director left the prison. He had been on duty for almost 26 of the last 36 hours dealing with various disturbances prior to Bristol. The Governor, Mr Smith also left then. He was to return at 10.00 the following morning.

The Retaking of the Prison

7.130   The commanders and their units were fully briefed on the intervention plan and took up their positions. Two sections under Mr McAllister approached A Wing by the Governor's passage. Two more sections under Principal Officer Benge went to the chapel entrance.

7.131   A third section under Mr Sunshine, a Governor 5 from Long Lartin, used a borrowed police vehicle in an attempt to reach an entrance at the other end of the wing. There was some confusion as to what went wrong with this aspect of the attack, but there is no doubt that it came under an onslaught of missiles thrown by inmates. As a result, it was difficult for the occupants to emerge with safety and two officers were injured attempting to do so. It had been intended that the vehicle would unload its occupants under the link bridge. This should have provided cover for the staff. Perhaps the vehicle went to the wrong entrance, or the officers may have left the vehicle from the wrong door - the side door and not the back door as had been intended. Whatever the cause, the result was that the officers tried to descend from the vehicle in the open without cover. After the two officers were injured it was decided that the unit should withdraw, which it did.

The Surrender

7.132   At this stage, Mr Yeomans and his C&R unit were in the hospital, having been on duty there during the night. During the course of the night, an inmate surrendered to the unit, coming through the hospital roof. He spoke to his "mates" in A Wing and assured them that they were not going to be ill-treated if they gave themselves up. This led to some 100 others coming across the roof. Thereafter a dialogue continued between A Wing officers who were members of the unit and inmates whom they knew from A Wing. Mr Yeomans formed the impression that more inmates would have come down if the water which had been sprayed on the roof had not frozen, so that it became too dangerous for them to take that route.

7.133   As the night went on, it became apparent that more and more inmates wanted to give themselves up - by 04.30 the number was perhaps 30 to 40; by 05.00 the number was between 70 and 90. It was clear to the members of the unit that the steam had gone out of the inmates; they knew the excitement was over and that they should call it a day. By the time the staff who were to be involved in the attack were assembling in the compound, well over 100 inmates wanted to give themselves up.

7.134   Mr Yeomans was unable to speak to control by his radio because it had been damaged. Instead, he spoke on the telephone. He informed control of the position. The initial reaction of the member of staff to whom he spoke was that this could be merely a ploy to defer the attack. The second telephone call Mr Yeomans made was received with a similar reaction. Mr Burton, the senior officer, then spoke on the telephone to Mr French. He also received a negative response.

7.135   At this time there were still a number of other inmates showing considerable violence. Water was being used to try and drive inmates back from the chapel roof. There were still inmates on the clock tower. There were also inmates on the roofs of B and C Wings. Inmates were throwing missiles from the high level bridge. However, after yet a further telephone call from Mr Yeomans' unit, Mr Wall decided to allow the inmates around the hospital to surrender.

7.136   In the meantime, Mr Yeomans had persuaded the inmates to remove the barricade between the entrance at the A2 landing and the hospital. They were assured that when the gate was opened they would see both Officer Marlow, who had been playing a part in the negotiations, and Mr Yeomans, whom they trusted. The barricades were removed and the inmates were allowed out two at a time. Altogether about 130 to 150 inmates came out in that way.

7.137   Two C&R units subsequently made sweeps through A Wing and at 08.27 the last two inmates were removed from the wing.

7.138   From the description given, it will be apparent that the part played by Mr Yeomans' C&R unit and by Mr Yeomans himself was very significant at different stages of the incident. Each one of them is worthy of considerable praise. Their courage and dedication is exemplified by Mr Yeomans' behaviour. He continued on duty until the incident was, for practical purposes, concluded notwithstanding that in the course of the incident toes on both of his feet had been broken (even though he was wearing boots with steel toe-caps). Mr Yeomans himself in evidence said that he had "never seen such bravery in all my life" as was shown by the members of his unit, everyone of whom had volunteered to try and rescue Mr Santley. It was indeed bravery that was shown by those men that night.

7.139   Once the C&R units had cleared A Wing of inmates, they then turned their attention to B and C Wings. They entered those wings. Again no resistance was shown by the inmates. Both B and C Wings were secure by 10.03. Five prisoners however remained on A and B Wing roofs.

7.140   At approximately 10.00 Mr Wall and Mr French stood down. Mr Rayfield, the Governor of Long Lartin, took over command of the prison.

7.141   The inmates who surrendered from A Wing were, in accordance with the arrangements which had been made, housed in D Wing. They were locked up four to a cell.

7.142   During the time that Mr Rayfield was on duty, there was a further disturbance among the prisoners in D Wing. Some prisoners were throwing missiles from windows and complaining about not receiving food. The delay was caused by difficulties in using the kitchen. Nevertheless, under the supervision of Mr Smith, who had returned to duty at 10.00, all the prisoners had been fed by 14.30. The incident in D Wing was quickly resolved by the deployment of a C&R team.

7.143 It was necessary finally to secure the surrender of the five prisoners on the A and B Wing roofs. At one stage the inmates moved onto the scaffolding around the clock tower, where they could be seen by the media and obviously obtained satisfaction from the publicity. Two specially trained negotiators from Long Lartin and Mr Pepworth, the Chairman of the Bristol Board of Visitors, sought to negotiate their surrender. Before agreeing to surrender they asked for a Doctor to be in attendance when they came down. Two of the five were not prepared to accept the prison medical officer. But they came down when the prison's locum arrived. They had all surrendered by 14.44.

The Board of Visitors

7.144 In addition to assisting with the negotiations, Mr Pepworth, the Chairman of the Board of Visitors, watched the prisoners being medically examined and saw them into their cells. He subsequently made three further visits to ensure that the prisoners whose surrender he had supervised were all right.

7.145 Mr Pepworth had arrived at the prison at 22.30 on 7 April and had witnessed the reception of the Dartmoor group of prisoners. He had left the prison at 01.45 the following morning after he had seen the prisoners settled into A Wing. He then attended at the prison again at 07.30 on 8 April because Mr French had asked that a member of the Board of Visitors should be present. He had seen breakfast being served on A Wing. At 09.15 he had arranged for Mrs Robin Radford, the Deputy Chairman, to take over for the rest of the Sunday.

7.146 After Mr Pepworth had heard of the start of the disturbance on 8 April, he and Mrs Radford returned to the prison at 22.20. They did not leave the prison again until 02.00. Mrs Radford returned at 05.40 on 9 April, and Mr Pepworth came back at 06.20. Both members of the Board were therefore present for extremely long periods at a time. Their active part in the resolution of the dispute was very much appreciated by the prison authorities and deserves to be highly commended.

7.147 Mr Pepworth and Mrs Radford observed no member of the prison staff behaving otherwise than with propriety. It is a satisfying feature of the handling of the disturbance that the inmates did not make any allegations of ill-treatment after the disturbance.

The Consequences of the Disturbance

7.148 Altogether 219 staff from other establishments had taken part in the incident. The staff displayed a high standard of professionalism notwithstanding the ferocity of some of the activities of the inmates who were on the roofs. They behaved as a disciplined force and were well led by Mr French and Mr McAllister and, after he took command, Mr Wall.

7.149 17 members of staff and 12 inmates were injured. By mid-day on 11 April over 300 inmates had been transferred to 13 other establishments.

7.150 In addition to the injuries which staff received, some of their personal effects were damaged. In that connection I trust that their claims for compensation have been handled in a different way from that of Mr McAllister. Because his own C&R equipment was trapped in his office in A Wing, Mr McAllister was wearing a lounge suit throughout the incident which was torn and ruined with water. His watch was also broken and lost and his shoes were ruined. He put their value at £430. He put in a claim and the Department offered £130 in full and final compensation. Not unreasonably, Mr McAllister was so disgusted by this offer that he declined the sum of £130 and told the department not to write to him any more. Those dealing with claims of this sort have a duty to protect public funds. However, the way Mr McAllister's claim was handled disclosed a degree of over-zealousness.

7.151   As an interim measure, staff coming off duty at the end of the incident were handed forms to fill in. This attempt at a de-briefing process was regarded as wholly inappropriate by exhausted members of staff and, although well-intentioned, was not well received. There was also some attempt to get staff together at the time, but they were too tired and were sent home. Officers complained that in some cases they were not de-briefed until six or seven weeks after the incident.

7.152   The principal psychologist responsible for the de-briefing accepts that the attempt at immediate post incident de-briefing was "very unfortunate". This was, however, due to the disorganisation in the holding area and the inadequate time to instruct the staff conducting the de-briefing sessions.

7.153   There were two proper de-briefing sessions arranged for the officers on 23 May 1990 and 5 July 1990. The results of those de-briefings were made available to the Inquiry and were helpful. One matter that comes through clearly is that it is of the utmost importance to keep staff fully informed of the way matters are progressing and to recognise the contribution which they are making. There has to be consideration given to better methods of conveying information. There was also a need to keep a tally of officers engaged in incidents since otherwise it may not be appreciated that a member of staff is missing. More formal arrangements are required to inform families of staff whereabouts and well-being.

7.154   Attention was also drawn to the length of time staff were on duty. With possible travelling time and short breaks or stand-downs, the average period on duty was 28 hours. The time varied from 9 to 56 hours. Twenty-eight hours is too long. When possible, the period on duty should not exceed 12 hours.

7.155   Very extensive damage was done to A Wing. Although the incident lasted nothing like as long, on inspection the condition of A Wing did not materially differ from that of the comparable wings at Strangeways. Some idea of the damage is given by the photographs 4-8 in Annex 7B. It will be observed from photograph 5 that the balustrading at the third level had been removed. It was thought that in addition to the balustrading being removed holes had been created in the landings which would provide traps for incoming members of the C&R teams, but this was not correct.

7.156   A striking feature was that despite the damage which had been done to the lavatory recesses and to other areas, the four cells which had been fitted with the experimental internal sanitation, in stainless steel units, were completely undamaged. As Mr Day said in evidence, it was as though "they, (the inmates) were trying to tell us something".

7.157   As a result of the incident, it would have cost £1 million to reinstate A Wing. However plans have now been made to refurbish A Wing in accordance with current standards and that will cost £3.5 million. Because of the scale of the work which, in any event, would have had to be carried out to A Wing whenever it was refurbished, the actual cost of the refurbishment was not materially affected by the damage. In addition, the refurbishment of B and C Wings will cost about £100,000.

Conclusions Specific to the Bristol Disturbance

7.158   These conclusions and comments must be read together with Section 9 which deals with the general lessons learnt from the April disturbances.

1.   The conditions in A Wing in particular were unacceptable. Some inmates such as those on Rule 43 on the wing, had negligible, if any, association. Many inmates were spending far too long in their cells, which, with four exceptions, were without integral sanitation.

2. As in other local prisons, escort duties had a significant effect on the regime at Bristol. As Mr Smith said in his statement, because of escort commitments there was not a week which went by without a workshop or activity having to close at some stage. The POA was also in dispute over manning levels. However the number of extra staff called in was reasonable in the circumstances.

3. The pattern of events during the week prior to 8 April indicated that the prison was unsettled (as was to be expected with the Strangeways disturbance continuing). However the staff were confident that if it had not been for the influx of the Dartmoor prisoners, there would not have been a serious disturbance. The Dartmoor prisoners were undoubtedly the catalyst which started the disturbance off. Without their presence that weekend could have passed without incident. Once it started, however, the Bristol inmates were all too ready to join in, as is confirmed by what happened not only in A Wing but in B and C Wings as well. Nonetheless, not all prisoners were antagonistic towards staff. There were several examples of inmates going to the assistance of staff. Unfortunately there was a sufficient number of hostile prisoners to turn what could have been a minor incident into a major riot. (The number of those who were hostile was probably affected by the transfer to Bristol of some prisoners who had demonstrated that they were control problems. The policy of transferring such prisoners requires reconsideration and will be reviewed in Part II of this report.)

4. I do not criticise the arrangements which were made for the housing of the Dartmoor prisoners when they arrived at Bristol. It is questionable whether even if they had been dispersed throughout the prison the result would have been any different. Once on A Wing, the staff appeared to have done everything that could be expected of them to contain the inmates peacefully. The fact that they were unaware of the trouble that these inmates had caused in the chapel at Dartmoor is most unlikely to have influenced events. The preparations which had been made against the possibility of a disturbance were appropriate. What happened illustrates the alarming speed with which an apparently stable situation can disintegrate. Even with a C&R unit on stand-by it can be impossible to restore the situation. Mr McAllister's decision not to allow the unit to intervene in A Wing when it arrived on the scene was perfectly proper.

5. The decisions which were made with regard to command of this incident illustrate the fact that not all Governors of prison establishments are going to have the qualities or experience which would make them the ideal commander of a serious disturbance. The Governor of Bristol came in to that category. But he had in Mr French, as his second in command, an energetic and forceful manager who was fully prepared to take control of the incident. The Governor wisely permitted him to do so until such time as more experienced assistance could be provided by the region. The Governor devoted himself with diligence to his chosen role. Mr French had himself been acting Governor until Mr Smith's appointment to Bristol. There is nothing to suggest that the arrangement of having the governing Governor in overall command while Mr French took direct control of the incident and the strategic decisions did not work well.

6. The initial uncertainty in the command arrangements had the consequence, that some time lapsed before Mr French could be fully in control of the situation. It was during this period that the decision was taken to remove the C&R team from the bridge to go to the assistance of Mr Santley. Clearly the rescue of Mr Santley was a matter of great urgency and the C&R team was needed for this purpose. However it should have been possible to have provided more support and direction to the staff in B and C Wings if there had been continuity of command.

7. The decision to evacuate B and C Wings was reasonable at the time it was taken, particularly bearing in mind the difficulty in communications.

However at that time support was already arriving at the prison. More staff might well have been able to have been deployed at B and C Wings if there had been continuity of command. Here the need for contingency planning which stresses the importance of containing a disturbance of this sort to part of a prison is relevant. It is a grave step for all staff to withdraw from a wing when a disturbance is taking place if the inmates are locked in their cells. It would have been preferable for the staff not to have left B and C Wings without first receiving instructions to do so. They should have informed the control room first of what they intended to do.

8. The ability of the prisoners to obtain access to the roofs of the chapel, A Wing and, eventually B and C Wings was again significant in the spread and gravity of the disturbance. Steps need to be taken to prevent a recurrence. It is important not to leave tools in a wing even when they are locked in a cell. As at Pucklechurch and Cardiff, the availability of tools can make what would otherwise be satisfactory protection of, for example, a roof, vulnerable. The speed with which the prisoners were able to remove the protective bars on the window giving access to the chapel roof and to break through the wall at the other end of the wing to gain access to the roof of the bridge, was almost certainly facilitated by the availability of those tools. Having regard to the design of the building, no other aspect of the external physical security of A Wing needs attention.

9. The same problems existed at Bristol as at Strangeways and all other establishments, with regard to keys. The one set of keys enabled prisoners to open all the cells in A Wing. There was also the problem about the size of the wings. In the refurbishment now being planned, it would be preferable if A Wing were divided into two separate self-contained living units. Staff also need to have easy and secure access to the roof zone and upper landings.

10. Neither the roof nor the pedestrian passageway of the bridge linking B and C Wings with A Wing was adequately protected. Particular attention should be paid to this problem and if a satisfactory solution cannot be found consideration should be given to removing the bridge entirely. So far as B and C Wings themselves are concerned, their construction falls short of category B physical security standards and consideration should be given to the appropriateness of their use for housing prisoners who require this level of physical security. If, however, a different method of categorisation to that at present adopted were to be used for remand prisoners (as is proposed in Part II) it may well be that the accommodation could be appropriate to hold those who require a lower standard of security.

11. The roof of A Wing and the chapel should be resurfaced with materials which will not provide such ready ammunition if prisoners again succeed in getting to the roofs.

12. There were episodes during the disturbance, and in particular in the attempt to rescue Mr Santley, when it was extremely fortunate that no member of staff lost his life. The attack by inmates on staff at times are appropriately described as murderous. At an early stage permission was given by the Deputy Regional Director for the use of water, but lack of pressure and difficulties with deploying hoses meant that in critical areas water was not available. In these circumstances the police could have been asked to consider whether they regarded it as appropriate to deploy any more forceful methods of physically intervening which were available to them. Although I certainly do not criticise the brave action which was taken to rescue Mr Santley, I am concerned that no greater protection could be given to the staff than their shields. In my view, in respect of the attacks to which they were subject, the law allows the use of greater force to protect them than was deployed. I recognise that it would have been tragic indeed, as could well have happened, if a life or lives had been lost because more forceful means of protecting staff were not available. What force should be

used would have to be decided in the light of the advice received and resources available, including those which can be made available by the police.

13. The events at Bristol illustrate the importance of the availability of water power which can be deployed by staff without relying on the fire service. Training and equipment must be provided to make this possible.

14. Consideration should be given to providing paramedic support to C&R units.

15. The part played by Mr Wall, and the complex considerations which have to be considered before making a forceful intervention, emphasises the need for governors who are fully trained and equipped to take tactical command in this type of situation. I do not consider that it is realistic to expect every governor of an establishment to be able to take tactical command of a major operation involving the deployment of substantial numbers of staff without appropriate training and experience. Although the Bristol staff and management acquitted themselves extremely well, the additional planning which Mr Wall felt was necessary illustrates the need for deep experience in the handling of this type of situation. With the Governor remaining in overall control, it should be possible to provide a commander of an incident who has the required training and experience at every establishment within a reasonable time scale. This is a matter which is also dealt with in Sections 9 and 12 of this report.

16. The way the inmates were prepared to surrender to their own officers, whom they knew, indicates that on a personal basis relationships between inmates and staff were better than could be expected in the conditions which existed. This reflects well on the professionalism of the staff who had to work in those difficult conditions and contributed to the speed with which the surrender took place.

17. Staff professionalism was also reflected in the way inmates were managed when they surrendered, despite the fact that the staff had been subjected to murderous attacks from the roofs of the prison.

18. There should be structured arrangements for keeping the families informed of their whereabouts and well-being of staff.

19. Where possible staff should not be on duty during a disturbance for longer than 12 hours at a stretch.

Section 8

Pucklechurch Remand Centre

Introduction

8.1   The riot at Pucklechurch Remand Centre took place on 22 and 23 April 1990. It was the last of the serious incidents which were examined by the Inquiry. It began some three weeks after the start of the Strangeways disturbance, a disturbance which was to continue until 25 April. The Pucklechurch disturbance was 13 days after the end of the Bristol riot.

8.2   Pucklechurch is a very different institution from the overcrowded Victorian local prisons at Manchester, Bristol and Cardiff. It held primarily male youths on remand. There were no mature convicted criminals serving long sentences. Unlike the local prisons, Pucklechurch was not used to hold inmates transferred from other establishments because they were control problems. Yet the violence which took place was every bit as bad as that which occurred during the other incidents, if not worse. A substantial proportion of the inmates were actively involved in the disturbance.

The Centre

8.3   The Centre is situated in a rural area approximately 8 miles from Bristol. It was opened in 1967 and built in two phases. The first phase was built in the 60's and the second in the 70's. (A plan of the Centre appears at Annex 8A.)

8.4   Pucklechurch had certified normal accommodation for 103 young males up to the age of 21, awaiting trial or sentence at the Crown Court or remanded for appearance at a Magistrates Court. Its catchment area for young male remands was part of South Wales and all of the South West of England.

8.5   At the time of the disturbance Pucklechurch was overcrowded. It held 124 male inmates. The authorised staffing level for the male part of the Centre was 56 unified grades, of which 55 were in post.

8.6   A few sentenced male inmates were held at Pucklechurch pending their allocation to other establishments and to undertake essential domestic work, such as catering. One of those who was to take a prominent part in the riot was a sentenced young offender who had been transferred to Pucklechurch so that he could be visited by his family.

8.7   There was a separate block of accommodation (marked 12 on the plan). It held 56 adult and young women, both sentenced and on remand. They did not take part in the riot.

8.8   The male accommodation was primarily in three wings, A, B and C ((34), (38) and (40) on the plan). In addition there was a segregation unit – D Wing ((39) on the plan). The wings are connected by a corridor running from A Wing in the East to C Wing in the West. That corridor has been nicknamed the M1 (marked 52 on the plan). Opposite the entrance to B Wing, that corridor forms a junction with another corridor, known to the Inquiry as the M4 (marked 51 on the plan). This leads to the main entrance to the block ((26) on the plan).

The Regime

8.9 As a Remand Centre which served a large area, the escort demands on Pucklechurch were particularly heavy. The unpredictability of the Court commitment made the management of the establishment and, in particular, the maintenance of a full regime, more difficult.

8.10 This was accepted by Mr Hall, the Chairman of the local branch of the Prison Officers' Association (POA). He considered that escort duties should be undertaken by a group of persons who were not fully trained prison officers. If his suggestion were followed, prison officers would have been able to concentrate more on the regime for inmates.

8.11 Mr Woolford drew my attention to Prison Rule 38(2). This allowed inmates to be discharged into police custody for production at Court. He said this Rule was frequently used to good effect. Mr Woolford also drew attention to the fact that, in his experience, Section 130 of the Magistrates Court Act 1980 was never used by Magistrates to refer Pucklechurch inmates to a Court closer to the Centre for subsequent remands. The use of this Section could have alleviated the burden on Pucklechurch.

8.12 There were other problems in providing a regime at Pucklechurch. The Centre had no workshop or vocational training courses. The unsatisfactory explanation for this was that it was a Remand Centre. The only work available was cleaning, kitchen work, assisting the works department in building and general maintenance and gardening.

8.13 Even the amount of gardening work available was less than it should have been. The majority of garden areas were outside the secure fence. It was not possible to employ remands to tend to these areas because they had no graded security categorisation. They were all regarded as requiring the equivalent of closed prison conditions. They could not therefore work outside the secure fence. As a result, prisoners travelled from Leyhill to tend these garden areas. This would not have been necessary if all the inmates had not been regarded as requiring closed conditions. There would have been a number of inmates at Pucklechurch who could have safely worked outside the secure fence.

8.14 Mr Woolford, a Governor 5 and the Head of Custody, told the Inquiry that, in his view, it would be possible to give a provisional categorisation to remand inmates at Pucklechurch. In support of this, he subsequently provided evidence that on four occasions over an eight month period he had carried out a test to find out the extent to which the staff on duty already knew the inmates who were received at Pucklechurch. Out of the average roll of 130, on each occasion between 65 and 85 of the inmates were personally known to the staff from previous periods of remand.

8.15 Mr Woolford considered that, within a short time after a remand hearing, it would be possible for the establishment to collect together the following information about an inmate: the bail certificate giving reasons for the refusal of bail, a social enquiry report, knowledge of the inmate based on a previous remand in custody, a list of previous convictions and a police statement of facts for the current charge.

8.16 This information would considerably assist a process of categorisation. Some such process could be of value since the Inquiry's investigative team reported that in Pucklechurch approximately 50% of those awaiting trial in the Crown Court had to wait more than five months for their cases to be heard. The categorisation of remand prisoners is considered in Section 12 of this Report.

8.17 HM Chief Inspector of Prisons (HMCIP), submitted a report on Pucklechurch in April 1989. It was based on an inspection which took place between 23 January to 26 January 1989. The Report stated:

"It was clear that the education department had not been playing its full part in the programme of inmate activities for some time.....The responsibility for the underuse of education facilities must be shared between the education staff and both local and regional management. The former should have shown more drive and initiative in promoting education, while local management should have provided the management structure which supported education staff and enabled them to produce a fuller programme. This highlighted the need for a Head of Inmate Activities and Services to ensure a balanced programme."

8.18   In June 1989, the prolonged absence of the Education Officer due to sickness led to his deputy being appointed acting Education Officer. She applied herself with energy and enthusiasm to the task of improving the educational programme. Her education staff consisted of three full-time teachers. Two spent almost all their time with the female inmates. The third worked half-time in the local college. There were also 11 part-time teachers who were employed on a sessional basis.

8.19   The male section of the Centre was able to use five classrooms and the library. Each weekday there were ten two-hour classes covering a variety of subjects, including computer training, art, life and social skills, and general educational topics. Young offenders of school age were required to attend educational classes, but for older inmates attendance was voluntary.

8.20   The acting Education Officer had tried to extend the education programme into the evenings. But it had not been possible to secure the agreement and support of the local branch of the Prison Officers' Association for this initiative.

8.21   Staff shortages had led to the frequent cancellation of daytime classes. It was seldom possible to hold more than 85% of the scheduled classes. Matters improved a little when agreement was reached to conduct classes without a discipline officer in attendance. Nevertheless, in the two weeks immediately preceding the riot, hardly any classes had been held.

8.22   The most successful part of the regime was that provided by the physical education staff. There was a well equipped gymnasium. It was staffed by one senior officer Physical Education Instructor (PEI) and one male and two female PEIs. The physical education department's boast was that every remand prisoner was given the opportunity to use the gym every day. Convicted prisoners had two hours compulsory PE each Monday and Friday. In the week, 150 inmates could be accommodated on a series of sessions either during the day or in the evening. Each session lasted one hour. This was clearly a very important feature of life at Pucklechurch. PE allowed the inmates to get out of their cells and have much needed exercise. It also provided them the opportunity to have a shower. A suggestion by one inmate (Inmate PG) that only 12 to 13 remands were allowed to go to the gym each day was not substantiated.

8.23   The general picture which emerges from the evidence, however, is of inmates spending long periods in cells without integral sanitation and in physical conditions which were, according to HMCIP's report, unimpressive. The communal washing, toilet and bathing areas needed refurbishment. Inmates were limited to one shower or bath per week, in addition to the shower after each session of PE. Normally, an exchange of clothing was also provided only once per week.

8.24   The target for the time inmates should spend out of their cells was set out in Pucklechurch's "contract" with the Region. It was 8.25 hours per day. The regime monitoring document showed that only 5.5 hours was being achieved.

8.25   In material provided to the Inquiry after the oral hearings, Mr Woolford showed that additional periods out of cell for activities such as meals, visits and bathing could increase this figure to approximately 8.5

hours. He rightly stated that he took no pride in this. He said that:

> "any out of cell time is unsatisfactory until we reach the point where the cell is reduced to a bedroom facility only and that the way forward for the Service, the inmates and for staff safety lies in high levels of activities coupled with good staff/inmate relationships".

I firmly endorse this view.

8.26 The lack of activity for inmates may be some explanation of the comparatively high adjudication rate at Pucklechurch. In 1989, the average number of offences per head of population in young offenders establishments was 3.5. At Pucklechurch it was 5.2.

The Management at Pucklechurch

8.27 The Governor of Pucklechurch was Mr David Leach. He joined the Prison Service in 1962. He had acquired considerable experience as an Assistant Governor in Borstal institutions and subsequently as the Warden of Blantyre House Detention Centre. He apparently had a good relationship with the staff and inmates generally. He had the strong support of the Chairman and Vice-Chairman of the Board of Visitors. He preferred a non-interventionist, supervisory style of management.

8.28 Mr Leach's head of Custody and the de facto Deputy Governor, was Mr Roy Woolford. Mr Woolford joined the Prison Service as a prison officer in February 1975. He was a most effective Governor 5. He had all the ability, energy and initiative required to perform the role which was delegated to him.

8.29 Although Pucklechurch is a relatively small institution, it had separate POA Committees for the female and male sections of the Centre. The Chairman of the male section was Mr Peter Hall. He had been in the Prison Service for some 15 years. He was at the time of the disturbance an acting senior officer. From the way he gave evidence, I have no doubt that he is a man of considerable ability and drive.

8.30 Mr Hall had constructive views about what should be provided for young inmates on remand. He made it clear in his evidence that he would have liked to have seen a considerable improvement in the regime at Pucklechurch. But he added the important qualification that this would require the additional staff which he considered necessary for his members' safety. In other words, in matters that did not directly affect his position as Chairman of the POA Branch, Mr Hall was liberal and flexible. In matters which affected the Association's interests, he would, where it was necessary, firmly adhere to the Association's policy, notwithstanding the consequences to the inmates.

8.31 Mr Hall's liberal approach to what should be provided for inmates was not shared by all the other staff. The approach of some of the staff was reflected by the remark, said to have been made jokingly by a member of staff, that "happiness is cell door shaped". In other words, this suggested that officers were only happy when inmates were locked into their cells.

8.32 Mr Hall firmly believed that most of the problems at Pucklechurch could be attributed to staff shortages. He claimed that in April 1990 Pucklechurch had one less officer than it had in 1987, when it went into "Fresh Start". The additional staff which it was agreed should be provided as part of the Framework Agreement had never been sent to Pucklechurch. (The Prison Service view was that it was not committed to providing the agreed proportion of replacement staff at each particular establishment, only nationally.)

The Effect of the Bristol Disturbance

8.33   The disruptive influence on Pucklechurch was not so much the continuing disturbance at Strangeways, but the disturbance at Bristol. In the course of his evidence, Mr Woolford vividly described the clamour which went up from the inmates when the news of the Bristol incident was first announced on the radio. Many of the inmates at Pucklechurch came from the same areas and background as the inmates in Bristol. Some would have been related to each other. Mr Woolford was of the opinion that if the inmates had not been confined in their cells when they heard the news on the evening of 8 April, they would have rioted there and then.

8.34   The inmates were subject to a restricted regime immediately after the Bristol disturbance. It involved controlled unlocking and other precautions. Management recognised, however, that it was important to relax the regime as soon as possible. Some degree of normality had been achieved by the weekend of 21 April.

Warnings of a Disturbance

8.35   During the week preceding 22 April, warnings had been received from inmates that there could be a disturbance. An inmate, who at that time was trusted by the management, reported that two named officers would be taken hostage by a group of inmates on A Wing. Neither of those officers was in fact Prison Officer Leary, who was to be the initial victim of the disturbance.

8.36   On Friday evening, 20 April, Senior Officer Gibbs had a conversation with Inmate PF. The inmate asked if there was going to be association that weekend. Mr Gibbs said that he was not sure because "we are short of staff." The inmate responded by saying, "If there isn't, then we are going to go straight through the fence." Mr Gibbs took this threat seriously. He completed a security information report (SIR) which, in accordance with the normal practice at Pucklechurch, was left in the Operations Office. In addition he informed the Principal Officer and Mr Woolford of its contents.

Staff on Duty over the Weekend 21/22 April 1990

8.37   It was decided to make arrangements for additional staff to be on duty over the weekend. This was in response to the information that had been received and because it was accepted that the inmates were unsettled.

8.38   The minimum staffing levels at the weekends were 14 in the morning and afternoon periods and 6 in the evening. This was increased to 18 in the morning, 15 in the afternoon and 8 in the evening. There was therefore on duty on the evening of Sunday 22 April: one gatekeeper; one senior officer (Mr Gibbs); and six other officers. Mr Woolford was the Duty Governor. He was not in the establishment after 17.00, but he was on call.

8.39   Mr Hall, the Chairman of the POA gave evidence that on Friday 20 April there was a request from Regional Office for two Pucklechurch staff to be deployed to the young offender institution at Usk for that weekend. One member of staff was to attend Usk on Saturday 21 April and the other on Sunday 22 April. Mr Hall says that he was concerned about this request. He recalls having a conversation with most of the management grades who were on duty on 20 April, including Mr Leach. He said he was told that it was an instruction from Region and not a request. Accordingly, the officers had to be provided.

8.40   The officers who were sent were, however, two off-duty officers. They received ex gratia payments at the rate of £8 an hour. The request did not, therefore, directly affect the staff on duty at Pucklechurch. Mr Hall suggested, however, that if £8 an hour could be paid for additional officers to be on duty at Usk, a similar payment could have been made for additional officers to be on duty at Pucklechurch.

8.41   Mr Hall said that on the same day, 20 April, when Mr Leach asked him how things were, he replied:

> "I think, sir, I should say, if you are not very careful you could be the next Governor who has no prison left to govern."

Mr Leach has no recollection of this conversation.

8.42   Mr Hall said in his evidence that on the Friday afternoon of 20 April it became apparent to him that the weekend manning was at the minimum staffing level. It was he who approached the Senior Officers (Mr Gibbs and Mr Bracey) and it was then that the arrangements were made for the additional staff to be on duty.

8.43   Mr Hall said that he also checked on what these additional officers would be required to do. He was assured by Mr Gibbs and Mr Bracey and by the Principal Officer, Mr White, that the officers were being:

> "brought on duty purely to bring the manning levels up to what we consider to be a safe manning level in view of the information that we have received from the inmates".

8.44   They were not intending that there should be any association on the Saturday and Sunday evenings. Mr Hall believes Mr Woolford was also present when this conversation took place.

8.45   Mr Woolford was, however, on leave on Friday 20 April and he has no recollection of such a conversation. I accept that Mr Woolford was not a party to this conversation. Mr Woolford pointed out that he would never have agreed to additional staff being brought on duty unless there were association. That was the purpose of having the additional officers. Mr Woolford regarded it as important for the stability of the prison that association should take place.

8.46   Until Sunday evening, 22 April, the weekend was uneventful. Mr Woolford went off duty at 16.00 on the Sunday. Thereafter, Mr Gibbs was the orderly officer in charge. There was a gatekeeper, two officers who were supervising association, three officers on patrol and a dining hall officer. The three patrol officers were involved in slopping out the inmates.

The Disturbance

i) The Attack on Prison Officer Leary

8.47   The dining hall officer was Mr Leary. From 17.30 on 22 April he was involved in a number of different duties. These included arranging for the kitchen staff to have showers and, in accordance with Mr Gibbs' instruction, allowing those on B1 landing to have association on their landing. The cell doors were left open for association, but the landing was secured by locking the gates giving access to it.

8.48   As was the usual practice, Mr Leary went to serve the tea to the inmates who were locked up in A Wing. A Wing has two storeys. He served the inmates on A1 Landing without incident. Mr Leary then started to serve the inmates on A2. A number of those inmates were housed two in a cell.

8.49   The majority of the inmates on A2 had been convicted and were awaiting sentence. (These inmates are uncertain about their future. They therefore tend to present more problems and to be more restless than the unconvicted inmates.) There were also on A2 a minority of sentenced prisoners. As already explained, these prisoners were at Pucklechurch to work in the kitchens or for some special purpose, such as to receive visits nearer to their homes.

8.50   Mr Leary was accompanied by two orderlies selected specifically for this purpose from the inmates who worked in the kitchen. This was the normal practice. While serving the tea, Mr Leary would not have been in sight or hearing of another prison officer.

8.51   Cells 2/1 to 2/6 were served as usual. Then Mr Leary moved to cell 2/7. By now it was approximately 18.35 on 22 April. The flap of that cell was open, indicating that the inmates wanted tea. Mr Leary noticed when he looked through the flap that both inmates were standing up. He assumed that this was because they were waiting to collect the tea.

8.52   As he opened the door, one inmate grabbed Mr Leary's pullover. The other demanded to know what had happened to a telephone call which he had requested. One inmate then put his left arm around Mr Leary's neck and shouted for someone to get Mr Leary's keys. His cell mate tried to do this. Mr Leary shouted to the orderlies to press the alarm. But they did not do so. Mr Leary's keys were secured by a chain to his trouser belt and he tried to hold onto them. However, in the course of the struggle, both he and his assailant ended up on the floor. The inmate shouted at him to give up his keys. Mr Leary then felt a punch on his back and someone trying to pull the keys out of his hand. He then started to lose consciousness.

8.53   The next thing Mr Leary knew was that he was lying in the cell. It was locked. His keys had been taken. He could hear what he described as "euphoria on the landing". He could hear the sound of plates being smashed. He heard inmates egging on other inmates, some of whom were in turn shouting to inmates in B Wing to smash up that wing. His impression was that by that time the majority of inmates on A Wing had been let out of their cells.

8.54   Mr Leary tried to open his cell window, but found that it had been tied up. So he took his truncheon from his pocket and smashed the window. He shouted towards the Central office where he thought Senior Officer Gibbs was located, but he did not get any response.

ii) The Sounding of the Alarm   8.55   At about 18.40 Mr Gibbs, who at that time was in the Centre, heard a cell call bell ring. He was busy with his paperwork. He assumed that one of the patrolling officers would answer it in due course, so he continued with his work. He next heard someone shouting from A Wing. He saw a cell window (which in fact was Mr Leary's cell window) being broken. He thought it was an inmate engaged in "smashing up". He decided to go down and see what was happening.

8.56   As he entered A Wing, Mr Gibbs saw inmates running down the stairs from A2 carrying broom handles and sticks. They surrounded him and told him to get his men and to get out. Mr Gibbs withdrew from the wing and tried to radio for help. However, his radio was dead and he discarded it. He shouted to two officers who had come from C Wing that there was a possible hostage and riot situation. Mr Gibbs then entered the Centre and locked the door behind him.

8.57   Mr Gibbs telephoned Prison Officer Scott at the Gate ((3) on the plan), and repeated what he had told the officers. He asked Mr Scott to phone as many people as he could think of for assistance. He said he would do the same from the Centre. There was a copy of the contingency plans in the Centre. Mr Gibbs started to telephone the numbers listed, which included that of Mr Woolford.

iii) The Association Room   8.58   The association room ((31) on the plan), was opposite the entrance to B Wing. At that time there were 35 inmates from B2 and C1 on association. They had been watching a video and were being supervised by Prison Officers Young and Rogers. Association had proceeded quite normally until the trouble on A Wing. However, when the trouble started on A Wing, another officer (Mr Fleming) entered the association room. He turned off the television and asked the inmates to go back to their cells. They would not do so. Although he does not remember this, Mr Gibbs then entered the association room and told the officers to leave and to lock in the inmates.

8.59   Mr Gibbs then sent two of the staff to see if they could contact Mr Leary. They did so. They managed to release him from his cell and take him to safety. Mr Leary was naturally extremely distressed. When the cell door had first been opened he thought that the inmates were returning and he jumped up to protect himself. However, one of the officers, Mr Fleming, reassured him. After talking to him for a few moments, was able to take him from the cell. The inmates did not try to stop them leaving. Up to this stage the inmates had shown none of the belligerence against staff which was to be a feature of what happened in the later stages of the riot.

iv) Mr Woolford Takes Charge

8.60   By 18.50 Mr Woolford had arrived at the prison. He took charge straight away. His immediate assessment was that it was worthwhile trying to confine the incident to the inmates in A wing. However, if this was to be achieved, it was essential to prevent the inmates who were in the association room from joining the disturbance.

8.61   Mr Woolford therefore went into the association room and took the "temperature". He concluded that the inmates would remain passive.

8.62   The A wing gate to the M1 could not be double locked, but at that stage Mr Woolford believed he would be able to hold the gate with staff who had riot shields. Mr Woolford returned to the operations room and telephoned for riot shields. He also asked the Regional Office for assistance. He then came out of the operations room.

8.63   Mr Woolford's assessment of the inmates on association was promptly proved to be wrong. The inmates on association joined in the disturbance. One of them even made an unsuccessful attempt to throw a fire extinguisher at him through the glass door of the association room. It was also clear that some of the inmates were already out of A Wing. They could well have provoked those on association to join in the disturbance.

v) The Evacuation and Spread of the Incident

8.64   In this new situation, Mr Woolford decided that the eruption could not be contained in A Wing. He evacuated the staff, together with the one inmate who was on Rule 43 and the inmates who were in the hospital. They were housed in the female block.

8.65   The gates which could be double locked were double locked. However the gates between the wings could not be doubled. Nor could the gate which gave the inmates access to the works department buildings ((20) on the plan) adjacent to A Wing. Both gates could be opened by keys in the possession of inmates. The inmates took advantage of this to obtain tools and oxy-acetylene cutting equipment. (The works department from which the tools were obtained was entered through wooden doors which, in any event, would have provided little resistance to a determined attack by inmates.)

8.66   The inmates made full use of the tools they had obtained. They were used to remove a window at the south end of the corridor in A Wing at the A2 level. They were also used to make a hole about a metre square in the north facing corridor wall. (It was an 11 inch cavity brick wall.) This enabled inmates to obtain access to the flat roof above the single storey M1 corridor. Once on the roof of the M1, it was possible for the inmates to get access to the other wings. It also gave them access to the flat roofs in other parts of the male prison, including the dining room, the association area ((42) on the plan), and the hospital ((28) on the plan). In this way they were able to take control of the whole block.

8.67   One of the inmates who gave evidence described how he saw other inmates using the oxy-acetylene equipment. He said that they had no idea how to use it. In view of this, he said, he agreed to use the equipment to stop them using it wrongly and blowing the prison skyhigh. With the equipment, he cut out some of the grills which protected the skylights in the corridors.

Those skylights were placed at regular intervals of about five metres along the length of the corridors. The majority of the skylights were smashed and had their grills removed. This was achieved partly by using the oxy-acetylene equipment and partly by using other tools obtained from the works department.

8.68   There were also holes made in other areas of the flat roofs. This involved breaking through the concrete slabs. They were approximately four inches thick and reinforced by standard steel square mesh. Using the oxy-acetylene equipment, a security window approximately six feet square was also removed to give access to the lawn in front of C Wing.

8.69   The inmates on the roofs used as ammunition slates from the chapel roof, parts of the coping which ran along the front of the roof, and other debris including pieces of porcelain, loose fixtures and fittings and the odd fire extinguisher, which was one of the most deadly missiles. The ammunition was thrown down on prison officers within the block by bombarding them through the skylights and the holes which had been made in the roof. Officers outside who came within range were also bombarded.

8.70   The inmates managed to obtain access to the drug cabinets in the treatment room. But the cabinet did not hold large quantities of drugs. It is unlikely that drugs played much of a part in what was to follow.

vi) The Arrival of Reinforcements   8.71   The staff who had been summoned to the prison started to arrive from about 19.00. By about 19.15 six staff were "kitted up" in C&R equipment. Their first task was to rescue a member of staff from a boiler room. When they had successfully done this, they assisted with the evacuation of the five or six inmates from the hospital. By that time there were about 120 inmates loose in the prison. Many were on the roof throwing missiles.

8.72   By 19.30 about 20 extra staff had arrived. At the same time the police arrived in force. Approximately 70 police officers with dogs secured the perimeter.

8.73   At 19.40 Mr Woolford reported to the South West Regional Office (SWRO). He told them that the perimeter had been secured by the police, that he had lost all male accommodation, and that he was trying to evacuate the 44 female inmates to Bristol where they were to be housed in police cells. His reasons for taking this last action were twofold. First, he wanted to safeguard the female prisoners. Although the double locks should have prevented the male inmates gaining access to the female block, the rioters had access to the yard adjacent to the female cells. The second reason was that Mr Woolford already appreciated that there would have to be some form of secure accommodation available in which to house the rioters when they were taken back into custody.

8.74   The transfer of the female inmates was no easy task. They were naturally reluctant to leave Pucklechurch at short notice (particularly as they were not able to take all their personal effects with them). In addition, the entrance to the female establishment was within range of missiles being thrown by the rioting inmates. The female inmates had to be protected by a canopy of shields provided by the C&R equipped officers.

8.75   The build-up of assistance was slowly continuing. By 19.55, Mr Woolford had about 30 officers under his command to deal with the estimated 120 inmates who were rioting. By 21.00 there were 40 officers. By 21.54, 54 C&R3 trained and fully equipped officers were available for deployment. This was not an unreasonable time scale bearing in mind the disturbance occurred on a Sunday evening.

8.76   At approximately 20.00, Mr Leach arrived at the prison. By that time Mr Woolford was very much in command. Mr Leach wisely decided to leave the control of operations in his capable hands. Mr Leach then took on what he describes as:

"a rather more overall role which had to deal with a number of issues: police, visitors and press".

8.77 This situation continued until Mr Alldridge, who was the governing Governor of Gloucester prison, arrived at Pucklechurch. He relieved Mr Leach shortly after 10.00 the next morning. When he arrived Mr Alldridge was briefed by Mr Leach and Mr Woolford and he decided to leave Mr Woolford in command.

vii) Preparations to Try and Retake the Male Block

8.78 SWRO sent to Pucklechurch Governor 5 Mr Fagg and Principal Officer Benge. They were both C&R instructors. When they arrived, they helped Mr Woolford to devise a plan to enable C&R teams to retake the male block. This was in accordance with instructions which Mr Dixon, the Assistant Regional Director, had given to Mr Woolford at about 20.30. Shortly afterwards, Mr Dixon gave a situation report to Mr Leonard, a member of the Deputy Director General's Office in Headquarters.

8.79 By 21.25 a plan had been devised. Mr Woolford rang SWRO. He reported that all the female prisoners had been evacuated. He described his intervention plan. This involved the use of 120 staff. Three teams, each of two C&R Units, were to be used. Two teams were to enter A Wing, one from the north end, the other from the south end of the wing. The third team was to enter the education block. They were to secure the M4 corridor from the main entrance to where it joined the M1 corridor which linked the wings. Four of the units were to sweep A Wing. They were then to proceed to B and on to C Wing. A follow-up group of 18 staff were to collect and take inmates back into holding cells. Mr Woolford expected that the majority of the inmates would wish to surrender.

8.80 At 22.06 refinements to this plan were discussed by Mr Woolford with Mr Dixon. Mr Dixon accepted the modified plan.

8.81 At 21.45, in order to avoid any prisoners who surrendered damaging furniture in the female establishment, Mr Woolford ordered Senior Officer Bracey to take six staff and strip all the female cells of all moveable furniture, but to leave a mattress in each cell.

8.82 These cells were accordingly stripped. But, contrary to Mr Woolford's instructions, the mattresses were removed as well. It may have been that some of these mattresses had been damaged, but there was no need to remove them all. Arrangements were subsequently made by SWRO to supply additional mattresses and blankets, but these were intended for use by the staff from other establishments and not the inmates. Mattresses were eventually put in to the cells but, not before they had been occupied by the surrendering inmates.

8.83 Initially Mr Sharley, a Principal Officer with the acting rank of Governor 5, performed the task of press liaison officer. However, Mr Cook, the Governor of Eastwood Park was sent to Pucklechurch by Region to take over this role. He did so from about 22.00.

8.84 While preparations were going ahead for the first attempt to retake the establishment, some inmates decided to surrender. By 23.48, 16 had been taken back into custody. Apart from the first few inmates who had been taken into custody very shortly after the incident began, all inmates who surrendered or who were apprehended were removed to the cells by staff using C&R techniques. These involved the inmate being held in wrist locks with one officer at each arm and a third holding the inmate's head. When restrained in this way, an inmate is bent forward. If there is full cooperation it should not be necessary for any pain to be inflicted, but to an onlooker the position appears to be and (as I know from personal experience, having sampled the treatment) is uncomfortable. If an inmate struggles or pressure is applied by those holding him, considerable pain can be caused.

8.85 While the C&R Units were still being assembled for the attack, a serious fire was observed in the Probation Office ((32) on the plan and to the north of A Wing). The Divisional Fire Officer, who was in charge of the Fire Appliances which were in attendance, was Mr David Hutchings. Various hoses had already been set up in front of the male prison blocks. But it became apparent that a main hose was required.

8.86   Accompanied by a C&R Unit, Mr Hutchings connected the main hose to a hydrant in front of A Wing. While he was doing so, he came under attack from inmates on the roof. Slates, bricks and masonry were thrown. Although Mr Hutchings was behind shields carried by prison staff, he was struck a number of times and once in the middle of the back, which caused him considerable pain. Some of the fire officers with him were also struck. Nevertheless, Mr Hutchings continued to set up the hydrant and only retreated when this had been achieved.

8.87   The hydrant was made operational. But, because of the danger to fire officers, no attempt was made to put out the fire in the Probation Office. It was left to burn itself out. The fire fighting equipment was never to be used by fire officers. But it was to be of considerable value when used by prison staff to fight other fires and also to restrict the activities of inmates (particularly those on the flat roofs).

viii) The First Intervention

8.88   SWRO were informed at 00.18, that the intervention was about to begin. It started shortly before 00.30 on 23 April. It was to be the first of two attacks. There is considerable confusion as to precisely what occurred during the two interventions, with conflicting stories by staff and prisoners. The following account sets out what I conclude happened.

8.89   The units seeking to enter A Wing found that access was impossible because of the barricades which had been erected by inmates and because of the fire which was still burning. Similar problems were faced by the units which were seeking to enter the M4 corridor. There were fires and barricades in that area as well, but not, as was suggested by the Prison Service in its written evidence, booby traps.

8.90   Having failed to gain access to A Wing, two units attempted to try and gain access by the south end of C Wing ((40) on the plan). However, a hole had been made in the wall of the corridor adjacent to C Wing through which inmates came out onto the open ground and attacked the units. They threw missiles from short range. At the same time other inmates on the roof of the corridor to C Wing threw missiles in support. An attack in earnest by inmates on a C&R team on open ground was something which had never occurred previously and the team were caught unprepared. It proved possible for the inmates to by-pass the unit's shields and attack the flank of the unit. Principal Officer Lothian, the Acting C&R Section Commander, suffered severe facial injuries and Mr Rogers injured his ankle. Both had to withdraw.

8.91   At 01.00 Mr Woolford reported to SWRO on the lack of progress and on the fact that there was a fire in A Wing. He judged that there was a hardcore of 60 inmates and that the remainder did not want to be involved. Shortly afterwards, because of the lack of progress which the units were able to make, they were ordered to withdraw. They did so at about 01.05.

8.92   Principal Officer Benge, the C&R Instructor who also played a significant role in the disturbances at Dartmoor and Bristol, described the level of violence by inmates at Pucklechurch as being more intense than that offered by the prisoners at either of the other two establishments. It was the most intense that he had ever had to face in a riot situation.

ix) The Lull Before the Second Intervention

8.93   Mr Woolford and his advisers, who were primarily Mr Benge and Mr Fagg, decided that additional C&R Units would be required if a second intervention was going to be more successful. The SWRO log records that at 01.20 on 23 April Mr Woolford asked the SWRO to arrange for a further three units to be made available.

8.94 Over the next four hours, staff who were in a position to do so had a period of rest and recuperation. The staff mess outside the establishment worked to capacity and officers' wives helped in providing sandwiches. During this period every member of the staff had a hot meal, soft drinks and cigarettes if they wanted them. As in other establishments, the staff involved and their families showed remarkable esprit de corps.

8.95 During the lull, more inmates gave themselves up. By 04.30 a total of 24 had surrendered. The inmates who were in A Wing also withdrew, no doubt because of the effects of a fire which was eventually extinguished by prison staff.

8.96 Just before 03.00 an explosion occurred in the male hospital ((28) on the plan). It was thought that a gas cylinder had exploded, but it proved to be the base of a tilley lamp. This caused considerable damage. At the time it was feared that the explosion may have resulted in a fatality, but this was fortunately not the case. After about an hour, the fire was extinguished. By 04.15 other fires which had occurred in different parts of the establishment had been put out.

x) The Second Intervention

8.97 During the night, a new intervention plan was devised, discussed and agreed with SWRO. The intervention was to start at 05.00. It was to involve 11 C&R Units. The first stage was to be an assault by four C&R Units through the main entrance into the M4. At the same time three units would attempt to gain access to A Wing and clear that wing of prisoners. It was then intended that two units from A Wing would proceed along the main M1 corridor to be joined by three units approaching down the M4 corridor from the main entrance. Two units would clear B Wing and three units would go on to take C Wing. Additional units would be used to deploy the hoses. The hoses were to protect the C&R Units entering the buildings by clearing the inmates from the adjacent roofs. Other C&R trained staff, protected by police shields and including women officers and dog units, were to take up position in the grounds in case any inmates should seek to escape.

8.98 In the meantime, the staff had been directing water onto the roofs. At 04.50 an inmate appeared on the roof of A Wing, held by two others, with a knife to his throat. The staff were told to stop using the water or his throat would be slit. The use of water was reduced and the inmates withdrew. It is most unlikely that this was anything more than a charade by the inmates concerned.

8.99 Additional units arrived from Oxford, Campsfield House and Exeter. At 06.00 the attack commenced. By this time it was light.

8.100 The rioting inmates abandoned both the Chapel and A Wing roofs in the face of the barrage of water from the hoses. But the units assaulting the main entrance were in difficulties. There was a substantial barricade and a great deal of smoke in the Reception Area ((27) on the plan). The inmates were still throwing down missiles from the Reception roof, the Hospital roof and the small flat roof above the main entrance. A third hose was deployed by another unit to keep inmates off the roof. Two reserve C&R Units were sent in to reinforce the attack on the main entrance.

8.101 By 07.00 units attacking A Wing had cleared that wing. By 07.15 the five units attacking the main entrance were inside the Reception Area. Both arms of the assault then proceeded to take B Wing, though difficulty was experienced on the second floor landing. Then, at about 08.45, the units began to move down the M1 corridor towards C Wing. They came under heavy attack through the corridor's skylights.

8.102 By 08.45 a total of 32 inmates had surrendered. Both C1 and C2 landings had been taken. It was however extremely difficult to gain access to C3 landing. This was because of the circular stairway which inmates were defending, while other inmates were throwing down missiles through the holes which they had created in the roof.

8.103   The units who had entered A Wing were under the command of Governor 5 Mr Waghorn. He was a trained C&R Section Commander. Having entered A Wing, his units were then engaged in seeking to retake C Wing. One of his units was sent down the M1 corridor past C Wing towards the kitchen/dining room.

8.104   In his evidence, Mr Waghorn described a barricade in the corridor near the Dining Room and how, when it was removed, inmates who were in the corridor shouted that "there's 60 of us and we are coming to get you." Mr Waghorn said that it was possible to see into the Dining Room/Kitchen area through glass in the corridor. He could see inmates moving about, but he could not say how many there were. (It is unlikely that there were as many as 60 inmates. It is more likely that there were 15 – 20.)

8.105   Mr Waghorn grouped his unit behind iron gates in the corridor which led down towards the kitchen/dining room. There were three units there. Mr Waghorn told the Unit Commanders that if the inmates charged at them that it was his intention, if it was safe to do so, to advance and see if it was possible to capture anyone. He did not, however, give any other instructions to the Commanders.

8.106   According to Mr Waghorn, the inmates did charge along the corridor, pushing a kitchen trolley in front of them. He said the inmates rammed the gates with the trolley, threw missiles and then battered away with broom handles and other weapons at the long shields which were being held up by staff.

8.107   Mr Waghorn gave instructions to the Unit Commanders to advance through the corridor gates. They did so, causing the inmates to retreat as the three units advanced.

8.108   Mr Waghorn says that he followed behind, but he did not actually see the units go in to the kitchen/dining room. Nor did he see what happened when they went in.

8.109   Mr Gibbs, the senior officer who had been on duty the previous evening, did, however, enter. He was C&R3 trained but, according to his recollection (which may be mistaken) he was not trained in C&R1 or 2. Mr Gibbs had found the experience of proceeding along the corridor very frightening indeed. He described the officers in his unit being bombarded through the skylights with missiles and having blankets soaked in oil being set alight and dropped upon them. The position had, however, improved when water was used on the roof to keep the inmates back.

8.110   Mr Gibbs confirmed Mr Waghorn's description of the inmates coming up from the area of the kitchen and dining room to do battle. But he said that, although the gates leading down to the kitchen had had their locks burnt off (presumably by use of the oxy-acetylene equipment) they were secured by the use of a pair of handcuffs. He said that the inmates built a barricade and set fire to it. A Commander called for bolt cutters, cut the handcuffs and said:

"Let's get down there before the fire really gets a hold."

8.111   Mr Gibbs described how the inmates retreated into the kitchen as the C&R Units advanced. Inside the door to the kitchen and dining room there was a large hole in the roof about five or six feet square. Mr Gibbs and the other members of the C&R Units created a canopy with their shields so that the units could pass under the hole. Then Mr Gibbs and the other members of the unit ran into the kitchen. He saw there was another hole in the roof, smaller in size, about 18 inches square, and situated close to where the kitchen joined with the kitchen stores.

8.112   Mr Gibbs said that the C&R Unit he was in then "just fell to pieces". He was with the leading group. When they went into the kitchen/dining room area there were still inmates present who were prepared to fight, even though they were outnumbered by the C&R Units. Hand to hand fighting followed.

8.113   Mr Gibbs put down his shield and his PR24 baton and seized an inmate who was dressed in a prison officer's uniform. According to his evidence, Mr Gibbs was frightened. He was not in control. He also described how two other inmates were dragged from the place in which they were hiding. He concluded by saying that "staff were going in every direction" and that the situation was "confusing" throughout.

8.114   The picture given by Mr Gibbs, while helpful, must be treated with caution as to its detail since, understandably, he clearly found the whole incident extremely stressful.

8.115   Mr Thomas was the commander of the second C&R unit. He did not believe there were any prisoners in the dining room when his unit entered. His unit therefore made for the kitchen. He ordered his unit to split. This should be a disciplined manoeuvre, but an officer broke ranks and jumped across the corner of the servery into the kitchen area. While I am not fully satisfied with the accuracy of this account either, it does give an indication that one officer at any rate did not follow the normal procedure.

8.116   After the kitchen and dining room had been cleared of inmates, the staff who were present were instructed to withdraw. The order for this came from Mr Woolford. However, Mr Waghorn thought that was a mistake. Supported by Mr Benge, he persuaded Mr Woolford to order the kitchen to be retaken. The order was given and the kitchen was reoccupied.

8.117   There is confusion about precisely how many prisoners were recaptured in the kitchen/dining room area, but the probability is six. Mr Waghorn was firmly of the view that those six inmates were taken into cells in C Wing. He was convinced also that they were searched in C Wing before being taken to the female prison block under C&R restraint. Mr Benge was equally certain that this did not happen. None of the inmates who gave evidence and who were apprehended in the kitchen area support Mr Waghorn. It seems therefore that Mr Waghorn is probably mistaken in his recollection.

8.118   The staff evidence about what happened in the kitchen is therefore confused. This is particularly unfortunate because evidence given by three inmates suggested that the inmates who were apprehended in the kitchen were subject to unnecessary violence. One inmate, who hid in a cupboard, described how he was beaten over the head with a truncheon. His evidence has to be treated with caution because he also described how he had been attacked when taken into the Hospital Wing. Having regard to the other evidence which I heard from the nurse who was on duty, his evidence as to what happened in the Hospital Wing is most unlikely to be true.

8.119   Other inmates also described being beaten up. They included three inmates who said they went into the kitchen in order to give themselves up. However, it was equally evident from inmates that missiles were being thrown through one of the holes in the roof (it is not clear which). One inmate described those missiles being thrown at an inmate who was wearing a prison officer's uniform because it was not realised that he was not a prison officer.

8.120   After the kitchen and dining room area had been retaken, C3 landing was also taken. During this period, prison officers used water to drive the inmates towards the dining room and kitchen roof area. For a time, one hose unit had been under a very heavy attack from missiles, but when the second hose was used this gave an effective crossfire of water. This use of water was of vital importance in retaking the block. It continued despite a formal objection from the Fire Service Union at about 12.50 on 23 April about the use of fire service hoses to control inmates.

xii) The Surrender

8.121 By the middle of Monday morning, 23 April, the position of the inmates was hopeless. It is surprising that they continued to resist. One explanation for the failure of some inmates to surrender, was that they were being intimidated by other inmates. This is corroborated by the log kept by the Board of Visitors. However, at the later stages, it is probable that inmates were being deterred from surrendering by the fear that if they did so they would be assaulted by staff. They said they saw inmates who were unhurt when they surrendered subsequently appear to be injured. They concluded that was because they had been assaulted after they had surrendered. Initially they also thought that the C&R units consisted of members of the police and not prison staff.

8.122 It is most unlikely that there were any assaults on inmates by staff while they were in the open area in front of the remand block and the female block. (I shall deal later with allegations of assault in the female block.) An explanation for the inmates' fears of assaults could be that they saw the surrendering prisoners being taken away in C&R holds, (as previously described), and that in the course of this some pain was caused. This can easily happen unless considerable care is exercised. Mr Woolford, at a later stage of the disturbance, appreciated this might be deterring other inmates from surrendering. He gave instructions that inmates, after they had surrendered, should be allowed to walk from the wing to where they were being assembled on the lawn accompanied by two officers. Unfortunately there is also some evidence of intimidating remarks being made by staff to inmates on the lawn, which, in view of its importance, I consider in some detail later.

8.123 Negotiations were conducted with inmates (but not until a late stage) by Mr Fagg, Mr Devaney and by Mrs Palmer, the Chairman of the Board of Visitors. They assured the inmates that the those who were surrendering were not being ill-treated. They said also that if the inmates came down from the roof in large numbers, no-one would put any C&R holds on them. They would be marched away together. Eventually, the remaining prisoners came down from the roof. By 13.40 on 23 April, the riot was over.

xiii) The Board of Visitors

8.124 Mrs Palmer, the Chairman of the Board of Visitors, had arrived at the establishment at 20.00 on 22 April. She was joined shortly afterwards by her Vice Chairman, Mrs Cooper, and by another member of the Board, Mr Fear. They stayed on duty throughout the night and kept a log of what was happening.

8.125 The log refers to the six inmates who were apprehended about the time the kitchen was taken. It describes the injuries of some inmates. It describes one as being "injured and taken to Prison Hospital". It says one had a "bloody right ear". Another's face is "covered in blood". Two more boys are recorded as having been brought in and taken to hospital – "one had blood all over the top of his head". Two other boys were brought in to the Prison Hospital "both bleeding". These entries are timed between 08.20 and 08.47 on 23 April.

8.126 An entry at the Board's log at 08.49 reads:

"A prisoner with severe head injuries taken out of female wing on stretcher – blood all over his face and head".

8.127 The final entry relevant to this matter is timed at 08.52. It reads:

"prisoner with nose and face injury leaves on a stretcher".

8.128 The Board members did not know how the injuries were sustained and so the log does not help on this. None of the inmates made any complaint at the time of being treated improperly. It was only during the interviews subsequently conducted on behalf of the Inquiry that complaints were made.

8.129 The Board of Visitors' log continues to provide a useful insight as to what happened later on Monday morning, 23 April. For example, at 09.06, the log records that a boy shouted that he wanted to see the Governor. He was greeted by swearing from officers. At 09.10 it records that:

"most of the boys are now on the roof of the kitchen and the escort areas. Roy Woolford establishes dialogue 'come down on my terms with no resistance and there will be no violence'. Boys say they want to come down."

(None however did so at that time.)

8.130   At 09.20 there is an entry in the Board's log that "two boys smash up cell" in the female block. At 11.23, it records one inmate surrendering. It records another surrender at 11.25. He is taken in by two woman officers and the log records that "one hugs him". The log also records (at 12.13) that an inmate who had surrendered indicated that inmates were being threatened by other inmates that they would be beaten up if they came down from the roof.

8.131   There is one longer entry in the log. It is:

"1.10 p.m.   Last 40 boys on roof reluctant to come down because they are afraid they will be beaten (by officers) Chairman of the BOV is asked to speak to them. Marilyn Palmer assures them that other BOV members are present and are watching them being put into cells. Also says that BOV will stay in the prison for as long as the prisoners want – all night if necessary. One boy says he will come down but not off the roof – he wants to come down inside the building. BOV says that she cannot guarantee his safety if he does that. Boys seem to be reassured and start climbing down from the roof. They are 'rubbed down' by one officer and then walk to the female prison in between two officers (not held). Officers form two lines to make 'corridor' for boys to be escorted down. BOV Chairman waits until the last boy is down and then follows them to the grassed area outside the female wing. One said 'She said she'd follow us – now where is she?' I assured him that I stood right behind him. Most of the boys now seem to be very *frightened*." (emphasis added.)

In her evidence, Mrs Palmer said that "apprehensive" would have been a better word than "frightened".

8.132   The log then goes on to describe how the inmates were allowed to sit on the grass if they wished. Mrs Palmer was joined by the Chaplain. The entry then continues:

"We are surrounded by officers; some making intimidating remarks to the boys."

8.133   Mrs Palmer was asked in evidence about the nature of the "intimidating remarks". She said:

"They were in the nature of winding up rather than serious threats. I certainly do not believe that they were serious threats and I think too much emphasis has been placed on that statement".

8.134   When she was pressed as to what was being said, she said:

"They (that is the officers) inferred that their arms and legs would be broken on the coach on the way home".

8.135   Mrs Palmer says that her reaction was to give the officers in question "a dirty look" and to say: "That really is not necessary".

8.136   The Board log then goes on to record that five inmates asked her "to write down their names and note that they had no injuries at 1.35 p.m.".

xiv) The Treatment of the Inmates in the Female Block and Hospital

8.137   The inmates on the lawn were seen quickly by Dr Mohammed Abdel-Aziz Abdel-Kariem (Dr Kariem) the full-time prison medical officer who was attached to Bristol prison. If an inmate needed medical attention, he was sent to the female hospital which had been prepared for inmates.

8.138 A very rough record was kept of the inmates who were seen by Dr Kariem and what treatment any was given. No full or proper record was produced to the Inquiry. The brief record which was produced indicated that the inmate who alleged that he had been assaulted in the kitchen and again in the hospital had one suture into the crown of his head rather than the nine he had said. The record also referred to another inmate who had complained of being assaulted. It records that he had:

"a cut to the right ear, black eye, loss of consciousness for two minutes".

8.139 This entry was in the handwriting of Sister Thomas, the nurse in charge of the Hospital Wing.

8.140 Those inmates who were not taken to the Hospital Wing, were taken to cells in A and B Wings of the female block. In order to accommodate the number of inmates some cells had to hold three prisoners.

8.141 The way inmates were treated in the female block gives rise to concern. First, it was alleged by inmates that inmates were struck while being taken to their cells. In one case, it was alleged that an inmate was struck when actually in the cells. Most of the allegations were based on what inmates said they saw through the cell door flap, or what they heard, rather than on direct evidence. One inmate contended that he was required to stand with his hands up against the wall of his cell while another inmate was brought in, who was then struck by the staff. There is no corroboration of the inmates' accounts, though their descriptions of what occurred are similar. Again, no complaint was made at the time by any inmate, although there were opportunities to do so.

8.142 It is possible that some of the screams and yells of pain which were allegedly heard by inmates could be attributed to the use of C&R holds. It is accepted that C&R was used for bringing some prisoners into the cells. Others screams and yells might have been deliberately misleading – "put on" by inmates who wanted to make out that they were being hurt. For the reasons I explained at the public hearing and set out in Section 2 of this Report, it is not possible for me to make any finding about these allegations. I am conscious, however, that my inability to do so could be unfair to staff who were not in a position to rebut these and other allegations which were made in public. This is, I am afraid, a limitation of an Inquiry of this sort - it is not practical to do more than record the fact of the allegations and the fact, which is equally important, that they are denied.

8.143 The second area for concern arises out of the strip searching of inmates. The clothes which they were wearing were removed and placed in heaps. No attempt was made to distinguish between one inmate's clothes and another, even though some of the clothing was the inmates' own property. They were not allowed to put back on any of the clothing. In addition, personal effects, including such items as watches and earrings, were taken away from the inmates. The reason for this is not clear. Again, no attempt was made to identify ownership of the items. By the hearing in Taunton on 18 July 1990, they had not been returned.

8.144 After the inmates had been searched, those whose clothes were wet were not provided with clothing immediately. The explanation put forward at the hearing was that this was because there was a shortage of clothing. There was only enough available for those inmates who were transferred to other establishments on the same day (23 April).

8.145 The Board of Visitor's Log makes it clear that clothes were only issued as and when inmates were shipped out on 23 April. It is not disputed that inmates who were transferred were not in all cases fully clothed. Some of these inmates were without underwear; others were without socks and shoes.

8.146 The inmates who remained at Pucklechurch complained that for a substantial period they were left without blankets or mattresses. As I have recorded earlier, blankets and mattresses were available in the establishment. The inmates could have been provided with them. There is no doubt that for a time they did not have mattresses. It is difficult, on the evidence, to be precise about how long this period was.

8.147 Mr Phipps, who was a Governor 5 from Leyhill Prison, arrived at Pucklechurch at about 09.30 on 23 April. He was placed in charge of the female block. He told the Inquiry that before he left the prison at 18.00 on 23 April he went into each cell. Each inmate had a mattress. Mr Phipps is mistaken as to at least one prisoner. I am satisfied that that inmate did not have a mattress until the following day.

8.148 Mr Phipps also indicated that the inmates who surrendered were divided into groups for the purpose of being searched. One group was the co-operative inmates. They were searched in their cells and their clothing was left outside their cells. The other group was those who were struggling. They were searched at the end of A Wing.

8.149 Inmates who gave evidence corroborated the fact that some inmates were searched in their cells. None of the staff, other than Mr Phipps, however, referred to the inmates being divided into two groups.

8.150 Mr Phipps' evidence was that within minutes of those inmates who were co-operative being searched, they were given blankets. This is, however, not agreed by the inmates. Mr Phipps' said that when he visited each cell and saw that each inmate had a mattress, he saw also that they had a blanket.

8.151 The log kept by the Board of Visitors has only limited entries relevant to these matters. The entry at 13.44 records that:

"BOV Mike Anthony felt it necessary to intervene on one occasion when he felt undue force was being used to put a boy in his cell".

8.152 There is also a suggestion in the log at 13.05 that Mr Phipps had tried to dissuade the Board of Visitors from watching the boys being stripped. Mr Phipps denied this.

8.153 Mr Alldridge took over from Mr Leach at 10.00 on 23 April. He stayed on duty until about 19.00 that day. Mr Alldridge did not concern himself personally with what was to happen to the inmates after their surrender. It appears from his evidence that he relied on what Mr Woolford had told him was intended to happen to them. Mr Woolford had, however, gone off duty by 14.30 on 23 April. (He had been continuously on duty for 26 hours.) According to one answer which he gave in evidence, Mr Alldridge did not regard himself as taking on the full responsibilities of the Governor. He said that Mr Woolford was the Governor in Charge. He was wrong as to this.

8.154 Mr Alldridge said that when he came on duty, he was principally concerned with setting up a new kitchen unit so that inmates could be fed. He did, however, visit the female block. There was a large number of staff in there, including some staff who were waiting to receive surrendering prisoners. He spoke to the doctor and the Ambulance Chief Officer. He asked the doctor about the injuries, which were one of his concerns, and spent some time talking to him. He saw two inmates, but he did not then, or at any other time while he was on duty, visit all the inmates who had been located in the female block.

8.155 Mr Leach came back on duty on Tuesday 24 April. He went into the female block, but he did not check the cells. He said in evidence that he was not aware that there was any problem about clothing or bedding. He said that he was first aware of there being a problem when he heard of a telephone call from Mrs Palmer. This was probably on Wednesday 25 or Thursday 26 April. Mrs Palmer had called the Centre as a result of being rung by the press. They were asking about an inmate who was said only to have been clothed in a blanket when he received a visitor at Pucklechurch.

8.156   In his evidence Mr Leach said that on hearing of Mrs Palmer's call, he went to the female block. He checked with staff. He was assured that all the inmates had clothing. But he did not check himself. Nor did he check at any date from that time until the last of the inmates were moved to other establishments on 1 May. He was quite unaware of the problem about the clothing until the Inquiry's hearing in Taunton on 23 July. Mr Leach said at the hearing that he believed that there had been an inmate who had received a visit in a blanket. But he admitted that he had not found out why that had happened or who was responsible.

8.157   I visited Pucklechurch with my Assessors on 1 May, shortly before the last of the inmates were transferred to other establishments. We saw some of the inmates in the female block. They were bewildered and frightened young men. One was dressed only in boxer shorts. The inmates, who were about to be transferred, said that they had not been told to which establishments they were being transferred and did not know what was to happen to them.

8.158   There remained also, long after the end of the disturbance, a problem with the clothing which had been removed from the inmates at the time they were put into the cells in the female block on 23 April. A proportion of the clothing was obviously wet or dirty as a result of the incident. That clothing would have needed cleaning and/or drying before it could have been returned to inmates. However, on the undisputed evidence which was given to the Inquiry, proper steps to deal with the clothing had not been taken by the time of the hearing in July, either by the staff or by management.

8.159   Inquiries by two of my Assessors after the hearing revealed that at some stage prison officers put the clothing in black polythene bags. These were placed in the female inmates' workroom, which was not in use following the disturbance.

8.160   The inmates' personal effects were also separated from the clothing. Subsequently these items were listed by Senior Officer Inglis. The date of the list was 22 June 1990.

8.161   On 2 May 1990, the teachers who were using the workroom in the female block, had their attention drawn to the bags by the smell and the presence of flies. They investigated and found damp clothing. They spread the clothing out on the ground to dry. Some bags contained only shoes, others coats, jeans and shirts. The clothing was, for the most part, in good condition. Some of the items were valuable, including almost new trainers and leather and suede jackets. The clothing, after it had been dried, was replaced in the polythene bags.

8.162   On 24 July the clothing, still in the bags, was in the external passageway between the works department buildings. The bags were under a tarpaulin. The clothing appeared to be still in reasonable condition. Apparently, instructions had come from the SWRO that the items were to be destroyed, but the senior officers in the prison were reluctant to take this action in the absence of written authorisation.

8.163   It appears that some of the Pucklechurch inmates had petitioned about what had happened to their property. Apart from the personal effects, that property was being treated as if it was irrecoverably lost. The Prison Service was declining any responsibility for what had happened to it.

8.164   The Prison Service launched an investigation in August 1990. The inquiry was conducted between 9 August and 10 September 1990 by Mr Alderson, the Governor of Exeter Prison, on the instructions of Mr Dunbar, the Regional Director of the South West Region. Mr Alderson was required to investigate:

"The report that an inmate received a visit dressed only in a blanket on a date some time after the serious disturbance in April. If the report is found to be accurate, to determine the circumstances leading to the occurrence...."

8.165   In his report, Mr Alderson ascertained that the Pucklechurch main stores and their contents were still intact after the disturbance. This was contrary to what had been suggested at the public hearing in Taunton. The storeman estimated that there was sufficient clothing in the Pucklechurch store for some 200 inmates.

8.166   Other kit arrived from Eastwood Park Young Offender Institution and from Cardiff prison at approximately 16.00 on 23 April. It appears that the additional kit was obtained because, for some reason, it was not appreciated that there was already enough at Pucklechurch. The kit was used to provide kit for inmates on Monday 23, Tuesday 24 and Wednesday 25 April. The evidence suggests that the task of kitting out all the inmates was completed by the end of 25 April.

8.167   Mr Alderson concluded, as a result of his inquiry, that in fact the inmate referred to in his terms of reference did have a visit before he had been issued with clothing. This had been because a:

"judgment was made to give priority to the visit not to how he was dressed".

8.168   Mr Alderson went on to say that he could:

"find no evidence except his, however that he was naked under his blanket. On reflection from the highlands of hindsight, I am sure staff would agree he should have been given clothing first, particularly as reception is next to visits, and that all visits should have been managed that way."

8.169   Mr Alderson also concluded that he was:

"unable to identify a coherent compact structure for managing the aftermath of the riot."

8.170   The Governor also ascertained from some of the inmates that they had retained their own clothing after they had surrendered. They did this by stripping themselves down to their underpants, then hiding their own clothing and covering themselves with blankets.

The Regional Director's Surrender Plans

8.171   On 21 September 1990 the Regional Director for the South West Region, Mr Dunbar sent to the Inquiry a copy "of an emergency order extract which is being used as an example of best practice". He had sent the order to the Governors of establishments in the South West Region, with a copy to the Deputy Director General.

8.172   In his letter to the Inquiry enclosing the plan Mr Dunbar said:

"That traditionally contingency plans in the Prison Service have tended to concentrate upon effective management of the incident rather than ensuring proper procedures in the immediate aftermath".

8.173   The new order set out a procedure for dealing with the surrender of prisoners after a major incident. On 7 November 1990 the Prison Service issued to all governors a document covering much the same ground. (A copy is at Annex.)

The Governor's Recommendations for the Future

8.174   After the hearing held at Taunton, Mr Leach sent to the Inquiry a list of useful recommendations as to the action which he considered could be taken for the future. The list was based on his experience of the disturbance.

8.175   Mr Leach's list indicated that he had given considerable thought to the improvements which could be made to the handling of disturbances. He made a number of sensible and practicable suggestions. One of Mr Leach's recommendations was that there should be regular meetings between Courts, police and prison officials to improve the co-ordination of court work. There had already been an initiative at Pucklechurch to achieve this. It had proved beneficial. Mr Leach suggested, however, that this should not be left to individual initiative, but should be set up on a national scale. I agree. These matters will be dealt with in Section 12 of this Report.

Media

8.176   The violence which was occurring during the disturbance received vast coverage by the media. There was no evidence, however, to suggest that this affected the progress or duration of the incident. The disturbance was clearly a matter of public interest. There appears to be no ground for commenting on the attention which it received from the media.

The Consequences of the Disturbance

8.177   35 inmates and 41 staff were injured during the disturbance. In addition, if Pucklechurch is to return to its former use, repairs will be necessary as a result of the disturbance which will cost £1 million and take six months to complete.

8.178   A decision will have to be taken as to the future of Pucklechurch. It is possible that it may be decided that it should have a different role. Prior to the disturbance breaking out, Pucklechurch's role was under consideration. If it were to be changed, it would be refurbished at a cost of about £4.5 million over 12-18 months. (The majority of this cost would have had to be incurred even if the disturbance had not taken place.)

8.179   In a letter dated 16 November 1990, the Prison Service informed the Inquiry that:

> "it will be some time before we are in a position to reach a final decision on the future of Pucklechurch."

8.180   The same letter points out that, if the Centre continued its previous role, the former male cellular accommodation would need to be:

> "significantly enhanced, separate regime facilities developed – and where necessary, improved – and zoning would have to be introduced".

8.181   In the meantime Pucklechurch was being used to accommodate female remand prisoners and as a temporary holding centre to assist in moving prisoners around the South West more effectively.

8.182   The costs of the disturbance, however, cannot be measured simply by recording the injuries and the expenditure required to carry out repairs. The staff involved and the majority of the inmates had undergone a shattering and terrifying experience. The inmates had to be housed elsewhere. The majority were transferred to the local prison at Cardiff. This is not an appropriate place in which to house young offenders. Others who would, in the normal way, have been accommodated at Pucklechurch no doubt had to be housed in wholly unsatisfactory conditions in police cells.

8.183   Staff had also to work at other establishments, particularly Cardiff. They had daily to make long journeys to do so, which added to their stress.

8.184 Relations between staff and inmates were bound to be damaged by the ferocity of the incident. This relationship was no doubt not helped by the investigations which had to be made by the Inquiry into the allegations by inmates about staff conduct.

8.185 The Board of Visitors felt deeply aggrieved that, having spent long hours at the establishment during the disturbance for which they do not receive one penny compensation, their conduct should have been subject to detailed investigation at the Inquiry.

8.186 The members of the management team have had their shortcomings exposed to public scrutiny.

8.187 The disturbance will leave scars on all involved which will take a long time to heal.

Conclusions Specific to the Pucklechurch Disturbance

8.188 These conclusions and comments must be read together with Section 9 of the Report which deals with the lessons to be learnt from the disturbances which took place in April 1990.

1. There is no doubt the disturbance was planned. It was planned by an inmate who gave a statement to the Inquiry. It was decided not to call him as a witness, partly because of the likelihood of criminal proceedings being brought against him, and partly because it was felt that he would seek to exploit the opportunity to give evidence for his own purposes. He was an inmate who, having previously been looked upon with favour at the establishment, had become disaffected. He had lost his job as a cleaner and was bitter and revengeful, with clear hostility to a particular member of staff.

2. When Mr Leary entered this inmate's cell, there was nothing that Mr Leary could do to prevent what happened, including the loss of his keys. The question arises as to whether Mr Leary should have been allowed to perform the duty on which he was engaged without another prison officer accompanying him and when he was only accompanied by two orderlies. Mr Woolford in his evidence regarded this as being an error, but would not criticise Mr Gibbs, who was the senior officer on duty and who was responsible for allocating staff at the time.

3. Mr Gibbs, the evening orderly officer, detailed Mr Leary in accordance with the normal Pucklechurch routine. However, given that there was good reason to be particulary cautious and that he knew that extra staff had been brought on duty for that purpose, Mr Gibbs should have arranged for Mr Leary to have had the assistance of another officer whilst unlocking cells. There were sufficient staff on duty to have allowed him to have been supported in this way.

4. Mr Woolford, the duty governor, also had all the relevant information to indicate that there was a risk of an incident occurring that weekend. It would have been prudent to have given additional guidance to the evening orderly officer to ensure that all reasonable precautions were taken.

5. For the future, particularly where an establishment is known to be in the unsettled state that Pucklechurch was on 22 April, I consider that an officer performing Mr Leary's duties should have another officer, in sight or earshot, available to come to his assistance when unlocking a cell containing two inmates.

6. Even if a second officer had been present, (which would probably have prevented the incident taking place then) on the information available, it is clear that another opportunity would have been seized by the instigator to obtain keys. Once this had been done, the outcome is unlikely to have been different.

7. Once Mr Leary's keys had been seized, there was no action which could have been taken which was not taken to prevent the incident spreading. Unfortunately, by the time it was appreciated what had happened to Mr Leary, enough inmates had been released to ensure that it was not possible to contain the incident to A Wing.

8. It is a matter of concern that the loss of one set of keys again gave the inmates the run of a large part of an establishment and access to the tools in the Works Department.

9. There is an acute conflict as to whether the additional staff who were on duty were to be used for providing association. Whatever Mr White agreed when approached by Mr Bracey and Mr Gibbs, I accept Mr Woolford's evidence that he at all times intended that there should be association on the Sunday evening and that the association which in fact took place was that which he intended. I consider that Mr Woolford was correct to have arranged for association to take place that evening. If association had not been so frequently cancelled in the past, the riot might not have received the support which it did. There was some suggestion in the evidence that in the past association had been cancelled by members of staff who were not governors. If this was the case, then it should not have happened. The cancellation of association, particularly for young remand inmates, should be regarded as a matter of significance and the decision should always be taken by a person of governor grade.

10. The arrangements which were made for additional staff over the weekend were adequate having regard to the constraints on staffing levels.

11. It is regrettable that so many inmates were prepared to support the instigators. The Strangeways incident was still continuing that weekend and this might have encouraged others to join in. However, a more significant feature was the disturbance which occurred in Bristol, a city and prison with which a lot of the inmates at Pucklechurch had connections. Another factor was that, because of the disturbances in other prisons, the inmates' activities had been curtailed.

12. Escort duties were placing unacceptable burdens on staffing levels. Continuity of regime is extremely important and, as the unpredictable demands of escort duties were interfering with the regime, better arrangements than those which existed at Pucklechurch are needed. This question will be examined in Section 12 of this Report.

13. Some progress had been made to improve the regime at Pucklechurch. But conditions were still far from satisfactory for young men who had not been convicted. There was no sanitation in the cells. Some cells were having to be shared. Inmates were locked up for too long. Young and bored remand prisoners are likely to be candidates for any excitement. A substantial number of the inmates at Pucklechurch clearly did not think that the consequences of taking part were a sufficient reason for not joining the incident with enthusiasm.

14. The regime at Pucklechurch exemplifies the totally unacceptable approach, even in Remand Centres, which is adopted with regard to the provision of facilities and an active regime for inmates, particularly young inmates, on remand. The time out of cells was insufficient; opportunities to work were unnecessarily limited; attempts to develop the education programme were frustrated by staff resistance and the living conditions were not of a sufficiently high standard. These are matters which need wider consideration and will be dealt with in Part II of this Report. What can be said, however, is that the situation at Pucklechurch demonstrates that separate provision for remands does not necessarily result in satisfactory standards.

15. The degree of violence which the inmates displayed is disturbing. There was undoubtedly more than an element of the sort of hooliganism which is often associated with football matches. There was a feeling of hostility about the conditions in which the inmates were being kept.

16. Mr Woolford displayed leadership of the highest order, verve and ability in commanding the response to the incident. He accepts that he under-estimated the capacity of the inmates to resist the first intervention. He wrongly assumed that, on a show of force, the majority of the inmates would surrender. His error was partly due to his failure to appreciate the fear of the inmates as to what would happen to them if they did surrender. Mr Woolford, advised by Mr Benge and Mr Fagg overestimated the prospects of success.

17. Mr Benge and Mr Fagg had considerably more experience of the potential of C&R units than Mr Woolford. As Mr Woolford had their support and the support of SWRO, it was appropriate for him to embark upon the first intervention.

18. The incident makes it clear that there can be disturbances where a display of C&R units about to intervene will not bring a disturbance to an end. Indeed the display appears to have encouraged the inmates to behave more aggressively.

19. What happened at Pucklechurch emphasised the vulnerability of C&R units being outflanked in the open. Consideration should be given as to how units can defend their flanks.

20. The second intervention was successful, although there was resistance. But discipline broke down when the first C&R unit entered the kitchen. On Mr Gibbs' account, there can be no doubt that authorised C&R techniques were no longer being used. No authority had been given for the drawing of PR24's. The putting down of a shield and a PR24 in order to apprehend an inmate is not in accordance with practice. Allowance has to be made for the fact that the incident had been extremely frightening for the staff involved. Unless staff are highly experienced and well trained, discipline is likely to break down in these circumstances. While officers are part of a disciplined service, the fact that the staff had been subjected to exceptional stress cannot be ignored.

21. I do not make any finding that any specific officer used excessive force during the assault on the kitchen/dining area. But the way the matter was handled made the staff unnecessarily vulnerable to the allegations which were made.

22. Significant features of the disturbance were the size of the force which was required to intervene successfully and the hostility of the inmates. Such a force could not possibly be assembled from an establishment's own resources and resources had to be drawn from different parts of the region. Although the SWRO appears to have done all that it could to assemble the force, this was an exercise which, inevitably, took a substantial period of time. This enabled the inmates to establish control of the whole estab-lishment and to erect barriers which made intervention more difficult. The disturbance was resolved within a reasonable time having regard to the degree of hostility displayed by many of the inmates.

23. The use of water played a significant part in retaking the establishment. This use was fully justified in the circumstances.

24. Water would not have been so effectively deployed without the hoses provided by the Fire Service. During the disturbance the use of the hoses by staff was questioned. The present arrangements are contained in what is called the Dear Chief Officer letter of 5 August 1988. Those arrangements lack clarity as to when, if at all, it is appropriate for the Fire Service to make equipment available for purposes of controlling rioting inmates. It would be preferable if there was no ambiguity on this subject. Arrangements may be able to be made with the Fire Service that allow equipment which is not identifiable by prisoners as being the property of the Fire Service, to be made available by the Fire Service to prison staff. Where this is not possible, the Prison Service should have available its own equipment.

25. The police responded promptly and fulfilled their allotted role of guarding

the perimeter of the establishment satisfactorily. I record, but am not able to assess, the police's view that, although all services co-operated effectively, it would have been preferable if there had been a representative fire officer, ambulance officer and governor at the Police Control Point.

26. The police were able to help with the provision of additional shields, but even then 41 prison officers were injured, many on the legs and back. Some of these injuries were due to the lack of protective clothing. The arrangements for providing protective clothing and equipment were not adequate to cope with the demands of a disturbance of this scale.

27. No specific points arise in respect of the ambulance service. The service attended promptly and functioned efficiently.

28. Although C&R techniques are effective, they must not be used indiscriminately, but only with discretion. Mr Woolford was right to stop the use of C&R holds on surrendering inmates. C&R could and should have been used on surrendering inmates with more discretion earlier. I have little doubt that its indiscriminate use delayed the surrender of some inmates.

29. The treatment of inmates after surrender has to be criticised. Mr Leach should have exerted more control over the arrangements which were made for the surrender of inmates before he went off duty at 10.00 on 23 April. Mr Alldridge, after he took over command, should have done likewise. The mass surrender should have been more closely supervised and the undisciplined behaviour should not have taken place. It should not have been only the Board of Visitors who noted the unfortunate remarks referring to the breaking of limbs. The housing of the inmates in the female block was a demanding task requiring careful planning. It did not receive such planning.

30. Most staff up to that time had behaved in the most commendable way. It is regrettable that the picture should be spoilt by the irresponsible behaviour of a small minority of officers. There is no doubt that at the time the inmates were very frightened (I use that word advisedly) and even if the remarks made to them when waiting on the lawn were made in jest they could, and did, cause considerable fear to the inmates.

31. When considering these criticisms the long hours that management and staff had been on duty should be taken into account. Each member of management and staff must have been extremely tired and, as Mr Leach himself pointed out, close to exhaustion.

32. It would not be right to make any finding of undue force being used by any particular officer against any inmate in the female block. However, although the inmates' evidence was not by any means satisfactory, a clear picture emerges from the evidence as a whole that a few officers, I cannot say how many, were not showing the degree of professionalism that was shown by the majority of staff in their treatment of inmates. While I make no finding with regard to the allegations of violence, I consider it is possible that some of those allegations may be due to the inmates not appreciating that the officers were applying C&R techniques.

33. Bearing in mind the evidence as to how the inmates on the lawn were behaving before being taken into the female block, it is difficult to understand how, as Mr Phipps suggested, it was necessary to divide inmates into two groups, one group of those who were "struggling" and the other of those who were not. The evidence indicates that by the time the inmates were on the lawn, there was no sign of any wish to continue the fight, although no doubt a minority were still prepared to adopt a truculent attitude. If they had been handled properly, there should have been no need to treat a section of them as "struggling".

34. The way that mattresses were dealt with also indicates a lack of adequate supervision and concern. Removal of the mattresses could have been due to a misunderstanding, but, if this was the case, the misunderstanding should have been rectified earlier.

35. The treatment of the clothing and personal possessions of the inmates is

wholly unjustifiable. No explanation or justification has been given why personal possessions such as watches and earrings should be removed. If they were removed, more care should have been taken of them and of the clothing to ensure that they could be returned in due course. The handling of this matter at the time was unfortunate. The failure of local management to recognise that there was anything untoward until the public hearing nearly 13 weeks later, demonstrates a degree of neglect.

36. A similar criticism can be made of the failure in supervision in allowing a prisoner to attend a visit dressed only in a blanket, as the probabilities indicate he was. There can be no doubt he was wearing the blanket, the only issue is whether he had any clothes underneath it. The strong probability is that he did not.

37. I conclude from all the evidence I have seen that kit was supplied to all inmates at Pucklechurch after the disturbance had ended, but, except for those who were transferred in the first few days, it took the establishment at least two days to provide it. There was ample kit available in the establishment throughout this time. It is possible, however, that some inmates may have been reluctant to accept and wear the kit in lieu of their own clothing.

38. Even when the Governor was alerted to the situation by media interest, Mr Leach failed adequately to investigate the situation.

39. Once the shortcomings of dealing with the aftermath of the disturbance at Pucklechurch was brought to the attention of SWRO, they proceeded to investigate energetically what had happened and to take steps to ensure there was no repetition.

40. The experience at Pucklechurch makes it clear that guidance on best practice in dealing with the aftermath of an incident should have been issued to all establishments as a basis for the development of this aspect of their contingency plans. The Prison Service document of 7 November 1990 setting out such procedures deals satisfactorily with the action which needs to be taken.

41. There was no proper debriefing or counselling of staff after the end of the disturbance. If it has not yet been done, instructions should be issued detailing the steps which should be taken to look after staff welfare after a serious incident. They should provide for the sensitive processing and speedy settlement of claims for compensation in respect of items lost or damaged during an incident.

42. It was submitted on behalf of the Prison Officers' Association that it would have been appreciated if the Prison Service had sent a letter to each officer involved in the disturbance thanking him or her for their actual involvement "which was very often above and beyond the call of duty". I draw this to the attention of the Prison Service so that it can be borne in mind in the case of any future disturbance.

43. While, in the course of this report, I have indicated there could have been more action taken by the Governor, as in the case of other establishments allowance should be made for the absence of adequate training in the handling of an incident of this sort.

44. The Chairman and members of the Board of Visitors are to be commended for the long hours they spent at the establishment during the disturbance and the contribution they made to its resolution. They conscientiously kept a log which proved to be of great value in establishing what had happened.

45. In their evidence at the public hearing, the Chairman and to some extent the Vice-Chairman revealed a lack of objectivity in considering whether there had been any conduct on the part of members of the staff or management which was worthy of criticism. The Chairman, in particular, found it difficult to accept the need for the Inquiry to investigate how the Board had performed its important role during the course of the disturbance and whether its members had maintained the necessary

independence and impartiality. This could have been due to a lack of experience of an Inquiry of this sort and an undesirable lack of knowledge of the procedures which have to be followed. It also reveals the danger, which Boards of Visitors must always guard against, of the Board becoming too closely identified with management and staff.

46. Pucklechurch suffered from the same problems as other establishments in relation to gates and locks. This problem is dealt with in Sections 9 and 11 of this Report. Subject to this, I do not consider it necessary to propose a substantial increase in security in Pucklechurch, if it is to continue to be a Remand Centre for young offenders. I accept that if the Centre should have physical security to Category B standards, then major action is needed. I do not consider, however, that the ordinary remand inmate should be considered to need Category B security. This point is considered further in Part II of this Report. Pucklechurch needs security "firebreaks" (which I consider in Section 9) not enhanced cellular security.

47. Some inmates were on remand for far too long. Too many inmates were also being remanded for an excessive period after conviction while awaiting sentence. There is a need for closer cooperation between the Courts and the Prison Service to ensure that these delays are kept to the absolute minimum.

Section 9

Lessons From Part 1

Introduction

9.1   In this Section, I draw together the particular lessons which arise directly from the disturbances which have been examined in the earlier Sections of this Report. My objectives are twofold. First, to identify steps that can be taken to avoid a repetition of the series of events which led to those particular disturbances. Secondly, to ensure that the Prison Service's ability to respond to any such disturbances will be better in the future.

9.2   Each Section of the Report which deals with an individual disturbance includes conclusions and comments on that disturbance. I do not intend to repeat those conclusions and comments here.

9.3   The proposals I set out in this Section are important. I hope they are also practical. But, as this Section will show, they will only achieve my two objectives if they are acted on in conjunction with the wider proposals set out in Part II of this Report.

9.4   The disturbances took place in a cross-section of establishments. Three were at local prisons with a mixed population (Strangeways, Bristol and Cardiff). For a local prison, Strangeways was large, Bristol medium and Cardiff small. Dartmoor was a training prison. Both Glen Parva and Pucklechurch were youth remand centres. Glen Parva, which was a substantially larger establishment than Pucklechurch, was also a Young Offender Institution.

9.5   The disturbances examined did not include among their number a dispersal prison, a Category C prison or an open prison. However, an examination of the chronology of prison disturbances which occurred during the 25 days of the Strangeways' disturbance (which appears at Annex) shows that a large number of other disturbances were taking place during the same period. Among those disturbances were two at Long Lartin, which is a dispersal prison. In addition, there were incidents at Stafford, Wymott and The Verne, which are Category C prisons.

9.6   With the exception of Dartmoor, which does not contain remand prisoners, remand prisoners were involved to differing degrees in all the remaining disturbances. The male section of Pucklechurch mainly contained young men who were on remand. They exhibited more hostility and aggression towards staff than was exhibited at other disturbances, other than possibly Strangeways and Bristol. It would therefore be quite wrong to assume that, because prisoners are on remand, they do not have the potential for creating serious control and security problems. It would be equally wrong to assume that all such prisoners need the conditions of security to which they are at present subjected. The correct approach will be considered in Part II.

9.7   The public has had good reason to know to its cost over the last 20 years that the results of prison disturbances can be extremely serious. The events of April 1990 were only the last in a litany of serious disturbances which differed from the earlier disturbances only in their gravity and longevity.

9.8   In October 1969, 155 prisoners at Parkhurst barricaded themselves in association rooms taking seven prison officers hostage. In the struggle that followed, 33 prison officers and 22 prisoners were injured.

9.9   In 1972, there was a series of protests in a large number of prisons. At that time, such events were without precedent. The protests began peacefully, but ended in violence. The demonstrations had started as "sit-ins". The first was at Brixton prison in May 1972. They continued until August, by which time 41 different prisons had been involved. At the end of August, the mood became more ugly. Prisoners caused damage in disturbances at Albany, Parkhurst, Camphill and Chelmsford. Finally, in November of that year, Gartree prisoners attempted a breakout. Their attempt was foiled. But there followed two days of mayhem at Gartree, during which 18 officers were injured and considerable damage was done.

9.10   In the summer of 1976, prisoners at Hull occupied the roof of the prison and for four days had control of most of the establishment. Hull was out of commission for a year.

9.11   In October 1978, a further riot took place at Gartree prison. It resulted in damage which, for some time afterwards, reduced the certified normal accommodation of the prison by a half.

9.12   In 1979, there were further disturbances at Parkhurst and Hull, and a serious incident resulting in considerable controversy at Wormwood Scrubs. Fourteen officers and 60 prisoners were injured.

9.13   In 1983, Wormwood Scrubs and Albany prisons were again the scene of disturbances.

9.14   In 1986, there was a spate of disorder affecting 40 institutions. It involved all types of establishments – local prisons, remand centres, training prisons and youth custody centres. 45 prisoners escaped. There was more than £5m worth of damage and 800 prison places were lost.

9.15   In June and July 1988, there were riots at two training prisons, Haverigg and Lindholme. Buildings were set on fire and almost £1m damage was done. A dozen members of staff were injured and 23 prisoners escaped. There was a further disturbance at Lindholme in August 1988.

9.16   In 1989, there was a serious disturbance at Risley.

9.17   It appears that the pattern of serious disturbances in English prisons has deepened and widened. Until 1986, large scale disturbances occurred mainly at training prisons and, in particular, at high security dispersal prisons. But the latest series of disturbances in April 1990 indicates that, with the exception so far of open and specialist prisons, no prison can be said to be immune from a substantial risk of involvement in prison disturbances.

9.18   It is clear from this analysis, and from the evidence given before the Inquiry, that similar disturbances could have very well occurred at many other establishments across the country. A further catastrophe of the scale of Strangeways could have brought the Prison Service to the verge of collapse. This could have threatened the operation of many other parts of the Criminal Justice System. No-one should doubt the importance of achieving a more stable prison system than we have at present.

The Importance of Security, Control and Justice to a Stable Prison System

9.19   The evidence from Part I of this Inquiry shows that there are three requirements which must be met if the prison system is to be stable: they are security, control and justice. The implications of this finding for Part II of the Inquiry are discussed in Section 10.

9.20   For present purposes, "security" refers to the obligation of the Prison Service to prevent prisoners escaping. "Control" deals with the obligation of the Prison Service to prevent prisoners being disruptive. "Justice" refers to the obligation of the Prison Service to treat prisoners with humanity and fairness and to prepare them for their return to the community in a way which makes it less likely that they will reoffend.

9.21   There are two basic rules if these requirements are to be met. They are:

    i)   sufficient attention has to be paid to each of the requirements;

    ii)   they must be kept in balance.

9.22   If this is not done, then the system is unstable and so is more prone to disturbance and riot. The April 1990 disturbances were a consequence of the failure of the prison system to conform with these basic rules.

9.23   The breaches of the two basic rules arose principally because of failures to provide an acceptable standard of justice, and because of inadequacies in some of the Prison Service's arrangements for maintaining and reasserting control. If a repetition of what happened in April 1990 is to be avoided, then it is essential that this situation is rectified. This will not be easy. The Stage I evidence indicates there is no single cause of riots and no simple solution or action which will prevent rioting.

The Disturbances Demonstrate a Need to Pay More Attention to Justice Within Prisons

9.24   A recurring theme in the evidence from prisoners who may have instigated, and who were involved in, the riots was that their actions were a response to the manner in which they were treated by the prison system. Although they did not always use these terms, they felt a lack of justice. If what they say is true, the failure of the Prison Service to fulfil its responsibilities to act with justice created in April 1990 serious difficulties in maintaining security and control in prisons.

9.25   It is not possible for the Inquiry to form any judgment on whether the specific grievances of these prisoners were or were not well-founded. What is clear is that the Prison Service had failed to *persuade* these prisoners that it was treating them fairly.

9.26   It is significant that prisoners recently transferred from other establishments were centrally involved in all the incidents which precipitated trouble in the target prisons. One of the leading participants at Strangeways had, in the course of a mere 21 months in prison, been moved from establishment to establishment at least six times, usually for reasons of maintaining control in the prisons from which he was moved.

9.27   Another prisoner, serving a much longer sentence, after an initial period of turbulence in which he was moved from prison to prison, had settled reasonably well for four years at a dispersal prison. But he resumed his unsettled behaviour at the Category B prison to which he was moved on recategorisation. At the time of the riot, he had only recently been transferred to Strangeways.

9.28   The inmate whose actions precipitated trouble at Glen Parva had very recently been moved in. He was then further from home and was said to be homesick for visits from his family.

9.29   At Dartmoor, one of the leading participants in the troubles had been in at least nine different prisons in the course of a three year sentence. He had only recently been transferred into Dartmoor. He was held there under the part of Rule 43 which is used to segregate prisoners in the interests of good order or discipline (GOAD).

9.30 The riot at Cardiff appears to have been precipitated by the actions of an inmate only recently moved into the prison from Bristol for control reasons. The Bristol disturbance again seems to have been set off by men recently moved in, this time from Dartmoor. At Pucklechurch, one of the inmates whose actions seem to have precipitated the riot had only recently been transferred there for the purpose of receiving accumulated visits.

9.31 All this evidence cannot prove that the movement of prisoners is in itself conducive to riot. Many prisoners are moved, be it for reasons of control or otherwise, without a riot resulting. But the evidence is suggestive. In all the cases studied, the precipitating incidents which set off riot involved those who had been recently transferred.

9.32 The Inquiry also received theoretic evidence from several sources which suggested that frequent moves for prisoners could be a source of instability and lead to disturbance. At the first of the public seminar hearings, Dr Grubin of the Institute of Psychiatry said:

"prisons are places where people live; they are the inmates' homes".

He reminded the seminar that moving home is inevitably a stressful experience. He argued that, wherever possible, prisoners should be controlled by the use of different small units within individual "community" prisons.

9.33 Professor Bottoms, in some interesting theoretic papers based on research at Long Lartin and Albany prisons, stressed to the Inquiry the importance of a stable and predictable environment for prisoners. He regarded this as a form of "social crime prevention" within prisons. Social structures depended on repeated routines of behaviour. Frequent moves for prisoners must make it more difficult to achieve such stable and predictable routines ("Situational and Social Approaches to the Prevention of Disorder in Long-Term Prisons"; Bottoms, Hay and Sparks).

9.34 The evidence before the Inquiry, therefore, suggests that a transfer against the wishes of a prisoner is one of the most resented actions which the Prison Service can take. It is made worse when the prisoner feels that he has been given no satisfactory explanation for that transfer, and when the transfer results in his being further away from his home. Such transfers can appear to the inmate to be unjust, and, in the way they are effected, may leave deep scars of resentment. In view of this evidence, in Part II (Section 12) of the Report, the issues raised by the Prison Service's use of transfers as a control mechanism for disruptive prisoners is considered in greater detail. Proposals are made which are intended to reduce the possible adverse effects of transfers.

9.35 It can also be said, on the basis of the evidence from all six disturbances, that the incidents which at the start involved only a few inmates, spread because they found ready support from many more inmates. Without that support, the disturbances would not have spread and would have been more readily resolved. Broad support for the instigators contributed to the seriousness of the incidents. At Strangeways, Pucklechurch, and possibly Bristol, although not all the inmates supported the disturbances, such support appears to have been widespread. The disturbances spread to almost all parts of each prison.

9.36 A contributory factor to the spread of the disturbances at Strangeways and Bristol was the way in which the disturbances were handled, in particular the decision by staff to vacate certain areas of the prisons. It was at those two establishments, together with Pucklechurch, that the hostility was the greatest and the damage was the most intense. At Glen Parva and Cardiff, where the disturbances were most effectively contained, the inmates were the least discontent, and the damage was the least extensive.

9.37   The evidence of prisoners is that they will not join in disturbances in any numbers if they feel conditions are reasonable and relationships are satisfactory. These are matters of justice which the Prison Service must address more closely. They are fundamental to maintaining a stable prison system which is able to withstand and reject the depredations of disruptive and violent individuals. These are matters which must be resolved if we are to have peace in our prisons. They are considered in Part II of this Report.

The Disturbances Demonstrate the Importance of Maintaining Security and Control

9.38   There are undoubtedly within the prison system of this country a number of prisoners who, given the opportunity and whatever the conditions within the prison, would seek either to escape or to be disruptive. No improvement in the conditions of containment will alter this situation.

9.39   For this group of prisoners, a reasonable and effective degree of security is needed. The prison system has to be managed in a way which will enable the required degree of security and control to be provided.

9.40   But even for these prisoners, it is important that a proper balance is struck. No more security safeguards should be applied than are strictly required. No more control should be exercised than is necessary. Excessive security and control can have the opposite effect to the ones desired. Prisoners will feel unnecessarily oppressed. They will feel a genuine grievance which will attract sympathy and support from their fellow inmates.

9.41   Most precautions which are taken for reasons of security assist also with control. It is therefore important to recognise, as does the evidence on behalf of the Prison Service, that the means used for maintaining security and control are not mutually exclusive.

9.42   In the rest of this Section, I identify the particular areas of control which my consideration of the evidence under Part I of this Inquiry has shown need fresh examination.

A Control Categorisation for Prisoners Is Not Practicable

9.43   There is already a system of categorising prisoners according to the security risk which they are thought to pose. This was introduced following the Mountbatten Report into Prison Escapes and Security in 1966. The system ranges from the highest security grading, Category A, to the lowest, Category D. Prisons themselves are graded according to the category of prisoner they are able to hold at the right level of security.

9.44   I have considered whether, alongside this system of security categorisation, there needs to be a separate system of control categorisation to reflect the degree of risk a prisoner is perceived to present to the maintenance of control in a prison.

9.45   The present security categorisation is a poor indication of possible control risks. Many prisoners who attract a high security categorisation, because they may present a risk to the public if they escape, present no appreciable risk of disrupting the life of the prison. Within a secure environment, they could be given a good deal of freedom.

9.46   On the other hand, there are some prisoners who present no appreciable risk to the public if they escape, but who present acute control problems within the environment of the prison. They may need to be held in conditions and to be treated in a way which are not justified by their security categorisation.

9.47   A control categorisation system would be a way of avoiding any distortion in the way the criteria for security categorisation are drawn up and used. It would clearly mark the procedures and arrangements which may be necessary for dealing with a disruptive prisoner. It could, if properly deployed, encourage the Prison Service to provide more relaxed living conditions in a closed prison for some prisoners, who must be held in conditions of high security, but not necessarily of tight control. A set of consistent criteria could also ensure that judgments in relation to control problems are made in a more consistent and objective way.

9.48   I have been persuaded, however, that the problems of such a system would not be easy to overcome. The evidence suggests that a prisoner who creates control problems in one prison, may behave with complete propriety in another. There is, as far as I know, no objective system for identifying potentially disruptive prisoners. Any categorisation system would, therefore, either be subjective, and objectionable on that account, or it would, in effect, involve applying a label after the event – shutting the door after the horse has bolted. Prisoners who are being held in Special Units or in segregation units under Rule 43 for the good order or discipline of the establishment, do not need to be given a further label.

9.49   A system of categorisation could also be either unnecessarily complex and bureaucratic, or it could be so simplistic as to be unfair. It would not be helpful to introduce a system which required a prisoner to be held in less favourable conditions than his colleagues unless there was good substantial evidence to justify such treatment. Establishments need to find a wide variety of ways of dealing with prisoners whom they identify as potential control problems. An attempt to deal with the cause of the problem – whether it arises from the life of the prison or from outside – may be more effective in deterring disruption than spending time reviewing the prisoner's control categorisation.

9.50   Accordingly, I do not propose the introduction of a system for control categorisation. If, in the future, an objective and easy to operate system for identifying potentially disruptive prisoners were to be developed, then the weight of the argument could change. There would still, however, be the need to ensure there were adequate safeguards to prevent the system being an instrument of injustice.

Security Information Reports Must Be Completed and Properly Submitted to Governors

9.51   The Prison Service in its evidence, said that there is the need for:

> "sound arrangements for gathering, collation and dissemination of intelligence".

9.52   The Prison Service's evidence refers to draft revised guidance on the use of SIR forms. The revised guidance makes it clear that the information can be passed orally. It states:

> "the task of raising an SIR form lies with the security department itself....where *the quality of the information justifies it*". (emphasis added).

9.53   This qualification on the responsibility of the security department to complete an SIR form gives rise to concern. An SIR should be raised in respect of all information which may affect security and control within an establishment, without regard to its apparent quality. If it does not affect security and control, no action is required. If it does, action may be required and it should be the subject of the SIR procedures.

9.54   The efficient working of a proper security information system can depend upon building up a picture from a number of small items of information. If what appears to be an unimportant item is not recorded, someone taking over responsibility for security can be deprived of a vital piece of the jigsaw which goes to make up that picture. The draft should be revised in the light of these comments. The importance of this subject was emphasised by the breakdown in the reporting of security information at both Strangeways and Cardiff.

9.55 A standard procedure should be instituted which makes the senior Governor on duty in the prison, or the most senior officer on duty at the time, responsible for ensuring that security information is properly recorded and disseminated. He should, therefore, when he comes on duty ensure that he is handed a written record of security information prepared by the officer responsible for security during the preceding shift. The Governor, or his substitute, should be responsible for ensuring that other Governors and officers are given any information it contains relevant to their duties. He should be personally responsible for ensuring that the record is properly maintained during his period of duty. He should be personally responsible for handing over that record, up dated in its turn by his officer in charge of security, to the most senior Governor or officer who relieves him.

The Disastrous Effect of the Loss of an Officer's Keys Must be Reduced

9.56 A central problem in many of these disturbances was the way in which prisoners who took keys from officers were able to use them to release prisoners from their cells throughout the establishment.

9.57 Precautions against keys being taken are needed. The methods of attaching keys to an officer's clothing should be reviewed. But this is not enough. A clear lesson of the disturbances is that it is no longer practical to continue the long standing tradition of staff, when on duty within a prison, normally carrying keys which will open the doors of all the cells within the prison irrespective of its size. The policy should be that a member of staff should only carry the keys which are reasonably necessary for performing the duties on which he or she is likely to be engaged during that officer's current shift. The details of this policy and its implications for the design of locking systems are discussed in Section 11 of this report.

Staff Must Initially be Expected to Withdraw From the Immediate Scene of a Serious Disturbance

9.58 The disturbances confirmed that in the case of a serious disruption, prison staff will almost inevitably have to withdraw. In normal conditions, it is neither practical nor desirable to have staff present in such numbers that, in the event of any riot, they could immediately restore control. No prison could exist equably under such a requirement. A riot should be a rare and unusual event.

9.59 This makes it all the more important, however, that a suitable procedure has been drawn up and that plans have been prepared which staff can follow if they have to withdraw. There must be proper physical barriers to avoid staff having to withdraw further than necessary from the immediate seat of the riot.

9.60 It makes it important also that staff should not withdraw unless the immediate circumstances make this unavoidable. Withdrawal should normally be made on the instructions of a senior officer or governor, having weighed all the circumstances, including the safety of the prisoners who will remain. The varied experiences of Bristol and Manchester showed the importance of not withdrawing staff prematurely. The experience of Cardiff showed the value of staff withdrawing to a defendable barrier.

There Should be Security Firebreaks to Which Staff Can Withdraw and Which Staff Can Hold

9.61 The disturbances showed that any disturbance must be contained within as restricted an area as possible.

9.62 I propose that the position to which prison staff should withdraw in the case of a serious disturbance which they cannot control should be identified in the course of contingency planning and training within an establishment. It should be a place which is capable of being held securely, at least for a reasonable period, to allow for support to arrive. It must therefore be somewhere where there are gates or doors which are of sufficient strength to withstand reasonably prolonged attack by prisoners.

9.63 Preferably the gates or doors should be electrically operated or have locks which cannot be opened by keys which the prisoners could have obtained from an officer on the wings or units. In other words, the gates or doors are to perform a function which in the case of a serious fire is performed by a firebreak. The siting of the gates and doors will have to depend upon the physical characteristics of existing prison establishments.

9.64 I propose that, where this is possible, there should be a security "firebreak" at the entrance to each unit within the prison establishment. In addition there should be a "firebreak" at the entrance to each area of the prison where the number of prisoners who can be expected to congregate is in excess of about 70 inmates. The implications of this proposal for the Prison Service's building and refurbishment programme are considered more fully in Section 11.

9.65 Taking Strangeways before the riot as an example, there should have been secure gates (a "firebreak") from the Centre to each of the wings at each landing level, at all doors leading from the Chapel, and between the Main Prison and the Remand Prison.

9.66 Once security arrangements on these lines exist within a prison establishment, then it is clear what action staff should take in the event of a serious disturbance. They should withdraw to the nearest "firebreak". If this is reasonable, they should hold that area until they are given orders to the contrary. If there is more than one gate which has to be defended, then staff can be given the necessary instructions to ensure that they do not all congregate at one gate, leaving other gates unprotected.

Physical Security Should be Checked and, Where Necessary, Upgraded

9.67 A security strategy based on the holding of "firebreaks" until reinforcements can be provided is, however, worthless if the "firebreaks" can be bypassed. This is what happened at Strangeways and Bristol. Access to the roof must not be possible. The forms of roof security which existed within the wings at Strangeways and Bristol would have been perfectly adequate if they had not been able to be bypassed (in the case of Strangeways by obtaining access to the eaves above the Chapel; in the case of Bristol by breaking through a wall).

9.68 Protection of the means of access to roofs and their cladding should be brought up to current standards at all closed prisons. No higher standard is required.

9.69 At Bristol and Pucklechurch, and very nearly Cardiff, prisoners were assisted in moving from one part of the prison to another by being able to get hold of Works Department tools. These tools enabled the prisoners to bypass what security there was.

9.70   Building tools, equipment and other appliances which will assist prisoners to penetrate the security which is provided, should not be left unattended in accommodation units, even if they are in a locked cell or store.

9.71   The shortcomings in physical security, which I have been discussing, relate directly or indirectly to what the Prison Service in its evidence identifies as being:

> "the first means of maintaining security, the physical integrity of cells and buildings".

9.72   Security is only as strong as its weakest point.

9.73   I propose therefore that each establishment should check its physical security at frequent intervals. If defects are discovered, then they should not be left to be dealt with in the course of some general refurbishment. The degree of general physical security will depend on the security category of the establishment.

9.74   In local prisons, security has had in the past too low a priority. There is a need for a clear message to be conveyed to prisoners and staff within large local prisons that the prospects of prisoners again being able to over-run the whole of a prison establishment are very remote. This will discourage prisoners from attempting to repeat the April disturbances and assist in restoring the morale of staff.

9.75   I propose, therefore, that in local prisons any improvements necessary in the security of roofs, gates and locks, should be regarded as being a matter of urgency. Ideally, any necessary work on these matters should be carried out in conjunction with the refurbishment programme which is required to divide wings into acceptably sized units. However, the implementation of any necessary work on roofs, gates and locks should not be deferred in local prisons where refurbishment is unlikely to take place for some time.

9.76   Additional expense is involved in implementing this policy. However, in comparison to the consequences of not implementing it, that cost is modest.

There Must Be Improved Methods of Communication

9.77   At Strangeways, as at many other local and other prisons, the communications room was inadequately equipped. The communications room has to be at the centre of operations when a major disturbance breaks out. The proper handling of a disturbance makes it essential that those responsible for co-ordinating the response can find out what is happening, and can convey information to those who need to know. The standard of communications equipment in a closed prison's communications room should be much closer to that which exists in the control room of a dispersal prison. I recognise, however, that such a prison's communications room may not require the same level of staffing as that in a dispersal prison, except when there is an emergency.

9.78   Further work should be undertaken to improve the methods of communication within establishments and between establishments and Headquarters during a serious disturbance. Staff, as well as Headquarters, need to be kept informed of what is happening. There were clear shortcomings in both areas during the disturbances. This was especially true in the case of Manchester. The implications of what happened there are discussed in Section 3.

9.79   Other communications also need to be improved during a disturbance. I propose that, in the event of a serious disturbance, communication points are established within a reasonable period to help enquiries from families of both staff and inmates, and to enable members of staff to phone home.

9.80   The contributions which were made by the Probation Service, the Chaplaincy and voluntary services during and after the riots are to be commended. However, contingency planning should make provision for the Prison Service itself to make arrangements to ensure that communications can take place. The Prison Service has a responsibility to do what it can to alleviate the stress which is caused to those involved in a serious disturbance. It needs to pay more attention in the future, to debriefing, stress counselling and staff and family care following a serious incident. What happened both at Cardiff and Pucklechurch (in the one case in respect of a member of staff's claim and in the other in respect of inmates' claims) shows there needs to be sensitive processing and the speedy settlement of any claims for compensation following a serious incident.

There Must be Better Contingency Planning and Training

9.81   It is to be earnestly hoped that the Prison Service will not continue to be racked by serious disorder. But, having regard to what has happened, the Service must be prepared to manage a disturbance satisfactorily if it should occur.

9.82   What happened during the disturbances indicated there is a greater need for the training of those who are likely to be involved, at differing levels, in the management of a serious disturbance. As Mr O'Friel pointed out during his evidence, once a disturbance is taking place, events happen with a remarkable rapidity. I propose therefore that contingency plans, the exercise of those plans, and staff and management training in responding to a disturbance, should be developed to the level where the Prison Service can be satisfied that all those likely to be involved in a disturbance know what to do and how to do it. Just as it is necessary to have regular fire training exercises, so within establishments it is necessary to have exercises directed to dealing with major disturbances.

9.83   Contingency plans need to be regularly revised, up-dated and tested. They need also to identify what I have referred to earlier as the "firebreaks" within the establishment, and the importance of not letting the disturbance spread beyond the "firebreak".

9.84   The record of what happened at Pucklechurch after the end of its riot emphasises the importance of contingency plans making proper provision to deal with the aftermath of a serious disturbance. During a disturbance, staff can be subject to very considerable pressures. Unless careful and detailed arrangements are made in advance, things can go very wrong. In commenting on the Pucklechurch disturbance, I have drawn attention to the action which has already been taken by the Prison Service to ensure that all establishments have acceptable plans for handling the surrender of prisoners.

Boards of Visitors Should Have a Central Role

9.85   Regrettably, the disturbances disclose a pattern of failure to inform the Board of Visitors of a serious disturbance. It is an important part of the role of the Board of Visitors to attend a disturbance as soon as it is practicable. When they did attend, the Board members invariably made a valuable contribution. But there was evidence at both Pucklechurch and Dartmoor that principles need to be better understood and practices better developed.

9.86   I propose that the preparation of contingency plans and their exercise should closely involve the Board of Visitors. They should be clear about their role and responsibilities, and how they should be exercised. They should require a member of the Board of Visitors to be informed as soon as a disturbance begins.

The Prison Service Should Have the Capacity To Deploy Water During a Disturbance

9.87 The careful and proportionate deployment of water against prisoners is one of the most powerful weapons available to staff dealing with a disturbance. The Manchester riot showed that there was a need to review the existing restrictions on the circumstances in which water can be used and the authority required for its use. It may be appropriate for the Fire Service to make available equipment to the Prison Service during a disturbance if inmates could not identify it as belonging to the Fire Service (eg the lights at Dartmoor). This should be considered. I propose also that equipment, such as the Green Goddesses which were eventually made available at Strangeways, should be much more readily available in the event of a serious disturbance. Prison Service staff should be trained in advance in how the equipment operates and in the circumstances and manner in which it should be used.

Control and Restraint Techniques Will Need to Continue To Be Reinforced and Co-operation with the Police Maintained

9.88 The Service is fortunate in having developed such effective C&R techniques. Those techniques compare favourably to those developed in other countries which the Inquiry visited. C&R techniques are, however, still not fully developed. I was impressed on my visit to Lindholme by the enthusiasm and energy which has been shown by the national instructors to learn from the experience of the April disturbances. I am confident that those responsible for the C&R techniques at the present time will ensure that they are continuously improved.

9.89 At the time of the disturbances, the Prison Service was still in the transitional process of changing from MUFTI to C&R. The training of governors in C&R3 techniques and the provision of C&R equipment was inadequate. I understand that these deficiencies are already remedied or being remedied. There is a need for governor grades in particular to become more involved in C&R training in establishments.

9.90 In the year before the April 1990 disturbances, the Prison Service had embarked on a substantial programme to train officers in C&R techniques. The intention was that each larger establishment should muster from its own resources a C&R Section (36 officers) together with the requisite commanders and communication officers. Each smaller establishment was expected to muster a C&R Unit (12 officers) with its commander and communication officer. Sixty establishments were "section establishments" and 64 were "unit establishments". In addition, it was intended that a minimum of 20% more staff would be trained than the strict number required to make up a section or unit.

9.91 These targets involved training approximately 4,200 prison staff and then regularly providing refresher courses for those staff. At the time of the disturbances in April 1990, 3,234 members of staff had completed their basic training. In the light of the disturbances in April, I have considered whether there is a need to increase the general training programme for uniformed grades of staff. In my view, the fact that the Prison Service managed to cope with the April disturbances when the total training programme had not yet been completed, indicates that the original proposals were sensible and realistic.

9.92 It is better to have a reasonable number of officers who are trained to the required standard and who then have regular refresher courses, than to have a larger force that is not so well trained. As standards within the prison system improve, it is to be hoped that a reduction in the C&R training programme will be possible.

9.93 I propose that suitable members of hospital staff be selected for C&R3 training so that they can act as paramedics in the event of a serious disturbance. The need for paramedics to be part of the C&R complement was made clear both at Strangeways and at Bristol.

9.94 During the disturbances, there was considerable confusion as to the status of those coming from other establishments. There was confusion also about the identity of those who were in command at the establishment where the incident was taking place. I propose that all staff within a prison during an incident should at all times, whether wearing C&R equipment or not, clearly display their names and the nature of their job within the establishment. I leave it to be determined by the Prison Service precisely how this is to be done because it may have tactical implications. (Proposals about wearing identification during normal duties are made in Section 13.)

9.95 As a result of the April disturbances, the Prison Service is energetically pursuing the possibility of improving the C&R equipment which is at present on issue. This is obviously sensible.

9.96 It is desirable that the Prison Service closely co-operates with the police in the provision of equipment during a disturbance. The police may be in a position to provide specialist equipment which either the police or the prison staff could operate but which could not be expected to be carried by a prison establishment.

9.97 The availability of firearms was a matter considered by the Mountbatten Report and again by a sub-committee of the Advisory Council on the Penal System. While I recognise that situations could arise where firearms and other forms of weaponry may have to be used, I would not propose any alteration to the existing policy. If such weaponry has to be used, this should be a matter for the police.

Conclusion

9.98 In the course of my examination of the six disturbances, I heard criticisms of the way they were handled. I have proposed a number of changes here and in the preceding Sections which I hope will improve the situation. However, in general, in a time of great stress, the Prison Service staff at all levels acquitted themselves in an exemplary manner having regard to the degree of preparedness which existed and the resources which were available.

9.99 Only those involved in the disturbances can appreciate how difficult it is to remain calm and to deliberate coolly over every action in the face of the riotous conditions which existed. The bill for what occurred is large, but it could have been very easily much greater. That it was not is a tribute to the standards in general displayed by the staff and management of the Prison Service.

PART II

AND RECOMMENDATIONS AND PROPOSALS

Section 10

Imprisonment

Introduction

10.1   We start Part II of this Report by examining what should be the role of the Prison Service. The evidence given in Part I of the Inquiry made it clear that there was insufficient clarity about what the Prison Service should be doing and how it should do it. This affected the way prisons were run. Uncertainties about this were one of the underlying causes of the disturbances. They lay also at the heart of the problems identified in Part I about the way the disturbances were handled. A reassessment of the role of the Prison Service is needed to give a clear sense of direction and to help restore the confidence of some of its members which was damaged in the riots.

10.2   In this Section of the Report we also consider what action can be taken to divert from prison those persons who do not need to be there. This is important in its own right. It is important also because it should help reduce overcrowding. It should also enable the resources of the Prison Service to be deployed in the most effective way. It should itself ensure that the work of the Prison Service is not dissipated and that its role is brought into clearer focus.

10.3   All this can only be achieved, however, if the Prison Service is seen for what it is - an integral part of the Criminal Justice System. The implications of this need to be accepted and followed through. If the Prison Service is to be able to carry out its role effectively, closer co-operation and co-ordination between the different parts of the System are essential.

Identifying the Task of the Prison Service

i) The Convicted Prisoner   10.4   The Report of the May Committee of Inquiry into the United Kingdom Prison Services, published in October 1979, recognises the importance of a clear explanation of the role of the Prison Service. In order to identify what should be included in that explanation, the Report admirably traces the changes in penal policy over the last 300 years. It identifies the progression from a "separate" system of cellular isolation, which was regarded as being "morally beneficial" (by preventing contamination and by providing an opportunity for reflection and self-examination) to a treatment model (which should, in the words of the report of the Gladstone Committee in 1895, "have as its primary and concurrent objects deterrence and reformation").

10.5   The May Report records the loss of confidence in the 1970s in the possibility of imprisonment achieving the reform of the offender. The Report points out that, as confidence in the treatment model waned, no alternative philosophy commanding wide public support has taken its place. To fill this gap, the Committee proposed that the aim of the Prison Service should be to provide "positive custody" for convicted prisoners.

10.6   The May Committee explained what it meant by positive custody by suggesting that Rule 1 of the Prison Rules should be re-written in the following terms:

> "1. The purpose of the detention of convicted prisoners shall be to keep them in custody which is both secure and yet positive, and to that end the behaviour of all the responsible authorities and staff towards them shall be such as to:
>
> a) create an environment which can assist them to respond and contribute to society as positively as possible;
>
> b) preserve and promote their self-respect;
>
> c) minimise, to the degree of security necessary in each particular case, the harmful effects of their removal from normal life;
>
> d) prepare them for and assist them on discharge."

10.7 Rule 1 has never been re-written as suggested by the May Committee. It remains in its previous form:

> "1. The purpose of the training and treatment of convicted prisoners shall be to encourage and assist them to lead a good and useful life."

10.8 When Rule 1 is read with Rule 2, it is clear that the May Committee was not proposing fundamental changes. Rule 2 provides:

> "2(i) Order and discipline shall be maintained with firmness, but with no more restrictions than is required for safe custody and well ordered community life.
>
> (ii) In the control of prisoners, officers shall seek to influence them through their own example and leadership, and to enlist their willing co-operation.
>
> (iii) At all times the treatment of prisoners shall be such as to encourage their self-respect and a sense of personal responsibility, but a prisoner shall not be employed in any disciplinary capacity."

10.9 Both Rules 1 and 2 and the proposed "May Amendments" emphasise two important objectives. The first is that prisoners are to be contained with no more security than is necessary. The second is that prisoners are to be encouraged to lead a good and useful life.

10.10 The Prison Board's Statement of Purpose, which should be displayed at all prison establishments, states:

> "Her Majesty's Prison Service serves the public by keeping in custody those committed by the courts.
>
> Our duty is to look after them with humanity and to help them lead law abiding and useful lives in custody and after release."

10.11 The Statement of Purpose recognises that the Prison Service has three tasks: (a) to keep secure those whom the Courts put in their custody; (b) to treat those who are in their custody with humanity; and (c) to look after those in its custody in such a way as to help them to "lead law abiding and useful lives" (i) while they are in custody and (ii) after release.

10.12 The Statement of Purpose differs from Rule 2 in that it does not spell out expressly the obligation of the Prison Service to use no more security than is necessary to look after those in its custody. This is implicit, however, in the requirement that prisoners should be looked after with humanity.

10.13 The Rules, the May Committee and the Statement of Purpose are at one in categorically accepting that it is part of the duty of the Prison Service to assist the prisoner in the future to be a responsible member of society.

10.14   Many prison services in other countries have also adopted Statements of Purpose or, as they are sometimes described, mission statements. Although each statement has its virtues, we do not know of any which, in relation to convicted and sentenced prisoners, is an improvement on that of the Prisons Board. We do not suggest any amendment to the Statement of Purpose in relation to those prisoners. We do not, however, regard the Statement as being sufficiently comprehensive to cover remand prisoners. We will consider separately their position in the next part of this Section.

10.15   The Prison Service's Statement has the advantage of being succinct. It provides a useful structure for examining the role of the Prison Service. However it does not, and could not in so few words, fully explain that role. The May Committee Report assisted a fuller understanding of the role of the Prison Service by considering that role in its historical penal context. We propose to examine the Prison Service's role in the context of the Criminal Justice System. The advantage of this approach is that it makes it clear that, together with the Police, the Probation Service, the Crown Prosecution Service and the Courts, the Prison Service has a special responsibility for maintaining law, order and justice in society.

10.16   First, when the Prison Service "serves the public" by keeping in custody those committed by the Courts, it does so to further the objectives shared by all parts of the Criminal Justice System. This responsibility of the Prison Service is important and is not mentioned in the Statement of Purpose. It needs to be recognised. The Prison Service tends to be too introspective and not to coordinate its activities with other sections of the Criminal Justice System.

10.17   Secondly, it is fundamental to the Prison Service's position as part of the Criminal Justice System that it should ensure that prisoners are treated with justice in prisons.

10.18   The Courts send prisoners to prison because in their judgement justice requires that the prisoner should receive a sentence of imprisonment. Imprisonment is the gravest punishment which it is open to the Courts to impose. The Courts do not, as they did at one time for some types of sentence, specify what form that punishment should take. They do not sentence someone to hard labour, or corrective training. They leave it to the Prison Service to decide how to provide the conditions of containment which are appropriate for that individual, having regard to all the relevant factors, including the length of sentence which he has to serve.

10.19   If the Prison Service contains that prisoner in conditions which are inhumane or degrading, or which are otherwise wholly inappropriate, then a punishment of imprisonment which was justly imposed, will result in injustice. It is no doubt for this reason, as well as because any other approach would offend the values of our society, that the Statement of Purpose acknowledges that it is the Prison Service's duty to look after prisoners with humanity. If it fulfils this duty, the Prison Service is partly achieving what the Court must be taken to have intended when it passed a sentence of imprisonment. This must be that, while the prisoner should be subjected to the stigma of imprisonment and should be confined in a prison, the prisoner is not to be subjected to inhumane or degrading treatment.

10.20   The condensed language of the Statement of Purpose does not (at least to the ordinary reader) draw attention expressly to the importance of treating a prisoner with justice. The definition of the word humanity in the Shorter Oxford Dictionary makes no reference to justice. It does, however, refer to "human attributes..... that appeal to man". It is entirely acceptable to argue that the requirement to treat prisoners with humanity includes an obligation to treat them with justice. However, the two terms are not strictly synonymous. If a prisoner is provided with a dry cell, with integral sanitation and as much exercise, activities, association and food as he likes, many people would regard him as being treated with humanity. They would continue to do so even if the prisoner had a deep sense of grievance because he had been transferred from one prison to another without any reason being given and, the prisoner felt, without any satisfactory means of redress. That would be a failure principally of justice. Only at the extreme could it be properly interpreted as failing the test of humanity.

10.21   Part I of the Inquiry made it abundantly clear that, while some prisoners were angry over the physical conditions or food, there were others who were antagonistic and disruptive because they felt they had been treated unjustly and there was no independent person to whom they could turn for redress. They were aggrieved over a failure of justice.

10.22   The failure of the Statement of Purpose to refer expressly to the requirement to provide justice in prisons, is shared by Rules 1 and 2 and the proposed May Amendment. This omission is explicable when it is appreciated that the extent of the entitlement of a prisoner to justice has only been clearly developed by the Courts since 1979 (see *R v Board of Visitors of Hull Prison* [1979] QB). It is now clear that, contrary to what was previously contended, in spite of his imprisonment a convicted prisoner retains all his civil rights which are not taken away expressly or by necessary implication. If, for example, a governor does not treat a prisoner justly in disciplinary proceedings, the prisoner can obtain judicial review.

10.23   In extending the remedies available to the prisoner, the Courts are only reflecting what are regarded by society as minimum acceptable standards. Where an institution has the sort of power over an individual which the Prison Service has, that institution must at all times be conscious of the importance of justice. This requirement is underlined when the institution is part of the Criminal Justice System. In due course, the Prison Rules should be amended to reflect the requirement that prisoners should be treated with justice.

10.24   There is a third consequence of the Prison Service's position as part of the Criminal Justice System. The objectives of the Criminal Justice System include discouraging crime. A sentence of imprisonment is imposed by the Court partly in order to deter offending. The objective of deterrence implicitly includes the underlying purpose of reducing criminal behaviour. In so far as this is possible, and within the constraints imposed by the fact that imprisonment is inevitably coercive, the Prison Service should therefore, as part of its role, be seeking to minimise the prospect of the prisoner re-offending after serving his sentence. This is fully consistent with the Prison Service's duty "to help them lead law abiding and useful lives in custody and after release".

10.25   It is now generally accepted that, particularly with young offenders, there is a risk that a custodial sentence, instead of making it less likely that the offender will offend again, increases that danger. In 1986 the reconviction rates within two years were: for male young offenders 63%, for male adult offenders 42%, and for female offenders 34%.

10.26   These are disappointing figures. They are more so if the costs are taken into account. Non-custodial sentences cost about 5% of the cost of custodial sentences. (The average cost of custodial sentences overall for the year 1988/89 was £288.00 per week. The cost for male offenders ranges from £541.00 per week at a high security dispersal prison to £199.00 per week in an open prison. The comparable cost of a community service order was £15.00 per week, a supervision order £16.00 per week and a probation order £19.00 per week.) As there is no evidence that non-custodial sentences are not at least as likely to prevent reoffending as custodial sentences, in those terms, custodial sentences provide poor value for the public at the present time.

10.27   The evidence before the Inquiry suggests that at least part of the explanation for imprisonment not being more successful in preventing reoffending is that the prisoner has so little responsibility for what happens to him during the period of the sentence. It is also clear from the evidence which the Inquiry has received from prisoners, that the conditions which exist at present in our prisons causes a substantial number of prisoners to leave prison more embittered and hostile to society than when they arrived. They leave prison, therefore, in a state of mind where they are more likely to re-offend. Furthermore, the sentence tends to make it more difficult for them to obtain employment. And it tends to weaken their connections with their families and their local communities.

10.28   If it is to further the objectives of the Criminal Justice System, the Prison Service has to address these factors. In particular, if the second half of the Statement of Purpose is not to be subject to ridicule, the Prison Service has to tackle the problems which arise from the conditions and restricted regimes in many prison establishments and in particular in the local prisons.

10.29   In order to do so it must seek to minimise the negative effects of imprisonment which make reoffending more likely. It must require the offender to confront and take responsibility for the wrong doing which resulted in his having to serve a sentence of imprisonment. It must encourage the prisoner to take some responsibility for what happens to him in prison. It must seek to provide the prisoner with an opportunity to obtain skills which will make it easier to obtain and keep employment and enable him to maintain his family and community contacts. It must seek to ensure that life in prison will be as close to life outside as the demands of imprisonment permit. It must, above all, ensure, through these and other means, that the prisoner is properly prepared for his return to society.

10.30   In seeking to perform this difficult task, the Prison Service needs to work closely with the Probation Service. This will be particularly important if the proposals in the Criminal Justice Bill become law. Punishments will then be served partly in prison and partly in the community. As the Probation Service will be closely involved with the part of the sentence served in the community, it is also important that they are involved in the part of the sentence which is served in prison.

10.31   In their evidence to the Inquiry, the Central Council of Probation Committees complained that they;

"are dismayed and frustrated at the inability of the Prison Service in general and many individual institutions in particular to recognise the potential of the Probation Service to make an effective contribution in working with prisoners".

10.32   As the Council points out:

"the traditional aim of the Probation Service is to restore offenders to law abiding life and its main purpose is to reduce reoffending".

10.33   This is also part of the role of the Prison Service. It is therefore essential that the Prison Service and the Probation Service work together to achieve this common objective. For this purpose, the Prison Service must further the development of "through-care".

10.34   In underlining the importance of the second half of the Statement of Purpose, we are not suggesting that this justifies a return to what came to be known as the treatment model of imprisonment. The distinction between what was then the policy and what is now proposed, is that, under the former model, it was thought appropriate to sentence an offender to a custodial sentence for reformative treatment, as if being a criminal was a curative condition. This was, for example, very much the policy behind the sentence of Borstal training for young offenders and of corrective training for adults. However, while we would not suggest that an offender should be sentenced to imprisonment *for* reformative treatment, we regard it as part of the Prison Service's role to ensure, where this is practicable, that a prisoner, while serving his sentence, should have an opportunity of training.

10.35   There is a fourth requirement on the Prison Service in its role as part of the Criminal Justice System. It is fundamental to this role that it holds the prisoner securely. The Statement of Purpose does not expressly refer to security. However it is implicit in the words in the first part of the statement that the Service "serves the public by keeping in custody those committed by the Courts". The Criminal Justice System cannot operate effectively if the decisions that are made by one part of the system, in this case the Courts, are not effectively implemented by another part, the Prison Service. The public and the Courts have a right to expect that when a prisoner is sent to prison, he or she stays there until the proper time for his release.

10.36   The Mountbatten Report of 1966 identified the importance of security. It made the recommendations which resulted in the present system of security categorisation. Since then, security has played a more prominent role in the Prison Service. The security with which the Mountbatten Report was concerned was the security which prevents prisoners escaping. This aspect of security was not breached at any of the establishments which have been targeted by this Inquiry as a result of the April disturbances.

10.37   There is, however, another aspect to security. That is the *control* of inmates within a prison establishment. It was this aspect of security which broke down during April 1990, not only in the targeted establishments but in other establishments as well.

10.38   As the events of that month proved, the need for control is extremely important. It is important because of the harm which can be done to the staff, other inmates and to prison property if control breaks down. It is important because of the contribution control makes to security. It is important because, if the staff are to be in a position to act in accord with the aims of the Prison Service, then they must feel secure. Control also provides inmates with a sense of security. They need to be secure from being subject to intimidation by other inmates and from improper conduct by staff. Finally, if control breaks down, it demonstrates a break down of law and order which, as part of the Criminal Justice System, the Prison Service has a major responsibility to uphold.

10.39   The achievement of security in this wider sense of including control is important in Prison Service establishments. But the attention paid to security should not be at the expense of the other aspects of the role of the Prison Service. Part of the reason for this is because, as Mr Ian Dunbar, a member of the Prison Service, has made clear in his report, A Sense of Direction, the other aspects of the role will help to provide "Dynamic Security". This is as important to the security of an establishment as physical containment. Prisons are of their nature establishments to which offenders do not wish to go and where they must be held securely; but prisons need not make those who are serving sentences in them feel bitter, hostile or degraded.

10.40   Part of the present difficulties of the Prison Service can be attributed to the fact that, since the Mountbatten Report, the Prison Service has not been in a position to pay sufficient attention to aspects of their role other than security. Overcrowding, and the fact that the prison estate was largely insanitary and run down, has made it necessary for the Prison Service to expend too great a proportion of its energy in crisis management, coping with the consequences of overcrowding and lack of sanitation. It is only in recent years that Governments have been prepared to make the resources available to tackle the inadequacies of the prison estate. As a result, the prospects for the Prison Service are now better than they have been for many years. It should now therefore be possible for the Prison Service to have proper regard for what should be its full role.

10.41   The full role of the Prison Service, as explained in Section 9 of the Report, requires the Prison Service to address three aspects. They are: security, control, and justice within prisons. The three aspects complement each other. The Prison Service must give each its due weight. And it must maintain the proper balance between them. If security is breached and a prisoner is allowed to escape, that frustrates the sentence imposed by the Court. There is a failure of both security and justice. If sufficient control is not provided and prisoners riot, security is put at risk and the ability of the Service to provide conditions which accord with justice will be impaired.

10.42   A proper concentration on these three aspects of the Prison Service's role would accord with the intent of the Statement of Purpose. It would involve the prisoner being treated with humanity and being helped to lead a law abiding life while in prison and after release. It would further the objectives of the Criminal Justice System.

10.43   This is a challenging, constructive and worthwhile role. It involves the Prison Service making a recognised and constructive contribution to the Criminal Justice System's task of maintaining public order and justice. If the challenge is met by the Prison Service, it will result in the prison system making a more worthwhile contribution to society than it does at present. While it may not achieve the reform of many prisoners, it will at least give prisoners upon their discharge from prison a better opportunity than exists at present of their becoming law abiding members of the community, if they choose do so. It will also result in a more stable prison system, less vulnerable to repeated serious disturbances.

10.44   The achievement of this role, however, depends on there being a proper balance within prisons between security and control on the one hand and humanity and justice on the other.

ii) Remand and Unsentenced Prisoners

10.45   Everything which we have said in relation to convicted prisoners can be applied to the role of the Prison Service in relation to remand prisoners. (We include unsentenced prisoners in this description.) But it is not a full or sufficient statement of that role.

10.46   The Prison Service regards the Statement of Purpose as being appropriate for both convicted and remand prisoners. Even when due allowance is made for the need for brevity in a Statement of Purpose, we take a different view. We appreciate, however, that there is nothing in the language of the Statement of Purpose which cannot be applied to remand prisoners.

10.47   The Statement of Purpose, in its present form, is not appropriate to remand prisoners because it makes no reference to the fundamental distinction between remand and convicted prisoners. The distinction is that remand prisoners, unless and until found guilty, are presumed innocent. They are not therefore in prison as a punishment. The fact that prisoners on remand have to be presumed innocent has important implications for the Prison Service's role in relation to them.

10.48   The remand population is a significant part of the total prison population. Until recently it was an increasing part. The proportion of the total prison population made up of remand prisoners increased from 14% in 1975 to 23% in 1988, before falling to 22% in 1989 and the first five months of 1990. This represents an increase from 5,600 remand prisoners in 1975 to 10,500 in 1989, falling to 10,100 in the first five months of 1990. The majority of these remand prisoners were awaiting trial (82% of them in the first few months of 1990). The remainder are prisoners who have been convicted but are awaiting sentence.

10.49   Not all prisoners held on custodial remand are later given a custodial sentence. Criminal Statistics show that of those earlier remanded in custody who were tried at Magistrates' Courts in 1989, a quarter (26%) were given non-custodial sentences and 12% were acquitted. The remainder, the great majority, were committed for trial or sentence to the Crown Court. Even at the Crown Court, a later custodial sentence is by no means certain. Of those previously remanded in custody by Magistrates tried at the Crown Court in 1989, a quarter were either acquitted or were given a non-custodial sentence (6% acquitted, 19% given a non-custodial disposal). The remaining three quarters were given sentences of immediate custody.

10.50   The dramatic increase in the number of prisoners on remand is not primarily because of the increase in the number of prisoners remanded in custody. The number of receptions of untried and unsentenced prisoners in 1975 was 77,903 and in 1989 it was 77,435. The increase is primarily due to the duration of the period in custody. This in turn is linked to an increase in the proportion of those committed to the Crown Court (up from 15% in 1979 to 21% in 1989 - partly because more cases can be tried either way) and to an increase in the percentage of those convicted who are in custody (up from 12% following the Bail Act 1976 to 22% now).

10.51   The time spent in custody by remand prisoners is, therefore, affected by whether or not the case proceeds to the Crown Court. In 1989 in the Magistrates' Court, defendants remanded in custody throughout the entire proceedings spent on average seven weeks in custody. This was about half a week longer than in the three preceding years. The period may have increased slightly during 1990. In the Crown Courts, the national average time between committal and the start of the hearing for defendants remanded in custody was 10.1 weeks. In some cases this period was substantially longer. In 1989, 950 persons had been in custody for more than six months. There are some defendants who wait up to a year in custody before they are sentenced (there were 100 such defendants in 1989).

10.52   We have quoted these statistics because they show beyond peradventure why the Prison Service must have a clearly defined role as to remand prisoners. The figures make clear that it would be wrong to regard the Prison Service's role in respect of remand prisoners as being limited to making provision only for short term visitors. They also demonstrate how changes in what happens in one part of the Criminal Justice System (the Courts) affects another part (the Prison Service).

10.53   In Section 9 of this Report, attention is drawn to the prominent part played in many of the disturbances by remand prisoners. They are an unstable section of the prison population. This is connected with the conditions of their confinement.

10.54   It is beyond dispute that in the majority of prison establishments holding remand inmates, the regime for these inmates is wholly unsatisfactory. Because they are not in prison as a punishment, the regime for remands should be better than that for sentenced prisoners (if it needs to be of a different quality). Unhappily the position is all too often the reverse. Even where the regime for the sentenced prisoner is far from satisfactory, the regime for the unsentenced prisoner is still more impoverished.

10.55   The explanation for this travesty of justice is partly that it is the natural inclination of the Prison Service to devote proportionately more of its resources to the inmates who are the longest in custody. Frequently, because remand inmates are entitled to have daily visits, because they need to make preparations for their trial and because they are not required to work, the Prison Service appear to conclude that, on the whole, it is not worthwhile devoting resources to remands. In the language used at one of our seminars, they are allowed to sink to the foot of the pile.

10.56   It is necessary to redress the present unacceptable situation for remand prisoners. Section 11 of this Report deals with the way in which the Prison Service should accommodate the remand population and in Section 12 we refer to their management. However, in addition to what is said in those sections, we emphasise in the following paragraphs the special responsibility which the Prison Service has in relation to remand prisoners. It is and should be seen as a central part of the Prison Service's role.

10.57   This role includes ensuring that not only are remands' physical conditions satisfactory but that their special needs are also recognised. Remand prisoners are in prison because they have been refused bail pursuant to the provisions of the Bail Act 1976. That Act provides that a Court *may* refuse bail if there are substantial grounds for believing the defendant, if released on bail, would:

a)   fail to surrender to custody, or

b)   commit an offence while on bail, or

c)   interfere with witnesses, or

d)   otherwise obstruct the course of justice, whether in relation to himself or any other person.

10.58   In addition, a defendant need not be granted bail if the Court is satisfied that the defendant should be kept in custody for his own protection. (There is an additional ground in respect of the welfare of a child or young person.)

10.59   The remand prisoner is subject to imprisonment only for one or other of the reasons set out in the Bail Act. It must be part of the task of the Prison Service to ensure that the security of remand prisoners reflects and is consistent with the specific ground relied upon for refusing bail. In the admirably succinct language of one of our Assessors (Professor Morgan), culled from the Perrie Lectures for 1988:

"Defendants refused bail should suffer no greater loss of liberty, both in duration and in degree, than is necessary to secure the course of justice."

10.60   Until he is tried and convicted, the Prison Service has the task of preventing, so far as this is practicable, imprisonment interfering with the remand prisoner's ability to conduct his defence.

10.61   It must also be part of the task of the Prison Service to enable the remand prisoner to spend his time in custody in as constructive a manner as possible and, to the extent that this is practicable, to preserve his employment, family and community connections.

10.62   If a remand prisoner's circumstances change so that it seems he may no longer be a person who may be refused bail, it is the Prison Service's task to assist in having the prisoner's case brought back before the Court so that the Court can decide whether or not, in the new circumstances, bail should be granted.

10.63   We recommend, therefore, that there should be a separate Statement of Purpose or an additional paragraph to the existing Statement of Purpose. It should deal specifically with the different status of remand prisoners and the Prison Service's obligations which follow on from that different status.

10.64   It will be for the Prison Service to construct a statement which satisfactorily encapsulates the approach to be adopted. The policy which we would suggest that statement should reflect, however, may be summarised as follows. So far as this is reasonable, a remand prisoners' containment should reflect the following considerations:

a)   a remand prisoner is presumed innocent until found guilty. His custody should contain no more restrictions than those which are necessary to reflect the ground upon which he was refused bail under the Bail Act 1976;

b)   a remand prisoner should be enabled to prepare for his trial and to have access to lawyers, probation officers and the Court;

c)   a remand prisoner must be permitted to maintain his links with his family, friends and community;

d)   a remand prisoner should be enabled to attend to business and personal affairs, to preserve his employment and to proceed with any education or training;

e)   a remand prisoner should be encouraged to spend the period on remand constructively in accordance with his wishes. This should include access to exercise (including PE), education, training, work and religion;

f)   a remand prisoner should have access to welfare bodies, the Social Services and a bail unit.

The Prison Rules

10.65   In a number of sections of this Report we refer to particular amendments that need to be made to the Prison Rules. We propose here a more fundamental revision.

10.66   The Prison Rules were made in 1964 and have since been frequently amended. As the law exists at present, while a breach of the Rules cannot give rise to an action for damages, it can be the subject of a successful application for judicial review. In the period since 1964, the approach to the administration of prisons has changed fundamentally. It is essential that the Prison Rules should reflect the contemporary situation and that their meaning should be clear. We propose that consideration should be given to producing a contemporary and relevant set of Rules which are consistent with the European Prison Rules.

Limiting the Role of the Prison Service

10.67   The Prison Service has had to handle an ever increasing number of prisoners in wholly inadequate accommodation. As Professor Morris has recently written, "overcrowding has had a mesmeric effect" on the Prison Service. It has resulted in the energy and resources of the Prison Service being expended in trying to cope with a series of crises. But for overcrowding, there could have been more concentration on improving prisons.

10.68   By the end of 1992, the Prison Service anticipates that the total number of inmates will be in balance with the total certified normal accommodation (CNA) of prisons. If this happens, it will be a major step forward. It does not mean, however, that from that date the spectre of overcrowding will be forever banished. On the contrary, the population has been and will continue to be spread unevenly over the prison estate. The accommodation may not match the areas of demand. There are problems which stem from the way the CNA is calculated. What will happen in the future is uncertain, not least because of the effects on sentencing of the Criminal Justice Bill now before Parliament.

10.69   While, therefore, the future is uncertain, there is no doubt that the pressure of overcrowding has been, and perhaps will be for some little time, a strong spur to limiting the role of the Prison Service. Because it is under pressure, the Prison Service should not be required to hold more prisoners than is necessary. But, even if the overcrowding problem were to be solved, it would still be important to ensure, so far as possible, that only those for whom there is no alternative are in prison.

10.70   It is important to avoid subjecting anyone to the damaging effects of imprisonment unless this cannot be avoided. In addition, as we have already stated, prisons are expensive places to run. The fewer prisons that are needed the better. It is usually far cheaper to punish offenders in the community. Any resources which need not be incurred in meeting the cost of housing prisoners who do not need to be imprisoned should be saved. The savings can then be used more constructively, for example in trying to counter offenders' criminal behaviour. It is therefore important, as is generally recognised, to reduce the prison population to an unavoidable minimum.

10.71   The achievement of this desirable objective depends upon co-operation between the various bodies who play a part in the Criminal Justice System. In addition to the Prison Service, we are referring to the Courts, the Crown Prosecution Service, the Police, the Probation Service and, to a lesser degree, the Department of Health. In the next part of this section we will identify action which has been taken which diverts remand prisoners and offenders from prison as a result of cooperation between these bodies. We will urge an extension of this action.

10.72   We appreciate, however, that the major influence on the size of the prison population is sentencing by the Courts. What is an appropriate sentencing policy is subject to Parliamentary control. The Criminal Justice Bill at present before Parliament reflects the present Government's views as to what this policy should be. But the Courts still have a considerable discretion over when they should impose sentences of imprisonment and what those sentences should be.

10.73   In determining what sentence to pass, we consider that the Courts should be aware of all the sentencing options available. The Courts should be aware also of the conditions within our prisons. To assist them in doing this, we will later in this section propose that they should be provided with more information than they have at present.

10.74   To ensure that the Prison Service makes suitable plans for the future, and in particular, has available the quality and type of accommodation and regime which is needed, it is necessary to maintain close co-operation between the Prison Service and the other agencies in the Criminal Justice System. Co-operation should be particularly close between the Courts and the Prison Service. This is because the Courts are responsible for passing the sentences of imprisonment which result in prisoners having to be accommodated by the Prison Service. We therefore conclude this Section of our Report by recommending closer co-operation between the different bodies which form part of the Criminal Justice System. We suggest the creation of two new bodies which should help to achieve this co-operation. We seek to explain why these bodies are needed and, in broad outline, how they would operate.

Diversion from Prison

i) The Remand Prisoner   10.75   We start our consideration of whether there are inmates in prison who should not be there, with the remand prisoner. Considerable efforts have been made by the various agencies which constitute the Criminal Justice System to try and reduce the number of persons remanded in custody and to limit the periods they spend on remand. However, much more still needs to be done.

10.76   Some successful initiatives are being tried locally. They need to be applied throughout the country. Other initiatives could be improved. The Courts could do more than they do at present to divert remand prisoners from custody.

10.77   The number of untried prisoners fell from 9,811 at the end of September 1988 to 8,366 in February 1990. But the main effect of this fall was not to relieve the pressure on the prisons, but to relieve drastically the pressure on the use of police cells to accommodate such prisoners.

10.78   Subject to what we have just said with regard to numbers, we fully agree with what was said by the Rt Hon John Patten MP, a Minister of State at the Home Office, during his keynote speech of 11 September 1989 to the 1989 International Half-way House Association. Mr Patten said:

"The remand prison population has grown strikingly over the last decade. In 1979 it stood at around 6,100 whereas now, despite some recent improvements, it stands at about 10,700. This means that about a fifth of the prison population is made up of unconvicted and unsentenced prisoners. Not only has this growth contributed significantly to overcrowding in local prisons, but at times there has been a substantial and even more unwelcome overspill into police cells. This has placed an intolerable burden on the police, and provided totally unsuitable accommodation for defendants – all at great expense for the taxpayer. Overall a very poor bargain for everybody....

Bail decisions are a matter for the Court and there will inevitably be many cases where bail has to be refused for good and proper reasons. On the other hand, people should be remanded in custody only when this is absolutely necessary and for the shortest possible time."

10.79 The many initiatives which have been taken in recent years to try to tackle the problem created by the size of the remand population have on the whole been successful. Indeed the scale of their success suggests that there were, and almost certainly still are, a substantial number of people remanded in custody who should not be in prison. They come from areas where there is no alternative scheme in operation. They create an unnecessary handicap for the Prison Service. The problems created by the unnecessary remands need to be tackled from a number of different directions. Each involves co-operation between the Courts, the Crown Prosecution Service, the Probation Service and the Prison Service.

a) The Courts 10.80 From the discussions we have had with those who have provided evidence to the Inquiry, it is clear that insufficient status is given to whether or not to remand a defendant or to grant him bail. All too often, remands are dealt with hurriedly before the real business of the day. They can be dealt with by a single Magistrate or two Magistrates rather than a full Court. They can be dealt with hurriedly on Saturday morning.

10.81 It is often suggested that decisions about whether or not to grant bail in Magistrates' Courts depend on whether or not bail is opposed by the Prosecution. (It is partly because of this that, at the present time bail information schemes – to which we will refer – are structured on the basis of providing information to the Crown Prosecution Service.)

10.82 None of this is to criticise Magistrates. They usually have virtually no information on which they can differ from the bail submission made by the Crown Prosecution Service. This is a highly unsatisfactory situation. Magistrates would not regularly, if ever, sentence a defendant to imprisonment on the limited information which is usually available on a bail application. Yet frequently the question of whether or not to refuse bail has an important influence on the sentence which is eventually passed. The refusal of bail can result in a defendant, for example, losing his employment or his accommodation, both of which may be important considerations in determining his ultimate disposal.

10.83 We propose, therefore, that there should be a clear expectation that Magistrates should not make a final decision to remand a defendant in custody until they have received at least the information which will be available to the Crown Prosecution Service in those areas where a Bail Information Scheme is in operation. We would expect Magistrates to insist on more information than that which is made available at the present time to the Crown Prosecution Service where there is no Bail Scheme in operation. They should develop the practice of requiring a report on the community ties which the prisoner has.

10.84 In addition, we propose that Magistrates should attach considerable significance to whether or not the offence which the defendant is alleged to have committed is one which, if proved, would justify a sentence of imprisonment. While it is in order to grant bail irrespective of the likely sentence, to remand a defendant in custody for an offence for which he would never be sentenced to imprisonment can be questionable, unless there is some reasonable justification, such as possible interference with justice or a persistent failure to surrender to his bail or to comply with its terms.

250

10.85   We propose that information should be provided to Magistrates about where the defendant would be confined if bail was not granted and about what was the regime then available at that establishment for remand prisoners. In the majority of cases, remands from a particular Court will always be held in the same establishment. There should not be too much difficulty in keeping the Magistrates fully informed about that establishment and in drawing the Magistrates' attention to the fact that the establishment is overcrowded where that is the case. This is a subject to which we return later.

10.86   In their submission to the Inquiry, the Parliamentary All-Party Penal Affairs Group drew attention to the fact that the higher Courts do not give guideline decisions in bail applications (as they do in the case of appeals on sentence). The applications are dealt with in chambers by High Court Judges and so are not reported. This results in a failure to rectify any lack of consistency of approach in dealing with bail applications by the lower Courts. It also prevents the higher Courts laying down a policy on bail. The Group therefore recommends that there should be a review of the Bail Act 1976 or a mechanism established to enable guidance to be given by the High Court. There is substance in this point. We would propose that, in the first instance, consideration should be given by High Court Judges to adjourning some bail applications to open Court so that a reasoned decision can be given where an area of difficulty is identified and where guidance could be useful.

10.87   There is also a need to monitor vigorously the progress of cases involving defendants held in custody. Both the prosecution and the defence must be encouraged to reduce the period they need to prepare for trial to a minimum. The time limits which already exist need to be regularly reviewed to see whether they can be reduced. It is particularly important to have the shortest possible waiting time where a defendant is convicted but awaiting sentence. The experience of prisoners at Glen Parva and Pucklechurch, reported in Part I, is testimony to this.

b) Bail Information Schemes

10.88   These schemes featured prominently in the evidence of the Association of Chief Officers of Probation. The evidence records:

> "There has been a reduction in the remand population of 1,200. This has been influenced heavily by the Bail Information Schemes initiated by A.C.O.P. which, in the areas where they are in operation, have reduced custodial remands by 13%."

10.89   A Bail Information Scheme operates through the Probation Service providing the Crown Prosecution Service with verified information about a defendant. It involves interviewing defendants either before the first Court appearance or before the second appearance. The resultant reports enable the Crown Prosecution Service to take an informed view about whether to oppose bail. This in turn enables the Court to take an informed decision on whether to grant bail (assuming that the Court seeks to go behind and question the view of the Crown Prosecution Service).

10.90   Eight pilot schemes were monitored and co-ordinated by the Vera Institute of Justice throughout 1987. According to the evidence from the Association of Chief Officers of Probation, the findings were that Bail Information Schemes:

> "demonstrated their effectiveness by influencing the bail decision making process, in favour of bail, in a significant number of cases."

10.91   The scheme depends upon the co-operation of both the Crown Prosecution Service and the police. The expansion of the Court based schemes has been rapid. We propose that they should be established in all areas of the country.

c) Prison Bail Schemes

10.92   Prison establishments can also have a role to play in bail information schemes. Ideally, the schemes try to avoid an unnecessary remand in custody at the first Court appearance. Sometimes, however, there has been insufficient time to interview a defendant or to contact the source of information for verification. In either situation, there could be a remand in custody. Further work has to take place before the second Court appearance while the remand prisoner is in prison.

10.93 The work which is required during the intervening period can be conducted under a prison based scheme. The prison based scheme can take up from where the Courts based scheme may have left off, or it can play a primary role and, under it, defendants can be interviewed for the first time.

10.94 The schemes based upon the prisons are still at an early stage. We propose that they should be expanded as rapidly as possible. Dr Mair's Home Office research on a scheme in Wormwood Scrubs showed the important contribution the schemes can make. Significantly, this research found that key information about the bail/remand decision was not available to the prison or the prisoner. The project found that the Court did not in every case, as it should have done, provide to the defendant a note on the reasons for refusal of bail.

10.95 To operate prison-based bail units will involve training. There is now a national training course which is available for probation staff. It should be extended to members of the Prison Service who can then play a key role in this valuable probation-led initiative.

d) Bail Hostels

10.96 Magistrates are handicapped if they are placed in the position where they have to choose between unconditional bail on the one hand and custody on the other. The availability of bail hostels or other accommodation arranged by the Probation Service can be significant in assisting the Magistrates to come to a decision in favour of granting bail. Unfortunately, there are at present, as the Government appreciates, too few bail hostels. Additional resources of over £36m in capital and revenue have been secured to provide 1,000 new bail places at approved hostels between April 1988 and April 1993. This will obviously result in an improvement. We propose that consideration be given to bringing forward this programme, to which we attach the greatest importance.

e) Special Hostels

10.97 We propose that more special hostels be established to cater for those with drugs or drink related problems. Many hostels are not in a position or are unwilling to accommodate this type of inmate. They have needs which could be catered for in special hostels by or in association with agencies in the community. The same is true of the mentally ill or the mentally disordered. They frequently cannot be placed in ordinary hostels, but could be accommodated in hostels which have psychiatric facilities.

10.98 If more people with these problems could be diverted from prison, this would be especially beneficial to the Prison Service because of the demands this type of inmate makes upon the Service. We recognise that there will not be savings of the same order as will accrue from diverting a person from prison to an ordinary hostel. It may, indeed, cost more. However, the additional benefit to the defendant who needs a place at a special hostel and to the Prison Service of that need being met outside prison, in our view justify any additional cost involved.

f) Secure Hostels

10.99 These are hostels which, as their name suggests, would provide a regime which would be more controlled and more secure than that provided at a normal hostel. They do not exist at present. There is by no means the same enthusiasm for secure hostels as there is for the other hostels to which we have already referred. The existence of secure hostels could encourage the use of conditions of detainment which would be close to those in a remand prison.

10.100 The Home Office on 13 February 1989 issued a consultation paper on Bail Accommodation and Secure Hostels. None of the probation organisations that responded to the discussion paper was in favour of secure bail hostels, though some would have been in favour of further research. They were concerned that the boundary between bail and remand in custody would be

252

blurred by secure hostels.

10.101   We found convincing and would endorse the alternative approach which has been adopted in the Inner London Probation area and which was described to us by Mr Graham Smith, the Chief Probation Officer. He said that, within his probation area, there was a range of hostels which provided differing degrees of security. In his experience, without having any special category of hostel, it was possible in the Inner London area to identify a hostel which met the needs of any particular defendant who was a suitable subject to be granted bail on the condition that he or she resided at a hostel. It is important, if this approach is adopted, for the Magistrates in the case to be aware of the range of regimes available so they can name an appropriate hostel. In the Inner London area the Chief Stipendiary Magistrate told us that he would have welcomed more information about the choice of hostels which are on offer.

ii) Offenders

a) Hostels for Offenders

10.102   We have focused on the use of hostels for those on bail. But hostels can, of course, play a very important part in assisting the Court to adopt a form of disposal other than imprisonment. We propose an increase in the number of hostel places to be used for this purpose.

10.103   It would be valuable if hostels could be clustered with protected accommodation, to be provided in housing or lodgings. This would enable inmates to progress from hostels to protected accommodation and if possible to the community at large.

b) Public Interest Case Assessment

10.104   If action can appropriately be taken to divert people from being brought to Court, then they will not, on that occasion at least, end up in prison. The use of cautioning has proved to be successful in keeping many juvenile offenders out of Court. The experience of the Inner London Probation Service is that this has avoided the net widening affect of drawing offenders prematurely into the Criminal Justice System. It has also, according to the Association of Chief Officers of Probation's evidence "in many cases, reduced the risks of reoffending".

10.105   The use of cautioning has now been extended to all ages. The Probation Service has been considering how it can co-operate with the Crown Prosecution Service so as to make this diversionary scheme operate more successfully. An experiment took place at Horseferry Road Magistrates Court which again brought together the Probation Service, the police and the Crown Prosecution Service. The scheme was intended to identify defendants for whom prosecution might do more harm than good. During the experiment, the rate of discontinuance on public interest grounds at the Horseferry Road Magistrates Court increased from 1% to 7%. In a third of the 116 cases, where a background report was received by the Crown Prosecution Service, the prosecution was discontinued on public interest grounds.

10.106   This scheme would appear able to make a valuable contribution. We propose the expansion of diversionary schemes involving such co-operation between the Probation Service and the Crown Prosecution Service. It may well be that there would also be a role, possibly a limited role, for co-operation between the Probation Service and the Prison Service in obtaining information from defendants who have already been remanded in custody, when that information might be relevant to a decision that the prosecution should be discontinued.

c) Young Offenders

10.107   We have already referred to the special responsibility which the Prison Service has with regard to young offenders. This is an area which was highlighted by HMCIP's report (Review of Suicide and Self Harm – published December 1990). As indicated in that report, defendants under the age of 17 should not be in prison. It is accepted by the Home Office that the "unruliness" concept is "out-moded". There is to be consultation about what procedures should be adopted in the future. As the principle of avoiding remand in custody is now firmly accepted, there is no need for this Inquiry to anticipate the outcome of that consultation.

d) Fine Defaulters

10.108   The number of fine defaulters at any one time who are within the prison system is now, fortunately, small - about 520. Their effect upon the prison system, however, is far greater than that number would suggest. There is a substantial number of fine defaulters who are sent to prison in any one year. In 1989, almost 17,000 people were received into prison (well below the peak of 24,500 in 1982). The Gloucestershire Probation Service collated the numbers going to prison from their area between August and December 1983. They found that "up to half of all people going to prison in this area, get into prison by the back door being committed for fine default". The number of fine defaulters in Strangeways over a year was equally significant.

10.109   The Government has decided to introduce the unit fine in the Criminal Justice Bill at present before Parliament. The objective of the unit fine is to ensure that fines reflect the offender's ability to pay. The Government has also decided that income support should be able to be attached for the payment of fines, in addition to any earnings.

10.110   It has been argued before us that there is a very strong case for saying that the time has now come when imprisonment for fine defaulting should be abolished, except possibly in those cases where the defendant deliberately places his resources beyond the reach of the Courts. In all other cases, if the fines cannot be recovered by an attachment order, it has been argued that they should be recovered, wherever this is appropriate, as a civil debt. We understand from "Deduction from Benefit for Fine Default" by Moxon, Hiddersen and Sultan that in Sweden (where previous rates of imprisonment for default had been high) imprisonment for default has nearly been eliminated, while a high level of payment has been secured.

10.111   If a defaulter has earnings, the earnings can be attached. There should be no need to imprison him or her. If he is dependant on income support, that support can, if appropriate, be attached. Again this is no need for imprisonment. If he has other income or property, the fine should be recovered by distraint or made recoverable as a civil debt. In such cases, the cost of the alternative of imprisonment is out of proportion to the sums involved.

10.112   The practical implications of abolishing imprisonment for fine defaulters are, however, significant. If the proposals now before Parliament are implemented, the combined effect of unit fines and deductions from income support should be very significant. The researchers to whom reference has been made estimated that 13,000 out of the 17,000 defaulters in 1989 were eligible for deductions. If the law had already been changed, they estimated that the great majority would have paid their fines by deduction. If these figures prove to reflect accurately the position if the law is changed, the problem will be largely resolved.

10.113   In these circumstances, we would suggest that the way forward is to await the implementation of the proposals in the Criminal Justice Bill, if they are approved by Parliament. Once they had had an opportunity to demonstrate their effect, we propose that an experiment should be mounted in limited areas to assess the practical implications of removing the threat of imprisonment. It would then be more possible to judge whether many Magistrates and others are right in considering, as they do at present, that imprisonment is an essential final sanction to secure the payment of fines.

e) Money Payment Supervision Orders

10.114   The Gloucestershire Probation Service states in its evidence, that "money payment supervision orders are a bind". But, as that Service also recognises, the involvement of probation time on a discriminate basis to assist those who, without some intervention, will be likely to end up as prisoners is very much needed. The Gloucestershire Probation Service therefore provides such assistance. So long as imprisonment for fine defaulting continues, we would encourage this sort of intervention.

f) The Mentally Disordered Offender

10.115   This group of offenders has always been a particular problem for the Prison Service. The majority of these offenders, if the facilities were available, would be dealt with more appropriately elsewhere than in prison. All too frequently, however, the Courts find themselves without an alternative to prison.

10.116   On 10 July 1990, the National Schizophrenia Fellowship, the Howard League, the Prison Reform Trust and the National Association for the Care and Resettlement of Offenders (NACRO) wrote a joint letter to the Home Secretary. They expressed their concern about the presence in prison of large numbers of mentally vulnerable individuals. They urged the Home Secretary to take a number of steps to divert such people from the Criminal Justice System. In addition, they asked the Home Secretary to improve the standard of care for those who are mentally disordered while in custody.

10.117   The Government recognise that action is needed substantially to improve the present situation. A significant survey has been conducted by Professor Gunn, at the request of the Home Office, into the extent of mental disturbance among the prison population. The Government has accepted the recommendations of the Inter-Departmental Working Group for Mentally Disturbed Offenders in the Prison System in England and Wales. A Steering Committee has been formed with the Home Office, the Department of Health and the Health and Social Services with a view to determining whether changes are needed in the current provision of services and how any such changes should be promoted. The Home Office is funding jointly with the Mental Health Foundation three projects organised by NACRO.

10.118   The evidence before the Inquiry suggests that there are a range of other initiatives which should make a positive contribution to minimising the number of mentally disordered people within the penal system. We describe these in the following paragraphs. We propose that they should be continued and developed further.

10.119   The Inquiry was pleased to note that the Home Office has issued guidance to the Courts, Prisons, Police and the Probation Service drawing attention to the statutory powers which enable mentally disordered offenders to be diverted from the Criminal Justice System (Circular 66/90 of 3 September 1990). The circular urges that the powers should be used wherever possible and to their fullest extent.

10.120   The Department of Health indicate that there is "some evidence" of a considerable diversity in the use of these powers. It gives an example of one locality where it was estimated that the Courts involved accepted only 50% of the recommendations made by psychiatrists for hospital orders rather than prison sentences. It notes that the degree of liaison and co-operation between health authorities and the Courts varies between different areas. The Department of Health proposes to draw the attention of health and social services authorities to the Home Office guidance. We know that those sentencing this category of offender can be faced by a lack of knowledge of the non-custodial options which are available. We believe the circular, if read and heeded, should be of considerable value.

10.121   The Department of Health accepts that, although expanded and developed in recent years, the services that are at present available for the mentally disordered do not work as well as they should in meeting requests for treatment from the Courts and the Prison Service. Nor do they result in the most appropriate placement of offenders. The Department acknowledges the need for research. This need should obviously be met.

10.122   The Department of Health also refers to action:

"being taken to establish more effective links between the Courts, the Prison Service and Prison Medical Service and the Probation Service, and

255

health and social services authorities - both at a planning and at an operational level".

10.123   We agree that more effective links are required. Our proposals for a Consultative Council and Local Committees, to which we refer later, could make a useful contribution to improving co-operation in this area.

10.124   Action is also needed to ensure that more accommodation is provided by regional health authorities. There is a clear need for more regional secure units and more medium secure facilities where the mentally disordered who cannot be accommodated in the ordinary local and regional psychiatric hospital can receive treatment.

10.125   The report "Mentally Abnormal Offenders", chaired by the Rt Hon Lord Butler of Saffron Walden in October 1975, proposed that there should be 2,000 beds in secure units. The Department of Health target had been 1,000 beds. However, the unhappy position is that at present there is only a maximum of about 600 beds available - "a maximum" because some of those beds may not be able to be used because of shortage of staff.

10.126   The special hospitals, of which there are at present four, provide the highest level of security available within the hospital system. Only the most dangerous patients who require treatment for mental disorders are admitted to these hospitals. On the evidence before the Inquiry, there do not appear to be any serious difficulties in finding a bed for offenders who need this type of secure hospital. The only difficulty that can exist is with regard to arranging the transfer of patients to the hospitals.

10.127   Here Manchester Prison, prior to the disturbances, provided a desirable precedent. Dr Campbell led a team, including three other consultant forensic psychiatrists. He paid regular visits to the prison. As a result, he was able to ensure the speedy transfer of prisoners to a special hospital or, if that standard of security was not required, to the regional secure unit at Prestwick Hospital where he was based.

10.128   In its submission, the Law Society suggests that section 35 of the Mental Health Act 1983 is largely unworkable. This was corroborated by other evidence to the Inquiry. Section 35 enables Courts to remand the accused to a hospital specified by the Court for a report on his mental condition. The Law Society drew attention to the difficulty of persuading any hospital to take a mentally disordered defendant. There is also the difficulty of identifying offenders who would be suitable for this form of remand. This regularly results in mentally disordered offenders being remanded in custody for the purpose of medical reports, when they might more suitably be remanded to a hospital.

10.129   This problem was the subject of research conducted by Dr Philip Joseph during 1989. He concluded that the practice of remands in custody in such cases was wasteful of Court and prison resources and grossly inefficient. Frequently it resulted in what he described as "a merry-go-round". A Court appearance would be followed by a further remand in custody because the psychiatrist was unable to prepare a report and because very little information was available to enable the psychiatrist to form a proper judgement.

10.130   To stop this sort of "merry-go-round", a psychiatric assessment service was established at two Inner London Magistrates' Courts, one at Bow Street and the other at Marlborough Street. The psychiatric "on-call" service is available two sessions per week and referrals are accepted from the Magistrates, Probation Officers, Duty Solicitor or sometimes the police officers. If admission to hospital is indicated, an approved social worker and a second Doctor is readily available to attend. Because the scheme is Court-based, the duty psychiatrist has access to a great deal of information. He has access to the Crown Prosecution Service file. The duty Probation Officer is available to provide background information. The duty Solicitor is there to give advice if necessary. Another advantage is that there is an opportunity for the Magistrates' Court to consider any submission from the Crown Prosecution Service for discontinuing the prosecution.

10.131 The results of this experiment have been very positive. Of the defendants assessed, the case against some 35% has not been proceeded with because it was decided that prosecution would not be in the public interest. A scheme of this nature can also ensure a proper use of section 35 of the Mental Health Act 1983.

10.132 A variant of this scheme operates at the Peterborough Magistrates' Court. There, if a person is identified at the Magistrates Court as being likely to need psychiatric assistance, the Court telephones the District Hospital. The Hospital arranges for a nominated duty consultant psychiatrist to examine the person in the cell. A report is then prepared the same or the next day. That scheme has also proved successful, despite the fact that there are limited local psychiatric facilities and there are problems in placing persons thought to be dangerous.

10.133 There are other schemes as well on the same sort of lines. In North West Hertfordshire, a multi-skill assessment panel makes the assessment. At Horseferry Road Magistrates' Court in London, a psychiatrist and a community forensic nurse from the Riverside Health Authority are available on one morning each week. They can refer offenders to the out-patients services provided by that Authority.

10.134 These schemes are referred to in the guidance circular 66/90. They are, however, experimental. There should be a thorough assessment of their respective virtues so that those which are found to have a wider application can be extended. For example, it may not be practical or economical to provide the services at every Magistrates' Court. Courts could be grouped for this purpose and mentally disordered offenders transferred to a Court providing this service where this is necessary. (For this suggestion we are grateful to the Chief Metropolitan Stipendiary Magistrate.)

10.135 We have given this brief survey to provide some indication of the activity that already exists. Professor Gunn's survey will provide much more reliable information as to the scale of the problem in the sentenced prison population. The problem could even be greater in the remand population, which his survey does not address. However, work on the remand population and an analysis of its mental health is currently being carried out by Dr Adrian Grounds of Cambridge.

10.136 It is, however, clear that there will remain for the foreseeable future, a significant problem for the Prison Service in accommodating mentally disordered offenders. We propose that the Prison Service should therefore recognise the special responsibility it has for those in its care who suffer in this way.

10.137 There is a need also to recognise the problems of mentally handicapped offenders. They are not treatable. The provision of hostels and sheltered accommodation can make a substantial contribution to diverting them from prison. We propose that more hostels and other accommodation should be available for mentally handicapped offenders. The Government should provide further support to the voluntary bodies who are prepared to take on the responsibility of running hostels or sheltered accommodation for the mentally handicapped.

10.138 The Prison Service must recognise, however, that it will continue to have to provide for a number, perhaps quite a large number, of mentally handicapped prisoners. For them, survival in prison is especially difficult. They need to be located with particular care. They create an additional responsibility for the Prison Service. We propose that the Prison Service should ensure that clearer and more specific attention is paid to them.

iii) Conclusion

10.139   The disparate initiatives to which we have referred are all inspired by the need to divert, in some cases from the criminal system and others from the prison system, those who need not be subject to those systems. In the majority of cases, this Inquiry can do no more than note the initiatives and their possible benefits. Taken together, they could have considerable impact.

10.140   These initiatives have a further significance to this Inquiry. They demonstrate what can be achieved by co-operation between different agencies involved in the Criminal Justice System. The need for a close and effective relationship between these agencies is a matter to which this Report attaches great weight. It is necessary to find an appropriate mechanism for assisting that co-operation. That is the issue to which we now turn.

Providing the Sentencing Court with More Information

10.141   Within the Criminal Justice System, the actions of the Courts have the most direct impact on the Prison Service. If the Prison Service does not satisfactorily perform its role, this can seriously affect the Courts. In counting the costs of the disturbances referred to in Part I, the consequences to the Courts in adjourned and delayed trials cannot be ignored. It is, therefore, extremely important that the Prison Service should be aware of the needs and problems of the Courts. It is equally important that those involved in administering justice in the Courts should appreciate what is happening within the prison system.

10.142   Great strides have been made in recent years in training Judges and Magistrates who are responsible for passing sentences on offenders. The time spent on training is, however, still limited. Part of that training involves making some visits to prisons. High Court Judges and Court of Appeal Judges who sit in the criminal division are not required to make any visits to prison establishments, but many do. When Judges and Magistrates visit prisons, however, they may have little, if any, opportunity to learn the views of prisoners.

10.143   It is unlikely that more than a small minority of the judiciary had any real knowledge of the appalling conditions in local prisons which contributed to the disturbances in April 1990. The information about prison conditions available to those who pass sentences, and about what actually happens to those who are sentenced, is still modest.

10.144   This needs to be remedied. We propose Judges and Magistrates should be given general information about the conditions within prisons to which those whom they have remanded in custody or sentenced are sent. If the prison is overcrowded, this is something of which the sentencer should be aware. They need to know about the regime to which they are likely to be subjected.

10.145   Judges and Magistrates need to know the likely facilities for education, training and treatment. They should know what the prospects are of prisoners going to Grendon prison, or an open prison, or an overcrowded local prison, and what will happen to the prisoners while they are there.

10.146   Judges and Magistrates need also to know the cost implications of the actions which they propose to take. They should have the opportunity to take these into account, to the extent to which they consider this is appropriate, when deciding on whether a person should be deprived of his freedom.

10.147   Judges and Magistrates need also to be aware of the alternatives to imprisonment, how their success compares with imprisonment and the comparative costs.

10.148   Sentencers should be kept abreast of the experience of other countries. It is relevant to know that England has the highest rate of imprisonment in proportion to its population in Europe. It is relevant also that, according to the evidence put before the Inquiry, the former state of West Germany had, at one time, a similar rate of imprisonment to that in England. In West Germany there has been a marked reduction in the use of imprisonment without any increase in the level of crime. They have been closing prisons rather than building more.

10.149 It is relevant also that in the Netherlands, according to Professor Downes, the prison population in 1950 was proportionately much the same as that in England. But by 1975 the Dutch prison population, as a proportion of the general population, had fallen to less than half that in 1950. In England and Wales, on the other hand, it had doubled. Yet the crime rates in both countries were very much the same in 1950 as in 1990 (although they grew at different rates during the interim period). These are all matters of which sentencers should be aware.

10.150 We propose that much of the information which we believe is needed and to which we have referred should be provided to the judiciary by the Prison Service. The Judicial Studies Board is already involved on a limited scale. It could provide the machinery for making available to the judiciary the additional information which we consider the Prison Service should provide.

10.151 Some sentencers still take the view that what happens to a prisoner after sentence and the state of our prisons are of no concern to them when deciding what course to take in relation to defendants who appear before them. Some Magistrates' Clerks are still advising Magistrates to this effect. We would suggest that this approach is wrong and should be authoritatively stated to be wrong. To be provided with information does not interfere with the independence of the judiciary. Such information is needed in order to perform satisfactorily the sentencer's difficult and demanding task of deciding whether someone needs to be deprived of his or her liberty and if so for how long.

10.152 There is nothing new in principle in expecting Courts to be aware of the availability of any disposal which they might wish to make. Before a Court makes a community service order, the Court has to be satisfied that it will be possible to arrange for the offender to carry out work under the community service scheme in the area in which he lives. Before an interim hospital order is made under section 38 or a hospital order under section 37 of the Mental Health Act 1983, the Court has to be satisfied that arrangements have been made for the offender's admission to a hospital within 28 days of the order.

10.153 There is, of course, no statutory requirement that, before a defendant is remanded in custody or is sent to prison, the Courts must ascertain whether there is room available in the prison to which he is to be sent. We do not suggest such a requirement. Nor are we suggesting that the Court should decline to send prisoners to prison, either under sentence or on remand, if the Court is fully satisfied that that is the only proper course open to it. We are, however, suggesting that justice and common sense requires that the Court, in coming to that conclusion, should have some real appreciation of the implications of the order which is being made. Before making an order remanding a prisoner to Brixton or Leeds prisons, it is a requirement of the proper exercise of justice that the state of those prisons should be known by the Courts responsible for making that order.

10.154 Courts need therefore to have a realistic appreciation of the pressures which exist within the Criminal Justice System and of the resources available to it. The capacity of the system and the regime which it is possible to provide to prisoners depend in part upon the resources which the Government of the day makes available to the Prison Service. They depend also on the time in which it takes to deploy those resources, for example in changing the size of the prison estate. But if, without any regard to the accommodation which is available at the time, the Courts were to send more and more prisoners to prisons, in the absence of any safety valve (such as would be provided by executive release) there will come a stage when the Prison Service will be overwhelmed by the task with which it is faced. There will then be a risk of a repetition of the situation which occurred in April 1990. Such a situation would be contrary to the interests of the public, the Criminal Justice System as a whole and each part of that system. It is for this reason we will in Section 11 suggest that there should normally be a limit on the number of prisoners in each prison.

10.155   The Prison Service's Standing Order 8 B1 and 2 notes that there are no requirements for Governors to provide Courts regularly with reports on prisoners before trial or after conviction. But if a Court requests a report, the Standing Order provides that the Governor should co-operate "by providing the information requested as far as possible". The Standing Order notes that copies of the Governors' reports will be made available to the defence by the Court.

10.156   We propose that consideration should be given to requiring the Prison Service to provide routinely for the sentencing Court a report on the manner in which a remand prisoner had behaved while in custody. If our proposal is accepted, consideration should be given to the report being made available to the defendant as a matter of course. The prospect of such a report could be a strong incentive to a remand prisoner to behave responsibly and constructively. If this were the case, it would reduce the risk of remand prisoners again becoming involved in riots. The report could affect the sentence imposed on the prisoner if he is convicted. The preparation of the report would be a new and important responsibility for prison staff. There would need to be safeguards to prevent abuse, and the subjects covered by the report would have to be discussed between the Prison Service and the Courts. It may be that pilot schemes monitored by the Local Committees to which we will refer later would be a sensible test of the merits of the proposal.

A Forum for Consultation Within the Criminal Justice System

10.157   We have already referred to a number of initiatives which are taking place which depend on co-operation between more than one agency within the Criminal Justice System. The Prison Service has not been in the van of those taking forward that co-operation. We have already noted that, because of the nature of its task, the Prison Service tends to be inward looking. It fails to see itself as playing a central role within the Criminal Justice System. The same comment can be made about other agencies within the Criminal Justice System.

10.158   The Prison Service must recognise and accept a more central role. The Prison Service is directly affected by any change in sentencing policy. The strategic planning of the Prison Service can be seriously affected by any change of policy by the judiciary. It is affected by the Courts' approach to bail. It is affected by changes in the nature and extent of alternatives to imprisonment.

10.159   For their part, as we have already explained, sentencers need to know about the circumstances and conditions of prisons. The work of the Courts is dependant upon a steady flow of prisoners to and from prisons. The transfer of prisoners has to work smoothly if trials are not to be interrupted or delayed. As has been shown in Part I, the demands of the Courts on prisons can be very disruptive of their regimes.

10.160   There is therefore a need for the judiciary and the Prison Service to co-ordinate their separate roles. This does not at present happen to the extent it should. The Prison Service certainly bears no greater responsibility for this than the Courts.

10.161   There is a need also for closer co-ordination between the Prison Service and the Probation Service. The Probation Service is being required to play an increasing role in the Criminal Justice System. In addition to its other duties, it makes an essential contribution, both while an offender is in prison and when he is granted parole. The Probation Service should work as closely with the Prison Service as it does with the Courts.

260

10.162 It has been suggested that there is a need for a common language between the Probation Service and the judiciary. We would suggest that there is also a need for a common language between the Prison Service and the Probation Service. In some foreign jurisdictions, there is a correction service which is responsible for both the Prison Service and the Probation Service. While not suggesting this is an example which this country should be required to adopt at this time, we do suggest it is essential for these two Services to cooperate closely.

10.163 The ways the Crown Prosecution Service organises its work and its policies also have implications for the Prison Service. For example, questions relating to the period prisoners spend on remand and, more importantly, the number and nature of prosecutions which there are likely to be at any one time, all affect the number of prisoners likely to have to be accommodated. The Prison Service needs to know the Crown Prosecution Service's plans. For its part, the Crown Prosecution Service needs to be aware of the practical implications of its decisions on the Prison Service.

10.164 The Crown Prosecution Service will also be influenced in its decisions about prosecution by what will be the consequence of a decision not to prosecute. Will he or she be likely to be a danger to the public? The public interest case assessments and the bail information schemes, which we have already described, show the scope and the need for the Crown Prosecution Service, the Courts and the Probation Service to work closely together.

10.165 The Department of Health is also involved, for example in matters relating to the mentally disordered offender. The Courts have to decide the best disposal for a mentally disordered offender. That decision is directly affected by the number of places that there are in special or secure hospitals. The Courts' policy must also be influenced by the facilities which are available within general hospitals and in the community.

10.166 The number of mentally disordered offenders who are likely to be sent to prison is also manifestly of importance to the Prison Service. It affects not only the need for accommodating such offenders, but also the need to provide them with medical services. In his Perrie Lecture on 18 October 1990, Dr Grounds commented on "the extraordinarily indirect way in which prisons and hospitals communicate". That problem must be overcome.

10.167 The geographical areas into which the Prison Service had recently been reorganised do not fit in any way with the organisation of the Probation Service, the Court Service, the Crown Prosecution Service or the police. We do not suggest that the Prison Service ignored this point in the way it drew up its areas. But we emphasise that there is at present no formal structure in which it is possible collectively to discuss the problems which this scale of re-organisation may create for the other agencies involved in the Criminal Justice System.

10.168 We are aware of the links which exist already. A series of trilateral meetings have recently been developed between the Lord Chancellor, the Home Secretary, and the Attorney General. Similar meetings have been held by officials. There are also ways in which the judiciary can be informally consulted on the sort of issues we have identified.

10.169 At the present time, however, to use the words in his evidence to the Inquiry by Sir Brian Cubbon, a former Permanent Secretary of the Home Office, there is a "major geological fault" in the prison landscape. He argued that the "fault" was the unpredictable and volatile size of the prison population. He suggested that it was necessary for sentencers to take greater account of the capacity of the prison system. We agree there is such a geological fault in the system. In our view it lies across all the agencies in the Criminal Justice System. It is a failure of co-operation. It shows itself in gaps in communication, in the necessary co-ordination, and in the wider consideration of developments in the Criminal Justice System.

10.170 We recommend that this "fault" be bridged. The form of the bridge would have to be determined by those who would have the responsibility for setting it up. Opinions can differ as to the form it should take and who should be involved. Our proposal is but one of a number of possible models. We propose that a national forum should be established to consider at the highest level the interaction of each of the agencies to which we have referred. It should consider matters affecting either the Criminal Justice System as a whole or affecting more than one of the agencies which form a central part of that system. The evidence before this Inquiry has shown that such a body is needed to address the strategic issues which result from the inter-face between the Prison Service and the other parts of the Criminal Justice System. Those issues cannot be addressed in isolation. They must be seen within the context of the work and objectives of the other agencies and interests, not least the judiciary.

10.171 It may be helpful if we indicate that a possible membership of this body would include a very senior judge as a representative of the Lord Chief Justice and possibly the Permanent Heads of the Home Office and the Lord Chancellor's Department and the Head of the Crown Prosecution Service. The Director General of the Prison Service would be a member. The Department of Health would also need to be represented at a very senior level, but it may well be that, because of that Department's specialist interest in the Criminal Justice System, its representative would not need always to attend. There should also be a senior representative of the Probation Service. It would be necessary to consider who that representative should be since our probation system is not a national system, but we do not envisage any real difficulty in identifying a suitable and acceptable person. A representative of chief officers of police would also need to be identified. If an issue were to be considered by the body which affects Magistrates, then an appropriate Magistrate could be co-opted.

10.172 The senior member of the judiciary should be chairman of the body. This would be in accord with all the representations which were made to the Inquiry on this subject. Indeed the Chief Probation Officer for the Inner London Area said that unless such a body were chaired by a senior member of the judiciary, it would not achieve its purpose.

10.173 The judiciary have a unique part to play in the operation of the Criminal Justice System. We suggest that it is right that they should be seen as central to its workings. They should be able to exercise their independent status to ensure that information relevant to the Criminal Justice System is produced and disseminated. They should be able to ensure that the implications of initiatives and developments on other parts of the system are properly identified. There are of course many ways at present in which such co-ordination takes place in an *ad hoc* way between other agencies and informally and bi-laterally with the judiciary. But there is, at present, no co-ordinated body involving the judiciary. That is a failing. To have groups considering the work of the Criminal Justice System without the judiciary playing a central part is to play Hamlet without the Prince.

10.174 We appreciate that there has been a natural concern to safeguard the independence of the judiciary. This is an important feature of our constitutional system. However, the existence of a body on the lines we have discussed would not have any implications for the independence of the judiciary. As the Lord Chancellor, in an address to the Magistrates' Association on 19 October 1990 said, "independence does not mean isolation".

10.175 The title of the body is unimportant, but our suggestion would be a Criminal Justice Consultative Council. It would have to be staffed and resourced by a government department, presumably the Home Office.

10.176 The precise terms of reference and constitution of the body would have to be determined by its members. But, as we envisage it, it would have no executive authority or collective voice. Its authority would stem entirely from the interests which it represents and it would report back separately to them.

10.177   To an extent, what it achieves would depend on the contribution of those involved. The nature of the problem which we have described is such, however, that we believe it would be able to make a practical and immediate contribution to improving mutual understanding and the necessary degree of co-operation and co-ordination within the Criminal Justice System.

10.178   The body would achieve this objective by identifying issues and areas which needed to be examined. It would receive reports from its members on developments and proposals in their area of operation and responsibility. It would arrange and encourage the identification and collection of information. It would be made aware of the resources available to and the priorities of each of the agencies in the system, including the Prison Service. It would oversee the development of the Special Conferences which are at present held on aspects of the Criminal Justice System and any more structured arrangements which might be developed for those conferences. It could assist the development of a prison system which met the needs of other parts of the Criminal Justice System and which operated strategies which were consistent with and supportive of those of other agencies within the system. It would also be responsible for overseeing the Local Committees to which we are about to refer.

10.179   It will be clear from this description that the Council is in no sense a Sentencing Council. It could not and would not be intended to perform such a role. That is a wholly different matter which is not part of this Inquiry's remit or the case for this body. Nor, of course, would it be a throwback to the Advisory Council on the Penal System which operated in the 1970s. That had a wholly different membership and different purpose.

10.180   This would be a body which would ensure that there was a proper exchange of information within the Criminal Justice System and a careful consideration of developments within that system. It would identify and encourage useful initiatives. It would threaten the position and responsibilities of none of those involved. It would promise a better attuned and better informed Criminal Justice System. These are, in our view, worthy and necessary objectives.

The Local Committees

10.181   While the Criminal Justice Consultative Council would be concerned with problems which would have an affect on the Criminal Justice System as a whole, there is also a need for co-ordination at a lower level. We recommend the establishment of Local Committees. A Local Committee should, within its locality, primarily be concerned with practical problems thrown up because of the interfaces between the various services involved in dealing with crime.

10.182   Some of the new initiatives which have recently taken place where offenders, as a result of co-operation between the different agencies, have been able to be diverted from prison have started in a single locality. The Criminal Justice Consultative Council could have the task, where appropriate, of encouraging the general extension across the country of such initiatives. But it would be for the Local Committees to encourage the implementation of the initiative in their area.

10.183   There are always regular problems of a local nature which affect the Courts, the Prison Service, the Probation Service, the Crown Prosecution Service and the local health authority. These could be resolved within the Local Committees.

10.184   Local Committees would supplement the variety of Court Users Committees which exist at present. These Committees are established under a variety of titles in some areas of the country. They exist in about 40 of 72 Crown Court Centres and have a differing selection of members. They are generally (according to evidence provided by the Lord Chancellor's Department) found to be of value. They improve local co-operation and provide means of solving local problems. The Committees we propose would have a wider focus, a higher status and a different membership. In particular, unlike the Court User Committees, they would involve the judiciary.

10.185   The Local Committees we propose could replace the existing Regional Liaison Committees. These are presently chaired by a Circuit Administrator and include a representative of the Lord Chancellor's Department, the Crown Prosecution Service, the Home Office, the Police, the Prison Service, the Probation Service, and the Justices' Clerks Society. These meet once or twice a year and are valuable. But they differ from our proposal in that they have no judicial representation. Nor are they part of a wider structure which the proposed national Consultative Council would provide.

10.186   However, it would be unwise to be dogmatic about the level of operation of the Local Committees. Because of the lack of co-ordination in the organisational structures of the member agencies, it is very difficult to achieve an appropriate match. We would, however, envisage that the Chairman would be the resident judge, or, as he is sometimes known, the senior judge of a large Crown Court complex, or his representative. The Circuit Administrator would be a member. The representative of the Prison Service would be the Area Manager or a Governor 1 within the locality. The Chief Probation Officer would be a member, as would the senior representative of the Crown Prosecution Service in the area and a very senior policeman in the area. We would also expect the Magistracy to be represented on the Committee, perhaps by a Magistrates' Clerk and a chairman of a local bench.

10.187   The Local Committees can be expected to identify initiatives of their own as well as following up proposals and approaches from the Consultative Council. Over a period of time, the Committees would carve out the limits to their role which are appropriate in a particular locality. As with the Council, we would expect the Local Committee to be very much a master of its own procedure and of its area of operation.

10.188   We attach the greatest importance to bridging the failures in communication, co-ordination and consideration which the establishment of the Council and the Committees should achieve. They would help to ensure that all the agencies involved, including the Prison Service, were able to contribute to a successful and respected Criminal Justice System. The ultimate aim of all those involved should be a reduction in crime. Unless the whole of the Criminal Justice System co-ordinates its efforts in fulfilling this aim, the full potential for reducing crime will not be achieved.

Section 11

Buildings

Introduction

11.1 This Section of the Report deals with the buildings in which the Prison Service accommodates prisoners and the conditions which those buildings provide. The way in which the buildings are designed, their state of repair and decoration are important to management, staff and prisoners alike. They can significantly affect the atmosphere of a prison. As the Inquiry was repeatedly reminded by members of staff on our visits to prisons, the conditions in which prisoners live are the staffs' working conditions. Poor conditions result in disaffected prisoners. As a result, the staff have not only to put up with the problems created by the design of the prison, they have also to cope with the problems created by uncooperative prisoners.

11.2 Poor physical conditions are not, however, a necessary or sufficient excuse for a badly run prison, or for poor relations between those who live and work within the prison. The quality and attitude of the management and staff are more important than the buildings. In many prisons in England and Wales (including, in particular, Manchester and Bristol before the disturbances) staff, against the odds and despite having to cope with unsatisfactory buildings at the time of the disturbances, have been trying to make prison a less destructive experience for inmates. But squalid physical conditions make their task more difficult.

11.3 There are vast differences in the quality of prison buildings. Some are of acceptable design, well maintained and suitably located. Others are dilapidated, damp, insanitary and subject to infestation. In the face of these conditions, and under the pressure of overcrowding, the Prison Service has embarked on a series of refurbishment schemes and a programme of building new prisons, both at considerable expense.

11.4 We know from the evidence we have received that some organisations are sceptical of this building programme. They argue that overcrowding is on the way to being solved, and that an overkill in provision is dangerous. They contend that, if the space is there, the Courts will fill it. We share forcefully the wish of these organisations to see a reduction in the prison population, but we cannot accept the implication that this should be achieved at the expense of proper conditions for prisoners and staff.

11.5 It is premature to suggest that there should be a moratorium on new prison building. We recognise and accept that the plan, for the time being at any rate, must be one which involves giving a high priority to a combination of refurbishing and improving existing prisons, while at the same time having a well planned programme for building new prisons. The aims of the plan should be to remove from the prison estate prisons which are unsuitable for use and to ensure that there is sufficient accommodation to hold the projected prison population in reasonable conditions.

11.6 In the light of this conclusion, in this Section of the Report we:

    i)   identify some of the broad principles which the Prison Service should take fully into consideration when carrying forward its programme for the improvement of the prison estate;

ii)   consider the extent to which it is practicable to give effect to these principles when refurbishing and converting existing prisons;

iii) draw attention to the importance of the Prison Service having a clear policy as to what it wishes to achieve within a new or refurbished prison; and of communicating that policy to those involved in planning the construction work;

iv)   stress the problems created by lack of hygiene, sanitation and overcrowding and identify ways in the future of reducing the risk of overcrowding in any particular prison.

The Broad Principles and How to Give Effect to Them

i) The Size of Accommodation Units and of Prisons

11.7   *The first principle is that normally prisoners should be accommodated in prison units of approximately 50/70 prisoners. The prison itself should not hold more than 400 prisoners, though when this is necessary there can be more than one discrete prison within a larger prison.*

11.8   This principle is derived from one of the lessons identified from Part I of this Inquiry. The evidence which the Inquiry received from sources in the United Kingdom and from abroad confirmed it. It makes good sense both from the point of security and in respect of the regime for prisoners. The evidence suggests that if these figures are exceeded, there can be a marked fall off in all aspects of the performance of a prison.

11.9   We recognise that present prisons are not built on these lines. But it may often be practicable to divide larger blocks or wings into the smaller-sized units we recommend.

11.10   Prisons which can accommodate more than 400 prisoners should be managed as separate prisons, each of about 400 and with their own governors, as we will explain in more detail later. This was largely what was happening at Strangeways in the case of the remand and the main prisons, although the principle was not fully developed and the population in both prisons exceeded 400. Strangeways provides, however, an illustration of the concept of prisons within a prison, under the overall control of a Governor 1.

11.11   The figures which we have given cannot be justified on any statistical basis of which we are aware. They are based upon the combined experience of some of those who have been responsible for managing prisoners for many years. They take into account the fact that questions of security and control cannot be divorced from the relationships which exist between prisoners and staff, or from the regime within a prison. They give due allowance to the need to be realistic about resources. We accept that greater economies could be found from a larger scale prison. But these economies have to be set against the costs which flow from the increased risk of a loss of control.

11.12   Prisons and units established in accordance with the figures which we have recommended, should enable good relations to be maintained between staff and inmates, a constructive regime to be provided, and proper and effective management of the prison as a whole to be maintained, at a realistic cost. They provide for a prison to have at least six and possibly eight accommodation units. This number of units permits the flexible use of accommodation. We attach considerable importance to this. It should enable differing regimes to be provided within the prison establishment. If properly managed, these should provide opportunities to motivate prisoners by giving them a sense of progress through their sentence.

11.13   The Prison Service has already addressed these issues in drawing up its building design requirements. These are contained in the Prison Service's Prison

Design Briefing System (PDBS) which was published in October 1988. One of the objectives of the PDBS is:

> "to bring together and up-date existing guidance and instructions relating to prison design and construction in such a way that the process of providing new prisons may be expedited and made more cost effective".

11.14   The Inquiry received evidence from a distinguished panel of architects on behalf of the Royal Institute of British Architects (RIBA). The panel welcomed the PDBS as a substantial step in the right direction.

11.15   We endorse strongly the general "concept base" of PDBS. As the PDBS makes clear, it was produced to meet an urgent requirement and it was based on the American New Generation design. The New Generation design (as RIBA told us) is a response to a particular system of management of a prison establishment. The system involves accommodating prisoners in small units.

11.16   The PDBS recognises the need to divide the inmate population into "small, identifiable groups" which are "self-contained" and planned with "separate living areas", which will provide "greater flexibility", encourage "inter-personal relationships" and "lead to a safer more relaxed atmosphere and climate". The PDBS explains that the advantages of its approach are:

> "Greater flexibility since all house units do not need to be run in the same way. Regimes and activities can then be varied between the separate houses to suit particular needs. The facility to segregate groups of the inmate population within the prison then becomes available and enables both remand and sentenced prisoners to be more easily accommodated within the same prison but assigned to separate housing units."

11.17   The PDBS proposals are based on a prison having a capacity for 600 prisoners, divided into groups of between 40 to 60, with a group of 50 providing a good balance. The PDBS describes the figure of 600 as being "the optimum balance between the need for effective relationships and control of prisoners and economies of scale". The total of 600 within a prison is a higher number than we regard as ideal. However, a prison of 600 prisoners can be operated as two prisons. This is what we would like to see happen if a prison is designed to hold that number.

11.18   The PDBS also assumes that there should be two groups of 50 inmates which would make up a separate housing unit of 100, each of which would have its own staff team. This approach results in units somewhat larger than we would regard as ideal, though it does provide groups or sub-units of a size with which we are in accord. The grouping of two sub-units as proposed would have advantages from the point of view of economy. We do not criticise this aspect of PDBS, although our preference would be for a lower total than it at present contemplates.

11.19   The PDBS is intended to assist with the design of existing prisons "wherever practicable". The disturbances in April showed the need to reconsider the size of the existing larger local prisons. Manchester prison held 1,647 prisoners on 1 April 1990, but was overcrowded. Other local prisons, such as Birmingham, have been built for far larger numbers than we consider desirable and are, in addition, overcrowded. Many contain wings which hold about 100 prisoners.

11.20   For the immediate future, local prisons will have to continue to be used for housing more prisoners than we would regard as desirable, even when not overcrowded. We are content, however, that they should continue to be used as part of the prison estate since many are conveniently situated for prisoners families and for the courts. But we propose that, if they are to remain in use, these prisons must be brought up to a satisfactory standard. They must provide reasonable conditions for prisoners. They must also provide adequate security and control.

11.21   We have seen the recommendations of the Prison Service Review of Physical Security and Control Arrangements in Establishments following the disturbances of April 1990. The report confirms the advice we have received that in the majority of establishments, if not all, it is possible to sub-divide the existing accommodation units or wings in a way which is approximately in accord with the approach to size which we recommend.

11.22   The review recommends in relation to Victorian prisons, that:

> "any accommodation block/wing with a CNA in excess of 120 should be sub-divided into two separate, self-contained accommodation units".

That recommendation, while it is based solely on security and control considerations, is in accord with our approach, although we would prefer to see the figure of 120 reduced.

11.23   We have also seen and had explained the imaginative proposals of the Prison Service for the refurbishment of the main prison at Manchester. This indicates that, while retaining the best features of a Victorian prison (the design, the strength of the fabric, the good lighting and airiness provided by the high ceilings and lofty galleries) it is possible to create manageable units of a size which we would regard as acceptable.

ii) Separate Units in Relation to Security

11.24   *The second principle is that an appropriate balance needs to be maintained between the requirements of security and the adverse consequences which can result from an over-oppressive atmosphere within prisons.*

11.25   It is important that, where a prison is made up of a number of small accommodation units, as we have proposed, each accommodation unit should be designed to enable any disturbance within it to be confined within that unit. It is equally important that, if a disturbance occurs outside a unit, it should be possible to prevent it spreading to within the units. Subject to the difficult question of what locking systems are needed, the redesign of the main prison at Manchester fulfils these requirements.

11.26   The Review of Physical Security, to which we have referred, makes it clear that it should be possible to achieve the necessary standards of security when a Victorian prison wing is divided. Roof and ceiling security can be provided. It is possible to make provision for separate and secure access by staff to all levels of the building. Steps can be taken to protect adequately areas in which vulnerable prisoners are housed. Protection can also be provided for pharmacies and treatment rooms where this is needed.

11.27   While generally welcoming the contents of the Review, we emphasise that it is important that care is taken in the design of security measures to avoid creating an atmosphere which is oppressive. Such an atmosphere can in itself lead to a hostile reaction from inmates.

11.28   Sensible and reasonable security precautions, on the other hand, should have a constructive effect. If staff feel secure and in control, they will be more relaxed in their dealings with inmates. Inmates also need to feel secure from other inmates. If they do not, their sense of insecurity will have an adverse affect on their conduct.

11.29   We do not consider it desirable to canvass the detailed security proposals contained in the Review. However, Mr Lynch, the architectural adviser to the Inquiry, has carefully considered that Review.

11.30   Mr Lynch has commented that the proposed subdivision of prisoners into small manageable groups:

> "should help to promote a more stable atmosphere in a prison, and should also help to foster a setting where the day-to-day relationship between prisoners and staff should improve and become more purposeful. In

addition, the conditions for any large scale disturbance will be limited by vertical sub-divisions of the wings".

11.31   Mr Lynch has drawn attention to a number of structural features which could be modified so as to have a less oppressive impact on inmates. He has also made a number of valuable comments about the visual impact of a number of the security measures proposed, offering alternative suggestions. He has commented that the need for the physical separation of vulnerable prisoners may become less essential with the move to smaller more controllable living units – a point we consider further in Section 12.

11.32   Mr Lynch's comments on the Review have been supplied to the Prison Service. We suggest that those comments are taken into account in implementing the Review's proposals. Subject to those comments and what we have yet to say with regards to locks, if the PDBS approach to security and the Review's proposals are followed, the standard of prison establishments should be satisfactory both from the point of view of security and control.

11.33   We have not considered it necessary to consider the principal form of security in a prison establishment, that is the perimeter wall and/or fence. A feature of the disturbances at the establishments targeted was that no prisoner escaped. This appears to indicate that this aspect of security was satisfactory. However, the Prison Service Report 1989/90 indicates that 161 prisoners escaped from closed establishments during that year. There was a rash of escapes at the beginning of 1991. Both show that security requires continual vigilance.

iii) Locking Systems and Keys

11.34   We bring together under this heading our third, fourth, and fifth principles.

11.35   *The third principle is that where a prison has separate accommodation units, the access to and egress from those units should preferably be controlled by electrically operated gates. Alternatively, the gates should have locks operated by a different key from ones used on the gates onto other units and they should be able to be doubled.*

11.36   *The fourth principle is that while the locks on the cells in the same unit can be operated by the same cell key, the locks on the cells in different units should require the use of different keys.*

11.37   *The fifth principle is that in each establishment, where this is possible, interior lines of defence should be identified which can be secured by suitable gates with double or electrically operated locks.*

11.38   These principles stem from the experience in the disturbances. The disturbances show what can happen when a prisoner obtains possession of a bunch of keys. Without what are referred to in Section 9 as "firebreaks", a whole prison can be overrun. Part I of this Report makes clear that the consequences are very grave and that a drastic reappraisal of the approach to locks and keys is needed.

11.39   At present there are four different classes of locks: (a) the cell lock (which is operated by a single key which can be used to unlock any cell within the prison establishment no matter how large); (b) the class 1 lock, (the only lock which can be "doubled" – "doubled" means that, by using a special key, the master pass key, which is not carried by staff when on normal duties, the throw of the bolt can be extended and cannot then be unlocked by a normal pass key. Class 1 locks are generally used for locking gates between the exterior and interior of a building); (c) the class 2 lock (which is fitted inside the secure perimeter of a building, in general to all control doors and gates; it is of the same size and strength as a class 1 lock, but it has a different pattern of key and it does not have a doubling facility); and (d) the class 3 lock (which is fitted to offices, stores, staff locker rooms, staff toilets etc).

11.40   Staff normally carry keys which will open all locks, except a class 1 lock

269

after the double lock has been applied. This description indicates the general rule. There are special circumstances in which it is not followed and not all these keys are carried at the same time. The normal situation, however, is that, if a prison officer loses his bunch of keys to a prisoner, unless the double locks are applied (where this is possible), inmates can obtain access to any part of an establishment. That is the disadvantage of the present policy. The advantages of the present policy are its simplicity and the fact that it enables staff to move readily from one part of the prison to another and (especially in an emergency) to assist in locking or unlocking prisoners in a part of the prison in which they do not normally work.

11.41   While recognising the advantages of the present system, we propose that the present policy should be changed. The policy should be that staff should carry no more keys than are necessary for the proper execution of the duties they are performing during their current shift. The manner in which staff perform their duties under "Fresh Start" should mean that it should be possible to identify in which parts of a prison establishment a particular member of staff will be performing his duty on a particular shift.

11.42   If those duties can be broken down so that some can be conducted with a lesser number of keys then, where reasonably practicable, arrangements should be made to enable this to be done.

11.43   The locks on the cells in different units should require the use of different keys. We appreciate that this may create operational difficulties, but we think it should be possible to devise ways of overcoming them.

11.44   Some of the problems of moving without keys, in particular between different units and parts of the establishment, could be overcome by the judicious use of electric locks. They have the advantage that they do not need to be opened by keys, which can find their way into the possession of inmates. Electric locks are not easily compromised. This is a matter of some general importance. During the past three years there have been a total of 18 instances of class 1 and class 2 locks being compromised. As a result locks had to be changed, at a cost of £308,000. (This figure does not take into account labour costs, because locks are fitted using direct labour.)

11.45   Among the disadvantages of electric locks are that they are expensive and, it is alleged, they go wrong. But the principal disadvantage if they are applied to cell doors is that they could adversely affect the relationship between staff and inmates which results from staff having personally to unlock inmates. Many Governors and staff attach considerable importance to this. On the other hand, when there are shortages of staff, electric locks can be very helpful, particularly in relation to giving access to night sanitation. They increase security and avoid the frustration caused by the failure of staff to answer bells. Any problems of reliability can be overcome by a manual override, which allows a key to be used.

11.46   The PDBS provides for manual locking systems. However it contemplates that in certain situations electric locks should be fitted. After the experience in April 1990, more attention should be given to the possible use of electric locking. We propose that tests should be carried out to evaluate the advantages and disadvantages of electric locking systems when compared with conventional systems.

11.47   This approach is supported by the Prison Service Review of Physical Security. It recommends that further consideration should be given in Victorian prison establishments to the introduction of an electric locking system designed to control access to each accommodation unit from a central secure control point. The Review also recommends that further consideration should be given to the introduction at establishments built in the 1960/70s of electric locking systems that include the provision of access to night sanitation. We support both recommendations. We stress the comment made in the Review that an electrical system can provide the opportunity to exercise total control over all movements within an establishment. The system also overcomes the problem, which arises in connection with double locks, of finding a readily accessible but still secure location at which to store a doubles key when it is not being used.

11.48   So far, we have concentrated on locks in accommodation units. There are other areas of an establishment where inmates congregate. Our general approach to security requires that any disturbance in an area of this sort should be able to be confined to that area. Subject to an establishment being of sufficient size, it should have an interior line of defence beyond which inmates do not usually go in large numbers. This would require gates at the entrances to such areas (for example the Chapel at Manchester). The gates would need to have locks which cannot be compromised by the loss of an officer's keys. They should have either double or, preferably, electrically controlled locks. Any keys to these locks should not be carried by staff when they are in the units or in other parts of the prison where these keys are not immediately needed. Each establishment should be individually examined with these requirements in mind.

iv) Community Prisons

11.49   *The sixth principle is that, where this is practical, prisons should be community prisons sited within reasonable proximity to, and having close connections with, the community with which the prisoners they hold have their closest links.*

11.50   The local prison is a well-established part of the prison system. Strangeways, Bristol and Cardiff are typical examples. Their primary task was conceived as being to serve the local Courts. For this purpose, they were to hold remand prisoners and newly convicted and sentenced prisoners until those prisoners who had been sentenced to longer periods of imprisonment were transferred to training or dispersal prisons.

11.51   The evidence in Part I of this report makes it clear that the role of local prisons has been substantially extended. They have begun to be rather what we have in mind when referring to community prisons. They contain a cross-section of the entire prisoner population, from those on remand to those serving sentences up to and including life imprisonment. They contain young offenders as well as adult prisoners.

11.52   There has also been a tendency for the same development to take place in training prisons. Over the last 15 years, a number of training prisons, such as Reading, Lewes, Hull, Rochester, Chelmsford and Preston, have assumed a local or part local role. The Prison Service noted in a response to a request from us:

> "It is possible to envisage a considerable blurring of the distinction between local and training prisons with much greater scope for holding sentenced prisoners closer to home. Indeed something of this has already begun: Bristol, Lewes and Norwich in the adult sector and Feltham and Glen Parva in the young offender sector combine both local/remand centre and training functions. Brinsford, Bullingdon and Elmley are all being built to a plan of this kind."

11.53   There is a very real advantage to prisoners in being in a local prison. The location of the prison enables them to receive regular visits from their families. Transport into the urban centres, where the local prisons are located, is also usually satisfactory. Even if the prisoner's home is some distance away, visits can still be reasonably practical. This explains why, although the conditions within many local prisons are far from satisfactory and in some cases appalling, prisoners are still anxious to remain in those prisons and are unwilling to accept a transfer to a prison which offers better conditions, but which is more remote.

11.54   The fact that the prisons are "local" means that they are close to the Courts which they serve. They are usually built in urban centres, as are the Courts. The majority of prisoners in a local prison are therefore reasonably close to the Court which will try and, if they are found guilty, sentence them. The prison is usually accessible to the lawyers who represent them at the trial and on any appeal.

11.55　It can help if the staff in a prison came from the same area as the prisoner. This is more likely to happen in a community prison located near to its catchment area. This will make it easier for the staff to understand and relate to their prisoners. This was a feature of the evidence relating to the Cardiff disturbance. The staff referred to the Dartmoor prisoners as being very different from the Welsh prisoners with whom they were used to dealing. This added to the staff's problems. The Welsh staff's rapport with the Welsh prisoners was one factor in bringing the disturbance to a relatively early conclusion.

11.56　The fact that the prison is within reasonably close proximity to the prisoner's home has further advantages. It assists in preparing a prisoner for release and when he is released from prison. Arrangements can be made more easily to ensure that, as far as is practical, he will receive support when he returns to the community. Accommodation or jobs will be more easily found. The probation officer or the prison officer involved in a pre-release scheme will be in a much better position to assist. Medical treatment, education and training can be more effective. There is a greater chance of maintaining continuity of a person's treatment or training course between the prison and his home base. Parole should work better.

11.57　Our recommendation for community prisons should help also to meet one of the Prison Service's own concerns. In the Prison Service's Annual Report for 1989/90 under the heading "Links with the Community", the Report states:

> "Staff in the service make considerable efforts to encourage prisoners to stay in touch with their families and keep links with the community generally. Inmates are prepared for their return to society – to lead law abiding and useful lives – in a variety of ways. In helping to forge these links staff also strengthen the role of the Service itself in the community."

11.58　The case for a community style prison is further strengthened when it is recognised that the majority of the prison population are in prison for a relatively short period of time. A substantial proportion are in prison on remand (although, as we have argued in Section 10, for longer than we would like). Of those who are sentenced (including fine defaulters) approximately 55% are serving sentences of six months or less, 80% 18 months or less, and 97% 4 years or less. (These percentages are calculated before taking into account remission or parole.) In such cases, there should be as little break with the continuity of life in the community as is compatible with the sentence of imprisonment.

11.59　We recognise that the principle of localisation was considered and rejected by the May Committee. The Committee foresaw practical problems of location. It regarded overcrowding as being the principal problem. It argued that this policy would involve spreading the overcrowding more widely, although not so intensely, because overcrowding was then, as now, concentrated predominantly in the local prisons. The Committee's Report stated:

> "We could not support increased localisation, with the consequent damage to some well-resourced and imaginatively run regimes in the training prisons, unless we could see some substantial counter-balancing advantage."

11.60　Since the May Committee reported, the position has changed. First of all, the Prison Service expects to overcome the overcrowding problem within the next few years. Secondly, there is now an extensive building programme of new local prisons. Eight are planned altogether, of which six are nearing completion. A new local prison, Belmarsh, is planned to open in the Spring of 1991 in Woolwich, London. Thirdly, in recent years the Prison Service has increased the number of prisons with local functions from 24 to 33. Finally, the recent disturbances have made it clear that it is no longer appropriate to have a wholly different level of regime in local prisons from that which exists in training prisons. The Prison Service accepts that the regimes within local prisons will have to be improved.

11.61 There is one further important factor which was identified from the disturbances considered in Part I of this Inquiry. Section 9 identifies the disturbing effect which the transfer of prisoners had on prisoners. If community prisons are provided with small units, that should enable a broader range of regimes to be offered within prisons nearer to the prisoner's home. The Prison Service should then be able to plan a prisoner's sentence in a way which avoids his being moved so far from the community from which he comes. This could avoid the unsettling effect of a transfer away from his locality.

11.62 We therefore recommend that the Prison Service should adopt a policy objective of accommodating the majority of prisoners in community prisons. Local prisons already largely conform to this policy. Training and dispersal prisons frequently do not. With time, however, and by careful strategic planning of the prison estate, it should be possible to extend this policy in the long term to the majority of prisons.

11.63 In the long term, therefore, we envisage the majority of prisoners being held in prisons near to their homes. There would still need to be some specialist prisons, for example, Grendon prison, and some, such as Dartmoor and on the Isle of Wight, would need special consideration, but otherwise we would expect the principle of localisation to have precedence.

11.64 Initially, the principle should be applied to the accommodation of prisoners serving shorter sentences or those prisoners who are coming towards the end of long sentences and who are being prepared for their return to the community.

11.65 We do not confine this principle only to male sentenced prisoners. If, and only if, local prisons are arranged in living units with the necessary degree of separation which we have proposed, it should be possible, at least until the estate can be reorganised, to hold young offenders and remand prisoners and, provided the security is fully up to standard, women prisoners in the same local establishment. It must be preferable to have women in a wholly secure and separate block under their own governor and staff and with full access to families within a local prison near to their home rather than, as at present, to have to hold them many miles from their homes and families. (We discuss the position in respect of remand prisoners more fully later.)

11.66 One way in which we think the Prison Service would be able to achieve the objective of community prisons is through the clustering of establishments within a particular locality or area. Within the cluster, it should be possible to provide the range of services and conditions which prisoners need. This would enable young offenders, remands and women prisoners to be held separately. It should also provide for the full range of security categories and for the full range of sentence lengths.

11.67 In the first instance, it may be that this can only be achieved by clustering prisons over geographical areas which are wider than the ideal. But if the policy objective is clear, then the Prison Service should be able to look for opportunities to reduce the area of the cluster, while still providing for the full range of conditions necessary for the majority of prisoners in each area.

11.68 A community prison system based on clustering prisons would have implications for the way the areas assigned to Area Managers have been drawn. Ideally, and in time, each Area Manager should be responsible for at least one "cluster" of prisons.

v) Visits   11.69 *The seventh principle is that there should be satisfactory facilities for visits including an adequate visitors centre.*

11.70   We have drawn attention to the importance of the prisoner's links with the community outside the prison. Visits from his family and friends are usually the main manner in which these links are maintained. We discuss the extent of visits in Section 14. In this part we consider visiting facilities. In view of the priority which we attach to visits, it is important that the facilities for visits help to make the visit successful. Regrettably, in many of our older prisons, the conditions which exist in the visiting area are far from satisfactory. They can be tawdry, uncomfortable, cramped and oppressive. It is important that, when a scheme for refurbishment is to take place, suitable attention is paid to providing a better environment for visits. The area should be brightly decorated. The furnishing, while simple, should be comfortable. There should be areas for children to play.

11.71   Attention must also be paid to where visitors are to wait before they are admitted to the visits area. They should not be left to wait outside the prison without any protection from the weather. Staff, prisoners and their families have stressed to the Inquiry how concerned they are when visitors, often accompanied by young children, are left standing outside the main gate to the prison in cold and wet weather. This should not happen. Usually the best way this problem can be tackled is by having a visitors centre. A centre can provide somewhere where visitors can wait. It can offer advice on social and welfare problems arising out of imprisonment. We propose that a visitors centre should be properly furnished and have facilities for addressing social and welfare problems.

vi) Accommodating Remand Prisoners

11.72   *The eighth principle is that, unless they consent to different arrangements, wherever this is practical, remand prisoners should be accommodated in separate prisons or in separate units which are treated as separate prisons, from prisons or units occupied by convicted and sentenced prisoners.*

11.73   Rule 3 of the Prison Rules provides:

"(2) Unconvicted prisoners shall be kept out of contact with convicted prisoners as far as this can reasonably be done."

11.74   In addition Rule 3 of the European Prison Rules provides:

"In principle untried prisoners shall be detained separately from convicted prisoners unless they consent to being accommodated or involved together in organised activities beneficial to them."

11.75   The rules identify the correct policy which should be implemented. The Prison Rule is qualified in its terms. The European Prison Rules set out a principle. In the future, the qualification to the Prison Rule 3(2) should become less important. Both sets of rules, however, have to be viewed in a broad commonsense way. They are intended to protect remand prisoners, not prejudice them.

11.76   The policy which the Rules establish is that remand prisoners should be accommodated separately. That does not mean they must never come into contact with sentenced prisoners, but that they should, in addition to having separate accommodation, normally have separate activities. At some establishments this policy can and is being implemented now. At others, remand prisoners would suffer if the policy were to be rigorously applied.

11.77   Approximately one-third of our prisons now hold remand prisoners. It would not be practicable in the short term to remove remand prisoners from these establishments. Nor would it be practicable to reallocate the prisoners within these establishments so as to enable what is a mixed prison to become solely a remand prison.

11.78   As the Part I evidence indicates, many remand prisoners are housed in local prisons which are extremely large. These prisons would be unsuitable for use solely as remand institutions. Local prisons do, however, have the important advantage for remand prisoners of being close to family, solicitors and courts, as we have already explained. From a location point of view, the local prisons are probably preferable to the alternatives which could realistically be made available.

11.79   The great disadvantage about the housing of remand inmates in mixed establishments is, as we have indicated in Section 10, that experience, in this country and abroad, shows that remand prisoners tend to receive the most impoverished regime of all inmates. It should be possible to avoid this happening. If the steps are taken by the Prison Service which we will identify later in this Report, we would expect that, even in mixed establishments, the remand prisoner will receive the conditions to which he is entitled as a matter of justice because of his status.

11.80   In the future, when the policy of separate accommodation has been reflected in the building of new establishments, the position will be different. The aim then should be that remand prisoners should be held in prisons which, while entirely separate from prisons for sentenced prisoners, will be within the community "cluster" of prisons which we have earlier described. In the shorter term, however, the policy should be that, where remand prisoners cannot be housed in separate prisons, and unless they consent to different arrangements (for example, to meet a special need) they should be housed, wherever this is practical, in separate units from those occupied by sentenced inmates and those units should be treated as separate prisons.

vii) Shared Accommodation   11.81   *The ninth principle is that a prisoner should normally be entitled, if he so wishes, to have a cell or room to himself.*

11.82   *The tenth principle is that dormitory accommodation is undesirable.*

11.83   Section 14(1) of the Prison Act 1952 provides that:

"the Secretary of State shall satisfy himself from time to time that in every prison sufficient accommodation is provided for prisoners."

11.84   Section 14(2) of the Act states:

"No cell shall be used for the confinement of a prisoner unless it is certified by an (officer) that its size, lighting, heating, ventilation fittings are adequate for health....."

11.85   Neither of these provisions has in practice provided adequate protection against overfull and unsuitable accommodation. The physical state of some of our prisons is damning testimony to those conclusions. We consider later in this Section sanitation, hygiene, and overcrowding. Having set out the rules which apply, we examine here the practice in relation to shared accommodation.

11.86   We endorse the policy in relation to accommodation which is set out in the European Prison Rules. The main provisions are as follows:

"14.1 Prisoners shall normally be lodged during the night in individual cells except in cases where it is considered that there are advantages in sharing accommodation with other prisoners.

Where accommodation is shared, it shall be occupied by prisoners suitable to associate with others in those conditions. There shall be supervision by night in keeping with the nature of the institution."

11.87   The United Nations Standard Minimum Rules contain similar requirements.

11.88   The Prison Rules 1964 do no more than require that the certificate referred to in Section 14(2) of the Act should specify the maximum number of prisoners who can be confined in a cell or room (Rule 23(2)).

11.89   The European Prison Rules do not have the force of law. However, it is the policy of the United Kingdom to support the Rules. In a circular dated 26 April 1988 to the Governors of all prison establishments, the Prison Service, while acknowledging that at the present time it does not comply at all establishments with the Rules which have been cited, at least gives general support for the principles behind them.

11.90   None of these Rules contains an unqualified requirement that an inmate should be entitled to occupy a single cell. In the Netherlands, it is, however, a fundamental principle, to which their Prison Service attaches the greatest importance, that a prisoner should be entitled to have a cell to himself. The same approach is adopted at Oak Park Heights in Minnesota. We believe that this should be the policy in this country as well.

11.91   There are security and control as well as management problems when more than a single prisoner occupies a cell. This was stressed by the Warden of Oak Park Heights and confirmed by the initial events which contributed to the disturbances at Cardiff, Glen Parva and Pucklechurch.

11.92   We were therefore pleased to note that the PDBS provides that each sub-unit should have 46 single cells and only 2 double cells. This appears to us to be a sensible division of accommodation.

11.93   There are some prisoners for whom a double cell might be preferable. But prisoners should not normally be required to go in such cells if they do not want to do so. (This approach must be subject to qualifications where there are special circumstances which dictate a different approach – for example in the case of a prisoner who is a known suicide risk. The reasons are set out in HM Chief Inspector of Prisons' Review of Suicide and Self Harm.)

11.94   The Prison Service is at present in no position to provide this level of accommodation in all its existing establishments. This should, however, be the standard at which it should aim.

11.95   It should be the aim of the Prison Service to phase out as soon as possible the use of dormitory accommodation. Dormitories provide no privacy for an inmate and enable the stronger inmates to exploit the weaker ones in a manner which is wholly undesirable. In expressing these views, we are echoing the evidence given to us by Mr Cavadino, who said during one of our public seminars:

> "I think many of us feel that dormitory accommodation is a disaster from many points of view, not only because it deprives people of privacy but because it is a recipe for intimidation, bullying, extortion, blackmail, and for disruption of the kind that can lead to riots. The Prison Department has increasingly accepted that and has moved towards changing dormitory accommodation into cubicular accommodation particularly in the adult system. But there are still a substantial number, particularly, young offender institutions with dormitory accommodation and many of us feel that as well as setting a date in the foreseeable future for ending slopping out it would be desirable to set a date in the foreseeable future for the end of dormitory accommodation in the prison system."

11.96   The Prison Service should consider setting a target date for ending dormitory accommodation and the sharing of cells, unless the prisoner consents or there are special circumstances which make it appropriate, in the interests of the prisoner, that he be required to share a cell.

viii) Access to Sanitation

11.97   *The eleventh principle is that prisoners should have access at all times to sanitation.*

11.98   *The twelfth principle is that adequate and suitable provision should be made for the requirements of staff.*

11.99   Rule 17 of the European Rules provides:

> "17. The sanitary installations and arrangements for access shall be adequate to enable every prisoner to comply with the needs of nature when necessary and in clean and decent conditions."

11.100   In response to Rule 17, the Prison Service has stated in the circular of April 1988, to which we referred earlier, that the provision of access to sanitary facilities is an important part of its programme.

11.101   This is a subject which has been commented upon in the strongest terms by the current Chief Inspector of Prisons and by his predecessors. The Report on Prison Sanitation of February 1989 commenced by referring to a comment made by the Chief Inspector's predecessor in 1984. He described the position at that time in terms which would be equally applicable to some prisons today. Successive Chief Inspectors have made it clear that they regard the practice of slopping out to be uncivilised, unhygienic and degrading.

11.102   During our visits outside the United Kingdom, with the exception of a segregation unit, we came across no prison in which slopping out was practised. The evidence which we received from staff and inmates from prisons in this country makes it clear that this is an aspect of our prison life which they find intolerable. It is extremely damaging to the morale both of prison staff and inmates and undermines the relationship between them.

11.103   In the Chief Inspector's Report of February 1989 it is stated that:

> "With the full co-ordination by all parties, conversion programmes could be set up simultaneously in a number of establishments and starting dates could be scheduled for the rest. Such a programme, using the DOW designed sanitation schemes described.....could.....be completed within seven years."

11.104   The Prison Service annual report for 1989 indicates that, during the course of that year, 600 lavatories and wash basins were installed in existing cells. This was in addition to the 1,100 places at existing establishments which were given access to sanitation as part of major building and refurbishment work. The Report stated that, by the end of March 1990, 53% of CNA places would have access to night sanitation. The plans at that time were to increase this to over 75% by the end of 1993-94.

11.105   In our view the stage has now come when Ministers should make a firm commitment. We recommend that Ministers should publicly set a timetable to provide access to sanitation for all inmates. The commitment should be to a date which is as early as is practicable, bearing in mind the priority which should be given to the programme. It should not extend beyond the date referred to by the Chief Inspector, that is February 1996.

11.106   It should be practical to give the commitment. The timescale in the Report on Prison Sanitation was reached after the fullest co-operation between the Inspectorate and the Prison Service Works Department and has never been questioned.

11.107   A commitment of this sort is not one which Ministers would normally readily make for prisons. We recommend it because, in our view, this is an exceptional situation requiring exceptional action.

11.108   When Courts send prisoners to prison they are entitled to expect that the prisoners will be treated in accordance with the Prison Service's "duty to look after them with humanity". The Prison Service itself is anxious to be proud of the fact that it fulfils that duty. However, to lock up prisoners for long periods at a time with no alternative but to use a bucket for their basic needs (which then has to remain in the cell, sometimes for many hours) is manifestly inconsistent with and makes a mockery of that duty. It is not just. The commitment we have proposed would remove a practice which is a blot on our prison system and which undermines the justice of the sentence which prisoners are serving.

11.109   Secondly, we would wish the Prison Service to investigate the introduction of procedures which, until such time as the main target is met, would allow prisoners to come out of their cells at night in order to go to the lavatory in their wings or units. We have in mind, particularly, the most overcrowded local prisons where there may at present and for some time to come be two, or even three prisoners in a cell, who are required to use a bucket or pot to relieve themselves. We propose that each Governor whose establishment has some cells with integral sanitation and some without should be instructed to arrange (so far as this is practical) the occupation of the cells without sanitation so that as many as possible of those cells are occupied by a single inmate.

11.110   In addition, we propose that all Governors should consider with their Area Manager and their staff whether it is possible, with the addition of some extra staff and until such time as the promised integral sanitation is installed, to unlock inmates from cells without sanitation in controlled numbers and under supervision during the course of an evening and before, say, mid-night. It would be impractical to unlock such prisoners at these times on demand, but rotas might be established so that prisoners would know broadly when they were likely to be allowed to go to the lavatory.

11.111   We believe, from their written evidence, that the Prison Officers' Association would wish to join with the Prison Service in finding imaginative and cost effective ways of meeting this objective in as many prisons as possible, for the sake of the staff as well as the prisoners. The Prison Service should bend its mind to this in the knowledge that, with the rapid spread of integral sanitation in accordance with a specific target date as we have recommended, the increased staffing commitment at any establishment would be short-lived.

11.112   So far, we have concentrated on the need for access to sanitary facilities by inmates. Mr Deering, Chairman of the Board of Visitors at Pentonville, has pointed out in his evidence that staff as well as inmates are short of sanitary facilities. According to Mr Deering, in Pentonville an already modest provision of facilities for staff was reduced as a result of the introduction of female officers who have to have their own toilet facilities. He points out that D Wing of the prison has been refurbished so that the 350 inmates are each provided with their own toilet suite. However, the refurbishment did not make any provision for staff toilets. This does appear to be an unfortunate situation. In all refurbishment schemes, the needs of staff should be fully borne in mind.

ix) Hygiene   11.113   *The thirteenth principle is that standards of hygiene should be commensurate with those in the community.*

11.114   Rule 15 of the European Prison Rules provides:

"15. The accommodation provided for prisoners, and in particular all sleeping accommodation, shall meet the requirements of health and hygiene, due regard being paid to climatic conditions and especially the cubic content of air, a reasonable amount of space, lighting, heating, and ventilation."

11.115   In its response to Rule 15, set out in the circular of April 1988 to which we have already referred, the Prison Service acknowledges that its aim is in full compliance with this rule.

11.116   A circular of 10 October 1990, addressed to Governors, is headed "PRISON BOARD PRIORITY 1991/1992 – HYGIENE IN PRISONS". The circular commences with this statement:

"The conditions within which prisoners live are central to the Prison Service Statement of Purpose which places on all of us a duty to look after them 'with humanity'. The priority we afford to hygiene standards throughout establishments is a crucial element in this and our aim must be to achieve standards at least equivalent to those generally sought in the community. Our responsibilities to staff are no less important".

11.117 The circular makes it clear that the priority which it identifies is in addition to the programme to end slopping out. The initiative is welcomed and needed.

11.118 We are particularly pleased to note the references to equality with standards in the community and to the needs of staff as well as inmates. Both staff and inmates have given us horrendous descriptions of infestation problems in prison establishments. We have had descriptions of the action which has to be taken by prisoners to block up every nook and cranny in their cells to try and prevent the invasion which would normally occur during the hours of darkness. We received a description of walls eaten away behind gleaming metal sheets in the kitchen at Wandsworth Prison, which is now to be the subject of an extensive refurbishment programme.

11.119 On 1 April 1992, as a result of the Food Safety Act 1990, prison establishments will be open to inspection by local authority and environmental health officers. They will have the right to inspect all areas where food is stored, prepared, served and eaten and waste disposed. While the Prison Service, as part of the Crown, will remain immune from prosecution, from then on it will be open to environmental health officers to issue an improvement notice for compliance within a given period, or to issue a prohibition notice ordering the cessation of a particular practice. It will then also be possible for the health enforcement authorities to seek a declaration for non compliance from the High Court identifying the conduct of the Crown which would amount in the case of others to a criminal offence.

11.120 The Prison Service's circular gives examples of objectives in hygiene improvement which might be adopted. They include improvements with regard to kit control, the provision of an improved laundry service, and effective programmes for the riddance of pests and for the deep cleaning of kitchens. It also refers to one of the consequences of lack of access to night sanitation. It suggests an objective should be to make arrangements for the disposal of:

> "excreta ejected from cell windows and the reclamation of underwear and clothing used as wrappings for these 'parcels'."

11.121 The circular identifies what is needed. If a sustained programme of the type referred to in the circular is implemented, then it should lead to a substantial improvement. A programme of this sort has been needed for a substantial period of time. The circular, and the refurbishment which is taking place or which is about to take place in a number of kitchens, are an indication of how effective even a modest change in the law can be. Management must ensure the programme is maintained.

x) Accommodation for Board of Visitors

11.122 *The fourteenth principle is that prisons should always contain accommodation which can be set aside for use by the Board of Visitors.*

11.123 In many prison establishments at present there is no accommodation which the Board of Visitors can regard as its own. We consider that there should be provision in all new prisons and in refurbishment schemes for such accommodation. The room need not be large, but it should be of a size to enable the members of the Board who are likely to attend the prison at any one time to meet, discuss problems and keep their papers. It should also be properly equipped. Boards of Visitors should not be dependent upon the management or staff of establishments making their accommodation and equipment available to the Board. The provision to the Board of its own accommodation will be one way of helping to ensure that the Board is perceived by inmates as independent of management.

xi) Conclusion 11.124 These fourteen principles, already long, are not intended to be comprehensive. They arise from the evidence which the Inquiry has received. They are directed particularly to the wider lessons learned from the April disturbances. If they are followed, they should provide standards of buildings, accommodation and conditions which are less likely to be conducive to riot.

11.125 In the remaining part of this Section, we examine two different subjects: the relationship which the Prison Service should maintain with professional advisers and the central issue of overcrowding.

The Relationship between the Prison Service and Professional Consultants

11.126 The prison building and refurbishment programme is, by any standards, substantial. It is in real terms larger now than ever before. In the year 1989/90, spending on prison buildings rose to £362.9m, from £190.3m in the previous year. Of that, £231.6m was allocated to work on new prisons and £122.7m to work on existing establishments. A programme on this scale requires careful planning and monitoring. It requires the close involvement of professional advisers.

11.127 The evidence before the Inquiry suggests that relationships between the Prison Service and external consultants are not what they should be. A body of consultants, who have in the past been involved in the prison building programme, told us that, if they criticised the Prison Service's approach to its building programme, this would lead to their losing the prospect of any further instructions. It is not possible for us to come to any conclusion as to whether or not there is any justification for this belief. However, the Prison Service needs to address the fact that this fear exists among responsible consultants. It must be made clear that there is no question of consultants being victimised as a result of making critical comments.

11.128 While we warmly welcome the PDBS, it must not, in the words of the RIBA submission, be regarded as being written in "tablets of stone". This is not what the authors of the PDBS intended. The PDBS has to be adapted by the architect of each specific project in the light of the constraints which are applicable to that project and the use to which the building will be put. To enable this to be done, clear guidance must be given to all those involved in a project about the Prison Service's plans for the running of the particular establishment. Only if the policy is clearly stated, will the most effective design be achieved.

11.129 The PDBS will need to be continually reviewed and modified in the light of experience. We propose that there should be in the Prison Service a multi-disciplinary design group, which includes a senior architect, for this purpose. There also needs to be research conducted into the effectiveness and efficiency of different designs. The Prison Service must make it clear that it attaches great importance to good design. We propose, therefore, that it establishes satisfactory lines of communication with consultants who are, or who are seeking to be, involved in the prison building programme.

11.130 Within the Prison Service the body responsible for the delivery of the programme is the Prison Building Board. That Board has three professional experts among its members, an expert engineer, a quantity surveyor and a financial expert. It has no architect. It does, however, receive reports from panels of experts in the Directorate of Works. Those panels include architects (although not necessarily ones who are members of the RIBA). 90% of the design work of a particular prison, however, will usually be contracted to outside architects. In this way there is, or should be, a feedback to the Prison Building Board of the experience of independent architects.

11.131 The RIBA would welcome an architect on the Prison Building Board. Indeed, they would like to see that Board headed by an architect. It is clear that an architect could make a contribution to the Board's deliberations. However it is not possible to come to the conclusion that the Board cannot properly function without the presence of an architect, particularly having regard to the expert advice available to the Board. We do not, therefore, endorse this recommendation of the RIBA. However, those responsible for the composition of the Prison Building Board will no doubt take into account RIBA's recommendation when they come to make future appointments to the Board.

11.132   We were pleased to receive from the Prison Architecture Research Unit, at a late stage, amplification of earlier evidence which it had given in which the Unit stressed the key role that users should have in the design of prison buildings. The Unit's evidence set out the principle in terms with which we agree. It said:

> "The principle that buildings do not work nor give value for money when there is neither understanding of connections between operation and design nor common purpose between designers and users and amongst users themselves is particularly true for jails where the potential for human confrontation is always present."

Overcrowding

11.133   In any examination of the use and suitability of prison buildings, it is necessary to consider the relationship between the number of prisoners the Courts send to prison and the amount of accommodation within the prison estate to hold them. The Prison Service can assist by making the best possible use of the available accommodation, but in the end the sentencing policy of the Courts and the amount of accommodation available are the decisive factors as to whether or not there is overcrowding within the prison system.

11.134   Sentencing policy is not a subject for this Inquiry. This part of this Section concentrates on ways of avoiding the accommodation available to prisoners being misused by overcrowding. Even if new prisons are built which lead the world in their quality and design, little, if anything, will be achieved if they are allowed to become grossly overcrowded.

11.135   In a contribution to one of the seminars, the Director General of the Prison Service described the effect of overcrowding on the Prison Service. He said that it was his belief:

> "that the life and work of the Prison Service have, for the last 20 years, been distorted by the problems of overcrowding. That single factor has dominated prisoners' lives, it has produced often intolerable pressure on the staff, and as a consequence it has soured industrial relations. It has skewed managerial effort and it has diverted managerial effort away from positive developments. The removal of overcrowding is, in my view, an indispensable pre-condition of sustained and universal improvement in prison conditions."

11.136   Later the Director General added:

> "for improvement to be solid and service-wide, the canker of overcrowding must be rooted out."

11.137   We unreservedly endorse the Director General's assessment of the effect of overcrowding and of the importance of resolving the overcrowding problem in the future.

11.138   The Director General also indicated that, if the present trend in the prison population continued, and the prison building programme produced in the order of 10,000 additional places, as he expected, then the Prison Service would be likely to move from a shortage to a surplus of accommodation in about two year's time.

11.139   This assessment is based upon the use of the certified normal accommodation (CNA) of a prison as an appropriate measure of the accommodation which is available within a prison establishment. It is based also upon comparing the total population of all prisons with the total of the CNAs of all prisons. It therefore makes no allowance for the fact that the population may not be evenly spread throughout all prison establishments. (Thus, while some prisons are still overcrowded, other prisons are well below capacity.) It does not address the question of what the standard of accommodation should be. It does not take into account that, at any one time, part of the accommodation included in the CNA will be out of commission for repairs, refurbishment or redecoration. However, after making allowance for all these factors, we accept that the improvement to which the Director General draws attention will be significant. It is essential that as soon as possible the number of places available should be brought into line with the size of the prison population which needs to be accommodated.

11.140   Nothing is, however, static. Even if overcrowding is banished in accordance with the Director General's timetable, it is necessary to ensure that there is no return to the present situation. Once banished, it must not return. Inmates and staff must in future be protected from the corrosive consequences of overcrowding which the Director General so eloquently identified.

11.141   Accredited Standards, to which we will refer in Section 12, will have a part to play. In addition, we recommend the laying before Parliament of a new Prison Rule to take effect at the end of 1992 (the date by which the system is intended to be in equilibrium). The Rule should provide that no establishment should hold prisoners in excess of its CNA. Because there may be short-term and unexpected fluctuations, the Rule should provide that any one establishment may exceed its CNA by 3% for a period of no longer than a week in any three calendar months. It is necessary also to provide for emergencies, such as that which occurred with the Manchester riot. The Rule should therefore provide that, in exceptional circumstances, an establishment can exceed its CNA for a period longer than seven days, or in excess of 3%, if the Home Secretary has first issued a certificate specifying the increase in the maximum number of prisoners in excess of the CNA which may be accommodated at that establishment, the period for which they can be so accommodated up to a maximum of three months, and the reasons why they have to be so accommodated. The certificate should be renewable. The Home Secretary should be required by the Rule, at the time the certificate is issued or renewed, or as soon as possible thereafter, to lay a copy of the certificate before both Houses of Parliament, together with a statement drawing attention to its terms.

11.142   Subject to the general and limited exception, only if an appropriate certificate has been made would the Rule permit the number of prisoners to be increased above the CNA of any prison establishment. If there is an increase, it would be limited to that provided for in the certificate and would be for no longer than three months, although such a certificate should be renewable by the same process.

11.143   The object of the procedure will be to make it clear that the Home Secretary is contravening the Prison Rules if he does not comply with the certificate procedure. Such non-compliance could form the basis for an application for judicial review. If a certificate were issued, and there were no exceptional circumstances, then the certificate would not provide a defence to an application for judicial review.

11.144   The laying of the certificate would ensure that Parliament was informed of the situation and could make its views known. Any unnecessary issue of a certificate, or unnecessary prolongation of its terms, should result in Parliamentary criticism.

11.145   The certification process which we have recommended will not provide an impenetrable defence against overcrowding. It should, however, reduce the risk of gross overcrowding reoccurring. It should help to avoid overcrowding again becoming endemic to the system.

11.146   From the end of 1992, there should anyway be no excuse for regular or endemic overcrowding on any scale. But this objective depends on the Prison Service's forward planning working properly to identify changes in the prison population in sufficient time to anticipate those changes. The Consultative Council or similar body to which we referred in Section 10 should be able to assist the Prison Service in this task.

11.147   Proper forward planning should involve the Prison Service building into its accommodation requirements an appropriate safety factor to make provision for demands over and above the expected average population. The safety factor should allow for the fact that some accommodation will always be temporarily out of use. It should allow for the week by week variations in the prison population which are bound to occur and which can be reasonably forecast (for example, changes due to seasonal factors). The Prison Service cannot be expected to hold all those whom the Courts send to it in acceptable conditions unless it makes a reasonable provision for such contingencies.

11.148   The Prison Service has established a national Tactical Management and Planning Unit to help in this task. It started work on 25 September 1990, as a consequence of the senior management reorganisation in the Prison Service. One of the functions of the Unit is to identify changes in population and to keep those changes under much closer view than previously. According to the Prison Service's evidence:

> "it will allow more comprehensive analysis of the categories of prisoners' sentence length and home area, to feed into the planning process enabling better informed decisions on how the estate could better meet population needs, what types of new prison places are required in future years and where they would be most usefully located".

11.149   It is too early yet to say whether the Unit will meet these objectives. We consider, however, that the creation of this Unit would appear to be a step forward. The Unit should receive the resources and support from the Prison Service which it needs to meet its objectives.

11.150   If our recommendation for a new Prison Rule is accepted, we would expect the Prison Service to try and manage the prison estate in a way which will not require the Home Secretary to involve Parliament. It would be an incentive to good management. We hope, therefore, that the Home Secretary would not need to use the certification process. We hope also that the prison population will continue to fall; and that the planned accommodation, with the necessary contingency reserve, will suffice.

11.151   If our expectations of maintaining a proper equilibrium in the Prison Service are not fulfilled, then there is also the Home Secretary's power of executive release under Section 32 of the Criminal Justice Act 1982. The power given by that section is a wide one, but there are considerable disadvantages in its use. However, in our judgment, there could be circumstances when the use of that power would be justified to prevent a repetition of the overcrowded conditions which exist now in some of our prisons and which in April of this year existed at Manchester Prison.

11.152   Police cells should not be used as an expedient to prevent over-crowding. The Inquiry visited the police cells at Manchester (the Central Detention Centre). While police officers appeared to be doing their best to make the prisoners' conditions tolerable, the conditions were in fact wholly unaccept-able. The night before the Inquiry's visit, 101 prisoners had been held in 73 police cells. The cells had no natural light, they were small, they had an objectionable smell, they were overheated and without sanitation. The amount of exercise which the prisoners could have each day was limited to 20 minutes. The exercise area was a cage of modest size on a flat roof patrolled from above by a doghandler. The prisoners spent the major part of the day locked in their cells. They were not allowed radios.

11.153 When the Inquiry visited, some remand prisoners had been in the cells for over two weeks. We were told that it was the practice for convicted prisoners to be held in these conditions for no more than a week.

11.154 The cost of the use of police cells is also a matter of concern. For the six months ending 31 August 1990, the estimated cost of holding prisoners in police cells was £25,175,000, of which about £20,725,000 was in respect of the North Region and was therefore probably due largely to the disturbance in Strangeways. The Prison Service had also to meet the costs of improvements to police cells which were necessary during this period, which was estimated at £60,000.

11.155 We propose that there should be a limit placed at the first opportunity upon the time a prisoner, whether on remand or under sentence, can be kept in police cells on behalf of the Prison Service. We suggest the maximum period should be four days. Even then, this is too long if the conditions are of the quality which existed in Manchester, which were wholly inappropriate and inconsistent with the requirements of justice. They were appropriate for holding prisoners for hours not days. This proposal should be reflected in a new Prison Rule.

11.156 The Director General drew our attention to the effect of overcrowding on industrial relations. An illustration of that effect is provided by the industrial action which the Prison Officers' Association has taken from time to time since the disturbances of April 1990. This has led to prison officers refusing to admit prisoners to certain prisons over and above a number which the Prison Officers' Association itself identifies. The reason given by the Prison Officers' Association for taking this action was its belief that if the action were not taken, prison staff would be at risk and the conditions within the prisons would be even more intolerable than they already were.

11.157 The consequence of the prison officers' action, however, was that prisoners were kept for substantial periods in police cells which were not designed for holding prisoners other than for short periods. Conditions in these cells were frequently worse than those which existed in the cells in prisons to which the prisoners had been refused entry.

11.158 It is not a reasonable exercise of power for the Prison Officers' Association itself to determine what is the proper maximum accommodation of a prison. Nor is it reasonable for the Prison Officers' Association to seek to enforce that decision by industrial action which involves refusing admission to those sent to prison by the Courts. It is inconsistent with the concern which the Prison Officers' Association has for the treatment of prisoners that its members should take action which they are aware will result in prisoners being subjected to the conditions which exist in some police cells.

11.159 It must be recognised that it is the duty of society and therefore of the Government of the day to provide the resources necessary to accommodate all prisoners in humane and acceptable conditions. Since such conditions cannot be produced quickly, the fulfilment of this duty requires careful planning based on the best possible projections of the likely prison population. This places responsibilities on Government, on the Prison Service and on all parts of the Criminal Justice System, including the judiciary. Together they must ensure that the best information is available to make accurate plans which make efficient and effective use of the resources which must be provided.

Section 12

Management

Introduction

12.1   There is a most remarkable dichotomy within the Prison Service. The dichotomy is between:

    i)   the high calibre and deep commitment of the majority of Prison Service staff, at all levels. They have an immense sense of loyalty. They have a warm sense of camaraderie with their colleagues. They want to see improvements within the prison system; and

    ii)   the dissension, division and distrust which exist between all levels of Prison Service staff. They labour under a blanket of depression. They lack confidence in the value of what they do. They harbour a deep sense of frustration that the effort which they are devoting to the Service is not appreciated.

12.2   Repeatedly the Inquiry was informed by staff that they believed the Inquiry was the Service's "last chance". It was a "last chance" to resolve the dichotomy before, in these members of staff's eyes, it was too late.

12.3   Part of the explanation for this situation is the disturbances which took place in April. Another explanation is the series of managerial changes to which the Service has been subjected. These changes have convinced some staff that management is more interested in reorganisation than the men and women who make up the Service.

12.4   While not underestimating the scale of the problem, the Inquiry is convinced that it is solvable and that the prospects of the Service for the future are probably brighter now than they have been for a very long time. The improvements in the physical conditions within prisons which are about to take place, and the management changes which have already taken place, should provide the foundations for creating a Prison Service which is wholly different from that which exists at present.

12.5   The Inquiry has been immensely impressed with the amount of thought which has been given at all levels to how improvements can be made to the Prison Service. There are numerous examples in particular prisons of what can be achieved by staff when they are properly motivated. But the creative energy and commitment which exists in abundance within the Service require to be properly directed. There is a profound desire for more visible leadership.

12.6   This Section and the remaining two Sections of this Report are intended to address this critical problem. As will appear from what follows, the one thing which is not needed is more change to the structure of management within the Service. There is however a case for a limited structural change in the relationship between the Service and Ministers. We consider that this needs to be marked by a more developed "contract". There is also a need for a change in the tone or approach to management within the Service. This Section deals with both these subjects. It also examines the existing "contract" between the Prison Service and establishments and recommends that "contracts" should be provided between the Governor of each establishment and his prisoners. In Section

13, we recommend similar "contracts" for staff. This Section considers too the Service's management of race relations. And it refers to the arrangements for escort duties and to the role of Boards of Visitors.

12.7 There is a quite distinct managerial problem with which this Section also deals. That is how to manage groups of the prison population which present special difficulties for the Service.

Senior Management Reorganisation

12.8 Over the last 20 years, the Prison Service has been subjected regularly to management reviews. In 1969, after the report of a Management Review Team, a wide ranging reorganisation of Headquarters' structure took place. Four regions were created, each with its own Regional Director and management team. But the Service remained a very closely integrated part of the Home Office.

12.9 In 1978, a Committee of Inquiry into the United Kingdom Prison Services (the May Committee) was set up following a series of industrial disputes. Among its terms of reference was an obligation to examine and make recommendations upon the organisation and management of the Prison Services.

12.10 The May Committee reported in 1979. Not all the May recommendations were implemented. But the Prison Service followed the underlying objective of that Committee, which was that the Prison Service should have a clear corporate identity, yet remain within the Home Office.

12.11 In 1980, the membership of the Prisons Board was changed so that its membership was increased from six to twelve. The new Board consisted of the Director General, the holder of the newly created office of Deputy Director General, the four Regional Directors, the four Headquarters Directors, and two non-executive Directors.

12.12 In 1984, a new framework for the accountability of establishments was introduced by Circular Instruction 55/84. This led to a substantial increase in the responsibilities entrusted to the Regional Directors and to a shift in their relationship with Headquarters (HQ). Each Governor was made directly accountable to his Regional Director as his immediate line manager. The Regional Director was in turn accountable to the Deputy Director General, and through the Deputy Director General to the Director General and finally to the Minister. As a result of the new framework, an annual "contract" was to be made between each Governor and his Regional Director. This "contract" was intended to define the functions of each prison establishment and to set the objectives which each establishment was to achieve over the following 12 months.

12.13 Over 1987 and 1988, the "Fresh Start" package of reforms were introduced. As the Home Office states in its evidence, this package "dramatically altered" the structures within prison establishments. The Governor became the head of a senior management team from which there were clear lines of command down into every area of the establishment. Prison officers and Governor grades were unified into an integrated structure in which all the staff were salaried. National shift systems were abolished and overtime was to be phased out.

12.14 On 3 February 1989, the then Home Secretary announced that there would be a Review of the organisation and location of the Prison Service above establishment level.

12.15 The result of the Review was published on 10 August 1989. On 11 January 1990, following a period of consultation, the then Home Secretary (Mr Waddington) announced that he had accepted the main conclusions of the

Review. The Prisons Board was to be restructured. The Home Secretary said that what was needed was:

> "a new structure which will enable it (the Prison Service) to operate with maximum efficiency and effectiveness as a single national organisation accountable to Parliament through the Home Secretary for the custody and care of inmates".

The Report identified as its "central message" that "the Prison Service needs to become a more managed organisation".

12.16 This objective was to be achieved by having nine members on the Board: in addition to the Director General and two non-executive members, they would be the Director of Building and Services, the Director of Prison Medical Services, the Director of Personnel and Finance and the three Directors who were to have operational as well as policy responsibilities. (The three Directors were the Director of Inmate Administration, the Director of Custody, and the Director of Inmate Programmes.) The office of Deputy Director General was to be abolished.

12.17 Between the three Directors just mentioned and establishments there were to be Area Managers. The number of Area Managers was initially to be 14, but was subsequently increased to 15, each of whom was to be responsible for approximately nine establishments. It had been planned that a small number of Area Managers would be appointed from people who had not been former prison governors. In the event, the first Area Managers were all appointed from among those who had had operational experience within the Service.

12.18 Following the disturbances in April 1990, the Prison Governors' Association, which had argued strongly against its recommendations during the consultative period, urged that implementation of the Report should be adjourned. Despite this, the then Home Secretary (Mr Waddington) decided to continue with its implementation. The reorganisation took affect on 25 September 1990. In giving his reasons for rejecting delay, the Home Secretary explained that he considered that the uncertainty this would cause would be damaging, especially at a time when the Service was most in need of determined leadership.

12.19 As part of his announcement of 11 January 1990 accepting the recommendations contained in the Report, the Home Secretary also announced that more work, in particular on personnel matters and the handling of inmate grievances, would be devolved to establishments and regional offices; that the whole of Headquarters up to and including the Director General would in due course be relocated to the Midlands; and that work would begin to determine whether, and if so when, the Prison Service should become a "Next Steps" executive agency.

12.20 Shortly after the Inquiry began to gather evidence, it became clear that the structural changes in the management of the Prison Service which had taken place previously and which were now proposed, were having an unsettling effect upon establishments. There were complaints that the Prison Service was being subject to too many doctrinal changes.

12.21 In its report, the May Committee had observed that:

> "We cannot escape the conclusion that many of those employed in the Service feel a deep sense of dissatisfaction with the organisation and management of it as a whole and that a gulf has grown up between the establishments in the field and the staff who work in them on the one hand and headquarters at the Home Office in London on the other".

12.22 The managerial changes which have taken place since 1979 have done nothing to reduce this deep-felt sense of dissatisfaction. In many establishments there is a strong feeling of distrust of Headquarters. The Review of August 1989 accurately summarises the position in these terms:

> "Headquarters divisions are widely criticised by Governors for appearing to operate in isolation from each other and pursuing their own areas of interest without regard to priorities or other divisions and establishments' needs....Governors see themselves as being bombarded by a confetti of paper from people who do not understand their problems, each giving unconnected and sometimes conflicting instructions. Those in the field are, for their part, seen by headquarters to select and modify or reject these instructions at will. Failure to implement policy does not appear to attract censure and, even more importantly, is not always even recognised because information systems and follow up procedures do not provide adequate feedback. Headquarters divisions are frustrated working in a vacuum and are uncertain of their role in ensuring that policy is carried out and to a satisfactory standard. Where failure to implement does not come to light, the chosen remedy is often simply to issue further and even more prescriptive instructions.
>
> The result of these tensions is in many cases mistrust between headquarters and the field. This is exacerbated by the different background which characterises the two groups. Those whose careers are tied wholly to the Prison Service perceive generalist civil servants at headquarters as lacking commitment to the Service, because their tour of duty lasts only three or four years and their primary loyalties is thought to be to the career at the Home Office at large . . . . For their part, many headquarters staff see the field staff as narrowly concerned with the running of "their" prison or region preferably with the least interference from outside . . . . Many governors are thought to operate in an autonomous, if not maverick way, resistant to any suggestion that as agents to the Secretary of State they can be called to account for the extent to which they have implemented nationally agreed policy."

12.23 This distrust also exists within some establishments between governor grades and uniformed grades. The Prison Officers' Association in its evidence makes clear that it considers that this distrust is due to the manner in which "Fresh Start" has been implemented. It draws attention to the fact that, while there has not been a single pay-related dispute in the Prison Service for over three years, there have been more than 100 disputes relating to "Fresh Start". The POA alleges that a Governor is:

> "trapped between the justifiable demands of his staff for increased numbers and the refusal of the Prison Department to even meet its original promises".

12.24 On the Inquiry's visits to establishments and regional offices, considerable misgivings were expressed by many, but not all members of staff as to the appropriateness of the reorganisation. We were very conscious, however, of the need not to add to the Prison Service's uncertainty and confusion. Since the Home Secretary had decided to proceed with the implementation of the reorganisation above establishment level, we decided that it would be undesirable if we were to reconsider the merits of that reorganisation. It would have been impossible to have assessed how it was working on the basis of only a few weeks in operation.

12.25 The situation of "Fresh Start" is different: it was introduced in 1987 and 1988. We will consider its implementation and development in Section 13 of this Report.

The Director General

12.26 We received frequent complaints from both management and staff that there was a lack of visible leadership in the Service. These related to the Prison Service in general and specifically to the April disturbances. Sometimes these complaints were linked to a nostalgic backward look to the Prison Commissioners.

12.27 The complainants did not suggest any lack of personal qualities on the part of the present Director General (Mr Train) or the former Deputy Director General, (Mr Emes, who held that office until it was abolished). The evidence suggests that the problem was substantially due to the division of responsibility between the Director General and the Deputy Director General prior to the most recent reorganisation. The Director General, although the head of the Service, regarded himself as being primarily responsible for policy and for advising Ministers. He did not have an operational background. He was an administrative civil servant. The Deputy Director General, on the other hand, was the professional former Governor who was responsible for running the operational side of the Service. By agreement between the Director General and the Deputy Director General, it was the Deputy Director General who "ran" the Manchester disturbance. Except in connection with one interview on the radio, the Director General was never mentioned during the evidence on Part I of the Inquiry. .

12.28 In some respects, this division of the responsibility between policy and operations probably worked reasonably well. However (not always understanding the nature of the organisational structure) establishments expected the head of the Service, the Director General, to play the leading role. He did not do so. Nor was the Deputy Director General perceived to be doing so. No doubt this was partly because, as a result of his title as Deputy, he was not seen as being the leader, even though he in fact played a very authoritative role during the disturbances.

12.29 Reorganisation has undoubtedly resulted in an improvement. There is no longer a post of Deputy Director General. Past experience is still, however, relevant. In our judgement, it draws attention to the need for the Director General not to be regarded as a *Chairman* of the Board (which is the description given to him in the May and scrutiny reports). He needs to play the part that his title as Director *General* suggests. An operational service, such as the Prison Service, requires a leader who is not merely the Chairman of a management committee. It needs an operational head who is and is seen to be in day to day charge of the Service – who appears to lead and to answer for the Service.

12.30 The responsibilities of the Director General are threefold. First and foremost, he is the head of the Service and must be in day to day operational charge of it. Secondly he has responsibilities for advising Ministers, for developing and implementing policy and for managing the resources of the Service. Thirdly, it should be part of his task to develop the co-ordination and co-operation which is needed between the Prison Service and the other agencies within the Criminal Justice System. These are extremely onerous and important responsibilities.

12.31 A number of Governors consider that it would be a considerable boost for the morale of the Service if the Director General was a man who had had professional experience as a governor of a prison. It was only a Director General who had risen through the Service who would have the understanding of the problems of the Service which is ideally required in its leader. Although it is suspected that there is some rule preventing a "prison man" being appointed to the office of Director General, we are satisfied that the situation is quite the contrary.

12.32 We consider it unfortunate that no Director General with a background in the Prison Service has ever held the post of Director General. The approach should be only to appoint a person without experience within establishments if there is no-one with this experience who would do the job as well. We trust that in time a Director General who has risen through the ranks of the Service will be appointed.

12.33   We do not consider however that the case has been made for saying that it is *only* someone who has come up through the Service who could fill this responsible office. Equally, there should not be any feeling that the office has *always* to be filled by an administrative grade civil servant. The most important requirement is that the Director General should have the necessary administrative and leadership qualities to be the head of the Service. He should be the best man for the job irrespective of his background.

12.34   The fact that so far there has been no suitable candidate from the ranks of former governors for the post of Director General when that office has become vacant does, however, suggest that the Service is not going about the task of recruiting, training and promoting the senior managers of the future in the right way. Experience of other sections of the Criminal Justice System would be of value to governors who have the potential to be the Area Managers, Directors and Director Generals of the future. Conversely top class administrative grade civil servants need to be given some experience of the problems and challenges of running a prison. These are matters which we consider further in Section 13 of the Report.

The Relationship between Ministers and the Prison Service

12.35   The Home Secretary, assisted by one of his junior Ministers, is directly responsible and accountable to Parliament for all aspects of Prison Service work. It is convenient to see the statutory framework which creates this responsibility. Section 1 of the Prison Act 1952 provides that:

> "All powers and jurisdiction in relation to prisons which before the commencement of the Prison Act 1877 were exercisable by any other authority shall subject to the provisions of this Act, be exercisable by the Secretary of State".

12.36   The Home Secretary is responsible for the appointment and payment of members of the Prison Service. Section 3 of the Act provides:

> "(1) The Secretary of State may for the purposes of this Act, appoint such officers and servants as he may, with the sanction of the Treasury as to number, determine."

12.37   The Home Secretary is also responsible for the general superintendence of prisons and for their maintenance and the maintenance of prisoners. His officers are under a duty to visit prisons and "examine" the state of buildings, the conduct of officers, the treatment and conduct of prisoners and all other matters concerning the management of prisons. His officers are also under a duty to "ensure that the provisions of" the Act and any Rules, including the Prison Rules, are duly complied with. (See Section 4(1), (2) and (3) of the Act – the last requirement is important in indicating the extent to which the Prison Rules are legally binding upon the Secretary of State; although damages for breach of the Rules cannot be obtained, other remedies on application for judicial review may be granted by the Court.)

12.38   Under Section 5 of the Act, the Home Secretary is under a duty to issue an annual report which has to be laid before Parliament. The report must specify the accommodation of each prison and the average and highest number of prisoners confined in each prison. It must include particulars of work done by the prisoners at each prison. It must make a statement of punishments inflicted in each prison and of the offences for which they were inflicted.

12.39   There are a number of other provisions which place obligations upon the Secretary of State, but the statutory provisions already referred to make clear the intimate nature of the Home Secretary's statutory responsibilities in relation to the Service. In addition, the Act also indicates the extent to which Parliament is intended to be kept informed of the manner in which the Home Secretary's statutory duties are performed. (Unlike the Prison Rules, those duties can only be altered by statutory intervention.)

12.40 The personal responsibility of the Home Secretary for the running of the Service is not surprising. The Prison Service is responsible on behalf of the State, for all aspects of the lives of those in its establishments. It is clearly right that the Secretary of State should be able to exercise his responsibilities and to be accountable to Parliament for what goes on in prisons. Nothing we are about to say is intended to undermine that responsibility. Equally, there can be no suggestion that the Home Secretary does not have, and should not exercise, the widest powers of delegation. (See the recent case of *R. v. Secretary of State for the Home Department, ex parte Oladehinde* [1990] 3 W.L.R. 797 in the House of Lords).

12.41 There is nothing, therefore, in the statutory provisions which would prevent the Director General acting as the visible head of the Prison Service.

12.42 The Prison Service Review of Organisation and Location refers to the relationship between the Home Secretary and Parliament. It goes on to say:

> "the need to account to Parliament, often with a fast response, for the way in which the Prison Service discharges its business and uses its resources, demands a tightly structured, well co-ordinated organisation with clear lines of authority and direction and good information flows between all functions and levels of the Service."

12.43 Apart from the reference to "a tightly structured" organisation, we would endorse this statement. A tight structure is not necessary where there is good co-ordination and fast communication. As long as these two requirements exist in the Prison Service, we recommend that the relationship between the Prison Service and Ministers should be more clearly structured to allow the Director General to exercise the leadership and authority needed to run the Service.

12.44 This was described in evidence to the Inquiry as a "structured stand-off". We have interpreted this as meaning that the Prison Service should be more clearly seen as an operational organisation which can be expected to work under the clear leadership of the Director General to the policies, priorities and with the resources established by Ministers. Once those policies, priorities and resources have been established, the Prison Service should expect and be expected, to get on with the job. The Director General should expect to answer for his stewardship to Ministers and to explain the work of the Service in public through the media. Ministers would remain answerable to Parliament. In this way, the public and Prison Service staff should have a better understanding of and greater confidence in the operational efforts of the Service and in its professional leaders, while the authority and responsibility of the Secretary of State was recognised and maintained.

12.45 It will be seen that this is not a proposal, therefore, involving any material change to the constitutional relationship between the Prison Service and Ministers. It is a proposal to change the public's and staff's perception of the Prison Service and its senior management. It is a proposal to reflect with greater clarity the implications of the Director General's responsibility for the Service's day to day operations. It is directed to helping to resolve the dichotomy which we identified at the beginning of this section.

12.46 The means of achieving this change are already to hand. They need now to be brought together and used in a structure which will achieve the relationship we have described.

12.47 The Prison Service already prepares a number of documents which identify the priorities which it has been given by Ministers and the resources which are available to meet these priorities. There is already a document issued to Prison Service governors setting out Prison Service priorities for each year. There is also a document setting out the Prison Service's objectives over the coming years (The Prison Service Annual Planning Document). This is described in the Prison Service evidence to as a "sort of corporate plan". (We describe these documents more fully in a later part of this Section.) We recommend that, drawing on these documents, the Prison Service should prepare a document approved by Ministers which sets out clearly the tasks and objectives of the Service for the coming year and the available resources. This document should be published. It would be, in effect, a "compact" or "contract" between the Director General and the Secretary of State. It would differ from the present published Annual Report because, unlike that document, it would be prospective and not retrospective. It would also clearly focus on the Prison Service's tasks and obligations. The Annual Report could contain a section to show how far these had been fulfilled.

12.48   The Minister would be entitled to amend or change the broad policy or objectives at any time, but if he did so on matters affecting the substance of the document, this would require a degree of formality not required at present. There would need to be a new or amended "contract". It too would need to be published.

12.49   So as to give affect to Parliament's role, the "contract" could be laid before Parliament at the same time as the annual report on the Prison Service (which would continue to be prepared by the Director General) is presented to Parliament by the Home Secretary. They could then be considered with the Chief Inspector's Report, which is also required to be laid before Parliament by the Home Secretary under Section 5A(5) of the Act.

12.50   At the present time the Accounting Officer for the Prison Service is the Permanent Under Secretary of the Home Office. Among his responsibilities as Accounting Officer, he is responsible to his Ministers for the propriety and regularity of his department's expenditure, and for prudent and economical administration.

12.51   It is the Accounting Officer who will be called upon to appear before the Parliamentary Accounts Committee (PAC) and to answer questions of the PAC concerning expenditure and receipts.

12.52   Where an agency is established under the "Next Steps" initiative, the Chief Executive is normally appointed as the Agency's Accounting Officer. However, without agency status, it is possible to have an Additional Accounting Officer who is responsible for certain votes of a Government department. He is then personally answerable to the PAC for those votes.

12.53   We considered whether to propose that the Director General should be appointed as an additional Accounting Officer for the Prison Service. We do not do so. We understand that the affect of such an appointment would be completely to isolate the Prison Service's finances from the financial provision made for other parts of the Home Office. We are not convinced that a step of this magnitude is required in order to achieve the sort of role for the Director General which we envisage. The Minister, through the Permanent Under Secretary would, as now, delegate responsibility for the Prison Service's finances to the Director General. The Director General would, as now, normally be expected to accompany the Permanent Under Secretary to any meeting of the PAC which considered the Prison Service vote. The Director General can therefore be allocated distinct resources for the Prison Service and can be publicly answerable for the way they are deployed. That is the position we seek.

12.54   We suggest that consideration might be given to the rank of the Director General in the light of our proposals. At the present time he is a Grade 2 – a deputy under secretary. The May Committee, in addition to recommending that the Director General should become the Accounting Officer for the Prison Service (which we do not recommend), recommended he should be of Second Permanent Secretary rank. We do not see the rank of the Director General as being crucial to his publicly demonstrated position as head of the Service.

However, bearing in mind his additional responsibilities, if our recommendations are accepted, including those in relation to the Consultative Council, it is desirable that the Director General's rank should be reconsidered. We appreciate that the creation of a Second Permanent Secretary rank within the Home Office has implications which affect other departments of Government and it is partly for this reason that we make no proposal upon this question.

12.55 Whether or not the Director General becomes a Second Permanent Secretary, the relationship between Ministers and the Director General of the type we have identified, would enable the Director General to exercise the leadership which is appropriate on behalf of the Prison Service. This should make a significant contribution to filling the vacuum in visible leadership that many in the Service believe exists at present.

12.56 It might appear that we are implicitly indicating a view as to whether or not the Prison Service should have agency status. This is not our intention. We consider that our proposal that the Prison Service should have a "stand-off" relationship does not necessarily involve the Prison Service having agency status. The relationship which we envisage between the Service and Ministers could exist whether or not the Service has such status.

12.57 Mr Louis Blom-Cooper QC and Professor Terence Morris, in their evidence, strongly endorsed the arguments of those, like the Prison Reform Trust, who were in favour of agency status for the Prison Service. They contended that the history of prison administration and management since the abolition of the Prison Commission in 1963 "had been a discouraging one".

12.58 In its evidence to the Inquiry, the Prison Service made it clear that the question of agency status still remained to be considered by Ministers. The evidence identified, however, the relevant issues, some of which relate directly to this part of our proposals. In particular, the Prison Service said that, because it is so closely bound up with the daily lives and personal liberties of individuals, it is difficult for the "responsible Ministers" to keep a distance since the exercise of managerial discretion can and does impinge sharply and immediately upon the life of a subject of the Crown (albeit one in custody). The evidence adds that:

> "the fact is that sensitive issues affecting individuals are part of the warp and weft of everyday prison life: the crucial question is whether a hands-off regime can work in a so politically and constitutionally sensitive operational service".

12.59 While we recognise the force of these considerations, we would suggest that as long as Ministers receive all the assistance which they need from the Service in order to enable them to formulate policy and are kept fully informed about sensitive issues when they occur, it is possible for them, normally and on a day to day basis, to perform their very heavy responsibilities in relation to the Prison Service in a "hands-off" manner. In our view, it is desirable that they should do so.

12.60 We regard our recommendation as to the relationship between the Service and Ministers as being perfectly feasible either with or without Agency status. We therefore see no need to make a recommendation or proposal in relation to it. We recognise there are arguments both ways. The important thing is to have a relationship which particularly recognises the operational responsibilities of the Prison Service and the leadership provided by its senior management. We would not want consideration of that to get unnecessarily bogged down in issues relating to agency status which in our view are not fundamental to achieving that relationship.

The Prisons Board

12.61 The Prisons Board has no statutory recognition. Its task has been described in annual reports on the work of the Prison Service as being to monitor the performance of the Service and to act as a consultative forum:

"it is a source of authority behind any advice given to Ministers from an official on the Board or any decision that is taken by that official on the basis of consultation through the Board".

12.62 The Report of the Review of Organisation and Location notes this description. It goes on to say that:

"the Board is not collectively responsible and accountable for development and delivery of the Service's policy; these are discharged personally by staff exercising the delegated power of the Secretary of State".

12.63 The report later states:

"an organisation of the size and complexity of the Prison Service needs to have a committee of its top management to decide the Service's priorities, to oversee the development of policy, to secure commitment to the validation of decisions taken by individual directors and to monitor the Service's performance against the targets which have been set. Any action taken within the Service should conform to the priority set by the Board and to policies which it has endorsed."

12.64 If the Director General is to have the role which we have identified for him, then the Board, of which he is chairman, is and should be regarded by him as being a useful tool to assist him to perform his role. It must be his Board.

12.65 The Board helps to bring together both the operational and the policy aspects of the Service. It is essentially an advisory and co-ordinating body. The Board includes among its members all the Directors who have direct executive responsibility under the Director General for running the Service. The Director General could be expected to attach great weight to its collective and coordinated contribution to progressing the policy of the Service. But the ultimate decision about how to act or what to recommend to Ministers must be his. The extent to which the Board is involved in the operational and policy formulating functions of the Prison Service is bound to be affected by the judgment and management style of the Director General of the day. A former member of the Board suggested in evidence to us that the Board needed proper terms of reference if it was to become an effective forum for discussing issues at the highest level within the Service. It must be the task of the Director General to ensure that its terms of reference reflect clearly the role he wants it to perform.

Relations between Headquarters and Establishments

12.66 The distrust and lack of confidence which exists between the various levels of staff and management of the Prison Service have to be tackled. Together with the overcrowding and the impoverished regimes within some prisons, they explain why, despite the individual qualities of those employed in the Prison Service and the general desire to improve the situation, more progress has not been made.

12.67 Running prisons involves team work. Headquarters, area managers, governors and staff are all part of the team and have to work together. They would do so more effectively if it were recognised by all levels of staff that the leading edge of the Service is the staff on the landings, wings and units in prisons. All the rest are working to make that edge more effective. It is the responsibility of management all the way up the line to the Director General to support these staff and so to enable them to achieve the Prison Service's Statement of Purpose.

12.68 Management's job must be to ensure that establishments have the resources which are needed for this purpose and that staff use those resources effectively. As a distinguished contributor to the Inquiry told us:

"management is (or should be) an enabling process".

The relationship between Headquarters and establishments should be based on Headquarters *enabling* governors to govern. Governors should, in their turn, *enable* their staff to look after prisoners.

12.69 This was the role which the Regions were trying to play during the disturbances which have been examined during Part I of this Inquiry. This is no doubt also what management at Headquarters has been and is trying to do, but it has failed to get the message across. The message which is heard at establishment level does not sound like "it is only our job to help". What is heard in establishments is Headquarters, who are regarded overwhelmingly as being administrators without practical experience, telling very experienced governors and staff how to do the jobs which they have been doing for most of their working lives.

12.70 Headquarters must, of course, know what is going on in prisons. For that they need information and statistical returns. But when information is required by headquarters and when staff are tediously required to fill in monitoring returns, it has to be made clear that the object of the exercise is to help those who are responsible for delivering the service to the inmates to provide that service more efficiently and more effectively.

12.71 Headquarters must also be able to create and establish consistent policies and practices between prisons. That is their legitimate and necessary role. But these policies and practices need to take account of the practical requirements of running a prison. They need to help the ultimate aim of the Service, not shackle establishments into uniformity and inappropriate procedures. If policies are understood and are helpful to running a prison, they are the more likely to be operated sensibly and sensitively by governors and prison staff.

12.72 The Director of the Scottish Prison Service, during the Inquiry's visit to Scotland, identified his principal role as being one of support. That was the message that he wanted the staff to hear. The Director was not of course suggesting that he never had to take command, or that he never had to overrule those who were his subordinates. It was a matter of emphasis. It is an emphasis which we would endorse.

12.73 We therefore recommend that the Prison Service should aim for a situation where it is appreciated by the Service as a whole that management (and the framework of controls that have been created) only exist to *enable* Governors to govern and to provide support for staff, so that both Governors and staff can perform their tasks as well as possible.

12.74 To achieve this, there should be, increased delegation to establishments. This was favoured by the Prison Service's management review. Each establishment should, for example, have as much responsibility as is practicable for determining how its own budget is spent.

12.75 A vivid example of the need for this was provided when the Inquiry visited Birmingham Prison in April 1990. Birmingham (Winson Green) Prison is one of the local prisons which is struggling with the problems of overcrowding. Nonetheless, the governors and staff are seeking to improve the regime for prisoners and are committed to doing so. One problem which they have is in relation to association areas for unconvicted prisoners.

12.76 At present, it is the deplorable situation that there is no opportunity to offer association to unconvicted prisoners. We were told, however, that there were some rooms which could be converted to association areas at a cost of £400 or £500. If three officers were available, it would be possible to supervise association for two hours each forenoon and afternoon for about 80-100 prisoners per day in those rooms. Furthermore, if the unconvicted exercise yard were to be fenced off in the same way as the convicted prisoners' exercise yard was fenced off (at a cost of £11,000) staff who were used to supervise exercise could also supervise the association. The necessary supervision would therefore be met without extra staffing costs.

12.77 We understand that resources have now been made available and that work has commenced. But expenditure on this scale for a project which would have been good for the morale of both staff and inmates should have been within the discretion of management at establishment level.

12.78 During the course of visits made by the Inquiry to other establishments, we heard similar stories of useful initiatives being killed off before they could be put into effect or, what is worse, killed off after work on them had started, because of the establishment's lack of control over its own budget. It is to be hoped that a process of greater delegation will help to avoid the frustration which at present can be created by an establishment not being able to spend a reasonable level of resources in the way that it wishes.

12.79 We recommend therefore increased delegation of responsibility to Governors for the functions connected with the management of the prison. We recognise that Headquarters have to ensure that the establishment is using its resources effectively and efficiently and that the establishment is performing its allotted role within the programme which the Prison Service has set itself. But these objectives should not prevent a greater degree of delegation. They can be achieved by proper monitoring.

The Prison Service's Planning Document

12.80 Each year, in March, the Prison Service prepares its planning document. We have referred to it in explaining our approach to the relationship which should exist between the Prison Service and Ministers. We describe it in more detail here, on the basis of the Prison Service's evidence to us. We see this document as providing the basis for the "contract" between the Prison Service and Ministers to which we attach considerable importance.

12.81 The planning document covers a five year period: the current year, the year just about to begin, and three forward years. They are the years which will be the subject of the annual Public Expenditure Survey. The document sets out the framework of plans within which the Prison Service is and will be operating. The plans are conditioned by an agreed programme of goals for the Service. The agreed programme of goals is in turn given effect by strategic objectives.

12.82 In order to monitor the programme and progress towards the goals and objectives, the Prison Service has nine performance indicators. They are:

a) the percentage of the prison population held in accommodation designed for fewer inmates;

b) the proportion of the population held in non-prison department accommodation;

c) the percentage increase in the number of places previously without access to sanitation where conversion has taken place;

d) the increase in CNA;

e) the average hours of employment/education/other activities per inmate per week;

f) the number of escapes/absconds per thousand inmates a year;

g) operating costs per inmate;

h) staff costs per inmate;

i)   the number of inmate hours per staff hour.

12.83   At the present time, the indicators are somewhat crude. The performance indicators make no allowance for the quality of the conditions measured. This is a matter of considerable concern to those establishments where the performance is of very high quality. Employment for inmates, for example, can vary enormously within the Prison Service. Some forms of employment are monotonous in the extreme. In others, such as at Leyhill, there is a considerable variety of employment, some of which is very imaginative. It is to be hoped that, with time, the Prison Service will be able to develop more sophisticated indicators which are capable of assessing the quality of what is being achieved in the prison.

12.84   Having set out the strategic objectives, the planning document also contains short term objectives which set targets for the year ahead. Progress is measured against the short term targets.

12.85   In addition the document contains a budget statement for the coming year and a statement of resources needed for the three following years.

12.86   The higher objectives which the planning document contains are carried through into the work programmes which are used to assist the Prisons Board to set annual priorities. These are widely publicised throughout the Service.

12.87   As we have said earlier in this Section, the Prison Service describes this document as its "corporate plan". We see it better expressed as a "contract" because it is a document which establishes what Ministers expect of the Service and what they are prepared to pay for those expectations.

The Area Manager's "Contract" with Establishments

12.88   To carry forward these objectives at establishment level, "contracts" are drawn up between the Governors of establishments and their respective Area Managers. The Prison Service describe the system in their evidence as "management by contract". It is for this reason we have throughout used the word "contract" rather than "compact", which, bearing in mind it is not legally enforceable, might be a more accurate description of the document to which we refer than "contract". The system originated in 1984 with Circular Instruction 55/1984. The "contracts" were agreed annually with the Regional Director and now they are agreed with the Area Manager. The Governor reflects on his performance of the "contract" in his annual report to the Area Manager.

12.89   The "contracts" are intended to:

"set out clearly the functions of individual establishments, the level of service to be provided in respect of them, how this is to be met within the resources available and any objectives for change in respect of local or national (ie strategic) priorities required in the year ahead."

12.90   The "contract" is therefore meant to set out in simple terms what the establishment does in every area of activity. There should be standards of performance set out for each corporate objective and blocks of work are identified for which groups of staff will be responsible.

12.91   Circular Instruction 55/1984 identifies 22 functions to be included in the "contract" with the establishment, to which four extra support activities have to be added – staff; administration and finance; buildings; and plant equipment and services. The functions which all prisons perform are grouped under six general sub-headings: custody of unsentenced prisoners; the court commitment; custody of sentenced prisoners; security, safety and control; services and facilities for prisoners; and community links and preparation for release.

12.92   Some of the 22 functions describe external obligations (eg to ensure that prisoners are produced at court as required). Some are simply descriptive and do not indicate priorities (eg "to maintain a level of security appropriate to the prisoners who are or may be held at the establishment"). A few are normative (eg "to enable prisoners to spend the maximum possible time out of their cells").

12.93   A management manual was issued in January 1990 explaining, *inter alia*, how governors were to prepare their "establishment contract".

12.94   The contracts which the Inquiry has seen indicate that they differ quite considerably in detail. The Inquiry has seen examples of "contracts" which set out specifically what the establishment intends to provide for each inmate. For example, under Function 17 in the Gartree "contract" it is stated:

> "Time out of cell for all inmates in normal location will be nine hours each weekday and nine hours 45 minutes each weekend day";

> "Programmed regime activity (work, education, chaplaincy activities, PE) to be available for a minimum of 28.08 hours *per inmate* per week" (emphasis added);

> "Evening association will take place for two hours on Mondays, Tuesdays, Thursdays and Fridays and for two hours 30 minutes on Wednesdays, Saturdays and Sundays. . . . Daytime association will take place for seven hours 45 minutes on weekends and bank holidays."

12.95   The implication is that *every* Gartree prisoner, except presumably those who have formally been administratively deprived of it, *will* get association as described above and presumably can *expect* to get it. This is a feature of the "contract" to which the Inquiry attaches considerable importance for reasons which will become apparent when we set out our recommendation for inmates "contracts". The form which an establishment's "contract" should take should follow the admirable precedent provided by Gartree. They should not follow the example of other "contracts" we have seen, which are a mere statement of generalities.

12.96   As we have said, the establishment "contract" is not a "contract" in the legal sense. Neither the Home Secretary, nor the Director General, nor the Area Manager could intend it to be enforceable by action. It does, however, provide a valuable statement of what the establishment should be doing during the year ahead and what it will be seeking to do in the longer term. This should give the establishment a sense of purpose and provide a bench mark for assessing the performance of the establishment during the year.

12.97   A shortcoming in the "contract" which was pointed out to the Inquiry is that some "contracts", at any rate, do not place a reciprocal obligation upon the Service to provide the resources and support which the establishment will need if it is going to fulfil its task under the "contract". We propose that this shortcoming should be addressed so that there are clear obligations on both sides.

A Code of Standards

12.98   We received much evidence from individuals and organisations proposing enforceable minimum standards for prisons. The organisations included the National Association for the Care and Resettlement of Offenders (NACRO), the Prison Reform Trust, the Prison Governors' Association and the Prison Officers' Association.

12.99   In 1982 the then Home Secretary, now Viscount Whitelaw, asked the Prison Department to prepare a draft Code of standards as a basis for consultation. However, although the Government published a summary of building standards, it decided not to proceed with the task of preparing a wider

Code. It took the view that this would not advance the programme which it had in hand for improving conditions in the Prison Service.

12.100 Although the Government did not consider that a Code of minimum standards would assist, House of Commons Select Committees have on three occasions, 1983, 1987 and 1990, reiterated the desirability of enforceable standards within prisons.

12.101 There has been considerable research into minimum standards. The nature of that research has been admirably summarised in the evidence of the Prison Governors' Association. In particular, in 1989 Dr Sylvia Casale and Ms Joyce Plotnikoff produced a series of papers, Minimum Standards in Prisons, which set out a step by step programme of change over a period of eight years. The objective was to demonstrate that, given the political will and matching resources, minimum standards could be implemented in this country by 1996.

12.102 In its evidence on this subject, the Prison Service called attention to the fact that we already have some "minimum standards". These are the detailed and specific standards contained in the Prison Design Briefing System and some Prison Rules and Standing Orders. For example, Prison Rule 26(2) provides that every prisoner shall have a hot bath on reception and thereafter at least once a week. Prison Rule 34(2) lays down the minimum provision in respect of letters and visits for convicted prisoners. The Prison Service suggested that the establishment "contracts" to which we have just referred also set out standards.

12.103 However, as the Prison Service also accepts, these do not amount to a comprehensive or universal Code. They are not what is normally understood to be anything like a Code of "minimum standards".

12.104 The Prison Service recognises that there are obvious attractions in the idea of developing such a Code: it would provide a more objective test than exists at present of the standards which the prison system aims to achieve and against which delivery could be judged. But the Prison Service identifies a number of reasons for *not* adopting a Code. I summarise them as follows:

- a) if the Code was not legally enforceable, it would only be aspirational. No Government would endorse a legally enforceable Code which it could not comply with or which would require resources which it did not plan to provide;

- b) it is difficult to know what should be included in the Code – should it only deal with physical standards or should it deal with matters such as frequency of visits etc?

- c) would it be a universal Code? Would it be necessary to draw up a number of different Codes? Would it be likely that one effect might be to reduce the standards of some establishments, such as training prisons?;

- d) a Code is of no value unless the Government is going to provide the necessary resources. As has been indicated in recent years, improvements can take place without a Code;

- e) it would be an enormously complex and time consuming task to prepare a Code. There is no guarantee that the end result will lead to an improvement in conditions. It is therefore preferable for the Government to concentrate its efforts as at present on improving conditions.

12.105 We are not impressed by any of these arguments. There should be no difficulties in preparing a Code. The evidence before the Inquiry indicates, as is to be expected, that there is a considerable degree of common ground as to what should be included in the Code. The European Prison Rules 1987 and the United Nations Standard Minimum Rules for the Treatment of Offenders provide a general guide as to what the Rules should contain; although, in our view, a much more specific set of rules is needed than either of those Codes provides.

12.106   If the Prison Service were to consult the Prison Governors' Association, the Prison Officers' Association, the other bodies to whom we have already made reference, and the other individuals and bodies who took part in our public seminar which dealt with this subject, they would soon be provided with a shopping list of what is to be included. It would then be for the Prison Service to decide what aspects of imprisonment the Code should cover. A Code does not have to be exhaustive to be effective. It does not need to be cast in tablets of stone. The European Prison Rules themselves have been amended and if the Prison Service adopted a Code it would be sensible for it to be reviewed from time to time. Indeed we would expect that, as a result, the standards would progressively be raised.

12.107   So far as expense is concerned, the availability of resources would dictate the speed at which progress could be made. In the meantime, a set of non-enforceable standards would be a bench mark against which the need for improvement could be judged. Furthermore, financial resources are not the only type of resources which are required. There need to be a committed staff and management to achieve the necessary standards. A Code could be of value in helping them to identify the standards at which they should aim.

12.108   We therefore recommend that the Prison Service should prepare its own Code of standards which sets out what the Prison Service considers should be the standards which it should set itself to achieve. We do not consider it necessary or desirable ourselves to establish what that Code should cover. The Code should be drawn up after consultation, among others, with the bodies we referred to earlier. But we would expect the Code to cover the physical conditions in which prisoners are to be held, and the opportunities which they are to have while in prison. They should be sufficiently explicit as to be meaningful, but not so detailed as to be unrealistic or unhelpfully rigid. In the first instance, we envisage the same standards being applied to all establishments. They would be applicable to anyone who was in custody as a result of an order of the court.

12.109   For reasons which will become clear later, we suggest they should be known as Accredited Standards.

12.110   After the standards have been drawn up, the Prison Service should identify, in relation to each standard, when it is likely to be achieved by every establishment in the Service. The timescale would be dependent on the level of resources which is made available.

12.111   The targets would need to be drawn up in consultation with the establishments. Some establishments would be able to achieve them much quicker than others. It would be for the Area Manager, in consultation with the Governor, to decide how each establishment in his area was to meet each target and when. Initially an establishment might be given a limited number of target standards and dates. These targets, and the progress towards them, would be set out in the annual establishment "contract".

12.112   It would be desirable to find a way of marking an establishment's progress towards meeting the Code of standards. We recommend a system of accreditation. When an establishment reached any one of the standards, it could apply for a Certificate of Accreditation for the relevant standard. When it met them all, it could apply for Accreditation Status.

12.113   The progress towards Accreditation Status would be monitored by the Area Manager and the Board of Visitors. When an establishment was able to comply with one of the standards in the Code, this could be acknowledged by the Area Manager issuing a Certificate of Accreditation for that standard. When it met all the standards, it could apply for full Accreditation Status, which would be granted by the Home Secretary after receiving the advice of HMCIP.

12.114 If an establishment fell below the accredited standard after it had been granted a Certificate of Accreditation, then the Certificate would be withdrawn by the Home Secretary. We would envisage this would again be as a result of the advice of HMCIP – probably after one of his routine inspections.

12.115 In the United States, they have a well developed system of accreditation of this sort. A prison establishment in the United States takes pride in achieving the accreditation standard. It is a mark of quality which the staff and management of a prison establishment regard as a commendation. We see accreditation as helpful in this country to motivate establishments to achieve Accreditation Status and to give establishments a sense of satisfaction when that standard is achieved. From what we have seen of the dedication of the great majority of the staff and management in the Prison Service, we believe that establishments would want to raise their standards where this is practical so as to obtain a Certificate of Accreditation and would work hard to do so.

12.116 The Code would be of value also in planning the national strategy in the Prison Service "contract" and the local strategy reflected in an establishment's "contract". Those "contracts" would be the means by which the progress which is necessary to raise all establishments to Accreditation Status could be achieved.

12.117 The Accredited Standards would not be legally enforceable in the first instance. That is not their initial purpose. They are intended to provide a clear benchmark as to the level of standards which ought to be achieved and a means of encouraging the Prison Service to achieve them. They provide a basis for which resources can be sought and allocated. Until they are achieved, we do not think it is sensible or practicable to seek to make them enforceable, even prospectively. Once they are achieved, that will be the time to decide whether it is necessary to make the standards legally enforceable, having regard to the effect of prisoners' "contracts" to which we are about to refer. We would, however, expect that, at that stage, they would anyway be the subject of a Prison Rule and so enforceable by judicial review.

12.118 In due course, different or separate standards would need to be developed for different establishments. This would be the next step. Remand Centres and units for example, would be expected to provide different if not higher standards than exist in other establishments and units.

12.119 This should not create any difficulty. The Government is considering private sector involvement in the remand system. If the private sector is to be involved in the remand system, it is accepted by the Government that contracts "will have to set clear and enforceable standards". The Government is therefore going to be involved in preparing standards. There is no reason why the standards required of the private sector for remand establishments should be any different from those required of the Prison Service.

The Prisoner's "Contract"

12.120 A properly drafted establishment "contract" should identify what kind of regime the establishment should provide for the inmates within each of its units. There is no reason why a prisoner should not be informed of the terms of that "contract" or at least, in simple terms, those parts that are relevant to him. In addition, we recommend that each prisoner should be offered the opportunity of entering into a "compact" or "contract" with the establishment. In that "contract", the establishment would state, in as precise terms as possible, what it would provide for the prisoner. In return, the prisoner would agree to comply with the responsibilities which the "contract" placed upon him. Such a "contract" should apply both to sentenced and remand prisoners.

12.121 Unlike Accredited Standards, these "contracts" would not contain standards applicable across the board. They would reflect the standards and conditions which were specific to a particular establishment or unit in an establishment or, in some cases, to a particular prisoner. They would identify the accommodation and the aspects of the regime which the prisoner could legitimately expect would be provided for him at that establishment. At present, some establishments would be able to offer only a modest regime. Other establishments would be able to offer a regime which it would be hard to fault. However, over a period of time and as the conditions within the Service improved, what the prisoner could reasonably expect to receive under his "contract" with the establishment would also improve.

12.122 The prisoner would also receive progressively more under his "contract" as he progressed through his sentence. On the other hand, he could lose for a period of time some of the features of his "contract" in consequence of a finding of ill discipline. The "contract" would therefore be a way of introducing greater incentives into the system. The "contract" would be subject to regular reviews for those in prison for an appreciable length of time. We recommend that the period between reviews should be 12 months.

12.123 We recommend that Prison Rules should make provision for establishments to offer a "contract" to each prisoner in its care. The "contract" would not be drawn up in a way which would give the prisoner private rights (that is a right to damages) but it would, in a case which was appropriate, be dealt with by the grievance procedure and it could provide a platform for an application for judicial review.

12.124 The Area Manager and the Board of Visitors would be able to monitor the quality of the "contracts" offered by an establishment and the establishment's performance of the "contract". On his inspections, HMCIP could be expected to be interested in the quality of the "contracts" offered by an establishment and the way it was fulfilling its task under the "contracts" and, if appropriate, to comment upon them.

12.125 It may be suggested that an establishment would have every incentive to provide as little as possible under the "contract". For an establishment to adopt such an attitude would be highly unprofessional and not in keeping with the approach which the Prison Service can be expected to adopt. It is significant in this regard that both the Prison Governors' Association and the Prison Officers' Association are in favour of minimum standards.

12.126 However, if an establishment were minded to take this course, it would be the Area Manager's responsibility to point out the unacceptable nature of this conduct. The Area Manager would be responsible for ensuring that his "contract" with the establishment placed suitable specific obligations on the establishment for looking after its prisoners. If those same obligations were not reflected in the "contract" with the inmate, this would require explanation. If need be, the inmate could also take up the matter through the grievance procedure on the basis that the establishment had not included in his "contract" those matters which the establishment should. This could even amount to maladministration, which could give redress before the Parliamentary Commissioner. Finally, although this is less likely, there is a possibility in an extreme case that judicial review would be of assistance.

12.127 A prisoner could not be obliged to enter into a "contract", but it would be very much in his interest to do so. If he did not do so, he would still receive the ordinary regime in the prison, but he might not receive opportunities that were extended only to those who were prepared to take on the responsibilities laid down by the "contract". The "contract" could be developed, as in the Netherlands, by offering a prisoner more if he were prepared to submit voluntarily to obligations which he would not otherwise have, urine tests for drugs, for example, on returning from home leave. By refusing to enter into a "contract", the prisoner could lose the advantage of being able to rely on the "contract" to show that he had a grievance.

12.128   We believe it would be possible to introduce the idea of "contracts" for prisoners at the present time. We accept that, for the most part, the same "contract" would be offered to the majority of prisoners in one of today's prisons, particularly in local prisons. We accept, too, that some would look unacceptably poor. It is one of the merits of our proposal that, where this is so, the "contract" would bring it into focus. In some training prisons with long term prisoners, of course, the "contracts" would be much fuller and more explicit and would be tied into the sentence plans which the Prison Service at present produces for very long term prisoners and which it aims to extend to others (see Section 14 of this Report). In the course of time, as the standards of prisons improve, as we believe they must, that would be reflected and clearly marked by the standard of the "contract" prepared for each prisoner.

12.129   We attach considerable importance to developing a "contract" on these lines. It would underline both the prisoner's and the establishment's responsibilities in relation to the way an inmate serves his sentence. It could substantially improve the position of the inmate since it would make clear what were his legitimate expectations. It would enable him, if he was being transferred to another establishment which provided a lesser regime, to point out the disadvantage to him of such a transfer. It would assist in providing a structure to an inmate's imprisonment and it would be in accord with the principles of justice which we believe should exist within a prison. In particular, together with Accredited Standards, it would be the way in which standards throughout the Service could be raised to acceptable levels by identifying the precise services to be delivered to prisoners.

Prison Staff's "Contract"

12.130   There is one more "contract" which is required for the completion of the framework of management by "contract" which we would like the Prison Service to adopt. That is the member of staff's "contract" with the Governor of a prison. This "contract" is more conveniently examined in Section 13 of the Report, where we consider staffing issues.

Medical Services

12.131   Prisoners (and their families) must feel confident that the medical treatment prisoners receive in prison is of comparable standard to that which they would receive in normal life from the National Health Service.

12.132   The Inquiry has seen a considerable body of evidence which indicates that there is a failure to fulfil this principle. The Inquiry was not in a position to make findings as to individual complaints of inadequate treatment which were made by inmates. The evidence relating to Strangeways showed that there existed among prisoners a suspicion that largactyl was being used too frequently "down the block" for control reasons rather than for medical reasons. We obtained reports from the Director of Prison Medical Services on the allegation. It was categorically denied by those responsible for administering medical treatment at Manchester. However the evidence makes it clear that great care should be taken to ensure that regulations on the use of drugs are not only carefully and accurately followed, but that it is made clear to Boards of Visitors, Chaplains, and most importantly, prisoners, that the regulations are being followed.

12.133   Any rumour or accusation that any particular prisoner is being over-medicated should be taken with the greatest seriousness by prison management. Every effort should be made to communicate to relatives, friends and other prisoners the medical reasons and the necessity for any treatment given, subject only to the need to preserve medical confidentiality. In carrying out these tasks, it may well be necessary to involve medical professionals not connected with the Prison Service.

12.134   The Prison Service is considering at the present time a Report of an efficiency scrutiny of the Prison Medical Service. In considering that Report, the Prison Service should bear in mind the comments that we have made above. The Report contains detailed recommendations which are in accord with the general approach that we have suggested should be adopted. Having considered those recommendations, we do not regard ourselves as being in a position to form a detailed judgement on them.

Race Relations

12.135   At the seminars held by the Inquiry, a number of those from outside the Prison Service with authority in this field commended the positive approach which was being adopted by the Prison Service in respect of race relations. The Prison Service has already a policy statement on race relations which appears on the first page of the information book which is now provided to all male prisoners.

12.136   Racial prejudice is, however, a particularly insidious problem, as the Prison Service is well aware. Positive action has to be continually taken to prevent discrimination.

12.137   Home Office guidance on race relations in prison was first given in 1981 in Circular Instruction 28/81. It established a broad principle of equality of treatment, and suggested that establishments with a substantial proportion of ethnic minorities might find it useful to appoint a race relations liaison officer. Such an officer is now a regular feature of prison establishments. His main duties have been described by the Prison Service as gathering relevant information, disseminating that information, assisting with training, addressing the individual problem areas and liaising with the appropriate outside agencies.

12.138   A more comprehensive circular was issued in 1983 (CI 56/1983). This was followed in 1986 by a third circular, CI 32/1986. That circular established specific procedures for ensuring racial equality in prisons, including the assigning of particular responsibilities and setting out a check list for assessing progress. It also recommended the public statement which is currently displayed in prison establishments.

12.139   The most recent circular, CI 39/90, requires that the policy statement be prominently displayed; identifies those matters relating to race relations policies which must be included in the Governor's "contracts"; requires Governors to include in their annual reports specific information in response to a check list which has been provided; gives guidance and instructions on the composition and terms of reference of the Race Relations Management Team and on the training and job description of the Race Relations Liaison Officer; and announces the setting-up of a new Prison Service Race Relations Group.

12.140   These are all positive and useful developments. It is encouraging that the Prison Service has shown that it is keeping its policies under review and regularly developing and extending them. But there are still grounds for concern. The evidence suggests that the compliance by prison establishments with race relations policies is erratic. The monitoring returns from prisons indicate that there remains a significant proportion of prisons which fails to provide adequate details of equal opportunity provisions.

12.141   Complaints of racial discrimination from prisons are made regularly to the Commission of Racial Equality. At a race relations conference organised by prisoners at Long Lartin in 1990, considerable disquiet was expressed by prisoners themselves about race relations. The same complaints were made to the Inquiry when the Inquiry visited Long Lartin. It was indicated that race relations at other prisons were substantially worse than those at Long Lartin. In the course of his inspections, the Chief Inspector has found that there is an absence of consistency in the implementation of Prison Service race relations policies.

12.142   The conclusion which the Inquiry draws from the evidence which is available is that, despite the Prison Service's good intentions, there is still a need for considerable further progress if a satisfactory position with regards to race relations is to be achieved within prisons. It would appear that the methods of monitoring incidents which could have a racial content need clarifying, and that more energy needs to be devoted by the Prison Service to promoting its own non-racial policies. In making these observations, the Inquiry acknowledges the valuable submission which it received from Mr Navnit Dholakia.

The Management of Intervention During Serious Incidents

12.143   The control and restraint techniques which have been developed in this country are at least as good, if not superior, to those adopted in the countries which the Inquiry visited. The C&R3 techniques which have to be used in the course of a serious disturbance were shown to be, by and large, effective in the course of the April 1990 disturbances, as appears from Part I of this report. During those disturbances, the C&R commanders were confronted with new problems. Since those disturbances ended, national C&R instructors have had to try and find ways of overcoming those problems. It appears that they have made considerable progress in doing this.

12.144   The manner in which the national instructors have set about this task is very impressive. There can be no doubt that C&R techniques will continue to evolve and become more effective as the Service's experience increases.

12.145   There has already been considerable liaison between the Prison Service and other services in this area, but little joint training. In order to assist the process of improvement, it is essential that national instructors should continue to have the opportunity of liaising, and where appropriate training, with other services in this country who are engaged in similar activities.

12.146   In Part I, Section 9, of this Report, the importance of C&R training for prison officers and governors is stressed. As with other forms of training, C&R training is part of "non effective hours" – in other words, in calculating the appropriate staffing levels for an establishment, C&R training is grouped with sick and annual leave. As we make clear in Section 13, action is needed to protect training by setting aside hours specifically for it, including C&R training.

12.147   Part I of this Report already contains a number of comments as to what could be done to improve the Service's handling of a serious incident. Here we will concentrate on issues relating to the management of intervention in the case of a serious incident. For this purpose, we define a serious incident as an incident in which the control of part of or the whole of an establishment has been lost or is in danger of being lost and the Governor needs assistance to restore control or to manage the situation effectively.

12.148   One of the national instructors who played a significant role in a number of incidents, drew our attention to the need for a proper command structure for commanding an incident. He stressed that, in his judgement, command structures should depend on the suitability of staff rather than on rank. Based on his experience, he had come to the conclusion that the majority of Governors 4 and 5 were unhappy when placed in a command role, unless perhaps they had had some past experience in the armed services. (The same position could be achieved by training.) He indicated that Governors were trained as managers not commanders. Staff were very unhappy at taking command from commanders who were not fully trained in the techniques to be used. He concluded that national instructors should act as tactical commanders of incidents.

12.149 This is an aspect of the handling of incidents which requires attention. The solution to the command problem is not, however, to place more junior staff in command of their seniors. The answer lies in ensuring that there are senior staff with the necessary experience and training to take command at the appropriate level.

12.150 Since April 1990, the Prison Service has given considerable thought to the way disturbances should be managed under the new arrangements for senior management. The Inquiry has carefully examined the Prison Service's new procedures and facilities. We are satisfied that they are a considerable improvement upon those which previously existed and, subject to the matters dealt with specifically in this Report, are reasonably satisfactory. There is now an appropriate incident management suite in HQ and arrangements have been made to ensure that an HQ response can be mobilised rapidly.

12.151 The comments which the national instructor made about the need for properly qualified commanders apply equally to the advice available to HQ. It is essential that the HQ operational directors and their staff who manage incidents are kept fully abreast of developments in C&R techniques. This will enable them properly to assess the appropriateness of a proposed response by an establishment to an incident. In addition, in the case of a large scale serious disturbance, it is important that HQ should have available the expertise which national instructors provided to establishments during the April 1990 disturbances. It is desirable that at least two members of staff at headquarters of Governor 1 or 2 level have specialist training which qualifies them to be regarded as experts in the use and deployment of C&R techniques.

12.152 In establishments, the governing Governor is the normal commander of any incident. However, while it should be within the capacity of any governing Governor to deal with the sort of incidents which can be expected to take place from time to time in any establishment, the experience of the April disturbances indicates that this is not true for a large scale serious incident. The proper use of a substantial number of C&R units is closely related to a military operation. Not all governing Governors are suited to being the General in charge of such an operation.

12.153 In Scotland, where the same C&R techniques are used, the response to this problem is to create a self-contained command unit which has been specially trained for this purpose. The unit comes into an establishment when a serious incident is declared and takes over the command of the establishment for the period of the incident. This solution has been considered by the Prison Service. The Service's conclusion is that it should not be transplanted south of the border. The number of establishments and the distances involved are much greater in England and Wales.

12.154 While attracted by the Scottish solution, we accept that it may be possible to devise an alternative in England and Wales which would be equally appropriate. The Prison Service, having been made aware of our concerns on this subject, has sought to find "a mechanism" which leaves the authority of the Governor unchanged, but which gives him specialist operational support. The preliminary conclusion of the Prison Service is that the answer might be provided by the deployment of C&R Co-ordinators at strategic points around the country who would be at about Governor 3 level. The Co-ordinator would be responsible for advising the Governor on the strategy and tactics necessary for the proper deployment of C&R3 resources. He would be responsible for co-ordinating the necessary logistic support, preparing an intervention plan, commanding the intervention and drawing up and supervising surrender procedures.

12.155 This could well prove to be a suitable solution. There needs to be some laid down procedure which ensures that the actual handling of the incident is in the hands of someone who has the necessary experience and aptitude to direct affairs, while not interfering with the overall position of the governing Governor of the establishment. Unless a better way is found of meeting this objective, we propose that the Prison Service identifies and trains suitable C&R Co-ordinators to manage serious incidents under the command of the governing Governor of the establishment in which such an incident is taking place. This should avoid the danger of the status of the governing Governor being undermined when the incident is over. It should also assist HQ. They would know that an intervention plan had the seal of approval of an experienced Governor, who was properly trained in what can and cannot be achieved by the deployment of C&R units.

12.156   Such an approach should also give confidence to the commanders of C&R units. If, as we would expect would be the case, the Co-ordinator is supported by a principal officer of the experience and calibre of the present national instructors, this should ensure that there will be proper control of an intervention. It should also avoid training more governor grades than are necessary to the standard which would be required. But it would also be necessary to have in establishments a suitable number of Governors 4 and 5 who were trained to ensure that they could play a supporting command role.

12.157   The Scottish Prison Service is also able to deploy a fully equipped "C&R stores vehicle" which can be sent rapidly to an establishment where the serious incident is taking place. Again, the larger geographical area of England and Wales may make this initiative less attractive. However, while certain equipment can be provided to the Prison Service by the police, we propose that the Prison Service should examine carefully the Scottish experience in relation to the use of this type of vehicle since we believe, in a modified form, it could be of value south of the border as well.

Escort Duties

12.158   The evidence before the Inquiry indicates that escort commitments are one of the major causes of prisons failing to maintain consistency in the delivery of regimes. If the Criminal Justice Bill, at present before Parliament, is enacted, it will give the Home Secretary power to make in respect of any area arrangements for the provision of prisoner escorts to be performed by Prison Custody Officers, who have the necessary certificate for this purpose.

12.159   In their evidence to the Inquiry, the Prison Officers' Association accepted that during Stage I of the Inquiry it was "clearly shown" that Court escort commitments in establishments gave rise to problems which affected staffing levels and so had "devastating affects upon the regime". The problems lay in their "variable and unpredictable" nature. As a result, the Prison Officers' Association accepted that Court duties should form "a separate function within the Service".

12.160   The Prison Officers' Association contended with vigour, however, that it would be wholly inappropriate for escort duties to be contracted out to the private sector. As against this evidence, the Inquiry received evidence from private sector contractors explaining their capacity to perform these duties.

12.161   A number of prison officers who gave evidence to us made it clear that they would regret escort duty being taken away from prison officers. This was partly because they considered that prison officers were the appropriate persons to have those duties. It was partly also because they valued the escort duties as relieving the pressure of being continuously within a prison establishment.

12.162   We are concerned about the effect on prison regimes of escort duties to the Courts and other places, including to and at hospitals. We appreciate that Court business ought not to be disrupted by the late arrival of prisoners at Court, or worse their non-arrival. Court escort work must therefore have a priority. But because escort duties for prisoners are unpredictable, the requirement is uncertain. To meet it, the establishment has often to cancel activities which it does not regard as vital but to which prisoners attach considerable importance.

The activities which are cancelled tend to be those which are provided to inmates in an attempt to produce a more generous and constructive regime. Once such activities are provided, the inmate can legitimately expect that they will be regularly provided. It causes frustration and anger when instead they are cancelled at very short notice.

12.163 The May Committee considered in its Report published in 1979 whether or not there should be a separate escort service. The Report concluded that such a service could have "many attractions" and would allow prisons to operate more "stable and uninterrupted regimes even in local prisons". But the May Committee considered that a separate service would not of itself be more economical of manpower than the present arrangements. On the contrary there would be increased cost and there could be recruiting difficulties. The Committee on balance were of the view that at that time there was not a sufficient case for the establishment of a separate force. However, the May Committee considered that efficiencies could be achieved if the Home Office were to provide prison officers' services to the Courts on an agency basis, charging the cost to the Lord Chancellor's Department. The Report did not consider the option of a privately run service.

12.164 We think that the balance on the merits of having a separate service has changed since the May Committee reported. We propose the setting up of such a service. We do not consider it appropriate or necessary for the Inquiry to be drawn into the argument about whether the private sector should be involved in the provision of the services. This involves wider questions, including issues of a political nature, which are not necessary subjects for an Inquiry of this nature and on which we could not make a useful contribution.

12.165 The key element to our proposal is that the escort service would not deploy staff from prison establishments. The importance of maintaining the regime within prison establishments has become central to combating the deterioration in inmate relationships which can give rise to disturbances. The extra costs, if such there are, would be more than justified by a more stable environment in the prisons and by the assurance that the prison officers assigned to run a prison were there to do that job and not spending long hours out on the road or sitting, often unproductively, around the Courts.

12.166 The evidence which is before us does not enable us to give detailed guidance about how a separate service should be organised. Our proposal could be achieved by separately deployed staff within the Prison Service, or by a separate public sector organisation, or by the private sector. We would expect the officers undertaking escort duties to be properly trained in their tasks, but they would not be of the same range or complexity as the tasks of a prison officer in a prison. That fact would need to be reflected in the escort officers' terms and conditions.

12.167 We fully appreciate the extent of the burdens which listing officers at Courts already carry in order to perform their duties. But we consider that Courts' staff must recognise the importance of cooperating with the Prison Service, or any service providing escort services, so as to ensure efficiency in the use of resources.

12.168 We propose also that systems should be developed in co-operation between the Prison Service and the Lord Chancellor's Department which enable the location of prisoners to be taken into account when considering listing. If the Lord Chancellor's Department had a responsibility for part of the costs of transporting prisoners to the Crown Court and the Higher Courts, as the May Committee suggested, this could be helpful in securing greater efficiency in the use of prisoner escort services.

Board of Visitors

12.169 We pay tribute to the vital contribution of Boards of Visitors to the Inquiry. In addition to attending the seminars and attending upon the Inquiry when it visited different establishments, the Board members made 45 formal submissions, and many more informal submissions. The Coordinating Committee analysed those submissions in a most helpful way. In nearly every aspect of this Report, the Inquiry has considered a relevant submission from the Boards. Many of the suggestions which are contained in their evidence, such as that in relation to dormitory accommodation and the transfer of prisoners back to overcrowded local prisons for reasons of good order or discipline, are in accord with our own.

12.170   We have already acknowledged the part played by Boards during the disturbances which we considered in Part I of this report. In addition, in April 1990 there were many more minor disturbances in response to which the Boards of Visitors played a part. The way the Boards responded to the crisis which occurred within the prison system during the spring of 1990, and the assistance which the Boards have since given to this Inquiry, provide strong and sufficient grounds for supporting the continued existence of Boards of Visitors.

12.171   We have no doubt whatsoever that the public and the Prison Service have cause to be indebted to the Boards of Visitors. The Boards should be preserved. We are conscious, however, that their endeavours on behalf of prisoners are inhibited by the fact that a substantial part of the prison population does not recognise the Boards' members as being as impartial as they in fact are. We have, therefore, considered whether there are any changes which need to be made to their jurisdiction so as to increase the quality of their contribution.

12.172   We have already in Section 11 drawn attention to the need for Boards to have at each establishment separate accommodation which is put aside for their exclusive use.

12.173   We propose that Boards of Visitors should receive more resources than they do at present. The Prison Service's Annual Report for 1989/90 correctly described the main duties of the Boards as:

"watch-dogs for the Home Secretary – overseeing administration of the establishment and the treatment of prisoners".

12.174   At the end of March 1990, Boards had a complement of 1,603 members as against a total complement of 1,763. For that size body, the resources allocated during 1989/1990 for training, travel and subsistence were £307,000. The Prison Service recognises that if Boards are to perform their functions satisfactorily every member needs to receive more training. The present sums allocated by the Prison Service are wholly inadequate for these purposes. Boards need also to have adequate secretarial support and secretarial equipment of the right quality.

12.175   It was suggested at one of our public seminars that some members of Boards of Visitors should also be paid. We would not give priority to this suggestion. Many other bodies give of their time without payment. We would hope that even those members of the Boards who make the greatest contribution, would feel it was possible to maintain the proud tradition of all members of Boards giving their services entirely without financial reward.

12.176   The most difficult problem which the Inquiry has had to determine in relation to Boards is whether they should continue to perform both of their present roles: their watch-dog role and their adjudicatory role. For some time now it has been thought that the two roles are inconsistent and that the adjudicatory role in part explains the lack of confidence of some inmates in Boards.

12.177   At the time of the May Committee report, the majority of Boards' members was strongly in favour of retaining their adjudicatory role. Now it seems likely that the majority takes a different view. We have come to the conclusion, particularly having regard to the evidence given at the seminars, that the adjudicatory role should be removed. This proposal is in accord with our conclusion that in any event the disciplinary machinery needs substantial readjustment. The Boards would, however, still have a role to play in relation to modified grievance procedures and in respect of the disciplinary procedures, as we will explain in Section 14 of this Report.

12.178   We emphasise that we would not want the status of the Board of Visitors to be lowered in any way as a result of our taking this course. Indeed, we believe the reverse should be the case. We consider that the change should enable Boards to make an even greater contribution to the fair running of prison establishments.

12.179   If the Boards are to play an effective role, then there is a need for organisational improvements. The type of improvements which are needed were set out in the Report commissioned and funded by the Home Office Research and Planning Unit "The Watchdog Role of Boards of Visitors" by Mr Mike Maguire and Dr Jon Vagg in 1984.

12.180   We propose that there should be a President of the Boards of Visitors, appointed by the Home Secretary. The office and standing of the President would help to emphasise the independent nature of Boards. The President would be expected to develop more effective methods for recruiting new members to Boards. He or she could give guidance as to good practice to be followed by Boards and supervise the provision of training. The President would be a key figure in taking forward the role of Boards. In performing these duties, the President would work closely in conjunction with the existing representative bodies – the Co-ordinating Committee and the Association of Members of Boards of Visitors.

12.181   The recruitment of members of Boards is a matter of the greatest importance. They should be drawn from as varied a background as possible. The reliance on the personal recommendations of existing members of Boards should be reduced. It may well be that the Advisory Committee model which exists in relation to Magistrates could prove to be an appropriate precedent for what is needed in relation to the Boards. However, if the suggestion of a President is adopted, then this would be very much a matter for the President to consider in conjunction with the Boards and their representative bodies.

Prison Visitors

12.182   The part which prison visitors play within prisons does not always attract the attention which it deserves. Some Prison Visitors made valuable submissions to the Inquiry. Their role supplements that of the Board of Visitors. They can be particularly important in maintaining links between a prisoner and the community. To a prisoner who is feeling isolated, to have a "prisoner's friend" can be of great importance in assisting him or her to keep in touch with the outside world. The Chief Inspector has referred to the role of prison visitors in his Review of Suicide and Self-Harm published in December 1990.

12.183   We propose that better use should be made of the services of prison visitors. The Prison Service should encourage and seek to extend the involvement of prison visitors in the activities of inmates within prison establishments.

12.184   A submission to the Inquiry by a lay visitor to police stations, who happens to be a probation officer as well, compared the prison visitor's role adversely with that of the lay visitor. He suggested that the role should be extended to correspond to that of the lay visitors to police stations. Were it not for the existence of the Board of Visitors, such an extension would be necessary. However, bearing in mind the part played by the Board of Visitors within prisons, we do not see any necessity to make any recommendations for change. The National Association of Prison Visitors made no submission to the Inquiry that there should be any change in their role.

The Management of Sex Offenders

12.185   In this part of the Report, we consider prisoners who are either subject to Rule 43 for their own protection (OP) or who would be subject to Rule 43 if they were not in a Vulnerable Prisoners Unit (VPU). We will, however, refer throughout to sex offenders because it is primarily in connection with sex offenders that the problems to which we are about to refer arise. There are other prisoners who also require protection. Their circumstances can vary quite considerably. While what we have to say in relation to sex offenders may be applicable to them as well, this is not necessarily so. We recognise too that not all those in prison for having committed a sex offence require the protection provided at present under Rule 43.

12.186   The management of vulnerable sex offenders creates considerable difficulties for the Prison Service. The difficulties arise because of the hostility and aggression shown to these prisoners by other inmates. As the disturbance at Manchester vividly showed, the consequences of the attitude of other inmates to sex offenders can be grave indeed. Their lives can be at risk.

12.187   On visits to other establishments which were not the subject of Part I of this Report, the Inquiry was made aware of the extent of the depth of feeling which exists against sex offenders. At Lincoln Prison, for example, during the seminar which took place with inmates, a prisoner, who had otherwise being making responsible and sensible comments, made repeated and vehement complaints, which some other inmates supported, about the fact that two of the prisoners who were taking part in the seminar were on Rule 43.

12.188   Wandsworth Prison now contains approximately 450 prisoners on Rule 43 on three wings. On the doors of the cells of the cleaners on those wings (who are not on Rule 43) and at various other parts of the prison, there are notices put up by the prisoners saying "not on Rule 43". These notices are intended to protect the inmates within from the victimisation from which the "Rule 43's" would suffer.

12.189   The problem which exists in the British system is not shared by all prison systems. With one exception, it does not exist in the European countries which were visited by the Inquiry. It occurs in France, but to a lesser degree than in this country. It causes problems in Canada and the United States.

12.190   Within our penal system, some establishments have tackled the problem with some success. For example, at Grendon and at Leyhill, there is a substantial number of sex offenders who were previously on Rule 43 and who have been absorbed successfully into the prison community.

12.191   At Littlehey, an experiment is being conducted on A wing. Prisoners on A Wing agree to come off Rule 43 on the assurance that prisoners from other wings will have no access to that wing. 80% of prisoners on A Wing are sex offenders. Initially, they are not compelled to leave the wing. Within two weeks, however, they are expected to have settled in and to start to go out each day to the workshops, classes etc, moving about the establishment as necessary, unescorted like all other prisoners.

12.192   The Report by the Prison Service in 1989 on the Management of Vulnerable Prisoners (the VP Report) indicates that the prisoners on A wing clearly drew great comfort from being on that wing with others who had committed a similar pattern of offence. At the time of the VP Report, the experiment was still fairly new. Over the first seven months, ten inmates had been moved from A wing into the general population. What had already been achieved in that short period, in the words of the VP Report:

> "Demonstrates that it is possible, given the necessary facilities, strong management and staff commitment, to move Rule 43 (OP) prisoners from a deprived existence in local prisons to a virtually normal location with a

311

good regime in a training prison."

12.193   Although there are these examples of what can be achieved, there remains a very difficult problem with the majority of sex offenders. Rightly, the Prison Service is giving it considerable attention.

12.194   The terms of Rule 43 are as follows:

"43(1) Where it appears desirable, for the maintenance of good order or discipline or in his own interests, that a prisoner should not associate with other prisoners, either generally or for particular purposes, the Governor may arrange for the prisoner's removal from association accordingly.

(2)   A prisoner shall not be removed under this Rule for a period of more than three days without the authority of a member of the Board of Visitors, or of the Secretary of State. An authority given under this paragraph shall be for a period not exceeding one month, but may be renewed from month to month, except that, in the case of a person aged less than 21 years who is detained in prison, such an authority shall be for a period not exceeding 14 days, but may be renewed from time to time for a like period.

(3)   The Governor may arrange at his discretion for such a prisoner as aforesaid to resume association with other prisoners, and shall do so if in any case the medical officer so advises on medical grounds."

The counterpart for young offender institutions, Rule 46, is in similar terms.

12.195   Our principal criticism of Rule 43 is that it deals with two situations which are very different: (a) the prisoner who has to be removed from association because it is considered that he could have an adverse effect on good order or discipline in the prison; and (b) the vulnerable prisoner (among whom sex offenders are approximately 70%) who is not removed from association because of the harm which he could cause to other prisoners, but because of the harm which others will do to him.

12.196   It is unhelpful that the Rule should be applied to two very different categories of prisoners. What the establishment should be seeking to achieve in relation to the two categories is quite different. In the case of the prisoner separated for reasons of good order or discipline, the removal from association needs to be fairly strictly imposed if the object of the exercise is to be achieved. In the case of the vulnerable prisoner, on the other hand, it is accepted that any more separation than is necessary to protect the prisoner is undesirable. The object from the start should be to return the prisoner to association if this is possible.

12.197   In moderate language which hides the true horror of the situation, the VP Report acknowledges that being on Rule 43 "OP" is undesirable for prisoners, whether convicted or unconvicted. It deprives the prisoner of normal association. It can prevent access to facilities for work, recreation, and education. It overrides other considerations for appropriate allocation (including proximity to home). It keeps a prisoner's offence at the forefront of the minds of those who have to make assessments of him. Being on the "rule" has become a stigma. As the VP Report also states, "the only real benefit which derives from being on the rule is the physical protection from assault or intimidation which it provides for the prisoners concerned".

12.198   The National Association of Probation Officers, in their evidence, emphasised the disadvantages of Rule 43. They concluded by saying:

"Perhaps what is ultimately needed is the political will to abolish Rule 43. It is possible that its existence may be institutionalising and perpetuating the persecution of sex offenders. It provides many prisoners with a legitimised target for venting their frustration and anger."

12.199   At the time of the Manchester disturbance in April 1990, it is estimated that of the total national prison population, 3,160 prisoners (8%) were either held under Rules 43 or 46 for their own protection or were held in vulnerable prisoner units. Only 880 were in VPUs. The vast majority were therefore held in the sort of conditions which existed at Strangeways.

12.200   The growth in numbers has been substantially faster than the growth in the overall prison population. The VP Report shows that while the total male sentenced population increased by 17.4% over the period 1983-88, the number of Rule 43 prisoners increased by a massive 156%.

12.201   With this number of vulnerable prisoners, in the light of the experience of the Manchester disturbance, and following our discussions in prisons, including discussions with vulnerable prisoners who eloquently put to us the case for protection, we accept that there is no alternative at the present time but to take special measures to prevent sex offenders in particular, and vulnerable prisoners in general, from being subject to victimisation. But Rule 43 does not provide the appropriate form of protection which they need.

12.202   There may be exceptional circumstances where it is necessary to hold such people in isolation for a few hours or days while their position is sorted out. But every local prison will have a substantial number of prisoners who today are said to be on Rule 43, but who could and should be on locations where they are not deprived of association among themselves, even though they may be separated from the general prison population. It is preferable that the generality of sex offenders should be regarded as what they are. They are vulnerable prisoners who need special protection but who, subject to that, should receive association and a regime equivalent to that of other prisoners.

12.203   These arrangements need to be reflected in a new Prison Rule. We propose, therefore, that the existing Rule 43 (and Rule 46) should be amended so that they no longer refer to prisoners being removed from association in their own interests. We propose instead an additional rule that deals specifically with the position of such vulnerable prisoners. The new rule would need to be drafted so that it achieves three purposes:

> i)   it would place an obligation upon the Governor of an establishment to take such reasonable steps as he considers necessary for the protection of prisoners whom he considers are vulnerable to attack from other prisoners;

> ii)   it would authorise the Governor to remove from association, only to the extent which is reasonable, a prisoner who needs protection;

> iii)   it would make the exercise of the second purpose for which the rule is provided subject to the same safeguards as are now contained in Rule 43(2).

12.204   We shall later in this Section be proposing that in future the Area Manager and not the Board of Visitors should authorise the removal from association of a disruptive prisoner. We considered whether to propose a similar procedure for vulnerable prisoners, on the ground that the authority for taking the executive decision to remove from association should lie with the executive – in this case the Area Manager. We do not do so because we consider that an authorisation whose purpose must be to protect the vulnerable prisoner and never to punish him is fully consistent with, and a proper expression of, the Board of Visitors' "watch-dog role". The Board will be acting in support of the prisoner. Almost invariably the prisoner will wish to be segregated for his own protection. The involvement of the Board of Visitors should be to ensure that during the time the prisoner has to be segregated, the best method of achieving the required protection is pursued. In addition, it would be open to the prisoner to take any grievance he had about the use of the Rule, through the grievance procedure which we discuss in Section 14.

12.205   So far as the prisoner who falls within the second limb is concerned, the rule would have the advantage that the Governor is under an obligation to provide no more segregation from association than is reasonable. We would anticipate that, by use of appropriate circular instructions, the Prison Service would make it clear that the use of the second limb should be reserved for those cases which really required this specific action. This, coupled with the third limb of the rule allowing close monitoring by the Board of Visitors, should prevent its abuse. The two limbs of the new rule would reduce the number of prisoners which the Board of Visitors has particularly to monitor. This should enable the monitoring to be more effective than it is at present.

12.206   The new Rule would have other advantages. It should enable the majority of vulnerable prisoners to be dealt with under the general obligation contained under the first limb of the proposed rule. If they are dealt with in this way, the Governor would still be able to make appropriate provision for them, while making pejorative labelling far harder. The Governor should be able to take a wide range of actions and disposals which could be equally applicable to other prisoners.

12.207   The proposed Rule would also avoid the inappropriate use of the label of Rule 43. This is demonstrated by what is happening at Wandsworth. We can see no reason for describing the prisoners on G, H and K wings as being on Rule 43. We recognise that the problem of managing these prisoners would still remain. But the fact that they were not on Rule 43 would underline the unacceptable nature of their present regime. It might also assist, even if marginally, with the problem of moving prisoners from those wings to other establishments. At the present time, the Inquiry was told, Wandsworth regard it as futile to attempt to transfer any prisoner on Rule 43 (OP) who is serving less than four years.

12.208   A new Rule should also help to reduce the present practice of certain prisoners automatically seeking to be placed on Rule 43 because of advice which they receive at Court prior to their arrival at prison. And it would remove the present anomaly of having two separate categories of sex offenders: those who are held on Rule 43 and those who are held in the national and regional vulnerable prisoner units.

12.209   We appreciate that it may be suggested that the replacement of Rule 43 for this group of offenders will not of itself tackle the fundamental and underlying problem of the attitude of the general population to the vulnerable prisoner. We accept that this is so. It is to those issues we now turn.

12.210   We agree with the Prison Reform Trust that to encourage prisoners, in effect, to lie about their offences in order to survive on normal location, is no solution to this problem. We recognise the reasons for this advice being given. These prisoners can benefit if the nature of their offence is not known. However, we consider it is wrong for a Service whose purpose is to assist the prisoner to lead a law abiding life in custody and after release, to encourage prisoners to conceal the true nature of their offences. It should be possible for the Prison Service to deal with this problem in a more satisfactory manner.

12.211   When the Inquiry visited Grendon, it was suggested that there was a need for at least one more prison offering the regime which it does for prisoners, including those who, in other establishments, would be on Rule 43. We propose that there should be a further prison run on the lines of Grendon in a different part of the country. The new prison could make a material contribution to breaking down the culture which is so prevalent at present in relation to sex offenders. This is a culture which is not confined to inmates alone. It is also present among some prison officers. It is at least as important for those prison officers' attitudes to be changed as it is for inmates' attitudes to be changed.

12.212   Prisons such as Grendon should be used as training grounds and as examples of what can be achieved. The lesson to be learnt from Grendon is that if prisoners find that conditions are attractive within an establishment, they will be slow to risk breaking the rules of conduct which are firmly laid down in case this results in their being removed from the establishment.

12.213 We would hope also that, if the Prison Service adopts our proposal for accommodating prisoners in small units, the extent of the special protection which is needed can be reduced. Vulnerable prisoners do not usually create control problems. Small units could be used to house vulnerable prisoners with other prisoners within a liberal regime. Because of the liberal regime, other prisoners would not want to run the risk of losing the benefits of the regime by attacking the sex offenders. The closer supervision which can take place within a small unit should also assist in allowing association to take place between non sex offenders and sex offenders. If problems within the unit arise, it is the aggressor and not the vulnerable prisoner who may need to be taken out of association. In other words, within the local prison there would be, in effect, a mini Grendon.

12.214 We also propose that more attention should be given to treatment. Many of those who gave evidence, including the Prison Reform Trust and the National Association of Probation Officers, stressed the unsatisfactory situation which results from our present approach to sex offenders. All too often they are left with no company other than that of another sex offender.

12.215 We recognise that when Rule 43 prisoners are subject to assaults or worse, this makes them feel, with justification, that they are the victims. It focuses their attention on their own condition and away from what they have done to *their* victims. This situation cannot be allowed to continue. Those offenders need to be assisted to avoid offending again. They must be required to confront their criminal conduct.

12.216 Fortunately, there is now a much clearer recognition of this need. It was referred to frequently in the course of the evidence to the Inquiry. It has been encouraged by the work of such bodies as the Suzy Lamplugh Trust and by the conferences which they have held. It was recognised by Mr Emes, the former Deputy Director General of the Prison Service, who is now Director of Inmate Programmes, at one of our public seminars. He acknowledged that while there were already some 63 establishments undertaking some form of work, there was a need for co-ordination and co-operation between the various agencies which at the present time were involved in initiatives with sex offenders.

12.217 This was also recognised by the then Home Secretary (Mr Waddington) when he addressed the Prison Governors' Conference on 13 November 1990. The Home Secretary said:

> "Up to now the provision has been unco-ordinated, dependent upon individual initiatives, and inconsistent in approach – and it has not been properly evaluated. What we now have is the opportunity, and the resources to co-ordinate and develop our arrangements. We will be able to assess offenders after sentence, introduce sentence planning, evaluate the range of treatments, consider the resources necessary and then decide not only which treatments to develop and use but, just as importantly, how best they must be co-ordinated with treatment offered outside prison."

12.218 The Inquiry has received impressive evidence from the Gracewell Clinic, which sets out a proposed treatment programme for sex offenders in prison and in the community. We are not in a position to evaluate the effectiveness of the programmes, but having been given details of the cost, we think it would be desirable to evaluate the effect of the programme in practice.

12.219 The evidence which we have received, including that from prisoners, strongly indicates that treatment programmes can result in a beneficial change in the attitude of sex offenders. This at least improves their conduct while in prison. Certainly we can confirm from the evidence they provided, that many sex offenders appear anxious to receive and to co-operate with treatment.

12.220   While, therefore, for the time being vulnerable prisoner units and other steps to protect sex offenders must be accepted as being a regrettable necessity, the long term objective should be to achieve a situation where it is possible to accommodate sex offenders in the general prison community. Existing attitudes will have to be changed. Those in the general prison community need to be housed in conditions which make them feel they have too much to lose by misbehaving – even in relation to sex offenders. Smaller units will assist. In addition, if the Service is to be true to its Statement of Purpose, it has to place greater emphasis on the need to make therapy available so that sex offenders can be confronted with their offending.

The Management of Disruptive Offenders

12.221   However much progress is made to improve conditions within prisons, they will remain places where, if people were to be given the choice, they would prefer not to be held. The art of prison management is the art of managing effectively a potentially hostile and discontented population.

12.222   A community prison managed in small units with varied programmes reflected in each prisoners "contract" provides the best foundation for responding to unco-operative prisoners without recourse to force. However, even in the best run prison, there will always be situations where a particular prisoner can have a seriously disruptive effect upon the establishment. He requires control. It is the best method of achieving this control with which we are concerned in this part of this Section.

12.223   We need to address the problem of disruptive prisoners because of the part they played in the April disturbances. As Part I has shown, the presence of some such prisoners at Strangeways appears to have been a significant factor in the scale of the disturbance. However, prisoners can be disruptive without ever being involved in a riot. Conversely, prisoners who are not usually disruptive can be caught up in a disturbance and behave in a most disruptive manner. We are not concerned here with this latter category. We are considering here prisoners who, for reasons which it is often difficult if not impossible to anticipate, indulge in a pattern of disruptive behaviour, often of varying frequency and intensity.

12.224   We hope that if the changes which are needed in the Prison Service are implemented, riots of the sort we saw in April will become of historical interest only. But we cannot realistically hold out the hope that in future no more prisoners will seek to behave in a disruptive or unco-operative way in the prison system. The problems they present must therefore be addressed.

12.225   We do not believe there is a simple or easily identified cause of disruptive behaviour. The Prison Service in its evidence has usefully summarised the research evidence which considers the relationship between overcrowding and the risk of disturbance (which may or may not involve disruptive prisoners). It points out that the research is inconclusive. In Britain, most of the worst violence has in the past taken place in establishments which were not at the time overcrowded.

12.226   The experience in the countries abroad which we visited is instructive. In France there has also been a history of serious disturbance. In the United States, with its complex range of federal and state provisions, there are contrasts. Many states, including New York, have experienced considerable disorder. Other states, such as Minnesota, have not. West Germany and Canada, by contrast, are both countries where serious disturbances used to be prevalent, but which in recent years have moved into a more tranquil period. In the Netherlands, serious prison disturbances are virtually unknown.

12.227   This brief and simplified history can be contrasted with the nature of each country's prison system. In France, many prisons are overcrowded with apparently limited regimes. In the Netherlands there is a very enlightened prison tradition, as there is in Minnesota. The conditions in prisons in New York are inferior to those in Minnesota. In West Germany and Canada, conditions within the prison system have now substantially improved.

12.228   We accept that it may not be possible to isolate a single factor which foments disturbances, such as overcrowding. Nonetheless, the evidence before the Inquiry, and the impression of our experience from making visits overseas, strongly indicate that there is a close link between the nature of the regime, in the broadest sense of that word, and the risk of prisoners behaving in a disruptive manner which, in some circumstance, can lead to disturbances.

12.229   The quality of life for prisoners, and their experiences in and expectations of prison, are important also in determining whether any incidents which disruptive prisoners may cause will lead to a disturbance taking root and spreading.

12.230   Our reference to regimes covers more than what is on offer at a particular prison at a particular time. Prisoners can become embittered and disaffected as a result of an earlier experience, perhaps when on remand, or in the initial stages of their sentence in a cramped and restricted local prison. The experience can stay with them throughout their sentences.

12.231   The best of way of reducing the risk of disruption and disturbance is to improve the regime within a prison and to improve the way prisoners are handled within the prison system. An improved regime will also be the best way of ensuring that, if a disturbance starts, fewer prisoners are inclined to join in.

12.232   In a minority of prisons which the Inquiry visited, where conditions were good or had substantially improved, such as at Holloway, the prisoners made it clear that they would be against rioting because it could only adversely affect their conditions.

12.233   Unfortunately, in many prisons in England and Wales, some prisoners believe that the only way to obtain an improvement in prison conditions is by rioting. The Prison Service would do well to give that the lie by ensuring conditions meet the standards which, as we have argued, justice requires. But it is also necessary to make it clear beyond peradventure that there can be no excuse for any prisoner seeking to take justice into his own hands and exploiting violence for some assumed common good. There can be no doubt that many thousands of prisoners have suffered in their circumstances and conditions as a result of the disturbances in April. Violence is not the way to a better prison system.

12.234   The first aim of the Prison Service in considering the problem of disruptive prisoners, therefore, must be to reduce the potential for disruption to the minimum extent possible. Most "disruptive" prisoners are not necessarily disruptive for the whole of their sentence: they are influenced by the conditions in which they are held and by the choice and nature of the prison to which they are allocated. Some prisoners will not be used to non-violent ways of resolving difficulties or frustrations. The Prison Service's policy must be so to manage the prison system as to keep the number of disruptive and unco-operative prisoners to the irreducible minimum.

12.235   There would be less likelihood of prisoners creating trouble if they were content with the location of the prison which is holding them. It is partly for this reason, that we have recommended that prisons should be sited in close proximity to the communities to which prisoners belong. This is where they are likely to want to serve their sentences.

12.236   There would be less likelihood of disruption if prisoners feel they are part of manageably sized groups with staff they know. It is partly for this reason that we have recommended small units in prisons, which are easier to control.

12.237 There would be less likelihood of disruption if prisoners can take part in a regime with as many incentives towards good behaviour as possible and with as few disincentives as is practicable. The importance of incentives is a matter we consider in Section 14 of this Report.

12.238 It is also important that there should be an effective grievance procedure so that the prisoner is not labouring under an unnecessary sense of injustice. It is beneficial for the prisoner, wherever possible, to know why decisions are taken which affect him. For this reason, we have recommended that he should be given reasons for a decision which materially and adversely affect the circumstances of his confinement. The introduction of prisoner "contracts", which we referred to earlier in this Section, should help in providing the positive environment for the prisoner which makes disturbances less likely.

12.239 We would expect that, if implemented, these proposals will lead to a substantial reduction in the number of potentially disruptive and difficult to manage prisoners in the prison system. But there will always be some. There is at the present time and, to a lesser extent there will remain, a serious managerial problem in how to deal with a prisoner when he becomes disruptive. There are now various options open to the management of a prison establishment if the more conventional means of charging the inmate with a disciplinary offence, or relocating the inmate to another part of the establishment, are not appropriate or effective. We discuss these options in the following paragraphs.

i) Current Options

a) A Transfer Under Circular Instruction 37/90

12.240 The first option is a transfer under Circular Instruction 37/1990. This instruction replaced in September 1990 CI 10/1974, which governed the transfer of a number of prisoners associated with the April disturbances. An examination of the sort of action governed by the circular is therefore of particular relevance to the Inquiry.

12.241 Important general considerations and principles are set out in CI 37/1990. They apply to transfers which are made in the interests of good order or discipline. The circular instruction distinguishes between two types of transfer. The first is a short term transfer from a dispersal prison to a local prison, with the possibility of immediate segregation at the local prison. This is to provide a brief "cooling off" period of up to a month before, normally, the prisoner is returned to his dispersal prison. It is open to the Governor of the dispersal prison to explore the viability of the prisoner transferring to another prison. In exceptionally difficult cases, he may refer the case to a special unit selection committee so that it can consider putting the prisoner in a Special Unit (to which we will refer later). (This part of the circular superseded the arrangements which had previously been available under CI 10/1974.)

12.242 The other form of transfer covered by the circular is the medium term transfer of up to six months to normal location in a local prison. This procedure was previously operated by Regional Offices. The expectation is that the prisoner returns to his training prison at the end of the transfer period, although the options of transfer to another prison or of consideration for a Special Unit are also open.

12.243 The circular states that:

"the transfer (whether on a permanent or temporary basis) inevitably entails disruption to the inmate and, if, in the process it creates travelling difficulties for visitors, it may adversely affect the frequency of visits which the inmate receives".

12.244 It adds that the transfer can create strong feelings of grievance in the individual concerned. The circular makes clear that the resort to transfer is not to be made lightly. Special care must be exercised to ensure:

> "that no inmate is transferred as a form of punishment, and that – eg in the choice of other establishment or in the frequency of transfers – the arrangements are not so designed that they amount to a form of punishment or may reasonably be seen to do so".

12.245   The evidence before the Inquiry indicates that this second sort of transfer can cause particular problems for local prisons, particularly if a number of prisoners are transferred in this way at the same time. The circular states that the facility "must be used sparingly". We strongly endorse this caveat. The transfer is subject to the agreement of the Tactical Management and Planning Unit and their close scrutiny must be used to ensure that the procedure is being operated appropriately.

12.246   Because of the dangers, the circular requires that the transfer and the associated arrangements, must be based on reasoned grounds and must be defensible; and such reasoned grounds must be recorded on the inmate's record by the Governor.

12.247   In addition, an inmate must be told the reasons for his transfer so far as this is practical and as soon as possible. The circular requires that this should be done before or at the time of transfer, although it states that the prisoner has no absolute right to reasons. If it is judged that the giving of reasons may result in additional control problems during transfer, the circular suggests that it would be sensible for the giving of reasons to be deferred until transfer has been completed. But deferral should not be longer than 48 hours after the transfer unless, in a most exceptional case, the inmate's demeanour necessitates delay, in which case the reasons must be given at the earliest opportune time.

12.248   The circular deals also with the situation after transfer. Where a prisoner has been transferred from a dispersal prison to a local prison for a "cooling off" period, the expectation is that he will be held under segregation in the local prison. In such cases, the circular provides that the prisoner should not only be given reasons for his transfer, he should also be given reasons to explain why he is being segregated. The same conditions on timing apply for explaining the reasons for segregation as apply to explaining the reasons for the initial transfer.

12.249   The circular also requires that the reasons should be given in writing if the inmate requests this. The circular requires that the explanation should be as full as is reasonably possible, but should not include any material which should be withheld in the interests of good order or discipline (in particular any material which identifies or may tend to identify and thereby put at risk another inmate, or which it is undesirable to disclose in the interests of security).

12.250   The circular therefore recognises that any transfer from one establishment to another in the interests of good order or discipline can be unfair to the inmate who is transferred. It can be unfair because the transfer could adversely affect him to a material extent and he does not have the protection of a hearing which would be available to him if disciplinary action were to be taken against him. The circular seeks to ensure that any injustice or any risk of abuse of power is reduced to a minimum.

12.251   The circular adopts an exemplary standard in respect of the requirement to give reasons. (We shall be recommending that it would be desirable to apply this standard more generally.) If the inmate is at least given the reasons for the action, this makes the procedure fairer than it would otherwise be.

12.252   We recommend, however, an amendment to the provision that those reasons need not be given in writing *unless* this is requested by the inmate. We think it would be preferable, from both the establishment and the inmate's point of view, if they were *always* given in writing. If this were done, and the inmate were required to acknowledge its receipt, at least when the prisoner did so, this would avoid any dispute over whether he had been given reasons. While in relation to some decisions this would be administratively onerous, transfers are such a disruptive step for prisoners that the discipline involved in giving reasons in writing is appropriate.

12.253   If properly interpreted and operated, the Prison Service's circular should prevent a specially difficult prisoner being shunted from one prison to the next every few months. Other countries, including the Netherlands, adopt such a "carousel" approach for handling their most difficult inmates. We are not in favour of this solution. We endorse the Prison Service's policy of returning a difficult prisoner to his original prison unless, exceptionally, it is decided he needs to make a new start somewhere else or should go to a Special Unit. The Prison Service must closely monitor the operation of the circular to ensure that these exceptions do not come to be granted in a way which is tantamount to putting the most difficult prisoners on a "carousel".

12.254   Subject to what we have said above about the sparing use of short term transfers, and to what we will say about the way they should be operated and monitored, we accept that it is necessary for the Prison Service to have available these forms of transfer as a response to a specially difficult situation which the Governor is satisfied cannot be resolved – at least at that time – within his own establishment.

12.255   Professor Roy King has made a number of precise and specific recommendations in relation to the procedure which was then 10/74. Those recommendations have been met only in part by the new procedure and it is right that we should express our views about the other recommendations which were not adopted. Professor King proposed that there should be disciplinary proceedings before transfer. Having regard to the circumstances in which the procedure is now to be used, we do not regard this recommendation as being appropriate. Although the situation may be potentially explosive, no disciplinary offence may have been committed and the need for transfer could still exist.

12.256   Secondly, Professor King suggested that the procedure should not be used as an emergency procedure as at present and that transfers should be conducted on a planned basis. As we have reluctantly concluded that, at the present time at least, there is a need for an emergency procedure, it follows we cannot endorse this recommendation.

12.257   Thirdly, Professor King suggests transfers should be authorised by the local Board of Visitors. This recommendation would run counter to the policy which we have recommended, which is that the Board of Visitors should cease to have its present adjudicatory role. There would be a danger, if the Board of Visitors were to authorise transfers, that they would still be regarded by prisoners as making decisions which adversely affect them.

12.258   We are in partial agreement with Professor King, however, that, where possible, a member of the Board of Visitors should be at the receiving prison when a prisoner arrives. This proposal, where it is practicable, would be worthwhile. However, it would suffice if a transferred prisoner is seen by a member of the Board of Visitors shortly after his arrival at the receiving prison. We propose that in future one or the other option is followed.

12.259   We would also propose, in accordance with Professor King's recommendations, that whenever this is reasonably practicable, a medical officer should see a prisoner before he is transferred and certify him as being fit for transfer, and that he is seen as soon as reasonably practicable after transfer by the medical officer at the new location.

12.260   We regard these proposals as being in the interests of the prisoner who is being transferred. It is equally in the interests of the prison from which he is transferred and to which he is transferred. The potentially disruptive situations in which the procedure is now used could give rise to serious allegations which are easy to make but difficult to refute. It is important that there should be an independent means of assessing those allegations.

b) Transfer from a Category C Prison to the Local Prison

12.261   This is the second option. It is not covered by the circular instruction to which we have referred above.

12.262   A substantial body of evidence during Part I, particularly in relation to the Strangeways disturbance, indicated that the practice of prisoners being returned to local prisons from Category C prisons built up within the local prisons a body of prisoners who were particularly troublesome. They were in particular prisoners who were unsuited to the dormitories which provide the accommodation in some Category C prisons. The Category C prison found it difficult to control them. Frequently, the returned prisoners were extremely disgruntled by their rejection by the Category C prison. They took it out on the local prison to which they were returned. Their presence made harder any efforts the local prison made to provide a regime with a lighter touch.

12.263   We hope that if, as we have proposed, dormitories are phased out within a set period, the use of this form of transfer should become less frequent. Where such prisoners have to be returned to a local prison, particular care should be given to their subsequent allocation so that they do not get caught up in a recurring cycle of disruption, segregation and transfer which can be so damaging for them and for the prison to which they are sent. In the future, if the Prison Service establishes a "cluster" of prisons within a community area, as we have proposed, this should enable such prisoners to be dealt with in a way which avoids them entering such a cycle.

c) Segregation Under Rule 43 of the Prison Rules (Rule 46 of Young Offender Institution Regulations)

12.264   This is the third option for dealing with disruptive prisoners. It is a mechanism for taking action to avoid incidents within an establishment without recourse to a transfer. It involves the removal of the prisoner from association in the interests of good order or discipline under Rule 43 of the Prison Rules, or in young offender institutions under Rule 46 of the Young Offender Institution Rules. (For convenience we will refer here to Rule 43 as being a reference to both Rules).

12.265   Circular Instruction 26/90 deals with the procedure for removal from association of inmates under Rule 43. Like the Rule itself, it covers both removal for reasons of good order or discipline and removal for reasons of the prisoner's own protection. As we have already pointed out, we do not consider it appropriate for the same Rule to apply to the two very different situations.

2.266   So far as good order or discipline is concerned, the circular indicates that the rule is "designed to assist Governors to prevent trouble". Governors may use it in respect of "known subversive inmates". It can be used to anticipate a situation where an inmate could jeopardise control.

12.267   The circular makes it clear that, wherever possible, means should be used other than segregation under Rule 43. This is clearly right. (We do not, however, interpret this reference in the circular as suggesting that a transfer under the arrangements we have described above is preferable; in most cases, in our view, it is not.) While segregation under Rule 43 is not intended to be a punishment, the use of the Rule will almost invariably adversely affect the inmate who is made subject to it. In most establishments, anyone segregated under Rule 43 will be subjected to regime restrictions very similar to those undergoing punishment. As the circular acknowledges, "some restriction of regime activities will normally be inevitable" because of the inmate's separate location and limitations of accommodation, manpower and other resources.

12.268   The circular provides a guide to the factors constituting removal from association. It states that normal factors:

"are detention in separate accommodation without an acceptable degree of social contact with other inmates and deprivation of the opportunity to participate in recreation (including physical education), entertainment, education classes or work (where generally available)".

12.269 The Governor's power to authorise segregation under the Rule is limited to three days (72 hours). If a longer period is required, then authority must be sought from the Board of Visitors or, exceptionally, from the Secretary of State. The extension can then be up to one month or, in the case of an inmate aged under 21, the extension is up to 14 days. After the expiry of an extended period, there can be a further authorization.

12.270 We do not regard it as appropriate for the Board of Visitors to continue to give such authority. Whatever is the true position, when a Board member gives such authority, prisoners do not see him as acting to safeguard their interests, but as the arm of management. This is not consistent with or helpful to the Board's watch-dog role. We propose that, in future therefore, it should be the responsibility of the Area Manager to give the authority. We propose that more than one extension of 28 days (or 14 days for young inmates) should only be justified if the Area Manager is satisfied that there are exceptional circumstances for this course. The Board of Visitors should, however, carefully supervise and monitor the exercise of this segregation power.

12.271 The circular encourages the giving of reasons as a sensible practice, but makes it clear that this is at the Governor's discretion. In our view the circular should give firmer guidance. We can see no good reason for differing from the position which exists in relation to transfers from an establishment. We recommend that the Governor should be expected to give reasons in writing, at the time, or as soon possible after a prisoner is segregated under Rules 43 or 46. We recognise that there are likely to be a number of occasions when material must be withheld in the interests of good order or discipline, to protect security or other inmates, but *some* explanation is usually possible and, if not, a statement of this fact, which can if necessary be reviewed through the grievance procedure, is desirable.

d) Allocation to a Special Unit for the Control of the Disruptive Prisoner

12.272 This is the fourth option. A major part of the sentence for adult male prisoners serving a long sentence will normally be spent either in a training prison or in a dispersal prison. A minority of prisoners who create particular problems of control, can be allocated to a Special Unit.

12.273 In order to understand the part played by the Special Units in the present management of the long term prison system, it is necessary to know how and why the Special Units came into existence, and to understand their place in dealing with long term prisoners who present particular difficulties of security and control.

12.274 Prior to the Mountbatten Report in December 1966, there had been a number of well publicised escapes and a perceived lack of really secure prisons in England and Wales. The Mountbatten Report recommended that prisoners should be divided into four categories (A, B, C and D) according to the degree of security needed for their containment. The Report recommended also that there should be a single highly secure prison built:

> "to house those prisoners who must in no circumstances be allowed to get out, whether because of the security consideration affecting spies, or because their violent behaviour is such that members of the public or the police would be in danger of their lives if they were to get out."

12.275 The Mountbatten recommendation for security categorisation was accepted. However, the recommendation for the concentration of high security prisoners in a single new prison was not accepted. In its place the then Government accepted a recommendation of the Radzinowicz Committee's report "The Regime for the Long Term Prisoners in Conditions of Maximum Security" published in March 1968. This suggested that, instead of a policy of concentration, there should be a policy of dispersal. This involved Category A prisoners being dispersed among the larger population of prisoners at specially selected establishments which were to be known as Dispersal Prisons. The object was that, within the secure perimeter of the Dispersal Prison, a liberal and open regime could be established for all prisoners, including Category A prisoners.

12.276   Following the acceptance of this recommendation, the security at seven existing prisons, Albany, Gartree, Hull, Long Lartin, Parkhurst, Wakefield and Wormwood Scrubs, was increased so that they could provide the perimeter security which was necessary for the dispersal role. It was an expensive business. Later two purpose built maximum security prisons were built in the north (Full Sutton and Frankland) and Hull and Wormwood Scrubs ceased to be dispersal prisons.

12.277   The Radzinowicz Committee had also recommended that a small minority of prisoners should be dealt with in separate segregation units within a larger prison. They were the disruptive prisoners who needed to be removed from the general population of a long term prison if its regime was not to be disrupted.

12.278   Following the disturbances at Albany and Gartree in the latter part of 1972, the then Home Secretary, Mr Carr, announced, among other measures, the provision of two control units operating a strict regime within the existing dispersal system. Prisoners who were persistent troublemakers would be transferred to one of those units until such time as they could be safely returned to normal prison life.

12.279   The first of the control units was opened at Wakefield in 1974. It became the subject of civil proceedings. In October 1975, the then Home Secretary, Mr Jenkins, directed that, as the unit at Wakefield had not been used to the extent expected, no further prisoners should be admitted to the unit.

12.280   The policy of dispersal was considered again in 1979 by the May Committee. They concluded on balance that the arguments lay in favour of dispersal.

12.281   In 1983, in response to the continuing concern in the Prison Service about the dispersal system, the Prison Service's Control Review Committee was asked to consider what changes might be made to reduce control problems. The Committee's report on managing the long term prison system was published in 1989. The report:

> "tried to find ways of making the system more flexible, to increase the number of available options, and to avoid creating last resort situations from which prisoners may see no way out".

12.282   The Control Review Committee recognised that long term prisons, by their nature, would always contain many men who were aggressive, manipulative and hostile to authority. It noted that in some cases prisoners would present control problems which could not be dealt with in normal conditions. The Committee recommended that there should be a new system of what came to be known as Special Units. These were designed to cater for those prisoners whose behaviour did not respond to the inbuilt incentives of the better structured long term prison system which the Committee envisaged.

12.283   The Committee's recommendation for Special Units has been implemented. There are now three Special Units – at Hull, Parkhurst and Lincoln – and a fourth Special Unit is planned at Milton Keynes.

12.284   At present Special Units make only a small contribution to the Prison Service's response to problems of control. They cater for a very small group of prisoners. According to the Prison Service evidence:

> "Parkhurst C Wing has currently 18 inmates; it is not thought sensible to

try to manage a larger group even though the unit could accommodate more prisoners. The Lincoln unit is smaller, currently being occupied by six inmates and has a maximum of seven places. Hull has ten places and could accommodate up to 20."

12.285   So at the time of the Prison Service's evidence to the Inquiry in September 1990, the population in special units was 34 and could not rise to more than 45.

12.286   The Prison Service has established a research and advisory group to advise on the development of the Special Unit system. Professor Bottoms, of the Institute of Criminology at Cambridge, is a member of the group. In his evidence to the Inquiry, he pointed out that "neither prior experience nor prior research pointed to any very obvious ideal' solutions to the particular kind of prisoners" who should be allocated to the units. It has been necessary to proceed on a trial and error basis.

12.287   A research report prepared for the Home Office in 1990, which was submitted to the Inquiry in conjunction with Professor Bottoms' evidence, observes that:

"given the way that most dispersal prison Governors seem to operate, the special unit strategy can be said to have a limited relevance to their day to day operational needs".

12.288   Because the selection procedures for the Special Units are slow, they do not assist with the prisoner which a dispersal prison wants to be moved quickly. "The (rightly) slow and deliberate special unit selection procedure simply does not mesh very well with (the) .... operational imperatives." The research report also points out that there is a danger that the whole Special Unit strategy might overstate, by implication, the extent to which control problems in dispersal prisons are simply the product of "difficult" individuals.

12.289   In their evidence to the Inquiry, the Prison Service described the planned unit for Milton Keynes as catering "for those control problem prisoners who may require a more *structured* regime" (our emphasis) than the other three units offered and for whom the only alternative at present was long term segregation. This suggests that the Prison Service considers that there are already prisoners for whom the existing Special Units are not suitable. It may also be an indication that the Service is aware that the liberal regimes in the Special Units are resulting in invidious comparisons being drawn between the conditions in the Special Units and those in the normal system. There are indications in the evidence we have received that they may be sending the wrong message to prisoners by apparently placing a premium on bad behaviour.

12.290   From the evidence we have received, and from what we have heard on our visits and in discussions, it is evident that Special Units do not provide an easy or complete answer to the problem of dealing with the intransigently disruptive prisoner. The security is necessarily tight. Special Units aim to provide a generous regime to counterbalance their claustrophobic environment. But this, in turn, requires intensive staffing. There is difficulty in selecting the prisoners who should be accommodated in the Special Units. When prisoners have been allocated to Special Units, then it is difficult subsequently to integrate them back into a more normal prison setting. There is more than a philosophical difficulty about apparently providing the best conditions and facilities for those who behave the worst.

12.291   We accept, however, the case for some form of Special Unit within our prison system as it is today. The Units should not be intended for other than a small minority of particularly disruptive prisoners, who cannot be safely accommodated in any other way. The aim of the Units should be to return the prisoner to "normal" prison life before his release. The conditions and regime must reflect this. The present difficulties of the Units which we have summarised above, are not, however, likely to be overcome unless considerable improvement can be made to the generality of prisons on the lines we suggest in this report. Such improvements could have a dramatic effect on the need for and the number of such Special Units.

e) Conclusion

12.292 It will be clear from our examination of these four options that they all have shortcomings. Three involve uprooting prisoners from their prisons – itself a disruptive experience. The fourth involves a restriction on association and living conditions which should not be other than very short term. The exercise of these options should therefore be as restricted as possible, and, we propose, more restricted than at present.

12.293 At present, the local prison is the lynch pin of the transfer system. Its use in this way would be much more acceptable if prisoners were transferred to a specialist re-assessment and allocation unit in the local prison so that their situation and future allocation can be considered in depth. This would be much preferable to the local prison having to hold them either in segregation or in a normal wing or unit. A transfer for this purpose would be less likely to be viewed as a punishment.

12.294 If such an allocation procedure is to be successful, it would have to be restricted to those cases which warranted it. It would not be a cheap option. The general approach should be one where all prisons, except in exceptional circumstances, consume their own smoke.

12.295 The Prison Service is right to have in place the options which we have described, subject to the points we have made. It would be wholly wrong, however, to imagine that they were the whole or a sufficient response. The key lies in the management of the prison system as a whole and in the provision made for the generality of prisoners. That is why, in examining the April disturbances, we have felt it right to look at the wider issues covered in Part II of the Report.

12.296 It is essential that there is as broad a range of regimes within the prison system as is practicable. The small units policy which we recommend, coupled with community prisons, would be important. The aim must be to produce a prison system which can cope with disruptive prisoners in a way which does not allow them to bring the life of a prison to halt or to be rewarded by specially favourable treatment and conditions for trying to do so.

ii) The Use of New Generation Prisons

12.297 If the Prison Service is to be able to provide in the general prison system for all the prisoners it is required to hold, it must be able to provide prisons which can hold prisoners in reasonable conditions for long periods under the highest levels of security. Such prisons should be able to hold prisoners who present particularly intractable problems of control.

12.298 We have referred to the new generation prison design in Section 11. We consider that, if applied to prisons capable of dealing with prisoners presenting problems of either security or control or both, they would provide a valuable further option for dealing with disruptive prisoners. We visited such a prison in Minnesota – Oak Park Heights Prison.

12.299 The Control Review Committee's report of 1984 makes it clear that that Committee was attracted by the new generation design of prison. Both from the physical point of view and because of the regime which the design makes possible, we consider it has considerable advantages over the existing dispersal prisons.

12.300 Professor King has made a comparative study of Gartree, a dispersal prison of an older design, and Oak Park Heights. He has come to the conclusion that, apart from the staff at Gartree (who were regarded as being superior to those at Oak Park Heights) Oak Park Heights was found to be more satisfactory in virtually every respect. It was safer, more secure and more trouble free. It offered better education, training and contact with the outside world. It ran with fewer staff. Professor King says:

"There seems little doubt that Oak Park Heights achieved what must be one of the major objectives of any prison system – the provision of a safe custodial environment for staff and prisoners – much more effectively than did Gartree."

12.301   Professor King adds:

"Moreover the perception that Oak Park Heights was safe, whereas Gartree was not, was so deeply engrained in the consciousness of those who lived and worked in the respective institutions, that it became one of the overriding features of the field work."

12.302   This last conclusion was influenced in part by the design of Oak Park Heights. The design gave the staff there a greater feeling of security. This in turn assisted the staff in providing the environment (what Professor Bottoms describes as the "social climate") for reducing disorder.

12.303   The current Prison Design Briefing System is based on new generation principles. The Prison Building Programme could therefore provide for the introduction of a maximum security prison within the existing system which incorporates new generation principles. That prison could take the place of one of the existing dispersal prisons. The Inquiry understands this may well be the intention for Whitemoor Prison, which is due to be opened in 1991.

12.304   We recognise that it may be possible to provide a wider range of regimes and more opportunities for dealing with difficult-to-control prisoners within the present dispersal prisons. More easily separable units would help. But this will be more difficult than in a new generation design. The Control Review Committee was right to indicate that it would not be possible in our existing prisons to develop fully the approach to prison management which is adopted at Oak Park Heights. This is because the units within the prisons would not be self-contained in respect of services: in Oak Park Heights prisoners live in units below the workshop for that unit.

12.305   We propose, therefore, that, in conjunction with the findings of the Prison Service Working Party to which we have referred, and the research of Professors King and Bottoms, the Prison Service should consider earmarking at least one "new generation prison" for "dispersal" prisoners, including those who would probably now be housed in Special Units. If, in accordance with our proposals, more effective and varied regimes with varying levels of security are introduced in community prisons, then long term prisoners, who may still require at some stage in their sentence the high security provided by dispersal prisons, would be able to be moved earlier to community prisons. In such circumstances, the Prison Service would need to review the number of prisons in the dispersal system. It should be possible to reduce their number.

The Management of the Remand Population

12.306   We have already indicated in Section 10 of this Report what we believe should be the general approach of the Prison Service to all those in the prison system who are on remand. In that section, we recognise the difficulties that exist in achieving what common justice requires, namely that remand prisoners should be treated in a way which accords with their status as unconvicted or unsentenced prisoners. In Section 11, because of these difficulties, we proposed that, when practical, and where this can be achieved within the requirement that prisoners should be accommodated near to their homes, remand prisoners should be accommodated in separate prisons, or in separate units within a larger prison.

12.307   It is the task of management to ensure that the Prison Service performs the role we have identified for it in relation to remand prisoners. If, in addition to the broad needs of the remand population identified in Section 10, further guidance is required, it can be found in the Prison Reform Trust's recent publication on Regimes for Remand Prisoners by Dr Silvia Casale and Ms Joyce Plotnikoff. Unless special emphasis is placed on this task, all the evidence indicates that the regime for remand prisoners will be inferior instead of at least as good as, if not superior, to that provided for sentenced prisoners.

12.308   In the course of the evidence, all too often we came across instances where an activity was not offered to a remand prisoner because it was thought the prisoner would be there for too short a time; or because it was thought that he would be spending his time preparing for his trial; or because it was thought that he would be on a visit. These are limp excuses. With good management and a flexibility of approach, including offering activities and opportunities in short "modules" throughout the day, it should be possible to accommodate the special needs of a remand prisoner and give him the opportunity to taking some part in all the activities in the prison.

12.309   As there should be Accredited Standards for prisons, so should there be Accredited Standards for remand centres or remand units within prisons. A remand prisoner should be provided with a "contract" in the same way as a sentenced prisoner, as we indicated earlier in this Section.

12.310   There is a further matter of concern in respect of the remand population which goes to its management by the Prison Service. At the present time, the Prison Service is not managing the remand population as it should. This part of this Section focuses on how the situation can be improved. The core of our concern, and the key to improving the management of these prisoners, lies in the assumptions made about the degree of security which all remand prisoners require.

12.311   If a prisoner is on remand in a local prison, then, unless it is necessary for him to be provisionally regarded as a Category A prisoner, he is treated as though he were Category B. This approach was adopted because it avoids the need for categorising remand prisoners.

12.312   This categorisation, however, subjects all remand prisoners to a degree of security and control which is frequently unnecessary. There can be no doubt that, at the present time, there are significant numbers of remand prisoners held in custody in conditions of security higher than they require. This is wasteful of the resources of the Prison Service. It is also unfair for the prisoner. We hope that the use of remand in custody will be progressively reduced as an enlarged bail hostel system comes into operation but, despite this, we consider that an alternative approach is required to the categorisation of remand prisoners.

12.313   We recommend that all remand prisoners should be regarded as equivalent to Category C rather than Category B prisoners, unless there is reason to regard them as needing Category B or Category A conditions of security. The same principle should apply to young remand prisoners. We appreciate that, for the foreseeable future, at least, the majority of adult remand prison inmates will still be kept in Category B establishments. But the fact that they are regarded as being equivalent to Category C will underline the fact that they should not be subject to more security or for that matter, more control than is necessary. It will also enable the prison establishment to adopt a more relaxed approach to their containment. In the long run, it could lead to a saving in costs.

12.314   The nature of the offence with which the prisoner is charged, his record and any information which is available as a result of a Bail Information Scheme, should be sufficient in the ordinary case to determine whether an upgraded security categorisation is needed.

12.315   The Crown Prosecution Service might also be asked to identify cases where it believes particular care is required in relation to security. The prosecutor could inform the Court at the time that the question of bail is considered if he considers that the circumstances of the case merit particular security precautions. Unless the Court disagrees with this view, it should ensure that the papers are appropriately marked to indicate that there has been a statement of this nature made by the prosecution. It should be possible to have attached to the papers a short statement indicating the reasons why the need for additional security is suggested.

12.316 It may, at first sight, appear to be a marked departure to suggest involving the prosecution and the Court in questions about the degree of security in which a prisoner should be held. However, the prosecution and the Magistrate already have to consider whether, for example, a bail hostel would provide the necessary protection against court proceedings being disrupted. This task would be similar.

12.317 Between the prosecution, the Courts, the Prison Service and the Probation Service there should be ample information available to upgrade the security in which a remand prisoner is held where this is necessary. There needs to be close co-operation to ensure that this information reaches the remand establishment with the inmate. The Local Committees, which we have recommended should be established, should resolve this problem. We have considered the danger of a change of the sort we propose resulting in more defendants being remanded in custody. However, we do not consider that there is any real risk of this suggestion having this effect.

12.318 We would stress, however, that our recommendation is not dependent on co-operation from other agencies and the Court. The Prison Service can, if necessary, satisfactorily perform this task without such assistance. That this is so is confirmed in the evidence given by Mr Woolford, the Head of Custody at Pucklechurch, referred to in Section 8 of this Report.

12.319 We have considered carefully the forceful arguments which were put before us by a member of the Prison Service at one of our public seminars. There it was argued that it was not practicable to do more than at present to differentiate between the security and control needs of different remand inmates. We have set out the ways in which we believe the necessary information can be secured and deployed.

12.320 Circular Instruction 7/1988 confirms us in our belief that more can be done. That circular deals with the categorisation and allocation of adult male prisoners. It provides that all prisoners on remand awaiting trial or convicted and awaiting sentence, other than those provisionally categorised A, should be placed in a new category U (unclassified). After stating that category U prisoners should normally be assumed to require accommodation appropriate to Category B prisoners, the circular went on to say:

> "There is no reason in principle why an unconvicted or unsentenced prisoner (other than potential Category A's or those provisionally categorised as A) should not be held in Category C establishments if suitable facilities exist and if adequate information is available which shows that Category B accommodation is not needed for that prisoner – any obstacles are practical rather than of principle and Governors should proceed on this basis."

12.321 We believe the practical obstacles can and should be overcome. We believe that the great majority of remand prisoners at present in Category B establishments would be perfectly well accommodated in Category C prisons if those prisoners were correctly situated close to the communities in which the remands have their homes. This could be the case with Norwich Prison. Local prisons are Category B and are often at present conveniently located for remand inmates. But this is not sufficient reason for upgrading the equivalent security categorisation of remands. As long as the reasons are available to identify those prisoners who need a higher degree of security, in accordance with the principles we have identified, the remand prisoner's categorisation should be kept as low as possible.

12.322   The result of such categorisation should allow for more relaxed regimes for some lower category remand prisoners. If the unit approach which we have recommended is adopted, whether in a separate centre or as part of a larger prison, then within the improved conditions which are necessary for all remand prisoners, it should be possible to have some units with a more open regime than others. This would give effect to the principle that a remand prisoner is not subject to more control and security than is necessary.

12.323   We propose that there should be a proper induction programme for remand prisoners. The programme would primarily be conducted by prison officers, but probation officers would also need to be involved. It would incorporate the prison bail unit, which we discuss in Section 10, and would deal with all the remand prisoners' problems which have to be addressed. If the programme is conducted properly, it should provide the information which is necessary to decide whether any remand prisoner should be given a higher security categorisation and for his appropriate allocation.

12.324   We recognise that the Prison Service may not be able to implement this proposal for an induction programme immediately. It is a target at which the Service should aim. The acceptance of our recommendation for the categorisation of remand prisoners is not dependent on it.

The Management of Young Offenders and Young Remands

12.325   The management of young offenders present a special challenge to the Prison Service. The age of the inmates places a heavy obligation on the Prison Service to minimise the damaging effects of being in custody.

12.326   The number of very young offenders in prison has been declining steadily since 1981. There were 2,145 untried young prisoners under 17 received in 1979; the number had fallen to 1382 in 1989. Over the same period, the number of unsentenced prisoners for the same age group fell from 2,226 in 1979 to 416 in 1989.

12.327   Despite the loss during the April disturbances of young offender accommodation at Manchester and Pucklechurch, the Prison Service has announced the intended closure of 520 places at Campsfield House, Eastwood Park and Lowdham Grange. Nevertheless, in 1989 just over a fifth of the prison population were young offenders (10,390).

12.328   We hope that the size of the young offender population will continue to fall. We emphasise, however, that the reduction in population must not be regarded as a justification for not furthering the policy of having suitable young offender establishments close to the centres at which the majority of young offenders have their homes. Ideally, as we have said in Section 11, we see these being separate institutions within a community cluster of prisons close to each main centre or community. In the meantime, and in some far flung areas, it would be appropriate to hold young remands and, separately, young sentenced offenders in a larger prison holding also adults. But they should be in separate units with separate access to facilities, and each should be under their own governor with their own staff. They should not be in conditions of the sort described by HMCIP in his recent reports on Hull and Leeds.

12.329   It is particularly unfortunate if young offenders are locked up for long periods at a time and do not have sufficient activities to absorb their energy and develop their abilities. The fact that it is not appropriate to *send* young offenders to prison establishments for training does not mean that they should not *receive* training while at the establishments. They manifestly benefit from a wide range of educational opportunities. There is also the need for young offenders to accept responsibility for their offences and to prepare them for their return to the community when they finish their sentences. Courses need to be developed for young offenders resulting in the award of national vocational qualifications.

12.330   The 1989/90 Prison Service Annual Report sets out the Service's objectives for its young offender institutions:

> "The aim of young offender institutions – to prepare offenders for their return to society – is achieved through
>
> – providing a full programme of activities which help offenders to develop personal responsibility, self discipline, interests, skills and physical fitness. These activities include education, training and work and are designed to help offenders to get a job after release
>
> – encouraging links between offenders and the outside community
>
> – working closely with the services responsible for offenders after their release."

12.331   The evidence before the Inquiry indicates that at some establishments (admittedly not young offender institutions) young offenders' treatment did not accord with these aims. This was true both at Manchester and in the case of remands at Pucklechurch. It was not true of Glen Parva. We propose that the Prison Service should seek to apply to all young offenders, irrespective of the type of establishment at which they are accommodated, the objectives for young offender institutions set out in the 1989/90 Prison Service Annual Report. So far as appropriate to their different status, the same objectives should apply to young remands.

12.332   The Prison Service has a proud tradition in relation to young offenders. It goes back to the Borstal training system. Borstal training had two defects which led to its demise in 1982: it was an indeterminate sentence, and its very title personified the discredited concept of sending youngsters to an institution for the training which it had to offer. In some eyes, it was also regarded as too paternalistic.

12.333   The house system which existed in the Borstal institutions was in some ways similar to what we are advocating when we refer to the need for the prison population to be managed in small units. This is particularly important in a young offenders' establishment. We consider that small units would help also to further the use of personal officers for young offenders. The Prison Service is now currently attaching considerable importance to personal officers. There have been training courses for officers to help their inter-personal skills and a training manual together with a useful pocket booklet have been produced.

12.334   The Inquiry Team were impressed by the parents' support scheme at Swinfen Hall for young offenders who were detained for life. The scheme involved the families in discussing the future of these youngsters with staff and their personal officers. It was very much appreciated by parents. They had the opportunity of learning what was involved in the sentence, enjoying a meal with their son and his personal officer, and establishing contact with other families with the same problem. The relationship which was established by the family with the personal officer would obviously be important for the future. The scheme needs extending to other institutions and classes of young offenders and indeed to adult establishments as well, as normally the families of all prisoners are affected by the sentence.

12.335   Such initiatives, however, have to be backed by the necessary resources and, in particular, the necessary training and guidance. The Personal Officer scheme has been strongly endorsed by the Prison Service, but the August 1989 report on the Personal Officer Work in Feltham YOI makes it clear that without proper support, such initiatives are of little value.

12.336   Greater attention must also be given to the opportunities provided for young offenders on remand. The Prison Service acknowledges this. In its evidence it noted that:

> "a major concern should be the quality of regimes for those under 21 held on remand."

12.337   The need for a personal officer scheme for young people on remand is as strong as it is for convicted young offenders. Bail schemes also have a particularly important role in relation to young defendants.

12.338   The number of recent suicides in relation to young remands, including one young man who was at Manchester and played a part in that disturbance, is particularly worrying. This subject has recently been considered by the Review of the HMCIP published in December 1990. The Inquiry cannot usefully add to what is stated in the Review.

The Management of Drug Abusers

12.339   In its evidence, the Prison Service noted that between 2,000 and 3,000 inmates each year have been reported by medical officers as having some degree of dependence on drugs at the time of their reception into custody. In 1989, 1,159 drug addicts were notified by prison medical officers in accordance with the Misuse of Drugs Regulations 1973. But the Prison Service noted:

> "These figures are recognised as understating the scale of drug usage in respect of people sent to prison."

12.340   The Prison Service has shown us a draft of Professor Gunn's report on Mentally Disordered Prisoners. The report was commissioned by the Home Office and carried out by the Department of Forensic Psychiatry at the Institute of Psychiatry. It suggests that "drug dependence is the commonest psychiatric problem in sentenced prisoners". The report found that the facilities in prisons had failed to keep pace with the scale of the problem.

12.341   Professor Gunn's report points out that, with few exceptions:

> "prison doctors regarded drug and alcohol abuse as being outside their area of concern"

and that:

> "many prison medical officers lack interest or involvement in the care of substance abusers, whether their primary problem is drugs or alcohol".

12.342   The research carried out for the purposes of Professor Gunn's report was the most extensive ever conducted. It was however confined to the sentenced prison population only.

12.343   In referring to alcohol dependency/abuse, the report uses as its criterion: those for whom "treatment for a drink problem might be appropriate". For drug dependency/abuse, the criterion is: the "daily use of drugs of dependency during the six months period prior to the index offence". The figures do not include cannabis users.

12.344   On this basis, the percentage in Professor Gunn's sample for whom the primary diagnosis was alcohol dependency or abuse among adult males was 8.6%. Among male youths, it was 8.7%, and among females it was 4.4%. The respective percentages for a primary diagnosis of drug dependency/abuse were, 10.1% adult males, 6.2% male youths and 24.2% females. Based on his sample findings, Professor Gunn estimates that 20.1% of the adult male sentenced population may be diagnosed as dependent on or abusing substances (drugs, alcohol and, to a much lesser extent, pathological gambling) together with 15.8% of the sentenced male youth population and 28.9% of the sentenced female population.

12.345 The Royal College of Psychiatrists, in its evidence to the Inquiry, pointed out that it was not easy to treat alcoholism or drug dependency. The success rate was low. It would be lower still where there was little desire to co-operate. Nevertheless, the College said:

> "prison with its many hours of enforced inactivity and boredom for most inmates, could provide a window of opportunity to help these growing numbers of dependent people - the drug abusers, the alcoholics and the pathological gamblers, who now together constitute a fifth of our sentenced population. Self-help organisations such as Alcoholics Anonymous and Gamblers Anonymous already meet in many prisons. They need encouraging and their work extending – in many prisons there is a waiting list of weeks or months for the "Alcohol Class". Voluntary agencies working with drug addicts and others (such as Lifeline in Manchester) should also be encouraged to contribute their experience, enthusiasm, and links with resources outside the walls".

12.346 We were helped by evidence from Lifeline. They pointed out that the majority of drug users do not identify themselves on reception for fear of receiving different and unpleasant treatment as a result. In many prisons, drug users were placed in isolation for the period of their withdrawal, during which time they received no medication, or at least no medication which would be considered appropriate by the National Heath Service. Lifeline suggested that:

> "Contact between the Prison Medical Service and their NHS counterparts is rare."

12.347 Lifeline also drew our attention to the problem of the illicit use of drugs by prisoners, as did NAPO (the National Association of Probation Officers). NAPO told us that a Parliamentary Answer on the 20 March 1990 had shown that 617 needles or syringes had been found in prison by staff between 1987 and 1989. But Lifeline suggested that too much reliance should not be put on such statistics. Injecting equipment which was smuggled into prison was widely used, they suggested.

12.348 We are not in a position to confirm or comment upon these claims. However Professor Gunn's report says that, while this may be due to under-reporting, the results of his survey do not suggest that injecting is widespread among former drug users in prison. Most prisoners we spoke to in a number of different prisons and in private discussions suggested to us that so-called "soft" drugs, such as cannabis, were available to some prisoners. But there was much greater reluctance among prisoners to admit to the presence of the harder drugs referred to by Lifeline.

12.349 The problem of drug abuse had already faced a large number of the prisons we visited in Europe, apparently to a greater extent than in this country.

12.350 We have referred earlier in this Section to the units in some prisons in the Netherlands - drug free zones. They provide assistance and an improved regime to prisoners who agree to take part in the programmes and to avoid any use of drugs. Lifeline commended this system to us. They suggested that drug free units should also be open to non-abusing inmates to avoid the units turning into Rule 43 ghettos. We propose that the Prison Service should examine the experience in the Netherlands and similar initiatives in Sweden and the United States and, subject to that examination, should make provision for drug free units. Such programmes would depend on the Prison Service drawing fully on assistance from outside agencies with experience in dealing with such issues. They would be assisted, as we said earlier, if our recommendation for prisoners' "contracts" is implemented.

12.351 Professor Gunn in his report makes a number of recommendations in relation to alcohol and drug abuse and dependency. He recommends improving the training of all prison staff. He suggests greater efforts to co-ordinate and improve practice, which at the present time is "poorly developed, variable and fragmented". The report suggests that every prison receiving drug users should have available a standard opiate withdrawal regime similar to that found at Holloway Prison. The report considers that there is a need for therapeutic community treatment for both drug abusers and alcohol abusers. In relation to drug abusers, it suggests that this should be based on the Grendon model and that it should only be used for a minority of imprisoned drug users. (Although the report refers to a Grendon model, the report also notes that drug abuse is at present regarded as a "contra-indication" to acceptance at Grendon itself.)

12.352 Professor Gunn's report also refers to the need for liaison with treatment agencies in the community. It suggests that part of a prisoner's preparation for release should include offering to put the prisoner in touch with such agencies.

12.353 These recommendations in Professor Gunn's report appear to us to be sensible and we commend them. We would specifically endorse a further suggestion by Professor Gunn that there should be an individual, (we propose a prison officer) who is responsible for coordinating the services provided within a prison establishment and in the locality for drug and alcohol abusers.

The Management of HIV/AIDS

12.354 The Prison Service Medical Directorate provided us with a statement of current Prison Service policy in respect of HIV/AIDS dated March 1990. In summary, this provided that all inmates should be questioned on reception to discover whether they were "high risk". If it appeared that they were such a risk, they were referred to the medical officer for consultation and possible clinical investigation. Blood tests were available to any inmate who requested it, or where the medical officer advised it and the inmate consented. Inmates taking such a test would be counselled. Inmates who proved positive would be placed under a Viral Infectivity Restriction (VIR).

12.355 The policy statement said that staff with an operational need to know were informed of the presence and identity of inmates who had been placed by the medical officer under VIR. Information about such a categorisation might also be made available to the police and others in the Criminal Justice System.

12.356 In a separate note by the Prison Service Medical Directorate, they told us that under VIR arrangements, medical officers had discretion to place some limitations on the regimes for HIV infected prisoners. They should, for example, be in single accommodation, or in accommodation shared with other identified HIV infected prisoners, albeit on ordinary location. Most, if not all, would be excluded from work in the kitchen or other types of work carrying the risk of blood spillage.

12.357 The Medical Directorate told us that they were concerned that too many infected prisoners were kept in the prison hospital, or in a special wing or unit, instead of on normal location. The decision about the location of such prisoners was left to the discretion of local management.

12.358 The evidence we received expressed deep concern about the Prison Service's treatment of HIV prisoners. It was clear, as the Medical Inspectorate accepted, that many prisons were not meeting the Prison Service's own stated policy. This is:

"To provide as normal a prison life as possible for identified HIV infected prisoners who are well".

12.359 The Inquiry visited a small, dingy and airless basement unit at Wandsworth Prison which contained a number of inmates who either had HIV, or who were awaiting the results of HIV tests. Apart from an hour's exercise, visits to the Library and some classes, they were confined to this small area. They had a television and a small amount of weight lifting equipment. The only available work was a small amount of mail-bag sewing. The only redeeming feature of the unit was the apparently caring attitude of the prison officers on duty, who did what they could to alleviate the situation.

12.360 It is hardly any wonder that, given the prospect of such conditions, prisoners who may be concerned about the possibility of having the AIDS virus, may be reluctant to express that concern to the prison authorities. We could not imagine conditions more likely to deter a prisoner from doing all in his power to avoid revealing that he was or might be HIV positive than those we saw at Wandsworth. The conditions were a travesty of justice.

12.361 The aim must be to provide decent treatment and opportunities for HIV prisoners. The first way to achieve this must be by ensuring that staff are fully aware of the extent to which HIV presents a risk to themselves or to other inmates.

12.362 We were impressed with the approach which we saw at Saughton Prison in Edinburgh. The Prison had run an AIDS month during which every member of staff in the prison had received training. Every new recruit received AIDS education. Prison officers were used to train other officers. There were small leaflets available for both staff and inmates. Simple informative posters were in most of the prison wings. The result was that there was not, we understand, the same degree of ostracisation of HIV prisoners as we saw at Wandsworth.

12.363 A local initiative at Bristol Prison has also resulted in a greater awareness by staff of the needs of prisoners with HIV. A network of trained prison officer counsellors has been established. As a result of the programme, we understand that there has been a greater respect for the confidentiality of information about infected prisoners. We would like to see more support and encouragement of initiatives of this kind.

12.364 The Prison Service should give local prison management a clearer remit to meet their responsibilities in the way they deal with AIDS. Area Managers must ensure that the Prison Service's own policy is met. There should be increased efforts to educate prison staff. The examples of good practice we have described might usefully be extended.

12.365 There needs also to be a reassurance for inmates who test positive that they will be given the help and counselling they require. We propose that each prison should ensure that it has the necessary links with AIDS counselling agencies. We envisage such agencies providing skilled assistance to the contribution which prison officers themselves can make to this work.

12.366 The National Aids Trust, the National Aids and Prisons Forum and the National Association of Probation Officers recommended that the Viral Infectivity Restriction (VIR) should be abolished as far as it affected the management of HIV positive prisoners. In addition The National Aids Trust and the Aids and Prisons Consortium Project recommended that there should be a greater degree of confidentiality than exists at present. This evidence suggested that the identification of a prisoner with HIV/AIDS had no relevance outside the medical field. What was needed instead was proper education on health and safety procedures, and the implementation of those procedures.

12.367 We are clear from the evidence we have seen that the identification of prisoners who are HIV positive by placing them under VIR can result in their being unjustifiably segregated. We have received no evidence to justify these restrictions or to suggest that they are a necessary means of protection in prisons.

12.368 We were told that at Saughton Prison in Edinburgh there was no VIR or equivalent regulation and no formal or informal segregation of prisoners with

AIDS and HIV infection. We were impressed too that, when the VIR restriction was withdrawn at Bristol, 24 out of the approximately 500 prisoners at Bristol, were prepared voluntarily to disclose that they were HIV positive. This compared with Wandsworth, where only 12 of approximately 1,700 prisoners had identified themselves as HIV positive.

12.369 We have no evidence either that disclosure – on a "need to know" basis – to wing staff that a prisoner was HIV positive is necessary or desirable. We were told that the Prison Services in Europe (most notably France and Switzerland) applied the normal rules of medical confidentiality. At Saughton we were told that neither the Governor nor the prison officers would be given this information. Only the medical staff knew. If the prisoner was transferred, medical information about him was passed through the normal medical channels.

12.370 HIV positive prisoners must not and need not become the pariahs of the prison system. It is in the interests of the prisoner, the prison in which he is serving his sentence and the public that those prisoners who feel they are at risk of being HIV positive identify themselves and co-operate voluntarily with the carrying out of tests. Prisoners must be able to do so with the knowledge that, if the tests prove positive, they will be helped, not hounded. These must be the central objectives. Unless the Prison Service radically changes its approach there can be no hope of them being met.

12.371 The Prison Service's present policy on confidentiality and VIR is out of accord with the general approach which we have proposed. It could well be counter productive by encouraging prisoners to conceal the extent to which they are at risk. We are not in a position to form a final view on any medical aspects to the present policies. We note, however, that other jurisdictions appear to do well without them. These are matters on which it is clearly necessary to reassure staff and to provide them with clear training and advice. But, ultimately, the Prison Service, on the basis of the best medical advice it can get, must decide the policy. And it must ensure that establishments are not able to flaunt that policy by local practices or agreements.

12.372 We propose that, as soon as possible, there should be a thorough review of the present policies of the Prison Service in relation to HIV. The review should:

a) subject the present policies in respect of VIR and confidentiality to critical examination with a view to setting them aside;

b) identify the action which can be taken by establishments to encourage prisoners who feel that they are at risk of being HIV positive to identify themselves and cooperate voluntarily with the carrying out of tests;

c) draw up a programme of treatment and opportunities for HIV positive prisoners;

d) examine the best practices which already exist within the Prison Service and the Prison Service in Scotland for training prison officers and then draw up proposals to ensure that the best practices are adopted in all establishments;

e) consider the best way of achieving close cooperation between prisons and AIDS counselling agencies.

12.373 When the review has been completed, a new policy on HIV should be announced by the Prison Service. The importance of implementing that policy should be forcefully drawn to the attention of Area Managers and Governors.

Conclusion

12.374 We have in this Section tried to set out a general approach to management within the Prison Service. We have also dealt with a number of specific management problems which we consider require attention. We have not, however, dealt with the extremely worrying problems which exist with regard to the relationship between management and staff. That is a subject with which we will deal in the next Section of this Report. Nor have we dealt with the equally important problem of the difficulties which exist in respect of the relations between prisoners and staff (although the prisoner's "contract" may help here). That is a subject which our proposals in the final Section of this Report should help to address.

12.375   The questions which we have examined in this Section are, however, of central importance, not least to the problems which we address in the following Sections. Unless a change can be make in the tone of management above establishment level, it will be very difficult to achieve better relationships between Governors and staff and between staff and prisoners. The Prison Service is conscious of the need to improve the performance of management. It believes that the recent re-organisation will achieve this purpose. It will certainly have the effect of bringing Headquarters into closer relationship with establishments. However, unless it provides the visible leadership that staff and Governors are looking for, and provides them with the right level of support they need, it will be all the more difficult, if not impossible, substantially to improve the quality of relationships within prisons.

Section 13

Staff

Introduction

13.1   The Inquiry received a considerable volume of written and oral evidence from all grades of staff and their unions. The Inquiry has also had many meetings with members of staff during its visits to establishments. Many letters were also sent to the Inquiry by Prison Service staff. (They are reviewed at Annex 2E.) The Chief Inspector has immense experience of the attitudes of staff as a result of the many inspections of prison establishments which he has carried out.

13.2   The overwhelming impression created by this evidence is that the vast majority of the staff have a deep sense of loyalty to the Prison Service. They have a genuine desire to see conditions for prisoners improve. They would welcome the opportunity to play a much more constructive role within prisons than they do at present. We noted this in Section 12 in considering issues relating to the management of the Prison Service. It is equally relevant here.

13.3   Even before the Strangeways disturbance started, many members of staff (particularly in the larger prison establishments) were deeply disillusioned. They felt undervalued by the public and management. They considered that the Service lacked leadership. Many had initially high expectations of the "Fresh Start" initiative. They had been disappointed with the results. In a number of prison establishments, they were aware that staff/prisoner relations were deteriorating. Instead of respect, there was increasing hostility being directed towards them by a substantial proportion of the prisoners.

13.4   The Strangeways and other disturbances in April 1990 made the situation worse. This was true for the staff who were actually involved in those disturbances. It was true also for the staff at other establishments. Some of these establishments had very similar conditions. They felt the same thing could very easily happen there. Many were deeply shocked by what they saw at the scenes of the disturbances or on television. There was an understandable feeling of insecurity.

13.5   This was vividly explained to the Inquiry by some of the members of the staff at Durham prison. They described how they had to steel themselves to attend the prison at weekends. They were frightened of what would happen within the prison at weekends because there were so few staff on duty. (This state of fear was confirmed by the Governor of that prison during one of our public seminars.)

13.6   It is most undesirable that staff should have this feeling of insecurity and lack of confidence. There is much that staff can take pride in. They should be proud of the way in which they handled the difficult situation in many prisons before the disturbances. They should be proud of the way in which most conducted themselves during the disturbances.

13.7   These problems of insecurity must be tackled urgently if there is to be any real prospect of introducing the improvements to our prison system which are needed. Staff in this state of mind are unable to play their proper role.

13.8   We propose that management should make a clear statement announcing a change of emphasis in the priorities and management style of the Prison Service. We have already in Section 12 referred to the need for management to adopt a clearly supportive role towards establishments. In addition, there should be a change away from concentrating, or appearing to concentrate almost exclusively, on improving the machinery of management and on introducing new management techniques. The change would involve management attaching greater significance to management/staff relations. It should involve developing the role of staff, and in particular of prison officers, both in respect of their work in prisons and of their links with the wider community.

13.9   Management must make it clear to staff that in a modern Prison Service, the role of the prison officer must not be confined to the unlocking and locking of cells. It should be a skilled professional role within a disciplined service. It should involve the constructive care of prisoners. It should involve preparing them to return to the community in ways which will make it less likely that they will re-offend.

13.10   There has also to be a constructive and responsive attitude on the part of staff and their respective unions in relation to this change of emphasis by management. At the present, the field of industrial relations is pitted and scarred by the debris of numerous battles. Industrial relations have to move on to new ground. There has to be greater trust, respect and goodwill on both sides. Unless there is the necessary sense of respect between staff and management, there is unlikely to be the necessary sense of respect between prisoners and staff which is an essential feature of any successful Prison Service.

13.11   Our recommendation in Section 11 for separate and secure small units within larger establishments should help to restore the confidence of staff in their physical safety. Our recommendation in Section 12 that managers should support staff and "enable" them to perform their task of looking after prisoners should also help. The object is to achieve an atmosphere in which relationships between staff and management can improve. In this Section of the Report we identify a number of other steps which could be taken to achieve the same objective.

The "Fresh Start" Package

13.12   The "Fresh Start" initiative was introduced in 1987. It involved a fundamental reorganisation of prison officers' working arrangements and of management within establishments. It was intended to increase the job satisfaction of prison officers and to improve their relations with management.

13.13   "Fresh Start" contained many needed reforms. It provided an important platform for developments in the future. But, so far, it has failed to achieve its potential. This is, at least, in part due to the way in which it was introduced.

13.14   Professor King carried out a survey in a cross-section of prison establishments. In his written evidence to the Inquiry he concluded that:

"Whatever the merits of Fresh Start - and there are many - it was introduced in a manner that has left a legacy of deep seated mistrust between staff in the field and the Home Office. There seems little doubt that it has produced some improvements in line management and accountability although it has exacerbated problems of lateral and functional communication. As a result, they (staff) no longer feel identified with their institution let alone the Service and have become more compartmentalised. While staff have welcomed the package on hours and pay they report much less job satisfaction. The changes have done nothing to unify the Service, and it is evident that industrial relations problems have not gone away."

13.15 A title for a section of the Prison Officers' Association's evidence on industrial relations is "Them and Us". This title encapsulates part of the problem between staff and management. It is a problem which has clearly continued despite the "Fresh Start" reforms.

13.16 In order to appreciate why the situation is so unsatisfactory, and to identify possible ways in which the situation can be improved, it is necessary to understand why it was thought that a new staff initiative was necessary, the broad objectives of the initiative, "a Fresh Start", and how it was implemented.

i) The Nature of the "Fresh Start" Package, Why It Was Necessary and Its Objectives

13.17 "Fresh Start" was intended to be a bold and imaginative new initiative which would provide the much needed radical reform of the way in which prison establishments were managed and operated. The May Committee had considered that one of the major problems in the management of prisons was the excessive reliance on overtime. This was associated with the way an establishment was complemented and with the organisation of shift systems.

13.18 Prior to the implementation of "Fresh Start", there were two systems for arranging staff attendance. One was the Vee Scheme, which was designed to meet the special needs of local prisons. It provided a high level of staff attendance in the morning to conduct escorts, and a lower level of scheduled attendance in the evenings and at the weekends. The other was the Functional Group System which applied within training prisons, detention centres and Borstals.

13.19 The basic working week was 40 hours. Under the Vee Scheme, management could require officers to work up to 10 hours overtime each week. In fact, under both schemes, many more extra hours were worked. On average, officers worked 56 hours a week. Some officers regularly worked 70 hours a week. Overtime was endemic. It was relied upon as an alternative to recruiting extra staff and as a way of raising the level of staff take-home pay.

13.20 The need to maintain earnings by working overtime led to the widespread adoption of what were known as "Old Spanish Customs". They were of labyrinthine complexity. They were used to justify a massive quantity of overtime working.

13.21 There were, from time to time, attempts to improve the position (eg the centrally driven Manpower Control Project in 1970). But they floundered. They failed partly because of the complexity of the staff working patterns and requirements. These had been able to grow "like Topsy", because there was no objective standard establishing the range and quality of the activities to be performed in each type of establishment. Activities and arrangements differed from establishment to establishment. They were largely determined by the Governor and the local branch of the Prison Officers' Association.

13.22 The attempts to resolve the problems also failed because the reliance on overtime meant that the Prison Officers' Association were in an extremely powerful position. They could and did threaten that their members would reduce the period of overtime worked if changes were in prospect which were not thought to be in their members' interests. Since the running of the prisons depended on overtime, this was a powerful threat.

13.23 A further problem was the gulf which existed between the governor class and the prison officer class within prison establishments. They were separately recruited. They had distinct career patterns. There was little movement between them. The two classes led to fragmented areas of command. As the Prison Service says in its written evidence:

"Security and control issues gravitated towards the officers, headed by the Chief Officer, and regime and conditions issues towards the junior Governors. There was effectively a split between resource management and control of output.

339

What resulted was a structure of working practices which bore little relation to the needs and outputs of the Service. Increasing overtime did not improve productivity. All the signs were that on average prison regimes had deteriorated significantly during the 1970's and early 1980's."

13.24   During 1985/1986 the Prison Service commissioned a joint study with the firm of PA Consultants to analyse the situation. The study concluded that the Service could be maintained at the existing regime level with an immediate reduction of 15% to 20% in total officers' hours worked. The study team estimated that the extra capacity "could be between 10% and 30% or more in any particular establishment, probably around 15-20% for the Service as a whole". This reduction depended on the redesign of shift systems so that they matched the needs of the work to be carried out within an establishment.

13.25   Based on the PA/Prison Service study, and taking into account an earlier Internal Review of Management Structures and a Joint Home Office-Treasury re-examination of pay arrangements, the "Fresh Start" package of reforms was prepared. The package was complex and far reaching. It had three central themes:

i)   new working arrangements and management structures;

ii)   the creation of a unified single structure in place of the existing officer and governor classes; and

iii) a considerable improvement in salaries to be accompanied by an initial reduction in and subsequently the elimination of overtime.

a) The New Working Arrangements and Management Structures

13.26   A principal feature was that work should be organised in what the Prison Service describes as "functional blocks". These blocks were intended to provide clearly defined individual responsibilities and lines of accountability. The "blocks" were to be broken down into work groups, each the responsibility of a designated group manager. The same staff were to be deployed to each group who together would have a shared responsibility for meeting the group objectives. The proposal involved reducing the number of management tiers. It was intended that the package would unify control and responsibility for the management of resources and for productivity at all levels.

13.27   Many members of staff were in favour of the continuity in working which "Group Working" provided. But the Inquiry received complaints from staff that Group Working isolated them from staff working in other groups within the establishment. It was suggested that this resulted in a reduction in teamwork.

b) Unification of the Governor and Officer Grades

13.28   The existing governor grades and prison officer grades were to be replaced by a single unified system. This was to involve staff in grades numbered 1 to 8. Grades 1, 2 and 3 are the equivalent of Governors 1, 2 and 3. Grades 6, 7 and 8 are the equivalent of the existing Principal Officer, Senior Officer and Prison Officer grades. The grade of Assistant Governor and of Chief Officer I both became Grade 4. The grade of Chief Officer II and Assistant Governor II both became Grade 5.

13.29   In practice, this meant the abolition of the uniformed Chief Officer. He had traditionally played within the Prison Service very much the role of the Regimental Sergeant Major in the Army. His office was central to the way prisons were managed. The Chief Officer I, in particular, was held in high esteem by both officers and governors. The Inquiry received many expressions of regret for his demise.

c) The Abolition of Overtime to be Compensated for by Increased Pay

13.30   The "Fresh Start" proposals involved the complete phasing out of overtime. All grades were also to be salaried. So far as the new officer grades were concerned, they would have a conditioned 39 hour week in place of the previous conditioned 40 hour week. In addition, these grades were entitled initially to contract to work a further nine hours each week. This would qualify them for the Group Working Contracted Hours allowance. Not less than two days per week (at least one of which was to be a weekend day) were to be free from scheduled duty (in other words, rest days). Officers were not to be required to attend for scheduled duty on consecutive weekends, unless this was provided for under an approved local agreement.

13.31 It was possible on some weeks for an officer to work more than his weekly hours because of (a) unavoidable attendance (eg delay in returning from external duty or because of travelling time where part or all of the travelling time was outside the scheduled hours of the shift); (b) emergency attendance; (c) special attendance (eg the need exceptionally to be present for an adjudication or interview); and (d) having to ensure that minimum staffing levels were maintained.

13.32 Additional hours of this nature were to be met by time off in lieu (TOIL). There was, however, a provision to make ex gratia payments to staff following the attendance of the majority of available staff during a protracted emergency. (These payments were made in respect of the April disturbances.)

13.33 The nine additional contracted hours were to be phased out over five years. This was to be achieved under a framework agreement. The agreement was to require one hour to be phased out from 1 April 1988, followed by two hours from 1 April of each of the succeeding four years. From April 1992 all prison officers were, therefore, to be on a 39 hour week. As the additional hours were phased out, the Contracted Hours allowance was incorporated into basic pay (which was also to be increased each year) at half the current rate.

13.34 The Prison Service did not intend to replace all the contracted hours which were to be eliminated. The Service was to replace half the reduction in contracted hours by engaging additional staff. The rest was intended to be met by greater efficiency.

13.35 As the contracted hours were reduced, the Prison Service would therefore save the cost of one hour for every two hours lost. Eventually, the saving would amount to the equivalent of 4.5 working hours (50% of nine hours) for each officer.

13.36 In order to finance the considerably enhanced remuneration involved in the "Fresh Start" package, the Prison Service had agreed with the Treasury that there would be substantial efficiency savings. The savings fell into two categories. There was to be first an immediate saving of 15%, that being the lower percentage identified as immediately achievable by the PA/Prison Service Review. Secondly, there was to be a further reduction of 9% to reflect the Prison Service's view of what further savings should be possible. Together, the requirement, therefore, was that the Prison Service should achieve through efficiency a 24% saving in the use of staff hours over the five year period.

13.37 The agreement with the Treasury initially required the 15% improvement in efficiency to be achieved immediately on 31 March 1988 (by reducing the hours worked). It was recognised at an early stage, however, that this would be impracticable. The requirement was too stringent. It was, therefore, agreed that the 15% reduction in hours should be phased over three years. The targets were: 12% by 31 March 1988; 14% by 31 March 1989; and the final 1% by 31 March 1990. These targets were achieved. They were achieved by reducing the previous average of 56 weekly hours worked by prison officers to a new maximum of 48 hours and by controlling national recruitment levels. None of these hours was replaced by the deployment of newly recruited staff.

13.38 The efficiencies were not, therefore, limited to 15%. Nor were they limited to the 20% which was the upper percentage identified by the Prison Service/PA Study. As we have said, the targeted improvement in efficiency agreed with the Treasury was 24%. The way this is explained in the evidence on behalf of the Prison Service is as follows:

> "The framework and implementation efficiencies combine to give a target improvement by 1992/93 of around 24%. This reflects the PA Study's assessment of what could be achieved initially (15-20%) plus a managerial view of what could be expected to accrue in time as the new structures began to yield cumulative dividends."

ii) The Scope for Efficiency Savings

13.39   The POA in its written evidence disputes the assertion that there were at least 15% inefficiencies in the use of staff hours prior to the introduction of "Fresh Start". It points out that techniques which measure, for example, the flow of a car assembly line, cannot be related to the running of a prison. It points out, as an example, that the time taken when dealing with any particular inmate depends on the type of inmate and the nature of his problems.

13.40   The Association also points out that no attempt was made to ascertain that the approved staffing levels were set at the correct level. Nor was any appraisal made about whether the 15% efficiencies would ensure that the "staff in post" corresponded to the approved staffing levels at each establishment. The Association also argues that a theoretical inmate/staff ratio has no basis in reality because prisons function 24 hours a day seven days a week and officers work shifts, are subject to rest days and have off every other weekend.

13.41   These contentions of the POA have to be considered in the context of the steps which were taken by the Prison Service to determine the complements of establishments before implementing "Fresh Start". The Prison Service's written evidence deals with this. It states that before the introduction of "Fresh Start" the complement of prison officers for each establishment was determined by P6 Division in Headquarters on the basis of recommendations from Regional Directors.

13.42   The Prison Service was clearly not over-impressed by the Regional Directors' recommendations. The evidence says that the recommendations were based on inspections of establishments by regional manpower teams:

> "The results were, inevitably, subjective in the absence of clear and common organisational structures and they tended to be influenced by the overtime culture which then pervaded the Service".

13.43   The Prison Service evidence states:

> "In preparation for the changeover to the new arrangements, establishments were visited by Fresh Start review teams from regional offices. These teams which usually included an Assistant Regional Director and members of the regional manpower team, examined each establishment's requirement under the Fresh Start organisation structure and recommended a complement of governors, officers and other staff. The initial reviews of establishments were conducted at considerable speed and produced recommendations which were inconsistent with the implementation efficiency savings which had been identified in the PA/Prison Service study and which were integral to the Home Office/Treasury deal with the POA. This was one reason why it was decided, with Treasury agreement, to reschedule delivery of the planned efficiency gains."

13.44   The "Fresh Start review teams" were the existing regional manpower teams (also referred to in the quotation) augmented by an Assistant Regional Director.

13.45   It is apparent from the evidence that the exercise was not in accord with what the PA/Prison Service study had envisaged. Because of the desire to introduce the package expeditiously, an exercise which would have an important influence on the implementation of the package was not carried out satisfactorily. It was hurried and superficial. This was symptomatic of many aspects associated with the implementation of the "Fresh Start" package. Speed was of the essence. Matters of detail were intended to be sorted out later. It is necessary therefore to examine carefully the way the "Fresh Start" package was implemented. We do so in the paragraphs which follow.

13.46   The problems in relation to these efficiency savings were, therefore, as follows. First, since there appears not to have been a proper examination of the needs of each individual establishment, the efficiencies had to be achieved from the existing staff complements in any particular prison, regardless of whether those complements were or were not appropriate.

13.47   Secondly, the staffing inefficiencies which may have existed in different prisons were by no means uniform. Some prisons had been better managed than others. Within a well managed prison, the staff were likely already to be used efficiently. In which case, the 15% staff reductions, which were needed to achieve the necessary efficiencies, would bear hard upon that establishment. Even in the case of inefficient establishments, there were often problems, such as long term absenteeism, which it could not be hoped would be remedied overnight. The "Fresh Start" savings made no allowance for such problems.

13.48   The evidence before the Inquiry makes it clear that Governor grades shared these perceptions. One submission was from a Governor representing the views of all governor grades in his establishment. It states that:

> "regrettably, the basic calculation for savings was required of all establishments whether they had already achieved efficiencies, whether they had specialised functions, whether they were Category B, Category C or Category D establishments; whether they had a good record of staff sickness or a bad record. Sensible implementation would have allowed for all of these differences – a blanket saving was however required,....."

13.49   This was not quite the position. It was alleviated by Regional Directors being allowed to vary the arrangements at particular establishments, so long as across the Region as a whole, they delivered the necessary saving. This was an improvement. But the extent to which it assisted depended on how efficient the Region as a whole was. It depended also on the accuracy of the Regional Office's perceptions of the comparative efficiency of each of its establishments.

iii) How "Fresh Start" was Implemented

13.50   The submission from the Governors which we have just quoted also points out that the "Fresh Start" package "was marketed exceptionally well throughout the Service". The submission then states:

> "The full implications of the package, and clearer and often new interpretations, followed implementation, and this resulted in prison governors and prison officers believing that the Prison Department had 'moved the goalposts', and reneged on parts of the deal. This led to many Prison Service staff becoming resentful, feeling that they had been cheated and that they had been the victims of the use of 'weasel words'."

13.51   The Inquiry takes the view that this last paragraph accurately reflects the feelings of a substantial part of the Prison Service about the manner in which "Fresh Start" was implemented. We consider that these feelings are understandable.

13.52   On 3 April 1987, the Prison Service issued Bulletin No. 8. The Bulletin set out the details of the "Fresh Start" in its improved form. That Bulletin, including appendices, covered 28 pages in small but legible print. The Prison Service also published a simpler and shorter document called "A Fresh Start – the Revised Offer". There were also a number of other publications concerning "Fresh Start".

13.53   The "Fresh Start" package was the subject of a promotional campaign in the Prison Service. It was put to the Prison Service in May 1987 and was overwhelmingly accepted in Union ballots (over 90% of the Governors and over 80% of the officers being in favour).

13.54   It was not surprising that the new arrangements were welcomed. They involved considerably improved pay for fewer hours work. And the work was to be performed in a more socially acceptable way. On average, in 1990, a prison officer earned £16,000 for a 43 hour week (£18,000 in London) with a further pay rise pending on 1 April 1991. There were pay increases also for the more senior grades. In addition, officers living in quarters could apply for an interest free advance of salary to assist in purchasing quarters repayable over ten years. Alternatively, officers were able to buy their quarters at a discount.

13.55   There were also pension benefits. The shorter pamphlet ("Fresh Start -The Revised Offer") said that under the framework agreement "as officers' average working hours reduce from 48 to 39, the Group Working Contracted Hours allowance would be progressively absorbed into basic pay and therefore become pensionable".

13.56   Appendix B of that pamphlet states that:

> "for these guaranteed annual reductions in hours and pay increases, staff will be expected to contribute increased efficiency by accepting that present levels of workload will be undertaken with increases in staffing levels equivalent to half of the capacity represented by the number of hours lost each year."

13.57   Nothing else was stated in that document about the need for efficiency or the required reduction in hours. In particular, there was nothing in that document, or in Bulletin 8, about the substantial increase in efficiency which would be required to compensate for the reduction in working hours from an average of 56 hours to 48 hours.

13.58   With regard to the 15% efficiency figure, the Prison Service in its written evidence states:

> "The POA have for some time now maintained a position of rejecting the analysis of national officer staffing levels inherent in the hours reforms. This is formulated in a contention that the 15% implementation efficiencies were never an agreed part of the Fresh Start package. This does not tell the whole story. Although the efficiencies were not formally part of the agreement they were fully understood by both sides in the course of the negotiations leading up to Fresh Start. It was made clear that the initial reduction to a 48 hour week – the removal, in effect, of the hours which were judged to have been wasted under the old system – would not be at the expense of safety, security and regime levels. The PA study was explicit that the 15% reduction in officer hours could be delivered while maintaining and even improving outputs. It was also quite clear that there was no commitment to additional recruitment to replace any of the hours lost through the reduction to a 48 hour week in contrast with the explicit words in Bulletin 8 about the additional recruitment which would operate to compensate for half of the reduction in hours from 48 to 39 during the framework agreement."

13.59   This version of the facts has not been challenged by the evidence submitted by the POA. The POA, when asked to comment on this subject, sent to the Inquiry on 7 January 1991 an extract from an eight page document which they sent to their members prior to the vote on "Fresh Start".

13.60   This document indicates that the POA were unclear about the effect of the 15%/20% efficiency savings on staffing levels. This document did not make the position clear to their members, but went on to describe a "least favourable method" of interpreting the facts. This would result in "the intended saving of 15% to 20% identified by the PA Management Consultants".

13.61   The Prison Service, in a letter to the Inquiry dated 19 December 1990 and in response to our request, makes a number of points to explain its presentation of the efficiency savings. We do not propose to set these out here because they do not provide a justification for our concern as to the manner in which "Fresh Start" was implemented. They do, however, rightly draw attention to the fact that the efficiencies were only one aspect of the "Fresh Start" package. The Prison Service also points out that Bulletin 12, issued on 28 October 1987 after the package had been accepted by staff, explained that the efficiency target in 1987-88 had been reduced from 15% to 10%, and that the "starting assumption" of the PA Study, that 15% savings could be gained, meant that the 15% "ought to be achieved with staff in post".

13.62   The clear impression which emerges from studying the relevant documents is that, in order to obtain approval of a package of much needed reforms, the Prison Service was not anxious to draw attention to the extent of the efficiencies involved. In our view this was unfortunate. It contributed in part to the misunderstandings which existed across the board among staff and governors as to what was involved in implementing the "Fresh Start" package.

13.63   In addition, it is apparent from the evidence which was received by the Inquiry, that staff and governors were generally under the impression that the reduction in contracted hours worked at each establishment would be compensated for by the provision of new staff to be deployed at that establishment to make up for 50% of the reduction. In fact this was not the intention of the Prison Service. The intention was that the reduced hours would be replaced in the way that senior management (at that time Regions) considered would be appropriate. The Inquiry was constantly being told when visiting establishments that the Prison Service had not kept to its promise to provide them with more staff. Nationally, however, the Service could show the necessary increase had been provided. The general impression which staff and governors had was that staff resources were reduced to a much greater extent than they had envisaged. This produced a considerable degree of cynicism of the Prison Service's motive in introducing the package.

13.64   This degree of cynicism is understandable. The Inquiry received evidence from a Governor who was very much involved in training governing Governors and senior staff in preparation for the introduction of "Fresh Start". He records how, following the acceptance of the "Fresh Start" proposals, adverse feeling about "Fresh Start" quickly diminished. It was replaced by enthusiasm and demands for more information.

13.65   The training Governor was asked by staff where were the staff going to come from to replace those staff which would be lost as a result of staff working fewer hours. He reassured them. Staff believed the assurances which he and others gave because they were trusted and because the information on which the answers were based came from the appropriate division of Headquarters. He himself had no appreciation of the true level of economies which were being demanded. That was why he gave misleading answers. He states that it was only later that he became aware, as the result of a change of duties, that it was intended that there was to be a 10% reduction in the level of staff across the region he was then working in. As he put it, this had:

> "the effect of making a lie out of all the training that had been given to senior staff and group managers".

13.66   The training Governor goes on to say that over the following two years he had on numerous occasions to defend his credibility, and explain why he had told establishments "a pack of lies". He states that it was only with the publication of Briefing No. 17 in January 1990 that the correct position was fully set out about the 15% efficiency.

13.67   Briefing No.17 states under the heading "Efficiency Targets" the following:

"The new working arrangements introduced with Fresh Start were designed to help the Service to work more efficiently. *The offer that was finally made to staff and accepted overwhelmingly*, was based on achieving 15% efficiencies in staffing through more flexible working practices on the move to 'Fresh Start'. In addition the framework agreement requires more efficiency savings...." (emphasis added).

13.68   Even Briefing No.17 can be criticised, however, as misleading. Staff had not been told that the offer was based on "achieving 15% efficiencies". 15% efficiencies were not part of the offer which was accepted overwhelmingly, as the Briefing No.17 clearly suggests. Some members of staff may have deduced this because they knew the PA Report had suggested that there were 15%/20% inefficiencies, but they were not told. We do not know what percentage of staff would have voted for the package if they had been told of the 15% efficiencies. We judge, however, that they would still have voted in favour of the package because it was in their interest and in the interest of the Service that they should do so.

13.69   In general and simplified terms, the effect on Prison Service staffing levels of the requirement to achieve initially a 15% efficiency saving with no compensating increase in staff appears to be as follows:

i)   on 31 March 1987 there were 17,315 prison officers in post. They worked an average of 56 hours per week. During the initial period of "Fresh Start" the hours per week per officer were reduced from an average of 56 hours to a maximum of 48 hours. This meant that the 17,315 officers were working on average for eight hours less per week. Multiplying 17,315 by 8 produces a total reduction of 138,524 hours worked each week;

ii)   if one then divides that 138,524 by 48, assuming all the 17,315 officers opted to work the contracted nine hours, the loss is equal to 2,885 fewer officers on duty.

13.70   This level of saving in hours worked involved, therefore, a substantial reduction in the availability of staff. It is for this reason that we stress that it would have been preferable for the Prison Service to have made clear what were the implications of this aspect of the package. Bulletin 8, and in particular the publication by the Prison Service, "A Fresh Start' – the Revised Offer", should have drawn attention to the consequences of the reduction in the availability of staff which was to be needed to achieve the required efficiencies. It should not have stressed only the very attractive features of the package in relation to increases in salary and other benefits. If there is to be the necessary confidence maintained between staff and management, both must be frank and fair with each other.

iv) Regime Effects   13.71   There was also a problem because the promised improvements to regimes did not materialise. In many establishments, Governors and their staff were distressed to find that they were not, as they had anticipated, able to improve conditions for inmates. The reality of "Fresh Start" did not in practice live up to the rhetoric. There was no enhancement of regimes and no increase in job satisfaction.

13.72   Since 24% efficiencies were required to be achieved across the board over a five year period, mostly by reductions in staffing levels, it is clear that little, if any, improvement in regime would be likely to result from the "Fresh Start" package. In particular, improvements in regime would be difficult if not impossible to achieve in establishments which were already efficient in the use of the available staff. Reductions in staffing levels in those establishments were likely to result in a reduction in regimes.

13.73   This conclusion was confirmed by the evidence of staff who wrote to the Inquiry. The Inquiry analysed 242 letters received from staff which addressed the possible causes of the disturbances. By far, the greatest number (122) regarded staff shortages as being a cause of the disturbance. (See the fuller analysis in Annex 2E.)

v) Effects on Non-unified Staff

13.74   The non-unified staff, who were not covered by "Fresh Start", were also aggrieved by its introduction. Their pay and conditions of work were left behind. It was intended to have a "Fresh Start" Part II to cover non-unified staff. But the reality was much more modest than this group of staff had expected.

13.75   Their expectations were disappointed. As a result, they felt devalued and unfairly treated.

vi) Evidence from the Prison Governors' Association

13.76   The written evidence submitted by the Prison Governors' Association is highly critical of the "Fresh Start" package as a whole. We identify it separately because it summarises a number of the criticisms referred to above and because, coming from prison governors, it carries particular weight. The evidence states:

> "It is true that the basic pay has increased and that there is more time off work but much of what the Prison Officer admired and respected in the Prison Service has disappeared. The strong tradition of respect for authority which was personified in the Governor and Chief Officer has disappeared......Any man or woman who saw the pinnacle of their careers in the rank of Chief Officer now find that they can only realistically hope to achieve the junior governor grade ranks. They believe they have lost so much status and received so little in return.
>
> The new structure is intended to give group identity and loyalty but often leads to fragmentation. Officers do not work overtime but build up large amounts of TOIL. The regime and quality of life that they strive for on behalf of their inmates has in nearly all establishments diminished. The increase in staff the Department constantly proclaims has been eaten up by new establishments and so many long established prisons do not have enough staff to preserve the pre-Fresh Start regime, let alone implement an enhanced regime. Officers do not proclaim greater job satisfaction. In return for an individual shorter working week they see worse conditions for their inmates and lower staffing levels, leading to unsafe conditions. To top this off, they are tired of the Prison Service HQ failing, as they see it, to honour its promises and commitments. In short morale and confidence has been undermined."

13.77   With regard to the non-unified staff the evidence adds:

> "All these staff are a valuable resource and they have been alienated by the callous treatment handed out to them. Fresh Start had begun a process of unifying the Service, but the process was cut short before it had hardly begun. Those who have been left out in the cold, naturally feel that all they have to offer is second class and unappreciated. Be they industrial staff, farm staff, administration staff, whatever, they feel let down. If ever there were an example of poor personnel policy, the treatment of these staff must come high on the list."

13.78   That the Prison Governor's Association should put forward evidence in these terms gives rise to serious concern. It confirms that there is a management problem in relation to staff of the highest order which has to be addressed.

vii) Conclusion

13.79   Nothing that we have said in criticising the implementation of "Fresh Start" should be interpreted as a conclusion that it was misconceived. On the contrary, "Fresh Start" was much needed. The problems lay in the speed of its implementation and in the information provided to staff.

13.80   "Fresh Start" involved a substantial organisational change. Its too rapid implementation created a danger of managerial capacity being overstretched and staff tolerance being adversely affected. In the long term, this could prove very disadvantageous. Professor King's survey identified a drop in job satisfaction following the implementation of "Fresh Start". The reaction of staff was typified by members of staff indicating that "Fresh Start is great but the job is rubbish", or "the job is flat – it is like a bottle of pop with the fizz taken out". These are all indications that there was inadequate preparation and that the pace of change was too fast.

13.81 If the introduction of "Fresh Start" had not been so hurried and had been more sensitively implemented, and if management had been franker, possibly it could have achieved the improvements needed, without causing the disillusionment which in fact has resulted.

13.82 We have no doubt, therefore, that there were inefficiencies within the Prison Service which needed tackling. The overtime position was wholly unacceptable. There were a myriad of undesirable restrictive practices. Whatever the shortcoming of the way in which "Fresh Start" was implemented, both staff and governors, when pressed on the subject, would not wish to return to the pre-"Fresh Start" situation. They agree that basically "Fresh Start's" conceptual framework is sound and offers a constructive way forward.

13.83 However, if the benefits which should flow from "Fresh Start" are to be achieved, there is now a critical need to restore the confidence of governors and staff in the package. It is necessary to deal sensitively with the concerns which staff and governors still have about the consequences of "Fresh Start".

A Framework for Determining Appropriate Staffing Levels

13.84 Disputes over what should be the correct staffing levels within the Prison Service are nothing new. The proper complement for a prison establishment was a matter of controversy at the time of the May Committee's work. It remains so. So far, "Fresh Start's" contribution has been to exacerbate rather than resolve the problem.

13.85 In the course of the evidence during Part I of the Inquiry, and on visits to establishments, the Inquiry was told that, if there were only a relatively small number of extra staff at a particular prison, this would make all the difference between an over-taut manning level and a manageable one. While a perception of this sort may be a useful starting point, there must be a more structured approach to the problem. Without such an approach, arguments about staffing levels will continue to poison relations between staff and management. Those establishments which are most aggressive and strident in their demands will continue to appear to achieve the most generous allocation of resources.

13.86 The bulk of the cost of keeping someone in prison is accounted for by staffing costs. Of those staffing costs, approximately 70% are uniformed staff costs. It is, therefore, worthwhile devoting considerable time to allocating staff correctly.

13.87 The Prison Service stated in its evidence that by early 1989 it was clear to the Service that there was a need for a "rigorous initiative to evaluate work". It was necessary for management to identify and define work, to set standards and to monitor performance. It was crucial that a methodology was designed to ensure work was efficiently organised and resourced. The Prison Service proposed to achieve this by developing the analysis of the corporate objectives which were incorporated into the "contracts" between Area Managers and establishments which we referred to in Section 12.

13.88 The system involved breaking down the "functional blocks" of work in establishments and identifying the resources necessary to carry out that work. It involved then identifying each constituent element of the work involved, and giving to each element an average time value. This was to be assessed, preferably, in consultation with the staff actually doing the work and the appropriate trade union. Obviously there is room for differing views as to how long a particular task would take, but the Prison Service stressed that it was concerned with ascertaining "average times which reflect a wide range of actual possibilities".

13.89 When the work had been assessed in this way, the necessary staff attendance would be calculated so as to cover the work efficiently. It is said by the Prison Service that, although the process is work driven, it still allows for the legitimate expectations of staff that their work should be well organised, that they should have quality jobs, that shift systems should be "user friendly" and that work patterns should provide a good sequence of work and rest days.

13.90 This corporate objective process was launched in April 1990. The Prison Service acknowledges that much still remains to be done to ensure that the process is understood and applied rigorously in each establishment. However, the aim is for every establishment to have completed the procedure by 30 September 1991.

13.91 The Prison Service states that "regrettably at this time the Prison Officers' Association is urging its members not to cooperate with the process". The Prison Service says:

> "This is unfortunate in that the methodology provides what is critically lacking in the Service at the present time – a common language about work and resources. Put differently, it is the only means by which it will be possible to determine authoritatively whether the Prison Service is correctly staffed for its duties or not. Until the process has been completed, claims that there are staff shortages will remain unsubstantiated."

13.92 We agree with the Prison Service that it is unfortunate that the POA are not cooperating, a subject to which we will return later. We agree also with the Prison Service that some sort of exercise of this nature is essential. It is needed to achieve a sensible approach to staffing levels and in order to resolve the present deadlock. It is an exercise to which the POA can make a contribution. They can draw attention to the features of the prison officer's work which have to be taken into account in arriving at the appropriate average time figure to be introduced into the equation. The exercise offers opportunities to the members of the POA, which we understand they would welcome, to influence the development of a more positive programme for prisoner activity, to enhance the role of prison officers and to improve working conditions.

13.93 The Prison Service's method of seeking to achieve appropriate levels of complementing establishments has been vigorously criticised in the evidence to the Inquiry, in particular from the POA. But no better alternative has been proposed to the Inquiry. The POA suggest there should be a return to the system for establishing staff levels which existed before "Fresh Start". However, it would be unrealistic to apply a pre-"Fresh Start" mechanism to the changed situation which now exists as a result of the implementation of "Fresh Start". Furthermore, it is clear to the Inquiry that the method which was used pre-"Fresh Start" did not work effectively. There is no reason to think that what it could not achieve in the past, it will achieve now.

Staffing Levels at Weekends

13.94 We have already pointed out that the disturbances which this Inquiry has investigated occurred at weekends. Although at other establishments the disturbances were not of the same intensity, the evidence shows that, when an establishment expected trouble, they usually expected it over a week-end. One reason for this is that staffing levels are almost invariably at their most taut at weekends. Whether they are *too* low at a particular establishment will depend on what should be the complement at that establishment. We express no view on that without a proper assessment having been made.

13.95 Where staffing levels at weekends are lower than they are during the week (as they almost always are) this usually results in a reduction in inmate activities or activities being carried out with less supervision. If activities are cut down, then this results in the inmates becoming frustrated. If there is less supervision, there is more opportunity to give vent to frustrations which already exist. In either event, inmates are more likely to take advantage of the reduced staff presence to create a disturbance, if this is what they are minded to do.

13.96   An example of the effects of inappropriate staffing levels at weekends was provided by the report of a short inspection by Her Majesty's Inspectorate of Prisons in March 1990 at Stocken. The report points out that the staffing system seems to have been designed to maximise staff presence during the weekdays and to provide minimum cover at weekends. It produced 12 senior officers on evening duties during the week and only two at weekends. As a result of this minimal cover, there was no evening association at weekends.

13.97   We propose that the Prison Service should aim to achieve a situation where an appropriate programme of weekend activities should not be restricted by lack of staff on duty.

13.98   The Prison Service has to look after prisons and prisoners seven days a week, not five. The prisoners' needs are not reduced because it is a weekend. On the contrary, because workshops will be closed and because it is easier for families to make visits at weekends, the prisoners' demands on staff can be greater at weekends. Against this, there are, however, duties, such as escort duties, which are not usually required at weekends. The proper staffing levels at weekends need to be determined in the light of these factors and the guiding principle which we have proposed.

13.99   In order to decide the scale of the manning problem at weekends, taking account of the opportunities offered to prisoners at weekends and the staffing levels provided, an assessment has to be made of the position at the present time. According to the contributions which were made at the public seminar on these matters, no such assessment has yet taken place. Regime monitoring arrangements do not help in identifying regime activities provided at weekends as opposed to during the week. We propose therefore that an assessment should now be made of the management of prisons over the weekend. When the scale of the problem has been clarified it should be easier to determine what action should be taken to deal with weekends.

13.100   One of the features of "Fresh Start" was the commitment to provide staff with one weekend in two off duty. This is a commitment which we would regard as entirely proper. Staff who want to have weekends off duty should be entitled to do so.

13.101   Mr Fittall (Head of DPF1 in the Prison Service) said at one of our public seminars, that, as a result of other features of "Fresh Start":

> "We have moved very suddenly from a situation where the staff had strong incentives to work weekends, there was a lot of financial advantage in terms of double time and so on in being at work at weekends, to a situation in which staff have a strong incentive to want to be off work at anti-social times."

13.102   This has resulted in some establishments agreeing to arrangements with staff whereby they are only on duty one weekend in three (eg Lincoln) or one weekend in four (eg Durham). While it is possible with a "very vigilant managerial grip over the deployment of staff" (Mr Fittall's words) to have a satisfactory regime with one weekend in two off duty, we do not consider that it is possible to run a satisfactory regime with *more* than one weekend in two off duty, unless the staff who are absent are replaced by some other means.

13.103   Mr Mogg, the Governor of Durham, thought that one solution was to provide incentives for people to work at weekends. Another suggestion which has been made was that part time officers should be used at weekends. There could be a range of contract arrangements covering different quantities of hours, with different terms, for work at weekends, evenings or at nights, designed to suit both individuals and establishments.

13.104 Greater flexibility is required if the objective is to be met in a way which meets the domestic needs of full-time staff. We would hope the POA might therefore support such developments.

13.105 We accept that, among the options, it might prove necessary to offer financial incentives to staff who ought to work additional weekends. We would, however, be very unenthusiastic about that course if it can possibly be avoided. It would undoubtedly be expensive. It would also be contrary to the spirit of the "Fresh Start" package. It would need reconciling with the fact that, if staff work extra time, they are entitled to compensation in the form of TOIL. There are already suggestions by staff that, if they are required to work during what they regard as unsocial hours, they should have TOIL as well during unsocial hours.

13.106 We propose, therefore, that particular consideration should be given to other options (in addition to the rigorous management to which Mr Fittall referred, which is essential). These options should include:

    i)   the introduction of an extended shift pattern at weekends. It may be preferable for a member of staff to work longer hours when he or she is on duty at weekends and to have more weekends off, than to work shorter hours and to have more weekends on;

    ii)   the recruitment of part time staff, including prison auxiliaries, night patrols and retired prison officers to achieve satisfactory manning levels at weekends. Some staff might prefer to retire early from full time work and take on a "limited hours contract". We also draw attention here to what we say later in this Section about the employment of civilians;

    iii)   the provision of a higher rate of TOIL. For example, one hour's additional work during a weekend might qualify for 1 1/4 hours TOIL during the week. This could help to redress any imbalance between staffing levels on weekdays and at weekends.

Training and Education to Enhance the Role of Prison Officers

13.107 In Section 10 of this Report we draw attention to the Prison Service's role in limiting the damaging effect of imprisonment upon a prisoner. The Prison Service must ensure, so far as this is practicable, that the prisoner returns to the community in circumstances which reduce the likelihood of his reoffending. This requires a substantial change in the manner in which most prisoners are treated. This in turn requires a substantial contribution from prison officers. They will only be able to make such a contribution if they are properly trained.

13.108 For this reason, and because it could also improve the present state of morale in the Prison Service, we recommend that more attention be paid by the Prison Service to training. A greater commitment to training would also help to show that the Prison Service cares about its staff.

13.109 In its evidence, the Prison Officers' Association drew attention to the scale of training which staff received in the Netherlands. There, staff had systematic training over the first five years of a prison officer's career, and advanced training between the third and fifth year of his service. This provides an indication of just what is possible.

13.110 The Prison Service provides at present a new entrant prison officer training scheme. The scheme consists of an observation period during which new officers have a two week attachment to a prison located close to their homes. It is followed by a nine week residential training course at one of the Prison Service's colleges. It ends with a two week induction period at the establishment to which the officer is posted. If the periods spent at the establishments are constructively organised, then we believe the training gives a prison officer a reasonable introduction to his work.

13.111   The length of this course, by some European standards, is very short. In our view, it is just about adequate in length, although we propose that it should be extended when this is practicable.

13.112   Greater commitment needs to be shown, however, to in-service training. We recommend that there should be a better structure for training aimed at enhancing an officer's career development.

13.113   Training is important because it improves an officer's performance. The submission from the Governor of the establishment, to which we referred earlier, draws attention to the fact that new responsibilities were placed upon principal officers in consequence of "Fresh Start". But they were given no training to prepare them for these new responsibilities. As a result, some principal officers who are well capable of fulfilling the role find it difficult to do so. They take an excessive time over relatively simple and largely clerical tasks.

13.114   Training also assists in developing staffs' self-esteem and confidence, particularly if the training provides a qualification which is recognised both within and outside the Prison Service.

13.115   Training also has a role to play in helping to eliminate racial discrimination. It can address both the way staff relate to colleagues from the ethnic minorities, and the way that staff relate to ethnic minority prisoners. Such training is important in ensuring that the Prison Service continues to be vigilant in pursuing its non-discriminatory racial policies and is seen to be so by its staff.

13.116   Training can result in a prison officer having skills which result in the prisoners' attitude to the prison officer changing. If a prison officer is in a position to train a prisoner, or to assist a prisoner on an application for bail, this can create the relationship which is essential for the successful running of a prison.

13.117   There needs to be a flexible approach to in-service training. There should be opportunities to work with other agencies within the Criminal Justice System. If escort duties are no longer to be carried out by staff in prisons, then it will be important that the Prison Service gives staff the opportunity to become familiar with what happens in Courts. Prison officers need to work particularly closely with Probation Officers. Training to enable them to do this should be provided both inside prisons and in the community.

13.118   We propose that prison officers should be trained so that they can themselves train other officers. An example of what can be done was provided by the staff inter-personal training skills course which was being conducted at Saughton Prison, Edinburgh, during the Inquiry's visit to that establishment. The officers who were conducting the training had themselves been trained by the Scottish Health Education Group, who provided the training pack from which they worked.

13.119   Similar training was taking place about AIDS. Once again, prison officers were being trained by the Scottish Health Education Group so that they could then train other officers.

13.120   We propose that the Prison Service should compile a list of establishments which have developed a speciality so that those establishments can be used as training centres for training in that speciality. Officers would be transferred on short term secondment to learn the necessary skills from officers at the training establishment, so that they could then introduce the speciality in their own establishments. (Wormwood Scrubs provides an example in respect of lifers. The Garth shared working scheme and the Lindholme through-care regime are other good examples. An examination of the establishments which have provided Butler Trust Award Winners would give a guide to many more prisons which would be able to perform this role.)

13.121   The Prison Service should be committed to achieving a situation where each officer has, in addition to his ordinary duties, a special area of expertise. The expertise could be in any area of activity relevant to prison life, eg, physical training, education, drug or AIDS counselling, social skills, welfare, bail, C&R, prison industry or care of the handicapped or disabled.

13.122   We propose also that prison officers should have an opportunity to obtain qualifications which are recognised both within and outside the Prison Service. This is what is beginning to happen with training officers in Scottish Prisons. These officers receive a formal qualification through the Jordan Hill College of Education, as the result of attending a sandwich course over a year. The course is designed jointly by the College and the Scottish Prison Service. This has the attractive feature that the qualification is one which is recognised externally.

13.123   The possibilities of what can be achieved are illustrated also by the newly initiated Education Liaison Officers scheme at Lincoln Prison. The scheme, for which the Education Officer at the prison, Mr J Nichol, is responsible, should result in the Lincoln Education Liaison Officers obtaining a City and Guilds Certificate in the teaching of basic skills. This will be a recognised qualification to teach those prisoners who are illiterate, near illiterate or innumerate and could result in the officers obtaining teaching certificates.

13.124   The duties of the Lincoln Education Liaison Officers fit in neatly with their duties as members of the discipline staff of the prison. It is intended that, where possible, the Education Liaison Officers will act as escorts for prisoners attending classes in the Education Centre. They will then be able to assist at the Centre. In addition, they will provide assistance with prisoners on the wing, including counselling and career guidance.

13.125   It is hoped to achieve what the Education Officer calls:

> "a 'para-education' force which can be brought to bear upon the prison as a whole which is able to deal with all education, training and pre-vocational matters of concern to prisoners; and deal with problems quickly and efficiently."

13.126   Mr Nichol points out that the officers will have an opportunity of extending their job satisfaction and, if all goes well, their professional standing. Their involvement should also lead to a different perception on the part of prisoners of the role of prison officers. It will also extend the educational services to far more of the prison population. This is fully consistent with the increased emphasis upon education which we will discuss further in Section 14.

13.127   The Physical Education Branch (PEB) provides a further example of what training can achieve. The physical education officers (PEOs) at any prison enter the Service as ordinary officers. But they then receive training from the PEB which results in their becoming physical education officers.

13.128   In June 1989, the Central Council of Physical Recreation carried out a survey and found that, following "Fresh Start", there had been less weekend and evening PE for inmates. The Central Council recommended that consideration should be given to enroling as "special" prison PE officers, men and women from further education, schools and qualified people, to supplement staff in the evenings, at weekends and during holidays. In addition, prison officers could be trained to act as auxiliaries. The Central Council also recommended that those holding the PEB certificate should have the opportunity of obtaining a nationally recognised award. We believe that the Prison Service should consider these constructive recommendations from the Central Council. (The contribution which the Central Council made to the Inquiry illustrates the benefit to be derived by the Prison Service from working closely with outside bodies who have a special expertise in a specific area: in Physical Education – the Central Council; in sport – the Sports Council.)

13.129   One of the consequences of the disturbances in April, as we have already pointed out, is that staff feel vulnerable. C&R training can help here. C&R techniques give to prison staff confidence that they can take action if this is necessary. This in turn gives them confidence in their everyday relationship with prisoners. This is an important factor in helping to reduce the number and outcome of the occasions when staff resort to C&R techniques.

13.130   It is important therefore that there should be a continuing programme of initial C&R training followed by refresher courses. C&R training can also help to unify the Service. If, within the establishment, there is such training which is available to all prison officers (and other suitable members of staff) it can break down the barrier which group working under "Fresh Start" can otherwise be perceived to create.

13.131   Professor Thomas, a Senior Academic Adviser to the Prison Department, has drawn our attention to a range of education and training initiatives which the Prison Service is pursuing. He told us of work being conducted to ascertain the best way of supporting staff who wish to study for management qualifications, notably the MBA. There are also courses which are designed to enable staff to be prepared for senior appointments. These are excellent initiatives for which the Service deserves credit.

13.132   We appreciate, therefore, that at the present time many initiatives are taking place to enhance in-service training and the qualifications it offers. We welcome the initiative of the Prison Service in developing an Advanced Diploma in Criminology (Prison Studies) in consultation with the Open University. But that is an option which would not appeal to many. Other opportunities should be provided to cater for as wide a range of needs and attributes as possible.

13.133   Initiatives in training will not, however, send the right message if staff find that it is impossible in practice to take advantage of them. At the present time more humble, but very important schemes, such as the Personal Officer scheme are floundering in some establishments because of lack of time to undertake the necessary training.

13.134   The time allowed for training should be as generous as possible. We propose it should be increased progressively to three weeks (15 working days) a year when this is practicable.

13.135   While training has considerable advantages, we recognise it also has resource implications. Our proposal would increase costs. In our view, however, the investment required to ensure that staff receive proper training is fully justified.

13.136   The majority of training should undoubtedly take place during hours of employment. Such training should relate directly to a member of staff's work. An obvious example of this type of training would be C&R training.

13.137   But not all training need result in staff being taken away from other duties. As a result of "Fresh Start", the hours which staff are required to work have been substantially reduced.

13.138   There are forms of training which would benefit a member of staff and make him or her generally better equipped to perform his task, either now or in the future. But the training might not be regarded as being directly associated with the person's present duties. An example of this sort of training could be a course leading to a qualification in sociology, criminology or the law.

13.139   Some assistance is available to prison officers from the Prison Service to enable them to undertake suitable outside courses. The assistance takes the form of financial help with fees, travelling expenses and the cost of text books. The Service also provides special leave for private study and examinations. We propose that the Prison Service should encourage more prison officers to take advantage of this scheme.

13.140   The Prison Service has, therefore, to continue to address problems of training. The Prison Service has to make it clear in its promotion policies the importance it attaches to a member of staff acquiring additional skills, both of specific relevance to the Service and of a more general nature.

13.141   Few of these developments will be achieved, however, unless a proper and adequate amount of time is set aside for training. The "Fresh Start" package provides some allocation of staff time to training, which it unhappily refers to as "non-effective" time. In our view it is wholly inadequate. It is undesirable also that it should be lumped together with the allocation for sickness, absences and for staff leave. The result is that training always loses out.

13.142   This was brought into clear focus in correspondence in 1989 between the then Governor of Manchester Prison, Mr O'Friel, and the then Director of Personnel and Finance.

13.143   On 29 March 1989, Mr O'Friel wrote to the Director expressing concern about the position with regard to training. He indicated that, under the early days of manpower management, the formula in use required 20% to be added to complement to take account of sickness, leave and training. Of that 20%, ten working days, or two weeks, were allocated to staff training, and a further ten working days, or two weeks, to sickness. Mr O'Friel indicated that, since that time, there had been an increase in the annual leave. He was concerned at what was apparently an attempt to make provision for the additional leave at the expense of training. He asked to know the current position. He stated that "staff training is crucial to successfully taking forward the wide range of changes we are making at establishment level".

13.144   The Director replied on 25 July 1989, indicating that he had only been able to consider Mr O'Friel's letter "when other higher priorities allowed". He said:

> "it has also taken us some considerable time to think through the implications of the questions you raise".

13.145   The Director then, at some considerable length, set out his understanding of the position (the accuracy of which is in doubt in so far as he suggested that the ten days or two weeks to which Mr O'Friel referred included rest days). The effect of the figures he gave was that the notional annual allowance for training included in non-effective hours could not amount to any more than an average of seven days per officer, instead of the previous ten days per officer.

13.146   In a number of establishments, however, it is clear to us that an average of up to seven working days training per officer could not be achieved, since the sickness rate exceeds the national average sickness rate included in the non-effective time allowance. In practice, it will rarely be possible to increase the amount of training by moving officers from operational duties to training. What happens in practice tends to be the reverse. Officers are removed from training to operational duties.

13.147 We propose that the three weeks a year training which we have proposed for each officer should be "ring-fenced", so that the period allowed for training cannot be poached for other purposes.

The Conditions within Prison Establishments

13.148 If conditions within prison establishments are improved, then it is much easier for a member of staff to perform his duties. Whilst slopping out is degrading for a prisoner, it is also degrading for members of staff who have to supervise the operation. Overcrowding places greater stress on staff. The improvements in the physical conditions which it is hoped will take place over the coming years, should help to improve staff morale.

13.149 It is important to remember that it is not only the prisoners who need improved conditions. If staff are going to perform their tasks well, they must have suitable recreation facilities and suitable accommodation to perform the wider role now expected of them. Staff need offices in which to prepare reports. They also need accommodation for training, changing and rest rooms, and suitable toilet and showering facilities.

13.150 We propose therefore that the Prison Service should review the facilities for staff working in prisons and the importance attached to their improvement in prison refurbishment schemes.

The General Recruitment of Staff

13.151 The improvement in salaries of prison officers has made recruitment easier. Recruitment is dealt with nationally from Prison Service Headquarters. It is the responsibility of Prison Service Personnel Management Division (DPF2). The Division has to deal with between 20,000 and 30,000 applications each year. This involves some 65 staff. Some of the requirements for recruitment are those which apply throughout the Civil Service. Others are specific to the Prison Service.

13.152 Candidates for prison officers must be between 20 and 49 1/2 years of age. They must be in good health and have good eyesight. Men must be at least 5 foot 6 inches and women at least 5 foot 3 inches in height. (At the present time, sensibly, this requirement is under review.) They have to be prepared to serve anywhere in England and Wales and to work shifts and at nights. Candidates have to be of British or Commonwealth citizenship, a citizen of the Irish Republic or a British protected person and resident in the United Kingdom. They have to provide good references. A conviction is not, however, necessarily a bar to employment.

13.153 There is an initial sifting process, after which applications are passed to one of five prison officer selection boards. At this stage, the applicant is at present reminded that many of the vacancies for prison officers will be in London and the South East, where house prices are high. Applicants are asked to confirm that they fully understand that the prison officer grade is a mobile one and that they may be required to move home to take up their first posts. If an applicant confirms his "mobility", he or she is invited to take an aptitude test at a prison establishment near his home. The test has been specifically designed to measure a candidate's competence in the skills needed as a prison officer.

13.154 Those who are successful in the aptitude test are invited to an interview before the appropriate selection board. The board usually consists of a Governor and a Higher Executive Officer, or two Governors, trained in interview and selection techniques. There is an interview rating scale designed to identify how well a particular candidate meets the requirements. As a result of the individual members of the board's assessment of a candidate, a recommendation about appointment is made to the Personnel Management Division. Those who are successful are sent a provisional acceptance letter. They then have to have a full medical examination and other matters such as references have to be checked.

13.155 Although nationally there is no shortage of applications for prison officer jobs, there are problems over the recruitment of applicants from London and the South East. As a result, it has been necessary to post officers into that area, even though they have expressed a preference to serve elsewhere. (During 1989/1990 the Service informed all prospective candidates that, at that time, the Service was recruiting only for London and the South East, but the position has again changed.)

13.156 The Inquiry met a number of members of staff who were extremely disgruntled by having to live in London and the South East away from their families. This may be unreasonable in the light of the precautions taken by the Service, but it is understandable that, once in post, attitudes towards mobility change. The difficulties are almost invariably connected with accommodation. The amount of accommodation available for rent has been reduced. The Prison Service is looking again at this problem.

13.157 It is important that methods of helping staff are provided and where this can be done, a member of staff should know how long he is likely to have to serve in the South East against his preference.

13.158 About 12% of the applications which are now being received are from women. Female applicants can volunteer to work in male establishments and vice versa. The Prison Service told us in their evidence of September 1990 that 323 female officers were working in 66 male establishments, and 34 men were working in six female establishments.

13.159 We have no doubt that opposite sex working is beneficial within prisons. Many members of the staff of male establishments who were previously opposed to the presence of female officers, have changed their attitudes as a result of working with female officers. It is now generally accepted that the presence of female officers on landings has a beneficial effect. The evidence to Part I of the Inquiry confirmed that female officers in male establishments can help to reduce tension.

13.160 It would also be desirable if the number of officers who are members of the ethnic minorities closely matched their proportion in the population as a whole. This is far from being the position at present. Fewer than 1% of the Prison Service's total staff at present come from the ethnic minorities.

13.161 The new recruitment literature and advertising (some of which is placed in local and ethnic minority newspapers) highlights the fact that applications are particularly welcome from members of the ethnic minorities. There have also been commendable efforts made towards stimulating direct contact with potential recruits in areas with a high proportion of people from the ethnic minorities.

13.162 These initiatives are having an encouraging effect. Between January and June 1990, 1,170 applications (9%) to join the Prison Service were from the ethnic minorities. This compared with 294 (4%) in the equivalent period in 1989. However, only a small proportion of these candidates (as is the case with white candidates) are successful in their application. The present strategy, by itself, is going to need a very long time to produce the desired result.

13.163 In the course of one of our public seminars, Mr Trevor Hall, a community relations consultant to the Home Office, provided guidance which we regard as being sufficiently important to justify repetition in the Report. What he said was:

> "Why is it are we not able to attract black people in those areas to those prisons? I will say why that is not happening. For too long prisons have been closed to the local community in any meaningful and significant way.

You have to provide time – professional time – for officials at every level, from Director General down, to get out and meet the community and to gain the confidence of the community, and when that is seen to be happening then, as is happening to the police now, black people will begin to come forward. With all due respect to my colleagues, we expect black people to make a dramatic jump because we advertise in black newspapers and such like. They are not going to do it because there is a credibility factor. They are very concerned that initiatives so far have only been seen to be the flavour of the month. We have to be more consistent, we have to be more systematic, and above all else we need to set ourselves goals for 5, 10 years and not just a one year cycle."

13.164   Mr David Evans, the General Secretary of the POA, made a response which is equally important. We set out his reply as well:

"I am not absolutely positive as to what the answer is. I think it is fair to say that one of the points you made is very significant. There is a great reluctance to open up the establishment to the local community and I think in London in particular it is a particular problem and I think that some imaginative things need to be done there. I believe that governors locally and the POA locally must address that particular problem. I also think it is a problem for the trade union movement within the Prison Service and I do not think we ourselves have actually confronted the situation as it really is. I think between the trade union movement, the Prison Department and the local governors, I think we should begin to open up the establishments to the community as much as possible and certainly go more regularly out to the schools so that ethnic minorities can confront the prejudices that exist in the Prison Service."

13.165   In our view the evidence to which we have just referred provides guidance for the Prison Service, governors and trade unions which they should follow. We therefore propose that the Prison Service should review its methods of recruitment of members of the ethnic minorities.

13.166   With regard to recruitment in general, the Inquiry received evidence from a number of Governors advocating local as opposed to national recruitment. The Prison Officers' Association, on the other hand, were in favour of national recruitment.

13.167   The Inquiry accepts that it is to the advantage of the management of the Service as a whole for recruitment decisions to be made at Headquarters. But we propose that prison establishments should be allowed to play a greater part in assisting recruitment. This would build up the prison's links with its local community.

13.168   Establishments could provide an introduction to what the Prison Service has to offer in the way of a career. They could encourage visits by organisations which might be a source of recruitment. Prison staff could also play a part in identifying candidates. Although the applications are processed nationally, there is no reason why they should not be handled initially by the establishment. The establishment could provide additional information about an applicant, which could be useful for making decisions about his or her suitability. Where this is practicable, potential applicants from outside the Service could be given an opportunity of spending time working with a prison officer. Local initiatives should assist with the problem of encouraging applications from the ethnic minorities.

The Accelerated Promotion Scheme

13.169   This scheme is designed to select and develop the Prison Service's future senior managers. It is open to those who have degrees and to existing members of the Service (whether or not in the unified grades) under the age of

36. Selection is by means of passing a written qualifying test followed by two days of extended interviews. The interviews are modelled on those used by the Civil Service for the selection of "Fast Stream" administrative civil servants.

13.170   The candidate should appear to have the potential to reach at least the rank of Governor 2. At present, it is intended that candidates will move rapidly through the initial ranks to reach Governor 4 in six to seven years. From then, they would follow the same pattern as other staff, with the expectation that the ablest would reach Governor 2 in the next six to seven years.

13.171   The present plan for all members who join the scheme is that they should spend at least one year (two years for graduates/direct entrants) as a prison officer, two years as a principal officer at a different establishment, and two years as a Governor 5 at a third establishment. At the end of this period, they are to be automatically called to the promotion board to Governor 4, at which they will compete on equal terms with others who are not members of the scheme.

13.172   Members of the scheme who are not already prison officers receive initially the normal training provided for new entrant prison officers. They then have a training programme which is specific to the scheme. This includes a six months residential course at the Prison Service College.

13.173   The scheme is still very much in its infancy. The first group are currently undertaking their six months residential training prior to becoming operational principal officers in April 1991. Course 1 consists of 16 members (14 men and 2 women) of which 14 are in-service candidates. As of November 1990, Course 2 consisted of 12 members, all graduates/direct entrants from 1989. Course 3 consisted of six members.

13.174   The Prison Service says it is aiming for about ten successful candidates each year (a target we consider is too modest) but it would be ready to take more if they reached the high standard set. So far, the Service has not been successful in attracting a candidate from the ethnic minorities. The candidates tend to be equally split between the two sexes. In-service candidates tend to be in their late twenties or early thirties, while the graduate/direct entrants tend to be in their early to mid-twenties. The Inquiry has been provided with a copy of the pamphlet which is distributed to potential direct entrants. It is attractive and well designed.

13.175 It is clearly very important that the accelerated promotion scheme should be successful. It would be desirable for the Prison Service to try and ascertain why it has not proved to be more attractive so far. As the Prison Service obtains more experience, its recruitment techniques should improve. However, the evidence put before the Inquiry suggests that the period to reach Governor 5 level is, at four years, far too long. A year to 18 months may be a more satisfactory period.

13.176   It may well be that the Prison Service should follow the example of the professions and join the "milk round" which visits Universities and Polytechnics. It could help also if a university/college vacation scheme for future potential applicants was developed which gave some exposure to work in prisons. We believe the rewarding nature of the work could provide the best advertisement for the scheme. An opportunity to see staff at work could encourage enrolment.

13.177   In the future, the fast track entrants should be providing the leadership which the Service needs. We propose that the Prison Service should review the scheme to enable it to provide the right number and quality of candidates who are needed for the future.

The Prison Officer Development Scheme

13.178 It is important that all those who join the Service have an attractive career structure before them, with a sensible and fair ladder for promotion. One of the advantages of the unified grade system is that it should provide just such a ladder. This, we believe, will in the long term have the effect of bringing the governor grades and the officer grades much closer together. When the majority of the junior governor grades have made their way up through the ranks, there should be less of a "them and us" atmosphere.

13.179 There is also a need for the more able staff to receive accelerated promotion. At our public seminars, concern was expressed about the ability of the Service to produce the middle management of the future. The problem is that, by being required to take one step at a time up the promotion ladder, a member of staff can be deprived of the opportunity which he deserves of reaching middle management status.

13.180 We were, therefore, pleased to know that the Prison Service has been consulting the Prison Officers' Association and the Prison Governors' Association about a possible scheme which would enable officers who are nearly eligible for the accelerated promotion scheme to have the benefit of a "prison officer development scheme".

13.181 The Prison Service has suggested that one explanation for the ordinary promotion process being so slow is that it is necessary, if an officer is to be promoted, for him to pass the senior officer promotion examination. He is only allowed to sit that examination after having served for 5½ years. This goes some way to explain why the average age of those being promoted to senior officer between the years 1986-1987 was 40.

13.182 Thereafter, the rate of advancement cannot be faster than the seniority date established by promotion boards. The Boards consider who should be called for interview. Promotion boards set high store by seniority, reflecting the value placed on experience. Only the older officers are called.

13.183 The future of the senior officer promotion examination is, therefore, under consideration. The Prison Service has it in mind also to guide promotion boards to adopt criteria for interview which place less weight on seniority. The aim would be to introduce a new development scheme for the earlier promotion of able prison officers.

13.184 The scope and nature of such a development scheme is still subject to negotiation and it is not necessary to go into its detail. However, we would make it clear that we regard a scheme of this nature as a matter of great importance. We propose therefore that the Prison Service adopts an appropriate prison officer development scheme. This should help accelerate the unifying process between prison officers and governor grades. It will enable appropriate members of staff to pass through the ranks more rapidly, and therefore increase their prospects of promotion. It can only do good to the Service and its morale, as well as to its recruitment of good staff, if it can offer a reasonable route for progress and management responsibilities to its most able officers.

The Chief Officer

13.185 As we have noted earlier in this Section, we received a substantial body of evidence which regretted the demise of the Chief Officer. It was argued that the present unified grades had left an unfortunate gap which manifested itself in many ways: less discipline, less leadership, poorer management and a loss of identity. All these shortcomings were associated with the departure from the prison scene of this officer.

13.186 While we recognise the force of these feelings, we do not propose that the rank of Chief Officer should be revived. The existence of the rank would be in conflict with an objective of "Fresh Start", of which we approve, of unifying grades. We attach importance to there being an open line of promotion from the rank of prison officer to Governor 1 or 2 and above. The natural promotion of officers through those ranks will in the course of time make the greatest contribution to bridging the existing divide between prison officer grades and governor grades.

13.187 The Chief Officer would create a break in the ladder. His pivotal importance to the system in the past depended upon his being a person of considerable ability and experience. In the Prison Service of the future, the qualities which the Chief Officer manifested should be deployed at a higher level. The presence of the Chief Officer within an establishment would make it more difficult if not impossible to have the unified approach to staffing which we regard as being extremely important to the future of the Prison Service.

Uniforms

13.188 There is a considerable weight of opinion in favour of all staff within a prison establishment wearing uniform. Those who support this view would exclude only those engaged in purely civilian type work, such as that performed by clerical staff. Others would strongly endorse all members of the unified grades wearing uniform. In both cases, it is argued that the increased use of uniforms within establishments would have a cohesive effect. It would break down the barriers which at present exist between different grades and different types of staff.

13.189 The Prison Governors' Association has conducted a ballot of their members about the wearing of uniforms. This showed that over 60% were in favour of the governor grades wearing uniform.

13.190 Although we recognise the contribution which uniforms could make to bringing unified grades together, it has to be appreciated that unless staff who do not fall within the unified grades were also allowed to wear uniform, it would increase the gulf which already exists between them and the uniformed staff. In addition, there is a countervailing argument that uniforms tend to create a barrier between staff and inmates. It was partly for this reason that within Borstal institutions the staff did not wear uniforms.

13.191 We do not regard these factors as being sufficiently strong to justify staff who are at present in uniform ceasing to wear it. We consider, however, that the arguments against uniforms make a strong case for reviewing the nature of the uniform worn. The prison officer's uniform should be reviewed with a view to making it less militaristic than it is at present. We were impressed by the less formal uniforms which were worn by some prison staff on the continent. In the Netherlands, the staff who are engaged on security duties (who are a lesser grade of officer) wear a more militaristic uniform than the discipline officer staff who work with prisoners. Discipline officers wear a uniform which is very close to civilian clothing.

13.192 Uniforms cost money. We were told by the Prison Service that the cost of a male prison officer's uniform is currently £333.44 including VAT (involving an annual replacement cost of £122 per officer, including footwear). The cost of a female officer's uniform, is £359.97 including VAT (involving an annual replacement cost of £126 per officer, including footwear). The sums individually are not large, but would cumulatively be significant for the Service. Unless those members of a prison establishment who at present do not wear uniform were either to have to pay for their own uniform, or were to have the fact that they are to be provided with uniforms taken into account in considering what should be their salary, the cost of extending the wearing of uniforms in the Prison Service would either require significant additional public expenditure, or would have to be found from among other existing priorities. We do not think extending the wearing of uniform should have a priority claim on scarce resources.

13.193 There are, however, occasions when some form of "uniform" is necessary. It is necessary for senior staff who are actively involved in dealing with a prison disturbance. This is desirable to protect the staffs' own civilian clothing and to enable the rank and responsibilities of those involved to be seen clearly. Governor grades, and everyone else who is engaged directly in dealing with a disturbance, should wear the type of overalls now worn by C&R units. One problem during the April disturbances was that staff strange to the establishment were unable to identify who was commanding them. We have proposed in Section 9 that the rank of the wearer should be clearly identified.

13.194 On the other hand, there are duties which a prison officer may be performing which may be better performed without wearing uniform. If this is the situation, officers should be encouraged, but not compelled, to wear what is regarded as being the most appropriate clothing. This may have particular relevance in Young Offender Institutions or Remand Centres for young inmates. Personal Officer duties or welfare work shared with probation officers may be examples of work which is best performed in civilian clothes. We propose that the management of each establishment and its officers should be given a degree of discretion in deciding when prison officers should wear uniform.

13.195 We also propose the phasing out of peaked caps. The Prison Service should consider introducing or approving the wearing of some other sort of practical headgear, such as a beret, for outdoor wear in inclement weather. We do not consider that the wearing of headgear inside prison buildings creates the correct image. Staff should be discouraged from wearing headgear of any sort indoors.

13.196 There is a special problem in relation to peaked caps. Although this is now less common in some establishments, it is still the practice among some staff to slash the peaks of caps. The result, intended or not, is to create a menacing impression. We are strongly against this practice. Until our proposal to phase out caps is met, Governors and Area Managers should ensure that staff do not slash the peaks of their caps and that staff with such caps are issued with normal ones.

13.197 The identification of staff is important in normal times in prison as well as during a disturbance. We propose therefore that all staff, and all Governors within a prison, coming into contact with prisoners should display a label or badge which clearly gives their name and rank.

13.198 It will be clear from what we have said that we do not hold doctrinaire views about the wearing of uniforms. The general principle reflected in our proposals is that staff should wear the clothes which are appropriate to the work they are doing. We would not wish to see resources which could be deployed elsewhere to improve the Prison Service, spent in providing uniforms. We therefore reject the suggestion that governor grades, and those non-unified grades of staff who do not at present wear uniforms, should in future do so.

"Contracts" between Staff and Management

13.199 There remains some controversy as to what, if any, legal contractual rights a prison officer has against the Crown. We propose that in relation to the legal rights of staff, the Prison Service should make clear its understanding of the position.

13.200 The concept of non-legally enforceable "contracts", which the Prison Service has developed for the management of prisons, and to which we referred in Section 12, would also, in our view, benefit relations between staff and management in prisons. We propose that staff should have their terms and conditions of engagement in the establishment in which they work clearly set out in a document. This document would not be directly legally enforceable. It would however be relevant in an application for judicial review.

13.201   We do no more than indicate the broad outline of this "contract". What it would contain would vary from establishment to establishment. However, we would expect it to develop in a way which made clear the concern which the Service had for its staff. It would need to show that the Service took an interest in what was provided for its staff and equally that the staff had responsibilities to the establishment and prisoners.

13.202   We would expect that the "contract" would set out in clear terms what the member of staff's establishment would provide for while he or she was there. It would make clear the facilities within the prison which he, and if appropriate his family, would be entitled to use. It would set out the welfare and health facilities which were available and the opportunities which the officer would have for training, both within the establishment and within the community.

13.203   The "contract" would also indicate what the establishment expects the member of staff to contribute. In the same way as the new grievance procedure for prisoners provides time limits for a response by management, so should the "contract" give appropriate equivalent time limits for a response to complaints by individual members of staff.

13.204   The Central Council of Physical Recreation, in its review of physical education in the Prison Service, draws attention to the fact that, although new entrants, as part of the selection process, have to pass a medical examination and show a reasonably high standard of fitness, they are never again examined by the prison Medical Officer or tested for their physical fitness to continue to serve. The evidence suggests the Prison Service is at the present time making better provisions for the health and fitness of inmates than it is for its staff.

13.205   The Central Council's Review recommends that a minimum level of fitness for uniformed staff should be determined by the Prison Service. We propose that the Prison Service implement this recommendation. The standard of fitness required should be such as to enable the appropriate staff to respond quickly to alarm calls, to arrive at the scene in a fit physical and psychological condition to accept and give orders and then take appropriate action. They should be capable of training for and carrying out control and restraint.

13.206   The Prison Service would need to decide how an agreed level of fitness could best be quantified, achieved, monitored and tested. It would need to be clear what rehabilitative action should be taken for those falling below the required level of fitness. Reference to these requirements should be included in the "contracts". The merits of this proposal, however, are not dependent on the introduction of the staff "contracts" with establishments.

Non-Unified Staff

13.207   There is a regrettable tendency when considering the Prison Service to pay insufficient attention to the needs and contribution of the non-unified grades of the Prison Service.

13.208   The staff in these grades cover a very broad range of different activities. They are the chaplains, psychologists, the psychological assistants, the prison farm managers, medical officers, pharmacists, education officers, supply and transport branch staff, and architects and surveyors in the Directorate of Works, some of whom are members of the Institution of Professional Managers and Specialists (IPMS). They are the clerical, typing and secretarial grades, some of whom are members of the Civil and Public Services Association. They are the executive grades, some of whom are members of the National Union of Civil and Public Servants. They are the administrative grades, some of are members of the Association of First Division Civil Servants. They are the night patrols, civilian tradesmen, farm workers, storemen, boilermen and teachers and many more who play their part in the running of a prison.

13.209 All these members of staff make differing and potentially valuable contributions to the work of the Prison Service. They were all concerned in one way or another in the disturbances which are the subject of the first part of this Inquiry.

13.210 So far, these sections of the staff who work in prisons have not received the same benefit as unified grades received from "Fresh Start". We have already referred to the Prison Governors' Association's comments about the non-unified staff being "left out in the cold". This is the view reflected in the submissions made by some of the unions which we have identified above. We appreciate that the task of implementing "Fresh Start", and the reorganisation above establishment level, meant that some initiatives which are desirable have had to be deferred. We propose that priority should now be given to reviewing the position of the non-unified grades with a view to introducing a relevant improved package broadly comparable to that received by the unified grades under "Fresh Start".

13.211 Some of the tasks which prison officers perform at present can be performed equally effectively and more economically by other staff. If prison officers are to be in a position to play the enhanced role we consider is appropriate, they should expect that these tasks will be passed to others.

13.212 Naturally, the Prison Officers' Association would prefer any duties which might otherwise be performed by prison officers to be performed by prison auxiliaries, night patrols and storemen, who tend to be members of their union. However, while there is probably a growing role for these staff, there are other tasks which are being performed by prison officers at the present time which do not justify the involvement of these grades. Some of the tasks, such as running canteens, could be better performed by outside bodies.

13.213 We have heard repeatedly during the course of the evidence how the clerical burden has grown, in particular for the principal officers and governor grades. Clerical work could and should be performed by civilian staff.

13.214 We propose therefore that the Prison Service should adopt a more flexible attitude with regard to the use of all types of staff, including part-time staff. We recommend that the tasks at present undertaken by prison officers and governors should be reviewed to identify those which could be undertaken by other grades. If the prison officer grades are to be the highly trained and paid professional force which we would like to see, then they will have to be recognised as being too valuable a commodity to be squandered on inappropriate duties. These duties should normally be performed by less well paid staff to which they are suited.

13.215 This policy must not be taken to extremes. In any establishment there needs to be a certain prison officer presence for security and control purposes. It can happen that the use of prison officers can be justified on some duties which are otherwise inappropriate, because, by doing so, the necessary presence of the correct number of prison officers is maintained.

13.216 It is important that the sense of isolation among non-uniformed staff which has been an unintended consequence of the introduction of "Fresh Start" should be addressed. With the encouragement of Area Managers, this should be well within the capacity of the governing Governor of prison establishments. All staff should be kept informed of the objectives and achievements of the establishment. It should be made clear to all levels of staff that the establishment is concerned for their welfare. The staff "contracts" we have proposed should help with this. The message which needs to be promoted is that all staff are part of a team. Although they may work in different areas or different groups, the successful running of the establishment depends upon the input of the team as a whole.

13.217 So that non-unified staff can play their proper role within the team, it is important that they should be provided with their share of training. They should be given an opportunity of understanding what is involved in the tasks performed by other sections of staff within the establishment. They should be aware of security procedures. Contingency plans for an incident should make provision for them. They should be aware of what is required of them if an incident occurs.

13.218 We propose that an induction course be introduced for non-unified staff to enable those members of staff to make a greater contribution to the running of the prison. The fact that they have received such training would give them more of a sense of belonging to the team. The type of course we have in mind would be provided at the establishment.

13.219 The course would provide information and instruction on such matters as the organisational structure of the Prison Service; its relationship with the Home Office and Ministers; its aims and objectives; the roles and identities of key personnel at Headquarters and Area levels (the Director General, Directors, Area Managers and heads of divisions, etc.); the organisational, management and communications structure of the local establishment; the establishment's function and the nature of its prison population; an introduction to key personnel, including the Board of Visitors; details of the establishment's "contract" with the Area Manager and their role in fulfilling it.

13.220 Additionally, all non-unified grades should receive instruction in basic security and control procedures, including the use of keys; SIR procedures for the reporting of security information; relationships with inmates; the need for confidentiality; how and where to seek advice; what to do if taken hostage; the nature of local contingency plans and their role in the various types of emergencies which might arise.

13.221 Time spent in a wing or on the landings either during or after the induction course would be a valuable experience. It would help staff to get to know each other more quickly and would give the non-unified grades an insight into the routine of a prison officer's working life. All members of the non-unified grades should also be made aware of the techniques used to deal with control problems and should see the various C&R techniques demonstrated. They could also be offered the opportunity to volunteer for some elementary instruction in basic self-defence techniques.

13.222 A comprehensive local programme of the kind outlined above should be able to be contained within the equivalent of five normal working days, depending on the size and nature of the establishment. A programme of this kind would probably have to be organised on a modular basis, so that a post was not left unmanned for extended periods. Some establishments already run induction courses of this kind, but we have no doubt that more could be done at relatively small expense. It would be well worthwhile.

Cross Postings

13.223 We noted earlier that, so far, no-one who had not previously served in a prison had been appointed as an Area Manager. The Prison Service's initial intention was that some should come from a non-governor background. This feature of the reorganisation was subjected to substantial criticism, not least by the Prison Governors' Association, on the grounds that the post of Area Manager required previous Service experience in prisons. We recognise this argument. On the other hand, we believe it would be beneficial to the Service to have fresh blood being injected from time to time into the Service. One way to achieve both objectives would be to provide in the administrative grades of the Home Office sufficient "high flyers" who have had first hand operational experience within the Service.

13.224 We therefore favour the exposure of staff from other sections of the Home Office to conditions within prisons. Equally, we favour the exposure of "operational" members of the Prison Service to other sections of the Home Office and other criminal justice agencies. We propose that cross posting between administrative staff in the Home Office and operational staff in prisons should be increased.

13.225 As part of this initiative, the Home Office should consider preparing a suitable programme to enable administrative staff in the Home Office to spend an appropriate period working in a prison establishment as part of their career development. We would hope the programme would involve fast stream entrants and others with good promotion prospects. The programme might make provision for a short period spent working with a prison officer and with one of the lower governor grades. More senior administrative grades could be subjected to a similar exposure at a rather higher level. If this initiative were implemented, it should make it easier for an administrative grade civil servant of the correct calibre to perform the role of Area Manager in the future.

13.226 We propose that a similar programme be prepared to allow the possibility of secondment between other agencies within the Criminal Justice System and operational staff in the Prison Service.

Industrial Relations

13.227 The May Committee, in Chapter 10 of its report of October 1979, admirably summarised the history of industrial relations in the Prison Service. It is not therefore necessary to repeat it. It is, however, relevant to note that, in September 1975, the National Executive Committee of the POA delegated the power to take industrial action to local branches of the Association.

13.228 In its section headed "The Importance of Good Industrial Relations", the May Committee summarised its conclusions. It said:

"That something has gone wrong with relations between staff and local and central management is undeniable – evidence of distrust, alienation and suspicion occurred too frequently for the reality of that to be seriously in doubt – but for such a situation all must bear some degree of blame. Something must be wrong, for example, with the management style and approach (and approachability) of headquarters....Governors must, we believe, accept a positive responsibility for the improvement of day-to-day relations within their establishments........Finally, it is up to staff........to recognise.......that there are limitations on management's ability to make concessions in certain major areas, and that there is a need to make full use of negotiating channels before resorting to industrial action. This, we believe, is first and foremost in the interests of prison officers themselves."

13.229 Among the recommendations for improving the situation which the May Committee made were: that staff and management had to recognise their joint responsibility for improving the operation of the prison service; that, wherever possible, disputes should be resolved locally; and that an assistant or deputy governor should be delegated at each establishment as a channel for complaints and a trouble-shooter in the event of a dispute occurring.

13.230 Unfortunately, the May Committee's exhortations and recommendations did not result in any long term improvement in industrial relations. Indeed, industrial relations became worse.

13.231 In 1986, there was a serious escalation in the tension between the Service and the Prison Officers' Association. The primary issue was over the POA's contention that they were entitled to negotiate the safe manning level in any establishment. The Prison Service contended that the Service should be in a position to impose its will in case of disagreement. The POA balloted their members on taking industrial action. This produced an 80% vote in favour of industrial action among the 70% who voted.

13.232 Industrial action followed at Gloucester Prison on 25 April 1986. Officers took action in response to the action of the Governor in stopping the pay of two prison officers, who had refused to prepare a new staff detail.

13.233 On 29 April 1986, the Prison Officers' Association National Executive Committee instructed all branches to ban overtime from noon on 30 April for a period of seven days. That was only the second time in the history of the Prison Service that national industrial action had been called. There followed a wave of serious and damaging disturbances which affected 40 establishments. On 1 May 1986, the Prison Officers' Association called off its industrial action.

13.234 Her Majesty's Chief Inspector of Prisons prepared a report into the disturbances. That report was presented to Parliament on 16 July 1987.

13.235 One consequence of the disturbances was that the Prison Officers' Association and the Prison Service agreed to a new interim "Cubbon" formula to be replaced by a new Dispute Procedure. The Cubbon formula takes its name from a letter written by Sir Brian Cubbon, the then Permanent Under Secretary at the Home Office, to the General Secretary of the Prison Officers' Association. Prior to this, there was no formal procedure for settling disputes. They were discussed locally.

13.236 The Cubbon formula was replaced on 1 October 1989 by a new Dispute Procedure which had been agreed between the Prison Service and the Prison Officers' Association in August 1989.

13.237 The Dispute Procedure provides a framework for the discussion of local disputes. It stresses that industrial action should be a last resort and that any disputes should be resolved as quickly as possible at the lowest appropriate level. If a dispute cannot be resolved locally, the dispute is referred upwards, finally ending up at national level.

13.238 When a local dispute is declared, either side must give 21 days notice of its intention to invoke the procedure. During this period, the status quo should prevail to allow consultation to take place.

13.239 The new Dispute Procedure has not achieved any substantial reduction in industrial action. Indeed, neither did the disturbances in April of this year. Nor did the appointment of this Inquiry.

13.240 We set out in Annex 13A the record of industrial disputes in the first ten months of 1990. Table 1 contains a list of prison establishments where there have been industrial disputes between 1 January and 30 October 1990. The second table lists prisons where prison staff have threatened to refuse or refused to admit prisoners in consequence of industrial disputes since 1 January 1990. The lists were given in answer to a question by Lord Harris of Greenwich in the House of Lords on 30 October 1990. Both lists are depressingly long.

13.241 There is at present no general agreement between the Prison Service and the Prison Officers' Association that industrial action will not be taken until alternative methods of resolving a dispute have been exhausted.

13.242 In the case of a limited class of disagreement, that is a disagreement where either party "wishes to withdraw from or revise a local agreement", the Dispute Procedure states that the status quo will prevail. In the case of a collective grievance, while there is a provision for no industrial action to be taken within 21 days of the grievance being notified to management, there is no agreement not to take industrial action thereafter.

13.243   The agreement between the Prison Officers' Association and the Prison Service provides that the agreement should be reviewed by both parties at the end of 12 months. The history of industrial action since the date of the agreement shows that there is an urgent need to attempt to make it more effective. In particular, we propose that there should be an agreement between the Prison Service and the Unions that no industrial action will be taken in prison establishments until all the procedures for resolving disputes have been exhausted. Where a dispute is still capable of being resolved by negotiation, irrespective of the legal position, it is irresponsible and unprofessional for prison officers to take industrial action which will affect prisoners.

13.244   There is a body of opinion which is firmly of the view that industrial relations can only be improved if industrial action by prison officers is made unlawful. It is contended that it is inconsistent with the position of the Prison Service as a disciplined service, and inconsistent with the role of the Prison Service, for industrial action to be permitted. It is suggested that the position should be the same as that with the police. Industrial action should be made unlawful. This is not a contention which was advanced by the Prison Service.

13.245   We accept that there may come a time when this question will have to be re-examined. It is self-evident that industrial relations within the Prison Service are in a sorry state. However, on the assumption that the Prison Officers' Association is a union entitled to the protection which applies generally in the law to trade unions, we would not open that door at this stage. We are aware, as a result of the Inquiry's visit to France that, in that country, the fact that prison officers are forbidden by law from taking industrial action has not prevented industrial action by prison officers.

13.246   We take the view that industrial action by prison officers should not be made unlawful at this stage, not because of any difficulties in enforcing such a law, but because, notwithstanding the history, we consider that it is still possible substantially to improve industrial relations by agreement. It is preferable for improvement to be reached in this way rather than by involving the law.

13.247   Conditions in prisons have significantly contributed to the present hostile state of industrial relations, just as they have contributed to souring relations between staff and prisoners. As a result of "Fresh Start" and the prison building programme, we believe that, with good sense on both sides, it should be possible to enter into a new era for industrial relations. There must be a willingness on all sides to achieve that improvement. In our view, the Prison Officers' Association should be given a further opportunity to show how they respond to improved conditions.

13.248   We are encouraged to take this view because we found from the Inquiry's visits to establishments that those places with satisfactory conditions and constructive regimes appeared more likely than other, less well endowed prisons, to have satisfactory industrial relations.

13.249   It should now be possible to enter an era when the conditions within our prisons are substantially improved, not only for prisoners but also for prison staff. The role of the prison officer also needs to be given new meaning. In this Section we have tried to identify how that role can be developed. We have only indicated an outline. We have not sought to provide the detail. This is the task of both the management and the unions. With the economic situation as it is at present, it must be clear that the resources that can be devoted to the Prison Service have to be constrained. It is in the interests of the staff which the unions represent, as much as management, that those resources are used to best possible effect. They cannot be without close co-operation between management and unions.

13.250   We have noted the constructive evidence which we have received from the Prison Officers' Association both at national and local levels. We have been impressed by the calibre of the representatives of the Association at all levels.

We feel that the Prison Officers' Association should have the opportunity to cooperate in bringing into effect the improvements which they recommend by encouraging their members and branches to support those improvements.

13.251   The POA's members will gain immeasurably from the improvements in conditions which we would like to see. But those improvements are largely inter-dependent. They are a package. The Prison Officers' Association cannot be selective as to the improvements which they would like to see implemented if there is to be a substantial change in the situation. An improvement in the cooperation between the Prison Service and the Prison Officers' Association is a significant part of that package.

13.252   Apart from overcrowding, which present projections indicate should not be as large a problem in the future as it has been in the past, staffing levels are perhaps the biggest cause of industrial unrest. It is for this reason that we urge the Prison Officers' Association to reconsider their present policy of recommending their members not to co-operate with the work of establishing appropriate staffing levels through the process of identifying corporate objectives. There is still time to co-operate in this work. A change of policy on this matter would enable the Association and their members to take an important step towards improving the present position.

13.253   The Prison Officers' Association in their evidence stressed the failure of the Prison Department to consult as they should. What the Prison Officers' Association and the other unions have to appreciate is that, just as at present they do not feel they can trust the Prison Service, so there are those in the Service who feel they cannot trust the unions not to be reactionary and destructive in relation to any change which involves a contribution from both management and staff. This distrust has to be tackled by both sides.

13.254   In saying this we have focused on the prison officers' union, as we have throughout this part of Section 13, since it is between that union and the Service that the distrust on both sides is the greatest. However, everything we have had to say is equally relevant to other unions.

Conclusion

13.255   We recognise and acknowledge the quality of the men and women who have the responsibility of manning and running our prison establishments. For too long now, they have had to perform their duties in bad conditions. These conditions made their task immeasurably more difficult. They may help to explain the fact that, although staffing levels have increased significantly, there has been no corresponding increase in regimes: indeed they have deteriorated. The staff/prisoner ratio has advanced from 1:7 in 1947, to 1:6.3 in 1950, to 1:4.8 in 1960, to 1:3.4 in 1970, to 1:2.5 in 1980, and to 1:2.3 in 1989. The benefits have not been felt by prisoners on the wings and in the cells of our prisons.

13.256   If the uniformed staff are prepared to co-operate with the fresh approach which we have identified, then the Prison Service will need to recognise that, for a short time at any rate, additional staff will be required. They will be needed in order to meet the requirement for additional training and for some of the other initiatives which we have proposed in this and other Sections. We consider that the more stable Prison Service which should result will in due course lead to fewer staff having to perform the functions they do at present. They can be used on more constructive duties.

13.257   It will be for the Service to determine how the additional staff requirement can be made available. An extension in the period required to achieve the "Fresh Start" economies would be a possibility. This would assist those establishments which contend that the economies are making it impossible for them to provide even their present regimes. It would go some way to resolving the problems of establishments which have incurred vast amounts of

TOIL for their staff (thousands of hours). Another or additional approach would be to recognise that the "Fresh Start" economies were related to the then prevailing level of activity in establishments. If it is accepted that there is a need for that level to increase, an increase in the number of staff available at the time when these tasks need to be carried out, may be justified.

13.258   We have therefore made a number of suggestions in this Section and in the other Sections of the Report aimed at bringing about a dramatic change in relations between management and staff and in the climate of industrial relations in the Prison Service. Together with "Fresh Start", they should help to transform the conditions of service of prison officers. They should give them a new standing and a new sense of pride in their profession, more job satisfaction, better prospects of promotion and greater security.

13.259   Prison officers must, however, appreciate that they are already an expensive commodity. They will become more so as a result of the enhanced training we have proposed – more expensive than their civilian (and at present sometimes better qualified) counterparts: teachers, probation officers, administrators and tradesmen. Prison uniformed staff have therefore to justify the additional expense which is involved in our proposals by their additional commitment to the transformation of our prisons.

13.260   If uniformed staff show the additional commitment required, then the additional expense will be justified. It will demonstrably provide a more efficient and effective Prison Service. It will be a Service whose work makes it less and not more likely that prisoners will offend again; a Service which is free from the riots of 1990 and the immense expense which they involved.

Section 14

Prisoners

Introduction

14.1   We started Part II of this Report by considering what should be the task of the Prison Service. We set out and endorsed the Prison Service's Statement of Purpose as a succinct explanation of that task. We noted that there were two limbs to the statement; the need (a) to keep secure those committed by the Courts to the custody of the Prison Service, and (b) to look after them with humanity and to help them lead law abiding and useful lives in custody and after release.

14.2   Prisoners are central to both parts of this task. During the April 1990 disturbances, the Prison Service successfully kept prisoners in custody – as required by the Statement – by preventing their escape. There were failures, however, in the control of prisoners, as we have shown in Part I. But the April disturbances showed even more fundamental shortcomings. These were in relation to the second limb of the Prison Service's task – to look after prisoners with humanity.

14.3   The letters which the Inquiry received from prisoners, both from those in the prisons where there were disturbances which we studied in detail, the target prisons, and from many other prisons throughout the country, made very clear the Prison Service's shortcomings in this last respect. One prisoner wrote:

> "It is obvious if prisoners are treated like animals, sworn at, degraded and psychologically toyed with week after week, they in turn lose respect, not only for their tormentors, but for society at large (that is why there is a large proportion of recidivists). Over the past two months I have heard several groups of prisoners talking about rioting here because of the food and other grievances. We can accept the punishment but not the mental torture."

14.4   This letter reveals one prisoner's relationship with the Prison Service. We do not suggest that it accurately reflects the experience of all prisoners in prisons; or that it is an accurate and fair description of life in prison. Prisoners are bound to look at their conditions in prison through the eyes of people who are forced to be there against their will and who inevitably tend to see their actions in the most favourable light. But this letter is a reminder that many prisoners are under considerable stress while they are in prison. Matters which others might be able to take in their stride become problems which prey upon prisoners' minds. If such problems are not recognised and dealt with, they can fester and eventually result in an explosion of violence.

14.5   In considering how the Prison Service can more successfully perform the second limb of its task, we are not seeking to achieve more comfortable surroundings, greater luxuries or increased privileges for prisoners for their own sakes. To think that would be fundamentally to misconceive the argument. We are seeking to ensure that a prisoner serves his sentence in a way which is consistent with the purpose behind the Court's decision to take away his liberty and his freedom of movement, while ensuring he is treated with humanity and justice.

14.6 There are two central propositions which need to be recognised if the proposals in this Section are to be seen in their proper context. The first self-evident proposition is that custody involves the loss of liberty. The result is that the prisoner is ultimately in the power of and under the care of the State. For the most part, he will be in prison for 24 hours a day, every day of the week. It is difficult for the prisoner, even if there is a satisfactory grievance procedure, to make good the failures of the State to make adequate provision for him. Even if the prisoner is granted permission to leave prison, he remains attached to the prison and knows that further sanctions will follow if he does not return in time.

14.7 The inability of a prisoner to provide for himself carries with it a high level of obligation and responsibility on the part of the Prison Service on behalf of the State. It carries with it implications for the Prison Service's claims on resources. If the Prison Service does not or is not in a position to arrange the necessary level of care for prisoners, no-one else will.

14.8 The second central proposition is that, at some time, almost all prisoners will be returned to the community. The imposition of a prison sentence is often seen as the end of the story. It is not. When a prison sentence is passed, the person is taken out of the community to which he or she will eventually return. On return, the prisoner will have been influenced in some way by his or her experiences in prison. It is unavoidable, as we have argued in an earlier Section, that the natural consequences of a sentence of imprisonment, unless remedial action is taken, will be a deterioration in the ability of the prisoner to operate effectively and lawfully within society. The Prison Service can contribute to that deterioration or seek to minimise it. Its duty is to minimise it and, in the words of the Statement of Purpose, help prisoners "lead law-abiding and useful lives in custody and after release".

14.9 The Prison Service, cannot, of course, ensure that prisoners are processed into law abiding citizens. But the Prison Service can and should make it clear to its prisoners that the prison system works fairly. It should give each prisoner every opportunity to serve his or her sentence in a constructive way. It should not treat prisoners in a way which is likely to leave them in an embittered and disaffected state on their release.

14.10 The Prison Service has to live with these prisoners during their time in prison. The rest of the country lives with them afterwards. We cannot afford to lock them up and forget them. We must ensure that the Service makes proper use of the time which a prisoner spends in prison, and the best use of the money available for keeping him or her there. The aim must be to reduce the likelihood of prisoners re-offending after their release.

14.11 The considerations which have guided us so far in this report have guided us also in examining the situation of prisoners when in custody in our prisons.

14.12 A central consideration is the concept of responsibility – the responsibility of the Prison Service for its prisoners, and of prisoners for what happens to them while in prison. The Courts have held the prisoner responsible for his or her offence and decided that imprisonment, and only imprisonment, is the just sentence. After his release, a prisoner will continue to be held responsible for what he does and for the conduct of his life – like any other member of the community. So far as this is practicable, the position should be the same while the prisoner is in prison.

14.13 Prisoners should therefore be encouraged to take as full a responsibility as is possible for the conduct of their sentences. This is not easy in an institutional setting. The State, as we have explained, must take ultimate responsibility for their conditions in prison and for the opportunities that are given to them. But one way to prevent the deterioration of prisoners in prison, is to prevent a creeping and all pervading dependency by prisoners on the prison authorities.

14.14 Prisoners must, therefore, be given the opportunity to make choices. They must be held accountable for those choices. Prisoners must come to recognise that it is for them to make positive use of their sentence. They should have a responsibility for how they serve their sentence and for how they will live after release. It is right that the Prison Service should provide every opportunity for prisoners to exercise that responsibility. The Prison Service must also ensure that those who do not do so in a constructive and co-operative way are held responsible for this as well.

14.15 Responsibility carries with it the obligation of respect. That can be in short supply within the prison system. Some prisoners, in their letters and conversations, have been quick to show that they do not respect some prison officers.

14.16 Earlier sections of this report have identified incidents which demonstrate that some prisoners have little respect for each other. They seek to scapegoat sex offenders so that, within the prison system, they have someone on whom the majority can look down – someone who can be seen as the target for abuse and worse.

14.17 There are, of course, as we have said, no immediate and quick answers to such problems. But a relationship based on mutual respect is unlikely to grow in prisons until prisoners feel that the authorities are treating them with respect as individual human beings. It is by creating an atmosphere of mutual respect within prisons that relationships between prisoners and staff will be improved.

14.18 To show and receive respect involves much more than expecting prison officers to be nice to prisoners. (Though the desirability of calling a prisoner by his name should not be ignored.) It requires that prisoners be treated in prison in a manner which demonstrates to them that the Prison Service pays more than lip service to its responsibilities to treat them with humanity. It is no good asking a prison officer to respect an inmate if all he can do is unlock him from his cell for a short time so that he can empty his pot. It is no good expecting the prisoner to respect the prison officer, or the system which he represents, if that is all he can look to the prison officer to provide. It is often said that respect is earned. It must be recognised that what is earned also has a cost.

14.19 There must also be justice in our prisons. The system of justice which has put a person in prison cannot end at the prison doors. It must accompany the prisoner into the prison, his cell, and to all aspects of his life in prison.

14.20 The Inquiry has considered carefully the evidence from those who wish to translate this principle of justice within prisons into a system which introduces the judicial process into almost all aspects of prison life. That is not our intention. We have been told often enough in evidence from prisoners and from prison officers that prisons run on goodwill and mutual co-operation. That must continue and increase. But that will only be achieved if prisoners, as well as staff, feel that the system is itself fair and just. Justice needs to be built in to the operations of the Prison Service, not imposed by the Courts.

14.21 The securing of justice in prisons is not only in the interests of prisoners. It is vital that the Prison Service should have the reputation for being fair and for providing in a fair manner a suitable service for everyone for whom it is responsible. Any organisation which must, as the Prison Service does, ultimately impose its will on people under the powers given it by Parliament, needs, in its own interest, to ensure that it is able to show that it uses those powers with discretion and with fairness.

14.22 This Section, therefore, seeks to apply these considerations to a number of different aspects of a prisoner's life. We will seek to show that a prisoner's time in prison should provide a clear sense of progress from reception to discharge. We shall suggest that such progress should provide incentives to prisoners to behave responsibly. We shall examine the role of education, training and work in the arrangement of the prisoner's sentence, and the contribution which pay and private cash can make. We shall look at the way in which basic essentials like food and clothing are inevitably important aspects of the way a prisoner believes he is treated in prison. We shall consider ways in which the prisoner may retain ties with the family and community to which he wishes to return. We shall address the ways in which prisoners can be consulted, and can have their grievances considered. And we shall consider the place of disciplinary proceedings in the running of a prison.

Incentives and Disincentives

14.23   It seems to us incontrovertible that prisoners are likely to behave more responsibly, and to make the best use of their time in prison, if they feel that their responsibility and effort will be in some way rewarded. Those who have a high investment in the system are not likely to seek to destroy it.

14.24   There is already an elaborate system of so-called privileges for prisoners provided under Prison Rule 4 and its equivalent for Young Offender Institutions – Rule 7. Prison Rule 4 provides:

> "There shall be established at every prison systems of privileges approved by the Secretary of State and appropriate to the classes of prisoners there, which shall include arrangements under which money earned by prisoners in prison may be spent by them within the prison".

14.25   Prison Rule 4 has to be considered in conjunction with Standing Order 4. The Standing Order identifies privileges for which inmates are eligible wherever they are located (Section A), and privileges for which inmates are normally eligible where conditions permit (Section B).

14.26   Section A of the Standing Order identifies facilities for making purchases and the items which may be purchased. These include newspapers, books, radios, smoking requisites, wrist watches, battery shavers and personal toiletries. Unconvicted inmates may spend as much private cash as they wish on such purchases. Convicted inmates may spend up to a certain limited amount of private cash in any 12 month period – the Governor has the responsibility of telling each inmate what the current level is. The Governor is given discretion under the Standing Order to allow the purchase of items not specifically listed in the Standing Order. There are restrictions on the number of publications which can be purchased – one daily and one weekly newspaper and two periodicals.

14.27   Section A of the Standing Order also allows inmates to be issued with a general notebook and a drawing book and sets out other privileges, including the right to enter a public competition provided that a fee is not required.

14.28   Section B of the Standing Order identifies discretionary privileges, including personal possessions, in-cell activities and association. It provides that certain articles may "normally be retained" by the inmate. These include photographs, greeting cards, wedding rings, pencils, pens and ink, a wristwatch and a crucifix and other religious articles. The Governor may also "in certain locations" allow inmates to have such things as a battery shaver, a vacuum flask, a battery operated record player or cassette player (without recording facilities), a floor mat, curtains and a caged bird. If conditions permit, the Governor may allow the playing of games in cells and inmates may also be allowed to engage in a hobby.

14.29   The Standing Order also states that association with other inmates is an important privilege. Every inmate is to be given the opportunity to have association, unless there are grounds for denying it to him.

14.30   In evidence to the Inquiry, the Prison Service said that Standing Order 4 is presently being reviewed to set out more clearly those privileges that prisoners should normally expect to be available at all establishments, and to specify more precisely the extent of Governors' discretion in providing or withholding such privileges. Such a revision is clearly needed, if only because the Standing Order does not distinguish satisfactorily between privileges for which inmates are eligible wherever located, and those for which they are normally eligible where conditions permit.

14.31   We would, however, go further. First, we propose adding to the existing "privileges" a provision permitting a prisoner have a suitable television set in his own cell.

14.32   Secondly, we suggest that, for the most part, it is incorrect to describe these provisions as privileges. They are, or ought to be, the normal expectation of all prisoners in prison who have not had such facilities withdrawn for clear and good reasons. This is more than a matter of semantics. In the past it has been argued on behalf of the Prison Service that privileges imply something which prisoners are given out of grace or favour. It should not be a matter of grace or favour that prisoners are allowed to associate, or that they are able to buy books, newspapers, or have radios.

14.33   We recognise that the Prison Service's device of using the word "privileges" may be to avoid the prisoner having a legally enforceable personal right to these privileges. The Prison Service may wish to avoid them being seen as entitlements because, if that is how they are seen, then the Prison Service is committed to providing the resources to deliver them.

14.34   We recognise that some of these facilities, in particular association, cannot always be achieved, for example, because of staffing difficulties or some unexpected contingency. But the answer to this problem does not lie in claiming that association is a privilege. The Prison Service needs only to recognise the position as it is at present under the law. The prisoner has no legal personal right to be provided with "privileges", however they are termed. But it can be, and it should, be the duty of the Prison Service, where practicable, to provide them. That duty can only be legally enforceable by the discretionary remedy of judicial review. A description should not be used to describe them which is inconsistent with this duty. In circumstances where, for example, there are good reasons for not having association, then it should be possible and reasonable to explain to prisoners why this is the situation.

14.35   We propose therefore that Prison Rule 4 and its associated Standing Order be amended to make clear the facilities which should normally be provided for prisoners. The amendments should recognise that these facilities should no longer be provided as privileges, but as a prisoner's normal expectation. Some of these facilities, which are not to be regarded as being part of the prisoner's basic standard of life may, however, be restricted as a result of disciplinary proceedings, as we shall explain later.

14.36   Thirdly, by giving Governors the degree of discretion which is at present open to them in deciding what "privileges" to grant and what not to grant, the result has been the creation of a system which many prisoners see, with justification, as arbitrary. The evidence before the Inquiry suggests that this has led to a deep sense of injustice and grievance.

14.37   Prisoners do not understand why, for example, curtains can be allowed in one establishment, and not in another of the same security category. The Inquiry heard, in taking evidence in Part I, a long and heartfelt explanation by one prisoner of a dispute with a prison officer over him having a box of tissues. The dispute eventually led that prisoner to spending time in the segregation unit. The problem, according to him, was that the prison from which he had come allowed him to have a box of tissues in his cell – and his present prison did not. He was not prepared easily to give up his tissues.

14.38   Such things may seem petty, but they are important. In this case, it led to a sense of grievance which was a factor in the disturbance which followed. Arbitrariness of this sort can lead prisoners to a feeling of unfairness and powerlessness which is unhealthy for the life and stability of the institution.

14.39   We propose, therefore, that there should be a more measured and careful approach to the provision of facilities for prisoners. The aim should be to provide consistency of treatment between different prisoners and different establishments of the same type. When there is a difference of approach, the prisoner must be given a reasoned explanation for it.

14.40   We have considered whether the provision of such "privileges" should form the basis of an incentive system. Should a prisoner only be allowed a newspaper, a periodical, or a radio, once he had earned such things through his own good behaviour and application in prison?

14.41   The matter was considered in discussion at one of our public seminars. We understood the argument of those, including Mr Rutherford of the Howard League, who said that prisoners should not be made to jump through artificially created hoops. If it is right that prisoners should be enabled to read newspapers, or to make their cells more comfortable and better equipped, then they should be permitted to do so without artificial distinctions being made.

14.42   A system of personal and minor incentives would be hard to administer fairly and without fear of prejudice. It would put an additional burden on prison officers in trying to form nice judgements about who could have what privilege. It would risk itself becoming a disincentive rather than an incentive to good behaviour.

14.43   These facilities are best seen as a way of providing all prisoners with ways of improving their living conditions. The facilities should only be at risk of being lost as a penalty within the prison disciplinary system. (The way in which that system should operate will be discussed later in this Section.)

14.44   Incentives need to be built in to the prison system not tacked onto it. There need to be ways in which, to quote the Prison Service's Control Review Committee Report:

> "Incentives can be deliberately developed as a matter of policy in order to make security down-grading and progression through the system a consistent and psychologically credible process".

14.45   The Control Review Committee noted that:

> "the best approach to control is to build incentives into the system but that, paradoxically, most of the identifiable privileges tend to be concentrated in the high security prisons. We have heard of prisoners deliberately misbehaving so that they are not down-graded to category C and moved to a less comfortable establishment. . . . What is needed is an overview, which the Prison Department is not presently geared to deliver, of the roles and objectives of establishments of different kinds, and the way they interlock."

14.46   We share the Control Review Committee's approach. We propose that there should be a clear and established sense of progress through the prisoner's time in prison. It is understandable that the Control Review Committee concentrated on long-term inmates. But a sense of progress should apply equally to any prisoner serving a sentence, and to remand prisoners. It should be possible for each prisoner to have the incentive of knowing that he or she will build up a record of activity and behaviour during his time in prison which increasingly allows him greater freedom and greater opportunities until such time as he is discharged. Any regression during a prisoner's time in prison should be as a result of his own behaviour. Such a set-back should be temporary. In time, he should have the opportunity to get back on the ladder of progress.

14.47   We propose that it should be the responsibility of each prison to make coherent provision for the prisoner's progress through his sentence in that establishment. The prisoner's "contract" which we recommended in Section 12 should be the way to record that progress. It should be the responsibility of Prison Service Headquarters to ensure that there is consistency between what each prison offers.

14.48 The nature and range of the facilities which will provide for the prisoner's progress will depend on the type of prison itself. But we would envisage, for example, that the following arrangements might apply in a local prison established as a community prison and in small units on the lines we have described in Section 11. There might be in one unit of the prison a careful induction programme; in another, an ordered day which is likely to be relevant for short-sentenced prisoners; and in a third, a programme which is likely to be relevant to those starting on a long sentence. In some units it may be possible to keep prisoners who are particularly involved in, say, full-time education; others might be principally for those on vocational training or industrial work.

14.49 There are likely, in such a prison, to be prisoners who have shown that they do not need to be locked within their cells, except at night. We saw such units for long term prisoners in Saughton Prison, Edinburgh, which illustrated what we have in mind. There, long-term prisoners were being given considerable freedom to move about the unit and collectively arrange their own routines.

14.50 There will also need to be, as we have explained in Section 12, a part of the prison which can hold in much less open conditions those who have shown that they are not, for the present at least, prepared to accept any trust placed in them and behave responsibly.

14.51 There must also be separate provision, as we have explained in Section 10, for any remand prisoners.

14.52 The conditions in category C prisons, in particular, must be made more acceptable if allocation to them is to be seen as a sign of progress and not as a punishment for good behaviour. We have already proposed in Section 11 that the use of dormitories in category C establishments should be stopped. This would remove a powerful disincentive. It is necessary also to ensure that prisoners are able to move to category C prisons and open prisons at the right time in their sentence.

14.53 We propose that much fuller use should be made of open prisons. They have lower running costs, so there are considerable resource benefits in increasing their use. They should not be seen, as some prisoners see them today, as the preserve of white collar criminals. This is a false apprehension, but the Prison Service could do more to counter it. Equally false is the belief that, because more offenders are being diverted from prison, there is a dearth of suitable prisoners for open conditions.

14.54 We found a strong and, we believe, well founded belief among management at Leyhill Prison that they could, without too much difficulty, find from within reasonable distance, enough prisoners suitable for the open conditions they provide, in effect, to fill a second establishment.

14.55 We do not propose that all prisoners must as a matter of course end their sentence in open conditions – although there is logic in the argument that they might do so, since they will shortly be in the open community. Where an open prison is part of a local "cluster" of different types of prisoners, as described in Section 11, then prisoners can conveniently progress to open conditions. In other circumstances, we recognise that there may be a case for returning some prisoners to a local or community prison towards the end of their sentences. This would allow them to take advantage of a pre-release employment scheme, or to be near the Probation Service and others who will supervise and assist them on release. But there are many other prisoners who are not yet in the last weeks of their sentences who should be more readily considered for open conditions. It should be the responsibility of each Area Manager to satisfy himself that the category C and category B establishments in his area are not unnecessarily "hoarding" those suitable for open conditions, however convenient it is to the governors of those establishments to have around the establishment prisoners they trust. That trust must be transferred to a wider body of prisoners.

14.56 Our approach to incentives has informed most of our consideration of the issues we shall deal with in this section. It is fundamental to our approach to the organisation and planning of a sentence. It will inform our approach to education, training and work and, in particular, to pay and private cash.

Induction, Discharge and Sentence Planning

14.57 The evidence which was before the Inquiry shows, with remarkable unanimity, that prisoners should have sentence plans and that there should be proper induction and discharge procedures. There is also little difference of view about what sentence plans should contain and what the induction and discharge procedures should be. The problem is how they can be achieved, and how fast.

14.58 The Prison Service evidence sets out what should be the position in every prison. We were told:

"First, each establishment should have specific arrangements to receive new inmates to meet their immediate needs and, inter alia, plan their regime. The arrangements may be described variously as reception or induction and may include a Work Allocation Board (which may still in some cases be called Labour Allocation). One of the purposes of these arrangements is to establish what kind of work (there being an obligation on sentenced inmates to work) and other activities (which are voluntary) an inmate will do. During this period inmates will have an opportunity to say what they would prefer to do and in the better establishments will be encouraged to do so".

14.59 The Prison Service added:

"These arrangements work very much better in some establishments than in others. Many establishments have an induction course lasting up to a few days, while others have arrangements that are much less formal and take much less time. Moreover, the arrangements are constrained by what activities are available and the current situation on overcrowding, resourcing and specific local difficulties. But it is part and parcel of the general development of sentence planning, personal officer schemes and improved officer/inmate relationships that inmates should be consulted about their regime and for them to be able to exercise some choice where this is possible."

14.60 The Prison Service evidence identified the creation of a new Directorate of Inmate Programmes as a way of taking forward the concept of sentence planning. Mr Emes, the new Director of Inmate Programmes, spoke at one of our public seminars of his priorities for developing sentence planning. Following the introduction of sentence plans for young offenders in 1988, he proposed, that sentence planning would be introduced in April 1991 for all prisoners serving ten years or more. He was hopeful also that the Prison Service could add to that one other group, probably sex offenders, and begin sentence planning for them at the same time.

14.61 At the same seminar, Mr Cavadino, of the National Association for the Care and Resettlement of Offenders, explained the way he saw arrangements being made for the whole of the prisoner's time in prison and for his release back to the community. The first stage in the process was to assess the prisoner's immediate needs:

"That means that when somebody is received into prison there should be an initial interview which will look for example at whether steps need to be taken immediately to protect his or her accommodation, to arrange for housing benefit, to cover the tenancy for the period in prison, to see whether the employer has been informed about the reception into prison if the offender has got a job."

14.62 This initial assessment was relevant to every person coming into prison, including remand prisoners.

14.63 The second stage was, in Mr Cavadino's view:

"the systematic assessment of the prisoner's needs in relation for example to education, training, work, medical needs and other types of needs in prison: and planning during the sentence to try to meet those needs in the course of the regime that the prisoner goes through".

14.64 The third stage involved not simply planning training while in prison, but planning what was going to happen when somebody left prison. Mr Cavadino proposed that there should be a specific release plan. The plan should cover such areas as "housing needs, employment, education, medical care, finance".

14.65 Mr Cavadino argued also that prisoners should be involved, to the maximum extent possible, in determining their own regimes. That partly involved individuals determining their own sentence plan, through what he described as "negotiation with staff".

14.66 The Prison Officers' Association's evidence was consistent with much of this approach:

"All prisons should offer a service to individual prisoner which includes an interview on admission to identify immediate problems in the community caused by the prison sentence and to seek to ameliorate them; a programme of activities to help the prisoner pass the sentence constructively; and a programme of preparation for release for each prisoner which should start well in advance of release and should cover housing, employment, education, medical care (including help with addictions) and finance."

14.67 The POA added:

"A comprehensive system for preparing prisoners for release has implications for both resources and the training of prison officers".

14.68 The POA proposed that:

"Each prison should be required to make a statement outlining its policy and practice regarding the content of the regime including preparation for release. In consultation with the Probation Service and voluntary organisations which can contribute to prisoners' resettlement, each prison should introduce a system for implementing its preparation for release programme which should include access to advice giving services, adequate written information and relevant training courses".

14.69 We would endorse the approach adopted by both Mr Cavadino and the POA. We propose that there should be well prepared and relevant reception and induction programmes for all prisoners, including remand prisoners.

14.70 We have in mind the following procedures. A prisoner on reception should be able to discuss his immediate worries with a prison officer. That officer must have the time to arrange any necessary immediate action in response. This is not the moment for counselling, sentence planning, or helping the person to come to terms with his sentence or his remand in custody. It is the moment when any necessary action has to be taken to ensure, in the graphic description of Mr Bartell during one of the public seminars, that the prisoner's budgerigars at home are fed. This is not a flippant point. Someone may need to be alerted at home to take care immediately of the house or flat, and to look after the children. There needs to be a facility for doing such things immediately on reception.

14.71   There should then follow a period of induction. The length of the induction may vary, but it should not be artificially squeezed into a few days, let alone a few hours. Some induction periods may need to run into a few weeks, depending on the length of the sentence and the complexity of the prisoner's position. Prisons will wish to keep their induction prisoners together in a particular part of their establishment. As we have said, in the local community prison we have proposed, we would see one of the small units being assigned to this work.

14.72   The work in an induction unit is ideally and properly suited to prison officers. They may need, as the Prison Officers' Association has suggested, some additional training. But we have no doubt that most officers at least will have the aptitude for the task. A constructive involvement with a prisoner at the induction stage, will provide a sound and valuable foundation for improving relations between prisoners and staff. An imaginative induction programme should draw on services and agencies from outside the prison, but the programme should be arranged and run by prison officers under the guidance of the senior management of the prison.

14.73   During the induction procedure, the prisoner's personal officer would need to be identified. While a personal officer may not be practicable for the shortest stay prisoner (ie a prisoner who will be at the prison for less than 28 days), we propose that in all other cases – for both remand and sentenced prisoners – each prisoner should have a personal officer. He or she would be a prison officer. The personal officer would be the officer to whom the prisoner could turn for particular assistance or advice. The officer should have a particular interest in the prisoner's "contract" and any sentence plan. A personal officer system already applies in young offender institutions, as we have noted in Section 12. It should be extended to the adult system. If the personal officer system is to work effectively, some care will need to be given to allocating the prisoner to an officer who is likely to be able to relate to him. It would be for the wing or unit manager to monitor the way each officer's "caseload" worked in practice.

14.74   The induction period would essentially focus on the inmate's time in prison and on what problems might need to be resolved once he was released. The prisoner must contribute to all parts of that process. It will be during this process that the "contract" to which we referred in Section 12 will be drawn up and explained to the prisoner. We would not see it as a matter requiring negotiation, to use Mr Cavadino's word referred to above. But it should certainly involve discussion and consultation. A prisoner is far more likely to co-operate during his time in prison if he feels he has had a part to play in the way he spends his day. Equally, it is impossible to impose a release plan on a prisoner. If it is to work at all, he must be involved in and in some way committed to it.

14.75   We propose that the Prison Service should work towards the time when all prisoners serving a sentence of 12 months or more can be given some form of sentence plan in addition to their "contract".

14.76   For a prisoner serving less than 12 months, if the prisoner's "contract" is developed by the Prison Service over a period of time in the way we would hope, a separate sentence plan should not be necessary. The distinction between the "contract" we have recommended and the sentence plan, is this. The "contract" is the short term document which, as well as setting out the conditions in which he will live, describes what is to happen to the prisoner during the period immediately following the making of the "contract". We have in mind that it would need to be reviewed each year. The sentence plan, on the other hand, is the long term plan covering the whole period of the prisoner's sentence, be it two years or ten years. It may require variation or amendment. It may have to be replaced. But the new or revised plan would still deal with the whole of the remainder of the prisoner's sentence.

14.77   Remand prisoners would not normally be in custody for more than 12 months. In their case, the "contract" would deal with the matters which would otherwise need to be included in a custody plan. We accept that remand prisoners face a greater degree of unpredictability than most sentenced prisoners, but that cannot be a reason for not providing them with as clear guidance as possible on the arrangements which can be made for their time in prison.

14.78   We recognise, from what Mr Emes said, that sentence plans are not going to be introduced overnight. In the last two years, since sentence plans were introduced for young offenders, the Prison Service has concentrated on other matters, in particular the implementation of Fresh Start and senior management reorganisation – to both of which we have referred in earlier sections. We believe that greater priority must now be given to the way prisoners spend their time in prison, and to the work which is undertaken in prison to prepare them for their release. If Mr Emes' target is met, it will have been three years between the introduction of sentence plans for young offenders, and the introduction of sentence plans for prisoners serving over ten years, and, perhaps, for sex offenders. The time scale for extending the introduction of sentence plans to other prisoners should be substantially shorter than this.

14.79   There needs to be a greater focus on preparing plans for the prisoner's release. Depending on the length of the prisoner's sentence, these plans should be included in his "contract" or in his sentence plan. The release arrangements will be the final stage of a strategy which should apply throughout the sentence. The strategy should be aimed at preparing the prisoner for his return to the community.

14.80   Preparations for release will attract a particular importance if the proposals in the Criminal Justice Bill at present before Parliament are implemented. Dr Fowles, a member of the Parole Board, noted this in evidence at one of the public seminars. He said that:

"People who are going to be serving sentences of four years or more will in fact need planned careers throughout their time in custody. . . . . Without an effective prison system behind it, then the new system is not going to function at all."

14.81   We were pleased to observe that the Prison Service is well aware of this point. In its written evidence to the Inquiry, referring to the work of the Probation Service in prisons and in the community, it said that:

"major changes in this work will be needed if the Government's proposals for early release set out in chapter 6 of the White Paper [the White Paper entitled "Crime, Justice and Protecting the Public"] are to be implemented successfully. Work to tackle offending behaviour and to help the offender to resettle in the community will have to begin in the custodial part of the sentence. There will need to be a thorough assessment of each offender at the beginning of the sentence, followed by the drawing up of a programme aimed at meeting the objectives of preventing and reducing offending and helping the offender resettle successfully on release. This, in turn, implies a structured framework within each establishment for multi-disciplinary work with prisoners."

14.82   We agree with the Prison Service's assessment. In particular, we agree with it about the need for careful co-ordination, involving other agencies, including the Probation Service. We agree with the Prison Service that sentence programmes or plans will be the way to tackle this. We propose that the Prison Service should now make the necessary arrangements to implement its proposals for sentence programmes so that they are ready at such time as the Criminal Justice Bill may itself be implemented. Those arrangements should then provide a sound basis for developing such procedures for all prisoners.

14.83   We commend also the Prison Service's intention to establish Pre-release and Development courses run by prison officers in every establishment by the financial year 1991/92. We were impressed by the planning and preparation of the courses we saw on our visits. We believe that they will provide a good service to prisoners and a valuable way of enhancing the work of prison officers.

Education

14.84   It has long been recognised that education has an important contribution to make to a prison's regime. This is reflected in the Prison Rules and in particular Prison Rule 29. Rule 29(1) provides:

> "(1)   Every prisoner able to profit from the educational facilities provided at a prison shall be encouraged to do so."

14.85   Education in Prison Service establishments is provided by inviting Local Education Authorities to supply teaching staff, with the related professional and administrative advice, support and supervision. Payments to Local Education Authorities for teaching services had risen from £10.85m in 1985/86 to £21.20m in 1989/90. The Prison Service told us that:

> "After allowing for inflation this is an increase in spending in real terms over five years of over 50%".

14.86   In addition, we understand from the Prison Service evidence, that the total number of student hours rose from 5.56m hours in 1987/88 to 6.8m hours in 1988/89 and again to 7.75m hours in 1989/90.

14.87   This appears to be a remarkable improvement and a lot of hours. But it must be remembered that these hours are spread unevenly over a large number of prisons and an even larger number of prisoners. We met many prisoners on our visits to establishments who told us that, even at these increased levels, educational provision was woefully inadequate. There were long waiting lists to join classes. Even those who succeeded in being accepted for a class could not be sure whether they would be able to attend it – classes were frequently cancelled because, prisoners were told, there was no prison officer to escort them to the education rooms.

14.88   There were similar views expressed by prisoners who wrote to us. Prisoners were particularly resentful that, in their view, education was not given a high enough priority and was too often cancelled because of staffing problems. Some of the letters also suggested that education programmes should be different. They should provide more sex education, social skills, vocational training and literacy classes. On the other hand, those whom we met in prisons on education courses were almost universally appreciative of the provision. It is clear from the evidence before us that they were the lucky ones.

14.89   What counts, therefore, is not just the number of hours available for education, but the number of inmates who can have access to it.

14.90   The Prison Service in its written evidence stated that on average during 1989/90 17% of inmates (over 8,000) were involved in full-time education and training. In addition, on average there were 20,000 student hours each week in evening classes. The Prison Service told us, however, that the number of evening classes available had been reduced due to an increased emphasis on full-time education during the working day. The Service noted that a considerable number of inmates also studied in their cells using Open Learning materials with tutorial support when required.

14.91   Open learning was also clearly of assistance in providing educational opportunities for remand prisoners. The Prison Service also told us that "the development of modular courses often of very short duration is seen as providing the best way forward in developing education opportunities for remand prisoners. The growing availability of high quality open learning materials, with which inmates can study at times to suit themselves with tutorial support as and when needed, should also play a major part in enhancing the education programme available to remand prisoners". We agree with the Prison Service that this is the correct approach for remand prisoners. We wish there had been more evidence of it being implemented in practice. We propose that the Prison Service should make increased provision for modular education courses, in particular for remand prisoners.

14.92   In considering these issues, we received substantial assistance from the evidence of, and from meeting the House of Commons Education, Science and Arts Committee. The Committee provided us with copies of the first report from its predecessors for the 1982/83 session on Prison Education and the Second Report from the Committee for the 1986/87 session, also on Prison Education.

14.93   The 1983 Committee had made 23 recommendations in its report, including proposing greater consultation with Local Education Authorities about the provision of facilities. It proposed also a new Prison Regimes Act, which would provide that a prisoner should have, throughout his sentence, the right of access to education. The Committee proposed that there should be rules made under the Act to provide for the remuneration of prisoners undertaking full-time education at a rate equal to that earned in prison industries. These recommendations for a Prison Regimes Act were not accepted by the Government.

14.94   In its Report published on 6 May 1987, the Education, Science and Arts Committee reaffirmed its belief in the value of education in prisons. The Report made some 35 recommendations. It reiterated the case for a Prison Regimes Act. It recommended that funding should be increased from what it calculated in 1985/86 to represent 4.7% of the total operating costs of penal establishments to 7%. (The Committee told us when we met that this would represent today about £50m – on any terms a very considerable increase over the current levels.) It recommended also a major programme to encourage and enable all those prisoners in need of basic education to receive it. This programme should involve prison officers as well as teachers.

14.95   For the reasons which we have explained in Section 13, we are particularly attracted to the Select Committee's recommendation that prison officers should be more closely involved in prison education. We will refer to this later in this Section. Because we have attempted to structure our proposals in a way which avoids having to rely on legislation, we have not included among our proposals the Committee's recommendation for a Regimes Act.

14.96   We were helped also by evidence from HM Senior Chief Inspector of Schools. The Inspectorate undertakes "a limited amount" of inspection of prison education at the invitation of the Prison Service. It involves, typically, visits to some 20 or so prisons each year. The Senior Chief Inspector's evidence emphasised the importance of the attitude of prison managers and uniformed staff towards education and training. The attitude varied between establishments – the more enlightened recognised the potential of education and training. Others had what the Senior Chief Inspector described as "more negative attitudes".

14.97   Mr Steel, one of HM Inspectors, contributed to the discussion at one of our public seminars. He identified the need for clear objectives and a thorough needs analysis of all people entering prisons. But he placed particular emphasis on inter-disciplinary work, involving collaboration between the various specialisms within a prison. He said:

> "We have noted with interest and a great deal of excitement that in a number of situations there is an increase in the inter-discipline training where prison officers, probation officers, education staff, governor staff, works staff will come together, and in those situations the training appears to be more integral."

14.98   We agree with Mr Steel. We propose that education should be seen as an integral part of the life of prisons. It should be integrated with the other activities and opportunities on offer.

14.99   We have deliberately addressed education before considering work because we believe it is necessary to signpost a change in the balance of the relationship between work and education. Both need to be seen as making sensible and practical provision for the training of prisoners. This training should not be treated as being solely an end in itself – it should also be designed to increase the competence and confidence of prisoners on release, and to improve their opportunities for finding work and a place in society.

14.100   An effective education programme in a prison should be able to be integrated with the education a prisoner would receive in the community on his release. This is particularly important for remand and short sentence prisoners. In the case of some prisoners, if the prisoner's and the Prison Service's investment in education and training is to be realised, the prisoner should be able to continue that education and training on release. It is the Prison Service's responsibility to ensure that any probation officer supervising the prisoner on release is aware of this aspect of the prisoner's time in prison. It is also the Prison Service's responsibility to ensure that the prisoner is given clear and effective guidance about the ways in which he may continue with education and training following his release, and about the organisations in the community who are there to help him to do so.

14.101   We recognise the dangers of being too optimistic about the prospects of rehabilitation, whether through education, training, or any other facility provided in prison. But whether the argument is approached from the point of view of control within the prison; or from the point of view of the prisoner who wishes to feel that he is making some constructive use of his time in prison; or from the view of those who believe that every prisoner should be given an opportunity to find a better alternative to repeated recourse to crime, the arguments all point the same way. The argument in favour of extending educational opportunities as far as resources will allow is overwhelming.

14.102   We propose, therefore, that education should be given an equal standing to work within the activities of the prison. They should come together in seeking to provide useful and recognised qualifications for prisoners which take account of their wishes and their intellectual capabilities and aspirations. Education should not be imposed – other than for those young offenders for whom it is already a statutory requirement. The problem as we see it in prisons is not dragooning people into the classes; it is ensuring that the classes are not only provided, but that the prisoners who wish to attend can do so.

14.103   If our proposals set out in Section 13 in relation to the role of prison officers and staffing levels are met, then there should not be the same problem of getting inmates to classes. A separate escort service, as we propose in Section 12, should help avoid officers being taken off for these duties. If prisoners involved in full-time education can, for example, be accommodated in the same unit in a local or community prison, that should assist the problem of accompanying inmates to classes. It should also be possible for some prisoners to go to classes without close escorting. Except where the highest levels of security may be required, we see little case for any significant level of security supervision in education blocks. The prisons we visited in Europe did not seem to find a need for such intensive security cover.

14.104   We attach importance also to involving prison officers in the work of education departments. We were attracted to the scheme at Lincoln Prison, referred to in Section 13, for the appointment of prison officers as education liaison officers. We believe other prisons should follow this excellent example. We believe it would be welcomed by prison officers as another practical way of enhancing their work, on the lines we discussed in Section 13. It should enable prisoners to see prison officers in a more constructive light.

14.105   We consider also that the Prison Service should involve prisoners more in the education programme. That means they should be more fully consulted about not just the courses which are on offer, but also the courses which are not yet on offer but which would be of value to them. It means also that some prisoners with particular teaching skills or qualifications should be able to join in the teaching programme themselves – both during the day and in evening classes. We saw such classes being run by inmates during our visits abroad.

14.106   A remarkably ambitious approach to these matters was followed at Stillwater Prison in Minnesota. There prisoners ran for that prison and for a nearby open prison, a University education course for prisoners, bringing in teachers from the State University. This programme was funded by the prisoners themselves, who earned substantial sums writing computer programmes and by telephone marketing. This may be too entrepreneurial a precedent, but it does demonstrate the scope of what is possible with greater flexibility and imagination.

14.107   We have considered also the question of what payment should be made to inmates undertaking education. We shall examine wider aspects relating to pay and private cash later in this Section. At present, inmates on full-time education are paid at a standard rate, which is often less than they could earn in workshops. Both Mr Emes, the Director of Inmate Programmes, and Mr Coggan of the National Prisoners' Movement, argued at our public seminars that there was no reason why those in education should expect to be paid the same as those in workshops. But others, including the organisation Bridging the Gap, proposed that what that organisation described as the "financial disincentives to education", should be abolished.

14.108   We recognise, as Mr Coggan said, that those who embark on full-time education in the world outside prisons are likely to face a financial loss compared to their colleagues in full-time work. But we do not believe it makes sense to push the analogy with the outside world too far. Prison can never be exactly like the outside world. It is necessary to take into account the low levels of pay in prisons and the amount of pay prisoners require in order to meet what they regard as being the most basic necessities of life.

14.109   It must be also remembered that one of the Purposes of the Prison Service is to help prisoners "lead law abiding and useful lives in custody and after release". One way to meet both parts of that objective is to provide ready access and encouragement to prisoners to take education courses. The prison system should not provide disincentives to suitable prisoners taking education courses and training courses. A uniformly low rate of pay is such a disincentive.

14.110   We propose, therefore, that there should be a payment scheme which provides pay levels for those engaged in education which are commensurate to those earned elsewhere in the prison, including in workshops.

Physical Education

14.111   For many – but not all – prisoners, physical education is one of the most popular parts of the prison day. The Prison Service told us that during each of the last three years, PE programmes have exceeded five million inmate/hours of supervised physical activity. It calculated that that represented more than two hours of PE per week for every inmate held in custody by the Service:

> "Overall, nearly half of all adult offenders take a weekly, active part in the PE programme and, while for young offenders there is a compulsory element, about 60% of them volunteer to attend additional classes."

14.112   The Prison Service stated that:

> "PE has a clear role to play in fulfilling the Prison Service's functions of providing prisoners with as full a life as is consistent with the facts of

custody and to preparing prisoners for their release back into the community. It maintains or more usually provides a level of fitness in those who are confined through general or remedial classes. It helps to release the tensions and possibly to dissipate the aggression which confinement generates. For a number it develops or fosters interests in sporting or outdoor activities (such as Outward Bound, City Challenge, the Duke of Edinburgh's Award or the Drake Fellowship), in leadership (through the CCPR's Community Sports Leaders Award Scheme), in leisure skills which, if validated by NCVQ, can be the basis for constructive work inside and, it is hoped, outside the custodial environment."

14.113   The Central Council of Physical Recreation (CCPR) told us that they believed it should be a stated aim of the Prison Service that inmates should leave prison no less fit and healthy than when they entered. It is implicit in the Prison Service evidence that that is the objective. If it is not already clear, we propose that it should be made so.

14.114   But there is also a second aim of physical education, as the CCPR evidence recognises. We propose that, as well as providing inmates with exercise and ways of letting off steam, the PE programme should give priority to providing structured courses that can lead to qualifications. We were encouraged by the Prison Service's reference to the National Council for Vocational Qualifications. As the Prison Service itself says:

"In the 1990s anyone without NVQs will be at a distinct disadvantage in the labour market."

14.115   We would put it more positively than that. We believe that NVQs provide a very useful way of focusing effort, and of providing incentives and motivation for such effort. NVQs can be incorporated into physical education programmes. They can also be a feature of many other aspects of prison life, including work in industrial workshops, in horticulture, in agriculture, and in prison kitchens. NVQs can also assist prisoners after discharge. We propose that the Prison Service should continue to develop the NVQ courses in as many aspects of prison programmes as possible. These qualifications provide prisoners with some confidence in their abilities and some equality in the labour market on their release.

14.116   We commend also the CCPR Community Sports Leader Awards. These were discussed by both inmates and staff at the seminars we held in October at Lincoln Prison. They were welcomed by the inmates as a sign of an achievement which they could take with them on release. They were welcomed by the staff, including the PE instructors, as a way of engendering a sense of pride and achievement among inmates while they were in prison. We were told that 13 of the 14 prisoners at Lincoln who had taken a recent Awards test had passed. There had been a well of sympathy and support among other prisoners for the one prisoner who had failed. Such mutual support needs fostering. Attainable awards and certificates are a good way of doing so.

Work

14.117   Prison Rule 28 sets out the arrangements for work in prison. The two parts of the Rule which are particularly relevant for our purposes are:

"(1)   A convicted prisoner shall be required to do useful work for not more than ten hours a day, and arrangements shall be made to allow prisoners to work, where possible, outside the cells and in association with one another.

(5)   An unconvicted prisoner shall be permitted, if he wishes, to work as if he were a convicted prisoner."

14.118   In its evidence to the Inquiry, the Prison Service pointed out that Prison Service Industries and Farms (PSIF) was the biggest single provider of occupation for inmates. The evidence said that:

"It currently provides 16,000 employment places, at a net cost of £17m a year. In 1989/90, it provided 13.3 million hours of inmate occupation at an average cost per hour of £1.32."

14.119 Of these 16,000 places, 11,000 were in 250 industrial workshops. The product range included metal and wooden furniture, security grilles and gates, weaving, workwear, footwear, printing, brushmaking, injection moulding, concrete moulding, road signs and laundry.

14.120 In addition, the Prison Service said:

"Nearly 2,500 inmates work more directly for the private sector on a sub-contract basis. Such work will range from sophisticated printed circuit board preparation, through light assembly to packing".

14.121 A thousand employment places were also provided in 42 Prison Service laundries.

14.122 Prison farms, as well as providing 75% of the prisons' requirements of milk and 85% of eggs, produced a revenue of £2m by sales of surplus milk, pigs and other livestock. The farms provided employment to prisoners of varying abilities. They allowed 1,970 prisoners to take part in formal training schemes in 1989, which led to a total of 2,859 passes.

14.123 The Prison Service reported to us that:

"In the financial year ended 31 March 1990, provisional figures show that prison industries generated sales of £31m with a net cost of operating of £19.7m after charging all expenditure".

14.124 They reported also that:

"In the same period, the value of produce and services supplied by Farms and Gardens activities was some £32.8m at a net profit of about £2.2m."

14.125 The Prison Service evidence emphasised the value for money which prison industries provided. The Service provided some now fairly old comparative costings for the year 1984/85. These showed that each inmate hour spent in PSIF workshops cost £2.62. By contrast, each inmate hour spent in education cost £4.57. The Service told us that PSIF had been:

"described by the Comptroller and Auditor General, in a report for the House of Commons as one of the best buys' of regime activities for both cost and penological reasons".

14.126 The Prison Service said that what PSIF provided, which other regime activities did not, was:

"work which is subject to the disciplines of the market place. For many inmates this will be a new experience in itself: and one of the things that the Prison Service should be trying to achieve is to instil the habit of work into inmates with poor employment records."

14.127 One of the biggest sources of inefficiency, the Prison Service told us, was in under-use of PSIF resources:

"Net working hours in workshops increased from 20.9 per week on average in 1988/89 to 21.7 per week on average in 1989/90. But there is much more room for improvement."

14.128 Part of the explanation for shortened hours can be traced to the abnormal hours at which prisoners have their meals. Mealtimes dictate the timing of shifts. Habits have become ingrained, but they can and should be changed. Lunch does not need to be served at 11.00 to 11.30 hours. At Saughton

Prison Edinburgh lunch takes place at 12.30. Supper can be later than 16.00 to 16.30 hours. We recognise the problems this can create for staffing patterns, but it is a problem which surely can, and must be addressed through the corporate objectives process of setting staff levels which we consider in Section 13.

14.129   There are a variety of options open to management to suit the local situation. Prisoners could work in shifts and have their meals at different times. Meals could even be brought to their places of work where this is appropriate. The main meal could be taken at the end of the day instead of the middle of the day, as is increasingly happening already. We propose, therefore, that each prison should aim to reach a situation where the hours of work correspond closer to those in the normal world outside the prison.

14.130   There is also a continuing tension between the claims of workshops and the claims of other activities. The point was graphically illustrated by the Head of Prison Service Industries and Farms, Miss MacNaughton at one of the Inquiry's public seminars. She said:

> "A new engineering workshop actually costs half a million to set up. Now, I do not think that the Government is going to be in the business – I do not think most taxpayers would want them to be in the business – of setting up new engineering workshops if they were going to be used very little and only part of the time. . . . If you are looking at the principle of normalisation, you have to address the question whether you do actually want work in prisons to be measured by the normal commercial disciplines. If it is going to be measured by the normal commercial disciplines, then you are going to have make some very hard choices about investment and about the use you make of investment in relation to that activity. . . . The key thing is that once you have customers and once you have taken orders, you have to try to deliver on time."

14.131   We do not for a moment question the logic of this approach. Large capital investment must not be wasted. Orders must be met. But, as Miss MacNaughton herself very fairly recognised, this approach is based on the assumption that PSIF should run as an outside industry seeking to make profits for its shareholders. In this case, the shareholder is the Treasury, acting on behalf of the taxpayer.

14.132   We have reservations about this approach. We do not believe it is realistic to view prison workshops as a means of realising financial profits. We propose that workshops should instead be seen primarily as part of a planned programme of activities and opportunities for prisoners. Of course, they should not be run at a loss if that can be avoided. But equally the choice of industry and the capital invested should be strongly influenced by the need to provide constructive and purposeful employment in farm and workshop for as many prisoners as can usefully be deployed. It should be influenced also by the need to find work which is likely to assist the prisoner to find employment after release.

14.133   The fact that Prison Rule 28 makes work compulsory for convicted prisoners should not lead to work, regardless of its nature, having always first demand on the resources and staff of a prison. Each prison should seek to provide a range of work which meets the abilities and requirements of its population. There is a case for specialised prisons, like Coldingley, where the primary focus is on industrial work. But equally there can be other prisons, particularly local prisons, which should provide properly structured work as part of a planned programme for prisoner development.

14.134   We propose that this planned programme should bring together work, training and education in a way that provides the most constructive mix for the prisoners who are to be involved in it. Such a programme must also take realistic account of the need to provide prisoners to keep the establishment running – prisoners are needed to sweep the floors and clear up the grounds. But this should not be the sole work provided, nor should it be, as often it is now, seen as a long term assignment. It should be possible to plan a prisoner's day so that part of the time can be spent on education and part on suitably identified work, either in the workshops or assisting in the upkeep and cleanliness of the prison.

14.135   This integrated approach has considerable implications for the selection and organisation of industrial and agricultural work in prisons. It means, first of all, that prisons should identify work which provides opportunities for a range of abilities. We recognise the need for some work of a simple nature, such as packing and assembly, or the knotting of string into nets: but on our visits we have been as depressed as many of the prisoners to see intelligent and articulate prisoners, well able to perform really challenging work, kicking their heels in such workshops. This is more than just dampening to the morale of both prisoners and staff; it provides a sense of frustration and lack of worth which can only help contribute to an atmosphere of aggression in a prison.

14.136   We received a substantial number of letters from prisoners who characterised work as "slave labour". Work in prisons was monotonous, degrading, and soul destroying. An equal number of writers suggested that work should be made rehabilitative and meaningful. The more work is tied in to the education and training programme, and the more it leads to recognised qualifications and certificates of effort, the greater will be the incentive to work constructively. As a result, the more valuable will be the work when the prisoner comes to release.

14.137   We propose that there should also be a greater range of arrangements for work and type of work in prison establishments. We were helped by the evidence from the Apex Trust in coming to this conclusion. The Trust proposed that work should be made as relevant as possible through the involvement of outside employers and through co-operation with Training and Enterprise Councils. It proposed also that the Prison Service should fund partnership schemes between prisons, industries, and the specialist voluntary sector. In the report which the Trust sent to us entitled "A Working Future for Prisoners and Prisons" the Apex Trust noted that:

> "In assessing bids from the private sector, selection of contracts should take place not simply on cash criteria but on criteria which look at: training provision; stability of the enterprise; and the likelihood of inmates gaining jobs on release".

14.138   We noted Miss MacNaughton's perfectly correct words of caution at the public seminar. She said that she had been struck by an admission of the German delegate at the conference which led to the preparation of the Apex Trust's report. When the economy slowed down, private employers pulled out. The regime activity was lost very suddenly, with no obvious replacement. It is possible, however, to exaggerate that argument. Taken to extremes, it could be a recipe for no form of work or enterprise at all. It may be better to have worked on a contract and lost it, than never to have worked at all.

14.139   We recognise also that in the past there have been significant problems created by contracts being entered into which a prison could not fulfil. The result has been a substantial financial loss. Again the solution is not to deprive the establishment of any possibility of showing initiative. The solution lies in PSIF having the time to exercise a supervisory role in a constructive way. PSIF should be able to alert the establishment to the need not to be unduly exposed to the risks of the marketplace.

14.140   We commend, therefore, the approach advocated by Mr Mather of the Apex Trust in involving outside employers at a range of levels within prisons. He told the Inquiry:

> "The very first thing that employers can do is help and advise in getting the existing training and work to be reflecting the real needs and opportunities in the outside world and this involves the work of Training and Enterprise Councils where already some links are occurring between prisons and these

principally private sector led bodies. Secondly, and at the other extreme, there is the opportunity for employers to actually operate businesses within prisons, paying the rate for the job. I would say, looking at how this operates in other countries, you are probably talking about a maximum of 15% of the prisoner population being employed in that way".

14.141 We were impressed on the Inquiry's visits abroad by the way private employers were involved in prison workshops. In particular in Germany, we learned of major international companies which had set up workshops in both sentenced and remand prisons. We consider the American experience also to be relevant here. We propose that the Prison Service should look for greater opportunities for deploying private companies in prison workshops.

14.142 Work can also be a way in which the prisoner regards himself as making amends for his conduct. There is now a well established tradition of prisoners making a variety of goods, either to be used for charitable purposes or to be sold so that the proceeds can be given to charity. Many prisoners find work of this nature improves their self-esteem and enables them, in a meaningful way, to show remorse. We regard this as being a most constructive use of work. We propose that, wherever possible, there should be schemes, however small, which enable a prisoner to contribute to society by making goods for charitable causes.

14.143 We are doubtful that the objectives we have discussed in the preceding paragraphs are likely to be met under the present structure for work in prisons. PSIF, whatever its strengths, often appears to be seen in prisons as "the enemy": not by prisoners, but by the staff, and at times by local management. The problem appears to lie in the fact that PSIF provide the work, and the prison management is intended to provide the prisoners. The result is that PSIF, understandably, put considerable pressure on management to ensure that, whatever else happens, the workshops are kept up and running. Where they are not, they are threatened with closure.

14.144 Mr Mather of the Apex Trust, said at one of our public seminars:

"We need to have a great deal more concerted effort to open up the workshops. I believe the constraints there are not so much to do with lack of market, because PSIF have got a full order book and are having difficulties getting it all done. It is to do with management."

14.145 The management of workshops needs to be brought clearly within the prisons themselves. We propose that it should be the responsibility of each prison Governor to make the necessary provision for work as well as training in his establishment. We did not find convincing the argument put in the Prison Service's evidence that:

"It is unlikely that industries or farms at any but the most cottage industry' level could be completely managed from within establishments".

14.146 In management terms, there are dis-economies in running a large scale enterprise, as the chequered history of prison industries has shown. It is easier to manage and control an enterprise involving two or three workshops and a handful of contracts than it is one with a net cost of £17m a year.

14.147 Our proposal should also mean that Governors will feel personally responsible for the success of the workshops and enterprises which they have established. They will be able to work more closely with local employers and Training and Enterprise Councils to provide the most appropriate mix of work in their establishments. They will better be able to take account of the nature of their prisoners and the community in which the prison is placed. If our recommendation to develop community prisons is followed, this proposal should gain added relevance and significance.

14.148 This proposal would not lead to the end of PSIF. It would still have an important role. There would still need to be a central organisation, supervising and advising on contractual arrangements before contracts of any substance are entered into, monitoring results, and providing professional assistance. It should be open to an establishment to call on Headquarters for assistance in finding work. We understand this is the arrangement in the Netherlands. PSIF in some situations would be the consultants. In others it could be a partner. But the nature of the relationship between Headquarters and the establishment would change. The relationship we propose is fully consistent with the relationship between Headquarters and establishments which we describe in Section 12.

Pay and Private Cash

14.149   The evidence we received from outside the Prison Service was almost wholly critical of the low level at which prisoners were paid. Mr Anthony Heaton-Armstrong wrote:

> "Prisoners' pay is ludicrously low and compares unfavourably with that of their colleagues in some other European countries."

14.150   One prisoner, serving a life sentence said:

> "The wages paid to inmates are by any standards ridiculous. If you have no outside support, like most long term inmates, you have to supply yourself with everything like tobacco, toiletries, stamps, writing material, tea, coffee, food to supplement the prison diet from an average of £2.75 a week. If wages were put at a reasonable level, prisoners could help dependents on the outside financially. Why bring a man so low that he is picking up butts? Show him how much he can achieve instead of how low he can sink".

14.151   The Apex Trust said:

> "Current levels of pay provide little or no incentive for inmates to engage in work and training."

The Trust went on to say:

> "On average, a prisoner will receive £2.80 for a week's work. There can be few more powerful indications of the low value which is placed on inmate labour and work provided. Few can surely defend a system which paid inmates less than the sum received by many children in pocket money."

14.152   The Prison Governors' Association was no less scathing:

> "At present inmates' pay is unacceptably low. For example, a basket of goods that an inmate might reasonably wish to purchase from a prison canteen each week would require earnings of at least £8.00."

The Association recommended:

> "Inmates should be given substantially higher wages that would act as an incentive. . . . The PGA believe that the whole system of pay for work in prison should be reviewed and the aim should be to give a reward for their labours."

14.153   Nearly one in six of the letters we received from prisoners outside the target prisons expressed concern about the low amount they could earn. A number of writers suggested it should be made possible for inmates to save towards the future, to pay part of their keep or to help their families. One inmate compared unfavourably the pay scales for the unemployed in prisons to the pay for those in work in prisons. He said that a prisoner who stayed in his cell all day received £1.75. For a 30 hour week he was paid £2.20 – "I in effect work 30 hours for 45p". His modest proposal was that the £2.20 he earned should be added to the "unemployed" rate of £1.75 to bring him up to £3.95.

14.154   The Prison Service, in its evidence, stated in terms that:

> "Inmates are paid at pocket money levels for work done, from which they

may purchase items from the canteen."

14.155 There were a range of pay schemes which were:

"designed to recognise responsibility and aptitude and reward effort and productivity. All convicted inmates, as well as those unconvicted inmates who offer themselves for work, receive a basic weekly payment of £1.75 (known as flat rate basic) whether occupied or not. For those in work or following a regime activity such as education, various flat rate, piece rate and incentive pay schemes provide opportunities to earn up to a maximum of £5.87 per week in certain workshops and kitchens. A number of establishments, such as the dispersal prisons, have special pay schemes. Expenditure on inmates' pay in 1989/90 totalled some £6.6m, giving an average weekly rate of about £2.65 per prisoner. Rates of pay were last increased generally with effect from 9 April 1990."

14.156 Standing Order 6 provides that at each establishment there should be one or more approved pay schemes in operation determining the rates of prisoner's pay. There are six main schemes – a flat rate scheme; a piece rate scheme; a modified piece work scheme; a kitchen payment scheme; a scheme for unconvicted prisoners; and a dispersal incentive scheme. On the evidence provided by the Prison Service, it would appear, therefore, that the Prison Service has been able to devise six different schemes to cover a financial difference of about £4.00.

14.157 Given such paucity of pay, the amount of money which a prisoner can have sent into prison gains considerable importance. Unconvicted prisoners may spend as much private cash as they wish. Convicted prisoners may spend a total of £115 in each 12 month period and a further £75 on hobbies materials.

14.158 We have considered whether it is right to continue to allow families to send in private cash. This is a matter on which we propose no change. It is a proper reflection of the status of remand prisoners that it should be possible for cash to be sent to them from outside the prison. There are not the same grounds for permitting unlimited cash to be used by sentenced prisoners. There are clear disadvantages. It would provide scope for exploitation by the more wealthy prisoners, or of the wealthy by the more powerful. It would remove incentives for certain prisoners to take part in work and education programmes. It would place an extra burden on families. If the proposals which we will be making about pay levels are accepted, then the sending in of money from outside should become a less prominent feature of life in prisons.

14.159 There are strong arguments for providing additional pay for prisoners. We have referred to them in our references earlier to the evidence we have received. A reasonable level of pay enables a prison to provide a sensible level of incentives, reflecting more accurately a range of effort and achievement. Pay is often seen in life outside prison as some measure of a person's worth. It is understandable that a similar yardstick should be applied by prisoners to prison wages. The current payment levels suggest that prisoners have moved into a Toytown world where all values are deflated – except those in the canteen, where prisoners have to buy goods at today's prices.

14.160 A more realistic level of pay would also allow prisoners to exercise some of the responsibilities that will be expected of them on release. The only place where this operates in this country at present is the pre-release employment schemes, where prisoners hand their wages earned in outside work to the Warden each week. Deductions are then made to cover such things as social security maintenance payments to the prisoner's family, and a contribution towards the cost of hostel board and lodgings.

14.161 Many prisoners we spoke to wanted to feel that they were able to meet some of their financial responsibilities. Prisoners found no difficulty with the suggestion that, if they were paid a more realistic wage, they should make a contribution to Victim Support Schemes. Some enthusiastically welcomed the idea. One prisoner spoke movingly of wanting to be able to buy his child a present for her birthday as a way of retaining some respect for himself within his family.

14.162   There is no doubt in our minds that prison pay is a very substantial cause of disquiet and dissatisfaction within prisons. It is a disincentive to engendering the proper attitude to work among prisoners. It takes away prisoners' respect. It leaves them heavily dependent on families who are likely anyway to be having to struggle to cope. It cannot make sense in the context of prisons, or as a matter of social policy.

14.163   We propose, therefore, that prisoners should be able to earn at more realistic pay levels. This is not a proposal for lining the pockets of prisoners. It is a proposal for ensuring that prisoners are responsibly able to set aside money in order to meet some of their obligations and requirements. Prison life could be transformed if prisoners were paid at a level which allowed them to make some realistic disbursements from their earnings in prison.

14.164   As far as pay levels go, British prisoners are the poor men of Europe. This was clear from our visits overseas. Pay levels varied. We would not wish to suggest that we were able to conduct, or thought it necessary to conduct, any sort of scientific survey. But it is worth giving some examples. An inmate in the Bois d'Arcy Remand Centre in Paris working in a workshop could earn 100 francs a day (approximately £10). In the Modello Prison in Barcelona, it was possible for a hard working prisoner to earn up to about the equivalent of £40 per month. In De Marwei Prison, Leewaarden, long term inmates were paid the equivalent of £15 a week and short term inmates £7.50 – the disparity was being reviewed. In Oak Park Heights, Minnesota wages varied between 47 cents an hour (approximately 25p) and $2.20 an hour (approximately £1.10). In Joyceville Prison, Canada, pay varied between Canadian $1.60 to $6.70 a day (approximately 70p to £2.90) – with the metal workshop paying $4.50 *an hour* (approximately £1.95) from which prisoners paid $10.00 a week (approximately £4.30) for their board and tax.

14.165   The prisoners we discussed this with at the seminar at Lincoln Prison suggested that there should be maximum wage of £15. At present pay levels, it was very hard on people whose families could not afford to send private cash. One inmate said that even being able to send home £5.00 could help to give a man back his pride. The staff at Lincoln thought that £15 might be too high, compared with the money available to the average pensioner, but they all agreed that current pay levels were unsatisfactory.

14.166   The present position cannot, therefore, be sustained. Pay scales should be substantially increased. It is easier, however, to will the end than to establish the means. In its evidence to us, the Prison Service said that:

"Each 10p a week increase would cost the Prison Service £250,000."

14.167   The Prison Service noted that there had been a substantial review of these matters. The review had been considered by the Prisons Board in May 1990. This had led to the conclusion that a wider range of options should be considered and that further work should be commissioned to this end.

14.168   We welcome the Prison Service's wish to consider a wider a range of options. We propose that the Prison Service should set itself realistic and attainable targets for improving prisoners' rates of pay. Initially, the target should be to improve the money received by prisoners so that the most hard working prisoners can earn up to £10 a week – a level which is below that which, we understand, will result in the prisoner making social security maintenance payments. From the Prison Service's own figures, if the increase were to be from an average of £2.65 to an average of £8.00, then the additional annual cost would be £13.4m.

14.169 An average wage of £8 is still by any normal standard derisory. We accept that the sum required even to increase wages to this extent is nevertheless very substantial. But the cost of keeping inmates securely in prison is also very substantial. £13.4m would represent only about 1.7% of current annual expenditure on keeping prisoners in prison. It is a price that must be paid if a fair and challenging sentence is to be offered to prisoners.

14.170 There are ways of redirecting resources in order to meet the initial costs we have identified. On the evidence from the Prison Service which we have referred to earlier, prison industry appears to have operated at a profit of £11.3m in the financial year ended 31 March 1990. Farms and gardens appear to have made a net profit of about £2.2m. If these profits were invested in increasing prisoners' pay, then it would be possible to meet our proposal of an increase up to an average of about £8.00 on the basis of PSIF returns alone.

14.171 While some of our proposals in relation to work might be said to affect these profit levels, equally other proposals involving greater involvement of the private sector should of themselves increase pay levels for prisoners involved in such enterprises. If Mr Mather's evidence is correct, that could benefit up to 15% of all prisoners. For these prisoners, the maximum level of £10 would have to be reviewed. It might be reasonable for part of the wages of those prisoners to be retained. Some could go to their families. Some could go to other prisoners providing domestic services in the prison.

14.172 In the longer term, we propose that pay levels should be increased much more substantially. This would enable the prisoner to take greater responsibility in continuing to meet his obligations to his family and the community. He would then pay a sum equal to social security and maintenance payments to his family, plus some extra if he wished; he would be required to contribute to Victims Support Schemes; he might pay something towards his upkeep; he would be able to buy or rent additional goods for his cell, such as a television or a small computer system. A realistic wage would be a way of ensuring that the prisoner takes greater responsibility for himself in prison and outside.

14.173 We suggest in the review that it has announced that the Prison Service considers also a more radical option. This would allow inmates' pay levels to be set against an earlier release date or, for longer serving prisoners, an earlier date for parole review. We envisage there might be a scheme whereby, at the same time as a prisoner earned a reasonable wage level, the amount he earned would also qualify him for earlier release. The more he was able, by his application and effort, to earn, the more days he would build up. There might be a sliding scale which at the maximum allowed a hard working prisoner to earn early release from up to a twelfth of his sentence length (ie a month for each year served). Such a scheme would have the advantage that the prisoner would obtain early release by his own efforts. It would not be, as remission is at present, automatic and subject only to loss through bad behaviour.

14.174 The periods of time involved would need to be sufficiently modest not to affect the integrity of the sentence. And the prisoner would have to be of good behaviour, since otherwise he could lose his employment or be subject to disciplinary proceedings. Both could result in his losing the benefits of the scheme. By earning early release, or an early parole date with an increased likelihood of earlier release, the size of the prison population could be reduced by a figure which, taken overall, could lead to the closing of some prisons or at least some prison wings. This would produce real savings which could (depending on the scale of the incentive) cover, or contribute substantially to, the cost of substantially increased wages. It would not, in our judgement, in any way affect the safety of the public or the purpose for which the prison sentence had been passed.

14.175 We recognise that considerable thought would need to be given to such a scheme, and in particular to the way in which it could be operated fairly for all prisoners. But we commend it to the Prison Service for further consideration.

We have no doubt it would be extremely attractive to prisoners and provide a powerful incentive for good behaviour.

14.176   We emphasise that we do not consider our proposal for a progressive increase in wage levels depends on the acceptance of this scheme.

Kit

14.177   It is impossible to expect prisoners to have respect for themselves and to feel responsible for their conditions, if they are required to be dressed in ill-fitting, dirty clothing. Equally there can be little self-respect if prisoners have no opportunity to keep their clothes clean and tidy, and if they are not provided reasonably regularly with adequate clean bedding and towels. Such inadequate provisions clearly affect the morale of prisoners. It affects too the way they are treated by prison staff. It is difficult to show respect to a person dressed in somebody else's dirty cast offs.

14.178   Prisons are well aware of the affect such a turn out has on visitors. Understandably, those prisoners who came in prison uniform to give evidence at Part I in the Inquiry were, almost without exception, dressed in shirts whose new creases were still visible. Prisons as well as prisoners like to create a good impression. They should be given the means to do so.

14.179   In its evidence to the Inquiry, the Prison Service said:

> "The arrangements for the supply and control of clothing are intended to achieve a balance between providing sufficient for inmates to be properly dressed and maintaining effective control over public expenditure. A major problem in recent years has been the high level of issue of clothing, with large quantities of items being vandalised or destroyed".

14.180   The Service told us:

> "In some establishments, particularly locals, scales [relating to the issue of items of clothing] have proved insufficient for present levels of consumption and issues from central stores up to five times the authorised replacement scales are by no means uncommon. As a consequence the only method of overall control in recent years has often been the availability of stocks".

14.181   The Prison Service evidence said that new procedures were to be introduced which provided for establishments:

> "to forecast their own future needs and to have an agreed budget (notional, not cash) within which they will be expected to contain their demands on S&T [Supply and Transport] Branch."

14.182   The Prison Service told us that the present scales of, for example, underpants allowed:

> "For seven articles in use – that was two pairs in the inmate's possession, two pairs in the laundry, two pairs in the clothing exchange store and one pair both to cover losses, damages and condemnations: the annual replacement scale is three pairs. Local prisons were given a 10% uplift and remand prisons a 50% uplift in the articles in use scale to allow for the higher population turnover."

14.183   A memorandum issued from Supply and Transport Branch, who are responsible for clothing issue, on 21 January 1987 set out the minimum frequency for changes of clothing and bedding. It recommended changes of blankets every six months; of briefs (underpants), vests, shirts and towels twice a week; T-shirts, sheets, pillow-slips and pyjamas once a week; and the provision of three pairs of socks a week. On 18 December 1990, the Rt Hon Mrs Angela Rumbold MP, a Minister of State at the Home Office, announced a phased programme to increase the changes of underpants from a minimum of two per week to four per week.

14.184 There is a clear gulf between what the Prison Service knows it is providing and what the prisoners and prison staff know they are receiving. The Prison Service may have done its sums correctly on paper, but that is not how it is perceived in individual prisons. We have set out the recommendations and expectations so that those not familiar with life in prison will be able to measure the full width of the chasm.

14.185 As long as the Prison Service wishes to provide clothing for its prisoners, then it has an obligation to meet at least its own standards of issue which we have described above. We propose that the Prison Service must ensure that each prisoner has the clothing which, by the Prison Service's own standards, he or she requires. Individual prisoners should not have to pay for the depredations of other prisoners, or for any failures of prison management, to provide him with the clothes he needs. If that means that stocks, particularly in local prisons, should be increased, then the Prison Service should increase them.

14.186 We welcome the development of the personal kit system. The Prison Service evidence explained that, under this system:

"Inmates are issued with kit which carries a number specific to it and to the inmate. The inmate uses that kit until he is discharged or transferred."

14.187 A personal kit system was operating in some 55 establishments at the time the Prison Service sent its evidence to us in September 1990, and further schemes were under development. But the Prison Service suggested that personal kit systems were only practical in establishments which had a reasonably static population. They could not be used in local prisons.

14.188 We are not convinced by this argument. If the Prison Service accepts that a local prison population means such a high turnover that no-one can be issued with his own kit, then it is hard to argue that the demands in local prisons should be controlled by what its evidence describes as "the availability of stocks". Such a policy appears to mean that the Prison Service refuses to issue local prisons with additional clothing above a certain level, regardless of their immediate requirements. It is not reasonable to penalise tomorrow's prisoners for the acts of those in prison today.

14.189 The reality, however, is that prisoners, including remand prisoners, do stay for an appreciable time in local prisons. There is no reason why those prisoners should not benefit from a personal kit system. Many such prisoners may remain within the prison system, even if they are at some stage moved to other prisons. It should be well within the administrative powers of the Prison Service to arrange for a prisoner to take his own kit with him. We propose that personal kit systems should be introduced throughout the prison system.

14.190 There may be advantage in moving from notional to real budgets for Governors. This would allow them to take responsibility for their own purchasing, at least of some items of clothing. For example, if a Governor or an Area Manager could buy certain items of clothing cheaper than they could from PSIF, they should be able to do so. PSIF, even by its own standards, should not have, literally, captive markets. Nor is there any particular merit in national uniformity for its own sake.

14.191 Some of the problems with clothing are of the Prison Service's own making. They stem from its current requirement that all convicted inmates should wear prison uniforms. This rule does not, of course, apply to remand prisoners. Nor does it apply to convicted women prisoners, who have been able to wear civilian clothing for the last 20 years. In evidence to the Inquiry, the Prison Service told us that consideration had recently been given to whether there should be a change in policy to allow convicted male prisoners to wear their own clothing. The evidence said:

> "The arguments in favour of such a change, apart from treating male prisoners as favourably as their female counterparts, focus on the possible benefits in terms of prisoners' self-respect. The main reservations were on the effects on inmate employment: as many as 2,000 employment places could be lost depending on how many prisoners chose to wear their own clothes and on how successful PSIF were in developing other markets."

14.192   The Prison Service said that there would also be problems to be overcome with laundering and drying clothes, "in view of the present lack of launderette facilities", and with storing and exchanging clothing. Nevertheless, the Prison Service was considering the possibility of mounting a pilot scheme at one or more establishments to assess the advantages and disadvantages of a change in policy. We understand that the Prison Service is proposing a pilot scheme for Belmarsh Prison when it is opened in April 1991.

14.193   We commend the planned experiment at Belmarsh. We propose that, subject to the Belmarsh experiment, there should be a phased programme to permit male convicted prisoners the choice of wearing their own clothes. That choice might be available to all but top security prisoners or prisoners who are on the escape list. We recognise that such developments will take time. That should be to the good since it should allow PSIF to find other outlets for work, we would hope on the lines we have proposed elsewhere in this Section.

14.194   We propose, as an interim measure, that prisoners should be able to wear some of their own clothing. It should be possible for prisoners to be able to wear their own socks and underwear. This kit could either be laundered in the prison laundry under a marked personal kit system, or, ideally, could be laundered in washing and drying machines placed in units and wings. (We welcome the fact that such machines are planned for the redevelopment of Manchester Prison. They should be a normal part of the redevelopment brief for every prison.) In making this modest suggestion, we are doing no more than drawing attention to an approach which is already well advanced in dispersal prisons. In these prisons, prisoners (including category A prisoners) are already given considerable latitude about what they wear. Few wear prison uniform all the time.

14.195   We can see very little reason why there is not a much more relaxed policy about prisoners being able to wear their own shoes. Many of the prisoners we have met attach considerable importance to being able to wear their own training shoes as a mark of their own individuality and identity. We propose that they should be allowed to do so.

14.196   If, as we understand to be the case, there is concern about the suitability of prisoners wearing their own clothing at work, then we believe it is entirely possible, as happens in other countries, for prisoners to be issued with overalls or other work clothes to wear at work.

14.197   We believe that as many prisoners as possible should be able to wear their own clothes during visits from their families and friends. But we recognise the possible security difficulties which may have to be overcome. This consideration should not prevent prisoners being able to wear their own clothes at other occasions, for example in the evening when on association in their wings or units.

Food

14.198   The poor quality of the food served in prisons was a recurrent theme of the letters we received from prisoners. It featured in over a third of all the letters we received from prisoners in the prisons whose disturbances were not investigated. This was more than any other complaint.

14.199   The main complaint was that the food was said to be inedible. Some found the food monotonous. There were too many variations on the theme of stew. Many fewer complained about the quantity. Some thought there was nothing the matter with the food as it was supplied to the prison. It was the way it was prepared and served that was at fault. Food often arrived cold and was sometimes raw.

14.200   The Inquiry received similar responses when we visited prisons and spoke to prisoners. Most of the food in the prisons visited by the Inquiry was served from heated trolleys wheeled from the kitchen to the wings. It was then served out to the prisoner, who usually took it back to his cell to eat. We have to say from our own observations that what looked palatable and reasonably appetizing when we saw it presented in the prison kitchens, often took on a very different hue when we saw it at the end of its long journey to the prisoner's plate in his cell.

14.201   We visited some kitchens in which it was clearly extremely difficult for any standard of food and hygiene to be maintained. We refer to the poor conditions of some prison kitchens in Section 11. In such conditions, it is impossible to provide a satisfactory standard of hygiene or quality of meal.

14.202   In its evidence to us, the Prison Service said that the quantity of food for inmates was prescribed in nationally laid down dietary scales. These scales were last comprehensively reviewed in 1984. They were designed to provide a balanced diet and to meet Department of Health recommended daily amounts of food energy and nutrients. For the quarter ending 3 March 1990, the notional average food cost per inmate per week was £6.71. Dietary variations were available for Buddhists, Ethiopian Orthodox, Hindus, Jains, Jews, Mormons and Muslims. A vegetarian or a vegan diet could be authorised on request. Where rice was a basic item of an inmate's usual diet, long grain rice could be issued as a substitute for potatoes. The Prison Service evidence added:

> "Much has been done in recent years to improve the preparation and serving of food; a wider variety of food has been introduced and a choice of dishes is available in the majority of establishments. Where space has been available and where security permitted cafeteria and communal dining facilities have been introduced. Otherwise prisoners eat in their cells".

14.203   The Prison Service accepted in its evidence that "there are some serious shortcomings in standards". In the past two years, the Service had established a Hygiene Policy Review Committee to raise general standards. It had also conducted a survey of prison establishments in 1989 which confirmed the need to improve basic hygiene practices, pest control arrangements and buildings. It had issued a document in July 1989, and again in May 1990, giving advice to prisons on hygiene matters and covering the legal requirements. On the 10 October 1990 the circular (to which we refer under Hygiene in Section 11 of the Report) was issued announcing that Hygiene in Prisons was a Prisons Board Priority for 1991/2.

14.204   A nominated pest control officer, drawn from the works staff, has been appointed at each prison to introduce a management programme "of both proactive and reactive measures for pest control and to supervise the placement and monitoring of contracts". The Prison Service proposes to introduce a Pest Control Survey which will investigate what pests are present in each prison, the extent of the infestation and the estimated costs of work involved. The results of these surveys, the Prison Service told us, would enable Governors to negotiate suitable and effective pest control contracts. The contracts would allow the prison to get rid of current infestations and they would provide for maintenance to prevent reinfestation. These surveys and contracts would, of course, apply to the whole prison and not just to the kitchens and the food stores.

14.205   We strongly endorse the need to bring all prison kitchens up to tolerable hygiene levels. This will involve substantial expenditure, not just in pest control but also in rebuilding costs. The Prison Service is budgeting for this and we believe it is a right priority. Staff and prisoners in kitchens should not have to work in filthy conditions; nor should prisoners be served with food prepared in kitchens which do not meet acceptable health standards.

14.206 Prison kitchens employ about 2,500 inmates in the preparation, cooking and serving of meals. We have already in this Section commended the move to provide training and certificates for such inmates.

14.207 We do not underestimate the formidable task which faces the 600 or so uniformed officers who act as prison catering officers. We heard at Wandsworth Prison of the considerable problems of trying to provide three meals a day for 1,500 prisoners. The principal catering officer of Pentonville Prison was reported in the Guardian Newspaper on 24 November 1990 as saying:

> "The clock's our devil here. Breakfast must be ready to go out through those doors at 7.40 sharp. Lunch goes out at 11.15. Bang. 900 meals, all at once. Then dinner at 4.15, with a piece of cake or bun for the last thing."

14.208 The Inquiry heard from Mr Frost, the Governor 5 in charge of catering at Manchester Prison, during the public hearing in Manchester of the problems associated with introducing a choice of menu. He said:

> "The obvious problem is that when we initially tried to introduce a choice, if we were feeding 1,700 people they expected 1,700 of each choice to be provided instead of 850 of each."

A good meal created its own problems.

> "You see, for example, a very popular meal was chicken, which we put on every fortnight. . . . Now, in reality, if you are feeding 1,700 inmates, you have 1,400 who are meat eaters, because 300 are vegetarians. You only get an allowance for 1,400 inmates, and when there is an item such as chicken, or whole gammon steak, you find that your vegetarians are meat eaters."

14.209 Mr Frost highlighted also the problem of making the budget stretch:

> "To enhance a menu, to stretch it, and give it far more variety, I am given 23p per man per week extra. . . . The budget I have to work out is cash allowances which I spend on extras. Every single thing else we have issued".

14.210 We are not in a position to form a view on the dietary quality of the food supplied in prisons, or on its quantity. But we propose that consideration be given to looking again at the dietary scales which were last comprehensively reviewed in 1984. This should be done in consultation with the Department of Health. The aim would be to ensure that the Prison Service is providing the right types of food as well as the right amounts. The review might also consider the budgets which are provided to catering officers to ensure that, while not generous, they are at least fair.

14.211 We propose also that catering officers should be given greater discretion in the deployment of their budgets. The evidence to Part I of the Inquiry showed that the level of satisfaction with the food in Cardiff was attributed to the successful purchasing policy of the Cardiff catering officer. There should be an experiment in nominated prisons to discover what, if any, benefits result from not requiring a prison to take food from a central supplier, nor even from Prison Service Farms, if they are able to secure a more competitive and better deal locally. Such contracts would, however, need careful monitoring by the Area Manager and by PSIF to ascertain that they provided better value for money.

14.212 There is a substantial problem in the timing and the serving of meals. We have already referred to this in connection with their effect on the length of the working day in prison. We know from our own visits that the mid-day meal is served around 11.00. The last meal of the day is often around 16.00. There is then an extremely long gap, relieved often only by tea and a bun, until breakfast the following morning. Some prisons have amended their routine so that the main meal is at 16.00 and not, as previously, at 11.00. That is an improvement but not a solution.

14.213   We propose that the Prison Service examines critically staff attendance times so that meals can be served and taken at more sensible hours. Properly timed meals were achieved at many of the prisons we visited abroad. One prison we visited, for example, had a half an hour overlap of shifts at mid-day, so that prisoners could eat their meals at a more conventional hour.

14.214   There needs also to be an improvement in the arrangements for the eating of the meals. Too many prisons have moved over to dining in cells. This should be the exception when security considerations or physical conditions make it unavoidable, and not the norm in category B prisons. We note that the Prison Service design brief for new prisons allows a room for communal dining, but a clear policy is required to ensure that it is used for this purpose.

14.215   We think prisoners should be given the choice of where they eat. Some prisoners will wish to dine in their cells, as an opportunity to remove themselves from the hurly burly of prison life. Others will wish, and might be encouraged, to eat together. This should not only make it easier to keep cells clean, but should go some way to providing fresher food which has not had to travel so far. If our proposals for smaller units are accepted, that should make communal dining easier. But, having visited Scotland and overseas, we think the control risks of collective dining may be exaggerated.

14.216   The Inquiry was interested to see that prisoners and staff ate together at Otisville Prison in New York State. The Inquiry joined them for a meal with the Warden. The senior staff at that prison found it an excellent way in which they could learn what was happening in the prison. Prisoners approached them to discuss problems. Certainly, judging by our experience, the arrangement had a beneficial effect on the quality of the food. We do not believe such arrangements should be imposed, but it would, in our view, be a significant reflection of the quality of relationships within a prison if such an arrangement were to be instituted at some prisons in this country.

14.217   We propose therefore that there should be a return to the practice of making provision for communal dining and that prisoners should be given the choice of dining together or, if they so wish, and this is practicable, in their cells. If and insofar as staff attitudes or shifts are an impediment to this (as has been suggested to the Inquiry) then management must face up to their responsibilities and change those attitudes, and if necessary the timing of shifts.

14.218   We would not wish it to be thought that all prison food is universally awful. That is very far from the truth. We recognise that all those in institutions tend to complain about food. As one inmate at our seminar at Lincoln Prison who worked in the kitchens told us – inmates always wanted more: if you gave them steak and kidney pie, they would want mushrooms and roast potatoes. That is only human.

14.219   Nevertheless, we have seen more than sufficient evidence to conclude that conditions in kitchens and the quality of the food as it arrives on the plate must be improved. If the proposals we have put forward, and the action to which the Prison Service is already committed, do not lead to an improvement, then there would be a strong case for contracting out the catering and serving arrangements.

Family Ties

14.220   From all the evidence we have received, it is clear that what may broadly be described as family ties are matters of great importance to prisoners. The maintenance of family ties goes to the heart of a relationship that so far as possible should be protected when a prisoner serves his sentence.

14.221 A quarter of those prisoners who wrote to us from the prisons not involved in the disturbances which we investigated, commented on limitations on visits. Letters, telephones and opportunities for home leave were all referred to. They were clearly seen by prisoners as practical ways of retaining their link with their community and with their family.

14.222 The Prison Service well understands the importance of such contacts. It said in its evidence to us:

> "The Prison Service has given a high priority in recent years to strengthening inmates' links with their families. This is wholly consistent with the duty of the Service, expressed in the Statement of Purpose 'to look after [prisoners] with humanity and to help them lead law abiding and useful lives in custody and after release'. The maintenance of strong ties between inmates and their families is crucial to fulfilling both parts of this duty. It is also, specifically required by Prison Rule 31(1), which states that: 'special attention shall be paid to the maintenance of such relations between a prisoner and his family as are desirable in the best interests of both'."

14.223 The Prison Service added:

> "The disruption of the inmate's position within the family unit represents one of the most distressing aspects of imprisonment, and it is often compounded by a sense of guilt of having let the family down and fear of losing them altogether. Enabling inmates, so far as possible, to stay in close and meaningful contact with the family is therefore an essential part of humane treatment. In these terms alone the improvement of family ties must be a priority for the Prison Service. In addition, though, relationships with the family can contribute very positively on several levels towards the achievement of successful reintegration into society following release from prison. There is every reason to believe that the nature of a prisoner's relationships with his or her family will be an important factor in determining whether he or she will succeed in leading a useful and law abiding life on return to the community. The family can provide both the incentive and the pressure to change. The inmate who returns to a secure family relationship may not wish to jeopardise it again and there will be an added onus on him or her to find employment and steer clear of further trouble. Moreover, their presence around the offender can be a source of support, encouraging and discipline. All this must tend to reduce the likelihood of re-offending."

14.224 We agree with the Prison Service. The proposals which follow in relation to visits, leave, telephones and correspondence are directed to the objectives which are identified in its evidence.

Visits

14.225 The Prison Service evidence notes that:

> "Inmates generally prize visits above all other privileges."

14.226 We have earlier given our views on the Prison Service's use of the term "privilege". As will be seen from the Standing Order, visits are an entitlement – a right – not a privilege.

14.227 Under the Prison Service Standing Order 5A(3), the minimum entitlement for convicted adults is one visit every 28 days following a first visit on conviction. Visits to convicted inmates should last at least 30 minutes, but the Standing Order suggests that Governors should allow longer where circumstances permit. The Prison Service told us that it aimed to bring the minimum entitlement into line with convicted young offenders, which was two visits every

28 days. It was also considering the possibility of easing the week-end pressure by allowing the exchange of one week-end visit for two week-day visits.

14.228   For the unconvicted, there is a daily visit from Monday to Saturday, each lasting a minimum of 15 minutes. The Prison Service told us that Governors had recently been given the discretion, having taken account of the views of inmates and visitors, to aggregate visits, since "it is recognised that visits of this length may well be unproductive and unsatisfactory". Up to three persons, not including any children under ten, are normally allowed at each visit.

14.229   We commend the Prison Service target of increasing the frequency of visits for convicted prisoners to two visits every 28 days. But this should be a step on the road to a greater provision. We recommend that the Prison Service should work towards providing convicted prisoners with at least one visit each week.

14.230   We propose that the Prison Service should improve the conditions in which visits are held. We have referred in Section 11 to the value of building visitors centres, where visitors can wait before they go into the prison. We have also referred in Section 11 to the need to improve the size of and facilities at many visits rooms. Some improvements will require significant capital expenditure. But more could be done with the arrangement of furniture and the provision of plants, and by making toys available for children, to give a more homely and less oppressive atmosphere. There needs also to be a careful review of staffing levels in visits. We recognise the scope for bringing in contraband during visits, but this may be better countered by post-visit searching rather than by the creation of an oppressive atmosphere in the visits room itself.

14.231   We wish to see longer visits. Some prisoners came near to telling us that short visits were often worse than no visit at all. A 30 minute meeting every month is a slim basis for maintaining a family contact. A 15 minute visit every day for a remand prisoner is, as the Prison Service recognises, more than unsatisfactory. We recommend that the Prison Service should aim to increase the minimum length of visits for convicted prisoners to an hour. We recommend that the Prison Service should as soon as practicable offer remand prisoners the choice of having three visits of an hour each week, as an alternative to short daily visits.

14.232   Some families simply cannot afford the travelling costs entailed in a visit. There is, therefore, provision for assisted prison visits. Since 1988, the Prison Service itself has taken over from the Department of Social Security the running of the Assisted Prison Visits Scheme. The Scheme provides that visitors who are closely related to the inmate and on low income may be reimbursed travelling expenses from public funds. The Prison Service told us that the great majority of applications for such visits are turned round by post in under two days. There were about 62,000 claims in 1990. In the financial year 1990/91, the scheme is expected to cost nearly £1.5m.

14.233   We were pleased to learn from the Prison Service that the scope of the scheme had recently been extended. Convicted inmates are now able to receive an assisted visit on reception. Previously, they had become eligible for such a visit only after four weeks.

14.234   The Federation of Prisoners' Families Support Groups, in their evidence, proposed that there should be two financially assisted visits a month and not one as at present. If the Prison Service meets its objective of increasing the minimum entitlement for visits for convicted adults to two every 28 days, then it should follow that the Assisted Prison Visits Scheme should apply to both visits.

14.235   In evidence sent to us by the National Association of Prison Visitors, the South West Regional Secretary of the Association proposed that financial assistance with visits to convicted prisoners should be extended to remand prisoners. We believe the case for this is incontrovertible. Remand prisoners should have at least as good arrangements for visits from their families as convicted prisoners. We recommend, therefore, that the families of remand prisoners should be eligible for financially assisted visits. We understand that the Prison Service may extend this provision to remand prisoners in the next financial year. We urge them to do so.

Home Leave

14.236   The purpose of home leave, according to the Prison Service Circular Instruction on Home and Pre-parole Leave (Circular Instruction 9/1988) is:

"(a)   To help restore self confidence by placing trust in a prisoner under conditions of complete freedom; and

(b)   To help the prisoner to re-adjust to life outside prison by giving the opportunity to maintain links with family and friends and in the case of long home leave, to contact prospective employers and make firm plans for release."

14.237   Prisoners are eligible for a long home leave of five consecutive days if they are serving 18 months or more. A life prisoner is eligible if he has been given a provisional date for release and has not yet been admitted to a pre-release employment scheme. Long home leave can be taken at any time during the four months before the earliest date of release.

14.238   Short home leave is of a clear two days, normally but not invariably at a week-end, exclusive of travelling time. Eligibility for home leave varies according to the category of prisoner and length of sentence. Determinate sentence prisoners in category B prisons serving sentences of three years or more are eligible to apply for one short home leave, which may be taken not earlier than nine months before the earliest date of release. Prisoners in category C prisons are eligible to apply if they are serving determinate sentences of two years or more. The leave may be taken not earlier than the prisoner's parole eligibility date, and thereafter at six monthly intervals until the prisoner becomes eligible for long home leave. In open prisons, prisoners may apply if they are serving determinate sentences of 18 months or more, if they are life sentence prisoners with a provisional release date, or if they are life sentence prisoners without a provisional release date who have served nine months in open conditions. Short home leave in open prisons may first be taken not earlier than the prisoner's parole eligibility date (or, in the case of life sentence prisoners with a provisional release date, after four months in open conditions) and thereafter at four monthly intervals until the prisoner becomes eligible for long home leave.

14.239   There are separate arrangements for long home leave and short home leave for young offenders. Long home leave is available to young offenders serving determinate sentences of 12 months or more, and to those serving life who have been given a provisional date for release. A long leave is not considered until the trainee has completed at least three months from the date of his sentence. The leave should be arranged during the eight weeks before his earliest date of release. Short home leave arrangements distinguish between offenders in high security, closed young offender institutions and open young offender institutions.

14.240   There was a general consensus among the evidence we received that there should be an extension of home leave. This included the Prison Governors' Association, the Prison Service Union, the Parliamentary All-Party Penal Affairs Group, the Howard League and the Federation of Prisoners' Families Support Groups. It was also apparently the view of the Prison Service Control Review Committee. In its report published in 1984 (Managing the Long Term Prison System) it states:

"The Committee of Ministers of the Council of Europe recommended in

September 1982 that member states should grant home leave to the greatest possible extent, to prisoners in closed prisons as well as open ones. Home leave is, in fact, a matter on which the practices in this country are markedly more cautious than in the rest of Europe, so that, on the face of it, there is plenty of scope for response to the Committee of Ministers' recommendation on this point."

14.241   We agree with the Control Review Committee. We consider further that home leave should not be confined just to long term prisoners. We were pleased to see from the Prison Service evidence that home leaves had increased considerably in category C establishments – from 7,000 in 1987 to 12,000 in 1989. We believe there is considerable scope for further increases, in particular in category B establishments. To do so would help to restore the prisoner's self-confidence and allow him or her the opportunity to maintain family links. It would also increase a prisoner's sense of responsibility in prison. He would not wish to lose an opportunity for home leave by misbehaving. Prisoners need to be trusted in prison and, on release, will need to be trusted still further. It is entirely reasonable that they should be given opportunities for demonstrating that trust during the course of their sentence. It is in the public interest that prisoners should be able to take such leave.

14.242   Home leaves, perhaps more than anything else, are likely to break down the detrimental effect of long periods of incarceration. They can bring a greater sense of normality and of the outside world into the life of the prison. A substantial programme of home leave would also, as the Prison Service Union pointed out, ease the tensions and staffing pressures over week-ends.

14.243   We recommend, therefore, that there should be substantial increases in the number of home leaves granted, both long and short leaves. To achieve such increases will require significant changes in the conditions of eligibility and in the number of leaves each eligible prisoner is able to take. The Prison Service will be able to work out fresh arrangements in the light of this recommendation. We would expect, however, long leave to be available to prisoners serving sentences shorter than 18 months and that a larger number of such leaves might be taken earlier in the sentence. Similar criteria might operate for short home leaves.

14.244   There are prisons which have to be made more attractive to their prisoners to compensate for the disadvantages which they have. Dartmoor is one example. It is generally unpopular with prisoners, partly because of its location. We recommend that in the case of prisons which are inappropriately located and to compensate for their shortcomings, home and other leave should be permitted to prisoners there on a more generous scale than to prisoners at other establishments.

14.245   In devising fresh arrangements, the Prison Service should also consider arrangements for providing more day leave for prisoners. These can be useful for prisoners for whom, because of their circumstances, it would not be appropriate to grant home leave. They can help prisoners who may not yet be ready for home leave or who may not, at that time, need it.

Family Visits

14.246   We received representations that special arrangements should be made for what are now called private family visits and what in the past have been known as conjugal visits. The Inquiry saw the arrangements for such visits during our visits to the Netherlands, to Spain and to Canada. We noted the Scottish Prison Service document published in May 1990 about the management of the long term prison system in Scotland "Opportunity and Responsibility". It stated that it intended that a Working Group should examine the possibility of providing family visits for those category A and B prisoners who would not be eligible for home leave. The document noted that:

"In many Western European countries prisoners are now permitted private visits with their spouses and/or families for periods from between 3 to 48 hours at certain intervals in their sentences. We feel that the time has come to look at the advantages and disadvantages of providing such facilities within our system and a review will be undertaken."

14.247   In response to our request for the Prison Service's views on private family visits, the Service told us:

"To date we have not given a high priority to this issue, taking the view that it would be more profitable at this stage to concentrate on increasing, wherever possible, home leave entitlements, on extending the availability of card phones, on the development of visitors centres and visiting facilities and on the improvement of the Assisted Prison Visits Scheme – since all of these developments benefit a much larger proportion of prisoners than would be able to take advantage of a private family visit programme."

14.248   We agree that the priorities for the majority of prisoners should lie elsewhere, in particular in developing home leave on the lines we have recommended. But, as the Scottish Prison Service document recognises, there must still be some who will not be able to take home leave during the course of perhaps very long sentences. Overseas experience has shown that private family visits are no longer an unthinkable or eccentric exception. They can form a small but, for some prisoners, important part of the arrangements which ensure that they maintain links with the family to whom they may eventually return. If such visits were available, prisoners might be less likely to behave in a dangerous and disruptive way while in prison.

14.249   We propose that the Prison Service should make provision for private family visits, initially, at least, for prisoners serving long prison sentences who are not eligible for home leave.

14.250   In its response to us about family visits, the Prison Service also told us that it was examining the possibility of allowing children to visit for much longer than the normal visiting periods. The Service was considering, for example, a childrens' visit unit at the women's prison at Styal. We have noted that such a project was launched in January 1991 at Holloway Prison. This allowed children to visit for the whole day. We commend such projects. If they are successful, both for the child as well as the prisoner, then we propose that the Prison Service should consider extending such facilities to male prisons.

Telephones

14.251   Public telephones accessible to prisoners were a common feature of many of the prisons the Inquiry visited overseas. They were accepted by staff and prisoners alike as a natural part of the provision. In Rikers Island, New York City, down the length of the long wing opposite tiers of cells, each of which was covered by iron bars, there were telephones for the prisoners' use. Telephones were not therefore the preserve only of "new generation" prisons, or of those prison authorities with the most liberal traditions.

14.252   The Prison Service here fully accepts the value of telephones:

"With the introduction of cardphones for inmate's use, prisoners have much greater autonomy and freedom to contact their families when they choose; they no longer talk to their partners only when major problems arise, but simply to communicate and pass the time of day. The nature of communication by phone also means that inmates are in part restored to their role within the family unit; they can give timely advice or support, and help to make arrangements. In this way feelings of familial inadequacy can be reduced and inmates are able to take greater responsibility for their own affairs."

405

14.253 The Prison Service has put the case powerfully. Access to telephones increases links with the outside world. It also increases the prospects of prisoners taking and accepting their responsibilities.

14.254 The Prison Service told us that cardphones had been installed in all open prisons, and that the programme of installation in category C prisons was nearing completion. We note that their installation in category C prisons and the equivalent female and young offender establishments was authorised by a Circular Instruction in 1988, so they have been quite some time in coming. The Prison Service told us in September 1990 that a trial would start shortly at Winchester Prison, under which unconvicted inmates would be able to use phones. There would need to be careful safeguards, because of the greater security risks and particularly the need to protect witnesses. If the trial was successful, it was hoped that the arrangements could be extended to other local prisons and remand centres. The Prison Service told us also that consideration was being given to the conditions under which convicted inmates in category B (non-dispersal) prisons might in future be allowed to use cardphones.

14.255 The Prison Service has developed with British Telecom a prison cardphone which is not useable or purchaseable outside prisons. Expenditure on phone cards from an inmate's private cash no longer counts against the annual limit of private cash expenditure, and inmates are no longer restricted to two cards a month.

14.256 The Prison Service has advised Governors by Circular Instruction (CI 61/1989) that, where a telephone is installed, inmates should be given free access to it during association hours. Governors may impose a time limit for each inmate if this seems necessary. But it is also open to Governors to apply for the installation of an extra machine if the weight of use warrants it. Governors at closed establishments are required to put a notice by the cardphone to say that conversations are liable to be monitored by prison staff: the cardphone is provided for use only by inmates who consent to this. There are further arrangements to ensure, as far as possible, that telephone calls by prisoners to the Samaritans are treated in confidence.

14.257 The introduction of pay phones was welcomed in evidence to us by the Federation of Prisoners' Families Support Groups. But they said that there was a long way to go before its potential benefits were realised. Unlike some American prison systems, they noted that Prison Service policy was to exclude high security establishments. And access in lower security prisons was very variable.

14.258 The Parliamentary All-Party Penal Affairs Group recommended that access to telephones should be extended to the majority of prisoners. This was supported by the Prison Governors' Association. They told us:

"We take as axiomatic that prisoners regard continuing contact with family and friends as the single most important aspect of their imprisonment. Such contact is most effectively achieved through visits, home leave and through access to a telephone. In this respect the wide spread introduction of telephones would do much to help reduce tension among the prison population, and particularly so in respect of unconvicted prisoners".

14.259 The Prison Service is clearly moving towards the more extensive provision of cardphones. We propose that the Prison Service give more urgency to the extension of cardphones to all categories of prison and to all types of prisoner. It should not be another two years before cardphones are available to unconvicted prisoners, or to category B establishments. As long as dispersal prisons contain a mix of prisoners, allocated there rather than to other category B prisons, then arrangements should be made to give organised access to cardphones for prisoners whose security categorisation allows it. We recognise the problems of allowing free telephone access to high security prisoners. Nevertheless, we would wish to see a scheme developed which authorised telephone calls from such inmates to their families, unless there were good reasons for declining to do so. In the case of such calls, it should in most cases be possible to rely on staff supervision and monitoring to ensure that the facility was not abused.

14.260   We share the Prison Service's concern that prisoners who wish to speak to the Samaritans should feel that they can do so in confidence. This can be an important outlet. We propose that the Prison Service devise with the Samaritans a provision for a free call number so that prisoners could make calls to the Samaritans in confidence at public expense.

14.261   We have noted that there are separate arrangements for the use of official telephones by inmates where the Governor is satisfied that there are strong compassionate reasons for doing so, or when there is an urgent need to contact a legal adviser or consular representative. The arrangements are set out in Circular Instruction 50/1988.

14.262   We were surprised to see a provision in that Instruction that required a call to an inmate's solicitor to be supervised, but not monitored. There are rules for ensuring that the prison authorities do not read or overhear exchanges in letters and visits between an inmate and his solicitor when they relate to legal proceedings or related matters relevant to the prisoner (the matters are set out in detail in Standing Order 5). We propose that similar rules of privilege should apply to inmates speaking to their solicitor on the telephone. These rules should apply whether the communication is by a cardphone or by the use of an official telephone at the permission of the Governor.

Censorship of Correspondence

14.263   The Prison Service has taken steps in recent years considerably to reduce the extent and degree to which prison officers censor the letters prisoners send and those they receive.

14.264   The Prison Service told us that censorship was abolished in open _really_- prisons in 1986. It was reduced to a random sample of 5% in category C establishments in 1988. The Prison Service said:

> "Trials have also been taking place since February 1990 at Leeds, Norwich, Winchester and Maidstone to evaluate the possibility of similarly reducing censorship of the correspondence of unconvicted and category B (non-dispersal) inmates to a 5% sample...the results of the trial will be assessed shortly and then a decision will be reached on whether the change should be applied at other like establishments. Consideration will also be given to the possible scope for further reductions in censorship in the other types of establishment".

14.265   The Prison Service indicated that the reading of incoming and outgoing correspondence by staff will continue to be necessary in certain cases where the risk of abuse is high. But its evidence recognised the reasons for reducing routine censorship as far as possible:

> "It is, above all, an intrusion of privacy which is resented by inmates and their families and friends. Second, censorship may inhibit some letter-writers, which may cause things to be left unsaid or inadequately expressed, and this may mean that the letter does more harm than good. Third, while we believe staff generally do their utmost to deal with mail speedily, censorship inevitably slows down the process and limits the number of letters that can be exchanged, all of which causes tension and frustration. Finally, the censorship operation consumes a good deal of staff time which could be better used in other ways".

14.266   Under Standing Order 5, convicted inmates are allowed to send one statutory letter a week, at least one privilege letter for adults, and two for young

young offenders, and as many more such letters as are practicable. They may also send special letters – for example when they are about to be transferred, or where these are necessary for the welfare of the inmate or his or her family. Unconvicted inmates may send two statutory letters a week, as many further privilege letters as they wish, and special letters when about to be transferred or in connection with their defence.

14.267   In prisons where there are censorship restrictions, letters must not exceed four sides of A5 paper and inmates may not receive from outside more letters than they are allowed to send. These restrictions are removed where all or most correspondence is not censored.

14.268   There are two elements to the Prison Service control over the contents of correspondence. The first provides for an examination to ensure that the letter contains nothing illicit in or attached to the letter. It provides also for a check that any out-going letter is from the inmate to whom it was issued and on the appropriate paper. The second element is censorship proper, where the letter is read. Except for those in category A or on the escape list, or specially identified by the Governor, the letter censor is urged under Circular Instruction 9/1989 to do no more than establish quickly that the letter contains nothing unusual which warrants closer reading.

14.269   None of those who sent us evidence argued for an increase in letter censorship. The National Association for the Care and Resettlement of Offenders suggested there should be an end to censorship of letters for most prisoners. The organisation Justice sent us their report published in 1983 "Justice in Prison" which proposed that prisoners letters should not be censored, except on reasonable suspicion that they contained objectionable material, although they could be examined for contraband. The National Association of Probation Officers argued that the abolition of the censorship of letters should be explicitly stated as the right of any prisoner.

14.270   We would not go as far as the National Association of Probation Officers, but we accept the broad principle set out in the Justice Report. We have found in informal discussions, both with staff in this country, and in some other countries, an attachment, which we consider unreasonable, to continuing some form of censorship. We do not, for example, accept the argument that this is necessary in order to identify bad news and so cushion the blow for the prisoner. If the prisoner has not formed a relationship with staff to turn to them for assistance in such circumstances, then the time to establish that relationship is not after such a letter has arrived and been read in his absence by the prison censor. The greater use of cardphones in any event spells the death knell of the censorship system.

14.271   We propose that prisoners' letters should not be censored except on reasonable suspicion that they may contain objectionable material, or if the prisoner is placed in category A. We would hope that, since abolishing censorship is technically simpler than installing telephones, this considerable curtailing of censorship can move at a quicker pace.

14.272   It should still be possible for incoming letters to be *examined* (but not read). The procedure would be as described above under Circular Instruction 9/1989. We see no grounds for routinely examining out-going letters. It should, as we have proposed, be open to the Governor to authorise the censoring of a particular inmate's letters if he suspects they could contain objectionable material, or would do so but for the censorship. Where the Governor authorises censorship, the inmate should be told in advance, or, where security considerations suggest otherwise, as soon as possible after the censorship has commenced. It is consistent with the approach which we shall discuss below, that such reasons should be given to the prisoner for this decision, in writing when this is requested.

14.273   The considerable reduction in censorship which we propose should be a welcome abolition of an unnecessary intrusion on prisoners' privacy. It should also provide the opportunity for redeploying the staff involved to more productive and fulfilling work.

14.274   As part of our general approach of maintaining a prisoner's links with the community, we propose that the Prison Service should encourage prisoners to write more letters. To enable them to do this, there should be a reasonably generous provision of note paper and envelopes free of charge. Any limits on the number of letters a prisoner is allowed to write should be removed.

Communication with Prisoners

14.275   We wish to see inmates given a greater degree of responsibility in the conduct of their lives in prison. From this it must follow that prisoners should be drawn into the life of the prison. They should be able to contribute to and be informed of the way things are run. This is a matter of commonsense as well as of justice. If prisoners have a greater understanding of what is happening to them in prison and why, they are less likely to be aggrieved and become disaffected. This should, in turn, improve relations between staff and prisoners.

14.276   It is against this background that we consider the question of developing communications with prisoners, and whether there needs to be any more formal structures than there are at present.

14.277   We noted that some of these issues were addressed by the Prison Service Working Party on Dispersal Prison Regimes which reported in 1990. The Report said:

> "Throughout the category B estate there is not a great deal of inmate participation in the management of affairs. Some prisons have concentrated upon allowing inmates to have some say in catering, canteen or entertainment. In many ways it is no more than inmates being allowed to state preferences. The discretion of whether they are implemented remains with management. Experience has shown that inmates who are formally approached by management to represent others fail to do this, being more concerned to put forward their own individual interest or acting under pressure to represent a powerful group. This is a sensitive area in which Governors can only go as far as is consistent with a proper relationship between staff and inmate."

14.278   The Report went on to recommend:

> "That inmate participation should not be formally set up within the prison system but Governors should be encouraged to seek the view of inmates in those areas where it would be genuine representation".

14.279   There is no question that discretion to implement any proposals made by prisoners must remain with management. It is possible to envisage very limited circumstances in which responsibility for decisions is delegated by management to a group of prisoners. At a simple level, prisoners may be able to choose between two types of menu or, as was happening in one establishment we visited, whether the main meal of the day should be taken as lunch or dinner. But greater communication with prisoners cannot and need not carry with it any implication that prisoners are making the decisions. There can be no question of management, either prison staff or Governors, being over-ruled by those in their charge.

14.280   We are in no doubt, however, that there is room for improving communications with prisoners. We have met too many prisoners who feel they do not know what is going on or that their views have not been heard for them to be dismissed as a devious or disgruntled minority. The general situation was well summed up in a submission from probation officers at Wormwood Scrubs

Prison. They said:

> "Prisoners feel cut off from all sources of information. Often, they neither know what is going on in the prison nor what is going on at home. Of course, they hear rumours and official announcements about the wider world and the prison and they get letters and messages from home. But often the official pronouncements are either delayed or contradictory or nonsensical and the messages from home are often very much delayed because of the slow pace at which letters and messages move through the prison system. It would not seem unreasonable to suggest that prisoners should receive at least weekly bulletins from the authorities about policy changes in the wings where they live, if those policy changes will make any real difference to their daily routines".

14.281   We are aware that some prisons already run prison newspapers – the Inquiry was given a copy of the Leyhill News and of the Lincoln Prison magazine "Open Forum", both edited by prisoners. But the proposals by the probation officers at Wormwood Scrubs go further. They suggest weekly written bulletins. A weekly bulletin might be too frequent, but we propose that Governors should make arrangements for regular bulletins to be prepared in as clear language as possible about policy changes and changes in routine which affect prisoners at their establishment. It is right that prisoners should be told in writing what is going on.

14.282   This would deal only with communication one way. It is necessary also to provide ways for prisoners to communicate with staff and management above the normal one to one level. Professor King, prisoners at Long Lartin and Mr Ron Ward, the Vice Chairman of the National Association of Prison Visitors, suggested some form of prisoner representative Committees. Professor King suggested that they should be elected, presumably by the prisoners themselves. He saw the Committees being given regular opportunities to review "the Rules" with prison managers and to air grievances as and when they arose. Mr Cavadino of NACRO, at one of our public seminars, suggested a slightly different approach. He proposed there should be formal arrangements for prisoners to be represented on the Committees within establishments "on regimes, education, catering and other areas".

14.283   We saw examples of prisoners' Committees on our visits abroad. We met an elected prisoners' Committee at Joyceville Prison in Canada. That Committee believed there was considerable value in it conducting a dialogue with staff on behalf of inmates, and vice versa. It negotiated on inmate pay and on issues such as safety at work. The members said they had in the past been useful in persuading inmates not to go on strike. The Committee itself was elected every six months, and usually long-term inmates were elected. A member of the Committee told us that the members had a lot of respect in the establishment.

14.284   The evidence we received from various levels in English prisons was more sceptical. Inmates the Inquiry spoke to at Swinfen Hall, where there were wing representatives who had meetings with staff, complained that the representatives often just gave only their own views, and not those of the inmates as a whole. This view was broadly echoed by management at Leyhill Prison. Leyhill used to have Prisoners' Councils. They had been disbanded because they were thought not to be representative. Instead, we understand that the Governor holds an open forum about every six weeks.

14.285   The Prison Service's Director of Inmate Programmes, Mr Emes, at one of the Inquiry's public seminars asked, rhetorically, how much influence prisoners should have over the overall regime provision. His answer was:

> "More than they do now, but I do believe that it needs to be carefully regulated. We have, in the past, tried Prisoner Committees; for whatever reason, they were not terribly successful. One of the problems with having Committees is how do you get proper representation of prisoners on those

Committees – ones that they feel happy with? Is, perhaps, a better way, to have consumer research and regular questionnaires, asking inmates views over a range of issues?"

14.286 On the basis of the evidence we have seen, we do not propose formal Prisoners' Committees. If Governors feel that such a Committee would be helpful at their establishment and can be representative of the prisoners and of value in the running of the prison, then they should be free to encourage such a Committee. But we believe there should be a wider range of methods tried. We propose, in answer to Mr Emes' question, that Governors and Headquarters should, as a matter of routine, consult prisoners by questionnaires or other means about major issues of policy affecting them before decisions are taken. We understand that such consultation exists in the Scottish Prison Service and that the Prison Service in England and Wales is interviewing a sample of prisoners on the basis of a questionnaire. We think that consultation with prisoners should be seen by policy makers as an essential part of any study or review.

14.287 Questionnaires and consumer research are not, however, the sole answer. There need to be more direct and human contacts between prisoners and management in prisons. That can only be achieved through face to face meetings. We propose that each Governor in charge of a prison should make arrangements for meetings with groups of prisoners. They can take a variety of forms. It may be helpful for staff on wings or in units to have regular meetings. The meetings might be with informally established groups of inmates. In addition, the Governor in charge should ensure that, from time to time, he has meetings with different groups of prisoners within his prison, sometimes with prison staff present and sometimes without. He should identify some items for discussion in advance so that prisoners and staff have time to think about them.

14.288 The Governor's arrangements for communicating with prisoners, both ways, might usefully be set out in the prisoner "contracts" which we have described in Section 12. The form of those arrangements matters less, however, than the need to ensure that communication takes place.

Remedies

14.289 The European Court of Human Rights has set out succinctly a principle which is part of the law of this country. It is that "Justice does not stop at the prison doors". A feature of this principle is that "in spite of his imprisonment, a convicted prisoner retains all civil rights which are not taken away expressly or by necessary implication". (See *R v The Board of Visitors of Hull Prison, Ex parte St Germain* [1979] Q.B. 425, at pp. 454/5 *per* Sebag-Shaw L.J., and *Raymond v Honey* [1983] 1 A.C. 1, at p. 10, *per* Lord Wilberforce.)

14.290 A prisoner is entitled to access to the Courts and to bring civil proceedings or make an application for judicial review against the Home Office. As the law has developed so far, a prisoner cannot obtain damages for a breach of the Prison Rules, but the breach can be the subject for an application for judicial review. On the application, the Court can grant him relief. It cannot, however, grant damages (unless he can show some other private right has been infringed) or an injunction, which is not available against the Crown.

14.291 The prisoner can also make an application to the European Commission for Human Rights with a view to obtaining a remedy from the European Court of Human Rights.

14.292 It is also possible for a prisoner to make an application to the Parliamentary Commissioner for Administration through his Member of Parliament in respect of maladministration by the prison authorities.

14.293 Finally, the prisoner has the right to petition Her Majesty the Queen and Parliament. (There used to be the general right to petition the Home Secretary, but that general right has now been absorbed in part into the new grievance procedure to which we will refer later.)

14.294 It is essential that there should be this number of avenues of redress open to a prisoner. A prisoner, as a result of his being in prison, is peculiarly vulnerable to arbitrary and unlawful action. Those who are responsible for his imprisonment should be subject to the scrutiny and control of, in particular, the ordinary Courts of the land. The Courts are well aware of this. There has been, over the last 15 years, a greater willingness on the part of the Courts to exercise that scrutiny. For example, at one time it was thought that a governor's adjudications in disciplinary proceedings were not subject to judicial review. It has now been made clear by the House of Lords that this is not the position.

14.295 While scrutiny by these bodies outside the prison system is important, it is also important that there should be the appropriate structures within the prison system to ensure that justice does not stop at the prison doors.

14.296 In the course of this Report we have, from time to time, referred to both the need for justice and the need for fairness in dealing with prisoners. Fairness is a very important part of justice. However justice is a wider concept than fairness. If a prisoner is treated unfairly, then he will usually also be treated unjustly. Likewise, if he is treated unjustly, he will normally also be treated unfairly. However, justice involves more than the general requirement to act fairly in the circumstances of a particular case.

14.297 A Judge or, for that matter, a prison Governor sitting under the proverbial palm tree and applying his personal ideas of justice according to the case which he is then deciding, may be able to resolve fairly a problem which is presented to him or to her. But this is not the way in which justice should be achieved, either in society as a whole or within a prison. Proper structures are necessary in order to achieve justice. Within a prison in particular, it is an important requirement of justice that justice should not only actually be done but should be seen to be done. It will not be seen to be done if there is no proper procedure, if there are no established rules, if the prisoner is not made aware of those rules and if there is not, at least at the final stage of the process, recourse to an independent element.

14.298 A proper system of justice within prisons is important for every prisoner and everyone who has to work in prisons. If a prisoner does not perceive that he is being treated with justice, he will legitimately feel debased, he will bear a grievance, and he will be a difficult prisoner to control. The absence of justice can poison relations between prisoners and staff and ultimately play a part in bringing about the explosive situation which existed in some prisons in April 1990.

14.299 In other parts of this Report we have referred to different aspects of the need for justice in prisons. Here we will refer to a requirement to give reasons for decisions which adversely affect prisoners to a material extent, to the need for a satisfactory grievance procedure and to the arrangements necessary for satisfactory disciplinary proceedings.

Reasons for Decisions

14.300 There is no general requirement in our law that a body such as the Prison Service has to give reasons for its actions (see the recent as yet unpublished decision of the Court of Appeal in R v *The Deputy Governor of Parkhurst Prison and Others, Ex parte Hague*). Forceful arguments have been advanced that the law should be changed in this regard. However, we do not consider that it is necessary for us to contend for such a dramatic change. We consider it sufficient to suggest that the Prison Service should adopt the practice, as a matter of good and sensible administration and management, of giving reasons to a prisoner for any decision which materially and adversely affects him.

14.301 This may seem at first sight a heavy burden to place upon prison staff and the Prison Service. We do not believe this need be the position in practice. Take a typical example. Exercise or an educational class has to be cancelled. Instead of leaving the prisoner in his cell and not letting him know what has happened, the prison officer tells him that his exercise or class has had to be cancelled because a PE instructor or teacher is ill. If a prisoner is given a simple reason of this sort, explaining what has happened, it will not make the prisoner happy about the position, but it could avoid the sense of powerlessness and the sense of frustration which may otherwise arise.

14.302 Frequently, the giving of reasons will avoid recourse to a grievance procedure. The provision of reasons also has other material advantages. If a governor or other member of staff is required, as a matter of course, to give a brief explanation to the prisoner for conduct which materially and adversely affects him, then this requirement will deter arbitrary action. It will result in a better standard of decision making.

14.303 We have deliberately proposed that the giving of reasons should not apply only to situations which are of central significance in the life of a prisoner. Our proposal sets the hurdle lower than that. This is because we recognise a prisoner is always vulnerable to being subjected to an underground or alternative system of discipline. A prisoner who offends staff in some way can be maliciously subjected to a course of conduct which drastically reduces his standard of life in a prison. Yet no major decision can be identified which has this effect. For example, a prisoner may not be given his usual job, he misses out on exercise, he does not have the opportunity to go to the library. There may, of course, be nothing malicious about such actions. But the prisoner believes that there is. The need to give reasons can reduce the risk of abuse and can help to resolve any doubt in the prisoner's mind about whether the issue has been properly considered.

14.304 The Prison Service is already well aware of the importance of giving reasons. For example, the Prison Service's new grievance procedures require that reasons should be given. There is a requirement to give reasons in respect of some of the arrangements for the transfer of disruptive prisoners. We discuss in Section 12 why we consider that the reasons for such a transfer should be given to the prisoner in writing as a matter of course. We want to extend a process which the Prison Service has already begun.

14.305 Our approach to giving reasons, however, should not be regarded as inflexible. It would not be practicable to require the giving of reasons where this is not desirable in the public interest. For example, in the case of Category A prisoners, it may be necessary to defer giving reasons on security grounds.

14.306 No reasons are at present given for parole decisions. The Inquiry was repeatedly told by prisoners that they regarded the failure to give reasons by the Parole Board as being very unfair. We were pleased, therefore, to note from the annual report of the Parole Board for 1989, that the Board has changed its policy and now support the notion that reasons should be given. The Parole Board has written:

> "The Government's stated intention to move cautiously towards a system whereby prisoners are given reasons for parole decisions is welcomed by most members. We see this as a positive move and one which is now considered to be both necessary and desirable in the interest of fairness to the prisoner."

14.307 In the ordinary way, we would expect the reasons for any material decision to be given orally and for a prisoner to be content with them in that form. A prisoner should, however, be able to ask for the reasons to be produced in writing. If he does so, and the request is reasonable, the request should be complied with. We deliberately refer to a "reasonable" request because, in relation to many decisions, it would not be reasonable to make such a request. We would normally regard it as reasonable to make a request if the prisoner was considering formally invoking the grievance procedure. In such a situation, it would be an advantage to the prisoner and to the person to whom the grievance is addressed to have written reasons. The giving of written reasons avoids any dispute as to what they were.

14.308 We therefore recommend:

i) that a prisoner should normally be given reasons as soon as is reasonably practicable for any decision which adversely affects him to a material extent;

ii) that for decisions which have a particularly disruptive effect on a prisoner, like the transfer of a prisoner for reasons of good order or discipline, reasons or a statement should be given as soon as is reasonably practicable in writing as a matter of course; and

iii) that for other material decisions, the Prison Service should comply with a reasonable request by a prisoner that reasons should be given in writing;

iv) that a new Prison Rule should be made giving effect to these recommendations.

Grievance Procedures

14.309   If a grievance procedure is to be of value, the procedure must:

i) be straightforward. The prisoner must be able to understand and operate it;

ii) be expeditious. In many situations, unless this is the position, the remedy which it provides may come too late. There must therefore be appropriate time limits;

iii) be effective. It must be capable of providing the remedy which is needed;

iv) be independent. And it must be seen to be so.

14.310   A proper grievance procedure has much in common with a proper appellate procedure for disciplinary proceedings. This is not surprising since, by seeking to appeal from a disciplinary decision, a prisoner is responding to a disciplinary decision in very much the same way as he may respond to a decision of a different sort. It is for this reason that we will be recommending arrangements for considering grievances, and arrangements for considering appeals from disciplinary proceedings, which follow, in many respects, much the same course.

i) The History   14.311   Grievance procedures have been extensively examined over the past 15 years by various official and unofficial bodies. In 1975 there was a report by an independent Committee under the chairmanship of Earl Jellicoe. The Committee suggested that the Board of Visitors' duty to hear prisoners' requests and complaints could not be properly carried out if the Board also had the task of adjudicating in disciplinary cases.

14.312   In 1978, the House of Commons Expenditure Committee recommended that the system of petitioning to the Home Secretary should be thoroughly reviewed. This recommendation was supported in 1979 by the May Committee of Inquiry into the United Kingdom Prison Services. This recommendation has now been implemented.

14.313   In 1983, the British Section of the International Commission of Jurists

(Justice) in its Report "Justice in Prison", went further and called for an independent investigator (a Prisons Ombudsman). The Commission also recommended that the offence which existed at that time of making "any false and malicious allegations against an officer" should be abolished.

14.314   These views and concerns were brought together in a major Report by HM Chief Inspector of Prisons in 1987 entitled "A Review of Prisoners' Complaints".

14.315   The Chief Inspector's Report led to the establishment of a Prison Service Working Group in the autumn of 1988 to develop proposals for improving grievance procedures. The Group concluded early in its deliberations that certain restrictions on making complaints should be abolished. These restrictions were the disciplinary offence of making any false and malicious allegation, the offence of repeatedly making groundless complaints, and a provision that a complaint could not be made outside the prison system unless it was at the same time also made through the Prison Service's internal procedures. These restrictions were all abolished on 1 April 1989.

14.316   The Working Group finally reported in July 1989. The Report usefully lays out the procedures which existed at that time. They were the arrangements which existed at the time of the April 1990 disturbances. They continued until 25 September 1990. These arrangements allowed the prisoner to make an application to the wing manager or officer in charge of his or her landing; to the prison Governor or the Governor's delegate; to the Board of Visitors; to some staff at Regional Office or, by petition, to the Secretary of State.

14.317   The Prison Service told us that it kept no full central records of statistics relating to the grievance procedure. It noted, however, that the Working Group had estimated that there were some 290,000 landing, wing and Governors' applications made in 1988 and around 14,500 petitions to the Secretary of State.

14.318   The Working Group set out succinctly, and in our view accurately, the criticisms of the system that existed at that time. The principal criticism was that there was no provision for independent review: the power of remedy lay solely with the Governor and the Home Secretary. For this and other reasons, the Report found, as Part I of this Inquiry also found, that the present system lacked the confidence of prisoners.

14.319   The Working Group recommended that the internal grievance system should be reformed. The key elements were that more complaints would be dealt with at the prison, reasons would be given, and there should be an avenue of appeal to Headquarters. The Report estimated that the establishment of an independent Complaints Investigator would cost between £0.8m and £2.2m a year, with costs to the Department in responding to his inquiries ranging from between £0.3m and £1.2m. The Report believed that it would be sensible to implement its recommended changes to the internal system before establishing a Complaints Investigator. This was the approach which Ministers subsequently decided upon.

ii) The New System   14.320   Following a brief testing of pilot schemes, a new system on the lines recommended by the Working Group was introduced on 25 September 1990, the same day as senior management reorganisation above establishment level was implemented in the Prison Service.

14.321   The guidance which has been given to prisoners about the new procedure suggests a five step process to making requests or complaints within the prison. First, it counsels, "try talking first to your landing, wing, or personal officer. Lots of problems can be dealt with very simply and quickly in this way." Secondly, it advises an oral application. For this, a written record is made of the application and the landing or wing officer or wing manager is expected to discuss it with the prisoner on the same day. Thirdly, if the prisoner is still unhappy, he is advised to make a Governor's application. He is told that a senior member of staff will discuss it with the prisoner "usually within two days of your application".

14.322   Fourthly, the prisoner may raise the matter formally by making a written request or complaint. He is told that he "will normally receive a reply within seven days from the time the form [on which he has made his request or complaint] is returned. This will give you the full reply or tell you what is happening, and when you may expect a full reply. The reply will tell you whether or not your request has been granted or complaint accepted, and, if not, the reasons".

14.323   Fifthly, the prisoner is told that he may also apply to speak to the Board of Visitors at any time. The Board would normally expect the prisoner to have tried already to solve the problem by oral application or by written request or complaint to the Governor. But the Board would be able to look at any reply the prisoner had received or tell the inmate when he could expect to get a reply. The prisoner is told that the Board will let the prisoner know what it has decided to do about his request or complaint:

> "It could, for example, ask the Governor to think again about the decision which had been reached. Or it could bring it to the attention of the Area Manager or even the Home Secretary."

14.324   The prisoner is told that he may also take up the matter with the Area Manager or Headquarters. He may appeal to the Area Manager about a decision taken by the Governor. He may write a request or complaint about Prison "rules and regulations" or "reserved" subjects to the Area Manager or to other staff in Headquarters. He is told that parole, early release and adjudications are reserved subjects. There are further reserved subjects in relation to life sentence prisoners and category A prisoners. The prisoner is told that he should receive a reply within six weeks of his appeal, request or complaint being received. The prisoner is **also** told:

> "There is no appeal against a decision taken by Headquarters, but you can of course write to someone outside if you want to do so."

14.325   There is also a procedure for what is described as "confidential access". Confidential access enables a prisoner to write, using a sealed envelope, to the Governor, to the Chairman of the Board of Visitors or to the Area Manager.

iii) Our Proposals   14.326   We are in no doubt about the importance to be attached to having procedures which deal effectively and manifestly fairly with prisoners' concerns. No other conclusion could reasonably be drawn from the evidence we have received or from our discussions with prisoners.

14.327   A fair and ordered grievance procedure with proper avenues of appeal and clear reasons given will help to create a climate in which prisoners feel they can be heard. This should make the day-to-day life of the prison more relaxed and reduce the likelihood of disturbances erupting. Such a system must be, and must be seen to be, the answer to the sort of letters we received which said: "no-one listens to us"; and "no-one answers our questions". This was well recognised in the evidence presented to us by the Prison Officers' Association which says:

> "Prisoners are less likely to turn to, or gain support for, illegitimate methods of drawing attention to their grievances if the procedures for investigating complaints are speedy, thorough and manifestly fair".

14.328   From the evidence we received, and from the discussion at our public seminars, the new procedures seem to be generally welcome. They meet many of the concerns about the earlier, much more haphazard system. The keys to the problem lay in setting time limits and in providing reasons for negative decisions. We welcome the delegation of the initial consideration of complaints to establishments, while providing for appeals to go to the Area Manager.

14.329   But some changes are needed. In the following paragraphs we consider particular aspects of the grievance procedure which, in our view, require modification and development. In particular we will recommend the introduction of an independent element through the appointment of a Complaints Adjudicator.

(a) Confidential Access

14.330   The Prison Service explained to us in evidence that confidential access was meant to be a safeguard. It provided an "unfettered channel of communication between the prisoner and the recipient". But the recipient had discretion as to how the request or complaint should be handled. He might decide to deal with it personally, or he might ask another member of staff to consider the matter, or he might ask the prisoner to raise his or her request/ complaint in the normal way.

14.331   The "Information for Prisoners" on "How to Make a Request or Complaint" states:

> "You can write direct, using a sealed envelope, to the Governor, the Chairman of the Board of Visitors or the Area Manager. This is called confidential access. You should ask for a request/complaints form and a confidential access envelope. This will be marked "Prisoners' Confidential Access"....*Confidential access is meant to be used only if your request or complaint is about something which you cannot raise with prison staff (see Annex A for advice on complaints against staff).* It is up to the person whose name is put on the envelope to decide how to deal with the problem you raise. He or she may need to get more information or to investigate the problem and this may mean that others will need to be told. If you use Confidential Access you should explain on the form why you have done so. This will help the person receiving it to decide how best to deal with it."

14.332 Annex A states:

> "After you have made a complaint...(iii) the Governor will ask a senior member of staff to look into your complaint. He or she will ask you what happened. He or she will also talk to the member of staff you have complained about. If there are other people who saw what happened they will also be seen. All this takes time, so you must be patient. The investigation has to be thorough to be fair."

14.333   The guidance given to staff about confidential access, however, has a different emphasis from that given to the prisoner. The Staff Manual says:

> "It does not mean that matters will necessarily be kept in confidence between the recipient of the request/complaint and the prisoner, although there may be rare occasions when this would be right. In particular, however, allegations against staff will continue to be handled in accordance with the guidance given in CI 8/89 (amended to reflect the change of headquarters organisation...) which requires that a member of staff should be informed of an allegation made against him or her as soon as possible, and that if the allegation is in writing that he or she should be given a copy."

14.334   The Prison (Amendment) Rules 1990, 8(iii), and the YOI (Amendment) Rules 1990, 9(iii), both state:

> "A written request or complaint under paragraph (i) above may be made in confidence."

14.335   A complaint can hardly be regarded as being made in confidence if the recipient is required to inform the person about whom the complaint is made of the nature of the allegation made and to hand a copy of the complaint, if it is in writing, to that person. As a substantial number of complaints which are made in confidence are likely to be about staff, we propose that steps should be taken to remedy the present misleading position which does not appear to conform with the relevant Rules. Either the prisoner should be told beforehand the full position. Or, before a confidential complaint is handed to the member of staff, the prisoner should have an opportunity of withdrawing it.

(b) Access to the Governing Governor

14.336   The Circular Instruction issued to the Governors of all establishments on the new procedures (Circular Instruction 34/1990) says:

> "The guidance given to inmates makes it clear that there is no automatic right to see the governing Governor, who has discretion whether to hear an application personally or to ask another member of staff to perform his duty. However, prisoners may write to the governing Governor under confidential access."

14.337   Confidential access ensures that the governing Governor must see the letter, but not that he must see the prisoner. We consider that, whatever the size of the prison, the governing Governor must be known to prisoners and must be available to them. This is one of the lessons which arise from Part I of the Inquiry. We recognise that governing Governors may properly delegate the initial consideration of an application to a less senior Governor and that such matters should, if at all possible, be resolved at that level. But we propose that each prisoner who has had his application considered by a more junior governor should have the right to see the governing Governor on one occasion in respect of each particular application.

14.338   We recognise that this may put an extra burden on governing Governors, but we believe that the governing Governor should give the highest priority to the considerations and concerns of his or her prisoners. They may be managers, but they are also Governors. We are of this opinion notwithstanding our view that large establishments should be broken down for management purposes into smaller units, each with their own governor. In our view it has to be accepted that there will be occasions that a prisoner will not be satisfied unless he sees the head man. If the matter has previously been considered at a lower level, he should have the opportunity to do so. This may avoid an appeal out of the establishment to the Area Manager.

(c) Board of Visitors

14.339   We do not think it essential that Boards should expect prisoners "normally" to have gone to the Governor first before coming to them. (This guidance is set out in the advice given to prisoners, which we have referred to earlier as the fifth step to making a request or complaint within a prison.) We would not wish to place any fetter on the stage at which the Board becomes involved. The timing of the Board's involvement will depend on the nature of the complaint or request. With experience, the Board will be in the best position to judge when its intervention is most likely to be constructive.

14.340   We propose that, when the Board is involved, then its role should be two-fold. First, the Board is there to advise and assist the prisoner about his involvement in the grievance procedure. Secondly, if it considers this would assist, it should investigate the grievance itself and then make any comment or recommendation which it considers appropriate to the Governor, the Area Manager or to the Complaints Adjudicator (whose appointment we shall be recommending) depending upon who was considering the grievance at that stage.

14.341   We would not expect the Board, in ordinary circumstances, to make a recommendation which was adverse to the prisoner. If the case was one where the view of the Board was adverse, it would confine itself to informing the prisoner that it had decided that it was a case in which it could take no action. For the Board to make a recommendation which was adverse to the prisoner, could have the unfortunate result of creating the impression that it was siding with the establishment.

(d) A Complaints Adjudicator: An Independent Element

14.342   According to the evidence we received, the new procedure retains one significant gap. There is no avenue of appeal to an independent person. Most of those who submitted evidence, and who contributed to the public seminar, agreed with the Prison Reform Trust that:

"In our view, a Prisons Ombudsman – with a broad remit not just 'maladministration' as is the case with the Parliamentary Commissioner for Administration – should be established forthwith".

14.343 The Association of Members of Boards of Visitors agreed that the appointment of a Prisons Ombudsman, "would be a positive step forward". The Parliamentary All-Party Penal Affairs Group said that a Prisons Ombudsman:

"would provide a channel for investigating prisoners grievances which, as well as being effective, thorough and accessible, would also be conspicuously independent of the Prison Service".

14.344 The Prison Service was not against appointing some form of Ombudsman for Prisons, but neither was it for it. It did not think it necessary to make a decision now. It told us in written evidence:

"Once these changes [the new grievance procedures] have had a chance to bed down a more measured judgement can be reached on whether a Prisons Ombudsman is also needed."

14.345 We recognise the need to avoid continual upheaval, and to allow the changes already made time to have effect. However, the presence of an independent element within the Grievance Procedure is more than just an "optional extra". The case for some form of independent person or body to consider grievances is incontrovertible. There is no possibility of the present system satisfactorily meeting this point, even once it has bedded down. A system without an independent element is not a system which accords with proper standards of justice.

14.346 We hope that the new procedures will be effective in ensuring that complaints and concerns are dealt with satisfactorily at the lowest level possible. We do not want to see an overweeningly and unnecessarily cumbersome system which requires all decisions to be taken at the most senior levels, or which expects all those decisions to be challenged on appeal. Were that to be the case, the system would not be operating properly.

14.347 We would see an independent avenue of appeal as a last resort which the prisoner would know was available to him. In practice it may prove to be rarely used. But this would not detract from its importance. The influence of an independent element would permeate down to the lowest level of the grievance system. It would give the whole system a validity which it does not otherwise have. It would act as a spur to the Prison Service to maintain proper standards. It would encourage the resolution of difficulties in advance of an appeal.

14.348 We have considered carefully the form that such an independent element should take. We have concluded that it is possible and desirable that there should be an independent person able both to consider complaints about grievances, and appeals from disciplinary findings. We noted earlier that both types of decision could generate the same sort of response from a prisoner. They could also sometimes arise from the same set of circumstances. There is no benefit in unnecessarily creating distinctions, irrelevant to the prisoner and to the events which concern him.

14.349 We recommend that a Complaints Adjudicator should be appointed by the Home Secretary. The Complaints Adjudicator would have two distinct roles:

    i)   in relation to the grievance procedure, where his role would be to recommend, advise and conciliate at the final stage of the procedure;

    ii)   in relation to disciplinary proceedings, where his role would be to act as a final tribunal of appeal.

14.350 The Complaints Adjudicator would be expected to make an annual report on his work to the Home Secretary. We would expect the Home Secretary would lay the report before Parliament.

14.351 The person appointed would need to be someone of independence and standing. Given the nature of his task, we think he should be a barrister or solicitor of not less than seven years standing – in other words, a person who would be eligible for appointment to the bench. Such status would ensure his independence.

14.352 The Complaints Adjudicator would not be a Prisons Ombudsman. If there are satisfactory grievance and disciplinary procedures, then these procedures, together with the other avenues of redress which are open to a prisoner, should make a Prisons Ombudsman unnecessary.

14.353 We considered particularly whether an Adjudicator on these lines makes otiose an application to the Parliamentary Commissioner for Administration in respect of maladministration. We have been grateful for evidence from and a most informative discussion with the Parliamentary Commissioner and his Deputy. To close the avenue to the Parliamentary Commissioner would require amending legislation. We do not believe that such an avenue should be closed. It should still be possible for prisoners to complain through a Member of Parliament to the Commissioner when they believe the Prison Service has been guilty of maladministration. Because of the statutory limits on the Commissioner's jurisdiction, that may not apply to maladministration of the complaints procedure itself.

14.354 We have considered what staff the Complaints Adjudicator would require. It is difficult to anticipate the extent to which appeals will be referred to him. We anticipate as we have said, that the major influence of the Complaints Adjudicator will be to improve the decision making process. We do not anticipate vast numbers of cases coming before him. We suggest, therefore, that he should be provided in the first instance with limited support. He is not intended to be an expert on prison practice and we do not anticipate a need for assessors and advisers. We would suggest, in the first instance, that there should be a Chairman at Headquarters, with secretarial support. Across the country there should be about three assistant adjudicators who would be qualified lawyers. They too would need secretarial support. The assistant adjudicators would be able to make recommendations to the Chairman or, under authority delegated by him, resolve the appeals themselves.

e) The Complaints Adjudicator's Role in Relation to Grievance Procedures

14.355 We envisage the Complaints Adjudicator as being the last stage of the grievance procedure. Before applying to the Adjudicator, the prisoner would need to have made his complaint or application to the Governor, (or Headquarters in certain matters) and to have received a reasoned and negative reply; and then, for Governor's applications, to have applied to the Area Manager and to have received a further reasoned and negative reply.

14.356 We do not, therefore, agree with part of what Mr Cavadino of NACRO advocated during our public seminar. He suggested that prisoners should be able to "appeal" to the independent person at any time without having first exhausted the avenues of internal "appeal". That would be a recipe, in our judgement, for confusion and for unnecessary applications to the Adjudicator. The Prison Service should be given the opportunity, and should be expected, to consider and, we would hope, resolve prisoners' grievances before the prisoner activated the independent element.

14.357 The Complaints Adjudicator should be free to receive any appeal which is put to him by any prisoner, who has gone through these earlier stages. He should be free to determine his own procedure. He would be concerned both with the merits of the complaint and with the manner in which the decision giving rise to the grievance had been considered. It should be open to him to receive a report from the Area Manager, the Governor, or the Board of Visitors in relation to the grievance. If he considers it necessary, the Adjudicator could visit the prison and speak to the prisoner, staff, management and the Board. It would be open to him to seek to resolve the matter in a way that is acceptable to all the parties. Alternatively, it should be open to the Adjudicator to refer the matter to the Area Manager or to take no further action if he so wishes.

14.358 The Complaints Adjudicator would not have executive powers to over-rule the decisions of the Prison Service. He would, however, be able to make recommendations to the Governor, the Area Manager, Headquarters or the Director General. He would expect to receive a response to those recommendations within a set time limit. Unless there were special circumstances justifying this, we would expect his recommendations to be implemented.

14.359 If the Adjudicator were unhappy with the response from the Prison Service, then it would be open to him to make a report to the Home Secretary. It might be that the Home Secretary would agree that, in the normal course, a target time should be set for any response he gave to the Adjudicator's submission.

14.360 It would not be part of the Complaints Adjudicator's role to determine what should be the policy of the Prison Service with regard to prisoners generally. His concern would be with individual grievances and how they were handled by the Prison Service.

14.361 This may be a particular concern in relation to Prison Rules and Regulations and "Reserved" subjects. So far as these matters are concerned, we would prefer there to be no special restriction placed upon the jurisdiction of the Complaints Adjudicator. However in practice, we would not expect the Complaints Adjudicator to make recommendations which conflicted with decisions on the merits by Headquarters. He would regard his role in such cases as being a supervisory role. It would be similar to that performed by the High Court in judicial review, a role which primarily involves scrutinising the decision making process.

14.362 It would be necessary for the Complaints Adjudicator himself to establish time limits within which he should respond to the prisoner making an application to him. We would suggest that, following acknowledgement of the receipt of the application, he should aim to provide a substantive reply or a progress report within six weeks and, if further work is needed, at three weeks intervals thereafter. (We would expect a substantive reply always to be available within 12 weeks.) Each prisoner should receive a written reply to his complaint, with reasons for the Complaints Adjudicator's response and for any recommendations made. The Complaints Adjudicator should also report to the prisoner on the Prison Service's response to any recommendations he has put to the Service or to the Home Secretary.

Disciplinary Procedures

i) The History 4.363 The most authoritative source on the prison disciplinary system is the Report of the Committee under the Chairmanship of Mr Peter Prior. The Committee was appointed by the Home Secretary in May 1984 to examine the arrangements for dealing with alleged disciplinary offences by prisoners.

14.364 The Committee reported on 3 October 1985 with some 100 recommendations. Among those, it recommended that Governors should continue to deal with most offences against discipline; that Board of Visitors should lose their adjudicatory role; and that more serious charges should be heard by a newly established independent body to be called the Prison Disciplinary Tribunal. The Tribunal would consist of a number of panels, each with a legally qualified chairman and two lay members. A circuit judge would be appointed as President. Chairmen were to be solicitors and barristers of not less than seven years standing.

14.365   The Prior Committee proposed that a prisoner should have a right of appeal to this Tribunal when the Governor's punishment exceeded seven days forfeiture of remission. Offences could also be remitted to the Tribunal, when it would have a maximum punishment available to it of 120 days forfeiture. Where the prisoner appealed against a finding by the Governor, the appeal would be by way of rehearing. When the appeal was against the punishment only, the prisoner would have a right of access to the Tribunal. There would also be a system of appeals against decisions of the Tribunal to an Appeal Tribunal composed of the President and selected members of the Disciplinary Tribunal. The Appeal Tribunal was to give reasons for its decisions.

14.366   The Committee also proposed that there should be a new and clearer code of disciplinary offences.

14.367   The Government published its reply in a White Paper in October 1986 entitled "The Prison Disciplinary System in England and Wales". The Government announced that it proposed to accept the recommendations of the Prior Committee that Boards of Visitors should lose their disciplinary functions; that the disciplinary role and powers of prison Governors should remain substantially unchanged; and that there should be a new code of disciplinary offences. It accepted the idea of a Prison Disciplinary Tribunal, but suggested that the local panels should be lay people rather than that each panel should be headed by a lawyer. The White Paper estimated that the annual cost in 1986 of its more modest proposal would be about £0.4m, compared to the cost of the full Prior Tribunal of £0.9m.

14.368   The Government suggested that there should be a right of appeal to the local panels from the Governor's decision when more than 14 days forfeiture had been awarded. Judicial review should continue to be available as a last resort.

14.369   The Government announced its intention to bring forward early legislation to establish the new Prison Disciplinary Tribunal which it proposed.

14.370   It was not to be. There was what the Prison Service described to us as:

> "A subsequent failure to achieve consensus on the form a new Tribunal should take".

14.371   Some Boards of Visitors, perhaps then the majority, were concerned about the central proposal that they should no longer be involved in adjudications. They felt then, as some still feel now, that adjudications did not compromise their independence and were useful in giving them the knowledge necessary to fulfil their "watch-dog" role.

14.372   The Government's option of lay panels, with no legal chairmen, was not universally accepted as providing a sufficient way of ensuring that standards of justice were introduced in the consideration of serious offences in prison.

14.373   The Government decided, therefore, to stick generally with the present system. It met the Prior Committee's recommendations for a clearer list of disciplinary offences. And it introduced an experiment, to which we shall refer later, in providing Clerks of Justices to give advice to Boards of Visitors when they were adjudicating.

ii) The Present Situation

14.374   The present position, therefore, is that Governors and Boards of Visitors adjudicate on prison disciplinary offences. These offences are set out in Prison Rule 47 as amended by the Prison (Amendment) Rules 1989. Among the 22 offences set out in the Rules are such offences which could, in certain circumstances, represent a criminal offence – such as assault, fighting with any person, and taking improperly any article belonging to another person or to a prison. Other offences are clearly related to infringements of the institutional life of a prison – such as denying access to any part of the prison to any officer, or being disrespectful to any officer or person visiting a prison, or intentionally failing to work properly or, being required to work, refusing to do so. There are also "catch-all" offences – such as that the prisoner "disobeys or fails to comply with any rule or regulation applying to him", and "in any way offends against good order and discipline". It is also an offence if a prisoner "disobeys any lawful order".

14.375   In evidence to us, the Prison Service accepted that the first two of these catch-all offences gave critics cause for concern. The Service told us that Governors were encouraged to keep to a minimum the number of local rules and regulations which might form the basis of a charge that the prisoner had disobeyed or failed to comply with such rules and regulations. The Service considered also that, on balance, "the variety of offending behaviour within establishments" was such that an offence of offending against good order and discipline should be retained. But the Prison Service emphasised the importance of using specific charges wherever possible. This view was confirmed in a note of 12 April 1990 from the then P3 Division in Headquarters to the governors of all establishments. The note advised on the laying of disciplinary charges following the disturbances in early April. The note said that, as far as possible, inmates should not be charged with offending against good order and discipline. We are in full agreement with this guidance.

14.376   The decision about whether a particular disciplinary offence should be heard by the Governor or should be remitted to the Board of Visitors is a matter for the Governor. He is required to enquire into every charge not later than the next day after the charge is laid, unless that day is a Sunday or public holiday. The Prison Service's manual on the conduct of adjudications published in January 1989 (and available in prison libraries or for sale to prisoners at £2.50,) adds:

> "However, if the offence is sufficiently serious to warrant a punishment higher than the Governor has power to impose, he may refer the charge to the Board of Visitors, provided he is satisfied that there is a case to answer".

14.377   We received evidence from Mr Heap, the Clerk to the Justices' of Cardiff Court. Mr Heap was involved in the scheme for Clerks assisting Boards of Visitors. He had sent a questionnaire about the operation of the scheme to his fellow Clerks. (We shall refer to other aspects of this questionnaire later). Mr Heap told us that most of the 11 Clerks who had replied to his questionnaire had noted that the referral of a case by the Governor to the Board was seen by Board members as requiring a penalty in excess of the Governor's maximum. This confirms our own assessment, having spoken to Governors and Boards. This is clearly not a satisfactory basis on which to conduct an adjudication. We also received the distinct impression from some members of Boards that they would feel that they were letting down the prison if they did not find a charge proved.

14.378   The Governor, and to a much greater extent the Board of Visitors, have extensive powers to punish disciplinary offences. The most serious of those punishments, and the one which the Prison Service told us was the most commonly used, is forfeiture of remission. The Governor has a power to order forfeiture of remission to a sentenced prisoner for a period not exceeding 28 days, and the Board of Visitors for a period not exceeding 120 days. Consecutive punishments of forfeiture are possible for related offences, but the total may not exceed 28 days for the Governor or 180 days for the Boards of Visitors. For young offenders, the initial punishment is 28 days for the Governor and 90 days for the Board of Visitors; and for consecutive punishments, 28 days again for the Governor and 135 days for the Board of Visitors. An unconvicted prisoner may be awarded prospective forfeiture of remission, which would then have to be served if he were subsequently convicted and given an immediate prison sentence.

14.379   There are other penalties which, again, provide different scales for the

Governor and for the Board of Visitors. They allow the forfeiture of any privileges, exclusion from associated work, forfeiture of pay, cellular confinement and, for unconvicted prisoners, loss of the rights to books, writing materials and other means of occupation and, if found guilty of escaping or attempting to escape, of the right to wear their own clothing. Punishments may be suspended for up to six months, except, other than in special extenuating circumstances, in respect of forfeiture of remission.

14.380 Forfeiture of remission may also be restored, but before applying for restoration adult prisoners must spend nine months from the date of the offence, and young offenders six months, without losing any further remission.

14.381 The position about forfeiture of remission will change if the proposals in the Criminal Justice Bill at present before Parliament are accepted. This is because the Bill replaces the current system of parole and remission of sentence with new arrangements. These would provide for short term prisoners (those serving a term of less than four years) to be released once they had served half their sentence, and for long term prisoners (those serving a term of four years or more) to be released once they had served two thirds of their sentence. (Where the sentence is one of more than 12 months, the release is on licence.) In addition, long term prisoners could be released on licence at the discretion of the Secretary of State on the recommendation of the Parole Board once they had served one half of their sentence.

14.382 The Prison Service told us that, if these proposals were implemented, power to forfeit remission would be replaced by a power to award "additional days". The Prison Service explained the provision as follows:

> "The effect of the additional days would be to postpone the date on which a prisoner is released from *prison custody. However, neither Governors nor Boards will be able to extend the total length of the original sentence passed by the Courts*". (their emphasis)

14.383 The Prison Service added:

> "It is our intention to duplicate the current system by which loss of remission can be restored by Governors and Boards. Through good behaviour, a prisoner will be able to cancel out the additional days' awarded at disciplinary hearings."

14.384 Provisions on these lines have been included in the Criminal Justice Bill at present before Parliament.

14.385 We recognise the Prison Service argument referred to above that neither Governors nor Boards can extend the total length of the original sentence. So, on this argument, the award is not, strictly speaking, an additional prison sentence. That argument applies equally to the present system of forfeiture of remission. But that is not how it seems to prisoners, and with some reason. The fact is that a Board of Visitors can, for a single offence, keep a prisoner in prison for 120 days longer than he otherwise would spend. This at present is seen by the prisoner as the equivalent to him or her being awarded a sentence of imprisonment of nine months (in order to spend the same amount of time in prison, allowing for full remission). This length of sentence is beyond the range of powers available to the Magistrates' Court. The powers of the Board of Visitors are therefore very considerable.

14.386 We have already stated in Section 12 that we consider that the adjudicatory function of a Board of Visitors is not consistent with their watch-dog role. Because they conduct adjudications, Boards of Visitors are not seen by prisoners as fair or impartial. In the survey conducted by Mr John Ditchfield and Mr David Duncan for the Prior Committee, they found that:

> "Inmates clearly believed that the adjudicatory system was heavily biased against them and that the inclination of both Governors and Board

424

members was to believe staff, rather than them."

They added:

"Prison officers did not share this perception, but there was evidence that some Governors accepted the system to be biased in this general sense."

14.387 Significantly, as we shall explain, the survey also found that:

"When given the alternatives of having serious breaches of discipline dealt with by the Board of Visitors, the Governor (with increased powers of punishment) or an outside court, the majority of all four groups of respondents [that is inmates, officers, Governors and members of the Board of Visitors] preferred the outside court."

14.388 For less serious offences, the finding was that:

"A clear majority of inmates expressed a preference to have them dealt with by the Governor rather than the Board of Visitors even though the Board was perceived by them as being slightly less biased. The Governor's more limited powers of punishment was the main reason for this choice".

14.389 These findings confirmed the research by Mr Mike Maguire and Dr Jon Vagg on the Watch-dog Role of Boards of Visitors published in 1984. We referred to it in Section 12. They found that the majority of prisoners felt that Boards of Visitors' adjudications were controlled "behind the scenes" and were biased against them. They found also that a substantial number of staff interviewed (29%) said that they had witnessed some kind of procedural incompetence on the part of Board of Visitors members at adjudications.

14.390 There are two principal concerns with continuing with adjudications by the Boards of Visitors. First, as we have discussed in Section 12, we do not consider that it is possible or reasonable to expect a Board of Visitors to act as both watch-dog and as an adjudicatory body. That is confirmed in the research and in the Prior Report. From the evidence we have received and the discussions we have had, we believe that is now accepted by many members of Boards of Visitors. We wish to enhance and develop the work of Boards of Visitors as effective watch-dogs monitoring the system, and advising and assisting prisoners, staff and management. That cannot be achieved if they continue with an adjudicatory function.

14.391 We considered whether Boards should act as some form of appeal body against the decisions of the Governor. We were persuaded by the views expressed at the public seminar, including by a member of the Co-ordinating Committee of Boards of Visitors, that that would be seen as a return by the back-door to all the problems of maintaining the independence of the Boards of Visitors which exist at present. While, in our view, that is a misapprehension, we accept that that would be likely to be the view of the majority of prisoners, and that is not something we would wish to perpetuate.

14.392 There is a second reason why we have concluded that it is essential to remove this function from Boards of Visitors. We do not think it is reasonable to expect Boards conducting adjudications in prison, with the extensive powers they have been given, to exercise the procedural safeguards which are necessary for the proper discharge of such a function. We do not consider that the option of appointing a Justices' Clerk to assist a Board of Visitors' adjudicating panel, while useful, is the whole or a sufficient answer. The Prison Service established in November 1989 a one year pilot scheme starting in 13 establishments to assess both the practicality and the potential benefits of such an idea. This scheme has been independently monitored by one of our Assessors, Professor Rod Morgan and by Ms Helen Jones of Bristol University. In forming our conclusions, we have not had sight of or been briefed about that research. We received evidence, however, at one of our public seminars from the Clerk to the Justices' in Cardiff, Mr Heap, to whom we have already referred. He showed us the report which he presented at the seminar. That report, which, as we have said, was based on the replies from 11 of the 13 Justices' Clerks concerned, noted that there was:

> "An overwhelming majority of views that there was a closeness between members of the Board and prison staff."

14.393   It noted also:

> "In some institutions there were meetings prior to hearings, always informal, between members of staff and Boards. It is impossible to tell whether these meetings involved discussions of cases to be dealt with."

14.394   Mr Heap's report also concluded that:

> "Those who were ready to state a view indicated by considerable majority that the Board of Visitor did not use the same care in approaching LOR [the penalty of loss of remission] as Justices would have approached imprisonment."

14.395   This evidence confirms us in our recommendation that Boards of Visitors should no longer be involved in adjudicatory hearings. Nor should they adopt an appellate role in relation to these hearings.

14.396   Previous reviews came to similar conclusions. The problem has been to identify what should be put in the Board's place. It is on that rock that further progress has foundered. A good deal of the evidence we received suggested that the time had now come to introduce the Prison Disciplinary Tribunal proposed by the Prior Committee. Those who took this view included the POA, Professor Martin (who was involved in the preparation of the Jellicoe Report on Boards of Visitors to which we referred earlier), the Law Society, and the Prison Reform Trust. We heard powerful argument in support of this view at the public seminar.

14.397   We are conscious, however, that these ideas have been on the table for some time and have not been taken up. Cost is a factor. So is complexity. We have felt it right to go back to the basic principles and, from there, to adopt a different approach.

iii) Our Proposals   14.398   Our starting point has been a consideration of the place of disciplinary proceedings within prisons. We have examined the degree to which offences within prisons can be dealt with as disciplinary offences or need to be referred to an outside body. We have looked at the criteria which should apply. We have considered also the penalties which should be available within the disciplinary system.

14.399   The Prison Service, in its written evidence, stated that 95% of all charges are dealt with without reference to the Board of Visitors. In 1989, the Board heard 4,497 charges and Governors heard 81,215 charges. The Prison Service told us that the overwhelming majority of charges brought forward were found proven. In 1988, when Governors heard 80,478 charges and Boards of Visitors 4,119 charges, only 3,730 charges were dismissed. (These figures for charges heard, like those quoted above for 1989, included hearings started but not completed that year.)

14.400   We were also informed by the Prison Service that the 80,000 offences punished in 1988 represented an average of 1.6 offences per prisoner. The most commonly used penalty, as we have noted above, was forfeiture of remission, equivalent, at the maximum for a single offence, to a nine months prison sentence. The Prison Service said that:

> "In 1988, the amount of unsuspended forfeiture of remission awarded has been calculated as equivalent to approximately 600 to 700 of the annual average population".

14.401   This is an astonishing extra burden on the Prison Service. It needs to be controlled and relieved. The award of loss of remission on this scale, in effect keeping people in prison longer, will be brought into particular relief if the proposals we have described in the Criminal Justice Bill are implemented. The penalty then will clearly be seen to be additional days spent in prison.

14.402 If penalties equivalent to quite long prison sentences are required, then it is more satisfactory that they should be awarded by a Court. That would allow a trial which provides the full safeguards of the criminal law. Penalties of this length can only be justified by an infraction of the criminal law and not by a breach of disciplinary rules.

14.403 We consider that, in respect of offences committed in prison, a clear distinction should, therefore, be drawn between disciplinary proceedings and criminal proceedings. The former are proceedings which are properly brought with the limited objective of maintaining order within the confines of a prison. They should be subject to a level of penalties and a formality of procedure which is commensurate with that objective.

14.404 Criminal proceedings are brought in order to protect the public interest in enforcing and preserving public law and order. There the penalties may be higher, but the procedural safeguards must be greater. The fact that some disciplinary proceedings also involve the commission of criminal offences is not decisive. The distinction between the two situations was clearly drawn by Lord Justice Shaw in a judgment which marked a watershed in this area of the law in the case *R* v *Hull Prison Board of Visitors, Ex parte St Germain and Others* [1979] Q.B. 425, at pp. 454/5.

14.405 We recommend that all disciplinary proceedings should in future be conducted by a governor of the prison in which the alleged disciplinary offence took place. There is, in our judgement, no need in such cases, at the first stage of a disciplinary proceeding, for the charge to be heard by an outside body, be it a Court or a specially created tribunal. Furthermore, we consider that, for disciplinary offences, the present powers of punishment of a governor are adequate. The high scale of penalties at the present time in part reflect the practice of the Board of Visitors normally to impose a greater punishment than that available to governors. They are not, in our view, justified by the nature of the offences charged. Nor are there sufficient procedural safeguards to make just such a level of punishment. We therefore recommend that the greater powers of punishment which at present are exercised by the Boards of Visitors should be abolished.

14.406 It should continue, therefore, to be open to a governor to award forfeiture of remission, or, under the Criminal Justice Bill, added days, on the same levels as at present – a period not exceeding 28 days. But, as the facilities and opportunities for prisoners improve, as we have proposed they should, then there should be more recourse by a governor to punishments which involve loss of facilities and opportunities, rather than loss of remission or added days in prison. The problem at the present time is that a prisoner has little to lose apart from remission – that should not be the position in the future. As the improvements accrue, the facilities and opportunities will need to be reviewed from time to time, in order to determine which may be appropriately restricted as a result of disciplinary proceedings. Those which should be regarded as being part of the prisoner's basic standard of life should not be curtailed. The remainder would be at risk of being restricted. In this way, and in the fullness of time, we would look for the day when it would be possible first to reduce and eventually to abolish recourse to loss of remission, or the addition of days, in disciplinary proceedings.

14.407 We do not, therefore, agree with the provision at present in paragraph 41 of Standing Order 3D, which provides that forfeiture should be restricted to privileges which have been abused in the course of committing the offence. We propose that if a prisoner commits a disciplinary offence affecting the life of the prison, then it should be possible for him to lose a facility or an opportunity, even if he has not actually abused that opportunity or facility in committing his offence.

14.408   We are aware that the conduct of adjudications can be devolved by the governing Governor to another governor in the prison. We do not depart from that principle. But we believe that the Governor in charge of a prison should be prepared to consider offences which, if proved, are likely to lead to the imposition of the maximum penalties available. There could, therefore, in practice be a gradation of proceedings between junior governors and the Governor depending on the seriousness of the disciplinary offence being charged.

14.409   We accept that there are other offences committed by prisoners which, albeit committed in prison, raise issues as to the preservation of public law and order. They should be characterised as serious criminal offences. We recommend that cases which, because of their gravity, are not suited to be heard by a governor should be the subject of the same proceedings, and the same legal safeguards, as a criminal offence committed outside prison. We consider that there is unlikely to be a need, for a separate quasi-judicial authority to be established to consider these cases. There is no benefit to the administration of justice in establishing a separate authority. Such offences should be heard by the normal criminal Courts. If, however, our expectation proves wrong and, because of the number of cases involved, there proves to be a need for a special tribunal, that could be created at a later date.

14.410   We propose that consideration should be given, in particular in certain parts of the country, to establishing a special panel of Magistrates to hear charges in respect of criminal offences committed by prisoners. Consideration will also need to be given, in particular, to the prosecution of cases arising in the Isle of Wight, in whose small area there are three prisons.

14.411   Cases requiring the Courts to consider offences in prison could usefully be heard in or close to the prison where they were alleged to have been committed. However the public would have to have access, and there would be few prisons where this would be possible. Where there are arrangements, such as at the new Belmarsh Prison in London, which link the prison with a Court outside its walls, this could be achieved.

14.412   We recognise that there may in some cases be special factors applying to criminal offences committed in prison. In particular, as some evidence to us has pointed out, there may be difficulties about providing evidence to substantiate the charge. But that is a problem which relates to any proceedings of a serious nature, regardless of who is to hear it. The Prison Rules set out clearly that the standard for conviction is proof beyond all reasonable doubt.

14.413   We recognise also that the penalties available to the Court will be limited in range. In effect, given the position of the alleged offender in prison, the penalty is further imprisonment. We would envisage, however, that a case would only be brought before the Court when the prosecution considers that the offence was so serious as to justify such a penalty, if proved. If it did not, disciplinary proceedings would be in order before the governor.

14.414   The Crown Prosecution Service would in due course be able to establish guidelines for the sort of offences which in its view would merit bringing proceedings before the Court. The general law would apply to offences committed in prison and the fact that offences were committed by persons already in prison would be taken into account, to the extent appropriate according to law, in deciding the length of any sentence. In due course, sentencing guidelines could be given by the superior Courts if this was necessary.

14.415   It is not wholly unprecedented for offences committed in prison to be heard by the outside Courts. The Prison Service told us that in 1988, 220 charges were referred to the police. It is not possible for us to forecast precisely how many more cases than this would in future need to be referred to the police with a view to bringing charges before the Magistrates Court. We will seek, however, to provide a broad estimate.

14.416   We were helped in making this estimate by information provided at one of our public seminars by a Prison Service official, Mr Brian Caffarey. He told the seminar that from April to December 1989 there were 1,723 punishments of unsuspended forfeiture of remission over 28 days. Those were cases dealt with by the Board of Visitors. Of those 1,723 punishments, 1,200 related to absconds, and failure to return from home leave. In our view, these are matters which, in almost all cases, are most properly considered as disciplinary offences and should in future be dealt with by a governor.

14.417   If that pattern were repeated over a 12 month period, and if all such cases involving absconds and failures to return to prison were in future dealt with by a governor, there should be less than 700 cases which might fall outside the governor's jurisdiction. We believe, for the reasons we have set out above, that many more of such cases ought in future to come within a governor's jurisdiction. And we would expect that, if our proposals in this Report were implemented, the overall level of offending in prison would fall. The number of cases coming to Court is, therefore, likely to be manageably modest.

14.418   We have considered with some care the arguments which were put to the Prior Committee about the involvement of Magistrates' Courts in prison disciplinary proceedings. We noted that the Prior Committee believed that such a process had apparent attractions, but it decided against advocating it. We would set out the arguments more fully were it not for the fact that our proposals are not on all fours with those addressed by the Prior Committee. The heart of our proposal is that domestic disciplinary offences would in future be dealt with by a governor. Only the most serious criminal offences meriting a prison sentence would go to the Courts.

14.419   Under our proposals, questions about the appeal procedures for the most serious offences fall away. Appeals in respect of cases brought before the Courts would be dealt with through the normal judicial process.

14.420   Appeals from the decision of a governor, however, are a different matter. There needs to be some avenue of appeal, and, in our view, there must be an independent element to it.

14.421   In considering what structure is required, it is necessary to take into account that a governor would be dealing with domestic disciplinary proceedings aimed at maintaining law and order within the prison. He would be exercising powers of punishment commensurate with those proceedings.

14.422   Under our proposals, it is clearly right that every prisoner who is subject to a governor's adjudicatory proceedings, should have some right of appeal. We have explained earlier why we do not believe that that appeal should be to the Board of Visitors. We propose that it continues, as at present, to the Area Manager. It should be open to the Area Manager to review the conduct of a governor's adjudication, or if he deems it necessary, to hold a rehearing of the proceedings, with the prisoner present. The Area Manager should have the power to quash the decision or to amend, up or down, the penalty. (We envisage however that it would be rare for the penalty to be increased.) The Area Manager should also be able to order that compensation be paid to a prisoner for loss of prison wages suffered before a decision was set aside on appeal. (This power is available in some of the jurisdictions we visited abroad.) The sums involved would be small, but it would be a visible indication of justice being done.

14.423   We do not think it is necessary, given the nature of the proceedings and the penalties involved, for the prisoner to have a right to appeal to the Courts. He would have, as now, the right to apply for judicial review. He would, as now, be entitled to write to the Secretary of State. It would be, as now, open to the

Secretary of State to quash the finding and to amend the punishment, but not to rehear the case.

14.424 We recommend that, as an alternative or prior to writing to the Secretary of State, the prisoner aggrieved by an Area Manager's decision in respect of an adjudication should be able to appeal to the Complaints Adjudicator, whom we have described in the preceding parts of this Section. As we have already indicated, at that stage, so far as the prisoner is concerned, there is little difference from his position under the grievance procedure. A governor and the Area Manager have made decisions with which he disagrees. It is therefore appropriate that the same appellate body should be available. As with the grievance procedure, the Complaints Adjudicator would be a body of final resort.

14.425 The Adjudicator should again be the master of his own procedure. We would expect that he, or the assistant adjudicators acting on his behalf, would rarely hold a formal rehearing of the adjudication. Governors are already required to keep a record of the proceedings and the Adjudicator would be able to ensure he received all the material necessary to conduct a thorough review of the proceedings. The Adjudicator would be able to see reports from the Area Manager, the governor, the Boards of Visitors and the prisoner, and normally talk to the parties if he so wished. He would form his own view on the merits. He would then decide the appeal himself. Although he would have the power to direct a rehearing by a governor or the Area Manager, his powers would otherwise be the same as those we have proposed for the Area Manager.

14.426 The Complaints Adjudicator's powers would therefore differ from those available to him in considering grievances. It is right, and consistent with the principles of justice, that an independent element should be able to review and set aside findings which result in a prisoner staying in prison longer than would otherwise be the case.

14.427 The Complaints Adjudicator would instil an element of independence to the disciplinary procedure, as he would introduce such an element to the grievance procedure previously discussed. His ability to scrutinise the decision making process should ensure that the required standards were maintained by governors and Area Managers. This would be an expeditious and inexpensive process appropriate to the type of disciplinary proceeding heard by and the powers of punishment of the Governor.

14.428 We propose that there should be time limits for bringing disciplinary proceedings and for appeals. We commend the present time limit introduced by the Prison Service for bringing charges within 48 hours of the discovery of the offence. We propose that time limits should be set for appeals. As a guide, we would suggest that the prisoner should have a right to appeal to the Area Manager within 48 hours of a decision by the Governor, and to the Adjudicator within seven days from being notified of a decision by the Area Manager. We suggest that the Area Manager should have a target for determining an appeal in respect of a disciplinary offence. It should not be more than four weeks. We hope it would be considerably less. The Adjudicator may also wish to work to a similar timescale.

14.429 Boards of Visitors, as we have said, should not have a place in the conduct of disciplinary proceedings. But they would have a valuable role in relation to such proceedings. It would be consistent with their watch-dog role that they should be able to assist and advise the prisoner at the prisoner's request, in relation to governor's disciplinary proceedings and in relation to the prisoner's decision whether or not to appeal. It would be perfectly appropriate for the Board of Visitors, with the consent of the prisoner, to make representations to the Area Manager or the Adjudicator.

14.430 Their role may be the more important because, given the domestic nature of these proceedings, we do not propose that prisoners should have a *right*

430

of legal representation at these proceedings. We propose that the prisoner, at the discretion of the Governor, Area Manager, or Complaints Adjudicator should be allowed to bring with him to the proceedings either another prisoner, or a lawyer, or a prison officer.

14.431 We believe it would be fully consistent with the enhanced role of a prison officer which we have discussed in Section 13, that he should have the professional skill to act impartially as a friend of the prisoner in disciplinary proceedings. For the purpose of an appeal, the prisoner could seek the same assistance.

14.432 In the Inquiry's public seminar, Mr Coggan noted that any system of justice in prisons "takes no account at all of the underlying and informal justice which operates in the prisons" which, he suggested, ought perhaps to be called "the injustice system". The Prison Officers' Association were also concerned about what they described in their evidence to the Prior Committee of September 1984 (which they submitted as part of their evidence to this Inquiry) as the "underground" disciplinary system. Referring to court judgements opening up the prison disciplinary system to public scrutiny and judicial review they suggested that:

> "One possible consequence – one that we deprecate – will be to drive the disciplinary system 'underground' and replace formal adjudications with administrative segregation, relocations, and adverse parole reviews and so on."

14.433 We are in no doubt that the Prison Service has a duty to ensure that that does not happen. The Prison Service raised this spectre in their evidence when it said: "The punishments available at an adjudication are by no means the only sanctions available to Governors." The Prison Service referred to the Governor having available a number of so called "administrative" measures. These included location under Rule 43 for reasons of good order or discipline, or transfer under the provisions of Circular Instruction 10/74. We discuss both of those measures in Section 12.

14.434 The Prison Service is under a misapprehension to describe these as sanctions. They are, or should be, used only as necessary and as specific responses to the actions of prisoners. They must not themselves be used as punishments (as the Prison Service itself recognises in relation to transfers, as we note in Section 12). Nor must they be used as sanctions which are in any way the equivalent of punishments. If a prisoner has committed an offence meriting punishment, then disciplinary proceedings should be brought against him. Rule 47 provides ample scope for such proceedings.

14.435 This sort of misconception should become a thing of the past if our recommendation for more reasoned decision making is implemented. The best protection against underground sanctions is to require and expect the Prison Service at all levels to consider its decisions and to give the prisoner reasons for them. If the prisoner is not satisfied, he may then activate the complaints procedure.

Conclusion

14.436 Taken together, the recommendations and proposals in this Section build up into a substantial agenda for reform. We recognise that some would carry with them resource implications. In others, there would be savings. We are not in this Section proposing an approach which is diametrically opposed to the direction which the Prison Service is already taking. We are suggesting building on the work the Prison Service has started.

14.437 Our suggestions are directed to one of the themes which has run through this report, the theme of justice in prisons secured through the exercise of responsibility and respect. The achievement of justice will itself enhance security and control. These themes must come together in the programmes provided for prisoners and in the way they are treated in prison. They must come together also in what is expected of prisoners coming into the prison system.

14.438 The Prison Service has concentrated in recent years on structural and management issues. It must now concentrate fully on the prisoners in its care. The proposals in this Section are intended to assist it in achieving this. Were these proposals to be followed, then we believe that they would substantially influence the way prisoners come to view the prison system. While not preventing all disruptions, they would marginalise those who claim they must resort to deeply damaging and costly disturbances on the grounds that there is no other way to have their voices heard.

Section 15

Recommendations and Proposals

15.1   This Section summarises the Report's recommendations and proposals.

15.2   Section 1 explains the approach adopted by the Inquiry in making its recommendations and proposals. We have recommended 12 major changes which the Inquiry would like to see implemented. We have proposed a number of detailed improvements which the Inquiry considers are necessary as a consequence of these recommendations.

15.3   We set out below the 12 recommendations which we make in Section 1. We amplify those recommendations, or parts of those recommendations in the part of the Section to which they relate. We summarise our proposals Section by Section.

Section 1: Overview

15.4   Our 12 recommendations are stated in paragraph 1.167. They are briefly explained in the subsequent paragraphs of that section.

15.5   *We recommend:*

> *1.   Closer co-operation between the different parts of the Criminal Justice System. For this purpose a national forum and local committees should be established (paragraphs 1.169 to 1.172);*
>
> *2.   More visible leadership of the Prison Service by a Director General who is and is seen to be the operational head and in day to day charge of the Service. To achieve this there should be a published "compact" or "contract" given by Ministers to the Director General of the Prison Service, who should be responsible for the performance of that "contract" and publicly answerable for the day to day operations of the Prison Service (paragraphs 1.173 to 1.178);*
>
> *3.   Increased delegation of responsibility to Governors of establishments (paragraph 1.179);*
>
> *4.   An enhanced role for prison officers (paragraphs 1.180 to 1.182);*
>
> *5.   A "compact" or "contract" for each prisoner setting out the prisoner's expectations and responsibilities in the prison in which he or she is held (paragraphs 1.183 to 1.185);*
>
> *6.   A national system of Accredited Standards, with which, in time, each prison establishment would be required to comply (paragraphs 1.186 and 1.187);*
>
> *7.   A new Prison Rule that no establishment should hold more prisoners than is provided for in its certified normal level of accommodation, with provisions for Parliament to be informed if exceptionally there is to be a material departure from that rule (paragraphs 1.188 to 1.191);*
>
> *8.   A public commitment from Ministers setting a timetable to provide access to sanitation for all inmates at the earliest practicable date not later than February 1996 (paragraphs 1.192 and 1.193);*

9. Better prospects for prisoners to maintain their links with families and the community through more visits and home leaves and through being located in community prisons as near to their homes as possible (paragraphs 1.194 to 1.196);

10. A division of prison establishments into small and more manageable and secure units (paragraphs 1.197 to 1.203);

11. A separate statement of purpose, separate conditions and generally a lower security categorisation for remand prisoners (paragraphs 1.204 to 1.206);

12. Improved standards of justice within prisons involving the giving of reasons to a prisoner for any decision which materially and adversely affects him; a grievance procedure and disciplinary proceedings which ensure that the Governor deals with most matters under his present powers; relieving Boards of Visitors of their adjudicatory role; and providing for final access to an independent Complaints Adjudicator (paragraphs 1.207 to 1.209).

Section 2: The Way We Worked

15.6 This Section describes the way the Inquiry went about its work.

Part I: The Disturbances

15.7 The proposals summarised below in respect of Sections 3 to 8 are limited to the specific disturbances dealt with by each Section. They need to be read with the proposals arising out of the general lessons learnt from Part I which are set out in Section 9 and summarised below.

Section 3: Manchester

15.8 *I propose that:*

Communications
1. During a disturbance, proper lines of communication should be maintained between the prison authorities and responsible voluntary organisations who are assisting (paragraph 3.348).

The Media
2. Press and programme editors should take appropriate action to ensure that long range microphones are not used to intrude into private conversations (paragraph 3.370).

Board of Visitors
3. The Home Office should accept responsibility for any liability by a member of the Board of Visitors to pay damages, as long as the member of the Board was acting in good faith (paragraph 3.378).

Emergency and Medical Services
4. There should be a system of accreditation for appropriate voluntary bodies so that it would be easier for the emergencies services to isolate those who seek to capitalise on a riot type situation (paragraph 3.348).

5. The Fire Service should have their own room in the Reception Area of the prison during a disturbance to brief fire brigade officers on arrival (paragraph 3.413).

6. The hospitals in the Manchester Area and the Greater Manchester Ambulance Service should consider, in consultation with the Prison Service, how to ensure more effective co-operation and the best use of medical resources in any future incident (paragraph 3.430).

7. The major incident plans of Ambulance Services should cover the possibility of riots in a prison in their area. They should be discussed and

ideally tested with the co-operation of the hospital authorities and the Prison Service (paragraph 3.431).

8. There should be continuous consultation and joint training between the prison establishment and the emergency services (paragraph 3.432 (39)).

Limits on Large Gatherings of Prisoners
9. There should be no arbitrary limit on the number of prisoners allowed to attend a chapel service. But as a general rule for an ordinary weekly church service on Sunday, for a prison with a mixed population such as that at Manchester, it would be preferable if the number of prisoners attending were less than 300. However it should be the responsibility of the Governor to decide how many prisoners should attend and his decision should be beyond criticism if he has considered the question properly (paragraph 3.432 (9)).

Command of a Serious Incident
10. The Commander at headquarters during a serious disturbance should avoid, so far as it is possible, being away from Headquarters, even to brief Ministers, while he is on duty (paragraph 3.432 (20)).

11. The person in command at Headquarters should be kept fully informed, but should recognise that his role is primarily supportive and supervisory, although in the final analysis he has a right of veto (paragraph 3.432(21)).

Handling of a Serious Incident
12. In any major incident it is important to try and deprive those taking part of food and water (paragraph 3.432(26)).

13. Further study should take place as to whether different negotiation tactics can be developed for use in riot situations which do not require an intervention force to be overtly waiting to intervene (paragraph 3.432(27)).

14. The use of loud noise and other methods of disturbing prisoners should not be used in the future until there has been a full evaluation of the value of such tactics and it is concluded that their use justifies the inconvenience they cause (paragraph 3.432(31)).

15. Guidelines should be drawn up after consulting the Prison Officers' Association, the Prison Governors' Association and the Boards of Visitors as to what matters it is appropriate for their members to make comments on during the currency of a serious disturbance (paragraphs 3.374 and 3.432(32)).

Scaffolding in a Prison
16. Any necessary scaffolding should be erected for the minimum period and should be as well protected as reasonable. In no circumstances should scaffolding be left lying around the establishment when not in use (paragraph 3.432(35)).

Section 4: Glen Parva

15.9 *I propose that:*

Personal Alarms
17. The Prison Service should test the viability of personal alarms for prison officers who by themselves unlock cells with more than one inmate in them (paragraph 4.115(7)).

Physical Security
18. The physical security of Glen Parva needs to be improved, taking account of the Prison Service's building priorities and the type of inmate intended in future to be held there (paragraphs 4.45, 4.81, 4.82 and 4.115(16)).

The Media
19.   At all establishments there should be at least one and preferably two Governor grades who have attended a training course on dealing with the media (paragraph 4.115(14)).

Delays in Sentencing Young Offenders
20.   Action needs to be taken to reduce the long waiting time for inmates who have been convicted but not yet sentenced (paragraphs 4.37 and 4.38 and 4.115(20)).

Section 5: Dartmoor

15.10   *I propose that:*

Board of Visitors
21.   There should be a laid down procedure for briefing the Board of Visitors (paragraph 5.170).

22.   The Board of Visitors should have the necessary facilities to fulfil its role readily available (paragraphs 5.173 and 5.174).

23.   The Board of Visitors should introduce a better method of explaining its role to inmates (paragraphs 5.183 and 5.199(19)).

24. The Board of Visitors should keep a record of all prisoners seen by its members and the complaints which they make (paragraphs 5.176 and 5.199(19)).

The Fire Service
25.   The respective roles of the Fire Service and the Prison Service as to extinguishing a fire inside part of a prison occupied by rioting inmates should be clarified (paragraph 5.199(15)).

Contingency Planning
26.   The contingency plans need to be revised (paragraph 5.199(3)).

Segregation Units
27.   The use of the segregation unit needs the closest attention and monitoring by the new Area Manager, the Governor and the Board of Visitors (paragraph 5.199(16)).

Relations Between Staff and Management
28.   The barrier between staff and management must be broken down. Management must make it clear that they will not tolerate reactionary attitudes (paragraphs 5.199(17) and (27)).

Food
29.   The time lag between the preparation of food and its consumption must be drastically reduced (paragraph 5.199(21).

30.   Consideration should be given to the staggering of meal times, to the introduction of eating in association and to the provision of dining rooms where this is possible (paragraph 5.199(21)).

Improvements to the Prison
31.   The programme for the refurbishment of the prison should be given the highest priority. If the prison is to remain in use, priority should be given to the provision of facilities to mitigate the effect of the climate, such as a sports hall. The refurbishment should include the division of the existing wings, integral sanitation, the enlargement of ventilation grilles into secondary windows so that the inmates can see out and dealing with the damp (paragraph 5.199 (24)).

Family Links
32.   Consideration should be given to how to improve prisoners' family links (paragraph 5.199(25)).

Dartmoor's Role
33.   Dartmoor should be given a clearly defined and positive role within

the prison system in which prison officers can be closely involved (paragraph 5.199(26)).

Section 6: Cardiff

15.11   *I propose that:*

Transfer of Prisoners
34.   Fuller information should be provided about an inmate who is transferred for control reasons (paragraph 6.78(3)).

Staff
35.   The age profile of the Cardiff staff and of the staff at other Welsh prison establishments should be examined to see if they have an undue number of older staff more prone to sickness than is desirable (paragraph 6.78(15)).

36.   Where an establishment has a high sickness level, this must be taken into account in assessing its staffing needs, subject to the establishment doing what it can to reduce the sickness levels (paragraph 6.78(15)).

Handling of A Serious Incident
37.   The Communications Room should have a dedicated telephone link to police headquarters (paragraph 6.78(19)).

38.   The local incident command and communications structure should be reviewed, with particular attention given to the location, organisation and manning of the incident command post (paragraph 6.78(20)).

Section 7: Bristol

15.12   *I propose that:*

Water Supply
39.   The practicality of improving the water supply to the prison should be investigated (paragraph 7.102).

Care of Staff During an Incident
40.   A record of officers engaged in incidents should be kept so that the absence of any member of staff will be appreciated (paragraph 7.153)

41.   When possible, the period on duty should not exceed 12 hours (paragraphs 7.154 and 7.158(19).

Refurbishment of Bristol
42.   In the refurbishment now planned, it would be preferable if A Wing were divided into two separate units and if staff were provided with easy and secure access to the roof zone and upper landings (paragraph 7.158(9)).

43.   Attention should be paid to the protection of the bridge between A Wing and B & C Wings. If it cannot be adequately protected, consideration should be given to removing it altogether (paragraph 7.158(10).

44.   Consideration should be given to whether B and C Wings provide adequate levels of security for Category B prisoners (paragraph 7.158(10)).

45.   The roof of A Wing and the Chapel should be resurfaced with materials which will not provide such ready ammunition if prisoners again succeed in getting to the roofs (paragraph 7.158(11)).

Section 8: Pucklechurch

15.13   *I propose that:*

A Single Officer Unlocking a Cell

46. An officer who unlocks a cell containing more than one inmate should be within sight or earshot of another officer (paragraph 8.188(5)).

Cancellation of Association
47. The decision to cancel association, particularly for young remand inmates, should always be taken by a person of governor grade (paragraph 8.188(9)).

Escort Duties
48. Better arrangements are needed for the organisation of escort duties (paragraph 8.188(12)).

Defending the Flanks of C&R Units
49. Consideration should be given to how C&R units can defend their flank when they are required to operate in the open (paragraph 8.188(19)).

Physical Security of Pucklechurch
50. It is not necessary to propose a substantial increase in security in Pucklechurch if it is to continue to be a Remand Centre for young offenders. Pucklechurch needs security "firebreaks", not enhanced cellular security (paragraph 8.188(46)).

The Trial and Sentencing of Young Offenders
51. There is a need for closer cooperation between the courts and the Prison Service to ensure that delays in bringing remand inmates to trial and in sentencing convicted inmates are kept to a minimum (paragraph 8.188(47)).

Section 9: Lessons From Part I

15.14   *I propose that:*

Security Information Reports
52. A security information report should be raised in respect of all information which may affect security and control within an establishment, without regard to its apparent quality (paragraph 9.53).

53. A standard procedure should be instituted which makes the senior Governor on duty in the prison, or the most senior officer on duty at the time, responsible for ensuring that security information is properly recorded and disseminated (paragraph 9.55).

Officers' Keys
54. The methods of attaching keys to an officer's clothing should be reviewed. Other proposals are made in Section 11 (paragraph 9.57).

The Withdrawal of Staff
55. A suitable procedure should be drawn up and plans should be prepared which staff can follow if they have to withdraw from the immediate scene of a serious disturbance. Withdrawal should normally be made on the instructions of a senior officer or governor (paragraphs 9.59 and 9.60).

Security Firebreaks
56. The position to which prison staff should withdraw in the case of a serious disturbance which they cannot control should be identified in the course of contingency planning and training within an establishment. It should take the form of a security "firebreak" at the entrance to each unit and area where the number of prisoners who can be expected to congregate is in excess of about 70 (paragraphs 9.62 and 9.64).

Physical Security
57. Protection of the means of access to roofs and their cladding should be brought up to current standards at all closed prisons (paragraph 9.68).

58. Building tools, equipment and other appliances should not be left unattended in accommodation units, even if they are locked in a cell or store (paragraph 9.70).

59. Each establishment should check its physical security at frequent intervals. In local prisons, any improvements necessary in the security of roofs, gates and locks should be regarded as being a matter of urgency. Any necessary work on roofs, gates and locks should not be deferred where refurbishment is unlikely to take place for some time (paragraphs 9.73 and 9.75).

Communication
60. The standard of communications equipment in a closed prison's communications room should be much closer to that which exists in the control room of a dispersal prison (paragraph 9.77).

61. Further work should be undertaken to improve the methods of communication within establishments and between establishments and Headquarters during a serious disturbance. Staff, as well as Headquarters, need to be kept informed of what is happening. Communication points should also be established within a reasonable period to help inquiries from families of both staff and inmates, and to enable members of staff to phone home (paragraphs 9.78 and 9.79).

62. More attention should be attached to debriefing, stress counselling and staff and family care following a serious incident (paragraph 9.80).

63. There needs to be sensitive processing and the speedy settlement of any claims for compensation (paragraph 9.80).

Contingency Planning and the Board of Visitors
64. Contingency plans, the exercise of those plans, and staff and management training in responding to a disturbance should be developed. Preparation of the plans and their exercise should closely involve the Board of Visitors. The plans should require the Board of Visitors to be informed as soon as a disturbance begins and they should attend a disturbance as soon as it is practicable (paragraphs 9.82, 9.85 and 9.86).

The Deployment of Water
65. The existing restrictions on the circumstances in which water can be used and the authority which is required for its use should be reviewed (paragraph 9.87).

66. Consideration should be given to the Fire Service making available equipment to the Prison Service during a disturbance which inmates could not identify as belonging to the Fire Service (paragraph 9.87).

67. Equipment to enable the deployment of water, such as the Green Goddesses, should be much more readily available in the event of a serious disturbance. Prison Service staff should be trained in advance in the use of the equipment (paragraph 9.87).

C&R Training for Paramedics
68. Suitable members of hospital staff should be selected for C&R3 training so that they can act as paramedics (paragraph 9.93).

Name Tags
69. All staff within a prison during an incident should at all times clearly display their names and the nature of their job within the establishment (paragraph 9.94).

Part II: The Prevention of Disturbances

Section 10: Imprisonment

15.15 *We propose that:*

70. A reassessment of the role of the Prison Service is needed in order to give a clear sense of direction (paragraph 10.1).

The Convicted Prisoner
15.16 *We propose that:*

71. The Prison Service should ensure that prisoners are treated with justice in prisons. In due course the Prison Rules should be amended to reflect this requirement (paragraphs 10.17 and 10.23).

72. The Prison Service and the Probation Service must work together to achieve the common objective of helping offenders to lead law-abiding lives (paragraph 10.33).

Remand and Unsentenced Prisoners
15.17 *We recommend that:*

There should be a separate Statement of Purpose or an additional paragraph to the existing Statement of Purpose dealing specifically with the different status of remand prisoners and the Prison Service's obligations which follow on from that different status (paragraph 10.63). – Recommendation 11.

15.18 *We propose that:*

73. It must be part of the task of the Prison Service to ensure that the security of remand prisoners reflects and is consistent with the specific ground relied upon for refusing bail; that, so far as is practicable, imprisonment does not interfere with a prisoner's ability to conduct his defence; that the remand prisoner spends his time in prison constructively and, as far as this is practicable, preserves his employment, family and community connections; and that, if his circumstances change, the case for continuing his remand in custody is brought back before the Court (paragraphs 10.59 to 10.62).

The Prison Rules

15.19 *We propose that:*

74. Consideration should be given to providing a contemporary and relevant set of Rules which are consistent with the European Prison Rules (paragraph 10.66).

Limiting the Role of the Prison Service

i) The Remand Prisoner 15.20 *We propose that:*

75. Successful local initiatives to reduce the number of people remanded in custody and the time they spend on remand should be applied throughout the country (paragraph 10.76).

76. There should be a clear expectation that Magistrates should not make a final decision to remand a defendant in custody until they have received at least the information available to the Crown Prosecution Service where a bail information scheme exists, and more information than is available to the Crown Prosecution Service where such schemes do not exist (paragraph 10.83).

77. Magistrates should attach considerable significance to whether or not the offence which the defendant is alleged to have committed is one which, if proved, would justify a sentence of imprisonment (paragraph 10.84).

78. Information should be provided to Magistrates about where the defendant would be confined if bail was not granted and about what was the regime then available at that establishment for remand prisoners (paragraph 10.85).

79. Consideration should be given by High Court Judges to adjourning some bail applications to open Court so that a reasoned decision can be given where an area of difficulty is identified and where guidance could be useful (paragraph 10.86).

80. The prosecution and the defence must be encouraged to reduce the period they need to prepare for trial to a minimum. Remand time limits need to be regularly reviewed to see whether they can be reduced. It is particularly important to have the shortest possible waiting time where a defendant is convicted but awaiting sentence (paragraph 10.87).

81. There should be Court-based Bail Information Schemes in all areas of the country (paragraph 10.91).

82. Prison-based bail schemes should be expanded as rapidly as possible (paragraph 10.94).

83. Consideration should be given to bringing forward the programme for expanding the number of places in bail hostels (paragraph 10.96).

84. More special hostels should be established to cater for those with drugs or drink related problems (paragraph 10.97).

85. As an alternative to secure hostels, Probation Services should provide a range of hostels with differing degrees of security (paragraph 10.101).

ii) Offenders   15.21 *We propose that:*

86. There should be an increase in the number of hostel places for offenders (paragraph 10.102).

87. There should be an expansion of diversionary schemes involving co-operation between the Probation Service and the Crown Prosecution Service to help the Crown Prosecution Service decide whether a prosecution need be brought in the public interest (paragraph 10.106).

88. An experiment should be mounted in limited areas to assess the practical implications of removing the threat of imprisonment from fine defaulters, if the proposals in the Criminal Justice Bill are implemented and once they have had an opportunity to demonstrate their effect (paragraph 10.113).

89. The range of initiatives being undertaken to minimise the number of mentally disordered people within the penal system should be continued and further developed (paragraph 10.118).

90. There should be research into the services at present available for the mentally disordered and how well they work (paragraph 10.121).

91. There should be a thorough assessment of the respective virtues of psychiatric assessment services to Courts so that those which are found to have a wider application can be extended (paragraph 10.134).

92. The Prison Service should recognise the special responsibility it has for those in its care who are mentally disordered (paragraph 10.136).

93. More hostels and other accommodation should be available for mentally handicapped offenders. The Government should provide further support to the voluntary bodies who provide these facilities (paragraph 10.137).

94. The Prison Service should ensure that clearer and more specific attention is paid to mentally handicapped offenders in its care (paragraph 10.138).

Providing the Sentencing Court with More Information

15.22 *We propose that:*

95. Judges and Magistrates should be given general information about the conditions within prisons to which those who may have been remanded in custody or sentenced are sent and the cost implications. They should also be kept abreast of the experience in other countries (paragraphs 10.144 to 10.149).

96. The Prison Service should be responsible for providing the necessary information to the judiciary, perhaps through the Judicial Studies Board

(paragraph 10.150).

97. Consideration should be given to requiring the Prison Service to provide routinely for the sentencing Court a report on the manner in which a remand prisoner had behaved while in custody (paragraph 10.156).

A Forum for Consultation within the Criminal Justice System

15.23 *We recommend that:*

There should be closer co-operation between the different bodies which form part of the Criminal Justice System. To this end there should be a national forum, possibly a Criminal Justice Consultative Council, to promote that co-operation at the highest level involving all the agencies in the Criminal Justice System (paragraphs 10.169 to 10.180) – Recommendation 1.

The Local Committees

15.24 *We recommend that:*

There should be Local Committees, possibly at a regional level, to promote the local co-ordination of the different parts of the Criminal Justice System (paragraphs 10.181 to 10.187) – Recommendation 1.

Section 11: Buildings

Building and Refurbishment Programme

15.25 *We propose that:*

98. High priority should be given to a combination of refurbishing and improving existing prisons, while at the same time having a well planned programme for building new prisons (paragraph 11.5).

99. The aims should be to remove from the prison estate prisons which are unsuitable for use and to ensure that there is sufficient accommodation to hold the projected prison population in reasonable conditions (paragraph 11.5).

The Principles

15.26 *We propose that:*

100. In executing its programme for the improvement of the prison estate, the Prison Service should take fully into consideration the following principles:

a)   normally prisoners should be accommodated in prison units of approximately 50/70 prisoners. The prison itself should not hold more than 400 prisoners, though when this is necessary there can be more than one discrete prison within a larger prison (paragraph 11.7);

b)   an appropriate balance needs to be maintained between the requirements of security and the adverse consequences which can result from an over-oppressive atmosphere within prisons (paragraph 11.24);

c)   where a prison has separate accommodation units, the access to and egress from those units should preferably be controlled by electrically operated gates. Alternatively, the gates should have locks operated by a different key from ones used on the gates onto other units and they should be able to be doubled (paragraph 11.35);

d)   while the locks of the cells in the same unit can be operated by the same cell key, the locks on the cells in different units should require the use of different keys (paragraph 11.36);

e)   where this is possible, interior lines of defence should be identified which can be secured by suitable gates with double or electrically operated locks (paragraph 11.37);

f) where this is practical, prisons should be community prisons sited within reasonable proximity to, and having close connections with, the community with which the prisoners they hold have their closest links (paragraph 11.49);

g) there should be satisfactory facilities for visits including an adequate visitors centre (paragraph 11.69);

h) unless they consent to different arrangements, wherever this is practical, remand prisoners should be accommodated in separate prisons or in separate units which are treated as separate prisons, from prisons or units occupied by convicted and sentenced prisoners (paragraph 11.72);

i) a prisoner should normally be entitled, if he so wishes, to have a cell or room to himself (paragraph 11.81);

j) dormitory accommodation is undesirable (paragraph 11.82);

k) prisoners should have access at all times to sanitation (paragraph 11.97);

l) adequate and suitable provision should be made for the requirements of staff (paragraph 11.98);

m) standards of hygiene should be commensurate with those in the community (paragraph 11.113);

n) prisons should always contain accommodation which can be set aside for use by the Board of Visitors (paragraph 11.122).

Recommendations Consequent on these Principles

15.27 *We recommend that:*

Normally prisoners should be accommodated in prison units of approximately 50/70 prisoners. The prison itself should not hold more than 400 prisoners, though when this is necessary there can be more than one discrete prison within a larger prison (paragraph 11.7) – Recommendation 10.

Each living unit should be divided from each other by secure gates, preferably electrically operated. Interior lines of defence should be identified in areas where prisoners congregate which can be shut off on similar lines. The locks on the cells in different units should require the use of different keys (paragraphs 11.35 to 11.37) – Recommendation 10.

Where this is practical, prisons should be community prisons sited within reasonable proximity to, and having close connections with, the community with which the prisoners they hold have their closest links (paragraph 11.49) – Recommendation 9.

Remand prisoners should be able to be accommodated in separate prisons or in separate units which are treated as separate prisons, wherever this is practicable (paragraph 11.72) – Recommendation 11.

Ministers should publicly set a timetable to provide access to sanitation for all inmates at the earliest practicable date not later than February 1996 (paragraph 11.105) – Recommendation 8.

Proposals Consequent on these Principles

15.28 *We propose that:*

101. Local prisons must be brought up to a satisfactory standard (paragraph 11.20).

102. Staff should carry no more keys than are necessary for the proper execution of the duties they are performing during their current shift (paragraph 11.41).

103. Tests should be carried out to evaluate the advantages and disadvantages of electric locking systems (paragraph 11.46).

104. The visitors centres which should be provided at all prison establishments, should be properly furnished and have facilities for addressing social and welfare problems (paragraph 11.71).

105. The Prison Service should consider setting a target date for ending dormitory accommodation and the sharing of cells, unless the prisoner consents or there are special circumstances which make it appropriate, in the interests of the prisoner, that he be required to share a cell (paragraph 11.96).

106. Each Governor whose establishment has some cells with integral sanitation and some without should be instructed to arrange, so far as this is practical, the occupation of cells without sanitation so that as many as possible of those cells are occupied by a single inmate (paragraph 11.109).

107. All Governors of establishments with prisoners who do not have access to integral sanitation, should consider with their Area Manager and their staff whether it is possible, with the addition of some extra staff, to unlock inmates from cells in controlled numbers and under supervision during the course of an evening (paragraph 11.110).

Consultants

15.29 *We propose that:*

108. The Prison Service should establish satisfactory lines of communication with consultants who are, or who are seeking to be, involved in the prison building programme. There should be a multi-disciplinary design group, which includes a senior architect, responsible for reviewing and modifying the Prison Design Briefing System (paragraph 11.129).

Overcrowding

15.30 *We recommend that:*

There should be a new Prison Rule to take effect at the end of 1992 to provide that no establishment should hold prisoners in excess of its certified normal accommodation. Some limited qualifications should be allowed to the Rule. Any more substantial derogation should be authorised by a certificate issued by the Home Secretary and laid before Parliament (paragraphs 11.141 and 11.142) – Recommendation 7.

15.31 *We propose that:*

109. Police cells should not be used as an expedient to prevent overcrowding. There should be a limit placed at the first opportunity upon the time a prisoner, whether on remand or under sentence, can be kept in police cells on behalf of the Prison Service. The maximum period might be four days. This proposal should be reflected in a new Prison Rule (paragraphs 11.152 and 11.155).

Section 12: Management

The Relationship Between Ministers and the Prison Service

15.32 *We recommend that:*

The relationship between the Prison Service and Ministers should be more clearly structured to enable the Director General to exercise the leadership and authority needed to run the Service. He should be ready to explain the work of the Service in public. There should be a published "compact" or "contract" between the Director General and the Secretary of State setting out the tasks, objectives and available resources for the coming year (paragraphs 12.43, 12.44 and 12.47) – Recommendation 2.

The Prisons Board

15.33 *We propose that:*

110. The Director General should ensure that the terms of reference of the Prisons Board reflect clearly the role he wants it to perform (paragraph 12.65).

The Relationship Between Headquarters and Establishments

15.34 *We recommend that:*

The relationship between Headquarters and establishments should be based upon Headquarters enabling Governors to govern and providing support for staff (paragraph 12.73) – Recommendation 3.

There should be increased delegation of responsibility to Governors for the functions connected with the management of the prison (paragraph 12.79) – Recommendation 3.

The Area Manager's "Contract" With Establishments

15.35 *We propose that:*

111. The "contract" between the Area Manager and the Governor should be a statement of what the establishment should be achieving during the year ahead and what it should be seeking to do in the longer term and of the reciprocal obligation of the Prison Service to provide the resources and support which the establishment will need if it is going to fulfil its task under the "contract" (paragraphs 12.96 and 12.97).

A Code of Standards

15.36 *We recommend that:*

The Prison Service should prepare its own Code of standards, to be known as Accredited Standards, which should be implemented by a system of accreditation and which should result in the award of Accreditation Status to each establishment – (paragraphs 12.108 to 12.119) – Recommendation 6.

The Prisoner's "Contract"

15.37 *We recommend that:*

Each prisoner should be offered the opportunity to enter into a "compact" or "contract" with the establishment. It would be the subject of a new Prison Rule. The "contract" would be reviewed annually with the inmate (paragraphs 12.120 to 12.123) – Recommendation 5.

Race Relations

15.38 *We propose that:*

112. Further progress needs to be made if a satisfactory position with regard to race relations is to be achieved within prisons. Methods of monitoring incidents which could have a racial content need clarifying and more energy needs to be devoted by the Prison Service to promoting its non-racial policies (paragraph 12.142).

The Management of Intervention During Serious Incidents

15.39 *We propose that:*

113. National C&R instructors should continue to have the opportunity of liaising, and where appropriate training, with other services in this country who are engaged in similar activities (paragraph 12.145).

114. Headquarters operational Directors and their staff who manage incidents should be kept fully abreast of developments in C&R techniques. Headquarters should have available experts trained in the use and deployment of C&R techniques (paragraph 12.151).

115. The Prison Service should identify and train suitable C&R Co-ordinators at Governor 3 level to manage serious incidents under the command of the governing Governor of the establishment in which such an incident is taking place (paragraphs 12.154 and 12.155).

116. The Prison Service should examine carefully the Scottish experience in relation to its use of a C&R stores vehicle (paragraph 12.157).

Escort Duties

15.40 *We propose that:*

117. An escort service separate from prison establishments should be set up (paragraph 12.164).

118. Systems should be developed in co-operation between the Prison Service and the Lord Chancellor's Department which enable the location of prisoners to be taken into account when considering the listing of cases (paragraph 12.168).

Board of Visitors

15.41 *We recommend that:*

The adjudicatory role of Boards of Visitors should be removed (paragraph 12.177) – Recommendation 12.

15.42 *We propose that:*

119. Boards of Visitors should receive more resources than they do at present (paragraph 12.173).

120. There should be a President of the Boards of Visitors, appointed by the Home Secretary (paragraph 12.180).

Prison Visitors

15.43 *We propose that:*

121. Better use should be made of the services of Prison Visitors (paragraph 12.183).

The Management of Sex Offenders

15.44 *We propose that:*

122. There should be a new Prison Rule which deals specifically with the position of vulnerable prisoners and which replaces the relevant part of Rule 43 (and Rule 46 in Young Offender Institutions). The new Rule would require the Governor to take such reasonable steps as he considers necessary for the protection of vulnerable prisoners and would authorise the removal from association of a prisoner only to the extent which is reasonable, and subject to the existing safeguards contained in Rule 43(2) (paragraph 12.203).

123. There should be a further prison run on the lines of Grendon in a different part of the country (paragraph 12.211).

124. More attention should be given to the treatment of sex offenders and to providing assistance to prevent their re-offending (paragraphs 12.214 and 12.215).

The Management of Disruptive Offenders

15.45 *We recommend that:*

The reasons for the transfer of a prisoner under circular instruction 37/90 should always be given in writing (paragraph 12.252) – Recommendation 12.

The Governor should be expected to give reasons in writing at the time or as soon as possible after a prisoner is segregated under Rules 43 or 46 (paragraph 12.271) – Recommendation 12.

15.46   *We propose that:*

125.   The transfer of disruptive prisoners to local prisons under circular instruction 37/90 should be used sparingly (paragraph 12.245).

126.   The other options for transferring or segregating prisoners who are thought to be disruptive should be exercised more restrictively than they are at present (paragraph 12.292).

127.   Where possible, a member of the Board of Visitors should be at the receiving prison when the prisoner arrives or should see him shortly thereafter (paragraph 12.258).

128.   Whenever this is reasonably practicable, a medical officer should see a prisoner before he is transferred and soon after his arrival (paragraph 12.259).

129.   It should in the future be the responsibility of the Area Manager and not the Board of Visitors to give authority to extend the segregation of a disruptive prisoner under Rule 43 of the Prison Rules or Rule 46 of the Young Offender Institution Regulations. More than one extension would only be justified if the Area Manager is satisfied that there are exceptional circumstances. The Board of Visitors should monitor and supervise the exercise of this segregation power (paragraph 12.270).

130.   Prisoners who are transferred to a local prison should be accommodated in a specialist reassessment and allocation unit in the local prison so that their situation and future allocation can be considered in depth (paragraph 12.293).

131.   The Prison Service should consider earmarking at least one "new generation prison" for dispersal prisoners, including those who would probably now be housed in Special Units (paragraph 12.305).

The Management of the Remand Population

15.47   *We recommend that:*

*All remand prisoners should be regarded as equivalent to category C rather than category B prisoners, unless there is reason to regard them as needing category B or category A conditions of security (paragraph 12.313) – Recommendation 11.

15.48   We propose that:

132.   There should be a proper induction programme for remand prisoners (paragraph 12.323).

The Management of Young Offenders and Young Remands

15.49   *We propose that:*

133.   The Prison Service should seek to apply to all young offenders, irrespective of the type of establishment at which they are accommodated, the objectives for young offender institutions set out in the Prison Service's Annual Report for 1989/90. So far as appropriate to their different status, the same objectives should apply to young remands (paragraph 12.331).

The Management of Drug Abusers

15.50   *We propose that:*

134.   The Prison Service should examine the experience abroad of drug free units and, subject to the outcome of that examination, make provision for drug free units in prisons (paragraph 12.350).

135.   There should be a prison officer responsible for co-ordinating the services provided within a prison establishment and in the locality for drug

and alcohol abusers (paragraph 12.353).

The Management of HIV/AIDS

15.51   *We propose that:*

136.   As soon as possible there should be a thorough review of the present policies of the Prison Service in relation to HIV. The review should:

a)   subject the present policies in respect of VIR and confidentiality to critical examination with a view to setting them aside;

b)   identify the action which can be taken by establishments to encourage prisoners who feel that they are at risk of being HIV positive to identify themselves and cooperate voluntarily with the carrying out of tests;

c)   draw up a programme of treatment and opportunities for HIV positive prisoners;

d)   examine the best practices which already exist within the Prison Service and the Prison Service in Scotland for training prison officers and then draw up proposals to ensure that the best practices are adopted in all establishments;

e)   consider the best way of achieving close cooperation between prisons and AIDS counselling agencies.

When the review has been completed, a new policy on HIV should be announced by the Prison Service and the importance of implementing that policy should be forcefully drawn to the attention of Area Managers and Governors (paragraphs 12.372 and 12.373).

Section 13: Staff

Introduction

15.52   *We propose that:*

137.   Management should attach greater significance to management/staff relations and to developing the role of staff and should make a clear statement announcing that it proposes to do this (paragraph 13.8).

Staffing Levels at Weekends

15.53   *We propose that:*

138.   An appropriate programme of weekend activities in prison establishments should not be restricted by lack of staff on duty. To assist in achieving this there should be a review of the management of prisons over the weekend, paying particular consideration to the options available to provide higher staffing levels at weekends (paragraphs 13.97, 13.99, and 13.103 to 13.106).

Training and Education to Enhance the Role of Prison Officers

15.54   *We recommend that:*

More attention should be paid to training by the Prison Service. There should be a better structure for training aimed at enhancing an officer's career development (paragraphs 13.108 and 13.112) – Recommendation 4.

15.55   *We propose that:*

139.   The new entrant prison officer training scheme should be extended when this is practicable (paragraph 13.111).

140.   The Prison Service should show greater commitment and flexibility in providing in-service training opportunities to cater for as wide a range of needs and attributes as possible (paragraphs 13.112, 13.117 and 13.132).

141. Prison officers should have an opportunity and be encouraged to obtain qualifications which are recognised both within and outside the Prison Service, and should be trained so that they can themselves train other officers (paragraphs 13.118, 13.122 and 13.139).

142. The Prison Service should compile a list of establishments which have developed a speciality so that those establishments can be used as training centres for training in that speciality (paragraph 13.120).

143. The time allowed for training should be protected and increased progressively to three weeks (15 working days) a year when this is practicable (paragraphs 13.134 and 13.147).

144. There should be a continuing programme of initial C&R training followed by refresher courses available for all prison officers and other suitable members of staff (paragraph 13.130).

The Conditions Within Prison Establishments

15.56   *We propose that:*

145. The Prison Service should review the facilities for staff working in prisons and the importance attached to their improvement in prison refurbishment schemes (paragraph 13.150).

The General Recruitment of Staff

15.57   *We propose that:*

146. The Prison Service should review its methods of recruitment of members of the ethnic minorities (paragraph 13.165).

147. Prison establishments should be allowed to play a greater part in assisting recruitment (paragraph 13.167).

The Accelerated Promotion Scheme

15.58   *We propose that:*

148. The Prison Service should review its accelerated promotion scheme to enable it to provide the right number and quality of candidates who are needed for the future (paragraph 13.177).

The Prison Officer Development Scheme

15.59   *We propose that:*

149. The Prison Service should adopt an appropriate prison officer development scheme (paragraph 13.184).

Uniforms

15.60   *We propose that:*

150. The prison officer's uniform should be reviewed with a view to making it less militaristic than it is at present (paragraph 13.191).

151. Governor grades, and everyone else who is engaged directly in dealing with a disturbance, should wear the type of overalls now worn by C&R Units (paragraph 13.193).

152. The management in each establishment and its officers should be given a degree of discretion in deciding when prison officers should wear uniform (paragraph 13.194).

153. Peaked caps should be phased out (paragraph 13.195).

154. All staff, and all Governors within a prison, coming into contact with prisoners should display a label or badge which clearly gives their name and rank (paragraph 13.197).

"Contracts" Between Staff and Management

15.61 *We recommend that:*

> *Staff should have their terms and conditions of engagement in the establishment in which they work clearly set out in a document which would not be directly legally enforceable (paragraph 13.200) – Recommendation 4.*

15.62 *We propose that:*

> 155. The Prison Service should make clear its understanding of what legal contractual rights a prison officer has against the Crown (paragraph 13.199).

> 156. The Prison Service should establish a minimum level of fitness for uniformed staff (paragraph 13.205).

Non-Unified Staff

15.63 *We recommend that:*

> *The tasks at present undertaken by prison officers and governors should be reviewed to identify those which could be undertaken by other grades (paragraph 13.214) – Recommendation 4.*

15.64 *We propose that:*

> 157. The Prison Service should review the position of the non-unified grades with a view to introducing a relevant improved package broadly comparable to that received by the unified grades under "Fresh Start" (paragraph 13.210).

> 158. The Prison Service should adopt a more flexible attitude with regard to the use of all types of staff, including part-time staff (paragraph 13.214).

> 159. An induction course should be introduced for non-unified staff working in prison establishments (paragraph 13.218).

Cross Postings

15.65 *We propose that:*

> 160. Cross posting between the administrative staff in the Home Office and operational staff in prisons should be increased and there should be the possibility of secondment between other agencies within the Criminal Justice System and operational staff in the Prison Service (paragraphs 13.224 and 13.226).

Industrial Relations

15.66 *We propose that:*

> 161. There should be an agreement between the Prison Service and the unions that no industrial action will be taken in prison establishments until all the procedures for resolving disputes have been exhausted (paragraph 13.243).

> 162. The Prison Officers' Association should reconsider their present policy of recommending their members not to co-operate with the work of establishing appropriate staffing levels through the process of identifying corporate objectives (paragraph 13.252).

Section 14: Prisoners

Incentives and Disincentives

15.67 *We propose that:*

> 163. Prison Rule 4 and its associated Standing Order should be amended to make clear the facilities which should normally be provided for prisoners.

The amendments should recognise that these facilities should no longer be provided as "privileges", but as a prisoner's normal expectation. They should include a provision permitting a prisoner to have a suitable television set in his own cell (paragraphs 14.31 and 14.35).

164. There should be a more measured and careful approach to the provision of facilities for prisoners. The aim should be to provide consistency of treatment between different prisoners and different establishments of the same type (paragraph 14.39).

165. There should be a clear and established sense of progress through the prisoner's time in prison. Each prison should be responsible for making coherent provision for such progress in that establishment. Prison Service Headquarters should be responsible for ensuring that there is consistency between what each prison offers (paragraphs 14.46 and 14.47).

166. Much fuller use should be made of open prisons (paragraph 14.53).

Induction, Discharge and Sentence Planning

15.68   *We propose that:*

167. There should be well prepared and relevant reception and induction programmes for all prisoners, including remand prisoners (paragraph 14.69).

168. Each prisoner who will be at the prison for more than 28 days should have assigned to him a prison officer as his personal officer (paragraph 14.73).

169. The Prison Service should work towards the time when all prisoners serving a sentence of 12 months or more can be given some form of sentence plan in addition to their "contract" (paragraph 14.75).

170. The Prison Service should make the necessary arrangements to implement its proposals for sentence programmes so that they are ready at such time as the Criminal Justice Bill may be implemented (paragraph 14.82).

Education

15.69   *We propose that:*

171. The Prison Service should make increased provision for modular education courses, in particular for remand prisoners (paragraph 14.91).

172. Education should be seen as an integral part of the life of prisons. It should be integrated with the other activities and opportunities on offer (paragraph 14.98).

173. Education should be given an equal standing to work within the activities of the prison. There should be a payment scheme which provides pay levels for those engaged in education which are commensurate to those earned elsewhere in the prison, including in workshops (paragraphs 14.102 and 14.110).

Physical Education

15.70   *We propose that:*

174. It should be made clear, if it is not already, that the stated aim of the Prison Service should be that inmates should leave prison no less fit and healthy than when they entered (paragraph 14.113).

175. Physical Education programmes should give priority to providing structured courses that can lead to qualifications. The Prison Service should continue to develop the National Council for Vocational Qualifications courses in PE as in many other aspects of prison programmes (paragraphs 14.114 and 14.115).

Work

15.71   *We propose that:*

176.   Each prison should aim to reach a situation where the hours of work correspond closer to those in the normal world outside the prison (paragraph 14.129).

177.   Workshops should be seen primarily as part of a planned programme of activities and opportunities for prisoners. This programme should bring together work, training and education in a way that provides the most constructive mix for the prisoners who are to be involved in it (paragraphs 14.132 and 14.134).

178.   There should be a greater range of arrangements for work and type of work in prison establishments. The Prison Service should look for greater opportunities for deploying private companies in prison workshops. There should be schemes, however small, which enable a prisoner to contribute to society by making goods for charitable causes (paragraphs 14.137, 14.141, and 14.142).

179.   It should be the responsibility of each prison Governor to make the necessary provision for work as well as training in his establishment in accordance with the advice and under the supervision of PSIF (paragraphs 14.145 and 14.148).

Pay and Private Cash

15.72   *We propose that:*

180.   Prisoners should be able to earn at more realistic pay levels. The Prison Service should set itself realistic and attainable targets for improving prisoners' pay. Initially, the target should be to improve the money received by prisoners so that the most hard working prisoners can earn up to £10 a week. In the longer term, pay levels should be increased much more substantially (paragraphs 14.163, 14.168 and 14.172).

Kit

15.73   *We propose that:*

181.   Each prisoner should have the clothing which, by the Prison Service's own standards, he or she requires (paragraph 14.185).

182.   Personal kit systems should be introduced throughout the prison system. There should be a phased programme to permit male convicted prisoners the choice of wearing their own clothes. In the meantime, prisoners should be able to wear some of their own clothing, including socks, underwear and training shoes (paragraphs 14.189, 14.193, 14.194 and 14.195).

Food

15.74   *We propose that:*

183.   Consideration might be given to looking again at the dietary scales which were last comprehensively reviewed in 1984 and at catering officers' budgets (paragraph 14.210).

184.   Catering officers should be given greater discretion in the deployment of their budgets (paragraph 14.211).

185.   Staff attendance times should be critically examined so that meals can be served and taken at more sensible hours (paragraph 14.213).

186.   There should be a return to the practice of making provision for communal dining so that prisoners can be given the choice of dining together or, if they so wish, and this is practicable, in their cells (paragraph 14.217).

Visits

15.75   *We recommend that:*

> *The Prison Service should work towards providing convicted prisoners with at least one visit each week. It should aim to increase the minimum length of visits for convicted prisoners to an hour (paragraphs 14.229 and 14.231) – Recommendation 9.*

> *The Prison Service should as soon as practicable offer remand prisoners the choice of having three visits of an hour each week, as an alternative to short daily visits. The families of remand prisoners should be eligible for financially assisted visits (paragraphs 14.231 and 14.235) – Recommendation 9.*

Home Leave

15.76   *We recommend that:*

> *There should be substantial increases in the number of home leaves granted, both long and short leaves. In the case of prisons which are inappropriately located, and to compensate for their shortcomings, home and other leave should be permitted to prisoners there on a more generous scale than to prisoners at other establishments. The Prison Service should also consider arrangements for providing more day leave for prisoners (paragraphs 14.243, 14.244 and 14.245) – Recommendation 9.*

Family Visits

15.77   *We propose that:*

> 187.   The Prison Service should make provision for family visits, initially, at least, for prisoners serving long prison sentences who are not eligible for home leave (paragraph 14.249).

> 188.   The Prison Service should consider extended visits from children to their parents in male prisons if the experiments in female establishments are successful (paragraph 14.250).

Telephones

15.78   *We propose that:*

> 189.   More urgency should be given to extending cardphones to all categories of prison and to all types of prisoner (paragraph 14.259).

> 190.   The Prison Service should devise with the Samaritans a provision for a free call number so that prisoners can make calls to the Samaritans in confidence at public expense (paragraph 14.260).

> 191.   Similar rules of privilege should apply to prisoners speaking to their solicitor on the telephone as are applied to their exchange of correspondence (paragraph 14.262).

Censorship of Correspondence

15.79   *We propose that:*

> 192.   Prisoners' letters should not be censored except on reasonable suspicion that they may contain objectionable material, or if the prisoner is placed in category A (paragraph 14.271).

> 193.   The Prison Service should encourage prisoners to write more letters by a reasonably generous provision of note paper and envelopes free of charge. Any limits on the number of letters a prisoner is allowed to write should be removed (paragraph 14.274).

Communications with Prisoners

15.80 *We propose that:*

194. Governors should make arrangements for ~~regular bulletins~~ to be prepared in as clear language as possible about the policy changes and changes in routine which affect prisoners at their establishment (paragraph 14.281)

195. Governors and Headquarters should, as a matter of routine, ~~consult prisoners by questionnaire or other means about major issues of policy affecting them before decisions are taken~~ (paragraph 14.286).

196. Each Governor in charge of a prison should make arrangements for ~~meetings with groups of prisoners~~. These meetings should include a provision for the Governor in charge to have meetings from time to time with different groups of prisoners (paragraphs 14.287).

Reasons for Decisions

15.81 *We recommend that:*

i) a prisoner should normally be given reasons as soon as is reasonably practicable for any decision which adversely affects him to a material extent;

ii) for decisions which have a particularly disruptive effect on a prisoner, like the transfer of a prisoner for reasons of good order or discipline, reasons or a statement should be given as soon as is reasonably practicable in writing as a matter of course;

iii) for other material decisions, the Prison Service should comply with a reasonable request by a prisoner that reasons should be given in writing; and

iv) a new Prison Rule should be made giving effect to these recommendations (paragraph 14.308) – Recommendation 12.

The Complaints Adjudicator: An Independent Element

15.82 *We recommend that:*

*A Complaints Adjudicator should be appointed by the Home Secretary with two distinct roles:

i) in relation to the grievance procedure, where his role would be to recommend, advise and conciliate at the final stage of the procedure;

ii) in relation to disciplinary proceedings, where his role would be to act as a final tribunal of appeal (paragraph 14.349) – Recommendation 12.

Grievance Procedures

15.83 *We propose that:*

197. Steps should be taken to amend the existing arrangements for confidential access by prisoners so that they are consistent with the relevant Rules. A prisoner should be told before he seeks to make a written complaint in confidence, that, if the complaint is against a member of staff, it will be shown to that member of staff. Alternatively, before the confidential complaint is handed to the member of staff in question, the prisoner should have an opportunity of withdrawing it (paragraph 14.335).

198. Each prisoner who has had his application considered by a more junior governor, should have the right to see the governing Governor on one occasion in respect of each particular application (paragraph 14.337).

199. The Board of Visitors should be able to advise and assist the prisoner about his involvement in the grievance procedure. The Board should be able, if it so wishes, to investigate the grievance itself and then make any comment or recommendation which is considered appropriate to the Governor, the

Area Manager or the Complaints Adjudicator, depending upon who was considering the grievance at that stage (paragraph 14.340).

Disciplinary Proceedings

15.84   *We recommend that:*

Boards of Visitors should no longer be involved in adjudicatory hearings (paragraph 14.395) – Recommendation 12.

All disciplinary proceedings should in future be conducted by a Governor of the prison in which the alleged disciplinary offence took place. The greater powers of punishment which at present are exercised by the Boards of Visitors should be abolished (paragraph 14.405) – Recommendation 12.

Cases which, because of their gravity, are not suited to be heard by a Governor should be the subject of the same proceedings, and the same legal safeguards as a criminal offence committed outside prison. They should be heard by the normal criminal Courts (paragraph 14.409) – Recommendation 12.

A prisoner aggrieved by an Area Manager's decision in respect of an adjudication should be able to appeal to the Complaints Adjudicator, as an alternative or prior to writing to the Secretary of State (paragraph 14.424) – Recommendation 12.

15.85   *We propose that:*

200.   If a prisoner commits a disciplinary offence which affects the life of the prison, then it should be possible for him to lose a facility or an opportunity, even if he has not actually abused that opportunity or facility in committing his offence. The nature of the facilities or opportunities which may appropriately be restricted in this way should be reviewed from time to time (paragraphs 14.406 and 14.407).

201.   Consideration should be given to establishing a special panel of Magistrates to hear charges in respect of criminal offences committed by prisoners (paragraph 14.410).

202.   There should continue to be a right of appeal from the Governor's adjudications to the Area Manager (paragraph 14.422).

203.   There should be time limits for bringing disciplinary proceedings and for appeals (paragraph 14.428).

204.   The prisoner, at the discretion of the Governor, Area Manager or Complaints Adjudicator should be allowed to bring with him to the proceedings either another prisoner, or a lawyer, or a prison officer (paragraph 14.430).

Signatories to the Report

Part I of the Report has been prepared solely by Lord Justice Woolf.

Part II of this Report has been jointly prepared by Lord Justice Woolf and by Judge Stephen Tumim.

This report is signed:

i)   in relation to Part I

The Rt Hon Lord Justice Woolf

455

ii)   in relation to Part II

The Rt Hon Lord Justice Woolf

His Honour Judge Stephen Tumim

31 January 1991

ANNEXES

Lord Justice Woolf's Inquiry into Prison Disturbances

ROOM 307 · HORSEFERRY HOUSE · DEAN RYLE STREET · LONDON SW1P 2AW · TELEPHONE 071 217 8541

Your reference
LJW 90 1/1/2

Our reference
1 May 1990

Date

from Lord Justice Woolf

Dear member of staff

I am writing to you since I believe you were a member of staff either at or sent to one of the prisons where there was a recent disturbance. You may therefore be able to help me with my inquiry.

I have been appointed by the Home Secretary:

> "To inquire into the events leading up to the serious disturbance in H.M. Prison Manchester which began on 1st April, 1990, and the action taken to bring it to a conclusion, having regard also to the serious disturbances which occurred shortly thereafter in other prison establishments in England and Wales."

Although I am appointed by the Home Secretary, I want to emphasise that this will be an entirely independent inquiry and therefore I am anxious to receive information from prison staff about these events. In particular I want to know your views:

1. As to what caused the disturbance at your prison.
2. What happened during that disturbance.
3. What was done to end that disturbance.
4. As to what action should be taken to avoid a disturbance of this sort occurring again.

You do not need to reply if you do not want to do so. If you do want to reply please put your answer in the enclosed envelope.

I will use your answer in order to decide whether I
should invite you to give evidence at the Inquiry either
by asking you to give evidence in writing or by attending
the Inquiry to give evidence orally, when you would be
questioned by lawyers appearing for the Inquiry and other
interested parties. You will not be made to give
evidence if you do not want to do so. If you are invited
to give evidence, you may want to consult your trade
union, if your are a member of one, about appearing
before the inquiry. The Director General has also
assured me that the Department would provide you with
advice and, if there were a potential conflict of
interest, would be ready to consider the provision of
independent legal advice at public expense.

Any answer you give to this letter will be used by me
only for the purpose of the Inquiry. At my request the
prison authorities have agreed that your answer will not
by used in connection with any disciplinary proceedings
except with your consent or where the answer reveals
evidence of such serious misconduct by a member of staff
as to make it clear that he or she was unsuitable to
remain in the Prison Service. You should however know
that there could be criminal or other legal proceedings
arising out of the disturbance and in connection with
those proceedings I could be ordered by the Court to
disclose your answer if the Court thought this was
required in the interests of justice. If I was ordered
to disclose your answer I would have to do so. Otherwise
I would only disclose your answer with your consent.

You may wish to know that I shall be holding a
preliminary public hearing in London on the morning of 14
May when I shall announce how I intend to conduct the
inquiry and will consider formal applications for
representation at the inquiry.

Please use the enclosed document for your answer which
should be sent no later than 18 May.

Yours sincerely

Lord Justice Woolf

LORD JUSTICE WOOLF'S INQUIRY INTO PRISON DISTURBANCES

You should reply no later than 18 May 1990

1.   Present Establishment

     Name

     Rank or Position

     Establishment in which disturbance occurred

     Your shift/duty, responsibility when the disturbance
     occurred.

2.   Write your statement below:

3. If invited to do so I would be prepared to give
    further evidence

       i)   in writing: YES/NO

      ii)   Orally: YES/NO

Date: _____

Signature: _____

Lord Justice Woolf's Inquiry into Prison Disturbances

ROOM 307 · HORSEFERRY HOUSE · DEAN RYLE STREET · LONDON SW1P 2AW · TELEPHONE 071 217 8541

Your reference
LJW 90 1/1/2

Our reference
1 May 1990

Date

from Lord Justice Woolf

Dear Inmate

I am writing to you since I believe you were an inmate at one of the prisons where there was a recent disturbance. You may therefore be able to help me with my Inquiry.

I have been appointed by the Home Secretary:

> "To inquire into the events leading up to the serious disturbance in H.M. Prison Manchester which began on 1st April, 1990, and the action taken to bring it to a conclusion, having regard also to the serious disturbances which occurred shortly thereafter in other prison establishments in England and Wales."

Although I am appointed by the Home Secretary, I want to emphasise that this will be an entirely independent inquiry and therefore I am anxious to receive information from inmates about these events. In particular I want to know your views:

1. As to what caused the disturbance at your prison.
2. What happened during that disturbance.
3. What was done to end that disturbance.
4. As to what action should be taken to avoid a disturbance of this sort occurring again.

You do not need to reply if you do not want to do so. If you do want to reply please put your answer in the enclosed envelope which I have arranged with the prison authorities will be sent to me unopened.

I will use your answer in order to decide whether I should invite you to give evidence at the Inquiry either by asking you to give evidence in writing or by attending the Inquiry to give evidence orally, when you would be questioned by lawyers appearing for the Inquiry and other interested parties. You will not be made to give evidence if you do not want to do so and if you are invited to give evidence I will arrange for you to be advised by a lawyer if you want advice.

Any answer you give to this letter will be used by me only for the purpose of the Inquiry. At my request the prison authorities have agreed that your answer will not by used in connection with any disciplinary proceedings except with your consent. You should however know that there could be criminal or other legal proceedings arising out of the disturbance and in connection with those proceedings I could be ordered by the Court to disclose your answer if the Court thought this was required in the interests of justice. If I was ordered to disclose your answer I would have to do so. Otherwise I would only disclose your answer with your consent.

I shall not of course be able to follow up individual prisoners' grievances other than where I consider that they may raise issues relevant to my work: if you wish to have your grievance pursued therefore you should also take it up through the normal channels available to you.

You may wish to know that I shall be holding a preliminary public hearing in London on the morning of 14 May when I shall announce how I intend to conduct the inquiry and will consider formal applications for representation at the inquiry.

Please use the enclosed document for your answer which should be sent no later than 18 May. If you wish additional paper the Governor has agreed to provide this. Your answer will not affect your ordinary letter entitlement.

Yours sincerely,

Lord Justice Woolf

LORD JUSTICE WOOLF'S INQUIRY INTO PRISON DISTURBANCES

You should reply no later than 18 May 1990

1.   Present Establishment

      Name

      Number

      Establishment in which disturbance occurred

occurYedr wing/landing/cell number when the disturbance

2.   Write your statement below:

3.   If invited to do so I would be prepared to give
     further evidence

          i)   in writing: YES/NO

          ii) Orally: YES/NO

Date: _____

Signature: _____

Lord Justice Woolf's Inquiry into Prison Disturbances

ROOM 307 · HORSEFERRY HOUSE · DEAN RYLE STREET · LONDON SW1P 2AW · TELEPHONE 071 217 8541

Your reference
LJW 90 1/1/2

Our reference
1 May 1990

Date

from Lord Justice Woolf

Dear member of staff,

I have been appointed by the Home Secretary:

> "To inquire into the events leading up to the serious disturbance in H.M. Prison Manchester which began on 1st April, 1990, and the action taken to bring it to a conclusion, having regard also to the serious disturbances which occurred shortly thereafter in other prison establishments in England and Wales."

I have written a personal letter to the individual members of staff who are likely to have first hand knowledge of the prison establishments referred to above. I am, however, anxious to have the assistance of any other member of the Prison Service who may have views on what causes disturbances in prisons; how they should be dealt with; and what action should be taken to avoid such disturbances occurring.

If you feel you have comments which you would like to make please write to me at the above address setting out your comments.

Although I am appointed by the Home Secretary, I wish to emphasise that this will be an entirely independent inquiry. Any response you give to this letter will be used by me only for the purpose of the inquiry but you should however know that there could be criminal or other legal proceedings arising out of the disturbances and in connection with those proceedings I could be ordered by the Court to disclose your answer if the Court thought this was required in the interests of justice. If I was ordered to disclose your answer I would have to do so.

Otherwise, unless your answer were to reveal evidence of such serious misconduct by a member of staff as to make it clear that he or she was unsuitable to remain in the prison service, I would only disclose your answer with your consent.

You may wish to know that I shall be holding a preliminary public hearing in London on the morning of 14 May when I shall announce how I intend to conduct the inquiry and will consider applications for formal representation at the inquiry.

Your reply should be sent not later than 18 May.

Yours sincerely,

Lord Justice Woolf

Lord Justice Woolf's Inquiry into Prison Disturbances

ROOM 307 · HORSEFERRY HOUSE · DEAN RYLE STREET · LONDON SW1P 2AW · TELEPHONE 071 217 8541

Your reference
LJW 90 1/1/2

Our reference
1 May 1990

Date

from Lord Justice Woolf

Dear inmate,

I have been appointed by the Home Secretary:

> "To inquire into the events leading up to the
> serious disturbance in H.M. Prison Manchester
> which began on 1st April, 1990, and the action
> taken to bring it to a conclusion, having
> regard also to the serious disturbances which
> occurred shortly thereafter in other prison
> establishments in England and Wales."

I have written a personal letter to all prison inmates
who are likely to have first hand knowledge of the prison
establishments referred to above. I am, however, anxious
to have the assistance of any prison inmate who may have
views on what causes disturbances in prisons; how they
should be dealt with; and what action should be taken to
avoid such disturbances occurring.

If you feel you have comments which you would like to
make please write to me at the above address setting out
your comments.

Although I am appointed by the Home Secretary, I wish to
emphasise that this will be an entirely independent
inquiry. Any response you give to this letter will be
used by me only for the purpose of the inquiry but you
should however know that there could be criminal or other
legal proceedings arising·out of the disturbances and in
connection with those proceedings I could be ordered by
the Court to disclose your answer if the Court thought
this was required in the interests of justice. If I was
ordered to disclose your answer I would have to do so.
Otherwise I would only disclose your answer with your
consent.

You may wish to know that on 14 May I shall be holding a preliminary public hearing in London at which I shall announce the way in which I intend to conduct the inquiry and will consider applications for formal representation at the inquiry.

Your reply should be sent not later than 18 May. The Governor has agreed to provide envelope and paper for your reply, which he will return to me unopened. Your letter will not affect your ordinary letter entitlement.

Yours sincerely,

Lord Justice Woolf

Letters from Prison

A summary of letters
written by prisoners and prison staff
to Lord Justice Woolf's Inquiry
into Prison Disturbances

Introduction

1. One of the first decisions made by Lord Justice Woolf, on his appointment on 6 April 1990 to carry out his Inquiry into prison disturbances, was to consult as widely as possible among both staff and inmates of prisons. Section 2 of the Report to this Inquiry ('The Way we Worked') describes how, on 1 May 1990, Lord Justice Woolf wrote personally to each member of staff who was in one of the six target prisons at the time of the disturbance and to each of the prisoners whom there was reason to believe had been present in one of the same prisons at the same time. At the time many inmates and staff of target prisons were widely scattered across the system as a result of the disturbances. New addresses were not always quickly and easily available, so a small minority of staff and inmates at target prisons would not have received a personal letter, but the vast majority did so.

2. In addition to these personal letters responses were sought more widely across the whole prison system. A top copy of a letter from Lord Justice Woolf was distributed to all establishments and offices in the Prison Service with a request that it should be drawn to the attention of inmates at all prison establishments and to all staff at establishments, headquarters or region.

3. Copies of the letters to staff at both target and non-target establishments are given at Annexes 2A and 2B of the Report to the Inquiry. Both asked for responses by 18 May. Responses began to flow in to the Headquarters of the Inquiry almost immediately. They reached their peak in the week 13 to 18 May but continued to arrive in subsequent weeks.

4. This summary covers all individual letters from staff and inmates received in answer to Lord Justice Woolf's invitations by the end of August 1990. It does not cover responses from groups of inmates, of which there were several, or formal submissions made by individual members of staff or inmates to the Inquiry. Where the same respondents wrote more than one letter these are dealt with as a single letter.

5. The material in the letters which covered actual happenings in the riots and disturbances was of great assistance to Part I of Lord Justice Woolf's Inquiry and has entered into the findings and Report of Part I of the Inquiry. However as well as providing information as to what happened during the disturbances, the letters from both staff and inmates contained particularly valuable information for Part II of the Report. It is this more general material which is presented and analysed in this report.

6. The analyses were carried out in three separate groups: letters from inmates in target prisons, letters from inmates in the rest of the system and letters from staff. Separate coding-frames (groupings of topics and themes covered in the letters) were developed for each set. Each is presented separately in subsequent chapters of this report.

Chapter One

Letters from Inmates of Target Prisons

1. At an early stage of his Inquiry, Lord Justice Woolf decided to pay particular attention to riots and disturbances which had occurred during April 1990 in six prisons: Manchester (Strangeways), Glen Parva, Dartmoor, Bristol, Cardiff and Pucklechurch. These six became known as "the target prisons". On 1 May 1990, Lord Justice Woolf wrote personally to all inmates of the six at the time of the riot or disturbance in that establishment. It is the responses to these letters which are described in this chapter.

2. Table 1 below gives the response rate from target establishments individually and as a group:-

	Total pop	Total letters	Percent response
Manchester	1647	259	16%
Glen Parva	778	75	10%
Dartmoor	607	90	14%
Bristol	572	118	20%
Cardiff	458	49	10%
Pucklechurch	115	16	13%
All target	4177	607	14%

The response rate varied from ten to twenty percent of inmates; Bristol and Manchester had the highest response rates, Cardiff and Glen Parva the lowest.

3. It is difficult to put the response rate into context and to say what could reasonably be expected. Many "direct mail" specialists in the commercial sector are delighted with a response of between one and five percent to any letter they send out, although of course the size of the response must vary with the interest of any communication to the group selected. That as many as one in five of the inmates of Bristol prison and almost one in five from Manchester responded to Lord Woolf's request for information, given all the difficulties of finding prisoners dispersed from their prison of origin and given the short time for response, will seem to many a striking and remarkable result. A lot of prisoners cared.

4. The personal material respondents provided entered into the evidence tested orally at Part I of the Inquiry and is covered in its conclusions. This report describes the material in the letters concerning the causes of the riots and ways of preventing them in the future.

5. In the following paragraphs an account will be given of letters from each of the six target prisons in turn and then the balance of responses over the target establishments as a whole will be considered.

I. Letters from Strangeways Inmates

I.1. 259 letters were received from inmates of Strangeways at the time of the riot; a response rate of 16%. The main part of most letters was taken up by descriptions of personal experiences in the riot. Many stressed how frightening these experiences had been:-

"I will never forget Strangeways as long as I live."

"Being in Strangeways at the riot was the most frightening thing that ever happened to me in my whole life."

"I have been out of Strangeways for six weeks now but I still have terrible nightmares every night about that disaster."

I.2. The same causes were named again and again. As one prisoner put it:-

"I can only put on paper what was discussed and spoken of at the time and reasons given and grievances aired. Most people were of the same opinion. Oppression, brutality, squalor, substandard conditions, ie food, minimum time out of cells, pathetic prison wages, lack of opportunities to use telephones, draconian visits, being sent to prisons far away from home where family and friends cannot visit."

I.3. The most commonly quoted single cause of dissatisfaction was "slopping out", together with other hygiene and sanitary problems. 143 of the 259 scripts received (55%) specifically mentioned this factor. The following quotations are typical:-

"At Manchester there are no toilets in the cells. If an inmate rang his cell bell over the dinner period, seven days a week he would receive no response from staff for that time period 1 hour 45 minutes. At night often nine o'clock the same rule was in force. A prisoner only receives attention in these periods by smashing cell furniture against the cell door – a common practice – especially if the prisoner is suffering from diarrhoea. We were only allowed one shower a week, even after working all day. The exchange of clothing (once a week) was only if clean items available. Sometimes there was clean underwear, sometimes there was not. A prisoner's bedding is never changed if it is blankets. But we were allowed to change one sheet a week. The quality of the wash would shock anyone outside prison."

"The toilets and washrooms were degrading and out of date and filthy. Time allocated to using them was very short. The water hot and cold that you got in buckets and jugs was used to wash your body, items of clothing and cleaning your cell. These same jugs, buckets, then had to contain water for drinking and washing knives, forks, spoons."

Complaints about the stench of pots in the cell and the impossibility of attaining normal standards of cleanliness, are repeated again and again. These sanitary conditions are felt as a repeated insult:

"If you treat us like animals, we'll behave like animals."

I.4. Many prisoners directly connect these difficulties with cleanliness and sanitation to overcrowding:-

"I believe Sir that Strangeways was built to house around 750 prisoners which I can believe. Now there were the number of 1600 in April. Looks like the Magistrates' Courts have gone berserk in dealing with offenders."

Another writes:-

"There are more than one reasons why the riot started in Strangeways.....but one is overcrowding. There should be at most two to a cell and toilets and washing facilities in every cell."

Overcrowding was the second most frequently quoted cause of complaint after sanitation and was specifically mentioned as a cause of riot in 131 of the 259 (50%) of letters received.

I.5. The next most frequent causes of discontent were "bang-up" (time locked in cell) and food. 112 of the 259 respondents (43%) mentioned the number of hours spent in cell as a prime cause of tension. "Twenty three hours a day banged up in our cells". This was often connected with complaints about the shortage or unavailability of work. Even those who felt themselves fortunate in having work thought long periods banged up and lack of work was a cause of frustration for others:-

> "Most of my 20 months in prison I have always worked. There are less fortunate prisoners who are not working and are locked up twenty three hours a day. I would like to say that there are a small minority who would like to be locked up, but most inmates want to work and there is just not enough work, or should I say jobs, to go round."

I.6.   Just over 100 of the letter-writers (103, that is 40%) complained about the Strangeways food. No one had a good word to say for it. Everyone who mentioned the food complained of it in vivid terms. The following quotation is mild compared to many:-

> "The riots were caused mainly through overcrowding, diabolical food, and disgusting sanitary conditions. The meals that we had to eat was mainly stew seven days a week. There was no variety in the meals."

Another prisoner remarked that Strangeways food was "worse than in any other prison I have been in." One man who had worked in the kitchens, wrote as follows:-

> "After being placed in the kitchen to work I can understand peoples feelings about food. I can well understand the difficulty of feeding 1600 inmates having been a chef myself, but this is a small excuse for the standard of food that came out of the kitchen."

Respondents complain of the Strangeways food in very similar terms:-"soya-bean stew", "cornbeef and swedes", "no vegetables only cabbage", "no vitamins", "uneatable", "always the same", "even the officers would complain for us".

I.7.   The next most frequently listed cause of complaint is 'staff attitudes', criticised by 72 respondents (27%). One writer complains "The attitude of most officers (not all) is to treat grown men as if they were little boys". Some respondents compare the attitudes of Manchester staff unfavourably with those of staff in other prisons:-

> "I did agree with the riot at Manchester because something had to be done. Because of the inhuman way they treated every inmate; like animals and not like human beings. I keep hearing the prisons are under-staffed but I have spent two years in Long Lartin prison which is the only prison where inmates are treated as human beings, allowed to think for themselves as far as prisons allow. It is not that the prison service wants extra staff, they want retraining to treat people as human beings."

I.8.   Not all respondents complained about staff attitudes. 24 respondents (9%) went out of their way to say that they had no complaints about staff and some of these respondents praise the regime in general. Some who had been in Strangeways before or had been there for a long time said they believed conditions at Strangeways to have improved:-

> "I had been held in Manchester for 23 months before the riot and can only praise the governor, Mr O'Friel for the work that he did in Manchester. He allowed more association periods, made sure that the majority of the inmates worked and there was a wide range of classes for us. Very few people were three to a cell."

But even this inmate who is positive on the whole adds:-

> "There is just one very common complaint about Manchester and that is the standard of the food. It was very poor to say the least. I believe that if riots are to be avoided in the future then food standards must improve."

I.9.   42 respondents (16% of the total) complained of the poor arrangements for visits at Strangeways:-

"Only one half-hour visit every 28 days. You end up totally alienated from your family."

Even the arrangements for those visits were thought to be poor. One prisoner, writing not from Strangeways but from the prison to which he had been moved, put it as follows:-

"I have found the officers here are much more pleasant about visits. At Strangeways my family were always kept a minimum of 60 minutes waiting to see me for 15 minutes and one or two officers would make smart comments about my fiancees looks ie 'nice looker' etc etc. If I complained about anything such as the length of time she had to wait they always said see the Governor or we're short-staffed or something. There seems to be even less staff on the Wing I am on now but there are never any problems."

I.10. A sizeable minority of respondents (32; that is 12%) commented on the arbitrary nature of justice they experienced as a cause of tension and bitterness. Some of the complaints are concerned with the justice of the courts:-

"Judges and Magistrates are giving out different sentences for the same crime. A lot of prisoners feel hard done to because there are no general rules or guide-lines."

"I think some inmates are not contented with the length of sentence received, they feel injustice and will look for any way possible to upset the prison system and its workforce."

Other comments concern justice within prisons:-

"I have in the past taken things up with the Board of Visitors plus I have petitioned on a number of things I see as my rights. All I have caused for myself is trouble......If you do go through the right channels for complaints you don't even get to see them, not given a petitions form. Or you are told 'Mess with us and we will mess with you'."

A few prisoners claim that discontent with the complaints procedure was a cause of the riot:-

"They was all shouting things like 'We have gone through all the right channels but they do not want to know the problems of the inmates.' For six days before the riots they was shouting on my landing, we take the right channels but they do not want to know."

One prisoner summed matters up as follows:-

"Prisoners had enough. Their complaints were taken no notice of so they did the only thing they knew and that was using force to show their feelings and I hope I will never see something as frightening as a riot again."

I.11. Most prisoners made some suggestions for avoiding riot in the future. By far the most common was to improve "conditions" in particular those of which they had complained. Some respondents made specific practical suggestions. No single suggestion was mentioned by more than a dozen prisoners in all. The following are some of the suggestions made:-

i) There should be some outlet for feelings or grievances other than the existing formal channels. One prisoner suggested regular group discussions on the Wing:- "Maybe have a member of the BOV sitting in on it instead of an officer to hear what wants changing and looking into. Maybe even a representative of the inmates taking notes and putting them forward to the Board. This could make people aware of problems concerning that particular Wing." Another suggested "Listening to prisoners grievances would help. Especially a collective body nominated. Take things seriously instead of just dismissing them out of hand as trivialities." Yet another writes "There is a complaints system in prison but it is intimidating towards the individual, if someone puts himself forward as a spokesman. He is looked on as a trouble-maker and like all trouble makers he is put on a dispersal draft (shunted from prison to prison). Why can't we have a prisoners council? Then the complaints could be put to the BOV or the Governor without fears of reprisal. I don't mean for the prisoners to run the prison, but just to air the views of the majority of non-trouble-makers."

ii) Some Rule 43 prisoners asked for separate prisons for Rule 43s:-"My personal opinion is as a Rule 43 prisoner every time a prison erupts the Rule 43s are going to get injured or killed. The only way to prevent this happening is to have a Rule 43 prison in the North, as they have Grendon in the South."

iii) Another prisoner suggested "more incentives and responsibilities." "Half remission is a good start. What about conjugal right for the good boys. More wages. Access to phones, TVs in cells, more gym, exercise, education." He points out that if such goods were available they would also be a means of control. Another prisoner comments "There was a documentary on about prisons in Sweden or somewhere. If it was like that it would work but that is up to the Home Office."

iv) Some prisoners make suggestions about security. Smaller prisons would be better. Or locking arrangements so the whole prison could not be taken over. Others (a few) think there should be more staff or that large gatherings of prisoners should be prohibited.

v) Some prisoners suggest "privatised bail hostels" or other ways of keeping remand prisoners out of locals. One says "Don't have prisons over-crowded with petty offenders", another comments "The whole judicial system has got out of proportion and it is time something was done."

I.12. The substantial set of letters from inmates of Strangeways, not only provided much information about the riot itself, but, as the above account has shown, presented strong views as to the problems which underlay the riot. Poor sanitation (in particular 'slopping out'), overcrowding and too much time in cell ('bang-up') were the three major complaints. The fourth most frequent complaint, made by over a third of the respondents, was of the quality of the food they were given. This was followed in terms of frequency by complaints about staff attitudes, and then about visiting arrangements. A minority of respondents went out of their way to say they had no complaints about the Strangeways regime or considered it to have improved recently. Another minority was disturbed about justice issues and believed these had contributed to the riot. A range of practical suggestions were made for improving matters, by far the most frequent of which was to improve conditions generally.

II.   Letters from Glen Parva inmates

II.1. The disturbances at Glen Parva were the second in the series of disturbances at target prisons. The Strangeways riot had begun on 1 April 1990 and the Glen Parva disturbance occurred on 6 and 7 April. There was a 10% response rate to Lord Justice Woolf's letter from inmates of Glen Parva. Since it is a reasonably large establishment (448 sentenced inhabitants and 330 remands) there were 75 letters to analyse. As with letters from other establishments, much of the content of responses was concerned with individual experiences. The following analysis concentrates on general judgements as to the causes of the disturbances and ways they could be prevented in the future.

II.2. 18 of the 75 responses (24%) had nothing at all to say as to the causes of the disturbances or ways of preventing them. Among the remaining 57 scripts, the most common response by far as to the cause of the riot was that it "kicked off because of Strangeways"; inmates were "jumping on the bandwagon." This was mentioned by 24 respondents (32% of those who wrote). Typical quotations are:-

"The main reason why Glen Parva had that riot on Unit 8 is because of what happened at Strangeways prison. There was a lot of talk about it in here when we all heard what happened, and the general attitude to it was 'Well done Strangeways' and 'Go on lads'."

"I think myself it was the Strangeways riot started this one. They were trying to copy."

Some prisoners wanted to point out that the riot was not just to be dismissed as "copycat". As one thoughtful respondent put it:-

"Everyday in one prison or another someone is thinking about causing a riot. They may discuss their thoughts with others or they may just keep them to theirselves but the potential is always there. All it needs is for one prison to start it. Once that happens the rest will follow. This method has been labelled 'copycat rioting' but it is far from that. Prisoners will not risk their paroles, remission or anything else for the sake of copying. It goes a lot deeper than that. Prisoners know that one prison rioting will not make any difference they also know that if they started it off other prisons will follow, because then an impact will be made on the public's mind so something may be done. So when the disturbance at Strangeways started other prisons knew that to get what they wanted they had to join them by creating a disturbance. The more prisons that helped the more chance they had."

II.3. A minority of respondents (among them some who thought the riot had been set off by Strangeways) made clear that they disapproved of the riot and thought it had been quite unnecessary:-

"I'm quite sure they done their protest for no reason whatsoever. In this YC the inmates had no reason to carry on like this what so ever because it is a cushy jail."

"All it was was a bunch of sappy little remands who wanted to get on the news. It served no purpose here because this establishment is a fair place to be. We get no bother from screws unless we chosen that bother."

There were six responses of this type plus four other responses saying good things about staff at Glen Parva; making ten responses (13%) going out of their way to say they thought a riot at Glen Parva not justified.....\"Glen Parva is one of the best conditions." One particularly thoughtful long response came from a young man who had been in prison ten months and claimed "I have been to six prisons on this sentence." He complained bitterly about the generality of conditions in other jails and thought riots to be necessary because of the conditions prisoners endure. However he added:-

"The Unit I am in here would never dream of rioting. I will explain why. The officers here do everything they can to make our time here as enjoyable as it can possibly be in prison. They will sit and talk and listen to you they will laugh and joke with you and they will be strict with you if need be. Everyone is treated equally and the same.....The officers here are the best I've ever come across, simply because they don't ignore you they actually try to find out if you've got any problems....."

The respondent then went on to describe a personal problem with which an officer had helped him and continued:-

"....the atmosphere on the Unit is always a happy one. I can't remember the last fight here. Its rare someone gets put on a minor report and its rarer someone goes down the block. 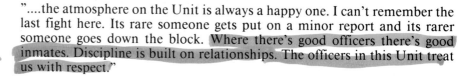Where there's good officers there's good inmates. Discipline is built on relationships. The officers in this Unit treat us with respect."

II.4. The most frequent complaint about conditions at Glen Parva was about food (15 responses; 20% of all those who wrote). However it has to be said that the comments about food did not approach the depth and bitterness of those from Strangeways. The matter is usually mentioned quickly and in passing. The following are typical comments:-

"The standard of food is very poor here as well as the quantity. Some mornings we would be able to eat our portions of cornflakes out of an

478

eggcup."

"The food is adequate here mostly but sometimes it is not enough."

However one or two are more cutting:-

"After a days work here at Glen Parva the inmate has only one thing on his mind. Food. So he collects his meals and wrinkles his face in disgust, the same food day in, day out, not only that it's not sufficient and he certainly wouldn't wish his meager portion of burned toast, lumpy potatoes, half-cooked vegetables, sloppy custard, sludge tea, fatty meat and gristle on his worst enemy.....The food is insufficient and he longs for Thursdays canteen where he can eat crisps and sweets etc."

One prisoner commented:-

"It's just a case really of adding more to some of the meals."

II.5.   Despite the positive comments about prison officers which have already been recorded, the second most frequent complaint about conditions made by Glen Parva respondents was of prison officer attitudes, criticised by ten respondents (13% of all who wrote). Even some of these criticisms were made in the context of other positive remarks:-

"We should be treated a lot better ie we should be treated like men and not children, we are put down too much and its getting worse. Glen Parva is one of the best prisons in England but the way things are going its reputation is going to get like Strangeways."

"Some of the officers could have a better attitude towards inmates. You get the odd few who spoil it. But we feel the lads who are quite decent are getting tarred with the same brush."

A few inmates are more critical. One, who admitted participating in the riot, wrote:-

"Officers treat inmates like outcast degenerate human beings which we are not.....The governors and officers are on a par with the Gestapo....I could go on for ever but I've got to stop and polish my Groups officers shoes. We rioted because we have got to get back at the screws who bully cheat and generally abuse us."

But it has to be said this response was exceptional. The more usual criticism was of petty rules....."Little stupid rules that they make up; not getting our proper rights which we are entitled to but don't get". Among "rules that are pathetic" one inmate quoted "No lending or borrowing, no more than four pictures allowed, no pictures on tables, lockers or wardrobe tops, no pictures of naked females allowed on display in cell."

II.6.   Nine prisoners (12% of all respondents) pointed to the special tensions suffered by remand inmates as a contributory cause of the disturbance:-

"The hanging around in limbo that remands feel makes them far more susceptible to riot."

"Us remand prisoners do not believe it is fair that if we want exercise we have to go to the gym and do workouts. We also only get association if we are willing to scrub floors. We should not have to do that when we are unconvicted."

"This is why I think it happened because of inmates waiting too long on remand to get sentence at courts for silly charges that they should not be in here for. If you do not want to work you get opted out of everything and you get locked up 23 hours a day and no activities."

"Remand prisoners are treated like they are guilty and they are not guilty until proven guilty. I would like to know why we are locked in our cells more hours than convicted prisoners."

II.7.   Three prisoners complained about poor access to medical care, three about the price of toiletries, three about grievance procedures, three claimed not to be out of the cell enough. Two prisoners said there were not enough showers, two criticised toilet arrangements and two insufficient clean clothes.

II.8. One respondent seemed to sum up the views of others as to how to prevent riots in the future:-

> "There's not really many things you can do as here at least we've got a toilet and running hot water in the cell. The officers are fair as I've already said. Its just a case of adding more to some of the meals. The disturbance here was I think pointless as we've not really got any argument that is worth complaining about. The disturbance here I think was just people thinking it was a good idea to carry the disturbance on to other prisons."

Another inmate commented:-

> "As to what should be done to prevent rioting again. First do not let inmates see TV when pictures of riot are being shown as that is like a trigger and I think that two people to a cell should be stopped. And you could have better security and more officers."

II.9. These letters from Glen Parva show a lower level of discontent than some other sets of letters and include many positive comments on the prison. Many respondents suggest the Glen Parva disturbances were chiefly dependent on those at Strangeways.

III. Letters from Dartmoor

III.1. The disturbances at Dartmoor began on 7 April 1990 and thus were the third in the series of troubles at target prisons. The population at Dartmoor was 607 inmates at the time of the disturbance of whom 90 responded to Lord Justice Woolf's invitation to write to him, a response rate of 14%. Once again the following summary concentrates on material in the letters on the causes of trouble and the ways to prevent them.

III.2. Only 11 of the 90 letters received (12%) failed to make any comment about the causes of the riot. By far the most frequently quoted cause of complaint was the "bad attitude" of staff. This was specifically mentioned by 35 respondents (39% of those who wrote). A typical comment is the following:-

> "Dartmoor seems to be still run as if it was the 1960s – a very totalitarian regime."

Letter after letter suggests that there is a "brutal attitude", "acrimonious atmosphere"; "staff are surly and arrogant". Some respondents take care to point out that there are many good staff, but even they agree there are problems. The following quotation gives the general flavour:-

> "The majority of staff here are decent ordinary blokes just earning a living and wishing to avoid unpleasantness. It is unfortunate that this majority is not more assertive because the reality is that there is an inner core of rather sad inadequate officers who are nothing more than bullies. Like all bullies they are cowards. I have certainly not witnessed any instances of physical bullying from them but their on-going attitude is one of belligerent intimidation, sheer bloody mindedness and abuse of their positions of authority. These men are invariably loud, use fuck or cunt in most sentences they speak and there is a banal sense of humour which if you don't happen to find amusing is an automatic black mark against you. For the most part they are idle. Work, apart from locking and unlocking doors appears to be one big hilarious tea-party. As you can imagine this gets a bit irritating from behind a door, particularly if you are unfortunate enough to want to use a lavatory..."

Several prisoners talk of the power of the POA in Dartmoor in order to criticise it:-

> "The Governor of this prison has had three votes of no confidence in him by his staff because he wants to improve conditions here."

A few prisoners make allegations of physical brutality; but more common are allegations of brutal manners, of insensitivity and laziness among what is said to be an influential minority of staff.

III.4. The second most common complaint of Dartmoor inmates is the quality of food, mentioned in 33 letters (37% of all responses). It was frequently described as meagre in quantity, monotonous, badly cooked and cold when served. One prisoner commented:-

> "The food is always cold due to the fact it is carried as far as a hundred yards through freezing corridors and across open spaces."

A prisoner who had been in Cardiff prison before Dartmoor and who had previous experience in catering compared the food unfavourably with Cardiff food and pointed to the success of a City and Guild training course used in the Cardiff kitchens. He suggested that if something similar could be arranged at Dartmoor, staff might take more pride in their work and the quality of the food would improve.

III.5. The alleged dirty and unhygienic state of the prison was a further cause of complaint at Dartmoor. There were 20 responses (22% of all letters) about different aspects of sanitation or hygiene. The recesses were said to be inadequate and dirty, showers too infrequent, clean kit too often not available.

III.6. A sizeable proportion of letters stated that the Dartmoor riot was in some sense caused by Strangeways. 19 responses (21% of all received) said things like "I suspect the prisoners here were expressing their solidarity with what happened at Manchester." One respondent, who was among the few not unduly critical of the Dartmoor regime, put it as follows:-

> "When Strangeways rioted, that started a chain reaction in a sense. Inmates saw everything on television news bulletins and photos on the front pages of newspapers. This prison may look dismal and may be isolated but the atmosphere is quite relaxed, so I myself could see no reason for starting a riot here. Admittedly the food is the worst I have seen in my life and the fact the visitors are searched before they enter the prison, which I believe is an infringement of human rights, Still I don't feel these are grounds for starting a riot."

III.7. Visiting arrangements were singled out for criticism by 16 respondents (17% of all replies). As one man put it:-

> "I think that the disturbance was caused by the inmates for the simple reason that most of them are too far from home to receive any visits."

III.8. Criticisms of the amount of time spent in cell were not as marked at Dartmoor, a training prison, as they were at Strangeways, a local prison. But six inmates did complain of the amount of "bang-up", eight more complained of the insufficient availability of work and another four of the lack of any facilities for rehabilitation.

III.9. The Dartmoor letters were so full of complaints that they had little to say on the means of preventing future riots, apart from the obvious strategy of reducing the causes of complaint. One or two inmates suggested that a media blackout on disturbances in other prisons, could help to prevent future riot.

III.10. The most frequently cited cause of riot in the letters from Dartmoor inmates was the "bad attitudes" of staff. This was closely followed by criticisms of the food. Sanitary and hygiene arrangements and visiting arrangements were also causes of discontent. About a fifth of respondents thought the riots were sparked off by Strangeways.

IV. Letters from Bristol

IV.1. The disturbances at Horfield (HMP Bristol) began on 8 April 1990 and hence were the fourth in the series of riots at target prisons. There were 572 inmates of Bristol at the time of the riot, of whom 118 subsequently wrote to Lord Justice Woolf. Lord Justice Woolf's letter of invitation to Bristol inmates unfortunately reached them rather late, and some respondents expressed scepticism as to whether their replies would get through and be read. In the event the response rate from Bristol was the largest from any of the target prisons (20% of all inmates) and included many long, helpful and thoughtful letters.

IV.2. 26 out of the 118 letters received (22%) had nothing specific to say as to the causes of the riot. Though many of these letters were detailed and helpful they concentrated on the events of the riot and the material they contained has been covered at the report of Part I of the Inquiry.

IV.3. The two most frequently named causes of riot in the Bristol responses were the "copycat" effect from earlier riots (32 responses; 26% of all letters) and the amount of time spent "banged up" in cell (31 responses; 26% of all letters).

IV.4. 32 letter-writers (26% of all scripts received) said that the riot was either a "copycat" disturbance or set off by the arrival in Bristol of prisoners evacuated from Dartmoor as a result of the riot there. 10 (8%) named only the general imitative effect stemming from preceding riots, 22 (18%) named the presence of ex-Dartmoor inmates as the main cause, sometimes also mentioning the "copycat" effect. The fact that the riot was named as "copycat" did not mean that it was not also seen as expressing grievances. One prisoner put it as follows:-

> "The disturbances at Bristol occurred via three major factors. One, that Strangeways had rioted and other prisons were having copycat riots. Two, that Dartmoor had had their riot and certain prisoners who were part of that riot were temporarily transferred to Bristol. Three, that life in prisons like Bristol up until recently has been very backward."

Another wrote:-

> "The prison riot at Bristol was a copycat of Strangeways but not just for the sake of it but in the hope people would stop and look at prisons in this country."

IV 5. The length of time spent banged up was complained of by 31 respondents (26%). "To be locked up 23 hours a day with nothing to do is mental cruelty" as one man put it. Some associated the problem with other difficulties for the prison regime, in particular the shortage of work:-

> "Shops have to close to send the officers on various escort duties. This leads to the locking up of inmates for 22 to 23 hours a day."

Some pointed to the effect of too much time in cell in causing irritation and frustration:-

> "To stop riots I think prisoners need more things to do and to have more free time (out of cell) and more evening activities so that they do not get so bored, irritable and restless."

IV.6. A minority of respondents complained about low and inadequate wages (10 scripts, 8% of responses):-

> "In Bristol the average is 3 pounds a week. Low wages encourage dealing in contraband and theft within the prison. The use of private cash means that family and friends are subsidising the prison service. Private cash is unfair to prisoners without outside access to money and often puts an additional hardship on prisoners' families. A realistic allowance should be paid to prisoners which would cover such items as batteries, toiletries, hobbies, tobacco or sweets."

IV.7.   After the effect of other riots and the amount of "bang-up", the most frequent complaints from Bristol were of poor sanitation and hygiene arrangements and the attitudes of officers.

IV.8.   Poor sanitation and hygiene arrangements were named as a contributory cause of riot by 28 letter-writers (24%). Slopping out was particularly resented but there were also complaints of too few showers, insufficient changes of clothes and general squalor. The following response serves for many:-

> "Each landing on A Wing at Bristol has two sit down toilets, two sinks, two separate urinals that cater for one person at a time. These have to be shared by around forty or more inmates. Prisoners are permitted to shower once a week but very rarely get a second weekly shower even after a day's work. Clothing change is once a week. Many prisoners are locked in their cells for 22 hours a day and when they wish to use the toilet have to use a little pot in the corner......to urinate in a cell is downright disgusting and humiliating."

IV.9.   26 of the letters (22%) criticised officer attitudes and named them as a source of discontent. The criticisms were of rudeness and verbal aggression rather than of any physical brutality. Often they are criticisms of "lack of communication between inmates and staff" to quote one inmate....."being treated not as an adult but as a robot". The following quotation is typical:-

> "Officers here are often loud and abusive for no reason at all and though the atmosphere was tricky they did nothing to soothe the situation, in fact I would say they actually provoked it."

There is not much sympathy for the thought that officers are over-worked:-

> "The trouble with officers is that they have not got much to do, so they sit about doing nothing. The trouble is they get used to doing nothing and then they can't be bothered when one of the cons ask for something."

One respondent recommended "better training for prison officers to raise them above their present status of being mere 'turnkeys' adding 'Then they would be able to relate to prisoners'."

IV.10.   Despite these frequent criticisms of Bristol staff, it should be noted that five letter-writers (4%) went out of their way to make positive comments on officers. "The staff here were a credit to the service" said one who was on Rule 43. Another respondent praised an individual member of staff who had persuaded him to join an Alcoholics Anonymous group which he felt had changed his life. An additional six prisoners (5%) made positive comments about the Bristol regime:-

> "There was no reason for any inmate to have taken part in this disturbance. Conditions on the wing were very relaxed. We have association every night and afternoon at weekend. Shower/bath every night and washing machine on the wing."

> "The inmates who got out on B Wing had no reason to take part as conditions are very good."

IV.11.   It appears that conditions within Bristol prison may have varied greatly. It is of interest that no less than 11 scripts (9% of all responses) point in particular to conditions on A Wing as a cause of riot:-

> "The general conditions in A wing were very tense before the riot. Bad for sanitation and all those on the Rule 43s."

> "Bristol suffered from poor conditions in A Wing. This was a slop-out wing.... the conditions were anything but sanitary and the wing was infested with cockroaches and mice."

> "The conditions on A Wing were very primitive although work was taking place to install showers and wash and toilet facilities in the cells, the latter was very much at the experimental stage."

Other letter-writers criticise the mix of prisoners on A Wing.

IV.12. After "bang-up", sanitation and officers' attitudes, the next most frequent complaints among Bristol letter-writers were of the food (20 respondents; 16%) and of overcrowding (19 respondents; 16%). Complaints about the food were usually routinised rather than detailed. "What more can you expect in prison?" one respondent put it. The overcrowding comments often occurred in connection with complaints about sanitation. One man experiencing his first time in prison put matters as follows:-

"When I discovered that three men had to share a cell of only 8 by 12 feet or thereabouts, I was astounded. A remand prisoner has no work, therefore he has to stay in the cramped stuffy cell with two other men, who he probably hates the sight of, for 24 hours a day. Many cells have only one chair or two chairs, or maybe no tables, so the inmates are forced to eat sitting on the bed. Try sitting on the lower bed of a double bunk and eating a meal. You too would become frustrated and angry. Mealtime over, he has to lie on the bed. Just for a change he could maybe sit on the bed. If he walks up and down the floor he is told to sit down or be put down. He has a head full of worry and problems about the forthcoming court case. One of the other inmates has a radio on at full blast, driving him crazy. He needs to use the toilet but the staff won't let him out and he daren't use the bucket or he gets beaten by the others. Wouldn't anyone get depressed?"

IV.13. Another group of letters draws attention to the particular tensions suffered by remand prisoners. This factor was mentioned by 14 letter-writers (11% of all responses):-

"There are too many people on remand in prison. Some people need to be held in custody because of the nature of their offence. But some prisoners don't.....and are being locked up 23 or even 24 hours a day with no one to talk to when they need help from outside. When a person is waiting for his trial he shouldn't be locked up all day."

IV.14. Problems with visits were mentioned by 12 respondents (10%). Visits were felt to be both too infrequent and too short. Prison officer attitudes during visits were also criticised. Two inmates complained that smoking during visits was no longer allowed.

IV.15. The major suggestion for preventing riots in the future was to improve conditions; that is to get rid of the causes for the complaint and tension which had been specified. A substantial sub-group (12 letters; 10% of responses) suggested that Rule 43s should be held in totally separate establishments. Those themselves on Rule 43 recommended this for safety reasons; others to reduce resentment and dislike of the Rule 43s. Individual thoughtful letters suggested a great range of possible other strategies including privatising prisons, setting up smaller prisons, devising a more incentive based system, segregating violent offenders, providing more clarity as to prison rules.

IV.16. The most striking feature of the responses from Bristol considered as a total set was the variety of responses within them. Prisoners on some wings spoke well of the prison and even expressed gratitude to prison officers. Conditions in other parts of the establishment gave rise to much resentment. About a quarter of Bristol respondents thought the Bristol riot was precipitated by Strangeways or by Dartmoor prisoners. The most frequently named causes of underlying discontent were the amount of time spent in cell, the sanitary and hygiene arrangements and the attitudes of officers. The food was disliked and both the amount of work available and the wages paid for it were criticised. Some respondents drew attention to the special difficulties of remand prisoners.

V. Letters from Cardiff

V.1. The riot at Cardiff prison began on 8 April, the same day as Bristol and concluded on the same day. There were 458 inmates of Cardiff prison at the time of the disturbance and 49 of them responded to Lord Justice Woolf's invitation to write to him. This is a response rate of 10%, together with that from Glen Parva the lowest response rate from the target establishments.

V.2.   Fifteen of the letters (30%) did not concern themselves with causes but were taken up with descriptions of the events of the riot. This material was very helpful to Part I of the Inquiry. The most frequently cited causes of the riot, taking the letters as a whole, were the amount of time in cell ('bang-up'), the attitudes of prison officers, sanitation and overcrowding.

V.3.   Twelve letters (24% of all responses) complain of too much time in cell; too little association or work. Three of these letters also complained of too little exercise:-

> "When the weather is boiling surely the inmates could sit or walk in the exercise yard?....Choosing between exercise or gymnasium is disgraceful. Everyone needs fresh air after 23 hours in a cell. But inmates also need the gymnasium – not a choice of either."

V.4.   Eleven respondents (22%) complained of officers' attitudes. But this number may give a wrong impression. The complaints were in no case of brutality, either verbal or physical, but rather of neglect or tensions. The following responses are typical:-

> "The disturbance started because of the officers they never gave us what we should have like television one hour a day we were lucky to have it three times a week."

> "From the time I was there there was a lot of tension with the boys and staff. The staff was edgy and not in a tidy state to do the job. I think they was worried because of the other prisons."

> "There is just not enough officers to man the overcrowded prison so if the prisoner has got any problems there is no-one for them to talk to."

Not all agreed that the problems of staff were due to under-manning:-

> "I do not see the demand for extra officers or staff, there are too many already, but I sincerely believe that attitude of present and future officers be strongly considered."

One man who complained of some officers, praised others:-

> "Sir I witnessed and received open hostility from certain members of staff. However I must stress a few members of the staff were very open and understanding to all. Three men in uniform were gentlemen. As for the others I must remain silent."

Four other inmates (8%) spoke well of officers. As one put it:-

> "There was still in my opinion a good relationship between prisoner and prison officer at Cardiff."

V.5.   Sanitation and overcrowding were often connected in responses. 10 inmates mentioned sanitation (20%) and nine (many the same inmates) spoke of over-crowding. The following quotation gives the flavour of the responses:-

> "The main reason for the riot in this establishment is overcrowding. Three inmates to a cell which was built to accommodate two. Toilet facilities for night time is still a bucket in the corner. The feeling a person go through which two other people are painfully trying to ignore the situation is humiliating to say the least."

V.6.   Eight inmates (16%) suggested the riot was a response to the media coverage of riots in other prisons:-

> "I believe the disturbance was a copycat effect after Manchester."

"It is my belief that the disturbance was the result of a very small number of inmates, two or three at most, deciding to emulate the prisoners at Strangeways."

V.7. As always in prisons food was a cause of complaint. But it is perhaps unusual that only 5 letters (10% of all responses) complained of the food and two responses (4%) described the food as good and above average.

V.8. Visits is another frequent cause of complaint and was mentioned in four letters, that is by 8% of respondents. Two respondents (4%) complained of low wages for work.

V.9. As for suggestions for preventing future disturbances, several suggested that a general improvement in conditions was the answer, two proposed that there should be swifter and more forceful action by prison officers:-

"When something happens in a prison it should be stopped straight away not let go on like Manchester, because I feel if Manchester was stopped in the beginning this wouldn't of happened in this prison."

V.10. Taken as a group the Cardiff letters appear less bitter than those from some other establishments. The major complaints are of the amount of time in cell, of sanitary arrangements and overcrowding and of the attitudes of officers.

VI. Letters from Pucklechurch

VI.1. There was a 13% rate of response to Lord Justice Woolf's letter from the inmates of Pucklechurch. But since Pucklechurch was a small institution of approximately 115 inmates in the male part of the prison, this means that only sixteen letters were received. One of these was clearly a spoof and one came from a female prisoner moved out of Pucklechurch as a result of the riot, leaving only fourteen letters to analyse.

VI.2. Of the fourteen Pucklechurch respondents seven (50%) did not mention any cause of the riot but confined themselves to describing events. Their evidence has been considered at Part I of the Inquiry. Two respondents said they could see no reason for the riot:-

"I didn't see any excuse for a riot.....the officers were fair plus it was an easy prison."

"There was no reason for it to start except to copy Bristol prison."

VI.3. The responses of the remaining five prisoners, who did address the question of cause, are summed up by the following response from one of them:-

"(1) Remand prisoners only got a half hour exercise a day and the convicted never got it at all. (2) When it was time to slop out we weren't given no more than five minutes which isn't long at all. (3) We were only given one shower a week. (4) We were only given a change of clothes once a week and one pair of socks and pants isn't enough for a week. (5) We only got three and a half hour association a week."

He also added:-

"The trouble was brewing up for quite a while before the riot started and it only needed one person to lead the way and the rest would follow, which was what happened."

VI.4. Though some respondents made allegations of staff brutality in the treatment of surrendering prisoners, there were no allegations of brutality by staff before the riot and only four of the 14 responses (28%) criticised the attitudes of staff in their day to day behaviour in the prison.

VI.5. One of the responses about the course of the riot may shed some light on the motivation of at least some rioters:-

> "It wasn't like a riot..... people were more interested in eating and smoking all they could get their hands on (same as me)."

VI.6. The Pucklechurch letters had little to say as to how to prevent riot. As one inmate put it:-

> "To say what action should be taken to avoid a disturbance like this occurring again I don't know because I have already said I don't know what started it."

VI.7. Unfortunately the Pucklechurch letters are too few in number to contribute greatly to our understanding of this disturbance, one of the most violent which occurred at the target prisons. There seem to have been reasons for a generalised low level of discontent.

VII. Summary and conclusion; target inmate letters

VII.1. As the above account has shown, inmates from different target prisons proposed different explanations of the causes of riots within their establishments. There was general agreement as to major factors, but differences in the frequency with which these explanations were put forward in different sets of letters. Any comparison of the findings across prisons must be carried out with care. From all prisons, letter writers were a self-selected group not a representative sample, and response rates from different prisons varied.

VII.2. In order to explore differences and similarities of response, the following table was prepared of all causes of riot named by more than 20% of respondents from any one prison. Results from Pucklechurch have not been included since the total set of responses from that establishment was too small.

Frequency of most commonly named causes of riot:-

	Strangeways	Glen Parva	Dartmoor	Bristol	Cardiff
Sanitation	55%	7%	22%	24%	20%
Overcrowding	50%	–	–	16%	18%
Bang-up	43%	4%	15%	26%	24%
Poor Food	40%	20%	37%	16%	10%
Poor Staff atts.	27%	13%	39%	22%	22%
Copycat	–	32%	21%	26%	16%

VII.3. The above table is suggestive. Six variables are most frequently cited as causes of disturbance – sanitation (which includes general hygiene factors such as shortage of showers or kit), overcrowding, 'bang-up' (too much time in cell, which includes insufficient work and association), food, poor staff attitudes and the copycat factor. The frequency with which all of them are named is very high indeed at Strangeways, (except perhaps for staff attitudes). At Glen Parva the copycat factor is most frequently named as the cause of the disturbance. Food is the only other variable named by 20% or more of respondents. At Dartmoor the most frequent complaint is of poor staff attitudes, closely followed by criticisms of poor food. The proportion of letter writers from Dartmoor who complain about staff attitudes (almost 40% of all letters) is higher than that at any other establishment, although it is a training prison and presents no complaints about overcrowding. Bristol and Cardiff present rather similar pictures. Both present frequent complaints about 'bang-up', sanitation and staff attitudes though at a lower level of frequency than at Strangeways. A lower portion of Cardiff than Bristol inmates name the copycat factor. The level of complaints about food at Cardiff is the lowest from any target establishment and at 10% of all responses, perhaps low for institutional food.

VII.4. These letters from inmates of target prisons give an illuminating picture of the problems of the prison system and suggest that it is well worth while asking inmates for their views.

Chapter Two

Letters from Inmates in the Rest of the System

1.   In the preceding chapter an account has been given of letters to Lord Justice Woolf from inmates of the six target prisons; Strangeways, Glen Parva, Dartmoor, Bristol, Cardiff and Pucklechurch. This chapter will describe the response to Lord Justice Woolf's letter from inmates in the rest of the prison system of England and Wales.

2.   603 men and four women from non-target establishments accepted Lord Justice Woolf's invitation to write to him. This represents a response rate of approximately one and a half per cent of the population of the non-target prisons. Not surprisingly, this is a lower response rate than that from the target establishments which varied between 10% and 20%. The letter to target inmates had been personally addressed and delivered. The request for information to non-target inmates was copied and distributed (often through being placed on a notice-board) through the governors of establishments. Bearing this in mind, a response rate of one and a half percent is a creditable response to an unsolicited request.

3.   Analyses were made to see how representative was the set of respondents of the prison population as a whole. The geographical spread of responses was wide. At least one man wrote from almost all adult male establishments. The only exceptions among the closed prisons were Lindholme, Downview and Erlestoke; and from among local prisons, Dorchester, Gloucester and Swansea. Albany prison provided most letter writers. Roughly 10% of its population at the end of April wrote individual letters. Letters were received from 5% or more of the population of Wakefield, Frankland, Bedford, Brixton and Norwich.

4.   An analysis of the sentence length of respondents as compared with that of the total prison population showed that respondents were more likely to be long-termers. There were four times the expected proportion of lifers or those with sentences over ten years among respondents. Similarly the responses were biassed towards older rather than younger men. Only 5% of respondents were under 21 as against 20% in the prison population as a whole. About a third of respondents were over 40 while those over 40 account for only 15% of the total prison population.

5.   Not unexpectedly given the bias towards longer sentences, there was also a bias among respondents towards those with more serious offences. Over half the respondents from non-target establishments were imprisoned either for violence or robbery.

6.   Only four of the letter writers were women. Their contribution was swamped by the male response but, apart from the fact that they seemed to view the establishments they were in more favourably than the men, they raised similar issues.

7.   Many respondents (14%) pointed out that they had wide experience of the prison system. Typical remarks were:- "in and out of prison for 30 years"; "I have spent all but one year of my life in prison since I was 17"; "what I have written is based on my 14 years experience in prisons – remand, dispersal and Category C – and my conversations with other prisoners". Another 19% named

two or more previous prisons they had been in. 6% said this was their first sentence, although this did not necessarily mean they had only been in one prison.

8.   Most of the letters were addressed personally to Lord Justice Woolf (who read all letters as soon as they arrived) and over one third of them expressed gratitude and appreciation for being given the opportunity to contribute to the Inquiry. Many pointed out that they had a great deal of knowledge about the problems of the system but had never before been consulted.

9.   Some letter-writers (46, that is 7% of all responses) were afraid that they might be "wasting their time" or that their letters might not be read. Some were suspicious that their prisons of origin did not wish them to write and were deliberately sabotaging the invitation to respond by displaying notices too late or too obscurely or by delays in providing paper, stamps and envelopes. "A number of prison officers here don't want prisoners here to write" said one man; and from the same prison another wrote "You won't receive many letters from this gaol because the inmates are scared of repercussions". Receipt of these letters intact belies some suspicions. Views of some prisons from which responses were sparse were also give by others who had moved on.

10.   The quality of the letters was high. There were twenty which could more accurately be described as essays or theses. Only ten letters were irritable or hostile. One only was wholly illegible. Fifty letters (8%) mainly aired personal grievances; but the great majority made serious general points based on personal experience.

Method of Analysis

11.   The analysis of letters from inmates of target prisons, reported in the previous chapter, was carried out by hand-counting the frequency of responses. Results had to be available for Part I of the Inquiry and there was no time for more elaborate procedures. There was more time for this analysis which was carried out completely separately. Every letter was carefully read and a note made of every topic raised. Gradually a list was built up of 54 separate topics which cropped up in the letters. These 54 topics were in turn classified under six theme headings. No response was classified under more than one heading. All data were computerised so counts could be provided of the number of times particular variables were mentioned, either by the letter-writers as a whole or by sub-groups of them.

12.   Because this analysis was carried out by an independent researcher completely separately from the analysis of the target inmate letters, a slightly different coding-frame (classification of topics raised) emerged from that used in the previous chapter. This is in many ways an advantage. The two sets of letters are different in nature. A special analysis had shown that target prison respondents approximated to the profile of the general prison population; non-target inmates were more biassed towards older and long-term inmates. Again target inmates had much to say about the disturbances which had afflicted their establishments and their comments might well have been affected by those disturbances. If it is wished to compare the frequency of responses among target inmates to that in this set of responses, it should be borne in mind that the definitions and boundaries of topic groups are not always exactly comparable in the two sets of data.

The Frequency of Responses

13.   Table 1 lists the 54 separate topics discerned in the letters and classifies them under six different theme headings. It also gives the numbers of letters in which each topic listed was mentioned or discussed, and also that number expressed as a percentage of the set of 607 responses. (Where two letters were

received from one prisoner, this was counted for the purpose of analysis as a single letter). The frequency with which a topic comes up in a set of responses such as this is a good guide to the salience of the topic for the respondents as a whole. It is hoped most of the topic names are self-explanatory, but in so far as they are not, a full account of the kind of responses they describe, together with representative quotations, can be found later in this chapter.

14. As Table 1 shows there were ten topics upon which at least 25% of the writers made comments. In order of the frequency of mention they are as follows:-

Poor staff attitudes	mentioned in 40%	of letters
Nature and grouping of inmates	,, 36%	,,
Poor food	,, 35%	,,
'Bang-up'	,, 34%	,,
Sanitation	,, 34%	,,
Cell conditions	,, 29%	,,
'Tension'	,, 27%	,,
Visiting arrangements	,, 26%	,,
Overcrowding	,, 25%	,,
Management	,, 25%	,,

15. Although for coding and analysis purposes counts were made of the frequency with which each separate cause of discontent was named, most letters cover many topics and do so in a way which closely interconnects them. The following letter exemplifies many:-

"It seems as if everyone in prison is pissed off about the same things. You will receive letters saying its because we only get one shower a week, one kit change, one visit per month until you have been convicted three months (no matter how long you have spent on remand). People will say the food is cold and there is no time for slop-out. They will complain about being locked in an 18′ by 12′ cell 23 hours a day, seven days a week.....You will be asked how you would like to piss in a bucket sometimes used by three other people and others before you. They will ask how you would like to have no choice as to who is thrown in with you – you have no say because you're just scum, another convict, a piece of shit.....They will also say that officers say nothing but 'bang-up', put in an application, see the Welfare, see the Governor, you're nicked! Never 'What can I do for you?'. The problem with the prison system is a simple one; its the prison system and the conditions you ask us to live in."
(30 year old; five year sentence)

Individual detailed complaints do not stand alone. They are perceived and presented as part of the whole general problem of prison.

16. The following sections of this chapter will describe comments made by inmates under the six theme headings given at Table 1 – conditions in prison, people in prison, the penal system, provision for prisoners, personal and family contacts and miscellaneous. No categorisation of such a varied set of responses can be completely successful, but the groupings used emerged from a close consideration of the letters on which they were based. No single comment has been categorised under more than one heading.

Theme I: Conditions in Prison

I.1. The separate topics listed under this heading are described below in order of the frequency of their mention by respondents. They are all interconnected; in particular the first five:- 'bang-up', sanitation, cell-conditions, overcrowding, and 'general conditions'.

i) 'Bang-up' I.2. The number of hours 'banged-up' (ie locked in) was mentioned by 208 (30%) of respondents and was often said to be a result of overcrowding or staff shortages. Some doubted whether so much bang-up was necessary:-

> "If you ask why bang-up you are told it is a shortage of staff but officers say they are bored when everyone is banged up, they have nothing to do. If it is a security risk to unlock everyone, why not one landing at a time, or even half. Such a gesture would ease tension and make inmates feel that something was being done to try and help."

The long bang-up is principally a feature of local prisons. Nearly half (47%) of all men writing from local prisons referred to long periods locked up; in most cases they talk of 18 to 23 hours out of 24.

ii) Sanitation I.3. Sanitation is here taken solely to refer to problems with lavatory arrangements. Even on this narrow definition (narrower than that used in the classification of letters from target inmates) problems of sanitation were named by a third of all respondents and by 40% of those writing from local prisons. Again and again respondents describe the squalor of using a bucket in a cell shared with others and 'slopping out' at a sluice next to washing places and sinks where eating utensils are washed. Slopping out is remembered and described with bitterness even by those who have moved on to open prisons.

I.4. Not only do men find the process degrading, it contributes to friction between staff and inmates. Inmates become resentful of officers who appear wilfully to refuse to let them out of their cells to use toilets or who limit the time allowed to slop-out:-

> "Not being in command of your bodily functions or mind causes frustration."

I.5. Graphic descriptions are given of hurling parcels of excreta from windows (a punishable offence) or somehow leaving them on the Wings in order to avoid spending the night with stench in the cell. Inconsistent rules about being able to purchase disinfectant and other toilet articles compound the problem.

iii) Cell Conditions I.6. 29% of all respondents specifically criticised the conditions in cells, often created by over-crowding and sanitation. The smell, the lack of privacy, the lack of choice of cell companion are all bitterly complained of. Other respondents criticise inadequate ventilation, ill-fitting windows, poor lighting, dirty and broken furniture and poor decoration.

iv) Overcrowding I.7. One quarter of all respondents referred to overcrowding. Half of these were from local prisons. A few suggested overcrowding was not necessary:-

> "Overcrowding is something of a myth. There are empty cells which are not used."

> "Overcrowding is given as an official reasons for unrest but actually it is being used as an excuse."

11 men in all (mainly from Category B prisons) did not consider over-crowding to be a main cause of poor conditions. But most respondents saw it as a very real problem for which they blamed either the courts or the government.

v) General Conditions I.8. As well as the above criticisms, 129 men (21%) criticised the conditions in prison in more general fashion. 99 men condemned the buildings variously as Dickensian, Victorian, antiquated, inhuman or in need of modernisation. Others spoke of problems such as the general lack of greenery, cold, humidity, low levels of heat, light or ventilation. The following comments are typical:-

> "Decent surroundings can make men calmer."

> "Not a blade of grass to be seen yet we are in the heart of the country."

41 respondents complained of dirt or vermin in the prisons; half of these responses were complaints of cockroaches, rats or other vermin.

vi) Washing Facilities I.9. 82 respondents (13%) wrote of problems connected with washing facilities.

491

Most felt that one shower a week was insufficient. Some respondents claimed they did not get even that. The availability of showers seemed to be a particular problem for those in local prisons. There were difficulties in getting towels. Concern was shown about the issue of razor blades, said to be limited to one a week.

vii) Clothing

I.10. Closely linked with concern about inadequate washing facilities were complaints about insufficient supply of clean clothing. As well as infrequent changes of kit, inmates complained of ill-fitting, poor quality and well-used clothing and of the restrictions on wearing their own clothes. In particular wearing secondhand shoes, socks and underwear was found distasteful. Some men complained there was no way to wash their clothes. Rules related to clothing were complained of; in one case refusal of permission to wear shorts in the garden, in another being not allowed to wear own clothes on visits. Several linked the poor quality and supply of clothing to a deliberate policy of degrading them and lowering their self-esteem.

viii) Building Programme

I.11. 34 men (5%) commented on prison building plans. Nine suggest speeding up the building programme and building more prisons. Two talked of upgrading existing prisons and two more of the need for good architectural design. Eight favoured smaller prison units or smaller wings or landings. Six suggested that building more and bigger prisons was not the answer. One wrote that such rebuilding is done for the benefit of officers not inmates; another suggested that re-building only helped Category A and B prisoners, said to be a tiny proportion of the population.

ix) Minimum Standards and Human Rights

I.12. 19 respondents (3%) suggested that the problems of prison conditions were so acute that human rights were being ignored and that some form of minimum standards should be implemented. They argued for a Bill of Rights or charter for prisoners which would be legally enforceable. Among these respondents were men who had already made contact with the European Court for various reasons.

x) Bedding

I.13. 17 respondents (2%) criticised the bedding available to prisoners. It was said to be unclean when issued and rarely changed. There were complaints of inadequate blankets in winter, broken beds and thin mattresses.

Theme II: People in Prison

II.1. A substantial set of comments in inmates' letters centered around people and human relationships. Topics categorised under this heading are described below in order of their frequency of mention.

i) Prison Officers

II.2. The largest number of comments were those about prison officers. This subject was mentioned in 294 letters; 245 of these letters (40% of all respondents) were critical and 49 (8%) favourable or neutral.

II.3. Of the 49 (8%) favourable or neutral responses, 39 were on the whole favourable and 10 neutral. The positive or relatively favourable comments included such remarks as "they do their best", "I am sorry for them", "they work under pressure". The responses categorised as neutral usually included some recommendation as to how prison officers should act: for instance "officers should be helpful"; "should be stricter - not allow inmates to run the prison" or "should not be moved so frequently so relationships could be developed".

II.4. The 245 (40%) critical responses can be divided into three sub-groups:-

a) 104 which complained mainly of 'brutality' or provocative and abusive behaviour;

b) 95 which stressed pettiness of mind, uncaring and belittling attitudes, 'breaking of the rules', indiscretion, favouritism and victimisation;

c) 44 which were concerned mainly with the quality and training of officers and in some cases their immaturity and questionable stability.

There were in addition five allegations of corruption among officers especially in relation to food. It should be noted that many critical letters qualified their remarks by saying that they were talking of "some officers" only.

II.5. The above division of critical responses can only be rough and ready. Some scripts cover a range of comments and different sub-groups shade into each other. The following extract from a 30 year old in a Category C prison exemplifies several complaints:-

> "The single and most important contributory factor in my opinion (in the causes of riot) – is the attitudes of prison officers.......What makes prison more difficult than anything is the often disgusting, ignorant and apathetic attitudes of prison officers. Any prisoner will know exactly what I am talking about. Being shouted at like a dog, being constantly verbally degraded and being belittled as part of the game. Nobody (unless of course they went in blue jeans and striped shirt) can understand just exactly what sinister goings on actually take place within a prison environment....a new world opens up to you. Officers bullying, telling lies at adjudications, disregarding rules. Prison officers seem to thrive on enforcing to the limit the often petty rules which constitute the prison rule book.....Generally the incidents I talk about occur more in local prisons than in dispersal or Category C prisons. I watched young recruited officers coming to the job with many good points, eg talking to prisoners, smiling, saying hello.....trying to help a prisoner if possible, even if that only meant opening the door to allow him to go to the toilet. However, within the space of a week or two these excellent attitudes were quickly and efficiently knocked out of all but the strongest willed by the old school of prison officer who growls and grunts like an animal."

II.6. Of the 104 responses in the first group, 58 used the actual word 'brutality'. In some cases they alleged witnessing brutality, in others to have experienced it. Most of the incidents described were related to segregation units and "being dragged to the block and beaten up". One man suggested that prison officers on the block form elite cliques which need to be broken up. Another defined brutality as "Home Office Approved Restraint Techniques used to the maximum". Apart from those who specified 'brutality', the rest of this group of 104 respondents complained of provocative, arrogant or abusive behaviour by prison staff:-

> "Officers can swear at and abuse prisoners. Under Rule 47 prisoners are nicked if they speak in the same way to officers."

II.7. In the group of 95 respondents who complained of pettiness or uncaring attitudes, many of the criticisms were of insensitive behaviour possibly intended as jocular:-

> "A prison officer will say 'I'm off home to my missus now; who do you think is going home to yours?'"

Officers were thought to have favourites, to cultivate influential inmates or to victimise others. Much conflict arose over rules perceived as petty and inconsistent. Some arose from sanitary arrangements:-

> "Here it is seen as a nicking offence to press the cell bell without an emergency."

The officers' behaviour was interpreted by many prisoners as designed to belittle them:-

> "There is a lot of discontent here about food, the surly attitudes of some officers and the constant psychological games they play. It is obvious that if prisoners are treated like animals, sworn at, degraded and psychologically toyed with week after week they in turn lose respect, not only for their tormentors, but for society at large...... We can accept punishment but not

493

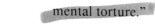

mental torture."

II.8.   The third group of comments about officers (44) related to their quality. Lifers were slightly more likely than other respondents to suggest the need for more training for officers. Other respondents described officers as either lazy, purposeless, paranoid, alcoholic, corrupt, needing psychiatric help, turnkeys only, or as having Dickensian or outmoded attitudes. One writer suggested that truncheons should be abolished; another recommended the wearing of identity badges by staff. One letter, signed by two inmates, said only:- "Who guards the guards?". The idea of personal officers is commended by two men, but another, who had a personal officer, said:- "He has only spoken to me three times in 17 months.".

ii) Nature and Grouping of Inmates

II.9.   220 of the letters (36%) discussed matters to do with the nature and grouping of prison inmates. These were either comments on how to treat defined sub-groups of inmates (134 comments; 22% of letters) or more general comments on the nature of the current inmate population and their problems (121 comments; 20% of scripts). Since some letter writers among the 220 discussed both topics, these two sub-groups add up to more than 220.

II.10.   Taking the comments on the general nature of the prison population and ways of dealing with it first, many writers were concerned to stress that prisons are run on the good-will of the inmates:-

> "What some prisoners want to do is stupid and frightening and I am sure you are aware that it is only the good will of prisoners in most gaols that allows the system to work.....this prison is a tinder box just waiting for a spark, as staff inmate relationships are nil."

Many stressed that the modern inmate is different:-

> "When prisons (locals in particular) were built and the rules laid down, life on the outside was not what it is now. When the prison regime was introduced those who were subjected to it did not leave behind such a quality of life as they have now. We live in a society today where we are encouraged to smoke and drink to strengthen the coffers of the exchequer and then are denied the one and can hardly earn enough to buy the other. The restrictions and rigidity one meets in prison constrict ones spirituality probably a lot more so than in the days of the birth of the present system.......it is not our fault that society and the quality of life have accelerated onward while the prison system has hardly moved at all."

II.11.   Those who commented on how to deal with special sub-groups of inmates often asked for more separation of different groups. "Mixing the good with the bad is a lethal mix" wrote one. The groups that they felt should be separated included remands from convicted men (13 letters), long from short term convicted men (16 letters), the young from the old (22 letters), and the first-timer from the experienced (five letters). Five letters suggested serious violent offenders, drug offenders and murderers should be segregated. The following responses are typical:-

> "When trouble comes it is old cons using the youngsters....if youngsters are put in the predicament of being away from home, they can be easily used. The youngsters get the blame while the old cons get their way. There are young men with too much energy to burn and pent up energy bursting to be released."

> "How hard it is to improve yourself or just protect yourself from deterioration when incarcerated alongside those who may be in a state of deterioration. Prison officer can't help in this because it is basically the survival of one's soul and good nature that is at stake."

Many letters discussed how to deal with Rule 43 prisoners. 39 recommended either segregation, isolation or castration. 12 believed sex offenders receive preferential treatment and are 'used' or 'planted' in return for favours. But more described the various hardships or 'torments' Rule 43 prisoners have to put up with. 20 respondents stated that ordinary inmates should not have to share their cells with the mentally sick, psychopaths or those suffering from AIDS....and believed that on occasion this happens.

iii) Management II.12. Management problems as against problems with particular officers were grouped as a separate category of responses. There were 129 letters (25% of all received) which commented on such issues.

II.13. 33 of these scripts commented on the role of the governor or governors. 22 described them as 'powerless' and thought it would be better if they could be put back in charge and 'run their prisons'. But not everyone agreed. One governor was described as arrogant, others as 'dictatorial', 'like royalty' or 'incompetent'. One man asked whether governors existed; he and others claimed never to have seen one. Some said the relationship between governors and prison officers was too close; others described disagreements between governors and the Prison Officers' Association:-

"The good intentions of Governors are sabotaged by the POA."

One man wrote that governors were helpful.

II.14. 36 letters made comments on the role of the government, 35 on the role of bureaucrats in managing prisons. The bureaucrats at the Home Office were thought to distance themselves from the prison scene and to adopt an "out of sight, out of mind" strategy. A typical letter criticises "faceless men in pin stripes who could not care less for inmates.". Many suggestions were made for improving matters. New guidelines should be evolved for managers, spot checks should be carried out regularly at establishments, there should be better arrangements for listening to staff and inmates.

II.15. Much of the criticism under this heading was general. 40 scripts discussed the part money and resources played in the situation. Others criticised what they saw to be inflexible and outmoded management attitudes. Management was seen as wilfully out of touch and refusing to listen to either pressure groups or prisoners.

iv) Manning II.16. The next largest group of responses grouped under the heading "People in Prisons" is the group dealing with manning problems in prison (129 letters; 21% of all letters). The letters in this group discussed staff shortages and the whole set of issues associated with the 'Fresh Start' industrial agreement.

II.17. 52 letters agreed that more officers were needed, especially at weekends, and that manning levels were too low for officers to be helpful. The rest of the scripts were more critical of the attitudes of the Prison Officers' Association. 12 men did not believe there were real shortages. 24 believed inmates were being 'used as pawns' by the POA. All saw disadvantages for prisoners in the argument between the POA and authority:-

"Some prison officers think they are above the governors and hold the threat of working to rule over the governor's head."

"Prison officers are in dispute over pay – less working hours, more warders. Prisoners are pawns on a chessboard."

"Since Fresh Start personal achievement for prison officers is no longer the norm."

v) Communication II.18. The next largest group of responses in this section referred to poor communications throughout the system. There were 105 such comments (17% of all letters). Typical remarks were:-

"No-one listens to us."

"No-one answers our questions."

"All communication has to be through formal channels."

"It is them and us throughout the system."

The vast majority of comments were on these lines. Only nine responses (four from Category C prisons) mentioned any signs of hope or improvement.

vi) Racism II.19. 28 of the letter writers (4%) made comments connected with race. Six men thought racial segregation in prisons would be a good thing and two claimed preferential treatment is given to black inmates. One black writer thought there was less racism in prison than outside; but 17 other writers complained of racism, both in prison and in the criminal justice system. One instance given is of the names of black or brown inmates being marked on Wing lists and only a certain proportion allowed on each Wing. A Muslim wrote of the difficulty of observing Ramadan in prison.

vii) Women Officers II.20. Seven of the writers commented on the presence of women officers. Their main anxiety was that it was degrading to have women present at the slop-out stations. They were all agreed on this.

Theme III: The Penal System

III.1. In making the many points described above many letter writers connected them with more general issues concerning the penal system as a whole. It is these responses which are now described.

i) Tension III.2. Many letter writers (167, 27%) believe that the penal system as a whole systematically creates tension. They argued that the tension which causes riots is not accidental, demanding a specific individual explanation on each occasion it arises. It is endemic in the penal system. The following quotation sums up these many responses:-

> "Disturbances are never planned. Prior to any large scale disturbance there is always a long period of dissatisfaction, tension and general bad feeling. Complaints of bad food, mail being lost or delivered late, excessive security searches, delayed visiting periods, violence in the segregation blocks – set the foundation for later, more physical and open conflict with prisoners and staff. Then a tendency to block attempts to see the No 1 Governor with complaints exasperates the prisoner. As they become more open in criticisms of the way in which prison is run, ghostings to distant prisons become a reality and remaining prisoners begin to feel that verbal protest will solve none of their problems and violent protest follows, usually after some trivial incident."

Again and again respondents point out that the current prison system inevitably causes such a build up of tension "like pressure in a pressure cooker".

ii) Rehabilitation III.3. 145 letters (24%) appealed for a purpose to be provided for prisoners by rehabilitative programmes. Many accepted that they were in prison as punishment, but argued that time spent deprived of liberty should be spent in learning how to manage better on the outside. 11 stated that prison now is a destructive and negative experience which makes it harder for men to go straight. 26 also pointed to the control advantages of some incentives within prison, which could be provided by rehabilitative programmes. They suggested goals could be tied to progressive privileges. Some asked for chances to "give something back to the community". One pointed out "When a man has nothing to lose you can't control him."

iii) Justice in Prison III.4. 135 responses (22%) concerned aspects of the justice system within prison. Grievances, petitions, applications and reports were all discussed. The general feeling is that inmates face a 'no-win' situation:-

> "No-one listens, they are never believed, decisions are always in favour of the officers. Officers thus believe they are above the law."

> "Petitions and applications are a waste of time: they are blocked, refused or

ignored as are complaints, for which additionally you may be punished."

iv) Rules and Regimes III.5. 116 letter-writers (19%) complained of the lack of clarity and pettiness of many prison rules and of inconsistency in their application.

"Prisons slack off rule-wise then tighten up again and tighten up even more and that aggravates inmates....."

Many believe prison officers can make up rules to suit themselves. Inconsistency between prisons is often noted:-

"Only stick deodorants allowed at Winchester and Wandsworth; only roll-on at Brixton."

v) Parole and the Lifer's Lot III.6. 97 prisoners (16% of all who wrote) expressed concern about parole; in addition 31 respondents (5%) raised the problems of life-sentence prisoners. 15 criticised the secrecy of parole or other reports. 49 described the 'wind-up' caused by inconsistencies and delays in the parole process. One wrote:-

"The phantom risk factor needs re-assessing to make parole eligibility a factor to be taken seriously. Then eligibility will become a control factor."

24 respondents complained of the lack of hope under current parole arrangements for those convicted of offences of violence. Ten men favoured the abolition of parole in favour of automatic remission. Two suggested that parole and remission should be earned and linked to rehabilitation. Eight men believed that they were kept in the dark about their tariffs and that these were neither properly explained nor understood.

vi) The Criminal Justice System III.7. 96 respondents (16%) criticised some aspect of the criminal justice system. Most references were to too many sentences, too long sentences, too many remands in custody, too little use of bail and other alternatives to prison. Others criticised the inconsistency of sentencing. Eleven talked of fabricated evidence and corrupt police. Another eleven wrote of failure of the courts to listen to probation officers and the use of 'tricks' to gain convictions at court.

vii) Theories of Punishment III.8. A substantial minority of letter writers (80; 13%) discussed the theoretic rationale and purpose of imprisonment. It was the older men and lifers who were more likely to produce such responses. 11 respondents argued that prison should be for reform not revenge. Two quoted Bentham. 14 held that British prisons were designed solely for punishment and urged that some other policy or purpose should be developed. 37 more argued that loss of liberty is the punishment and is sufficient punishment; more should not be added. One man argued for "more government investment in the discipline of criminology. There is a shortage of ideas.".

viii) Other Topics III.9. A number of other topics were categorised under the general heading of the penal system. None of them was named by more than 10% of letter-writers, and most by under 5%. The delays which were criticised by 53 respondents were mainly delays in the criminal justice system. The complaints about confidentiality and secrecy included some of lack of confidentiality within prison as to an inmate's offence or concerning his family circumstances and some of excessive secrecy about what was written on any reports about inmates. Complaints about strip-cells (12), strip-searches (8) and cell searches (7) were very strongly felt. Strip searches of visitors gave great offence. The use of strip cells for punishment was alleged and condemned. The majority of the 26 complaints on categorisation referred to the restrictions Category A status puts on visiting and letters. The responses concerning security issues suggested that these dominated all other considerations and made conditions too tight and severe. References to moves were infrequent (14 letters) and in most cases complained of personal experience. 12 men referred to poor arrangements for reception within prison and these letters describe some very bad experiences.

Theme IV: Provision for Prisoners

IV.1. This theme category overlaps somewhat with Theme I, Conditions in Prison. The reason for grouping the responses described in this section separately is that many letter-writers made the point that the strongest reaction of men locked up for a long time is boredom and that more could be done to reduce this boredom by providing better facilities. A range of improvements were suggested and it is those improvements, and the reasons why they were proposed, which are described in this section.

i) Food

IV.2. 35% of all respondents (218 letters) thought something should be done about prison food. Many pointed out that food is of great importance in prisons. It breaks up the monotony of the day and is one of the few things to which to look forward. Only four people said food was not a major cause of discontent. The rest agreed that prison food was monotonous and frequently disgusting.

ii) Activities

IV.3. Out of the 126 (20%) references to activities and association (which are not easily distinguishable) two thirds complained there is not enough and 12 more complained that cuts had been made. Some were dissatisfied with the nature of provision and ask for more TV, videos, sport, games or hobbies.

iii) Earnings

IV.4. 113 men (19%) were concerned about the low wages for work done. One lifer complained that his week's labour earned him "enough for paper and envelopes but not enough for a stamp". Many thought it would be helpful if inmates could pay for part of their keep or to help their families. It was also suggested that earnings could be used as an incentive.

iv) Work

IV.5. There were 100 references to work (16%), apart from the complaints about wages. 42 complained of the lack of work or its cancellation. 22 characterise the work on offer as monotonous or 'slave labour'. Another 23 suggest that work should be meaningful and could be rehabilitative. One man suggested that work should be optional but taken into account for parole decisions, others complained that work was awarded a low priority by prison officers or that there was no work for remands.

v) Exercise

IV.6. Of the 80 letters (13% of respondents) mentioning this factor, 48 were resentful of the limited amount of exercise allowed and most of the rest asked for better facilities. The importance of gym and exercise facilities in keeping men fit was stressed.

vi) Education

IV.7. Almost as many respondents called for better educational facilities as pointed to the need for better gym or exercise arrangements (78 respondents; 13%). Eleven were enthusiastic about the educational provision available to them, but 54 thought their provision inadequate, shabby and prone to cancellation. Three writers suggested pay for those on educational courses so they would be encouraged rather than penalised for undertaking them. Ten writers criticised the availability of books and one more said no-one had offered him the use of a library.

vii) Boredom

IV.8. 61 men (10%) complained specifically of boredom and under-stimulation. "I myself have now an in-depth knowledge of the behaviour patterns of urban pigeons" said one. Many respondents linked the occurrence of riots or disturbances to the desperate need for something to happen.

viii) Canteen and Private Cash

IV.9. 56 men (9%) said that current arrangements were a source of friction. Many pointed out that there was no uniformity between different prisons in rules as to what can be bought or brought in. 14 criticised what were seen as inflated prices in the canteen. 23 would like to be able to use more private cash with no ceiling. But others pointed to the inequalities between prisoners caused by private cash arrangements.

ix) Tobacco

IV.10. 48 letters (8%) referred to the problems of not being able to afford a regular supply of tobacco. Six claimed that 'tobacco barons' still existed in prison. More than one man was convinced that tobacco companies had offered to supply free tobacco to prisoners but that the government would not allow it.

x) TV in Cell   IV.11.   43 letter writers suggested that TV should be made available in cells. It would alleviate boredom and hence help control.

Theme V: Personal and Family Contacts

V.1.   The topics described under this heading all relate to a prisoner's personal welfare and his contacts with his family.

i) Visits   V.2.   The most frequently mentioned topic was visits (158 letters; 26% of all respondents). 65 prisoners, mainly remand prisoners and those in locals, complained of the length and frequency of visits. 31 men complained that distance from home made frequent visits impossible. 15 out of the 18 who recommended conjugal visits were long-termers. 13 men thought that more home-leave could be given. For some very long-termers this was a burning issue. The conditions for visits were generally deplored.

ii) Degradation   V.3.   So many letter writers (90; 15% of all letters) made specific use of this word to describe the effects of the prison system on them that it seemed worth coding and counting separately. Many connected the 'degrading' effect of prison with the propensity to riot - "Treat us like animals" (or sometimes "like dogs") "and we will behave like animals". Others wrote "All we ask is to be allowed to keep a little self-respect" or "to be treated like human beings". "We are stripped of our humanity". Comments of this kind came from all groups of prisoners but were particularly frequent among those on remand or those writing from local prisons.

iii) Help with Personal Problems   V.4.   85 respondents (14%) wrote of the difficulty of getting any help with personal problems while in prison. 47 men described feelings of helplessness; there was "no-one to talk to". Prison officers, it was felt, were not trained to help although they some occasionally tried to do so. One request for help was answered by a prison officer:- "I am not a Samaritan". The need for counselling or therapy was mentioned by 12 men. Probation officers were criticised by 19 men – "a waste of time, overloaded, useless".

iv) Mail   V.5.   Most of the 73 comments (12% of inmates) on this topic are about delays in receiving or posting mail. Some allege loss of letters or that they are withheld or tampered with as punishment. 24 respondents complain of the censorship of mail. 16 believe inmates should be allowed more letters or that there should be no restrictions on correspondence.

v) Medical   V.6.   67 men (11% of respondents) complained about medical services in prison. These complaints were among the most vehement and bitter in the whole set of letters, especially when based on personal accounts. 38 wrote of doctors who were "appalling", "a disgrace", "only in it for the money". Many believed that little or no help was offered to the mentally sick, drug addicts or sex offenders and there was concern over the presence in prisons of HIV positives and AIDS sufferers. Eight of the writers suggested transfer of the Prison Medical Service to the National Health Service or privatisation.

vi) Drugs   V.7.   There were 48 references (8% of responses) to drugs problems in prison. 21 respondents claimed drugs were regularly brought in. Eight referred to the use of drugs as a currency within prison. Three argued that drugs were beneficial because of their calming influence.

vii) Telephone   V.8.   39 respondents (6%) mentioned telephones, the great majority (35 responses) to say what a great need they meet, not only to maintain family contact but to contact solicitors. Some complain of lack of privacy when making calls and the allowance of calls is frequently considered insufficient.

viii) Home Leave and Property

V.9. 11 men (2% of respondents) think there should be more home-leave and that this would help to retain family ties. Another 11 (2%) point to difficulties in retaining ties with the world outside prison caused by restrictions on keeping mementoes such as photographs or small gifts.

Theme VI: Miscellaneous

VI.1. The first two topics grouped in this category concerned the media generally and the question of copycat riots. The view that riots were often caused by a 'copycat' effect was advanced in 13 letters (2% of responses). 49 letter-writers (8%) were concerned with the effect of the media on the view of prisons held by the general public. 21 thought media coverage of prisons "got it wrong" and encouraged the ordinary public to think conditions were too soft. It was also felt the media were guilty of inciting feelings against sex offenders. The media were thought to fuel the public perception of prisoners as "50,000 psychopaths". They were not interested in stories of injustices within prison and did not cover charity work done by prisoners.

VI.2. 50 letters made comparisons between prisons in this country and in others. A few had direct experience of prisons in other countries. Holland, Scandinavia, Germany, US, South Africa and Australia were among the countries with which English and Welsh prisons were unfavourably compared. Differences from Scotland and Northern Ireland were also referred to. It was said that in Scotland prisoners are now allowed to choose the prison to which they are sent.

VII: Summary and Conclusion

VII.1. This chapter has described fifty-four separate topics, grouped under six major themes, raised by prisoners from non-target establishments in their responses to Lord Justice Woolf's consultation after the riots of April 1990. It is based on letters from 603 men and four women writing from a wide variety of prisons.

VII.2. Inevitably in this grouped analysis, much has been lost of the freshness, eloquence and cogency of many individual responses, all of which were read separately by the Inquiry team. But something has also been gained. The grouped analysis allows us to see how common concerns expressed in individual letters are to responses from across the system.

Chapter Three

Letters from Prison Staff

1. So far this report has summarised the results of Lord Justice Woolf's invitation to the inmates of British prisons to help his Inquiry. It will now turn to the views of prison staff.

2. Staff were consulted by Lord Justice Woolf in the same way as inmates. Personally addressed letters were sent to all staff known to have been in target establishments at the time of the disturbances and a letter inviting responses from all other staff was copied and distributed (often through being placed on a notice-board) through the Governors of establishments. In total 350 letters from prison service staff were received in response to this invitation; 202 from staff in the target establishments, where riots or disturbances had occurred which were the subject of special study by the Inquiry, and 148 from staff elsewhere in the system.

3. The following table shows the origin of the 202 letters from target establishments and the percentage of staff from those establishments who responded. (Note that letters were sent to all staff; uniformed grades, non-uniformed grades and specialists. Figures for total number of staff in post at the relevant establishments were provided by Prison Department):-

Establishment	No.responses	No.staff	% response rate
Manchester	102	550	18%
Glen Parva	12	347	3%
Dartmoor	30	136	22%
Bristol	29	270	11%
Cardiff	19	219	8%
Pucklechurch	10	55	18%

At around 20% the response rate from Dartmoor, Manchester and Pucklechurch was impressive. It means that about one in five of the staff of the establishments at the time of the riot wrote personally to Lord Justice Woolf.

4. Considering the responses as a whole, they came from all types of establishment:-

        212 from Local Prisons or Adult Remand Centres;
        54 from Dispersal or Category B Training Prisons;
        35 from Young Offender establishments including remands;
        29 from Category C Training Prisons;
        5 from Category D Training Prisons;
        5 from Prison Service Headquarters;
        4 from Grendon;
        3 from Female establishments;
        2 from Prison Service College;
        1 from establishment not stated.

The heavy weighting towards local prisons was to be expected given the central focus of the Inquiry.

5. As with inmate letters, responses came in over a period of time. All letters

received were read carefully as they arrived by Lord Justice Woolf and his team. Many letters from target establishments were long, detailed and amounted to continuous personal logs of the respondent's experience in the disturbances or riots. These accounts were used at Part I of the Inquiry and have entered into its report. The formal analysis reported here, like the analysis of inmate letters reported in previous chapters, concentrates on general judgements made by prison staff, omitting detailed accounts of the course of events during the disturbances themselves.

6.   Inspection of the letters showed that the topics raised could be classified under three main themes:-

Theme I   – Causes of the riots and other disturbances;
Theme II – Criticisms of the management of the disturbances;
Theme III – Comments on the prevention of future disturbances.

All letters were analysed and computer coded and the following report is based on that analysis. Since there were fewer letters from staff than from inmates, it was possible to analyse responses both from target and non-target establishments together using the same coding-frame (ie grouping of themes and topics). Results are presented side by side below though it is made clear from which type of establishment responses came.

Theme I: Causes of the Riots and Disturbances

I.1.   Of the total 350 letters received, 242 addressed the question of causes. The following table gives the frequency of mentions of various causes across the whole set of letters from target and non-target establishments:-

Staff shortages	122 responses
Poor prison conditions	91 responses
Media coverage	61 responses
Transfers in	53 responses
Lack of discipline	51 responses
Lack of leadership	39 responses
Failure to take precautions	28 responses
Appeasement of inmates	26 responses
Prisoner mix	23 responses
Access to roof	22 responses
Locals too big	10 responses
Poor staff-inmate relationships	9 responses
Poor rehabilitation	9 responses
Parole process frustration	2 responses.

No other cause was mentioned in more than one letter. The following paragraphs discuss, with examples, responses under each code:-

i) Staff Shortages   I.2.   This was the most common response as to causes, given in 46 letters from non-target establishments and 76 from target establishments. Of these 76 responses, 53 came from Strangeways, 10 from Dartmoor, 5 from Cardiff, 3 each from Glen Parva and Bristol and 2 from Pucklechurch.

The largest group of letters offering this reason for the riot hence came from Strangeways. The following are some typical comments:-

"Staffing levels have been a constant thorn in our side, particularly since the advent of Fresh Start.....less staff available to handle the same numbers."
(Officer)

"Without a doubt one of the main factors in the riot at Strangeways was that inmates took advantage of reduced staffing levels." (Principal Officer)

"Reduction of staff to keep a low profile....lack of staff on duty even when knowledge of particular incident going to take place." (Senior Officer)

"Wrong priority was given to manning the prison on weekdays.... weekends appeared only to have been considered as a sort of aside." (Senior Officer)

"One crucial factor was the lack of staff at weekends. Some weekends there was not enough staff to lock up inmates from exercise or films. It was a frequent joke among inmates who'd say 'Ring the alarm bell boss and I'll bet you won't get two staff to respond'."
(Officer)

The same point is made again and again, sometimes with supporting figures, sometimes without.

I.3.   But it was not only Strangeways staff who criticised staffing levels. Responses from elsewhere are exemplified by the following letter from a Principal Officer at a small local prison in the south of England:-

"I feel that a local prison is never fully understood by the Prison Boards and Regional Offices. This one is extremely busy and runs at full stretch the whole time.....I thought that Fresh Start would be the making of the Prison Service as staff would be more relaxed with extra time off. For too long far too much overtime had been worked and a great deal of wastage occurred in every department. However the opposite now applies and staff shortages are getting desperate....this is prior to the summer leave period starting so the situation will only get worse. Add to this the daily cancelled productions, Crown Courts unmanned and basic searching tasks undone, and it becomes obvious that there is insufficient staff adequately to cover the establishment.....These problems are everywhere in locals." (Principal Officer)

ii) Prison Conditions   I.4.   This was the second most commonly quoted cause of riots and disturbances. It was mentioned in 91 staff letters; 47 of them from non-target establishments. At the target establishments, prison conditions were quoted as an underlying cause of riot by 29 staff from Strangeways, 8 from Dartmoor, 5 from Cardiff and one each from Bristol and Pucklechurch. The most frequently specified poor conditions were overcrowding, too much time in cell and poor sanitation. The following quotations are from Strangeways staff:-

"What caused the riot? Overcrowding. There are many iterations from inmates that they felt brutalised. This is true for staff also."
(Hospital Officer)

"There is a constant overload in such vital areas as catering, visiting arrangements, the maintenance of buildings and services. Too many inmates place too great a strain on all parts of prison routine.....The sheer size of the living-units at Strangeways is not on a human scale. When large-scale movement of inmates is underway the wing resembles a giant ant-hill.....The problem of sanitation is aggravated in the over-crowded prison. Manchester was engaged in a modest programme of integral sanitation in cells...... it was all too slow."
(Governor 4)

"Unsanitary conditions and overcrowding do not contribute to a calm and settled environment."
(Officer)

"There had been a lack of clean and sufficient supplies of prisoners uniforms over a period of some months ie no socks, underwear, shoes etc."
(Acting Senior Officer)

"Friction was caused by inmates not being able to get clean kit on bathing days."
(Officer)

"Stew had become a very regular meal much to the annoyance of inmates."
(Officer)

I.5. Prison conditions were also mentioned frequently in letters from staff in non-target establishments. The following is a typical example:-

> "One of the most degrading aspects of inmate incarceration is the one of slopping out. Most Victorian prisons have this procedure and it can only be removed by having in cell sanitation and single cell accommodation."
> (Principal Officer)

Several letters mentioned food problems as causing serious prisoner dissatisfaction. The following comment is perhaps particularly interesting:-

> "In this local prison we have a proportion of long term inmates who have been sent here from dispersal and training prisons for various reasons.... These prisoners are able to make comparisons between the food supplied in dispersal and training prisons and that supplied in local prisons and I have had complaints about the quantity of food we are able to supply from the local prison dietary scale. If food complaints played a part at Manchester, maybe the difference in dietary scales at different establishments could have been a factor...Catering Officers at locals should be given the opportunity to work from the same dietary scale as the dispersal prisons."
> (Catering Officer)

I.6. A thoughtful letter from a senior officer at a Young Offender Institution lists a series of points which he says "may appear trivial" but "because they concern the basics of life give an indication of the frustration under which staff and inmates live". They include:-

> "Insufficient cleaning equipment such as mops, brushes, cleaning agents. In a lot of cases mops are supplied with incompatible handles which makes them useless.......Tissue issue entitlement is three tissues per man per day which equals ninety tissues per month. The monthly issue is one box of tissues with ten tissues removed (contents 100 tissues, allowance 90). This creates work for staff and can be humiliating for the inmate.......The toilet paper issue is of very poor quality. In fact it can only be classified as inhuman. The issue of semi-soft toilet paper should be considered.....The razor blade issue if inadequate. Inmates are expected to use the same razor for seven days."
> (Senior Officer)

This officer considers that such trivial but consistent problems build up frustration which can reach serious levels.

iii) Media Coverage

I.7. This was the third most frequently quoted cause of the April riots and disturbances. It was mentioned in letters from all the target establishments and in some from non-target establishments in the following numbers: 17 responses from Dartmoor, 11 from Bristol, 9 from Cardiff, 7 from Manchester, Strangeways, 6 from Pucklechurch, 4 from Glen Parva, and 7 from non-target establishments. The Manchester letters mentioned the effect of continuous media coverage in dragging out the riot.

I.8. Dartmoor staff were those who most commonly mentioned the "copycat" effect. The following letters from Dartmoor staff exemplify this view:-

> "After the riot had occurred at Strangeways the inmates at Dartmoor prison followed all news of it avidly, especially watching Channel 4 news on TV at 7 pm, which they could watch on evening association. When they saw any inmates posturing on Strangeways roofs they would cheer and when they saw either police or prison officers they booed (I was on evening duty both Monday and Thursday when this occurred)."
> (Prison Officer)

> "It seems evident to me that both the disturbances at Dartmoor and Pucklechurch were copycat occurrences largely encouraged by the prolonged press and media coverage of HMP Strangeways."
> (Governor 5)

I.9.   However at least one Dartmoor respondent also observed:-

"To neatly package the Dartmoor riot as a copycat incident would in my opinion be a grave error."
(Principal Officer)

and another Dartmoor respondent wrote:-

"It is difficult to isolate the cause of the riot at Dartmoor from disturbances happening elsewhere in the service, most notably at Manchester......but they should also be put into the context of other riots and revolutions such as those in the Eastern Block and the London poll tax riot the night before the Strangeways riot....A large percentage of prisoners see themselves as either unjustly imprisoned or overly oppressed while in prison."
(Principal Officer)

By no means all of those who saw the media as a contributory cause to the riots, saw it as the main or only cause.

iv) "Transfers In"   I.10.   53 respondents named "transfers in" to a prison of troublesome inmates from elsewhere as a cause of riot. The majority of these responses came from staff at Manchester Strangeways who accounted for 37 of the 53 letters naming this cause. 11 letters from Bristol named the same factor. It was mentioned by three respondents from Cardiff, one each from Pucklechurch and Glen Parva but in no responses from Dartmoor or from the non-target establishments.

I.11.   The following are examples of responses from Manchester on this topic:-

"I have spent 12 years at this prison and I believe one of the major contributory factors which caused the disturbance was the coming together of like-minded inmates who as individuals are troublesome types, who collectively became a dangerous element.....The inmates I refer to as the dangerous element are those who are here under DPSG (Dispersal Prison Steering Group). These inmates are here as a result of disruptive behaviour at their previous prisons and an overcrowded local prison with few facilities is a heaven sent opportunity for them to manipulate the least bit of discontent amongst the population."
(Principal Officer)

"The prison in general had numerous trouble-makers who had been sent from other prisons, often the only entry on their record being suspected of being involved in or something or not suitable for such and such. They would be returned to us. It seems that Governors of establishments that we allocated to, only wanted model prisoners."
(Officer)

"Disruptive prisoners from many other establishments had been taken in."
(Senior Officer)

"Manchester was becoming a dumping ground for problem prisoners."
(Senior Officer)

v) Lack of Discipline   I.12.   This heading includes responses from staff which suggested that the root of the problem was a weakening of prison discipline. There were 53 responses of this sort, the majority of them from Strangeways. (27 from Manchester Strangeways, 15 from non-target establishments, 3 from Cardiff, 3 from Dartmoor, 2 from Bristol, 1 from Pucklechurch and none from Glen Parva).

I.13.   The following are some responses from Manchester:-

"As to what caused the disturbance firstly the overall softness of the prison regime. Inmates are given too much freedom, too much of their own way. To me personally it is heartbreaking to see how well they are treated, all the very best of facilities available, when ordinary hard-working people ie old age pensioners, are finding it hard to manage on their pension."
(Officer Instructor)

"Discipline in prisons had been eroded since Fresh Start. When inmates

were placed on punishment it did not act as a deterrent to others with some wanting to stay on the block because of separate cells."
(Officer)

"There's been a scaling down of discipline against prisoners over a number of years......running of the prison too easy."
(Senior Officer)

"Liberal regimes in local prisons don't seem to work due to the many categories of prisoners." *too many cates??*
(Officer)

"A liberal and relaxed regime has been operating in the prison since the introduction of Fresh Start. Due to this liberal regime inmates virtually had a run of the prison enabling them to wander around the prison unchecked. This freedom gave the disruptive element the opportunity to organise trouble."
(Officer)

"For the last few years regime improvement has been the war-cry of the Prison Service but this has not been matched by a firm commitment to maintain discipline. Powers of punishment have been eroded to the extent that some prison staff feel it is a waste of time instituting disciplinary proceedings....It is a disgrace that criminals are better protected in our society than our elderly and sick......The prison service should be run by people who know prisons not by people with degrees in sociology."
(Senior Officer)

Responses from other prisons concerning lack of discipline took much the same tone although they occurred less frequently.

vi) Lack of Leadership in Establishments

I.14.   This response was more common in responses from non-target than target establishments. 24 of the 148 responses from non-target establishments mentioned this factor but it was only mentioned by 9 respondents from Manchester, 3 from Cardiff, 3 from Dartmoor and by none from Bristol, Pucklechurch or Glen Parva.

I.15.   It is often connected in responses both with criticisms of the 'Fresh Start' initiative and with criticisms of staff shortages. Again and again the point is made that management structures within establishments are not working properly; sometimes this is thought to be because of Fresh Start systems, sometimes because of the abolition of the Chief Officer grade, sometimes because of poor management structures or shortage of staff. Whatever the reason given for the problem there is agreement that personnel management and/or leadership within establishments is weak. The following comments are representative:-

"Among the current problems creating tension are fragmented management structure....Fresh Start I was implemented overnight changing centrally controlled syste ms with Governors and Chief Officers managing the system through the Heads of Department giving continuity. Fresh Start introduced group working which proved to be a disaster. These groups are like headless chickens, normally managed by group manager at rank Principal Officer. These Principal Officers are not qualified to manage at this level. The prospects of promotion from Principal Officer to Governor 5 is very slim. This does not give the Principal Officer the incentive to produce good results."
(Industrial Manager. HPTO)

"The prison service is padding out its senior management structure and has lost the hands on approach to running a business."
(Principal Officer)

"When we had the Chief Officer there was a figure head, someone we could go to when troubles arose, he made on the spot decisions, liaised with the Governor. He was respected. A large proportion of Governor grades do not hold that respect."

(Officer Instructor)

"We need a reorganisation of the line management structure. There are too many Governors, therefore confusion about ultimate responsibilities etc. Chiefs should replace Governor 5 grades for the benefit of officers."
(Principal Officer)

I.16. The dissatisfaction felt with management often expresses itself as a yearning for the old Chief Officer grade. The Chief Officer is remembered with regret, in that he is felt to have provided more clear and acceptable leadership within the establishment than many believe they now receive.

I.17. The following bitter comment from an education officer at a non-target establishment, about to retire, sums up the feelings of many:-

"The present system ensures that there is no continuity of staff. Continuity is probably the most important single factor in ensuring regime stability. It seems to occupy most of the senior uniformed staff in office admin of time sheets and rotas, when they should be involve in inmate management. It seems to have introduced management systems which allow senior staff to avoid responsibility and has encouraged an attitude by senior management that makes too many concessions to inmates......inevitable consequence of loss of morale amongst uniformed staff who feel totally unsupported. So who cares?"
(Education Officer)

vii) Failure to Take Precautions

I.18. The frequency of this response in the entire set of proposed causes for the disturbances was almost entirely due to the frequency with which it was mentioned as a cause of riot by respondents from Strangeways, Manchester. In all 28 respondents mentioned failure to take precautions as a cause of riot and of these 21 came from Manchester, 4 from Dartmoor, 2 from Cardiff, one from Pucklechurch and none from Bristol, Glen Parva, or non-target establishments.

I.19. Of the 21 Manchester respondents naming this factor, all were in uniformed grades. The following is a typical comment:-

"Staff warnings of a major display of indiscipline were ignored or not taken seriously."
(Senior Officer)

The whole question of the response to warnings at Manchester was dealt with thoroughly at the Part I hearings of the Inquiry and is discussed in the main body of the Inquiry report. Staff comments and information were useful in this exercise and will not be reported on further here.

viii) Appeasement of Inmates

I.20. This response is connected with, but slightly different from that concerning lack of discipline. It includes suggestions that there had been insufficient punishment of previous rioters. Ten respondents from Strangeways named this factor as did 12 respondents from non-target establishments and three from Dartmoor. It was not mentioned by respondents from Bristol, Cardiff, Pucklechurch or Glen Parva. Typical comments from Manchester are as follows:-

"The management tried to have a liberal regime with the wrong type of inmate. Over the last few years a lot of rules and regulations were relaxed to appease inmates, ie remand prisoners being allowed to wear own clothes regardless of state ie training shoes track suits. At one time they had to be smart and have a jacket and proper shoes..... Inmates were allowed association and had videos on their own wing and allowed to wear basically what they liked. The more they were given the more they demanded."
(Officer)

"The lenient punishments given to inmates who misbehave means these awards do not act as a deterrent and staff feel it is not worthwhile placing an inmate on report."
(Officer)

507

The following response is from a non-target establishment:-

> "Take positive and immediate action....punish transgressors adequately. This sounds very simple but prisoners understand this. Not one prisoner was charged after the 1983 riots at Albany and this saps staff morale and encourages transgressors."
> (Senior Officer)

ix) Prisoner Mix

I.21. This suggested cause of riot was particularly frequently presented by respondents from Manchester, Strangeways. 14 of the 23 responses naming this factor came from Manchester, 8 from non-target establishments and one from Bristol. There were no such responses from Cardiff, Dartmoor, Pucklechurch or Glen Parva. There is some similarity to response (iv) above on "transfers in". It is the over-all nature of the prison population which is here complained of. Sometimes it is blamed on a failure to transfer out:-

> "Inmates at Manchester wait too long for transfers to prison of allocation."
> (Officer)

Other respondents commented that there were too many Category A prisoners in Manchester. The following response is typical of many:-

> "The factors involved included long-term and short-term prisoners conforming under the same regime; long-term prisoners staying a considerable time at Manchester before dispersal; not enough outlets for Category B prisoners to Category B prisons. Prisoners being returned to Manchester unsuitable for training prisons."
> (Principal Officer)

x) Access to Scaffolding

I.22. This was mentioned by 22 respondents, all from Manchester, Strangeways. All respondents were members of uniformed grades and what they had in mind was the scaffolding put up in Strangeways for purposes of refurbishment. The question of the possible role of the scaffolding in the Manchester disturbances was dealt with thoroughly at the Part I public hearings and is discussed in the Inquiry Part I report, so will not be commented on further here.

xi) Locals too Big

I.23. This factor was mentioned by ten respondents, five from non-target establishments, three from Manchester and one each from Dartmoor and Pucklechurch. The following comments are from Manchester:-

> "The age of the large Victorian prison is past..... The prison needs dividing into smaller units with self-contained facilities, feeding points, exercise yards, churches etc."
> (Officer)

Some respondents from non-target establishments also spoke of the need for smaller more manageable units in prisons and stated they felt the current size of many locals to be too large for good management.

xii) Poor Staff-inmate Relationships

I.24. Six respondents from non-target establishments named this as a contributory cause of riots and it was also mentioned by one respondent from Strangeways, one from Cardiff and one from Glen Parva:-

> "Prisoners need to be treated like human beings. Consult psychologists."
> (Prison Officer)

> "There's no doubt that some staff do not know how to relate to prisoners and can't be bothered to find out. So you just get a sort of low-level bullying manner. It is not an easy job and many staff are very good. But you can get bad traditions in particular establishments or parts of establishments."
> (Hospital Officer)

> "If morale is low then relationships suffer. Surely relationships must be the most important factor in maintaining calm in our prisons."
> (Governor 5)

xiii) Poor Rehabilitation

I.25. This was an infrequent comment and could possibly have been included under the topic of prison conditions; but a few respondents went out of their way to say that the lack of opportunity for a prisoner to improve himself or to learn anything of use to him after release set up frustrations which contributed to riot. Eight of the nine responses naming this factor came from non-target establishments and only one from a target establishment (Bristol). Some letters point to the poor effect on staff morale of a lack of belief in the possibility of rehabilitation. The following comment is typical:-

> "Many inmates deserve a second chance. Prison is not a punishment but a means towards rehabilitation. The Prison Service should be fighting their paymasters to provide and implement the changes that are required to provide such a system.....Employment of inmates is often regarded as a joke within the service. There is very little meaningful work on offer and there is also very little constructive training. Surely it is possible to find contracts financially viable to the Prison Service Industries and which are also beneficial to inmates in terms of real training?"
> (Officer)

xiv) Frustration with the Parole Process

I.26. This response was mentioned by two respondents only both from non-target establishments. Both pointed out that delays and frustrations in parole can create uncertainty, make prisoners hard to manage and are a possible contributory cause of riot.

Causes of the Riots and Disturbances: Summary

I.27. Fourteen separate identifiable possible causes of the riots and disturbances which were named by staff have been described and exemplified above. No other responses were mentioned more than once. Respondents comments on the causes of riot taken as a whole contain a great variety of emphases. Some staff concentrate on failures in discipline or management within the prison; others comment more on poor conditions for prisoners and the failure to offer any positive regimes. All who mention staff matters agree that there is a shortage of staff, many criticise line management.

I.28. It is impossible to read these judgements of staff as to the underlying causes of riots without being impressed both by the dissatisfaction of the majority of those who replied but also by their commitment and loyalty to the Prison Service.

I.29. It could be argued that the very circumstances of Lord Justice Woolf's letter to staff encouraged a negative reply; the invitation was asking them to comment on some of the worst riots in British prison history. Again it could be argued that only a minority of staff replied; possibly these were the malcontents. But the response rate (as that of inmates) was in fact quite high by the standards of "direct mail". Most responses were long, thoughtful and deeply felt.

Theme II: Criticisms of the Management of the Disturbances

II.1. In addition to requesting views as to the causes of riot, Lord Justice Woolf's letters requested staff views as to the management of riots and disturbances.

II.2. 77 of the 350 letters received contained criticisms of the way the riots or disturbances which occurred in April 1990 were managed. The following was the order of frequency of the various complaints made in these 77 letters:-

Delay or slowness in intervention	49 responses
Lack of C&R Equipment	31 responses
Poor communication between ranks	31 responses
Negotiation used inappropriately	14 responses
Poor communication with staff families	3 responses.

In so far as comments or criticism dealt with the detailed course of events in any one particular establishment, the evidence of the staff was considered at Part I hearings and is discussed in Part I of the Inquiry report. However since the factors mentioned may be seen to have general as well as specific applicability, a few brief notes are given below of the size and nature of responses in each category.

i) Delay in Intervention

II.3.   The great majority of the 49 responses concerning delay or slowness in intervention came from Manchester staff. No fewer than 37 letters from Manchester criticised the delay in mounting an assault. Typical of other responses were the following:–

> "The riot could have been stopped if the go-ahead had been given. Undoubtedly there would have been injuries but there would still be a working prison establishment at Manchester."

> (Prison Officer)

> "All I have to say is we took the prison back on the 25th day of the siege. The same result could have been achieved if we had been allowed to go in on the third day."

> (Officer)

II.4.   Four letters from Dartmoor staff also felt intervention in the riot had been too delayed, as did two letters from Glen Parva. The other nine letters making this criticism came from staff at 'non-target' establishments.

ii) Lack of C&R Equipment

II.5.   Of the 31 letters received which criticised a lack of C&R training, equipment or protective clothing, 19 were from Manchester, one each from Pucklechurch, Dartmoor and Bristol and nine from non-target establishments.

iii) Poor Communication between Ranks

II.6.   Of the 31 letters received which criticised weaknesses in the chain of command, in particular poor communications, 17 were from Manchester, two each from Dartmoor and Glen Parva and one each from Pucklechurch and Bristol. The remaining eight letters were from non-target establishments.

iv) Negotiations used Inappropriately

II.7.   Of the 14 letters received which criticised an inappropriate use of negotiations, 11 were from Manchester, one each from Glen Parva and Cardiff and the last from a non-target establishment.

v) Poor Communications with Family

II.8.   Only three letters were received which criticised poor communications during the riots with the families of staff and all three were from Manchester.

Management of the Disturbances: Summary

II.9.   The mass of criticism received from prison staff as to the management of the riots thus centred on the management of the riot at Strangeways, Manchester. The management of the riot is considered in detail in the report on Part I of the Inquiry. However the responses in this set of letters are of some interest in giving a quantitative picture of the factors staff believe to be important in riot management.

Theme III: The Prevention of Future Disturbances

III.1.   As well as being asked for views on the causes and management of the riots, staff were asked for their views as to the best means of preventing future disturbances. Of the 350 respondents from target and non-target establishments, 236 made some suggestion to prevent riots in the future and 114 did not address this question. Many of those who replied gave more than one suggestion. Responses will be described in order of frequency but since suggestions for the future were mostly given quite briefly, and in some cases reflect views already described as to the causes of riot, quotations will not be used to illustrate them.

510

i) Ensure There Are Enough Staff on Duty

III.2.   This was the most common suggestion for preventing trouble in the future, made by 103 of the 236 respondents who made some recommendation.

ii) Improve Conditions for Prisoners

III.3.   There were 86 separate responses in this category. Many who mentioned the improvement of conditions made more than one specific suggestion so the number in the following table (listing frequency of specific suggestions) adds to more than 86:–

Increase availability of work	58 responses
Reduce overcrowding	47 responses
Stop slopping out	45 responses
Provide rehabilitation	24 responses
Improve relationships	20 responses
Better food	13 responses
Better visits	11 responses
Better mail/phone access	3 responses
TV in cell	3 responses

The great salience given by staff to the availability of work is of interest.

iii) Ensure Prompt Use of Force

III.4.   41 of the 236 respondents suggesting ways of preventing trouble in the future listed this factor. 35 of these 41 responses particularly stressed the time element; the need for an instant use of force to regain areas where trouble had taken place. Many of these responses came from Manchester staff. 15 of the 41 responses recommended the use of different weapons such as CS gas, baton rounds, rubber bullets, stun grenades or water cannon.

iv) Better Equipment and Training

III.5.   40 of the 136 respondents making recommendations for the future pointed to the need for better C&R training and/or equipment. Training was mentioned by 26 of these respondents; equipment by 22.

v) Miscellaneous

III.6.   A range of other suggestions were made. 21 respondents pointed to the need to be able to isolate particular areas either through better management of keys or some other method. 16 mentioned the need to secure roofs. 43 said discipline within prisons should be stronger. 26 asked for the re-introduction of the Chief Officer. 28 thought that trouble makers should be more effectively segregated. 17 suggested there should be less reliance on custody; 12 that the parole procedures should be made less stressful. 19 asked for censorship of media coverage of riots. 12 thought Governors should be given more local control of their prisons, less oversight by Headquarters. 11 felt that in future Rule 43A prisoners should be held separately. Seven recommended improved grievance procedures. Two wished to see escort services to court privatised and three wanted the restoration of the death penalty. No other solutions were advanced by more than two respondents.

IV: Letters from Staff: Conclusion and Summary

IV.1.   This chapter has presented an analysis of the 350 letters from the staff of prisons received by Lord Justice Woolf before 1 August in response to his invitation to the staffs of target and non-target establishments to write to him. The analysis has covered the views of prison staff as to the causes, management and prevention of riots and disturbances.

IV.2.   Staff shortages and poor prison conditions were seen as pre-eminent causes of riot and the provision of adequate staff numbers and the improvement of conditions means of riot prevention. In addition a host of detailed points were made. Many staff (although a minority of all responding) thought discipline in prisons too slack. Almost all were critical of management and personnel practices.

IV.3.   A summary such as this cannot do full justice to the many long and thoughtful letters received from staff, as from inmates. All letters were read carefully and individually by Lord Justice Woolf and his team and entered into the thinking of the Inquiry. If this analysis adds anything it is an over-all summary of the balance of responses received.

Lord Justice Woolf's Inquiry into Prison Disturbances

Preliminary Public Hearing on Monday 14th May 1990

Statement by Lord Justice Woolf

1.   As you know, I have been appointed by the Home Secretary to conduct an Inquiry into prison disturbances. My terms of reference require me to enquire into the events leading up to the serious disturbances in Her Majesty's Prison, Manchester, which began on 1st April 1990 and the action taken to bring it to a conclusion, having regard also to the serious disturbances which occurred shortly thereafter in other prison establishments in England and Wales.

2.   When announcing my appointment in the House of Commons, the Home Secretary, on 5th April, 1990, made it clear that I was to have considerable discretion as to the manner in which I interpreted my terms of reference.

3.   At the outset, I should like to express my sympathy for those people and their families who have innocently suffered from these disturbances.

4.   The purpose of today's preliminary public hearing is threefold:

  First of all, to give guidance, so far as this is possible at this stage, as to the scope of the Inquiry so that those who are considering making written representations or giving evidence to the Inquiry will be in a better position to identify the issues which are relevant.

  Secondly, to indicate the character of and the procedure I propose to adopt at the Inquiry and the preliminary timetable, to which I will seek to adhere.

  Thirdly, to deal with the questions of representation of parties at the Inquiry and costs.

5.   I have already received considerable assistance from a number of interested parties, who I have consulted, and I have visited a number of prisons, including those at which the most serious disturbances occurred. I am also aware of the comments which have been made in the media as to the scope of my Inquiry. As a result, I am satisfied that a purely factual investigation of events during the disturbances at different prisons is not alone what is required. In my judgement, it is necessary, in order to fulfil my terms of reference, for me to conduct, not only an Inquiry into the immediate causes and the events during the disturbances, but also to examine, in depth, the underlying causes of those disturbances so I will be in a position at the end of my Inquiry to make, what I hope, will be sensible, reasonable and practical recommendations which will improve our prison system and help to reduce the risk of such disturbances occurring in the future.

6.   For this purpose, it will be necessary for me, not only to examine the situation in prisons where disturbances occurred, but also prisons where disturbances have not occurred, since they may provide lessons for the future as important as those where disturbances did occur.

7.   This is a substantial task, and I have given careful consideration as to how it

can be carried out in a way that will not only achieve the objects which I have identified, but will enable my Inquiry to be conducted expeditiously, as it is clearly important that the results of my Inquiry should be known as soon as possible.

8. With these objectives in mind, in addition to continuing a broad-ranging consultative process and continuing to visit penal establishments in this country and abroad, I propose to conduct the formal part of the Inquiry, in public, in two stages:

> the first stage will be confined to ascertaining the relevant factual events during six serious disturbances during April. Those disturbances occurred, in addition to Strangeways, at Bristol, Cardiff, Dartmoor, Glen Parva and Pucklechurch. Those establishments happen, in themselves, to provide a fairly wide spectrum of different categories of prison establishments;

> the second stage will deal with the broad ranging issues and underlying causes to which I referred earlier.

9. Fortunately, to assist me to conduct the Inquiry, the Home Secretary has agreed to provide me with considerable assistance. First of all, he has provided me with three Assessors, who are particularly well qualified to give me the help I need and from whom I have already received valuable advice. They are: Mr Gordon Lakes CB MC, who is sitting closest to me on the right, a former prison governor and former Deputy Director General of the Prison Service, who is regularly consulted by international bodies as to penal matters.

10. The second is Professor Rod Morgan of Bristol University, who is sitting to my right at the end of the row, who is a distinguished academic authority on penal matters.

11. The third assessors is Mrs Mary Tuck CBE, who, until recently, was head of the Home Office Research and Planning Unit and who is particularly suited to give me advice as to how to conduct the investigations which are necessary for the in-depth examination to which I have already made reference. Mrs Tuck sits one away from me to my right.

12. In addition, as has recently been announced, the Home Secretary, at my request, has invited His Honour, Judge Tumim, to join the Inquiry after the first stage has been completed. As is well known, as Her Majesty's Chief Inspector of Prisons, Judge Tumim has already played a significant contribution to improving our prison system. Her Majesty's Chief Inspector of Prisons has a statutory duty to enquire into our prisons and if he had not helpfully agreed to accept the Home Secretary's invitation, not only would I be deprived in respect of the second stage of the Inquiry of the benefit of his wisdom and experience, there also could have been a regrettable duplication of effort. In consequence of his appointment, there will be available to my Inquiry, the results of the research which has been and is being conducted by the Independent Inspectorate of Prisons. However, the fact that Judge Tumim is joining me for the second stage will not affect the scope of, or my approach to, the Inquiry. I have had an opportunity of discussing fully with Judge Tumim how I propose to conduct the Inquiry and he is in full agreement with the course which I propose.

13. Three members of the bar have already been instructed by the Treasury Solicitor to act as Counsel to the Inquiry. They are: David Latham QC, Mr Anthony Morris and Mr David Evans, who are sitting to my right. Together with the Treasury Solicitor, they will have the task of preparing and presenting the evidence for the Inquiry. In accordance with the now well established tradition, their role will be one of strict impartiality. In performing their role, I am pleased to be able to say they are receiving, and I am sure will continue to receive, the co-operation of the Chief Constables of the Police Forces who are responsible for investigating the criminal aspects of the disturbances. While this Inquiry will not seek to determine the criminal responsibility of an individual, or individuals, arising out of the disturbances, as the interests of the police and this Inquiry are

quite distinct, the co-operation to which I referred is extremely valuable to this Inquiry and I am very grateful for it.

14. Notwithstanding the considerable assistance to which I have already referred, I was concerned about a further difficulty in conducting this Inquiry which arises out of the fact that prisons are closed institutions to which the public cannot have unrestricted access. In many enquiries, it is possible for interested parties to investigate the facts for themselves. This is not so easy in the case of the present Inquiry and, therefore, in consultation with my Advisors, I decided to set up a small Inquiry team which, in addition to my Assessors, will consist of other members having the necessary experience, independently, to examine the facts for themselves and independently examine and check the Department's version of events. The report which the teams prepare will be made available in response to reasonable requests.

15. For their benefit and for the benefit of interested parties, I have drawn up a guide which indicates a list of some of the matters which the Inquiry may have to examine as part of the first stage of the Inquiry. The list does not purport to be exhaustive and can be extended as necessary. Copies of that list are also available attached to the statement which I am now making. I do, however, hope that the list, together with the reports of the teams will enable the background facts relating to many issues to be agreed. Copies of the guide are available and it deals with the possible issues under three heads: the position at a prison during the three months immediately preceding the incident, the facts of the incident and its aftermath.

16. In addition, I have tried to communicate with each member of the prison staff and each prisoner who was at each of the six prisons where the serious disturbances occurred. Because the staff and prisoners at some of the establishments where disturbances occurred have been dispersed – this is particularly true of Strangeways – ensuring that the letters were delivered to the intended recipient was made more difficult. I have also arranged for the contents of a more general letter, from myself, to be brought to the attention of other members of the Prison Service and other prisoners so they can also make any representations to the Inquiry which they wish. Copies of the letter to specific members, the staff and prisoners and the more general letters to staff and prisoners are also available. When those letters are read, it will be observed that I have indicated that any response to those letters will not be used for any purpose other than the purposes of my Inquiry without an order of a Court. I have not offered any immunity in respect of criminal proceedings. However, recipients are told that the response will not be used without his consent in any disciplinary proceedings, unless in the case of a member of prison staff the response shows that he has been guilty of serious misconduct, so as to make it clear that he, or she, is unsuitable to remain in the Prison Service. It is right that here I should acknowledge the very considerable support which the Inquiry has had from the Prison Service, who gave the Inquiry all the help which is needed in distributing the letters and making their contents known.

17. Finally, I should refer to the administrative support team with which I have been provided, ably led by the Secretary to the Inquiry, John Lyon, who sits to my left. They have cheerfully been working extremely long hours to very good effect and I expect they will have to continue working very long hours, I hope equally cheerfully.

18. It is proposed that stage 1 of the formal Inquiry will commence at a suitable venue in the Manchester area, if possible on Monday 11th June; that we will then proceed to take evidence for three weeks dealing with the Strangeways disturbance. There will then, if we run to time, be a week in which the Manchester evidence can be digested and the Inquiry will re-open in Bristol on 9th July and will then continue for two weeks to hear evidence relating to the serious disturbances which occurred at the named establishments in Wales and the West Country. After those two weeks, the Inquiry will move to London where the remaining evidence will be heard, including evidence relating to the

disturbance at Glen Parva. I would like to conclude the hearing of evidence for stage 1 by 3rd August. However, if this proves impossible, after a suitable break, the hearing of evidence will continue in London, so the taking of evidence can be finally concluded, so far as stage 1 is concerned, in September.

19. In the normal way, a day's hearing for stage 1 will commence at 10.00 am and finish at 5.00 pm. If I am satisfied the parties need Friday for preparing their evidence for the following week, I would be prepared not to sit on Friday. If, initially, I agree not to sit on Friday, I would reconsider the position if we are not making the required progress, and that is both a threat and a warning. Any application on this point should be made to me at the end of today's hearing or before 11th June to the Treasury Solicitor.

20. Although I will take into account all written representations which I receive, and I stress that the accumulative effect can be very important, it will not be sensible to call as witnesses all those who can give relevant evidence. It would be, for example, pointless to call a witness who can merely repeat the evidence of another witness where the evidence already given is not in dispute. The advantage of having Counsel to the Inquiry is that they can help to ensure that only the necessary evidence will be given orally before me.

21. All witnesses who give oral evidence are to be regarded as being called on my behalf in order to elicit the facts, and not as called by any particular party. For the most part, witnesses will be called and examined by Counsel to the Inquiry. No witness shall be called to give evidence unless he or she has first provided a written statement. Once a witness has been examined, there will be an opportunity for cross-examination, but I would make clear that cross-examination will be subject to such limits as I think is necessary to impose in the interests of fairness and proper expedition.

22. If and when any substantial allegation is to be made against a person or body at the Inquiry, that person or body should be informed of the allegation by the Treasury Solicitor. The substance of the evidence supporting the allegation should be given in good time to the Treasury Solicitor. If the allegation is to be pursued at the Inquiry, the substance of the allegation will be given to that person or body by the Treasury Solicitor so that they have an opportunity to deal with it by cross-examination or by evidence. Counsel to the Inquiry will be responsible for seeing that this aspect of the procedure is followed.

23. The second stage of the Inquiry, which is designed to enable recommendations for the future to be made, will be conducted on seminar lines. For this purpose, I propose, in due course, to try and identify topics which can be the subject of papers, which will be dealt with at the hearing for the second stage, which will be heard in London. I would welcome suggestions as to the issues which should be tackled during the second stage.

24. From the visits and consultations which have already taken place, it is clear that among the underlying factors which may increase the potential for disorder in our prison system are overcrowding in our prisons, the conditions in which many prisoners are held, the regimes with which they are provided, the number of and conditions for remand prisoners, the size or design of some of our prisons, the manner of response to incidents and the methods used for achieving control of prisoners and the management of prisons and their staff. I will be looking to the prison department, staff associations and the various bodies interested in the activities of prisons and those who have studied the issues to provide me with written contributions which, while they may deal with other matters, will consider these factors. I anticipate that the contributions will deal with factors such as:

> Firstly, the make-up of our present and projected prison population, whether there are categories of persons who are being imprisoned who do not need to be in prison and whether some prisoners should be held in different conditions. The sort of matters I have in mind are the adequacy of

bail hostel schemes, the time that some unconvicted prisoners are held on remand, whether persons refused bail might be subject to less restrictions on their liberty and the scope, for example, for diverting certain offenders from prison.

Secondly, the sort of establishments and regimes we need for the population which has to be held in prison, staff/prisoner ratios and relationships, security and control, the number, size and role of local prisons, the treatment of different groups of prisoners, including sex offenders, inadequates and the mentally ill, the adequacy of arrangements for dealing with prisoner complaints and the methods for ensuring that custodial conditions do not fall below the proper standards.

Thirdly, what is the sort of Prison Service what we need to run our prisons, including career structure, conditions of service and the role of prison officers and other personnel, and the best method of fulfilling escort and court manning commitments and responding to operational emergencies and the relationship between headquarters and management and staff?

25. Where at all possible, I would like to have written submissions in relation to Stage 1 by 21st May and in relation to Stage 2 by 1st September next.

26. As soon as I am in a position to do so, I will identify the subject matters of the seminars which I referred to as forming part of Stage 2. I anticipate the seminars would take place in October. The written submissions, which I receive for the purpose of the second stage of my Inquiry, will be taken into account for the purposes of my Inquiry, irrespective of whether or not they deal with the subjects selected for discussion at the seminars. It will not be until the conclusion of the second stage that it will be possible to determine the areas where it would be appropriate for myself and Judge Tumim to make recommendations.

27. I fully recognise the interest that the Press will have on behalf of the public to report what takes place at the Inquiry. It is my intention and desire to give every assistance that can properly be given to enable them to perform this function. For this purpose, I propose, save in exceptional circumstances, that copies of statements made by a witness called during the first stage will be available to the Press as the witness is called to give evidence. However, there will be no television filming or photograph of any kind in the buildings where the Inquiry will take place during the hearings and there should be no sound recordings made of the proceedings. I would also ask the Press not to interview any witness to whom it has been indicated that he will be called to give oral evidence at the Inquiry until he has done so.

Representation

28. It is entirely a matter for my discretion as to which bodies or persons are allowed to be represented at the oral hearing. The Inquiry is different from all ordinary legal proceedings and there are no parties. However, there are individuals and groups of persons who have a real interest and it is right they should be allowed to be represented so that they may be able to cross-examine witnesses and make submissions. I would expect representations to be by lawyers, although I would consider other forms of representation where appropriate. A person or body who wishes to be represented must be prepared to show the necessary interest. If a number of persons have such an interest but there is no discernible difference between their interests, I would not necessary be prepared to grant separate representation and the correct course may be for them to be jointly represented by the same advocates.

29. So far as individuals are concerned, I will consider whether or not their need to be represented cannot be met by the Counsel instructed to assist the Inquiry or one of the interested bodies.

30. Any decision I make today about representation will not be final and I will

be prepared to entertain the application for representation at any time. The application should be made initially, in writing, to the Treasury Solicitor.

31. So far as the second stage of the Inquiry is concerned, because of the informal nature of the proceedings, I will expect that interested bodies will not find it necessary to be legally represented and that they can make their contribution by their officers.

Costs

32. There are no statutory provisions governing this Inquiry and therefore I have no power to order the payment of costs from public funds or by any parties. However, the Home Secretary has indicated to me, if I recommend that a party's costs should be met from public funds, unless there is good reason for not doing so, he will pay the costs reasonably incurred. When I do recommend payment, it will be on the standard basis. In the absence of the formal machinery of the Court for taxing such costs, the solicitor's bill will be taxed on an informal basis by the Treasury Solicitor's Department. I have already given an indication as to the position as to costs in the letters which I have written to members of the Department and to prisoners. There is no need for me to repeat what I have said in those letters. At the end of the each stage of the Inquiry, I will consider what recommendations to make. However, it may be helpful if I indicate that, for the first stage:

> Firstly, I am prepared to consider applications from members of the Department and prison staff to be represented independently and not by the department or the association of which they are members if there are some reasonable grounds for their not being so represented. If there are reasons for their not being so represented, it would not be fair to expect them to bear their own costs of representation; for example, if any member of the prison department staff or any prison officers have had notice of allegations which are being made against them and it would be reasonable for them to have personal representation, I will make the necessary recommendation.

> Secondly, I will also be prepared to consider making such a recommendation if I conclude that it would be reasonable for an individual to be represented but he is capable of being properly represented by an association already appearing at the Inquiry. The recommendation will be that the costs of that association, insofar as they are increased by having to represent that person, should be paid. If clarification is needed with regard to the position in relation to costs of any individual or body, I will be happy to try and clarify the position on receiving an application, in writing, which should be made in the first instance to the Treasury Solicitor.

33. With those preliminary remarks, I am now prepared to hear any application which anyone wishes to make for representation.

Lord Justice Woolf's Inquiry

Guide to Part I issues

This is a guide as to issues which will be considered for the purpose of part 1 of the Inquiry. I would emphasise that this is not intended to be an exhaustive list of the issues which will be considered. It is no more than an outline framework.

A) What was the position at the prison during the three months immediately preceding the incident in relation to:

    i)   staffing – authorised and in-post
                  – patterns of work at week-ends and bank holidays

    ii)   industrial relations

iii) nature of the prison population – Certified Normal Accommodation and daily average population by classification (legal status) and security category; Rule 43s; prisoners reallocated on control grounds

iv) physical conditions
   a) details of cell sharing
   b) vulnerability of roofs – internal and external
   c) congregation points
   d) sub-divisions of accommodation
   e) locking systems
   f) control/communications centre including CCTV etc
   h) location of sensitive documents eg prisoners main records
   i) security of canteens and drug cabinets

v) regimes for each section of the prison population:
   a) access to sanitation
   b) frequency of showers/baths and clothing availability
   c) exercise arrangements
   d) letters, visits and access to telephones
   e) work, vocational training and education including PE
   f) recreational association and films
   g) religious services
   h) personal possessions
   i) freedom of movement

vi) contingency planning
   a) staff training
   b) availability of equipment – control and restraint, communications etc
   c) familiarisation visits
   d) exercises – local, regional and national
   e) use of water for control purposes
   f) control of utilities
   g) plan of action in case of an emergency

vii) indicators of tension and remedial action
   a) adjudications and minor reports
   b) numbers reporting sick
   c) requests for Rule 43
   d) returned food
   e) staff absenteeism
   f) number of Governors applications, Board of Visitors applications and petitions
   g) Security Intelligence Reports and other warnings of impending trouble

viii) the availability of illicit drugs

ix) how were complaints/petitions monitored

B) Facts of Incident

   i) immediately precipitating factors, if any

   ii) what was done by
      a) prisoners
      b) the staff
      c) local management
      d) regional office
      e) headquarters
      f) other agencies (police, fire and ambulance services)
      g) media in covering the incident

   iii) injuries to staff and prisoners

   iv) Public Relations policy and application
      a) use of Home Office Public Relations Branch officers
      b) involvement of operational personnel

c) physical arrangements and briefing for media representatives
d) involvement of staff associations
e) communications with prisoner families

C) Aftermath

i) arrangements for surrender

ii) information for families

iii) redistribution/reallocation of the population

iv) staff arrangements – counselling, time off, emergency payments etc

v) immediate remedial action taken in the light of the incident – physical and organisational changes

vi) treatment of alleged ringleaders and participants eg hospitalisation, segregation, transfer etc

vii) press statements.

Lord Justice Woolf
14 May 1990

List of Names of those giving oral Evidence at the Public Hearings in order of Appearance

Public Hearings at Manchester

Mr E Clerk
The Reverend Noel Proctor
Captain Ian Ferguson
Mr B McCormick
The Reverend Peter Went *
Mr R Pogson
Mr D Goodale
Mr B Duffield
Mr J Johnson
Mr J Palmer
Mr A Zegveldt
Mr D Rigby
Mr M Andrews
Mr P Richardson
Mr S Collins
Mr F McKean
Mr D Reynolds
Mr S Parr
Mr W Oliver
Mr H Robertson
Mr S Verrall
Dr B Somasunderam
Dr P Walczak
Mr J Callaghan
Mr R Frost
Mr M Bell
Mr G Price
Mr M Unger
Mr I Serle
Mrs M Stewart
Mrs E Redfern
Dr I McCartney
Mr I McWilliam-Fowler
Mr P Hancox
Mr J Rutson
Mr G Morrison
Ms J Stewart
Mr H Wallace
Mr N Holliday
Mr I Boon
Mr G Underhill
Mr P Hewitt
Mr J Bancroft
Mr A Fagen
Mr D McNaughton
Mr B O'Friel
Mr R Halward

Mr B Emes
Mr T Bone
Mr A Papps
Mr P Chisnell*
Mr A de Frisching*
Mr W Elder*
Mr N Collinson*

plus 14 inmates
and 2 other witnesses who gave evidence in private

Public Hearings at Taunton

Dartmoor

Mr J Head
Mr H Coldwell
Mr R Comber
Mr W Green
Mr J Mawson
Mr A Dudley
Mr D Haley
Mr G Crook
Mr R Upton
Mr G Sheppard
Mr P MacLean
Mr A Taylor
Mr M Thacker
Mr M Sharp
Mr J May

plus 8 inmates

Cardiff

Mr D Smith
Mr B Lockley
Mr A Bartlett
Mr D Winters
Ms M Jones
Mr D Latham
Mr T Jones
Mr J Hutton
Mr L Serjeant
Mr O Williams
Mr M O'Brien
Mr S Eddy*
Miss S Ring
Mr A Rawson
Mr A Martin*

plus 2 inmates

Bristol

Mr M Knott
Mr C Wills
Mr A Harris
Mr P Helmore
Mr W Burton
Mr D Yeomans
Mr P Stevens

Mr M Marsh
Mr B Eveleigh
Mr D McAllister
Mr N Day
Ms S Wilks
Mr A French
Mr N Wall
Mr R Smith

plus 2 inmates

Pucklechurch

Mr A Fleming
Mr A Leary
Mr D Gibbs
Dr Abdel-Kariem
Mrs P Thomas
Mr G Fagg
Mr D Young
Mr B Cremin
Mr P Hall
Mr K Bennett
Mr M Scott
Mr D Waghorn
Mr J Alldridge
Mr T Sharley
Ms M Palmer
Mrs M Cooper
Mr P Cody
Mr B Ducker
Mr R Rawlings
Mr T Phipps
Mr M Rogers
Mr D Hutchings
Mr B Benge
Mr R Woolford
Mr D Leach
Ms M Benedict*
Mr R Pepworth*

plus 8 inmates

Public Hearings in London

Glen Parva

Mr J Rumball

Others

Mr J Hunter
Mr R Dixon
Mr M Thomas
Mr A Bracey
Mr J Doidge
Mr I Dunbar
Mr B Emes

* statements "read in" without witness being called

Lord Justice Woolf's Inquiry into Prison Disturbances

Statement on Part II Seminars - 29 June 1990

I propose now to make a statement on behalf of myself and Judge Tumim in relation to the public seminars which Judge Tumim and I will hold as part of the second stage of this Inquiry.

2.   I announced at the preliminary hearing of this Inquiry in London on 14 May that the second stage will deal with broad ranging issues and underlying causes. I gave a preliminary indication of the sort of factors on which Judge Tumim and I hoped to receive evidence. I announced also that we proposed to conduct public seminars during this second stage of the Inquiry and I undertook to identify the subject matters of the seminars as soon as we were in a position to do so.

3.   With Judge Tumim's agreement, I propose now to give an indication of the subjects of those seminars.

4.   We have been grateful for the very extensive ideas and proposals which we have received from very many sources in recent weeks on the matters which Judge Tumim and I might consider during the second stage of the Inquiry. That evidence has come from many organisations and individuals, including members of the prison service, prison inmates, academics, and others with a close and informed interest in prison matters.

5.   It has nevertheless been no easy task. The potential canvass is very broad: there are few tidy boundaries. Some issues are matters of complex fact. Others may seem a far cry form the roof of Strangeways. Self-evidently, not all matters, however important they may be, can be pursued within the format of a public seminar. The public expect a report, not argument without end. Equally, there is little merit in pursuing imaginative proposals unless they have been carefully tested. Public debate is a fine way to achieve that.

6.   The criteria, therefore, which Judge Tumim and I have followed in identifying our seminar topics are as follows:

> a)   The topics should be *relevant* to the prevention, management and control of the sort of serious disturbances within prisons which we saw in April and which we are charged to investigate;

> b)   the topics should be *central* to considering how to prevent such disturbances;

> c)   the topics should be matters where it is already apparent that no ready consensus exists and where public discussion will be helpful in finding a way through the different and conflicting approaches;

> d)   the topics should hold out the prospect of identifying practical recommendations achievable within a realistic level of resources.

7.   Accordingly, Judge Tumim and I propose to hold public seminars on the following five topics. They are:

i)   the tactical management of prisons and the prison population;

ii)   the need for active regimes, and how to achieve them;

iii) the administration and management of the prison service;

iv)   justice within prisons; and

v)   the relationship between prisons, other parts of the criminal justice system and other agencies.

8. Judge Tumim and I wish to emphasis that these topics form part only of our examination of the wider issues relating to prison disturbances. As I made clear on 14 May, we want to receive written evidence on any matter which those submitting the evidence consider to be relevant to our Inquiry. We have invited such evidence by 1 September. When we have received it, we shall consider it carefully and, guided by what we have seen, we shall provide before the seminars further guidance on the matters which we believe might usefully be discussed within each topic. We shall at the same time be considering carefully other very important issues which, while they may not come within the seminar topics, are nevertheless matters to which we must give the closest examination. An obvious example is security in prison establishments, but there are many others. We shall wish to make recommendations on matters on which we have received written evidence and which do not form part of the seminar discussions.

9. In addition to these seminars Judge Tumim and I will continue to have discussions with a wide range of those whose advice and guidance we need. We shall be testing ideas and challenging assumptions. We shall be looking for ways of including groups of prisoners in contributing to this second part of the Inquiry and in discussing with us the wider issues. We have already received much useful help in the letters which prisoners have written to us. We shall continue to ensure their voices are heard.

10. Finally, there is the question of representation. As I said on 14 May, I believe the informal nature of the seminar discussions should obviate the need for legal representation by interested bodies. I recognise, however, that the parties to this Inquiry who have already sought representation - with the exception, I dare say, of the Crown Prosecution Service - may wish to continue to have available the services of Counsel at these seminars. As to this I am prepared to receive representations. I must say, however, that, having consulted Judge Tumim, I should be more amenable to such applications if they carry with them an assurance that Counsel are being retained to advise and, on occasions, to ask questions clarifying the statements of other participants to the seminar, and that the officers of the organisations they represent will be ready to make their contribution to the discussions in their own way and in their own voice.

11. I am ready to hear any particular points which represented parties may wish to make at this stage.

Lord Justice Woolf's Inquiry into Prison Disturbances

Written Evidence Submitted to the Inquiry

Aids and Prison Consortium Project
Apex Trust
Association for Psychological Therapies
Association of Chief Officers of Probation
The Association of First Division Civil Servants
Association of Members of Boards of Visitors
Avon Ambulance Service
Avon and Somerset Constabulary
Avon Fire Brigade
Mr A Barrow
The Rt Rev Bishop of Lincoln
Mr L Blom-Cooper QC and Professor T Morris
Professor K Bottomley
Professor A Bottoms, Mr R Sparks and Mr W Hay
Bridgebuilders
Bridging the Gap (Leeds)
British Medical Association
British Pest Control Association
The Butler Trust
The Caesar Project
Campaign Against Lead in Petrol
Dr S Casale
The Central Council of Physical Recreation
Central Council of Probation Committees
Chief and Assistant Chief Fire Officers' Association
Civil and Public Services Association
Viscount Colville of Culross, Chairman of the Parole Board
Coordinating Committee of Boards of Visitors
Criminal Bar Association
Mr J Croft CBE
Sir Brian Cubbon GCB
Ms M Deitch
Devon Ambulance Service
Devon and Cornwall Constabulary
Devon Fire and Rescue Service
Mr N Dholakia, Commission for Racial Equality
Lord Donaldson of Kingsbridge, OBE
Professor D M Downes
Federation of Prisoners' Families Support Groups
Fight Racism! Fight Imperialism!
Fire Brigades Union
Dr A Fowles
Mr C Ganderton
Ms V Garner
Dr J Gomersall
Greater Manchester County Fire Service
Greater Manchester Metropolitan Ambulance Service

Greater Manchester Police
Greater Manchester Probation Service
The Reverend Brian Greenaway
Professor J Gunn and others in the Department of
    Forensic Psychiatry, Institute of Psychiatry
Professor E Hall Williams and Professor S McConville
Lord Harris of Greenwich
Department of Health
Mr M Heap
Home Office Departmental Joint Industrial Council
Sir David Hopkin, Chief Metropolitan Stipendiary Magistrate
Mr A Heaton-Armstrong
Hertfordshire Probation Service
HM Chief Inspector of Fire Services
HM Chief Inspector of Prisons for Scotland
HM Inspectorate of Schools
House of Commons Select Committee on Education, Science and Arts
Howard League
Mrs J Hughes
Lord Hutchinson of Lullington QC
Inner London Probation Service
Institution of Professionals, Managers and Specialists
Irish Prisoners' Support Group
Justice
Justices' Clerks' Society
Kent Unit for the Education and the Guidance of Ex-Offenders
    (East and West Kent)
Professor Roy D King
Koestler Award Trust
The Labour Party
Mr M Lacey
The Law Society
Leicestershire Ambulance Service
Leicestershire Constabulary
Leicestershire Fire and Rescue Service
Leo Orenstein Associates
Sir Montague Levine, HM Coroner, Inner London South District
Liberty
Liberty Trust
Lifeline Project Ltd
Lifeshare
Mr R Light
Magistrates' Association
Mr M Maguire
Manchester Aids Forum
Ms C Martin
Professor J Martin
Mr P Mawer
Mental Health Act Commission
Mental Health Foundation
Merseycare Trust Ltd
Merseyside Probation Service
Minimum Standards Group
National Aids Prison Forum
National Aids Trust
National Association for the Care and Resettlement of Offenders
National Association for the Care and Resettlement of Offenders Education
    Centre, Manchester
National Association of Fire Officers
National Association of Prison Visitors
National Association of Probation Officers
National Association of Senior Probation Officers
National HIV Prisoners Support Group

National Housewives Association
National Prisoners' Movement
National Schizophrenia Fellowship
National Union of Civil and Public Servants
National Union of Civil and Public Servants (Governors branch)
National Union of Civil and Public Servants
  (National Prisons Instructional Officers Group)
National Union of Civil and Public Servants (Prison Outstations Branch)
National Viewers and Listeners Association
New Bridge
The Northern Ireland Prison Service
Outlet
The Outsiders Group
Parliamentary All-Party Penal Affairs Group
Parliamentary Commissioner for Administration
Partners of Prisoners and Families Support Groups
Penal Affairs Consortium
Penal Reform International
Mr R Pencavel
Ms E Player and Ms E Genders
Ms J Plotnikoff
Portia Trust
Mr T Price, Director, The Gracewell Clinic
Prison Architecture Research Unit
Prison Fellowship for England and Wales
Prison Governors' Association
Prison Officers' Association
Prison Reform Trust
HM Prison Service
The Prison Service Charity Fund
Prison Service Union
Mr C Pyne, Coopers and Lybrand Deloitte
Quaker Social Responsibility and Education
Rational Corrections
Mr S Reading
The Rector of Liverpool
Dr R Reeves
Ms G Richardson
Royal College of Psychiatrists
Royal Institute of British Architects
Save Britain's Heritage
The Scottish Prison Service
Dr P Scraton
Selcare (Greater Manchester Trust)
Dr G Silverman
South Glamorgan Fire and Rescue Service
South Wales Constabulary
Mr Richard Southwell QC
Special Hospitals Service Authority
Staffordshire Probation Service
Suzy Lamplugh Trust
Mr D Swann
Thetford Ltd
Professor J Thomas
Transcendental Meditation National Headquarters
  (Maharishi Yogi)
Mr M Unger
United Kingdom Detention Services
United Nations Association
Uxbridge Magistrates
Mr L T Wilkins
Lady Williams
Professor C Wilson

The Lord Windlesham PC CVO
Women in Prison
Dr M Wright

Seminar A

Tactical Management of the Prison Population:
26 and 28 September 1990

1. The main question to be addressed, in this first of the stage II public seminars of the Woolf Inquiry, is the tactical management of the prison population. Is this currently carried out in the best and most sensible way, bearing in mind the need to prevent riots and disturbances?

2. Stage I evidence to the Inquiry has suggested that the mix of the population within prisons and the overcrowding within certain prisons, especially locals, may in themselves be conducive to riot. Current arrangements for categorisation and housing the prison population date back to the Mountbatten and May reports. Are there better ways of managing a prison population of the current size, even within the type of accommodation currently available, more likely to achieve an orderly prison system? Does the present method of progressing a prisoner through the system provide sufficient incentives for good behaviour? Can principles of tactical management be devised which would help the development of incentives?

3. It is proposed to break down the discussion into three parts, each taking one half-day. The last half-day could be available if needed.

Morning session: 26 September

4. The question for this morning's session is as follows:-

"How best can sentenced prisoners, including disruptive prisoners, vulnerable prisoners and those who are escape risks, be categorised and housed across the prison system? Are present arrangements for the use of the prison estate for sentenced prisoners the best that can be devised, bearing in mind the need to reduce riots and other disturbances?"

5. Preliminary analysis of stage I evidence suggests the following relevant findings:

– many in local prisons believe the mix of sentenced prisoners they hold is of its nature explosive;

– local prisons hold many prisoners transferred to them for control reasons (eg under Circular Instruction 10/74) and many other medium or long-term prisoners for whom places cannot be found elsewhere;

– some prominent among the rioters had a history of previous disruption within the system and previous disciplinary offences. Others had experienced previous periods of calm and ordered containment within the system;

– many prisoners do not fully understand and may be distressed by the way they are processed through different types of prison according to their security category. This distress can lead to disturbance;

– rule 43 prisoners are particularly at risk in riot situations.

6. In considering the question for this morning's session, participants should assume a roughly similar sentenced prison population to that now held. (There will be a chance to discuss whether any groups of prisoners should be completely removed from the system at a later seminar, seminar C).

7. Participants should also avoid entering more fully than is necessary into the question of the most suitable regimes for different types of sentenced prisoners. (There will be a chance to discuss the details of regimes more fully at seminar B on Active Regimes.)

8. They will also need to bear in mind that the question of tactical management of the remand population is being reserved for this afternoon's session.

9. In this morning's session, participants will first be invited to consider the tactical management of disruptive prisoners and of vulnerable prisoners. Is there such a thing as the disruptive prisoner? How should he best be housed within the prison estate? Are rule 43 and other arrangements for vulnerable prisoners suitable? Participants will then be asked to look at the tactical management of the sentenced population as a whole. Is individual sentence planning a good idea? Do current arrangements assist sentence planning? What is the role and function of the categorisation processes? Is the stress on security considerations alone justified? Could control categorisations usefully be developed? Should there be more categorisations to ensure that prisoners be held in the conditions most suitable to their requirements or should there be fewer categorisations and other rules so that changing requirements can be met? Is the dispersal system the most suitable arrangement? Are some of our prisons too large and can they be operated as a number of smaller units?

Afternoon session: 26 September

10. The question for the afternoon session is as follows:–

"Are the present arrangements for categorising and housing the remand population suitable? What improvements can be suggested in the interests of reducing riot and other disturbances?"

11. This question follows directly from the morning session. Once again participants should bear in mind that there will be further opportunities to discuss regimes and relationships with the rest of the criminal justice system at seminars B and C. The focus of this afternoon's discussion is categorisation and tactical management.

12. Preliminary analysis of stage I evidence has suggested:

– riots occur both in separate remand establishments and those shared between remand and other inmates;

– remand inmates in local prisons may have especially impoverished regimes and many participated in riots;

– the high security categorisation of remand inmates gives rise to dissatisfaction;

– inmates found guilty by the court but awaiting sentence were disproportionately involved among those participating in riot.

13. The seminar will wish to consider whether remand inmates should be accommodated in entirely separate establishments or units within establishments; whether there would be advantages in introducing some categorisation system for remand prisoners and if so how this could be administered; and whether it is possible to have an arrangement whereby a variety of different regimes can be provided within an establishment.

Morning session: 28 September

14. The question to be considered at this session is:–

   "To what extent is it possible to introduce in the prison system greater incentives for good behaviour?"

15. Preliminary analysis of stage I evidence has suggested:

   – that the present disciplinary system does not provide incentives to good behaviour;

   – prisoners feel they have little sense of autonomy within their prison careers; little to work for or achieve;

   – prisoners do not always feel rewarded by moves down-scale in security category.

16. The seminar will wish to consider whether present systems of prison management have neglected to develop incentives for good behaviour and relied too exclusively on punishment? What sorts of incentives could be devised? Should prisoners be required to earn privileged conditions and remission? What would be the implications for management of the whole prison estate and for the categorisation process of bringing in a more incentive based system? For which prisoners should there be sentence plans? What are the principal matters which should be contained in a sentence plan for a typical category B prisoner sentenced to over three years?

Afternoon session: 28 September

17. The afternoon could be available if needed.

Seminar B

Active Regimes: 2 and 5 October 1990

1. The first seminar in this series – on the tactical management of the prison population – considered the impact of the allocation of different types of prisoners within the prison estate on the propensity to riot or disturbance. The discussion covered such topics as prisoner categorisation systems, the movement of prisoners through the system, the need to make special provision for certain categories of prisoners and the need to build incentives into the system.

2. But whatever the overall system of housing prisoners and progressing them through the system, it has been suggested to us again and again that an over-riding priority is to provide active regimes for all prisoners, in whatever kind of prison they are housed, that inactivity and boredom play a part in producing disruptive behaviour.

3. This seminar moves on to consider the practical problems involved in providing active regimes.

4. The following paragraphs list specific questions to be discussed on each of the first three half-days of the two-day seminar. The last half-day could be available if needed.

Morning session: 2 October

5. The question to be considered at the morning session is as follows:-

   "What principles should govern the form of regime to be provided for the sentenced population and what can be done to ensure it is delivered, including what should be the role of the prisoner inside the prison."

6. Our provisional analysis of stage I evidence suggests:

   – the major complaint made by prisoners is of the amount of time "banged up in cell". Prisoners' letters, prison interviews and other evidence all point to the severe frustration built up in active young men by long periods of inertia and inactivity in cramped conditions;

   – much of the damage caused in the recent riots was caused by those who used the opportunity created by a loss of control to let off accumulated frustration and anger. Steady and active regimes can prevent the build up of such frustration and anger and hence minimise the chance of control problems escalating to riot;

   – since Fresh Start there have been serious efforts to increase time out of cell. Nonetheless for many prisoners time out of cell is still minimal. The reasons usually given are shortage of staff and control problems;

   – many prisoners do not have the opportunity of productive work and when they do the hours worked are usually short;

   – education is usually the first activity to suffer when there is pressure on the time or availability of uniformed prison staff;

– control problems can be caused by large gatherings of prisoners.

7. Should the guiding *principle* be:

    i)   to keep the prisoner busy;

    ii)   to provide activities which minimise the damaging affects of imprisonment;

    iii)   to prepare him for release.

8. How far should the individual prisoner be consulted about his regime? Can greater choice be introduced? Should any of these activities be compulsory? Should the regime be enforceable? And if so how?

9. What arrangements should be made for conducting regime activities? Should there be greater involvement of the prison officer, prison service specialists, outside specialists – or prisoners themselves?

Afternoon session: 2 October

10. The question to be considered at the afternoon session is as follows:-

"To what extent is it possible to provide an active regime for remand prisoners and what is the nature of regime to be provided?"

11. Stage I evidence has shown:

– remand prisoners were well-represented among rioters. Some riots were in specialised remand establishments;

– remand prisoners routinely have even poorer regimes than sentenced prisoners because of the difficulties of making adequate arrangements for a constantly shifting population and of the particularly heavy demands made on uniformed staff dealing with remand prisoners by the need to service the courts.

12. Does the seminar agree that the needs and problems of remand prisoners are different from those of sentenced prisoners and need to be considered separately? If so, what principles should govern the regimes of remand prisoners? Many of the same problems which arose concerning sentenced prisoners in the morning session will arise. But should the remand regime also bear in mind a greater need for remand prisoners to have access to the outside world, to family, friends, newspapers, legal advice? What implication do any such needs have for the provision of a remand regime? Should, for instance, remand prisoners be compelled to join in work, education or exercise programmes? If so of what nature? How much freedom should remand prisoners have to devise their own regimes? Are the needs of remand prisoners sufficiently different that they should be held in separate establishments? Do active regimes for remand prisoners raise the same problems of control as those for sentenced prisoners? What are the implications for resources?

Morning session: 5 October

13. The question to be considered at this session is as follows:-

"What specific provision should be made for inmates with special needs?"

14. The preliminary analysis of stage I evidence suggests:

– special sub-classes of prisoners may have particularly impoverished regimes;

– rule 43 prisoners in particular frequently have poor work and education opportunities because of the perceived need to keep them separate from other prisoners. They are also particularly at risk in times of riot, although they do not necessarily themselves create control problems;

– prisoners from ethnic minority groups may find the prison experience particularly difficult;

– the mentally or physically handicapped may have special problems and may be at special risk in disturbances.

15. At this session participants in the seminar are invited to consider what special arrangements, if any, need to be made in order to achieve active regimes for inmates with special needs. What principles should govern the allocation, if any, to any special regimes within the prison? How can the dangers of stigmatisation be avoided while at the same time meeting special needs? The seminar will consider in turn the principles which should govern the provision of separate regimes for any sub-category of prisoners and the special needs of rule 43 prisoners, of prisoners from ethnic minorities and of the handicapped.

Afternoon session: 5 October

16. The afternoon could be available if needed.

Seminar C

Co-operation with the Criminal Justice System: 19 October 1990

1. So far these seminars have considered prisons in isolation from the rest of the criminal justice system. But it is the system as a whole which controls:

    – the intake to prisons; the numbers and types of people held in custody;

    – the length of stay of prisoners within prisons; the systems of parole, remission, release dates;

    – much of the workload on prison staff, for instance in servicing the courts.

2. In addition the prison service interacts with other agencies of the criminal justice system in the treatment of offenders; in particular with the probation service, with voluntary organisations, the courts and the Health Service.

3. This third seminar in the series will consider the relevance of these relationships between prisons and the rest of the criminal justice system to the prevention of riots and disturbances within prison.

4. The discussion will be organised in two sessions; one in the morning and one in the afternoon.

Morning session: 19 October

5. The question for the morning session is as follows:-

    "Are there categories of inmates, such as the seriously handicapped, who ought not to be in the prison system?"

6. A preliminary analysis of stage I findings suggests.

    – some among those participating in riots had a history of mental illness;

    – some participating in riot were long-serving prisoners who had particular worries about their release date;

    – many who participated in riot were prisoners held on remand;

    – other participants in riots were prisoners found guilty by the courts but awaiting final sentence;

    – vulnerable prisoners such as those on rule 43 and those seriously handicapped were particularly endangered in the riots;

    – one of the major complaints of rioting prisoners was overcrowding within the system;

    – many prison staff were of the opinion that of recent years many prisons are housing a more difficult "mix" of prisoners than in previous periods.

7. Participants will be invited to identify the type of person, if any, whom they

believe should not be held in the prison system. By what principles should such a judgement be made? What other disposal than prison would be more suitable for such groups? How could they be defined and identified? How practical is it to think that institutions other than prison could deal with such groups? What would be the effect on costs? And on public confidence?

Afternoon session: 19 October

8. The question for the afternoon session is as follows:-

"What links should exist between the prison system and the courts system and the probation service?"

9. The preliminary findings of stage I of the Inquiry listed above as relevant to the morning session are obviously still relevant to this session. The way prisoners are treated cannot be considered wholly in isolation – they are influenced by their experience of other parts of the criminal justice system. The prison system is a part of the overall field of criminal justice and can only be expected to operate efficiently if that service is co-ordinated with others working as far as possible to a common set of objectives. Decisions on parole, remission, the date at which home-leave or time out on licence can be granted, are taken in a wider criminal justice system context. These decisions affect prisoners and prison management alike.

10. The session will be invited to consider:

– the particular areas in which co-operation between the prison system and other parts of the criminal justice system is likely to be most beneficial;

– what are the likely benefits of such co-operation? What are the difficulties in achieving it? For example, could such co-operation help to reduce the number of people on remand?

– are there tasks undertaken by the prison service which could more effectively be undertaken elsewhere – and vice versa?

– how can co-operation be achieved? Is any further machinery or mechanism necessary? At what level or levels is the machinery needed – national, regional, local? Are changes required to help ensure that the necessary co-operation is achieved?

Seminar D

The Administration of the Prison Service:
22 and 23 October 1990

1. Previous seminars in this series have discussed the tactical management of the prison population, the regimes experienced by prisoners and the relationship between prisons and other parts of the criminal justice system; all from the point of view of the need to prevent riots and other disturbances.

2. But whatever the policies on all these topics, nothing can be achieved unless the prison service itself is in good heart; well-staffed, well-administered and well-managed. Stage I of this Inquiry has demonstrated much devoted and excellent work by both staff and management. But it has also demonstrated much discontent and bitterness; deep disagreements between staff and management, disagreements and jealousies between different grades and types of staff and feelings of rejection and isolation among many who staff the system.

3. A two-day seminar clearly cannot address all the issues of prison management in detail. Nor would it be right to attempt to do so. The special interest of this Inquiry lies in trying to identify factors which have an effect on the tendency to riot and other disturbances. With this in mind, three separate questions have been identified for discussion on each of the first three half-days of the seminar. The afternoon could be available if needed.

Morning session: 22 October

4. The question for this morning's session is as follows:-

    "What should be the role of staff of prisons? How should they be recruited and what activities should they perform?"

5. A preliminary analysis of stage I evidence suggests:

    – some prisons studied had developed innovative schemes for shared working between uniformed and specialist staff which had been found helpful in reducing tensions and encouraging co-operation albeit on a small scale;

    – many, in both governor and uniformed grades, complain that too much time is taken up by administrative chores, the value of which is doubted, at the expense of time with prisoners;

    – the distribution of tasks between uniformed and non-uniformed grades and between these and other specialist staff, such as probation officers, education officers, physiologists and others, can cause difficulties, with each group believing the other puts problems in its way.

6. These findings suggest a need to go back to first principles. The seminar will be asked to consider what it believes to be the central function of all staff in prisons. What principles should be used to discriminate between the importance of various functions? What might these functions be? How much specialism do they imply? Is the current balance of specialists and other staff along the right

lines or does it need re-thinking? Do these findings have any implications for recruitment and training? What do they imply for the current divisions in the service between uniformed and non-uniformed grades, between Headquarters and prison establishment staff? Can unexpected exigencies with staff implications properly always be accommodated by time off in lieu.

Afternoon session: 22 October

7.   The question for this afternoon's session is:–

"How can a sense of leadership, purpose and corporate identity be provided for the prison service?"

8.   A preliminary analysis of stage I findings suggests:

– there were, at the time of this year's riots, some tensions between individual establishments and region and regions and Headquarters, which in some cases may have damaged necessary co-operative planning;

– despite this, the substantial logistical tasks of re-housing prisoners made homeless through riots and of deploying control and restraint teams across individual establishments to come to the aid of those in need, were accomplished with much efficiency and considerable success during the series of riots and disturbances. There was much evidence of corporate spirit and of establishments being willing and ready to come to each others' aid;

– many prison staff at all levels complain that they have an insufficiently clear sense of the ideals and goals which should infuse their work, despite the general welcome given to the Prison Service "mission statement";

– many establishments studied showed signs of serious tensions between uniformed and non-uniformed staff and of distrust of management by staff.

9.   The prison service is currently in a time of change. Reforms of recent years have already led to growing autonomy. The recent organisation review has led to a fresh structure, which became operational on 25 September. This new structure has been designed, among other things, to create a greater sense of leadership, purpose and corporate identity for the service. The seminar should take these new arrangements as given. There would be little point or value in re-considering them at this stage. Participants should confine themselves to discussing whether, assuming the new structures, they can make any further practical recommendations for improvement. How, for instance, can relations and communications between uniformed and non-uniformed staff, between establishments and Headquarters, be improved and developed? What level of information and service should Headquarters ideally provide establishments? How independent can or should be the status of a Governor? How best can the gulf between administrators and the professional prison service be bridged?

Morning session: 23 October

10.   The question for this morning's session is:–

"How should a proper complement of a prison establishment be determined?"

11.   The preliminary analysis of stage I evidence has shown:

– many prison staff at all levels, including senior Governor grades, believe that current levels of staffing are insufficient to combine the goals of security and an active regime;

– local arguments about minimum staffing levels appear to be endemic and to bedevil management freedom of action in calling in staff in the numbers needed at times of tension.

12. A short public seminar cannot hope to solve the endemic problems of setting suitable staffing levels for the many different establishments within the prison system. It is suggested the seminar could most usefully concentrate on questions of principle. By what principles should a sufficient staffing level be set? How technically should this be done? Through local or national negotiation? Or through the use of expert advice? Or by some combination of both methods? What lessons have other institutions or public services to offer? How can it be ensured that the interests of the prisoner are represented in any negotiations? How intimately are these issues connected with the risk of riot or disturbance? Is it right to accept any level of risk and if so can that level be defined?

Afternoon session: 23 October

13. The afternoon could be available if needed.

Seminar E

Justice in Prisons: 30 and 31 October 1990

1. This is the last in the series of five public seminars called by Lord Justice Woolf's Inquiry into the prevention of riots and other disturbances in prisons. So far the seminars have discussed the tactical management of the prison population, the question of active regimes, the relationship of prisons to other parts of the criminal justice system and the administration and management of prisons; considering all these issues in the light of their relevance to preventing riots.

2. In this last public seminar of the series we turn to the question of justice within prisons. Letters from prisoners have shown that they at least perceive this as an issue crucial to the prevention of riots. Discontent with justice within prisons is widespread and a constant cause of disagreement, anxiety and tension. Many rioters claim that their rioting was inspired as a protest against injustices.

3. Some would argue that prison is of its nature co-ercive. Men are not in gaol because they wish to be there, but because society has decided they must be there. A certain level of discontent may be inevitable; and it is unrealistic to expect that any prison justice system will escape resentment and complaint. Others would argue that precisely because prisoners have been imprisoned for their own offences against justice, it is of the first importance that they themselves should experience in prison what it is to be treated with justice. In this seminar we shall consider the relevance of prison justice issues to riots and other disturbances and consider whether it is possible that the quality of justice within prisons could be improved.

4. Once again the discussion will be organised around three questions; one for each of the first three half-days of the seminar. The last half-day could be available if needed.

Morning session: 30 October

5. The question for this morning's session is:-

"What are the necessary features of a satisfactory grievance procedure?"

6. A preliminary analysis of stage I evidence has suggested:

– prisoners complain that their lives are over-controlled by a mass of petty regulations, applied arbitrarily and inconsistently. Regulations vary from prison to prison or even within prisons on different Wings. Prisoners complain that they cannot understand or meet the demands made on them; that their grievances or complaints are dealt with in an arbitrary way; and that prisoners are not given reasons for decisions which affect them and do not even know how and when such decisions have been reached;

– some engaged in riots or disturbances have claimed that they had no other way of bringing their grievances to notice;

- Boards of Visitors are widely perceived as insufficiently effective and independent.

7. Grievance systems have been much studied and in one brief half-day session the seminar cannot expect to go over the whole agenda. Some familiarity with earlier discussions of the matter will be assumed. However documents such as the Prior Committee Report, the Home Office response, and the Home Office report on the Working Group on Grievance Procedures, show that there is still disagreement on fundamentals as to how to deal with this problem, disagreement already becoming evident in stage II evidence submitted to this Inquiry. Participants will be asked to consider first if any agree that the question of grievance procedures is relevant to the prevention of riots and other disturbances. Secondly, they will be asked to try to define the principles which should govern a good grievance procedure; paying particular attention to factors which would increase prisoner confidence, reduce friction between staff and inmates and hence discourage disturbances and protest. How could such a system be achieved while avoiding unacceptable levels of bureaucracy and cost, which could in turn raise fresh problems?

Afternoon session: 30 October

8. The question for this session is:-

"Is the present system of disciplinary proceedings appropriate?"

9. A preliminary analysis of stage I findings suggests that:

- punishment "down the block" or by withdrawal of remission is often perceived by prisoners as unfair and is a salient cause of complaint both among those who riot and others;

- uniformed staff sometimes complain of arbitrary changes in the levels of punishments administered by governors or the Board of Visitors. Sometimes these are felt to be too lenient and so set up a lax atmosphere which can give rise to control problems;

- the present system thus appears to have the confidence neither of staff nor of inmates.

10. Disciplinary procedures in prison, like grievance procedures, have been widely discussed of recent years. Once again some familiarity with earlier discussions will be assumed. The seminar will be asked to concentrate on areas where there are serious divisions in principle underlying the current debate. One of these is the extent to which external formal judicial authority should be brought in to control or advise on prison disciplinary proceedings. Is it possible to arrive at principles which should help settle this debate? And (a more empirical question) are there real gains, relevant to riot control, to be gained by bringing in more formal judicial review? Would these gains out-weigh the (probably large) cost in resource terms? Do participants have any view as to priority between say improved sanitary conditions and a more formal judicial review system? Are both equally important in their view to the prevention of riot or one more valuable than the other? Or are there principles which would dictate that one or other or both reforms should have absolute priority? Are the existing or the proposed powers of punishment of: a) governors and b) Boards of Visitors necessary and appropriate or excessive?

Morning session: 31 October

11. The question for this session is:-

"How should we seek to ensure the maintenance of minimum standards in the prison system?"

12. The preliminary analysis of stage I evidence suggests:

– a high level of discontent among prisoners and staff as to the conditions in which prisoners are kept in the prison system;

– a wide-spread belief among all involved (inmates and staff) that "conditions", not least over-crowding and bad sanitation, are a contributory cause of riots and disturbances.

13. Thus all are agreed that the achievement of some minimum level of standards would help to reduce riot. Where there is disagreement is on what that level should be and on how to ensure that it is achieved. Some will wish to argue for some sort of legal imposition and enforcement of minimum standards. But all would agree that to pass a law is not in itself sufficient to achieve change. The seminar will be asked to consider the role of the law in this matter and that of other strategies for achieving minimum standards.

Afternoon session: 31 October

14. The afternoon could be available if needed.

List of those who participated at the Public Seminars

Mr D Abellson	–	Coordinating Committee of Boards of Visitors
Ms K Akester	–	Liberty
Mr E Allison		
Mr J Anderson	–	The Howard League
Mr J Appleton	–	Coordinating Committee of Boards of Visitors
Mr P Ashman	–	Justice
Mr A Barclay	–	Prison Governors' Association
Mr A Barrow	–	Association of Chief Officers' of Probation
Mr J Bartell	–	Prison Officers' Association
Mrs S Black	–	Coordinating Committee of Boards of Visitors
Mr L Blom-Cooper QC		
Mr J Boddington	–	Prison Officers' Association
Mr T Bond	–	Prison Officers' Association
Professor K Bottomley		
Professor A Bottoms		
Ms L Bowles	–	Prison Governors' Association
Mr J Brindley	–	Lord Chancellor's Department
Mr B Bubbear	–	HM Prison Service
Mr B Caffarey	–	HM Prison Service
Dr S Casale		
Mr P Cavadino	–	National Association for the Care and Resettlement of Offenders
Mr P Chapman	–	PA Consultants
Mr G Coggan	–	National Prisoners' Movement
Mr D Cornwell	–	Prison Governors' Association
Mr L Crawford		
Ms F Crook	–	Howard League
Mr R Daly	–	Prison Governors' Association
Mr D Davidson	–	Coordinating Committee of Boards of Visitors
Ms M Deitch		
Mr N Dholakia	–	Commission for Racial Equality
Professor D M Downes		
Ms P Drew	–	Home Office Criminal Justice and Constitutional Department
Mr I Dunbar	–	HM Prison Service
Mr B Emes	–	HM Prison Service
Mr C Erickson	–	Prison Governors' Association
Mr D Evans	–	Prison Officers' Association
Mr W Fittall	–	HM Prison Service
Mr E Fitzgerald	–	Liberty
Mr H Fletcher	–	National Association of Probation Officers
Mr R Ford	–	Association of Chief Officers of Probation
Dr A Fowles	–	Parole Board
Mr C Fullwood	–	Greater Manchester Probation Service

Mr C Ganderton		
Mrs V Gant	–	Coordinating Committee of Boards of Visitors
Ms V Garner	–	The Law Society
Ms E Genders		
Mr K Gill	–	Central Council of Physical Recreation
Miss J Goose	–	Home Office Criminal Justice and Constitutional Department
Mr T Graves	–	Home Office Trade Union Side
Ms H Grindford	–	Howard League
Dr D Grubin		
Mr P Hall		
Mr T Hall	–	Community Relations Consultant
Mr T Hall	–	HM Prison Pentonville
Professor E Hall Williams		
Mr P Hancox	–	HM Prison Manchester
Lord Harris of Greenwich		
Mr M Head	–	Home Office Criminal Justice and Constitutional Department
Mr M Heap	–	Justices' Clerk, Cardiff
Ms K Heibst	–	Mental Health Foundation
Dr R Hood		
Mr K Horner	–	Coordinating Committee of Boards of Visitors
Mrs J Hughes		
Mr D Humphreys	–	National Union of Civil and Public Servants
Lord Hutchinson of Lullington QC		
Mr W Innes	–	HM Prison Service
The Reverend J James	–	HM Prison Grendon
Ms N Jameson	–	Fight Racism! Fight Imperialism!
Mrs M Jay	–	National Aids Trust
Mr W Jeffrey	–	HM Prison Service
Professor N Jepson		
Mr C Kay	–	Special Hospitals Service Authority
Ms A Kelmanson	–	National Aids Trust
Professor Roy D King		
Mr M Lacey	–	Association of Chief Officers of Probation
Mrs D Lamplugh	–	The Suzy Lamplugh Trust
Mr T Legg CB	–	Lord Chancellor's Department
Mr M Lewis	–	Prison Governors' Association
Ms S Lewis-Anthony	–	Interrights
Mr T Lidell	–	Association of Chief Officers of Probation
Ms J MacNaughton	–	HM Prison Service
Mr M Maguire		
Mrs B Major	–	National Schizophrenia Fellowship
Ms C Martin	–	Howard League
Professor J Martin		
Mr B Mather	–	Apex Trust
Mr P Mawer		
Mr R Mayes	–	Campaign Against Lead In Petrol
Mr E McGraw	–	New Bridge

Mr T Melia	–	HM Inspectorate of Schools
Mr L Mitchell	–	Home Office Trade Union Side
Mr M Mogg	–	HM Prison Service
Professor T Morris	–	Howard League
Mr M Morrison		
Mr C Newell	–	Crown Prosecution Service
Mr C Nicholls QC	–	The Bar Council
Mr L O'Callaghan	–	Civil and Public Services Association
Mr B O'Friel	–	Prison Governors' Association
Mr M O'Sullivan	–	HM Prison Service
Mr T Owen	–	Liberty
Mrs J Pitchers	–	Coordinating Committee of Boards of Visitors
Ms E Player		
Ms J Plotnikoff		
Mr W Preston	–	Prison Governors' Association
Ms H Price	–	Coordinating Committee of Boards of Visitors
Mr T Price	–	The Gracewell Clinic
Mr S Pryor	–	HM Prison Service
Mr P Quinn	–	HM Prison Askham Grange
Mr G Read	–	Association of Chief Officers of Probation
Mr J Reed	–	Department of Health
Ms M Rice	–	Afro Carribbean Mental Health Asociation
Mr K Richards		
Ms G Richardson		
Mr S Ridley	–	The Law Society
Mrs M Romanes	–	Magistrates' Association
Ms J Rowley	–	Apex Trust
Professor A Rutherford	–	Howard League
Ms L Savings	–	Institution of Professionals, Managers and Specialists
Mr C Scott	–	Prison Governors' Association
Mr S Shaw	–	Prison Reform Trust
Dr J Sim		
Dr J Sinclair	–	HM Prison Service
Mr E Smellie	–	National Association for the Care and Resettlement of Offenders
Mr G Smith	–	Inner London Probation Service
Mr R Sparks		
Mr J Steel	–	HM Inspectorate of Schools
Mr J Steele	–	Northern Ireland Office
Ms V Stern	–	National Association for the Care and Resettlement of Offenders
Mr G Stone	–	Kent Probation Service
Dr M Swinton		
Ms H Talbot	–	Association of Members of Boards of Visitors
Dr P Taylor	–	Special Hospitals Service Authority/Mental Health Foundation
Professor J Thomas		
The Reverend Peter Timms	–	Koestler Awards Trust
Mr C Train CB	–	HM Prison Service
Mr G Westall	–	National Schizophrenia Fellowship

546

Mr B Weston	–	Association of Chief Officers of Probation
Mr R Whitfield	–	Howard League
Lady Williams		
Mr C Wilson	–	Department of Health
Ms L Wilson-Crome	–	Association of Chief Officers of Probation
The Lord Windlesham PC CVO		
Mr P Winkley	–	Prison Governors' Association
Mr S Withers	–	Civil and Public Services Association
Professor M Zander		

Prison Seminar: Lincoln Prison

Discussion Guide: 16 October

1.   Throughout the month of October Lord Justice Woolf and Judge Tumim are holding a series of public seminars in London as part of their inquiry into prison disturbances.

2.   It is not possible to invite inmates to these seminars; and while certain prison service staff and their representatives will attend, this will not provide the opportunity for a direct practical discussion with prison staff.

3.   Yet Lord Justice Woolf and Judge Tumim are very aware, from the many letters already received by the Inquiry, that staff and inmates are perhaps the best source of practical ideas as to how the system could be improved, in order to make riot and disturbance less likely.

4.   They have hence arranged this one day seminar for a cross-section of inmates (in the morning) and prison service staff (in the afternoon) to discuss questions already known to be of great importance.

5.   The same questions will be discussed in the morning and in the afternoon; first with inmates and then with staff. The questions to be discussed are as follows:-

   1)   "Are there any ways in which the prison system could provide greater incentives for prisoners?"

6.   Many have suggested that the present system of control in prison is based more on punishment than rewards. Is this true? Should there be more rewards for good behaviour as well as punishments for disruptive or poor behaviour? Would this be wise? Is it practical? If there were to be more rewards for good behaviour what form should these rewards take? Would different incentive systems be needed for the long-term and the short-term prisoner? What problems might be caused? Might an incentive system simply lead to accusations of favouritism and injustice? Is it just to offer rewards to some prisoners and not others? What sort of behaviour should be rewarded? How could any reward or incentive system be managed? By whom?

   2)   "How can communication and relationships between prison service staff and prison inmates be improved?"

7.   Are there *policy* changes which are likely to improve relations between inmates and staff? Would prisoners' Councils help – consultative groups elected by prisoners – as happens in some other countries? What are the most important changes to help staff – training, greater involvement in inmates problems and preparation for release? What would be likely to make inmates less hostile to staff? Would matters be improved if prison officers had greater job satisfaction? If so, how could this be achieved? How practically can inmates benefit more from their time in prison?

8.   In thinking about these questions, Lord Justice Woolf and Judge Tumim are particularly interested in your own personal views as to practicalities and

possibilities. Those who live and work in prisons know more about what might really work than anyone else. Please try to think of positive suggestions for improvement. This is your chance to affect the future of the prison system.

9. Lord Justice Woolf and Judge Tumim will be accompanied at the seminar by their Assessors and the Secretariat, who will take a note of the discussion. But the names of contributors to the discussion will not be disclosed publicly and the persons who make particular contributions will not be named. This is because we want everyone taking part in the discussion to feel free to give their own personal opinion, not as a representative of some larger group but

List of Those Who Had Meetings With the Inquiry

Home Office

Permanent Under Secretary, Home Office
Criminal Justice and Constitutional Department
Criminal Policy Department
Police Department
Prison Service

Other Government Departments

Department of Health
Lord Chancellor's Department
The Scottish Prison Service

Official Bodies/Representatives

The Rt Reverend Bishop of Lincoln
Chief Metropolitan Stipendiary Magistrate
House of Commons Select Committee on Education, Science and Arts
Parliamentary Commissioner for Administration
Senior members of the police service

Staff Representative Bodies

Association of Chief Officers of Probation
National Association of Probation Officers
Prison Governors' Association
Prison Officers' Association

Non-Governmental Organisations

Association of Members of Boards of Visitors
Central Council of Probation Committees
Coordinating Committee of Boards of Visitors
Council of Europe Committee for the Prevention of Torture
The Howard League
Justices' Clerks' Society
Magistrates' Association
Mental Health Foundation
National Association for the Care and Resettlement of Offenders
National Association of Prison Visitors
National Association of Probation Officers
The Prison Reform Trust
Royal Institute of British Architects

Individuals

Ms U Banerjee
Mr F W P Bentley
Mr L Blom-Cooper QC
Professor A Bottoms
Dr S Casale
Mr J Croft CBE
Sir Brian Cubbon GCB
Lord Harris of Greenwich
Sir James Hennessy KBE CMG
Dr R Hood
Mrs J Hughes
Professor Roy D King
Mr H Mantel
Ms G Richardson
Mr G Smith
Mr D Thomas
Professor Vorenberg
Lord Windlesham PC CVO
Professor M Zander

Meetings Overseas

Official Bodies/Representatives

The Netherlands

Ministry of Justice, The Haque
Deputy Regional Manager of Prisons, West Central Netherlands
Deputy Regional Manager of Prisons, North and East Netherlands

Germany

Lower Saxony Ministry of Justice, Hanover
Federal Ministry of Justice, Bonn

France

Director of the Prison Service, Ministry of Justice, Paris

USA

New York City Correctional Commissioner, New York
Commissioner for Correctional Services, Albany
Commissioner of the Minnesota Department of Corrections, St Paul, Minnesota

Canada

Deputy Minister of the Ontario Provincial Correctional Services, Toronto
Federal Regional Deputy Commissioner, Kingston, Ontario
Commissioner for Correctional Services, Ottawa, Ontario

Individuals

Professor Pfeiffer, Hanover
Judge Volkart, Hanover
Judge Randall, St Paul, Minnesota
M. Favard, Paris
M. Errera, Paris

Visits made as part of the work of the Inquiry

Visits by the Inquiry to prison service establishments in the United Kingdon

England and Wales:

HMP Belmarsh (Woolwich)
HMP Birmingham
HMP Bristol
HMP Cardiff
HMP Dartmoor
HMP Durham
HMYOI Glen Parva
HMP Grendon
HMP Holloway
HMP Hull
HMP Leyhill
HMP Lincoln
HMP Lindholme
HMP Long Lartin
HMP Manchester(Strangeways)
HMYOI & RC Pucklechurch
HMYOI Stoke Heath
HMYOI Swinfen Hall
HMP Wandsworth
HMP Wormwood Scrubs

Scotland:

HMP Peterhead
HMP Edinburgh (Saughton)
HMP Shotts

Visits by the Inquiry to prison service stations in England and Wales

Prison Service Headquarters
C&R training school at HMP Lindholme
Midland Regional Office
North Regional Office
South East Regional Office
South West Regional Office

Visits by the Inquiry to Prison Establishments Overseas

Canada:

Ontario Correctional Institute, Brampton, Ontario
Vanier Centre, Brampton, Ontario
Joyceville Institution, Kingston, Ontario

France:

Bois d'Arcy Remand Centre, Paris

Germany:

Uelzen Prison, Lower Saxony
"Santa Fu" Prison, Hamburg
Cologne Prison, Cologne

The Netherlands:

Esserheem Prison, Veenhuizen
De Schie Remand Centre, Rotterdam
Over Amstel Remand Centre, Amsterdam
De Koepel Remand Centre, Haarlem
De Marwei Prison, Leeuwarden

Spain:

City Centre "Modello", Barcelona
Quatre Camins Prison, Barcelona
Carabanchel Prison, Madrid

USA:

Otisvile Federal Correctional Institute, New York State
Rikers Island (male), New York State
Rikers Island (female), New York State
Oak Park Heights Prison, Minnesota
Stillwater Prison, Minnesota

H.M.P. Manchester at 1 April 1990

1	Redgra Area on Croft Site	25	Offices	41	Cycle Shed	51	C of E Chapel
2	Workshops	26	Dog Handlers	42	'A' Wing	52	Portakabin
3	Future Development	27	Former Burial Ground	43	Toilets	53	Store
4	Gymnasium	28	'K' Wing	44	Exercise		
5	Workshop & Stores	29	Remand Visits Over	45	Former Hospital		
6	Laundry	30	Stores	46	Former Police Court		
7	Gate Lodge	31	RC Chapel	47	Officers' Mess		
8	Bridge to Croft	32	Staff Facilities	48	Exercise		
9	Sherbourne Street	33	Southall Street	49	Fence		
10	'C' Wing	34	Entrance	50	Gate to Croft		
11	Sports Hall	35	Gate Lodge				
12	Boiler House	36	Main Reception				
13	Toilets	37	Remand Reception				
14	'D' Wing	38	Officers' Club				
15	Exercise Yard	39	'F' Wing				
16	'H' Wing	40	Visits				
17	'B' Wing						
18	Toilets						
19	Kitchen						
20	Workshops						
21	'G' Wing						
22	'I' Wing						
23	'E' Wing						
24	New Hospital						

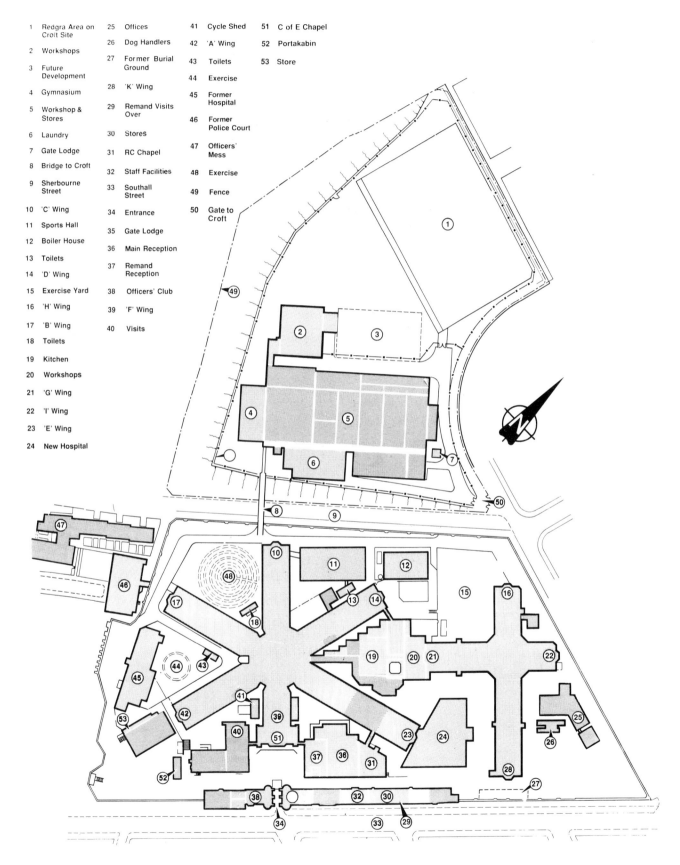

Photograph 1: The Roof Spaces at HMP Manchester

Photograph 2: The Roof Spaces at HMP Manchester

Photograph 3: The Roof Spaces at HMP Manchester

HM Highbank Prison

Major Disturbance Strategy

Stage I

Regain Control

- Staff withdrawal if necessary - staff roll taken.
- Senior Management informed.
- Assemble staff.
- Mount rescue team if necessary.
- Inform Region, request support staff.
- Establish Command post.
- Inform Press Office.
- Assemble local C&R III Team.
- Gain control of majority of Prison.
- Prepare for injuries to staff and inmates.
- Relocate passive prisoners.
- Extinguish fires if possible.
- Isolate incident area.
- Deploy staff to gather evidence.
- Appoint negotiators.
- Plan to relocate rioters.
- Prepare statements for Director and Press.

Stage II

Containment

- Receive staff from other establishments.
- Make catering arrangements for staff and passive inmates.
- Establish debriefing Unit.
- Plan to transfer rioters.
- Plan to transfer passive inmates if necessary.
- Plan for ongoing containment.
- Zone establishment and deploy staff accordingly.
- Arrange media handling.

Stage III

End of Incident

- Plan controlled surrender.
- Locate rioters.
- Assess damage.
- Transfer rioters.
- Transfer passive prisoners if necessary.
- Stand down staff.
- Full debrief of staff.
- Thank staff verbally.

Stage IV

Aftermath

- Establish normal routine, if possible.
- Clean up.
- Repair damage.
- Set up Investigation Unit to prepare disciplinary charges.
- Thank you letters to Public Services and establishments.
- Start internal inquiry.
- Interim reports to Region.
- Assess staff morale.
- If necessary, provide counselling and emotional support for staff.
- Initiate staff training programme if indicated.
- Control disciplinary hearings against inmates.
- Submit full report to Region.

HM Highbank Prison

Major Emergency Roles

Command Suite

Commander

In consultation with the Director, will determine the strategy to deal with the incident and ensure a successful conclusion as soon as possible.

Radio Officer

To control the radio network, and advise the Commander as necessary.

Telephone Officer

To sift and log incoming telephone calls, and pass outgoing messages as required.

Logging Officer

To log events in the Command Room.

Runner

To organise refreshments for the Command Team, and run messages for the Commander.

Senior Police Officer

Advise the Commander and co-ordinate police support.

Senior Fire Brigade Officer

Advise the Commander and co-ordinate actions of Fire Brigade.

Information Officer

In consultation with the Commander, to prepare situation reports, press releases, and pass information to staff.

Scene of Incident

Site Commander

On radio link up with Commander, to be the ears and eyes of the Commander and anticipate escalation of incident. To organise and control staff at the scene of the incident. To receive surrendered prisoners.

C&R III Commander

To carry out the strategy agreed with the Commander, and advise the Commander by radio as necessary.

Negotiators

To negotiate with prisoners as directed by the Commander.

C&R Support Group

To supply log keeper and radio officer for C&R III, and to receive injured staff and surrendered prisoners.

Operations Function

Operations Officer

To ensure that staff resources are utilised properly, inmate movements properly managed and evidence obtained in preparation for disciplinary charges.

Marshalling Officer

To meet staff arriving at the prison and direct them to assembly point.

Briefing Officer

To brief staff and support detached duty staff.

Staff Management Officer

To deploy staff throughout the incident.

Debriefing Officer

To obtain an accurate record of events during the incident.

Inmate Movements Officer

To record and control inmate movements throughout the incident.

Security/police liaison

Liaison Officer between prison and police.

Evidence Officer

To ensure that evidence is obtained throughout the incident to support the laying of disciplinary and criminal charges.

Staff Welfare Officer

Provide refreshments, meals and other facilities to meet the needs of prison staff and Public Service personnel.

Staff Officer Function

Staff Officer

Will advise the Commander, organise the Support Group and handle administrative matters.

He will deal with queries from the POA and BOV.

Head of Works

Will advise the Commander, erect structures as directed, and assess damage at end of incident.

Hospital Officer – Part Time Medical Officer

Establish a first aid post in hospital and treat injured staff and inmates.

Chaplain

Advise the Commander as required, and provide moral support to staff and passive inmates.

Probation Officer

Advise the Commander as required, and establish a unit to deal with queries from inmates' relatives.

Management Services

EO Discipline

Supply escorting staff with relevant inmate files.

EO Stores

To co-ordinate the deployment of all civilian staff.

AO Stores

Ensure that stores and equipment are available during and after the incident.

Head of Prison

To maintain, as near normal as possible, the regime in areas of the prison not affected by the incident.

Regional Representatives

Senior Liaison Officer (ARD)

Senior liaison officer will advise the Director and support the Governor as necessary. He will work with the media.

Support Group Liaison Officer (GIV)

Will co-ordinate the duties of detached duty staff and ensure establishments provides appropriate facilities and accommodation.

Management Services (ARD)

Assess need for equipment.

Regional Works Supervisor

Assist Senior Works Officer to access damage and obtain supplies.

Dogs

Co-ordinated by Regional Office and P5 Division.

Boards of Visitors

(a) To act as impartial observers throughout the incident.

(b) To conduct subsequent disciplinary proceedings.

CHRONOLOGY OF SIGNIFICANT OPERATIONAL EVENTS: 1–25 APRIL 1990

	Manchester	Establishments involved in other serious disturbances (see Note 1)	Other significant events
1 April	**11.00 am** Incident began in chapel. Main prison lost by 11.15 am.		**11.45 am** First reinforcements dispatched to Manchester from Leeds.
	12.15 am Remand prison lost.		**11.55 am** NRO incident control room opened – efforts continued all day to arrange reinforcements within the region and places for transferred prisoners.
			2.00 pm HQ control room opened – heavy involvement in national co-ordination of support for Manchester and places for prisoners.
	3.00 pm First batch of prisoners transferred out	**3.10 pm–4.45 pm** Demonstration at Hull.	**3.20 pm–8.45 pm** Demonstration at HMRC HMP Rochester.
	8.00 pm E Wing re-entered.		**8.25 pm–8.45 pm** Fire at HMP Kirkham.
	11.50 pm 676 prisoners had been transferred out; 200 –300 still at large.		
2 April	**00.10 am** Staff withdrawn from E Wing.		
	7.06 am 1,289 prisoners had transferred out; 142 still at large.	**8.50 am** Minor incident at HMYOI Stoke Heath.	**8.20 am** NRO began notifying courts of non-production of inmates. National operations room began co-ordinating arrangements for serving courts.
	10.00 am Remand prison regained – six prisoners surrendered.		

Manchester	Establishments involved in other serious disturbances (see Note 1)	Other significant events
		12.05 pm Minor incident involving 110 prisoners at HMRC Low Newton.
1.00 pm 120 prisoners still unaccounted for.		
3.00 pm Decision not to mount full scale attempt to retake main prison at that stage.		
3.32 pm Limited assault on kitchen successful.		
4.10 pm Home Secretary's statement		
		7.00 pm Fire in dining room at HMP Lindholme – four staff injured.
		7.15 pm Two prisoners on ledge at HMP Bedford
	9.00 pm Escape attempt and barricade at HMP Long Lartin.	
3 April 11.00 am Estimated 1,556 prisoners had been transferred out; 64 still unaccounted for.		
10.44 am Editor of Manchester Evening News involved as observer of negotiations.		
11.30 am Staff enter E Wing to divert attack by prisoners on staff in F Wing.	11.50 am Long Lartin incident resolved.	

Manchester	Establishments involved in other serious disturbances (see Note 1)	Other significant events
3.00 pm Prisoner Mr D White died in hospital.		
4.00 pm Solicitors involved as observers.		4.05 pm Bedford incident resolved.
		9.20 pm Attempted escape from escort en route to Wandsworth and Brixton.
4 April Negotiations continued.		1.10 am–2.30 am Hostage incident at HMP Stafford.
		9.45 am Officer taken hostage at HMP Durham.
10.25 am Remand prison searched.		
		10.50 am–11.02 am 70 prisoners in passive demonstration at HMP Full Sutton.
		8.00 pm Five prisoners barricaded at HMRC Brockhill.
By 8.45 pm, 31 prisoners surrendered during day.		
10.10 pm Officer Scott died in hospital.		
5 April 1.10 am Prisoners claim bodies in E Wing.		
		7.00 am Durham incident resolved.

Manchester	Establishments involved in other serious disturbances (see Note 1)	Other significant events
9.45 am 15 to 25 prisoners estimated still at large. Prisoner tried to address the public using a makeshift megaphone.		**11.40 am–12.45 pm** Inmate on roof at HMYOI Deerbolt. **2.00 pm** Brockhill incident resolved. Inmate on roof at HMP Wymott.
Home Secretary made further statement in Parliament, including announcement of Woolf Inquiry. During the day Fire Service hosed down areas of the prison.		**3.45 pm** Mr Mellor visited HQ Ops Room.
6 April **Overnight** Noise and powerful lights used to disturb sleep patterns and maintain pressure. Prisoners claim to have a month's supply of food.		**2.41 pm** Wymott incident resolved. Decision that all staff involved in C&R activities at Manchester should receive five days special leave with pay.
	7.20 pm Disturbance at HMYOI/RC Glen Parva.	
7 April 1.00 am Further attempts to		

Manchester	Establishments involved in other serious disturbances (see Note 1)	Other significant events
disconnect mains water supply.	02.46 am Glen Parva incident resolved.	11.05–8.00 pm Two inmates on roof at HMP Stafford.
5.20 pm Three prisoners surrendered.		
Afternoon – C&R teams explored E Wing 2nd level.	3.39 pm Disturbance at HMP Dartmoor.	
8 April One prisoner surrendered.		8.30 am Suicide reported at HMP Highpoint.
	08.50–12.10 pm Disturbance at HMP Cardiff.	Two overnight escape attempts reported by HMP Canterbury.
		10.30 am–10.40 am Passive demonstration at HMP Leeds.
		11.36 am–12.20 pm Minor disturbance at HMP Brixton – two staff casualties.
		2.30 pm–2.59 pm Inmate caused gas leak and evacuation at HMP Pentonville.
Late pm – Large quantities of water pumped into main centre to put out fires.	3.15 pm–4.10 pm Remand prisoners attempt to overwhelm staff at HMP Hull.	

Manchester	Establishments involved in other serious disturbances (see Note 1)	Other significant events
	6.00 pm Disturbance at HMP Bristol.	
	6.00 pm Dartmoor incident resolved (inmate remains on roof).	
	6.50 pm Disturbance at HMYOI Stoke Heath.	
		11.20 pm Disturbance at HMP The Verne.
9 April Decision taken to end use of loud music.		2.07 am The Verne incident resolved.
		12.05 pm–12.20 pm Demonstration at HMYOI Castington.
Two prisoners surrendered.	2.44 pm Bristol incident resolved.	
	2.50 pm Stoke Heath incident resolved.	
	2.55 pm–3.20 pm Passive demonstration at HMP Hull.	
	Prisoner remains on roof at HMP Dartmoor.	
		7.45 pm–10.45 pm 65 inmates barricaded at HMYOI Everthorpe. Four staff, three inmates injured.
10 April 5.00 am 50 officers entered C Wing with police. Prisoners attack with scaffolding poles. Four officers injured. Three prisoners surrendered. 15 prisoners thought to be still at large.	Prisoner remains on roof at HMP Dartmoor.	

Manchester	Establishments involved in other serious disturbances (see Note 1)	Other significant events
11 April 10.50 am Three further surrenders. 12 still at large.		
Funeral of Officer Scott.		
DDG and Regional Director visit prison.		
Night Prisoners move their base to top of rotunda.	**10.05 pm** Three more prisoners on roof at Dartmoor.	**10.00 pm** Hostage incident at HMP Swansea.
12 April Negotiation continued.	**1.40 am** Dartmoor incident resolved (One prisoner remains on roof).	**9.55 am** Swansea incident resolved. Plans for weekend staffing at Manchester.
		7.45 pm-8.40 pm 35 inmates barricaded at HMYOI Portland.
Night Fire bombs made from cooking oil thrown from roof.		
13 April Green Goodesses arrive. Authority given for use of water above ground level in accordance with existing policy.	Prisoners remains on roof at HMP Dartmoor	
Two prisoners surrendered.		
Ten prisoners still at large.		
14 April Prisoners threaten to fire bomb chapel.	**12.40 pm** Prisoner on roof at HMP Dartmoor surrenders.	
Installation of perimeter CCTV completed.		

Manchester	Establishments involved in other serious disturbances (see Note 1)	Other significant events
Night – noise activity suspended.		
15 April **pm** Noise used to prevent prisoners speaking to bystanders.		
16 April Officer hit by scaffolding pole.		
9.50 am Prisoner brought out on stretcher suffering from gastro-enteritis – one of the stretcher bearer surrenders, the other prevented from returning.		
17 April Governor instructed to draw up plan to retake the prison one wing at a time		**10.21 pm** Hostage incident at **HMP** Liverpool.
18 April Seven prisoners still at large.		**12.29 am** Liverpool incident resolved.
3.00 pm Prisoners broke through C Wing roof.		
3.00 pm DDG and Regional Director visited prison; decision not to mount dangerous attempt to regain E Wing.		**8.45 pm–9.00 pm** 36 inmates in passive demonstration at HMP Kirklevington.

Manchester	Establishments involved in other serious disturbances (see Note 1)	Other significant events
19 April Decision to consult Chief Constable of Greater Manchester Police.		**12.45 am** Seven Rule 43 prisoners escape from HMP Gloucester.
Much activity among prisoners in afternoon.		**8.15 pm** Hostage incident at HMP Camp Hill.
20 April C&R teams entered chapel to hose down bonfires, and remove parts of barricade.		**12.45 am** Camp Hill incident resolved.
21 April C&R teams again enter chapel and F Wing – forced to withdraw under heavy bombardment.		
Discussions with the Chief Constable of Greater Manchester Police.		
22 April Visit by Home Secretary. Discussions between police and Prison Service experts, led by DDG, in which means of gaining high ground is identified.	**6.35 pm** Disturbance at HMRC Pucklechurch.	**9.55 am–2.15 pm** Two inmates on roof at HMP Birmingham.
More Green Goddesses provided.	**8.50 pm** Hostage incident at HMP Long Lartin.	
23 April In light of weekend	**9.05 am** Long Lartin incident resolved.	

Manchester	Establishments involved in other serious disturbances (see Note 1)	Other significant events
discussions, Ministers agree that plan should be made to retake prison and conclude the incident. Mr Emes visits prison to supervise preparation of plan. Sir Clive Whitmore involved in discussions.	1.17 pm Pucklechurch incident resolved.	
3.12 pm Prisoner captured.		
24 April Preparations for assault. Efforts sustained to keep prisoners under pressure.		
25 April 9.00 am Operation begins.		
10.02 am One of six prisoners surrenders.		
6.20 pm Operation ends. Remaining five prisoners surrender.		

NOTE

1.   The establishments thus categorised are Bristol, Cardiff, Dartmoor, Glen Parva, Hull, Long Lartin, Pucklechurch and Stoke Heath.

572

HMP Manchester (Redevelopment Plan)

1. Empire Street
2. Remand Wings
3. Hospital
4. Tower
5. Dog Handlers
6. Future Demolition
7. Chapel
8. Stores
9. Main Building
10. Southall Street
11. Exercise Area
12. Works Department
13. Laundry
14. Kitchen
15. Entry Building
16. Industries and Inmate Training
17. Physical Recreation Centre
18. Workshops
19. Proposed Road Bridge
20. Sherbourne Street
21. Services Block Below
22. Staff Complex
23. Visitors Reception Centre
24. Great Ducie Street

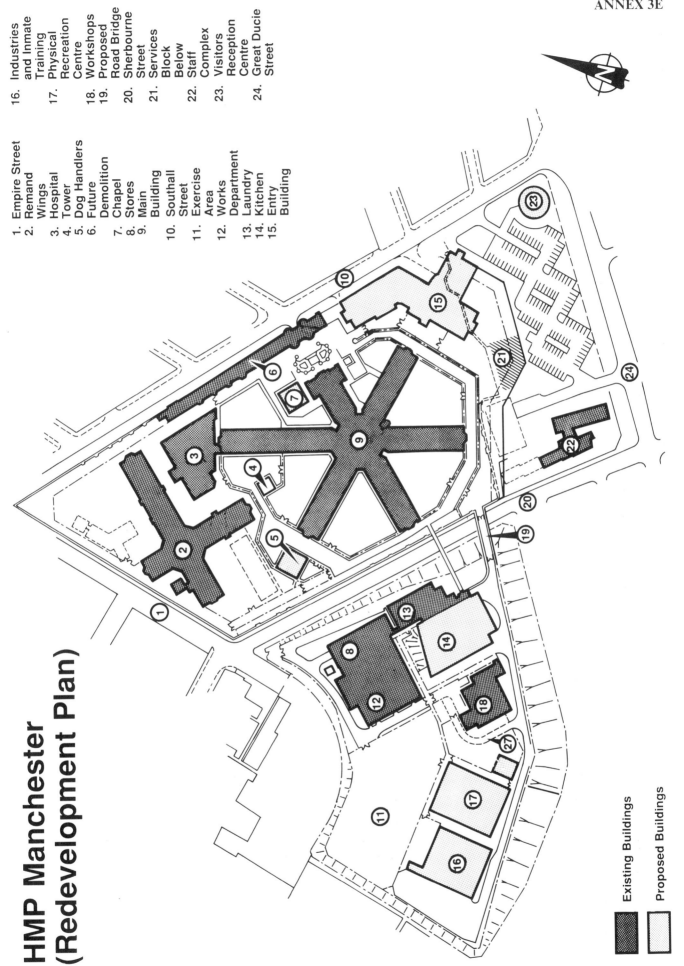

Existing Buildings

Proposed Buildings

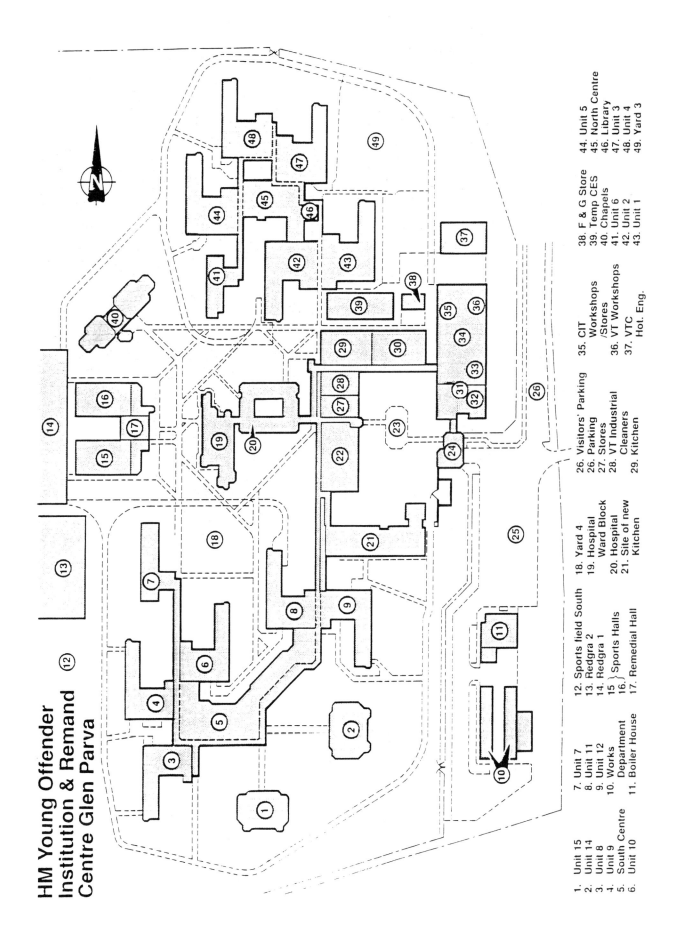

HM Young Offender Institution & Remand Centre Glen Parva

1. Unit 15
2. Unit 14
3. Unit 8
4. Unit 9
5. South Centre
6. Unit 10

7. Unit 7
8. Unit 11
9. Unit 12
10. Works Department
11. Boiler House

12. Sports field South
13. Redgra 2
14. Redgra 1
15. } Sports Halls
16. }
17. Remedial Hall

18. Yard 4
19. Hospital Ward Block
20. Hospital
21. Site of new Kitchen

26. Visitors' Parking
26. Parking
27. Stores
28. VT Industrial Cleaners
29. Kitchen

35. CIT Workshops /Stores
36. VT Workshops
37. VTC Hot. Eng.

38. F & G Store
39. Temp CES
40. Chapels
41. Unit 6
42. Unit 2
43. Unit 1

44. Unit 5
45. North Centre
46. Library
47. Unit 3
48. Unit 4
49. Yard 3

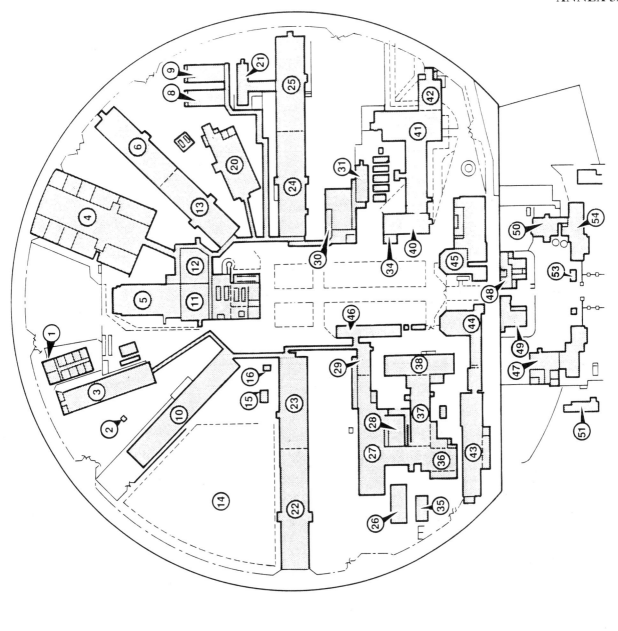

HMP Dartmoor

1. Offices/Dogs
2. Incenerator
3. AO's main store
4. E Wing
5. Reception /Cinema etc.
6. 'D' Wing
7. CIT Painters Workshop
8. CIT Painters Workshop
9. CIT Painters Workshop
10. Gymnasium
11. VT Workshop
12. Laundry
13. 'C' Wing
14. 'Red Gra' Area
15. Gym Equip Store
16. Boiler House
17. Kitchen
18. Bath House
19. 'G' Wing
20. 'F' Wing
21. 'A' Wing
22. 'B' Wing
23. CIT Workshop
24. Carpenters Workshop
25. Finished Goods
26. Stores
27. Clothing Exchange Store
28. Reception Canteen
29. Fire Station
30. Plant Store
31. Building Operations & Works Pipe Store
32. VTC Welding & Textile Shop
33. Textile Industry & Works Store
34. Chapel Ecumenical
35. Hospital & Education Block
36. Offices
37. Fabrication & Blacksmith's Shop
38. Visits
39. Governor's Office/Board Room & Staff Canteen
40. Gate Lodge
41. Probation Department
42. Former Dep. Governor's Quarters
43. Plant Fitters Shop
44. Visitors Waiting
45. Former Governor's Quarters Further Staff Mess
46. Orderly Room
47. Works Complex

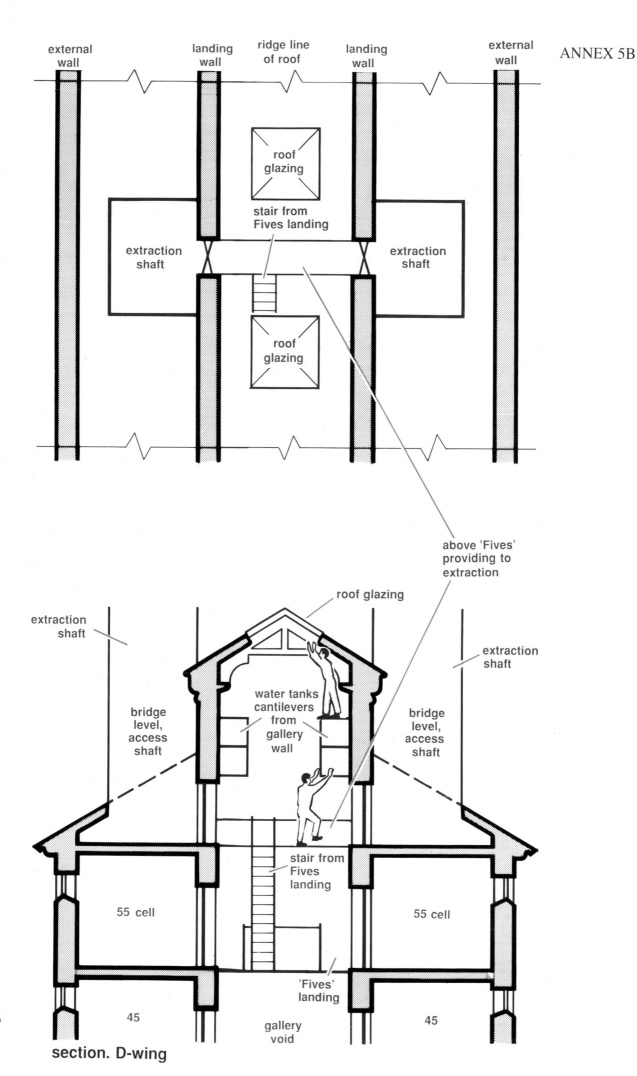

external
wall

landing
wall

ridge line
of roof

landing
wall

external
wall

roof
glazing

stair from
Fives landing

extraction
shaft

extraction
shaft

roof
glazing

above 'Fives'
providing to
extraction

roof glazing

extraction
shaft

extraction
shaft

water tanks
cantilevers
from
gallery
wall

bridge
level,
access
shaft

bridge
level,
access
shaft

stair from
Fives
landing

55 cell

55 cell

45

45

'Fives'
landing

gallery
void

section. D-wing

HMP DARTMOOR – BOV MAJOR INCIDENT PROCEDURE

General

1. The Governor or Duty Governor is to inform the BOV Chairman or in his absence the next member on the BOV "call-out" list, contained in the BOV Incident pack within the Governor's Incident Box.

2. On arrival at the Prison, the BOV member is to be briefed by the Governor or member of Staff detailed by him on the nature of the incident and the BOV task.

3. The BOV Incident pack contains an Incident Log, pens, note-books, blank rota sheets, BOV members telephone details and the detailed instructions for proceeding with the observing of the incident. The first BOV member to arrive is to start the log, recording all events observed noting the times, places, names of Staff and Inmates - giving details of the occurrence.

4. BOV members should observe all that takes place as far as possible, particularly at unlocking and during transfer of Inmates, also checking of property at the close of an incident. (Detailed instructions attached).

5. BOV members have no executive authority and must not attempt to assume it; they attend as independent observers of fact who are concerned to know what is happening; to safeguard the interests of the Staff and Inmates alike and to be in a position to report and comment on the incidents(s) from an objective viewpoint. Members must be fully conversant with the rules governing their role.

6. BOV members should not attempt to deal with complaints from Staff or Inmates during the incident, but should record the circumstances and issues arising for subsequent discussion and action.

7. The BOV should consider afterwards any action they may wish to take regarding the incident, eg by way of report to the Secretary of State, comments to the media, review of procedure with the Governor, etc.

8. BOV members may by invitation attend a Press Conference called by the Governor but should not take part in it:- Prison Department "Guidelines for BOV's during major incidents" DPS6 (81) 7 paragraph 4 refers.

9. A copy of these guidelines and detailed instructions are to be kept in the incident pack.

Chairman
Board of Visitors

MAJOR INCIDENT PROCEDURE –
DETAILED INSTRUCTIONS

STAGE ONE

1. a.   A request for BOV presence during an incident will normally be made by the Governor to the BOV Chairman, who is responsible for keeping the BOV Clerk informed as to his availability.

    b.   When the Chairman is not available, a local member should be contacted i.a.w the "Call out list" contained in the Governor's incident box.

    c.   The strength of presence is then to be rapidly agreed between the Governor/BOV Chairman/Member deputising (by telephone). During normal working hours, the BOV Clerk will telephone members as required, outside of working hours the Chairman/Member deputising will be responsible, and for organising a rota of members attending.

NOTE: By design the Vice Chairman and certain other BOV members will *NOT* be involved in the "Call-out", being required to remain uninvolved for possible subsequent enquiries/adjudications etc.

2.   BOV members who hear of the incident should:

    a.   *NOT* come into the prison but remain "On call".

    b.   *NOT* telephone the prison because of the danger of jamming the prison switchboard, keeping their own telephone free where possible to receive incoming calls.

3. a.   The first BOV Member to arrive at the Prison assumes the responsibility of Duty BOV Member until relieved.

    b.   The Duty BOV Member is to extract the BOV Incident Pack from the Governor's Incident Box and "Open the Incident Log". The Incident Log is to remain in situ, using the note-books when observing, writing up the Incident Log on return; own notes *ARE TO BE RETAINED* as they may be required subsequently.

    c.   The "Incident Log" forms the official record of what took place and when; it must be formally handed over by one Duty BOV Member to the next together with a verbal briefing – particularly with regard to any matters still be to be finalised.

4.   Relieving Duty BOV Members are to:

    a.   Formally take over the "Incident Log" on arrival and satisfy themselves that they are properly informed by the previous Duty BOV Member about the progress of events and all matters sill outstanding, thence

    b.   Report to the "Duty Governor" for a briefing by him.

5. a.   The activities of the Duty BOV Member must depend entirely upon the circumstances pertaining; while the incident is actually taking place – it will probably be necessary to observe from a distance and care should be taken to avoid any direct physical involvement as Staff will have to be detailed for your protection at a time when they may be urgently required for other duties. Ensure that the Governor knows of your whereabouts at **ALL** times so that you can be contacted quickly if it is necessary.

    b.   Make sure that you are kept informed at regular intervals of the progress of the incident; if there are casualties – Staff or Inmates – try to see them as soon as possible and record all relevant details, **but** be guided by the Governor and his Staff at all times as to where it is safe to go.

STAGE TWO

6.   a. When wings are being opened up the Governor may well request the presence of a BOV Member. In these circumstances you should let the Staff and Inmates know that a BOV Member is present and assist in any way that you can in the restoration of normal routine.

b. This is a critical time; those responsible for the incident may be on the look-out for retaliation from Staff, indeed may well try to provoke it if they feel that their efforts have failed. Inmates who did not participate, may fear retaliation from the ring-leaders and need protection from them. There may also be a large number of Inmates being actively helpful to the Staff, whose actions put them at risk from their fellow Inmates, their actions should be noted for future reference. BOV Members should also be aware at this stage of Staff that may be present on detached duty.

STAGE THREE

7.   a. During the next 24 hours, there may well be a number of transfers out of the Prison, you should endeavour to find out when these transfers are to take place, and make sure that you accompany each man from his Wing to the transfer area. Note his condition and identify yourself to him. (As a BOV Member.)

b. Remember you are the only independent witness of the Inmates condition at the time of leaving; if he shows any signs of injury, ask him about it and record his answers. If in any doubt ask for him to be examined by the Doctor before he leaves. Equally if he appears to be in good condition, record the fact, because your evidence on this point will be the Staff's main safeguard in the event of his making any subsequent allegations against them.

c. During this stage you should make frequent visits to the Wings, E Wing or other segregation area which may have been set up, the Hospital and other parts of the Prison as you consider necessary. Observe and record as much as possible of events taking place, ensuring that you see all of those known to have been involved in the incident, making your presence known – talk to as many people as possible.

d. Experience shows that this is likely to be the time of maximum tension, it is therefore important to remain objective and to avoid taking sides; if trouble does occur, observe and record what takes place, noting the time, place, and names of Staff and Inmates present and involved.

e. While you cannot sit subsequently on a panel adjudicating on a charge arising from a specific episode in which you were involved, you may well be called as a witness to give evidence.

STAGE FOUR

8.   a. Following the incident – the property of Inmates transferred out will be sent on to them, and again experience has shown that this is an area which often gives rise to subsequent queries.

b. You should ask to be kept informed about times of checking Inmates' kit so that you can be present while it is being done; any discrepancies should be noted, as should the names of those whose kit is in order.

9.   The Governor/BOV Chairman/Member deputising will decide when BOV presence is no longer required. The Board will then decide what further action is required regarding any Incident Summary, Reporting to the Secretary of State, etc.

J E DOIDGE

Chairman, Board of Visitors
HMP DARTMOOR

Distribution:

    The Governor
    Incident Pack (2)
    BOV Members
    BOV Clerk

HMP Cardiff

1. Adam Street
2. Playing Field
3. Garden Stores
4. Greenhouse
5. Hospital Exercise Yard
6. Hospital
7. Exercise Yard
8. Gymnasium
9. Chapel
10. D Wing
11. Craft Workshop
12. Reception (under)
13. Main Store (Training overhead)
14. Sandon Street
15. Works Department
16. Fitters Shop
17. Plasterers CIT Shop
18. Victualling Store
19. Clothing Exchange Store
20. Boiler House
21. Laundry
22. Bath House
23. Kitchen
24. Metal Shop (2)
25. Metal Shop
26. Tailors Shop 1 and 2 (overhead)
27. Tailors Cutting Shop (Training Shop overhead)
28. Main Exercise Yard
29. 'B' Wing
30. A Wing
31. Centre
32. Administration (Education overhead)
33. Main Reception
34. Old Gate
35. Knox Road
36. Former Visits
37. Gate Visits
38. Officers' Mess

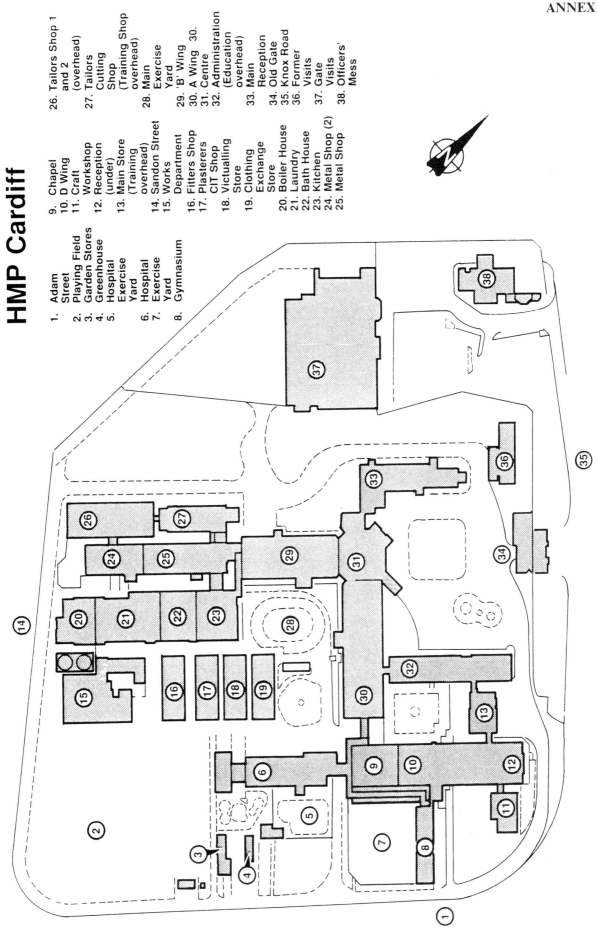

581

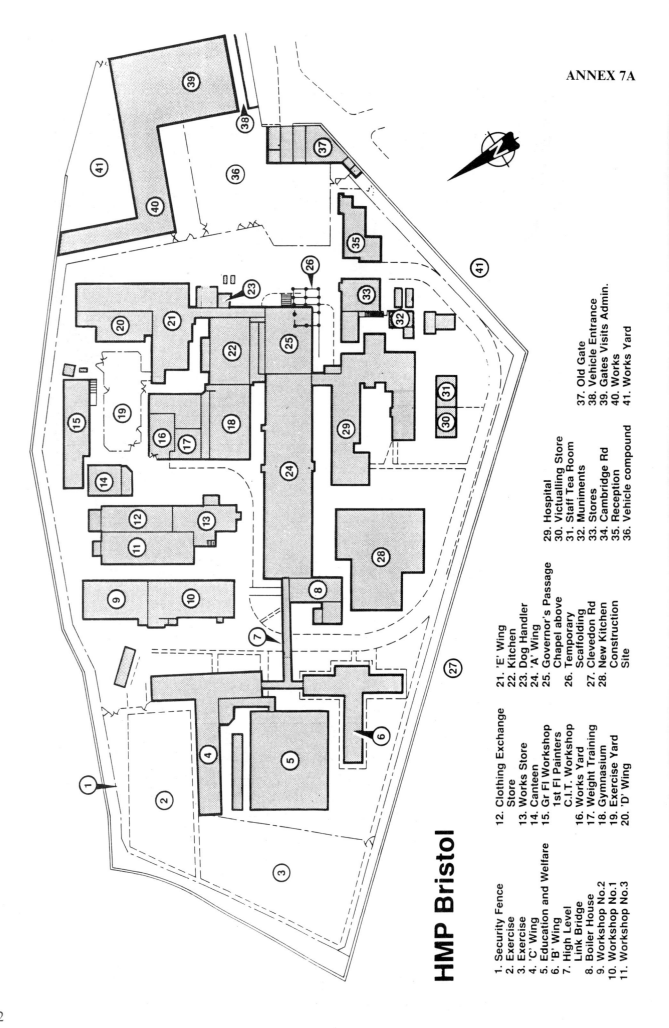

HMP Bristol

ANNEX 7A

1. Security Fence
2. Exercise
3. Exercise
4. 'C' Wing
5. Education and Welfare
6. 'B' Wing
7. High Level
   Link Bridge
8. Boiler House
9. Workshop No.2
10. Workshop No.1
11. Workshop No.3

12. Clothing Exchange
    Store
13. Works Store
14. Canteen
15. Gr Fl Workshop
    1st Fl Painters
    C.I.T. Workshop
16. Works Yard
17. Weight Training
18. Gymnasium
19. Exercise Yard
20. 'D' Wing

21. 'E' Wing
22. Kitchen
23. Dog Handler
24. 'A' Wing
25. Governor's Passage
    Chapel above
26. Temporary
    Scaffolding
27. Clevedon Rd
28. New Kitchen
    Construction
    Site

29. Hospital
30. Victualling Store
31. Staff Tea Room
32. Muniments
33. Stores
34. Cambridge Rd
35. Reception
36. Vehicle compound

37. Old Gate
38. Vehicle Entrance
39. Gates Visits Admin.
40. Works
41. Works Yard

Photograph 1: Bars Removed From Window

Photograph 2: Hole in 19" Brickwork

Photograph 3: Access to C Wing

Photograph 4: Damage to wings

Photograph 5: Damage to wings

Photograph 6: Damage to wings

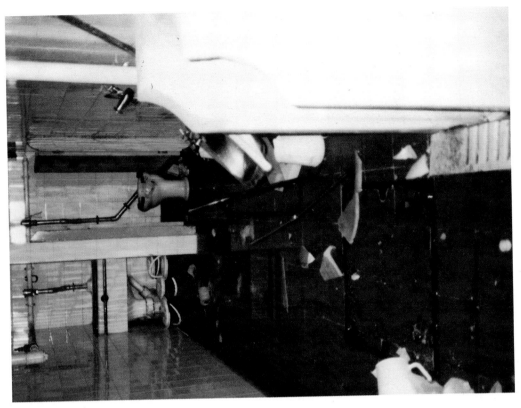

Photograph 7: Damage to wings

Photograph 8: Damage to wings

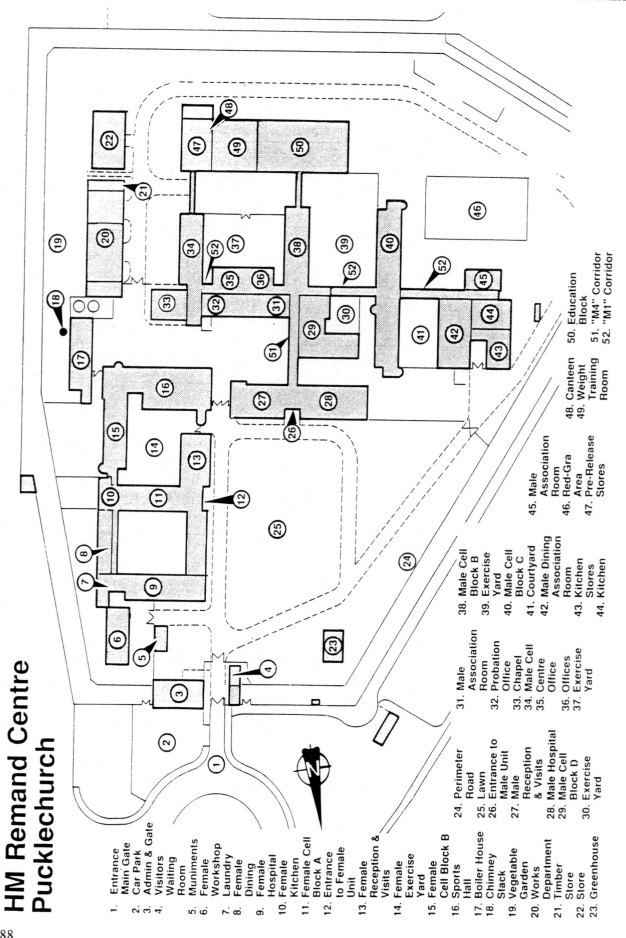

HM Remand Centre Puklechurch

ANNEX 8A

1. Entrance Main Gate
2. Car Park
3. Admin & Gate
4. Visitors Waiting Room
5. Muniments
6. Female Workshop
7. Laundry
8. Female Dining
9. Female Hospital
10. Female Kitchen
11. Female Cell Block A
12. Entrance to Female Unit
13. Female Reception & Visits
14. Female Exercise Yard
15. Female Cell Block B
16. Sports Hall
17. Boiler House
18. Chimney Stack
19. Vegetable Garden
20. Works Department
21. Timber Store
22. Store
23. Greenhouse

24. Perimeter Road
25. Lawn
26. Entrance to Male Unit
27. Male Reception & Visits
28. Male Hospital
29. Male Cell Block D
30. Exercise Yard

31. Male Association Room
32. Probation Office
33. Chapel
34. Male Cell
35. Centre Office
36. Offices
37. Exercise Yard

38. Male Cell Block B
39. Exercise Yard
40. Male Cell Block C
41. Courtyard
42. Male Dining Association Room
43. Kitchen Stores
44. Kitchen

45. Male Association Room
46. Red-Gra Area
47. Pre-Release Stores
48. Canteen
49. Weight Training Room

50. Education Block
51. "M4" Corridor
52. "M1" Corridor

588

PROCEDURE FOR DEALING WITH THE SURRENDER OF PRISONERS AFTER A MAJOR INCIDENT

At the termination of a major incident within the establishment the following procedure to deal with the surrender of prisoners will be adopted:

1. *The Commander will appoint a Surrender Area Manager* (normally of the rank of Principal Officer) who will:

    (a) *Establish the identity of each individual prisoner* who is surrendering by name and prison number and will initiate Part A of the Individual Incident Log (illustrated at Appendix A).

    (b) *Detail two uniformed members of staff, who have not been members of any Control & Restraint Team*, to escort the prisoner to a designated search area.

    (c) *Ensure that sufficient property bags and seals have been made available from Reception* to hold items of prisoners' property and, where necessary, items of clothing.

    (d) *Ensure that all items of clothing*, whether prison issue or civilian clothing, are itemised and searched.

    (e) *Ensure that all items of personal property* are placed in a property bag and sealed in the presence of the prisoner, the seal number being annotated on the property list. He or she will also ensure that all property removed from the prisoner is correctly stored in the Reception area in the appropriate property box.

    (f) *Ensure that the prisoner is allocated to appropriate accommodation (preferably cellular if available)* and that that has been kitted-out to the specified scale with sleeping, washing and toilet utensils.

    (g) *Ensure that there are sufficient full sets of clothing available* to issue to prisoners who have had theirs removed as a result of the "strip-search".

    (h) *When and where appropriate, liaise with the Senior Catering Officer* on duty to ensure that sufficient meals are available to feed each prisoner who has surrendered.

    (i) *Ensure that the Individual Incident Log* is fully completed prior to its being filed in the prisoner's Form 1150/2050.

2. *The "On-Call Doctor" will:*

    (a) *Medically examine each prisoner* so as to assess the extent of any injuries or marks and ensure that a Form 213 is raised, as appropriate.

    (b) *Record details of any treatment* which may be prescribed on the prisoner's IMR.

    (c) *Sign and date the relevant section of Part A* of the Individual Incident Log and, where appropriate, make comment.

3. *Arrangements should be made for a member of the Board of Visitors to:*

    (a) *See each individual prisoner* who has surrendered.

    (b) *Sign and date Part B* of the Individual Incident Log and, where appropriate, make comment.

4.   *A Senior Manager of a rank no lower than Governor 4 will:*

(a)   *See each individual prisoner* who has surrendered and ensure that:
i)   *Each prisoner has been medically examined* and been seen by a member of the Board of Visitors;

ii)   *Where appropriate, has had a meal;*

iii)   *Each prisoner is in possession of a complete set of clothing*, having been returned after the "strip-search" or being a newly-issued set of prison clothing.

(b)   *Sign and date Part C* of the Individual Incident Log and, where appropriate, make comment.

INDIVIDUAL INCIDENT LOG

Part A

Prison No:_____   Name:_____

Initials:_____   DOB:_____

Sentence:_____   EDR:_____

Incident:_____   Time of Surrender:_____

Time Searched:_____   Clothing Bag Seal No:_____

Property Bag Seal No:_____   Location/Time:_____

Time clothing issued:_____   Time Bathed:_____

Time Meal Taken:_____   Signature:_____

Rank/Position:_____   Date:_____

(TO BE COMPLETED BY HEAD OF MEDICAL SERVICES)

Time examined:_____   Comments:_____

_____

_____   Signature:_____

Rank/Position:_____   Date:_____

Part B (To be completed by Board of Visitors Member)

Time seen:_____   Comments:_____

_____

_____   Signature:_____

Rank/Position:_____   Date:_____

Part C (To be completed by Manager of Rank not less than Governor 4)

Time seen:_____   Comments:_____

_____

_____   Signature:_____

Rank/Position:_____   Date:_____

Prisons: Industrial Disputes

Source: Hansard 30 October 1990
[columns 1833-1834]

TABLE 1

Prisons with Industrial Disputes since 1st January 1990

Acklington	
Albany	
Aldington	
Ashwell	Settled
Askham Grange	
Bedford	
Blundeston	Settled
Bristol	Settled
Brixton	Settled
Brockhill	Settled
Campsfield House	
Canterbury	Settled
Cardiff	Settled
Channings Wood	
Chelmsford	Settled
Coldingley	
Dartmoor	Settled
Dorchester	Settled
Downview	Settled
Durham	Settled
East Sutton Park	Settled
Eastwood Park	
Featherstone	Settled
Feltham	
Frankland	Settled
Ford	Settled
Full Sutton	
Garth	
Glen Parva	
Gloucester	
Haverigg	Settled
Hindley	Settled
Holloway	Settled
Kingston	
Kirkham	
Lancaster	Settled
Latchmere House	Settled
Leeds	
Leyhill	Settled
Littlehey	Settled

Liverpool	
Manchester	
Morton Hall	Settled
The Mount	Settled
Northallerton	
Norwich	Settled
Parkhurst	Settled
Pentonville	
Portland	Settled
Preston	Settled
Pucklechurch	
Risley	
Rochester	
Rudgate	
Stafford	Settled
Stoke Heath	
Styal	
Swaleside	Settled
Swansea	Settled
Thorn Cross	
Thorp Arch	
Wakefield	Settled
Wandsworth	Settled
Wayland	Settled
Werrington	Settled
Wetherby	
Winchester	Settled
Whatton	
Wormwood Scrubs	
Wymott	

Prisons: Industrial Disputes

Source: Hansard 30 October 1990
[Columns 1834-1836]

TABLE 2

Prisons Which Have Threatened or Refused
Admittance of Prisoners Since 1st January 1990

Aylesbury
Bedford
Birmingham
Brixton
Campsfield House
Channings Wood
Chelmsford
Dartmoor
Dorchester
Downview
Durham
Exeter
Featherstone
Feltham
Full Sutton
Garth
Gartree
Glen Parva
Guys March
Highpoint
Hindley
Holloway
Hull
Latchmere House
Leeds
Leicester
Lincoln
Lindholme
Liverpool
Long Lartin
Onley
Pentonville
Portland
Preston
Reading
Risley
Shrewsbury
Swansea
Thorn Cross
Usk
The Verne
Wandsworth
Wayland
Wetherby
Wormwood Scrubs
Wymott

A.

Assistant Governor	– Now replaced by grade of Governor 5 (qv).

B.

BOV	– Board of Visitors (qv).
Banging up	– Locking prisoners in their cells (slang).
Block	– Segregation unit (qv) (slang).
Board of Visitors	– Members of the public appointed by the Home Secretary with a watchdog role. Also adjudicate on serious disciplinary infringements by prisoners.

C.

C & R	– Control and restraint. Range of techniques for handling incidents involving violent or recalcitrant prisoners.
C&R1	– Technique for handling a single violent prisoner or prisoners fighting.
C&R2	– Techniques for self-defence and for handling intermediate scale incident.
C&R3	– Techniques for handling large scale disturbance.
C&R team	– Three officers. Basic unit for C&R1.
C&R unit	– 12 officers plus a commander. Basic unit for C&R2 and 3.
CI 10/74	– Circular Instruction on temporary transfer of disruptive prisoners from dispersal to local prisons. Recently superseded.
CNA	– Certified Normal Accommodation. Intended to identify the number of prisoners which an establishment will hold without overcrowding.
Categorisation	– Assignment of prisoners to a security category.
Category A	– Prisoners whose escape would be highly dangerous to the public or to the police or to the security of the State.
Category B	– Prisoners for whom the highest conditions of security are not necessary, but for whom escape must be made very difficult.
Category C	– Prisoners who cannot be trusted in open conditions, but who do not have the ability or resources to make a determined escape attempt.
Category D	– Prisoners who can reasonably be trusted to serve their sentences in open conditions.
Category E	– Unofficial term for the Escape List or E List. Prisoners normally in Categories A or B (qv) presenting a high risk of escape who are temporarily made subject to additional security precautions.
Censor	– Prison officer responsible for censoring prisoners' incoming and outgoing mail.
Centre	– Central point from which wings radiate in many Victorian prisons. Term also used for central location in some other establishments.
Centre box	– Office on the centre. Used mainly for supervising movement and collating information.

Controlled unlocking	–	Process of unlocking prisoners in small groups.

D.

DDG	–	Deputy Director General.
DG	–	Director General. Head of the Prison Service.
Doubling	–	Use of special key to over lock certain gates or doors thereby preventing them being unlocked by the key normally used. (Also used to mean holding two prisoners in a cell.)

E.

Escort duties	–	Escorting of prisoners outside an establishment, eg to and from court appearances.

F.

Fours	–	Fourth landing (qv) (slang).
Fresh Start	–	Major reform of the Prison Service which restructured management, work patterns and complementing in establishments.

G.

Governor	–	Head of an establishment.
Governor 1	)	
Governor 2	)	
Governor 3	) –	Management grades in prisons (apart from some administrators and specialists).
Governor 4	)	
Governor 5	)	

H.

HMCIP	–	Her Majesty's Chief Inspector of Prisons.

L.

Landings	–	Floor levels, normally in galleried prisons, but term may be used in other establishments.

M.

MUFTI	–	Minimum Use of Force Tactical Intervention. Techniques for dealing with disturbances. Superseded by C&R3 (qv).

N.

NRO	–	Former Prison Service North Regional Office.

| Negotiators | – | Prison staff trained in negotiating techniques who speak directly to prisoners during an incident. |

O.

| Ones | – | First landing (qv), ie the ground or lower ground floor (slang). |

P.

PEI	–	Physical Education Instructor. A specialist prison officer (qv).
PGA	–	Prison Governors' Association. A representative body for prison governors.
POA	–	Prison Officers' Association. Trade Union representing prison officers.
PR24	–	Baton or stave carried on the belt by officers in a C&R unit (qv) for defensive use if required.
Petitions	–	Means by which prisoners could address grievances and requests to the Home Secretary under the former grievance procedure.
Petitions Register	–	Record of petitions.
Principal Officer	–	Most senior of the three grades of prison officer (qv).
Prison Officer	–	Uniformed discipline or specialist officer. Also used for basic grade prison officer.
Punishment block	–	Segregation unit (slang).

R.

Recesses	–	Area on each landing (qv) with washing and lavatory facilities.
Regime	–	The prisoner's complete lifestyle, encompassing the routine and programmes provided.
Region	–	Former Prison Service administrative unit.
Remand	–	Untried prisoner awaiting a further appearance in a Magistrates' Court. Loosely applied to all unconvicted or unsentenced prisoners.
Rule 43	–	Prison Rule under which prisoners may be segregated for their own protection or in the interests of good order and discipline.
Rub down	–	Search of a prisoner without removal of clothing.

S.

SIR	–	Security Information Report submitted by a member of staff.
SWRO	–	Former Prison Service South West Regional Office.
Segregation Unit	–	Accommodation for prisoners held under Rule 43 (qv), awaiting adjudication or for cellular punishment.
Senior Officer	–	Grade of prison officer (qv) between Officer and Principal Officer (qv).
Slopping out	–	Prisoners emptying their chamber pots at the recesses (qv).

T.

Threes	–	Third landing (qv) (slang).
Twos	–	Second landing (qv) (slang).

U.

Under centre	–	The lower ground floor under the Centre (qv).

V.

VPU	–	Vulnerable Prisoner Unit.

Printed in the United Kingdom for HMSO
Dd 0509504 2/91 C45 51-7934 (4682)